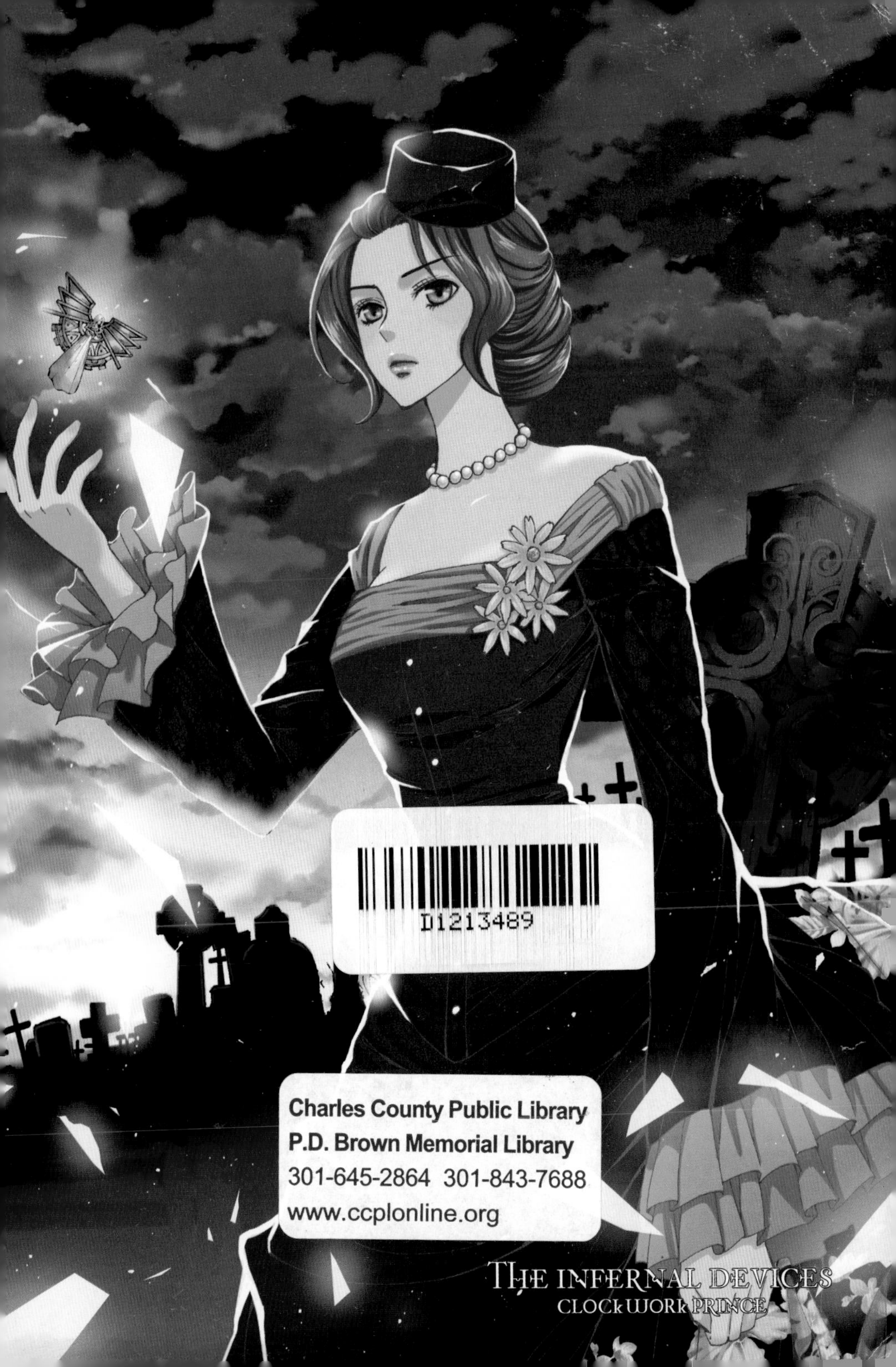
THE INFERNAL DEVICES
CLOCKWORK PRINCE

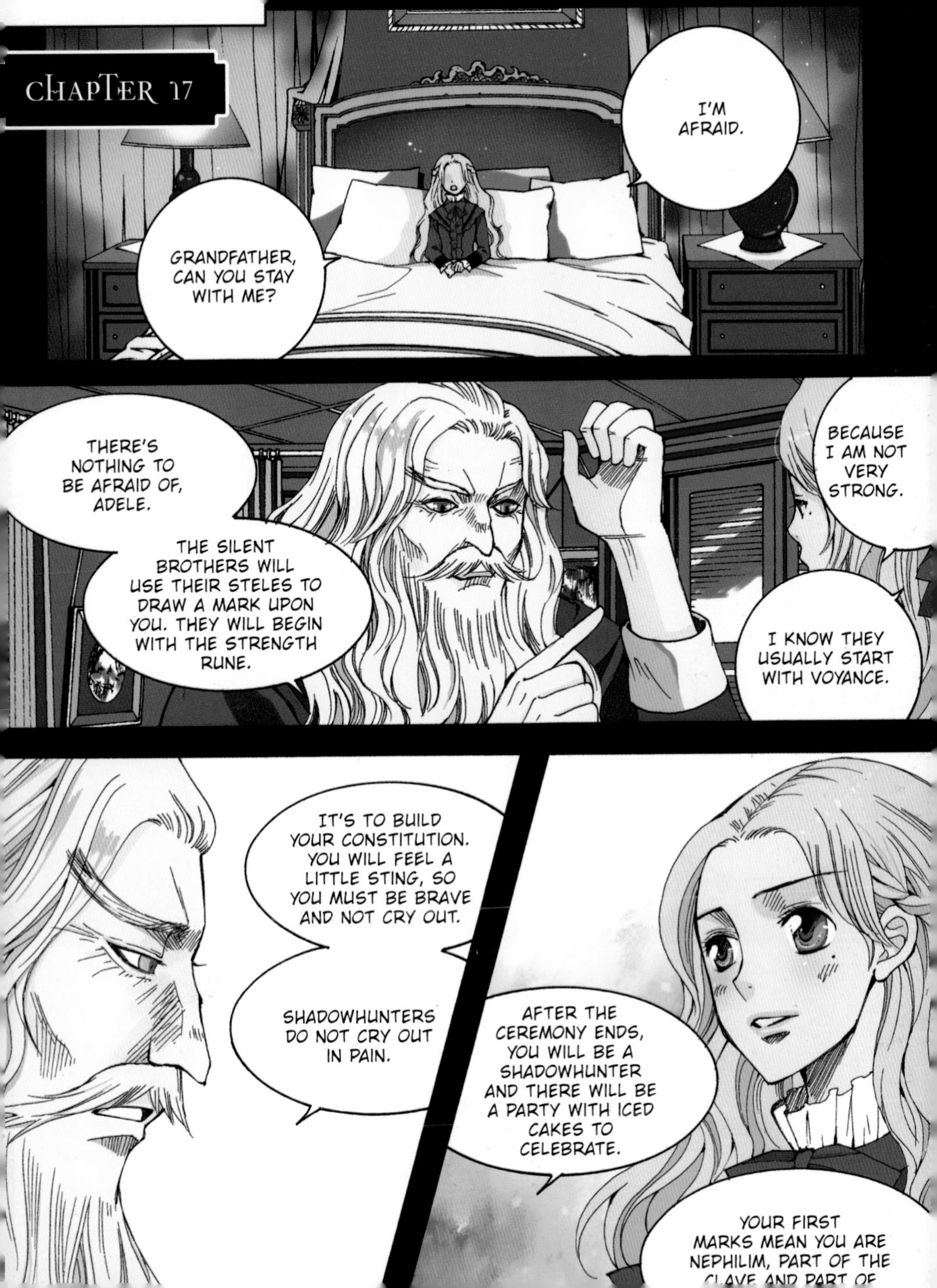
CHAPTER 17
GRANDFATHER, CAN YOU STAY WITH ME?
I'M AFRAID.
THERE'S NOTHING TO BE AFRAID OF, ADELE.
BECAUSE I AM NOT VERY STRONG.
THE SILENT BROTHERS WILL USE THEIR STELES TO DRAW A MARK UPON YOU. THEY WILL BEGIN WITH THE STRENGTH RUNE.
I KNOW THEY USUALLY START WITH VOYANCE.
IT'S TO BUILD YOUR CONSTITUTION. YOU WILL FEEL A LITTLE STING, SO YOU MUST BE BRAVE AND NOT CRY OUT.
SHADOWHUNTERS DO NOT CRY OUT IN PAIN.
AFTER THE CEREMONY ENDS, YOU WILL BE A SHADOWHUNTER AND THERE WILL BE A PARTY WITH ICED CAKES TO CELEBRATE.
YOUR FIRST MARKS MEAN YOU ARE NEPHILIM, PART OF THE CLAVE AND PART OF

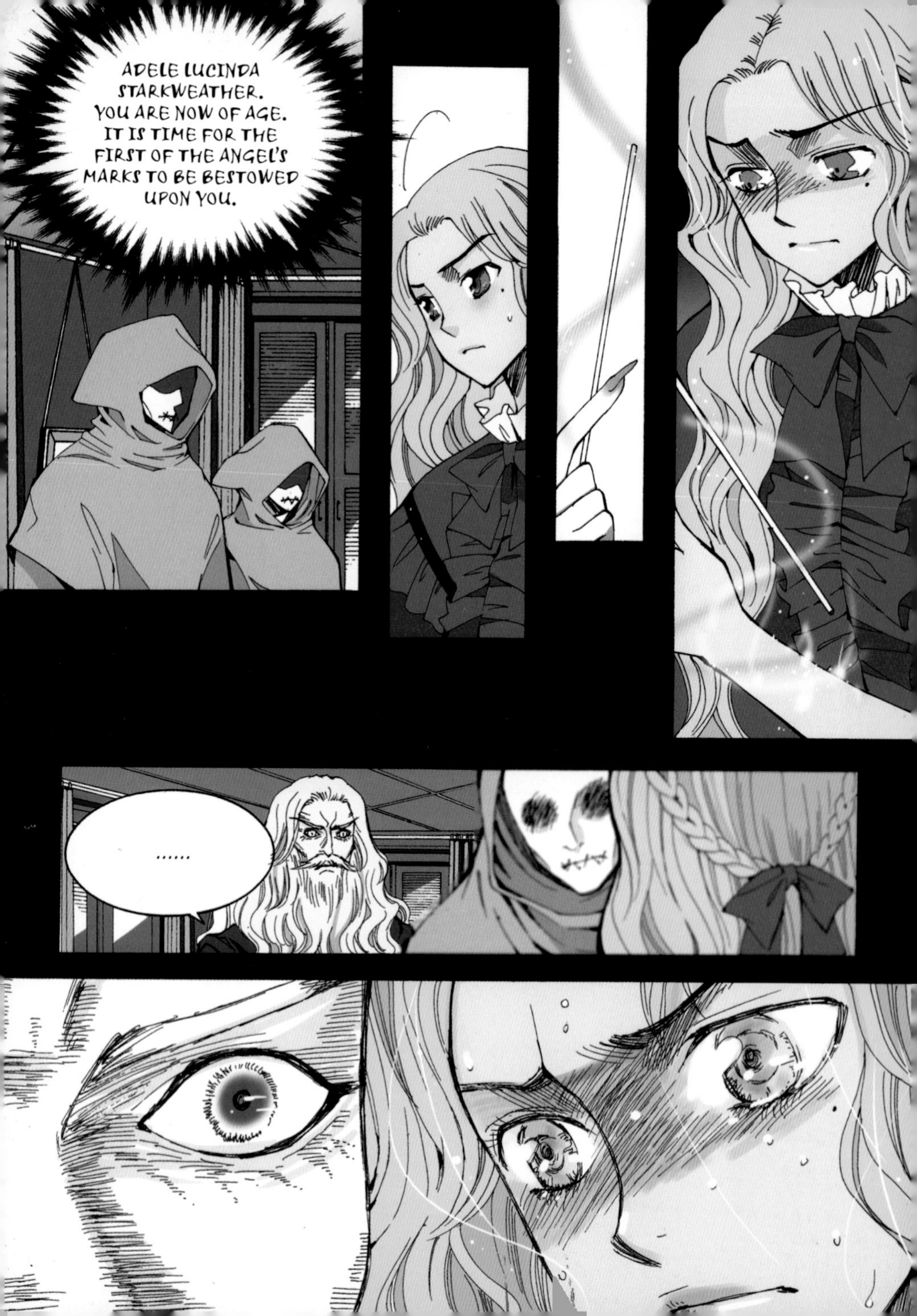
ADELE LUCINDA STARKWEATHER. YOU ARE NOW OF AGE. IT IS TIME FOR THE FIRST OF THE ANGEL'S MARKS TO BE BESTOWED UPON YOU.
......

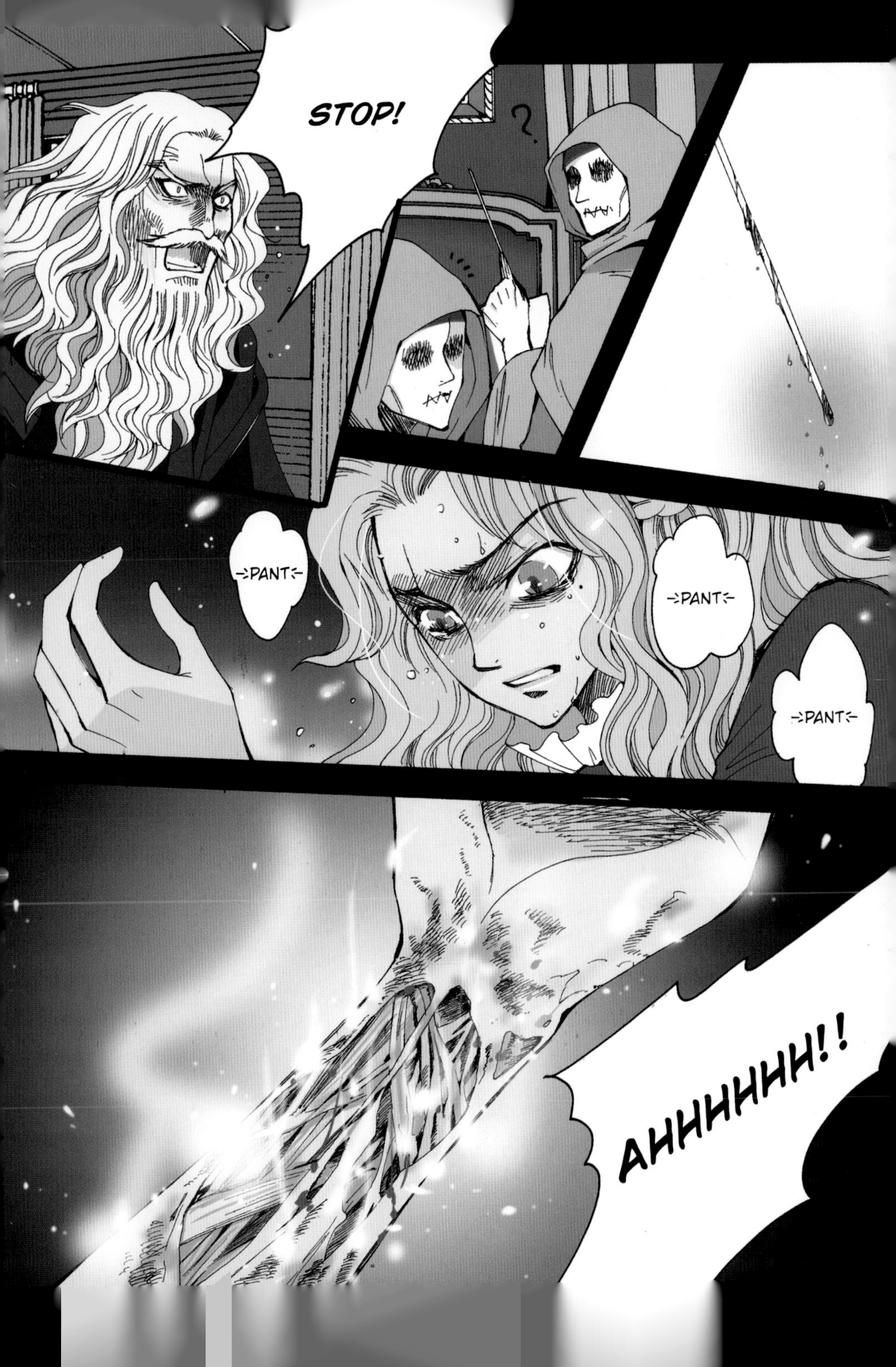
STOP!
?
-PANT-
-PANT-
-PANT-
AHHHHHH!!

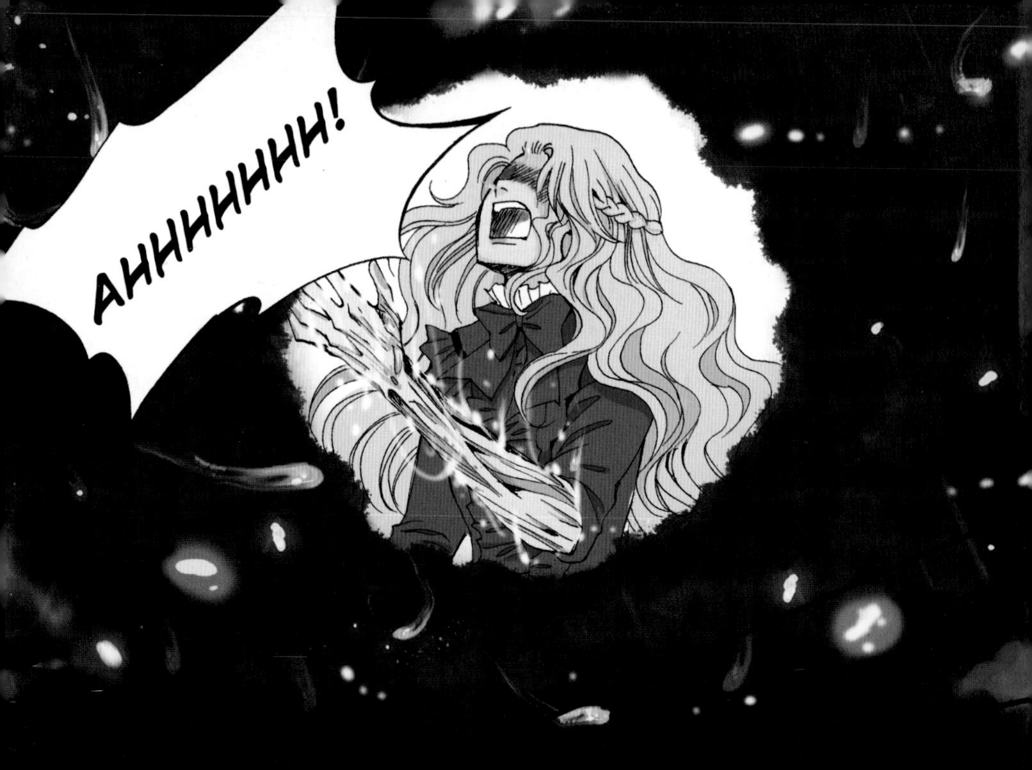
AHHHHHHH!

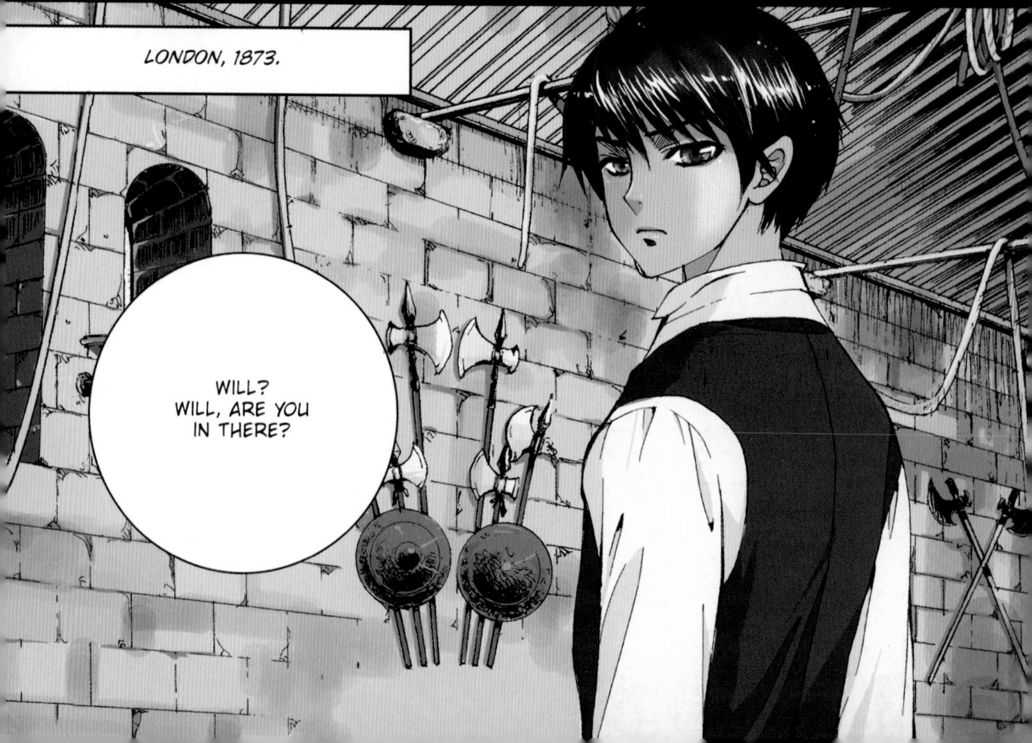
LONDON, 1873.
WILL?
WILL, ARE YOU
IN THERE?

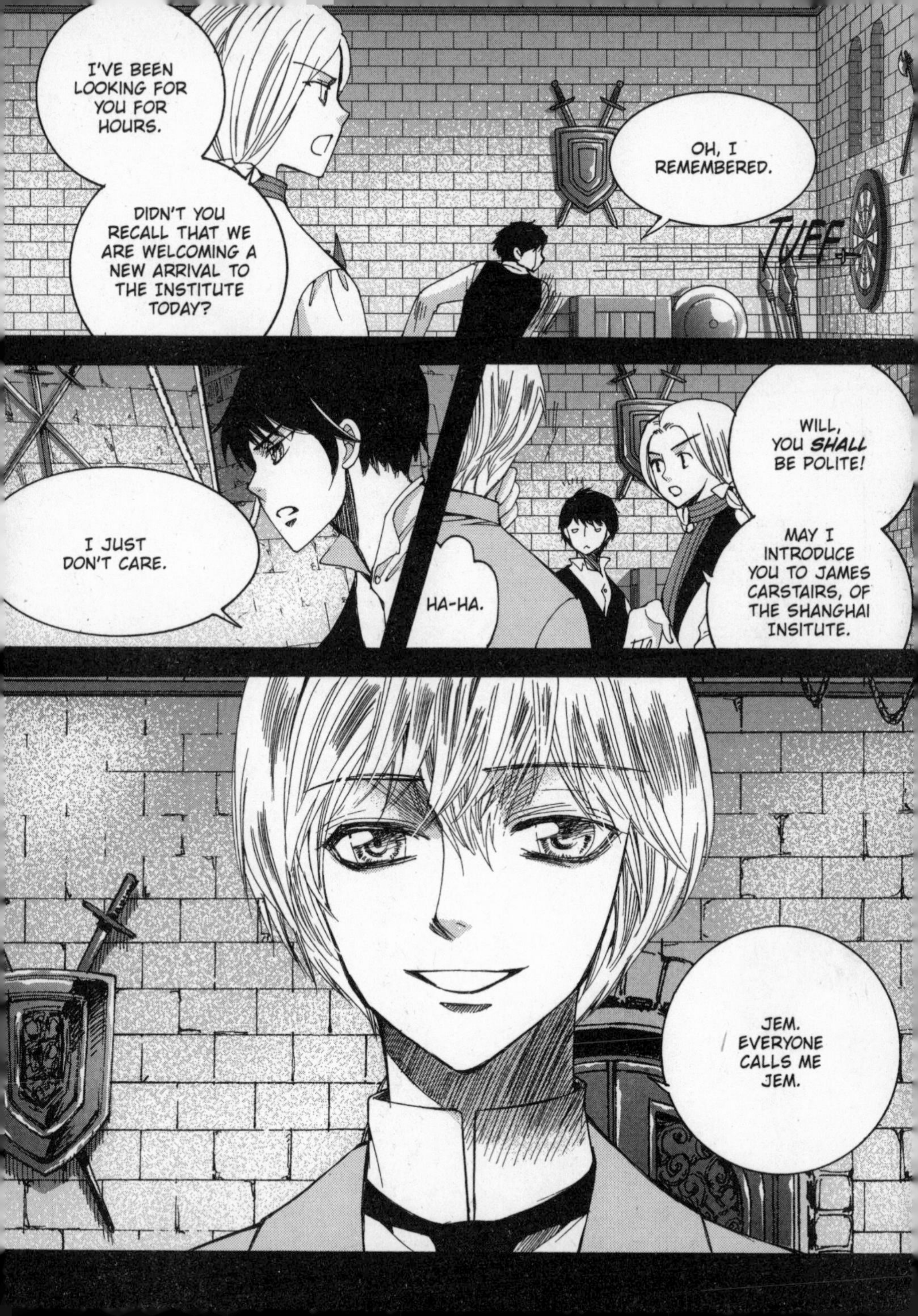
I'VE BEEN LOOKING FOR YOU FOR HOURS.
DIDN'T YOU RECALL THAT WE ARE WELCOMING A NEW ARRIVAL TO THE INSTITUTE TODAY?
OH, I REMEMBERED.
TUFF
I JUST DON'T CARE.
HA-HA.
WILL, YOU SHALL BE POLITE!
MAY I INTRODUCE YOU TO JAMES CARSTAIRS, OF THE SHANGHAI INSITUTE.
JEM. EVERYONE CALLS ME JEM.

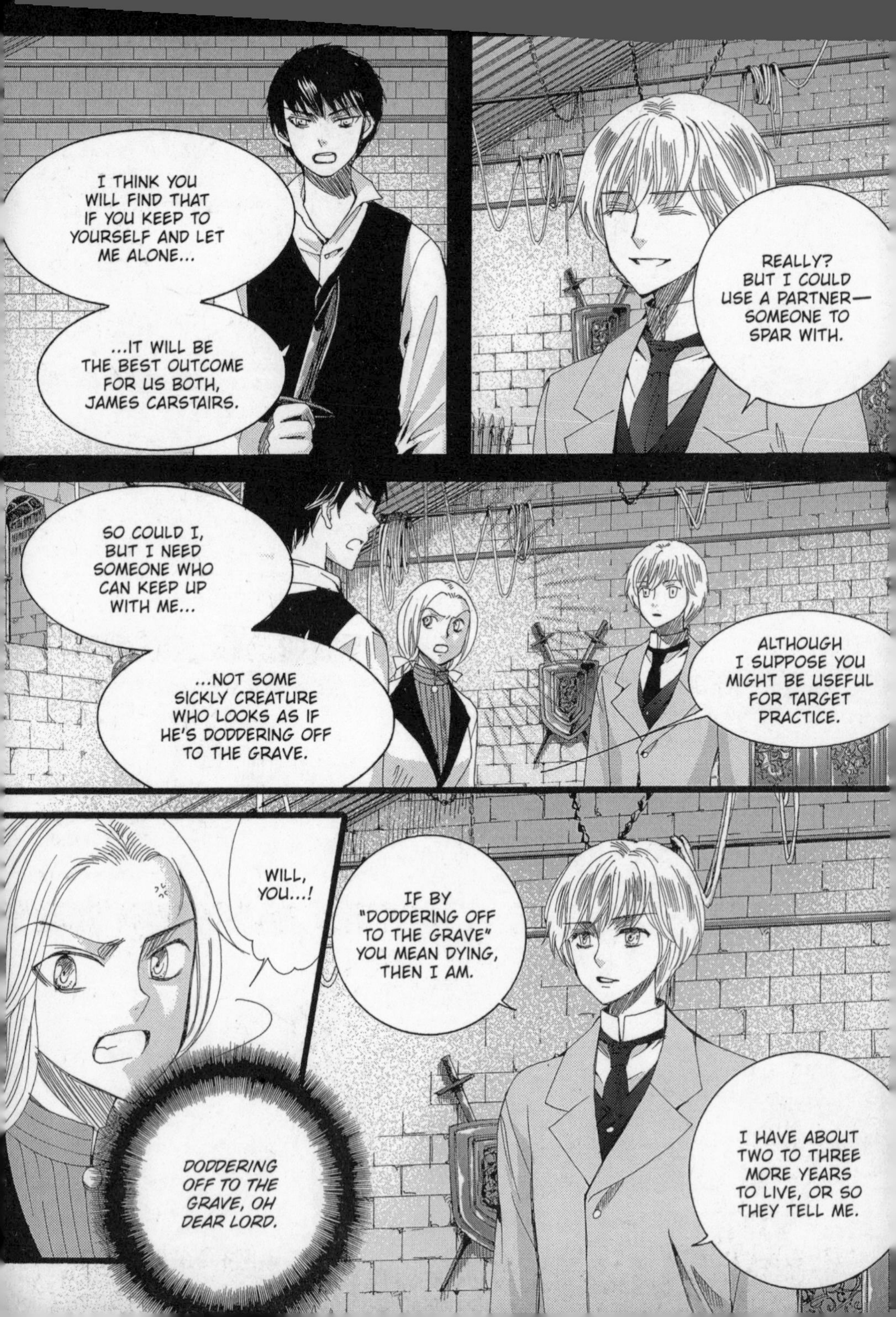
I THINK YOU WILL FIND THAT IF YOU KEEP TO YOURSELF AND LET ME ALONE...
...IT WILL BE THE BEST OUTCOME FOR US BOTH, JAMES CARSTAIRS.
REALLY? BUT I COULD USE A PARTNER— SOMEONE TO SPAR WITH.
SO COULD I, BUT I NEED SOMEONE WHO CAN KEEP UP WITH ME...
...NOT SOME SICKLY CREATURE WHO LOOKS AS IF HE'S DODDERING OFF TO THE GRAVE.
ALTHOUGH I SUPPOSE YOU MIGHT BE USEFUL FOR TARGET PRACTICE.
WILL, YOU...!
DODDERING OFF TO THE GRAVE, OH DEAR LORD.
IF BY "DODDERING OFF TO THE GRAVE" YOU MEAN DYING, THEN I AM.
I HAVE ABOUT TWO TO THREE MORE YEARS TO LIVE, OR SO THEY TELL ME.

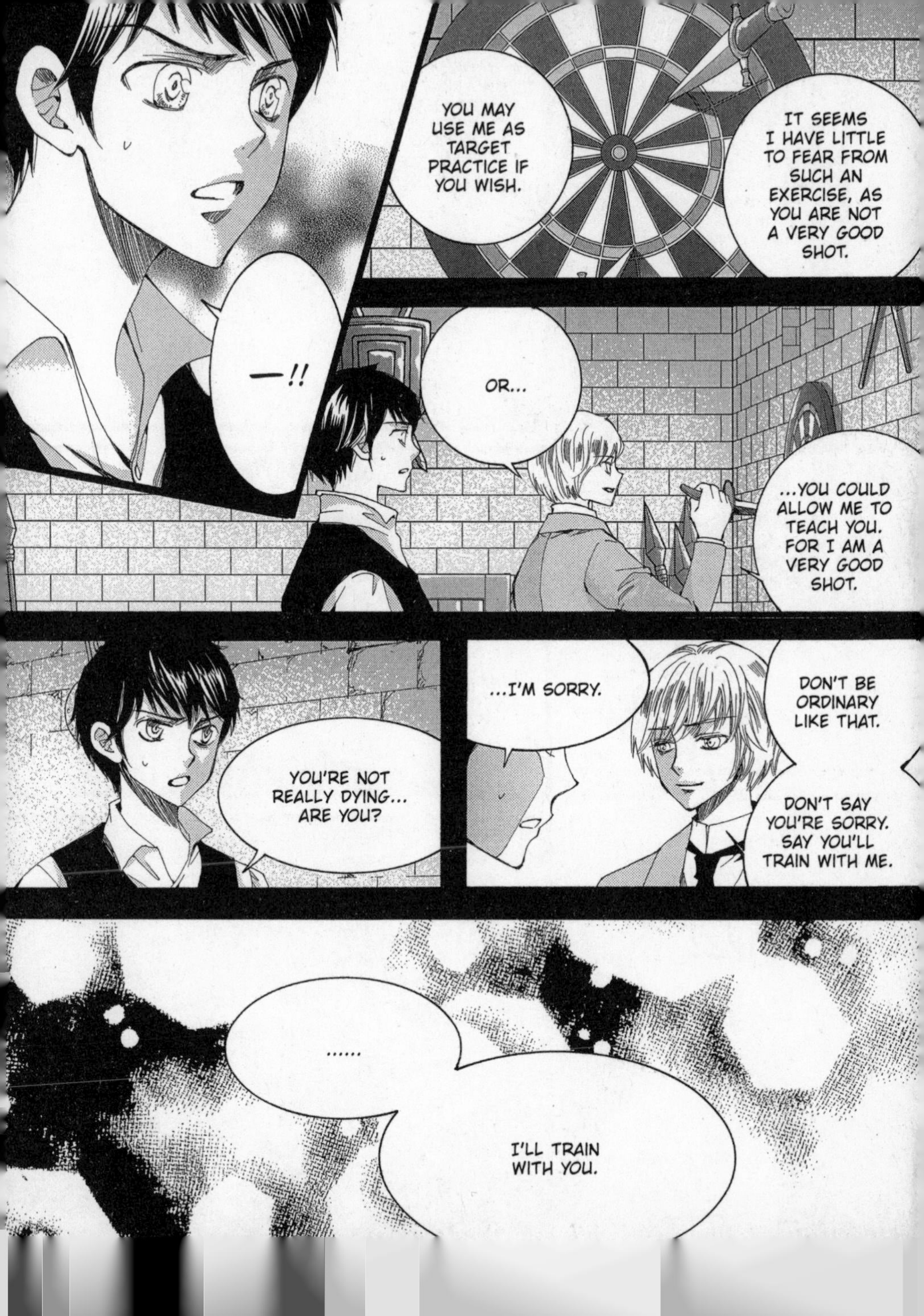
IT SEEMS I HAVE LITTLE TO FEAR FROM SUCH AN EXERCISE, AS YOU ARE NOT A VERY GOOD SHOT.
YOU MAY USE ME AS TARGET PRACTICE IF YOU WISH.
—!!
OR...
...YOU COULD ALLOW ME TO TEACH YOU. FOR I AM A VERY GOOD SHOT.
...I'M SORRY.
DON'T BE ORDINARY LIKE THAT.
DON'T SAY YOU'RE SORRY. SAY YOU'LL TRAIN WITH ME.
YOU'RE NOT REALLY DYING... ARE YOU?
......
I'LL TRAIN WITH YOU.

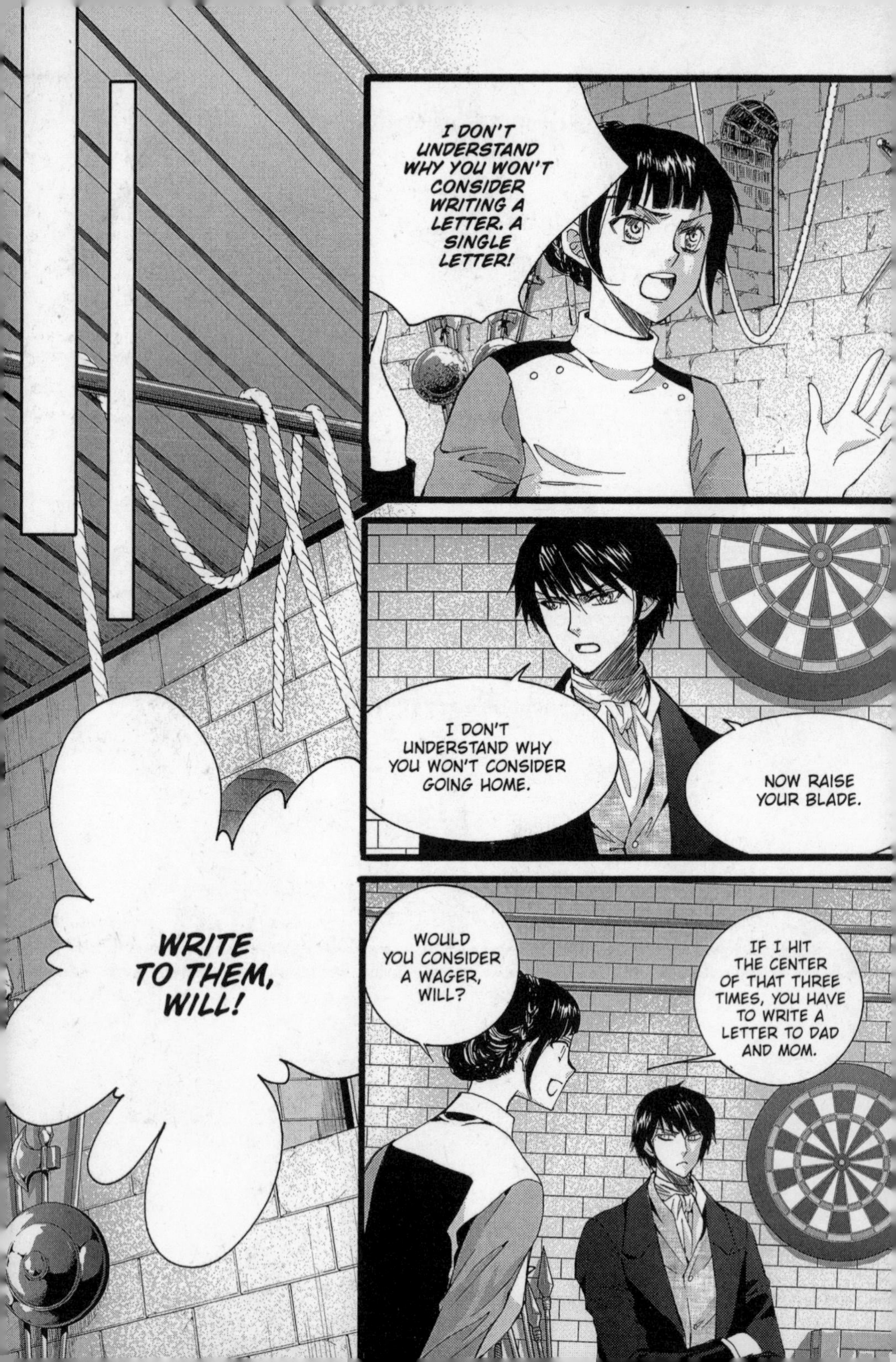
I DON'T UNDERSTAND WHY YOU WON'T CONSIDER WRITING A LETTER. A SINGLE LETTER!
WRITE TO THEM, WILL!
NOW RAISE YOUR BLADE.
I DON'T UNDERSTAND WHY YOU WON'T CONSIDER GOING HOME.
IF I HIT THE CENTER OF THAT THREE TIMES, YOU HAVE TO WRITE A LETTER TO DAD AND MOM.
WOULD YOU CONSIDER A WAGER, WILL?

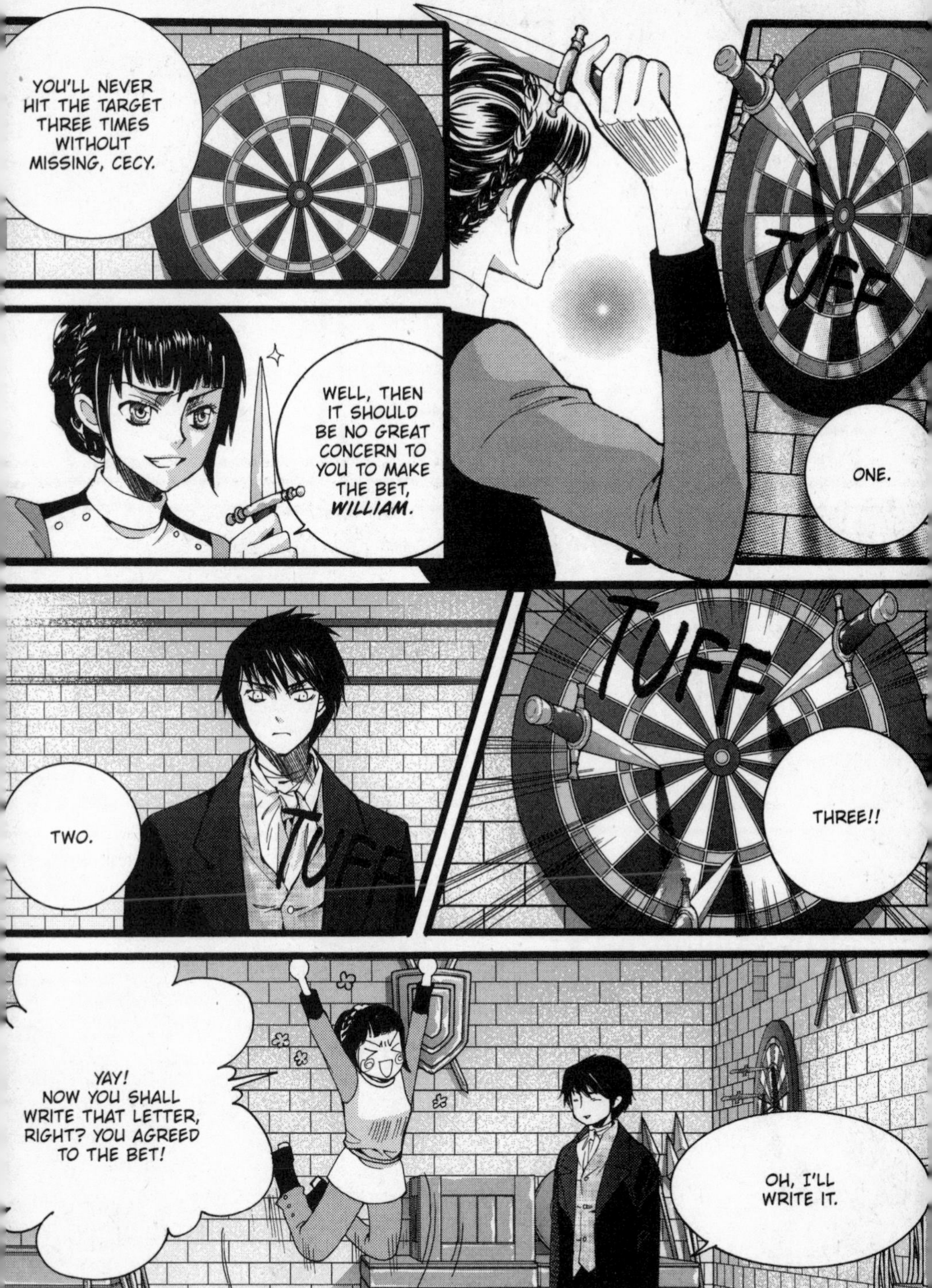

YOU'LL NEVER HIT THE TARGET THREE TIMES WITHOUT MISSING, CECY.
WELL, THEN IT SHOULD BE NO GREAT CONCERN TO YOU TO MAKE THE BET, ***WILLIAM***.
TUFF
ONE.
TUFF
TWO.
TUFF
THREE!!
YAY! NOW YOU SHALL WRITE THAT LETTER, RIGHT? YOU AGREED TO THE BET!
OH, I'LL WRITE IT.

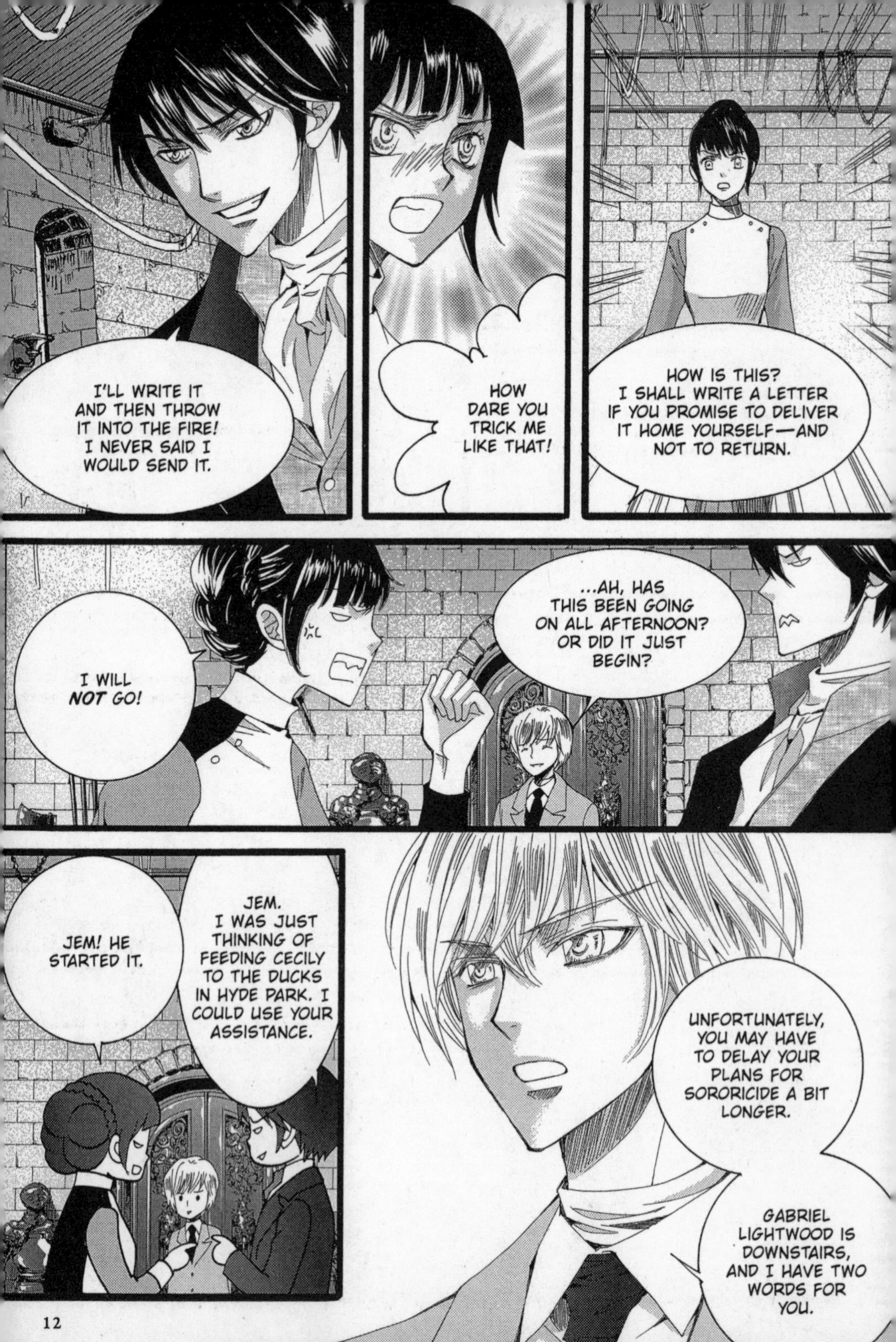
I'LL WRITE IT AND THEN THROW IT INTO THE FIRE! I NEVER SAID I WOULD SEND IT.
HOW DARE YOU TRICK ME LIKE THAT!
HOW IS THIS? I SHALL WRITE A LETTER IF YOU PROMISE TO DELIVER IT HOME YOURSELF—AND NOT TO RETURN.
I WILL *NOT* GO!
...AH, HAS THIS BEEN GOING ON ALL AFTERNOON? OR DID IT JUST BEGIN?
JEM! HE STARTED IT.
JEM. I WAS JUST THINKING OF FEEDING CECILY TO THE DUCKS IN HYDE PARK. I COULD USE YOUR ASSISTANCE.
UNFORTUNATELY, YOU MAY HAVE TO DELAY YOUR PLANS FOR SORORICIDE A BIT LONGER.
GABRIEL LIGHTWOOD IS DOWNSTAIRS, AND I HAVE TWO WORDS FOR YOU.

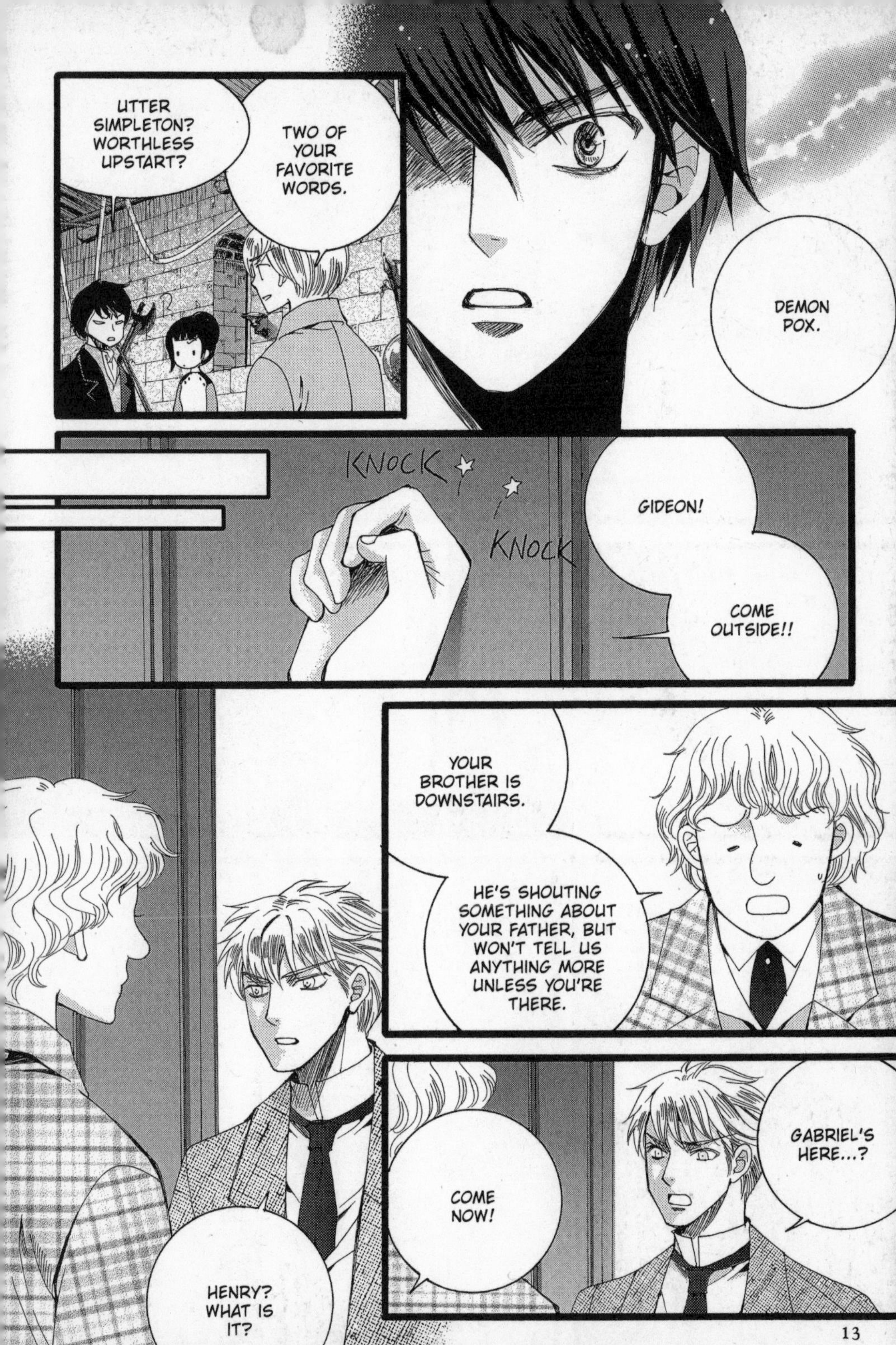
UTTER SIMPLETON? WORTHLESS UPSTART?
TWO OF YOUR FAVORITE WORDS.
DEMON POX.
KNOCK
KNOCK
GIDEON!
COME OUTSIDE!!
HENRY? WHAT IS IT?
YOUR BROTHER IS DOWNSTAIRS.
HE'S SHOUTING SOMETHING ABOUT YOUR FATHER, BUT WON'T TELL US ANYTHING MORE UNLESS YOU'RE THERE.
COME NOW!
GABRIEL'S HERE...?

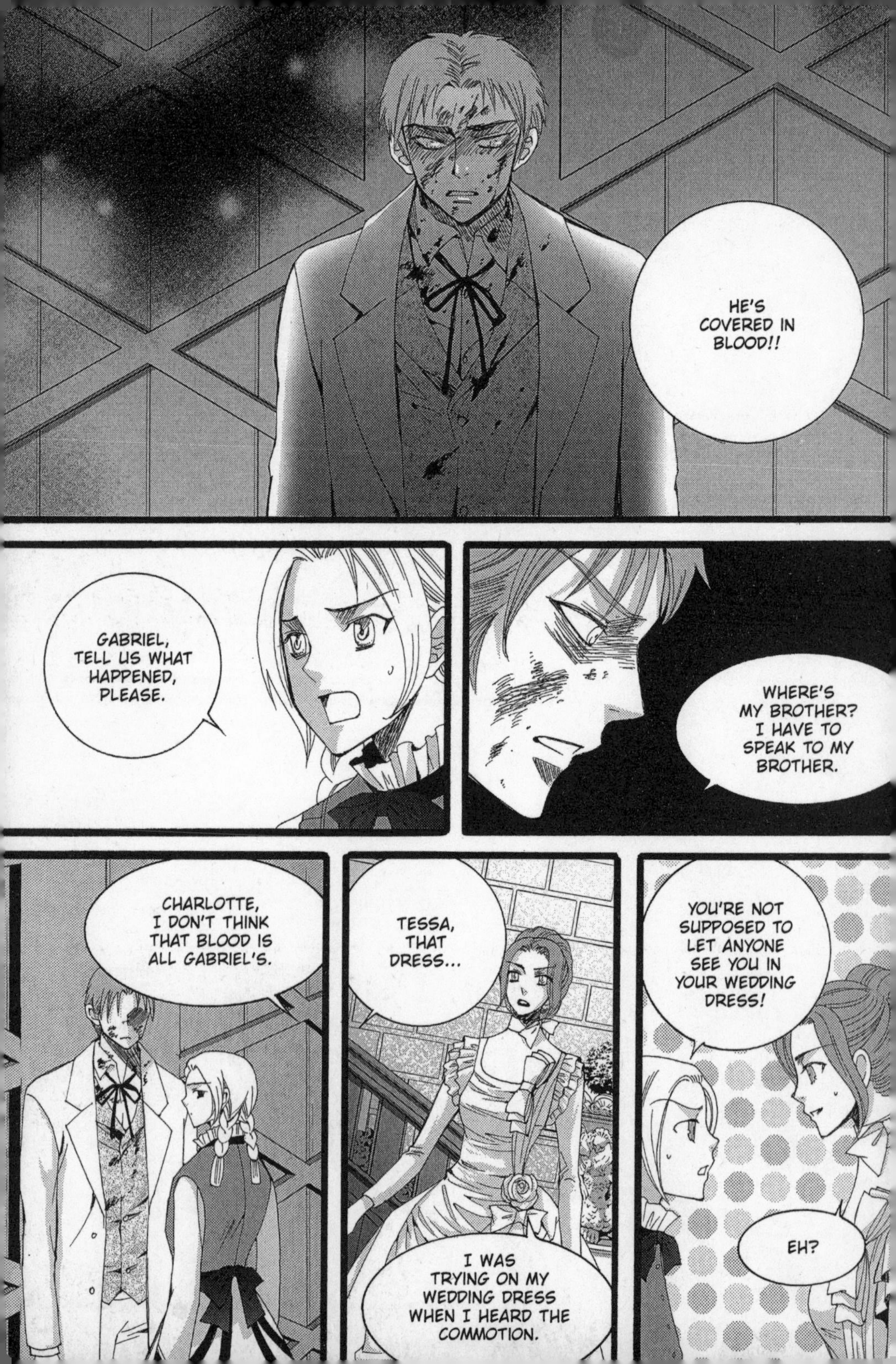
HE'S COVERED IN BLOOD!!
GABRIEL, TELL US WHAT HAPPENED, PLEASE.
WHERE'S MY BROTHER? I HAVE TO SPEAK TO MY BROTHER.
CHARLOTTE, I DON'T THINK THAT BLOOD IS ALL GABRIEL'S.
TESSA, THAT DRESS...
I WAS TRYING ON MY WEDDING DRESS WHEN I HEARD THE COMMOTION.
YOU'RE NOT SUPPOSED TO LET ANYONE SEE YOU IN YOUR WEDDING DRESS!
EH?

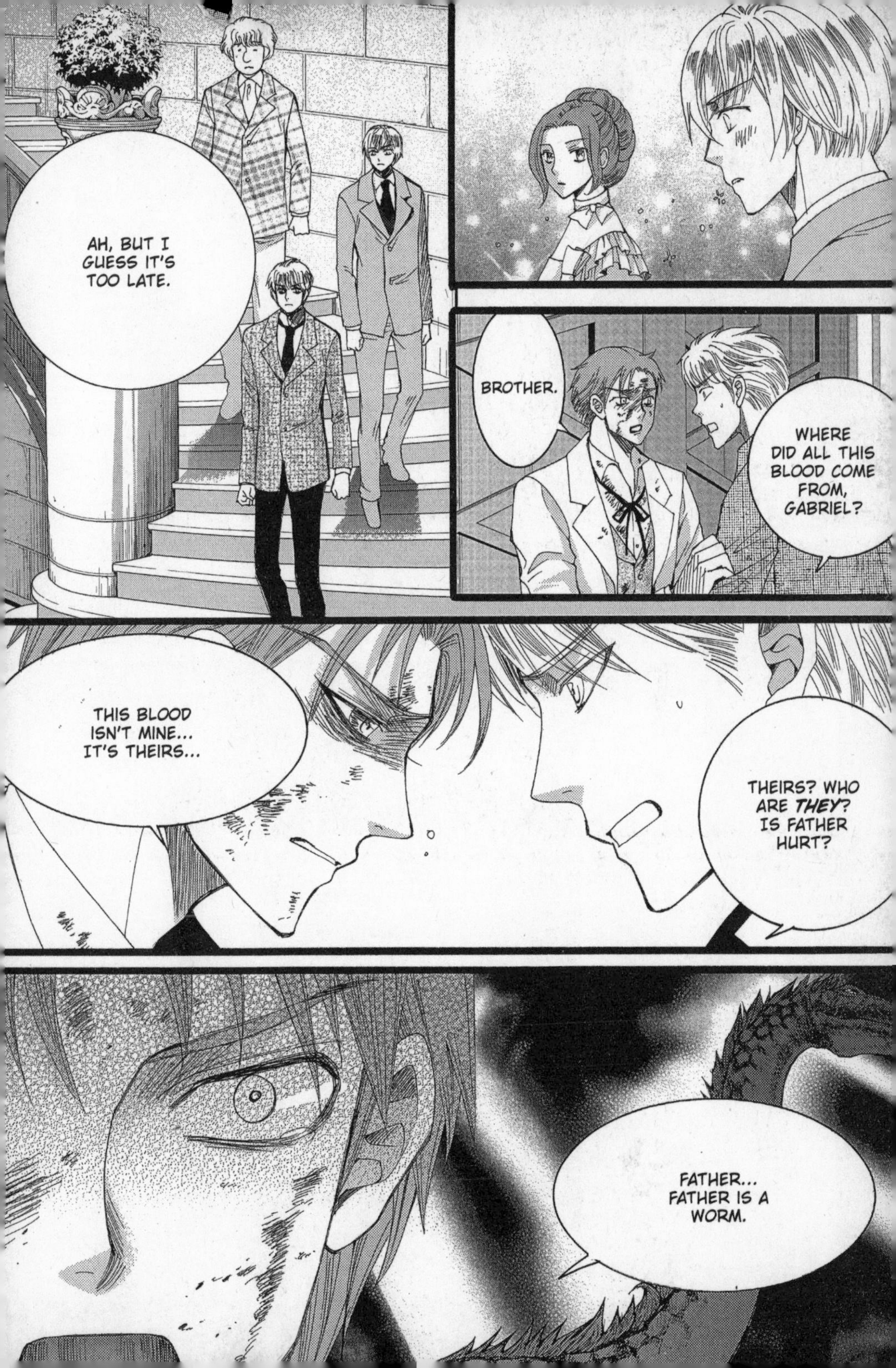
AH, BUT I GUESS IT'S TOO LATE.
BROTHER.
WHERE DID ALL THIS BLOOD COME FROM, GABRIEL?
THIS BLOOD ISN'T MINE... IT'S THEIRS...
THEIRS? WHO ARE *THEY*? IS FATHER HURT?
FATHER... FATHER IS A WORM.

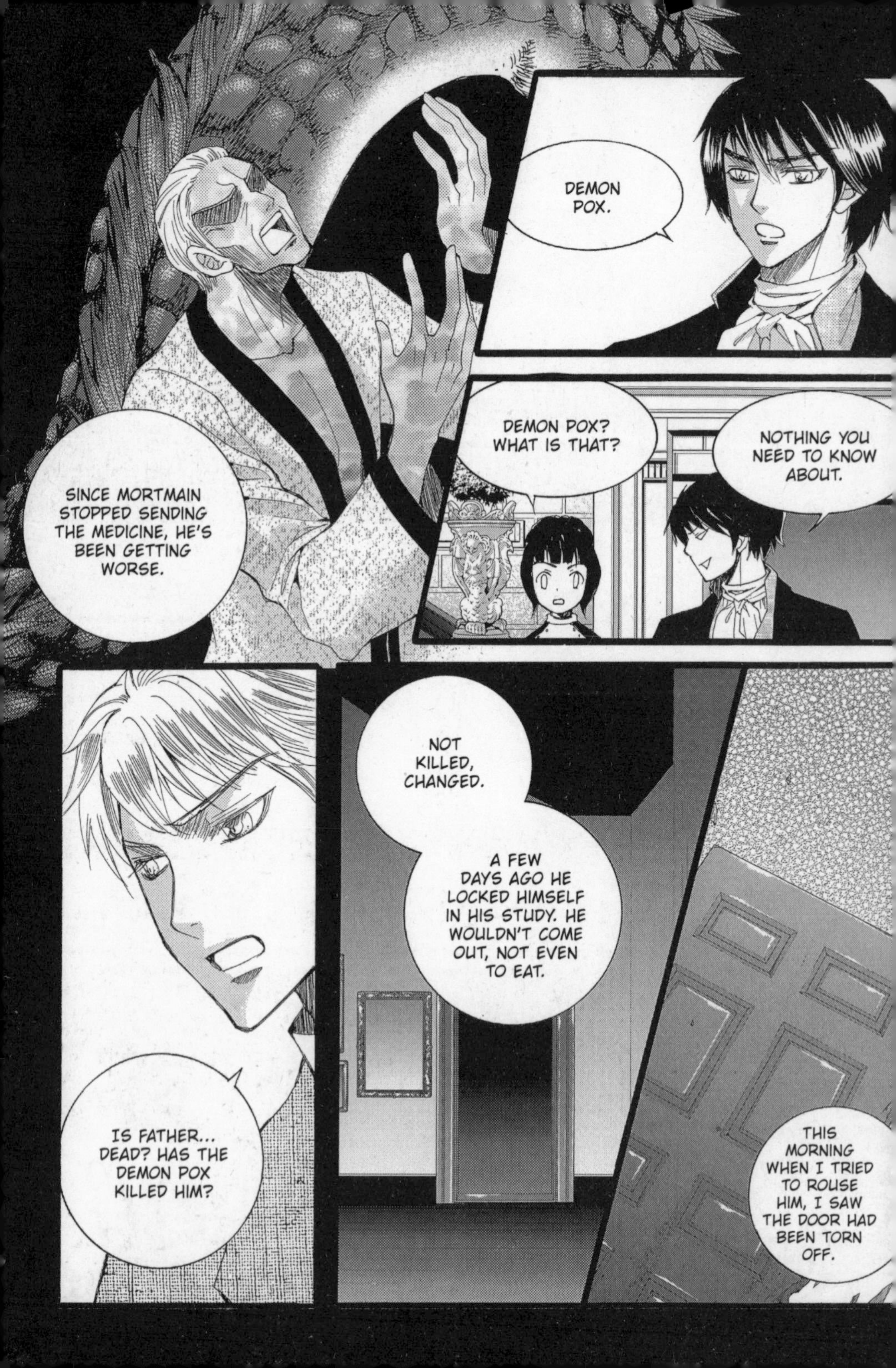
SINCE MORTMAIN STOPPED SENDING THE MEDICINE, HE'S BEEN GETTING WORSE.
DEMON POX.
DEMON POX? WHAT IS THAT?
NOTHING YOU NEED TO KNOW ABOUT.
IS FATHER... DEAD? HAS THE DEMON POX KILLED HIM?
NOT KILLED, CHANGED.
A FEW DAYS AGO HE LOCKED HIMSELF IN HIS STUDY. HE WOULDN'T COME OUT, NOT EVEN TO EAT.
THIS MORNING WHEN I TRIED TO ROUSE HIM, I SAW THE DOOR HAD BEEN TORN OFF.

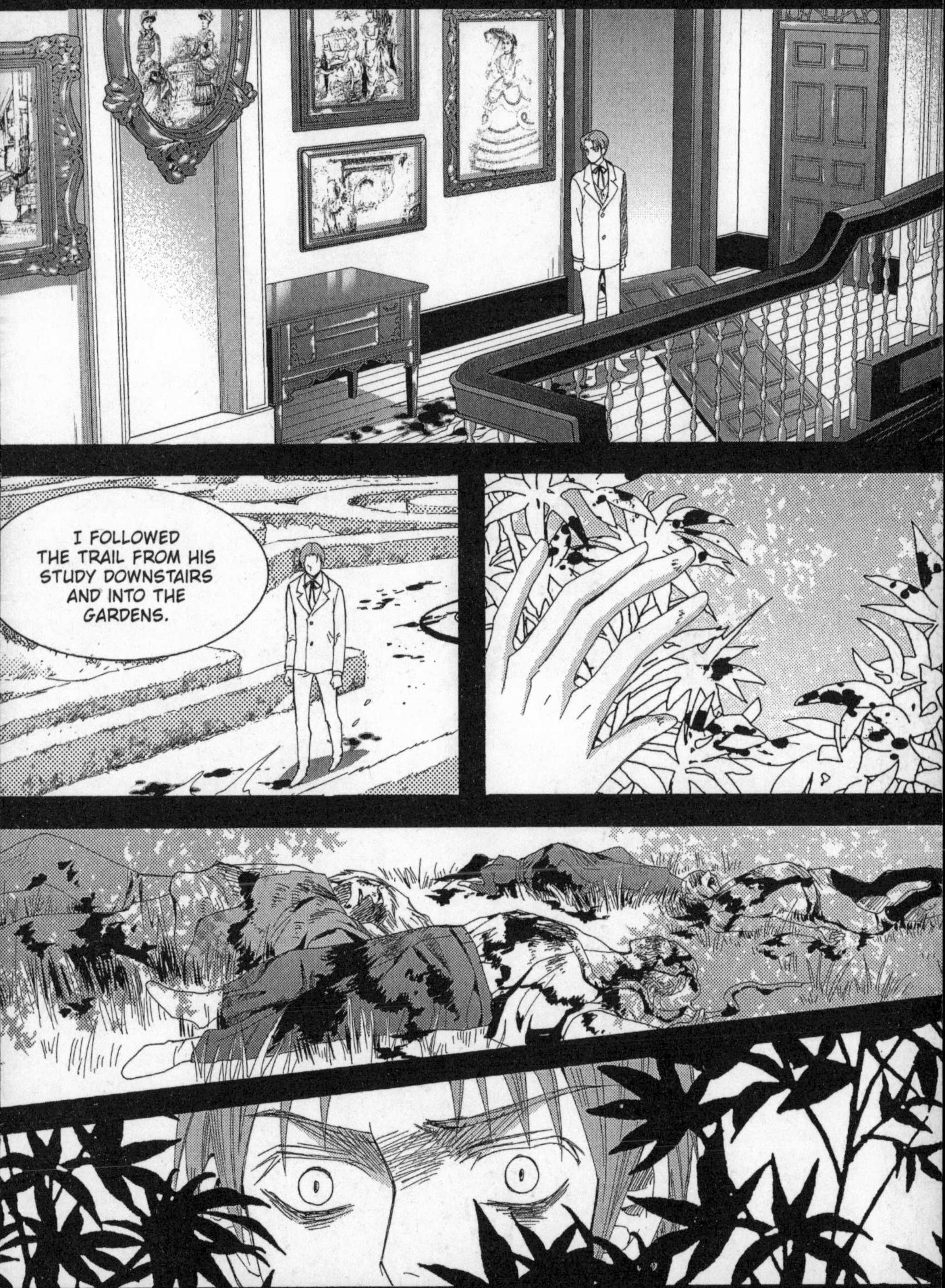
I FOLLOWED THE TRAIL FROM HIS STUDY DOWNSTAIRS AND INTO THE GARDENS.

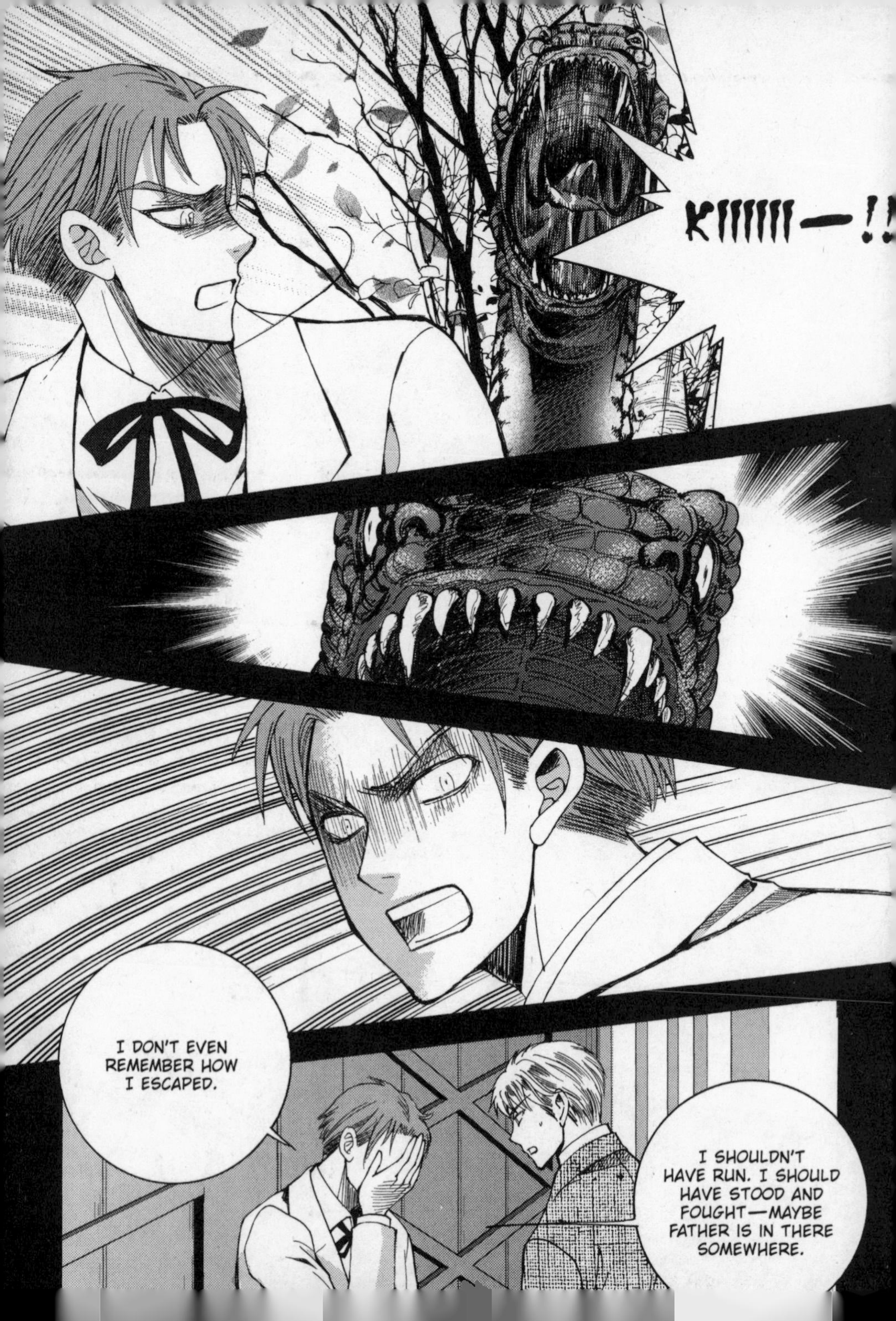
KIIIIII—!!
I DON'T EVEN REMEMBER HOW I ESCAPED.
I SHOULDN'T HAVE RUN. I SHOULD HAVE STOOD AND FOUGHT—MAYBE FATHER IS IN THERE SOMEWHERE.

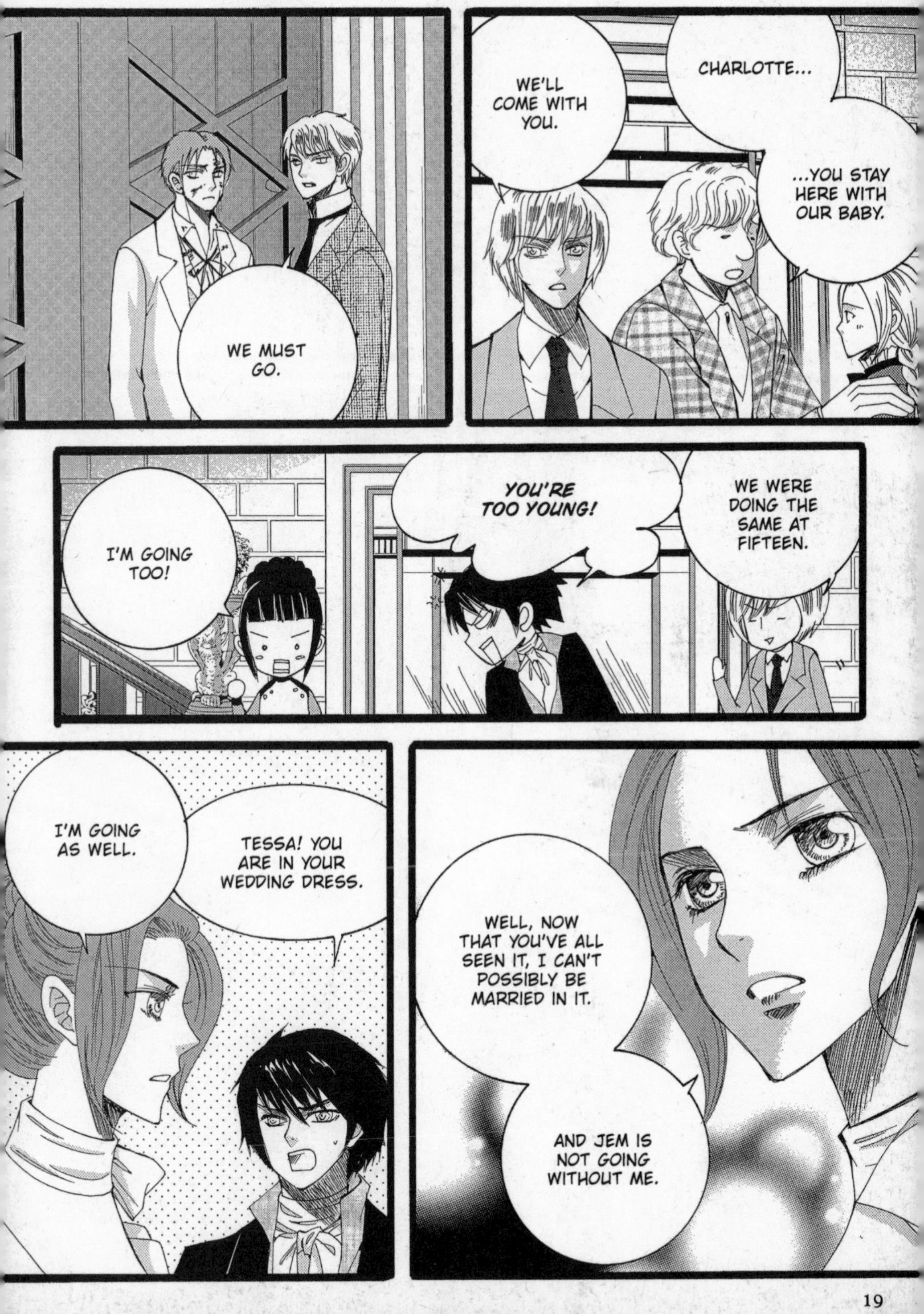
WE MUST GO.
WE'LL COME WITH YOU.
CHARLOTTE...
...YOU STAY HERE WITH OUR BABY.
I'M GOING TOO!
YOU'RE TOO YOUNG!
WE WERE DOING THE SAME AT FIFTEEN.
I'M GOING AS WELL.
TESSA! YOU ARE IN YOUR WEDDING DRESS.
WELL, NOW THAT YOU'VE ALL SEEN IT, I CAN'T POSSIBLY BE MARRIED IN IT.
AND JEM IS NOT GOING WITHOUT ME.

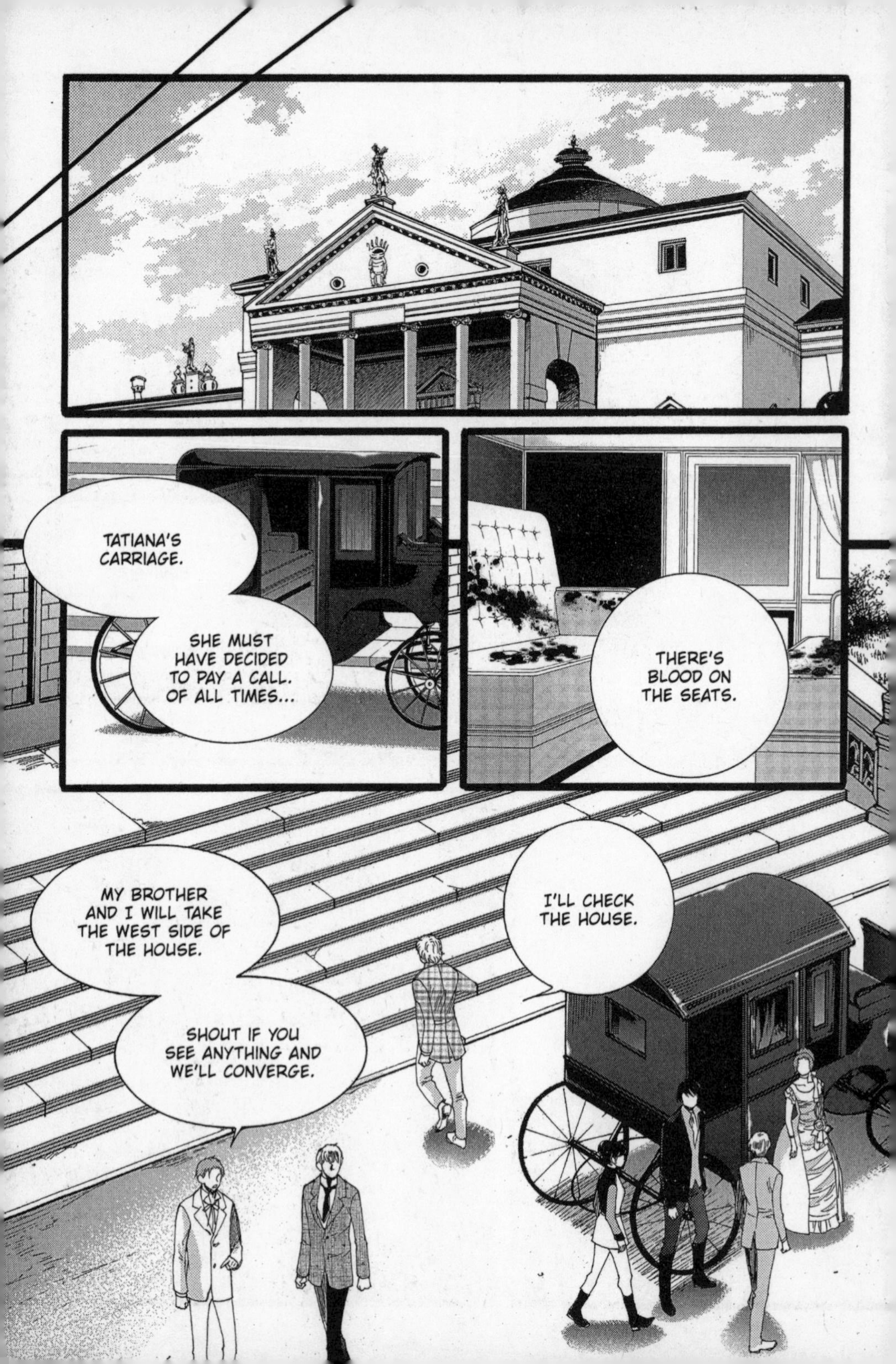
TATIANA'S CARRIAGE.
SHE MUST HAVE DECIDED TO PAY A CALL. OF ALL TIMES...
THERE'S BLOOD ON THE SEATS.
MY BROTHER AND I WILL TAKE THE WEST SIDE OF THE HOUSE.
SHOUT IF YOU SEE ANYTHING AND WE'LL CONVERGE.
I'LL CHECK THE HOUSE.

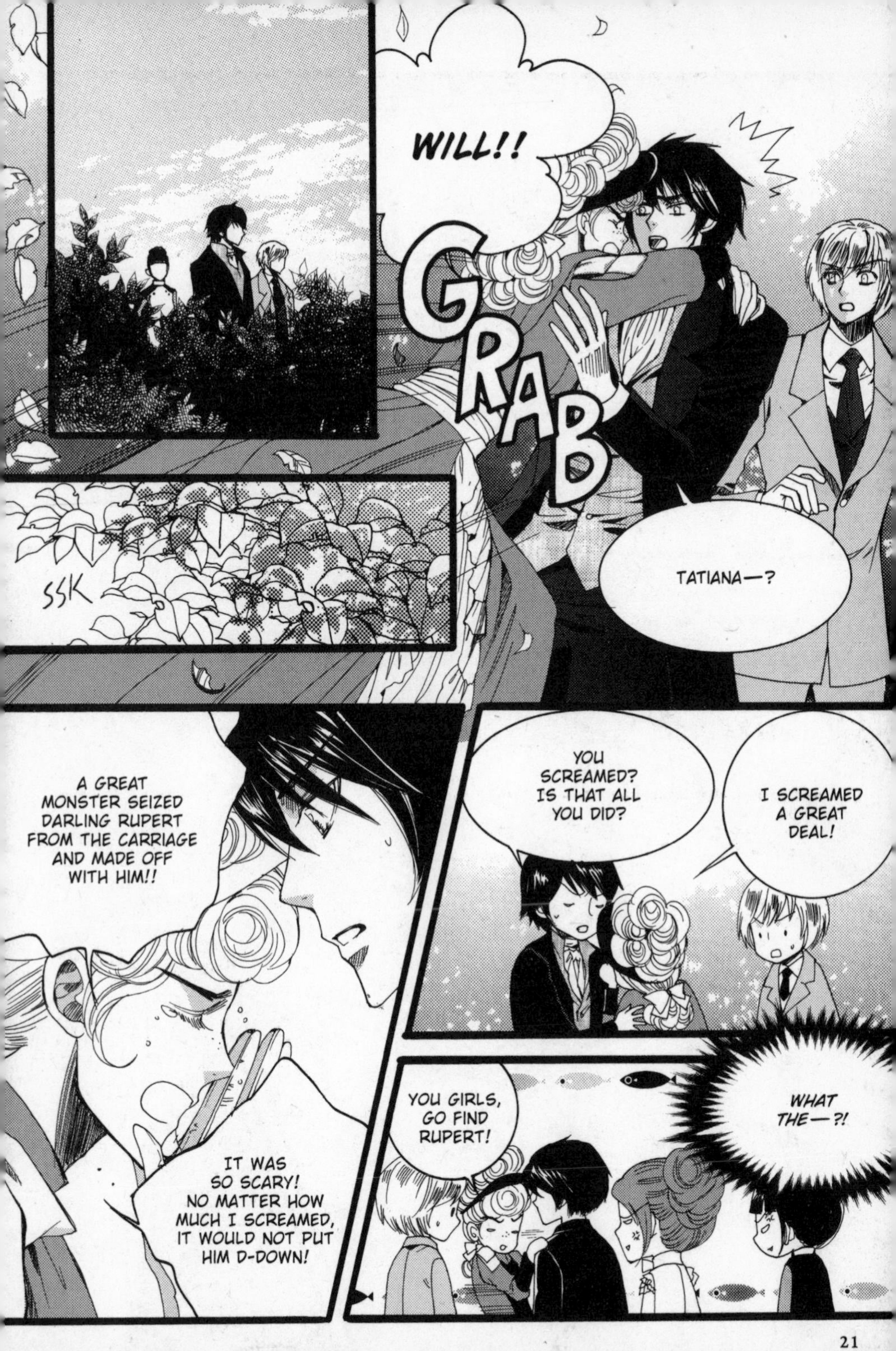

SSK
WILL!!
GRAB
TATIANA—?
A GREAT MONSTER SEIZED DARLING RUPERT FROM THE CARRIAGE AND MADE OFF WITH HIM!!
IT WAS SO SCARY! NO MATTER HOW MUCH I SCREAMED, IT WOULD NOT PUT HIM D-DOWN!
YOU SCREAMED? IS THAT ALL YOU DID?
I SCREAMED A GREAT DEAL!
YOU GIRLS, GO FIND RUPERT!
WHAT THE—?!

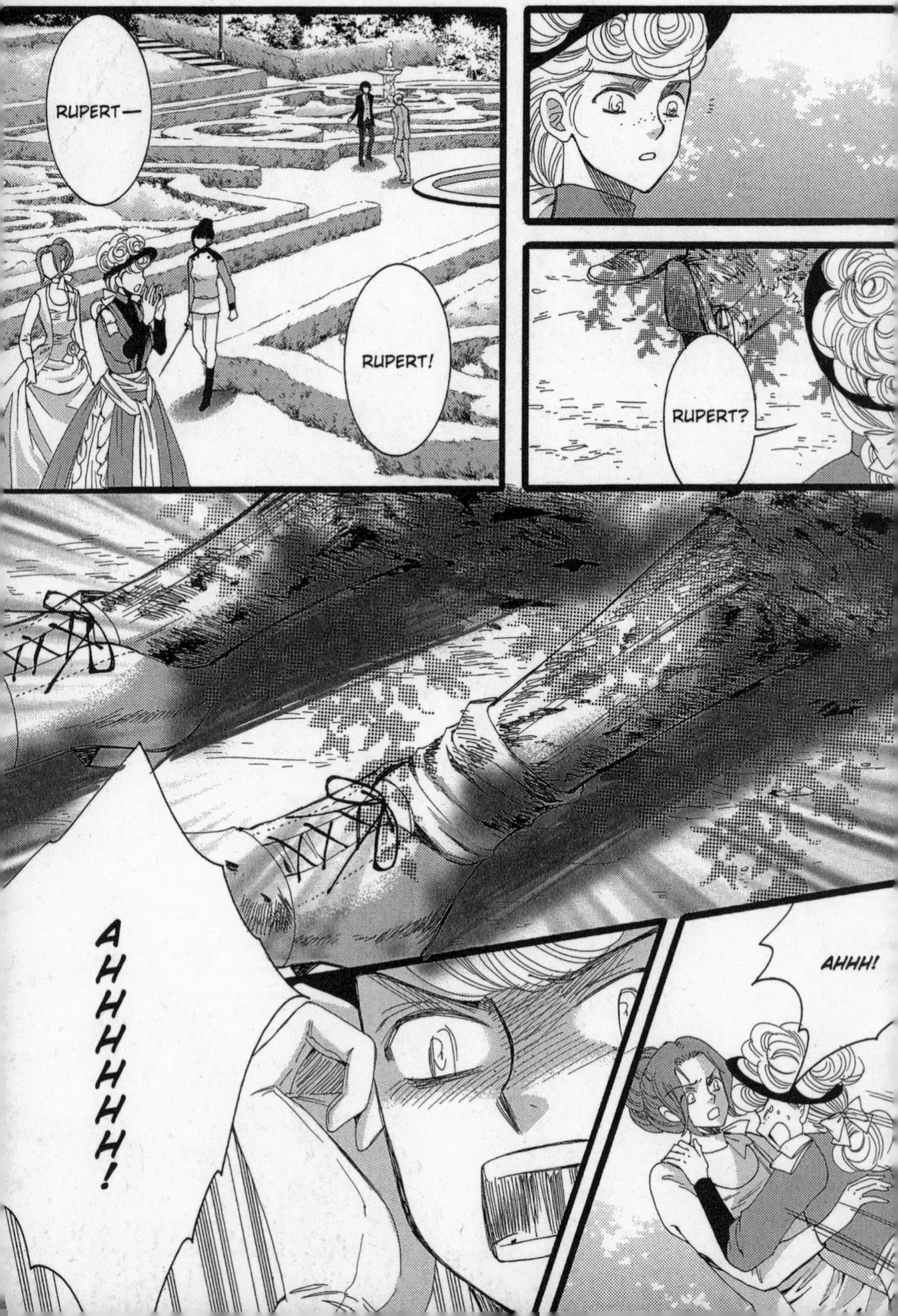
RUPERT—
RUPERT!
RUPERT?
AHHHHHHH!
AHHH!

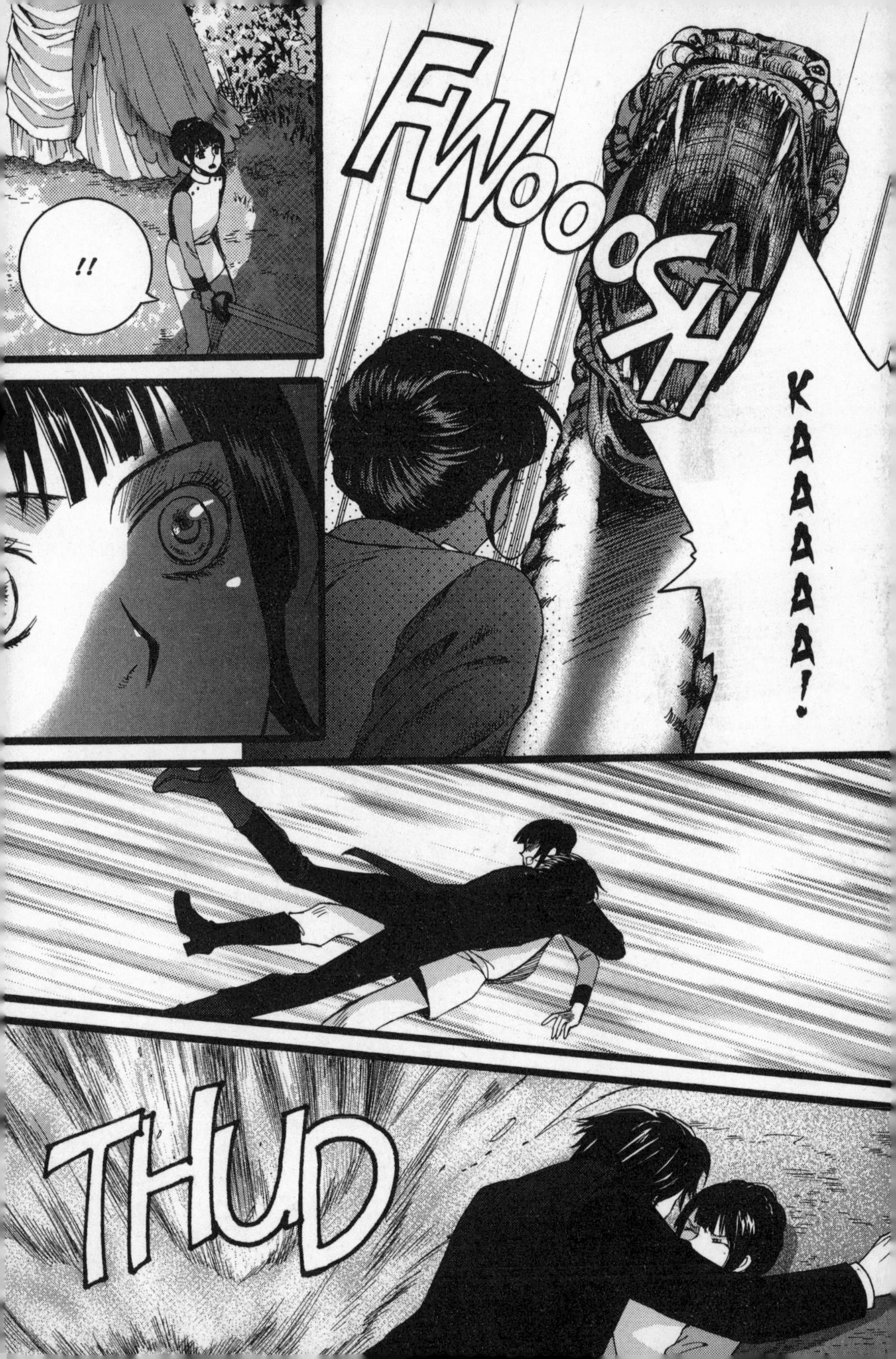
FWOOOSH
KAAAAAA!
!!
THUD

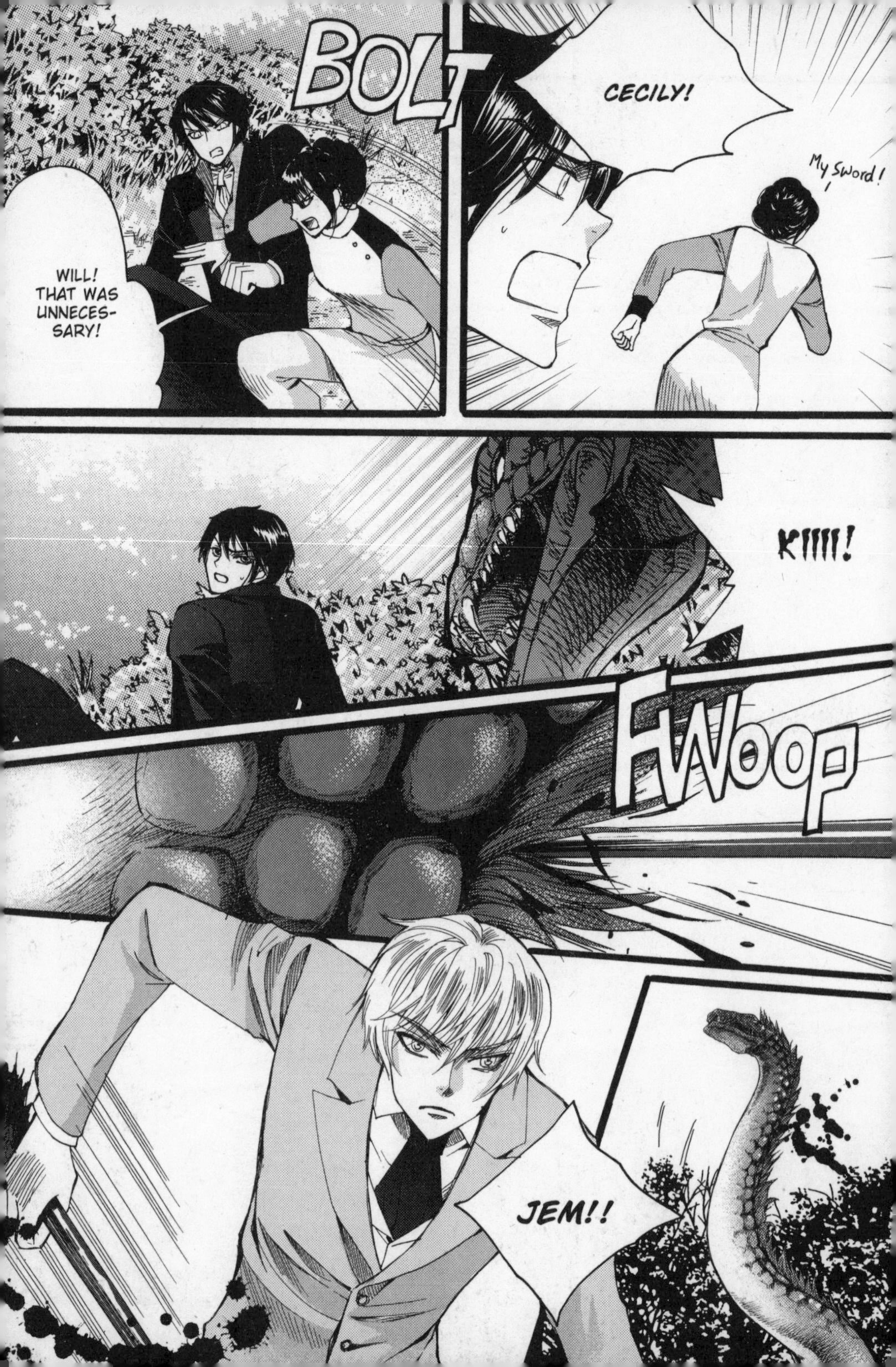

BOLT
WILL! THAT WAS UNNECES-SARY!
CECILY!
My Sword!
KIIII!
FWOOP
JEM!!

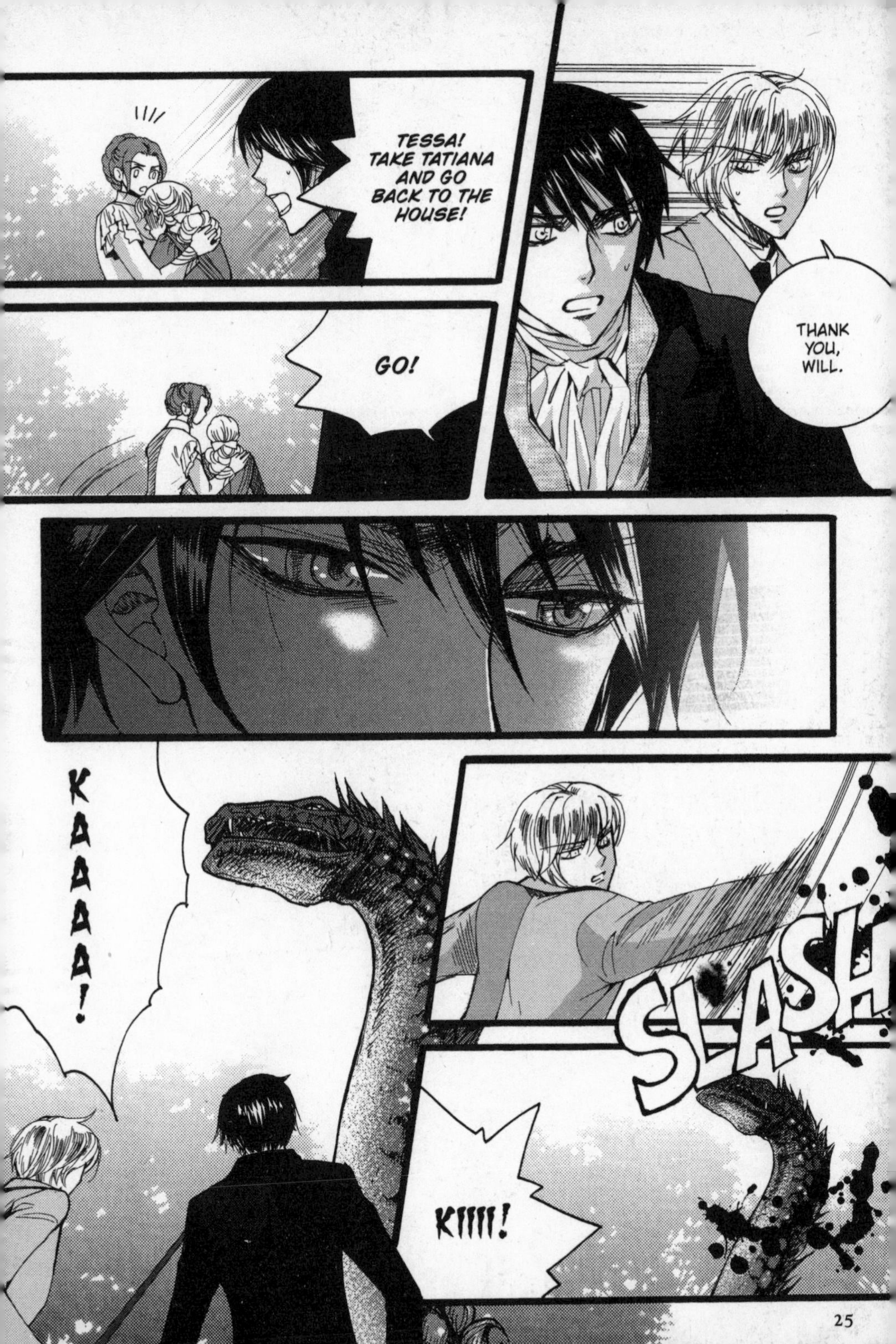
!!!/
TESSA! TAKE TATIANA AND GO BACK TO THE HOUSE!
GO!
THANK YOU, WILL.
KAAAAA!
SLASH
KIIII!

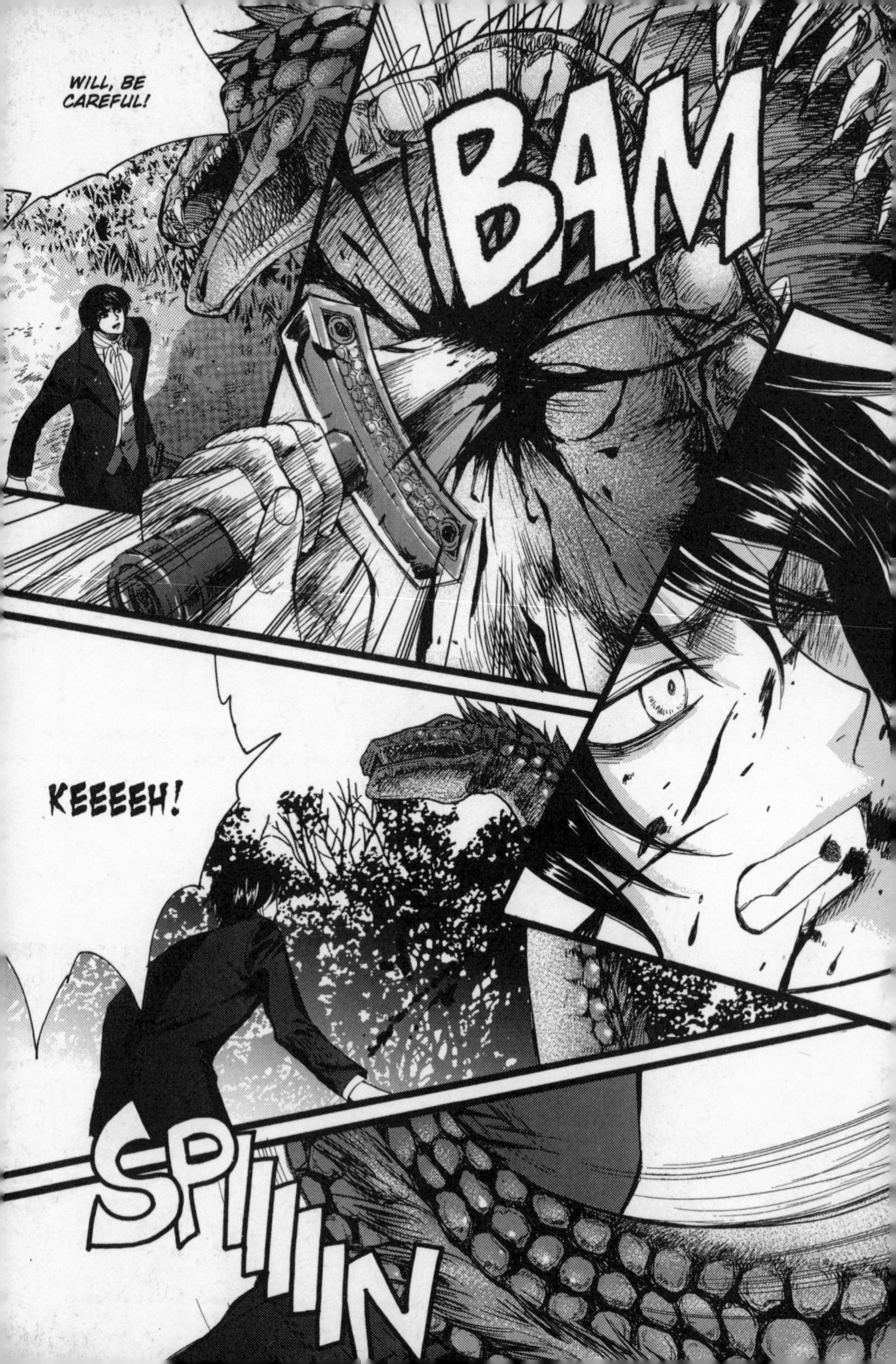
WILL, BE CAREFUL!
BAM
KEEEEH!
SPIIIIN

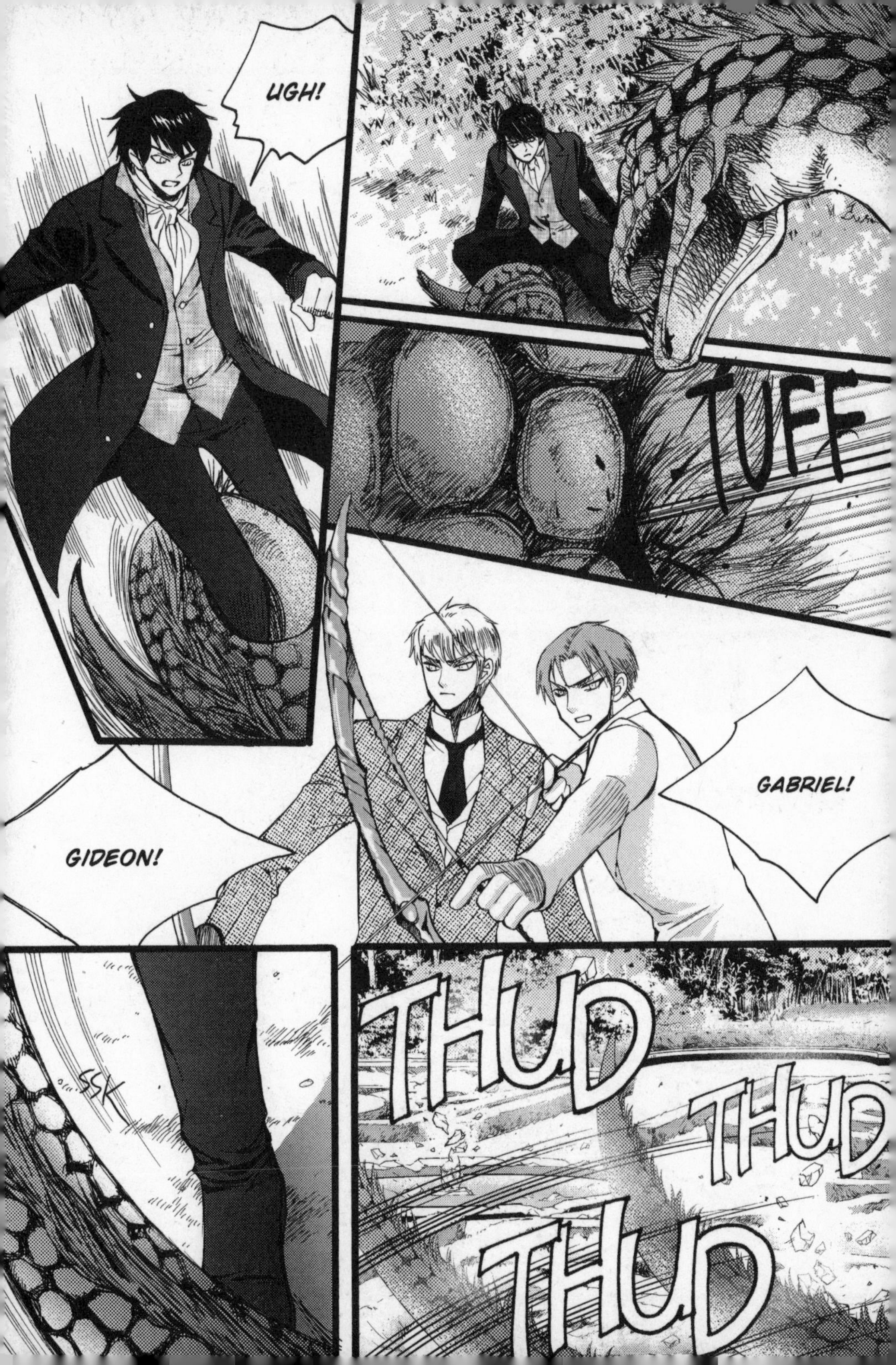
UGH!
TUFF
GIDEON!
GABRIEL!
SSK
THUD
THUD
THUD

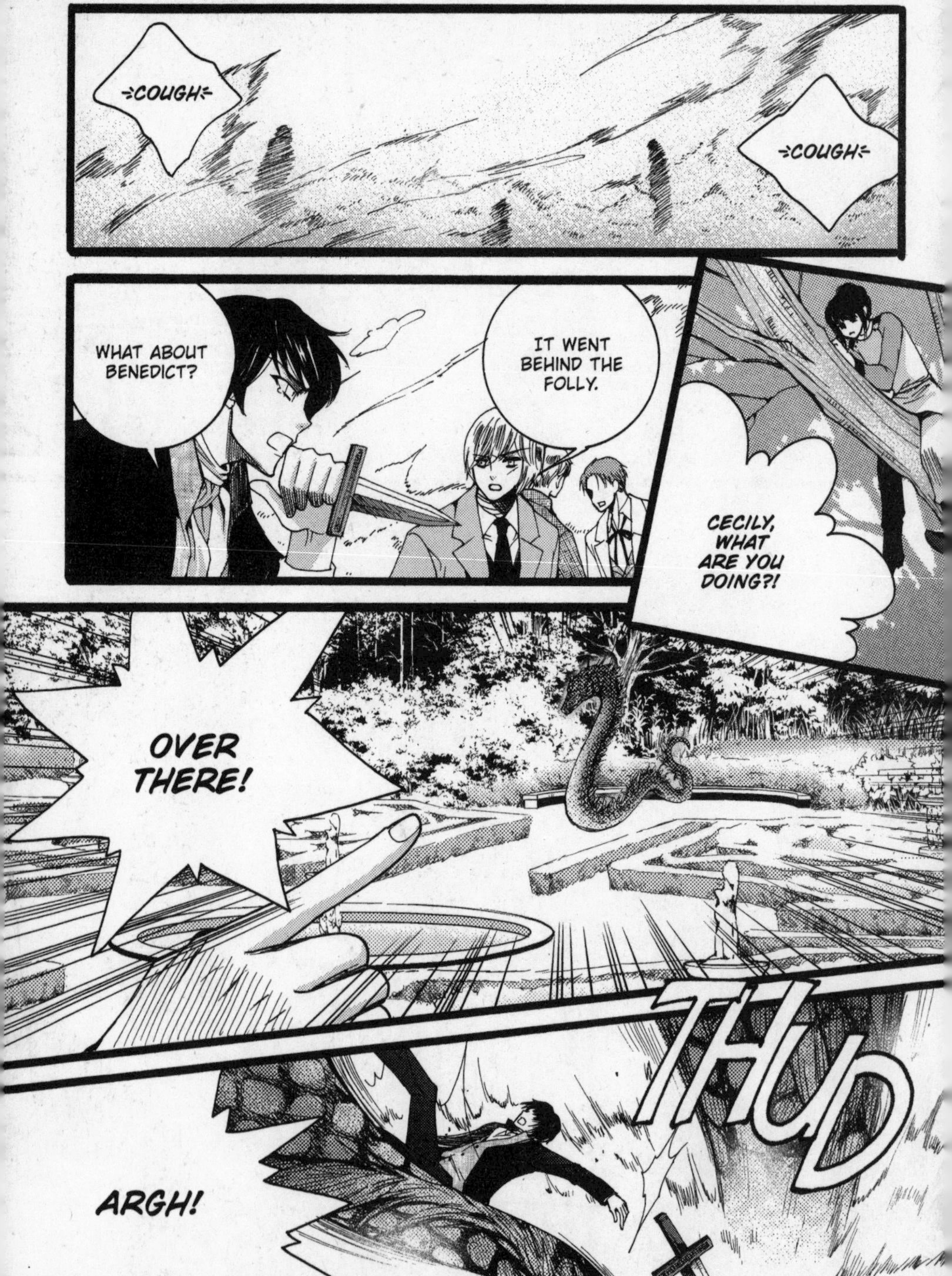

COUGH
COUGH
IT WENT BEHIND THE FOLLY.
WHAT ABOUT BENEDICT?
CECILY, WHAT ARE YOU DOING?!
OVER THERE!
THUD
ARGH!

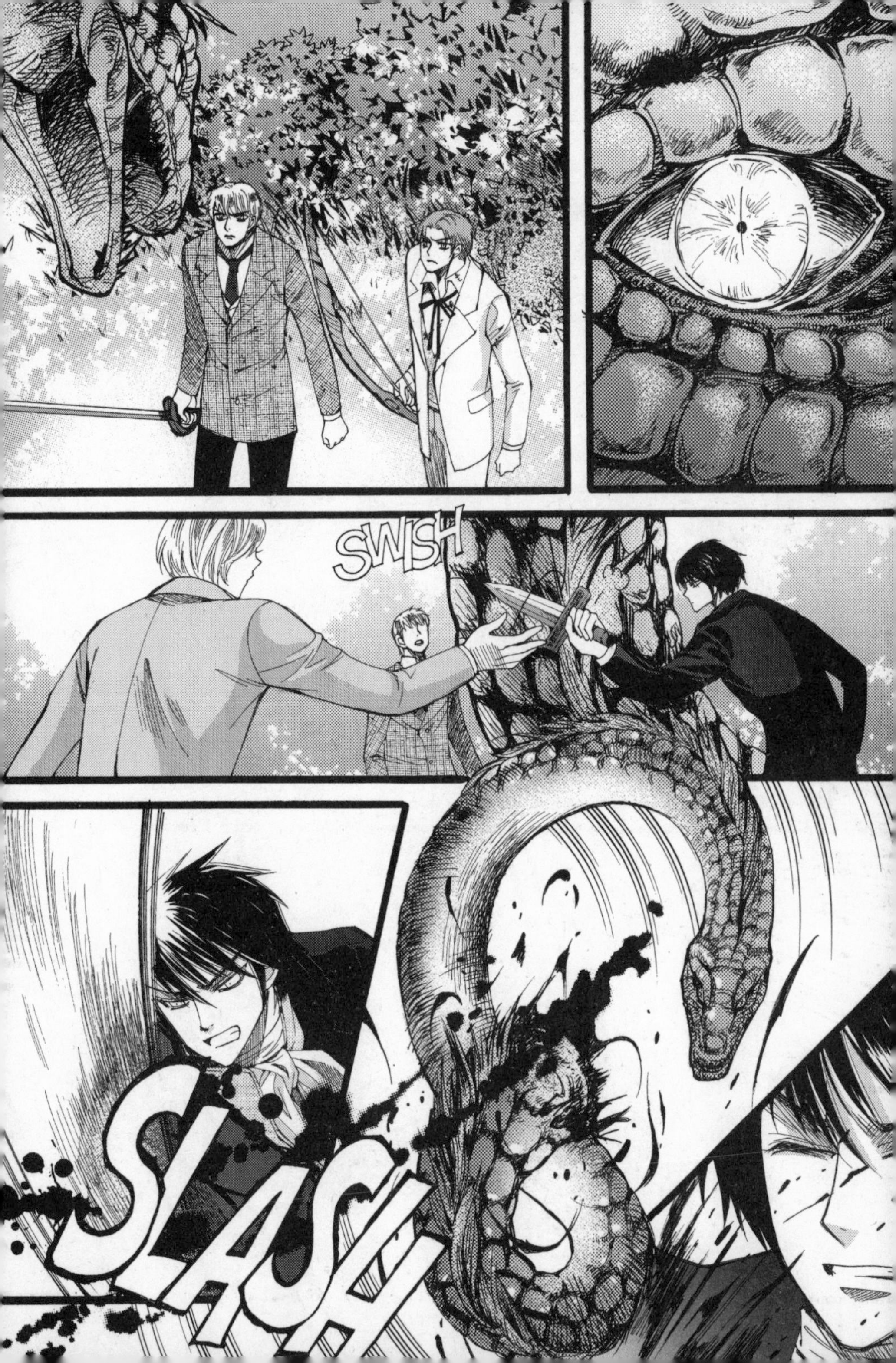
SWISH
SLASH

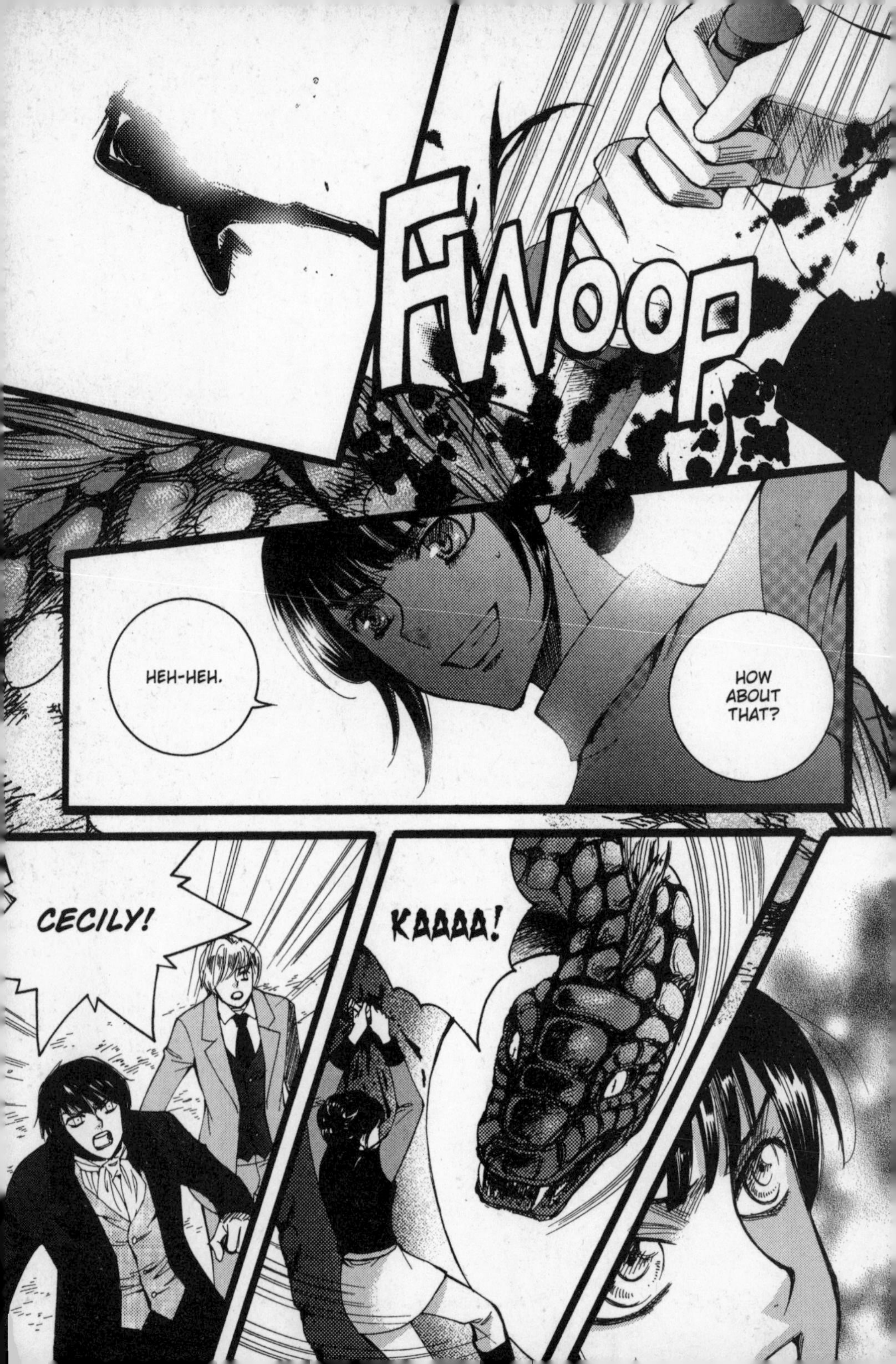
FWOOP
HOW ABOUT THAT?
HEH-HEH.
KAAAA!
CECILY!

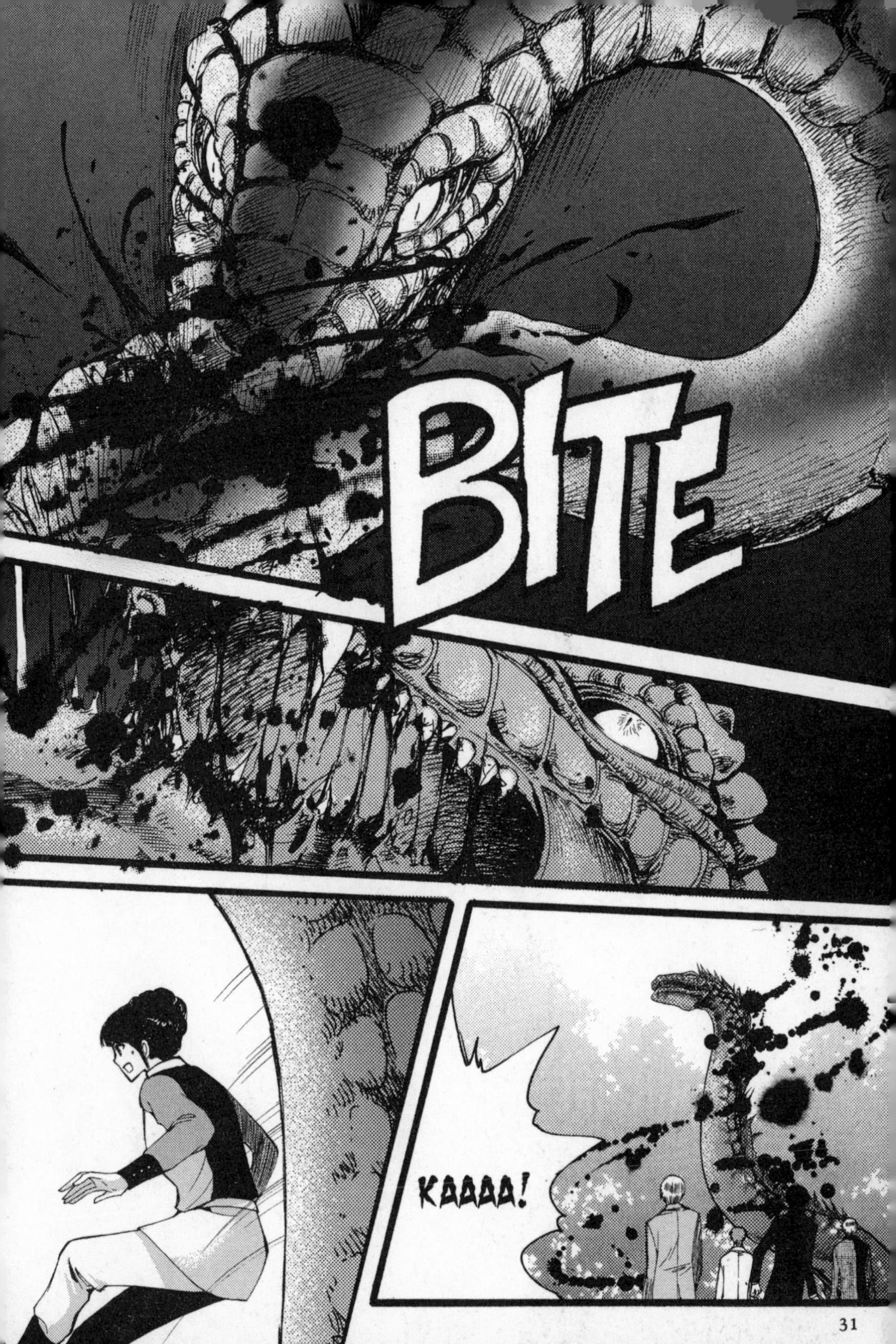
BITE
KAAAA!

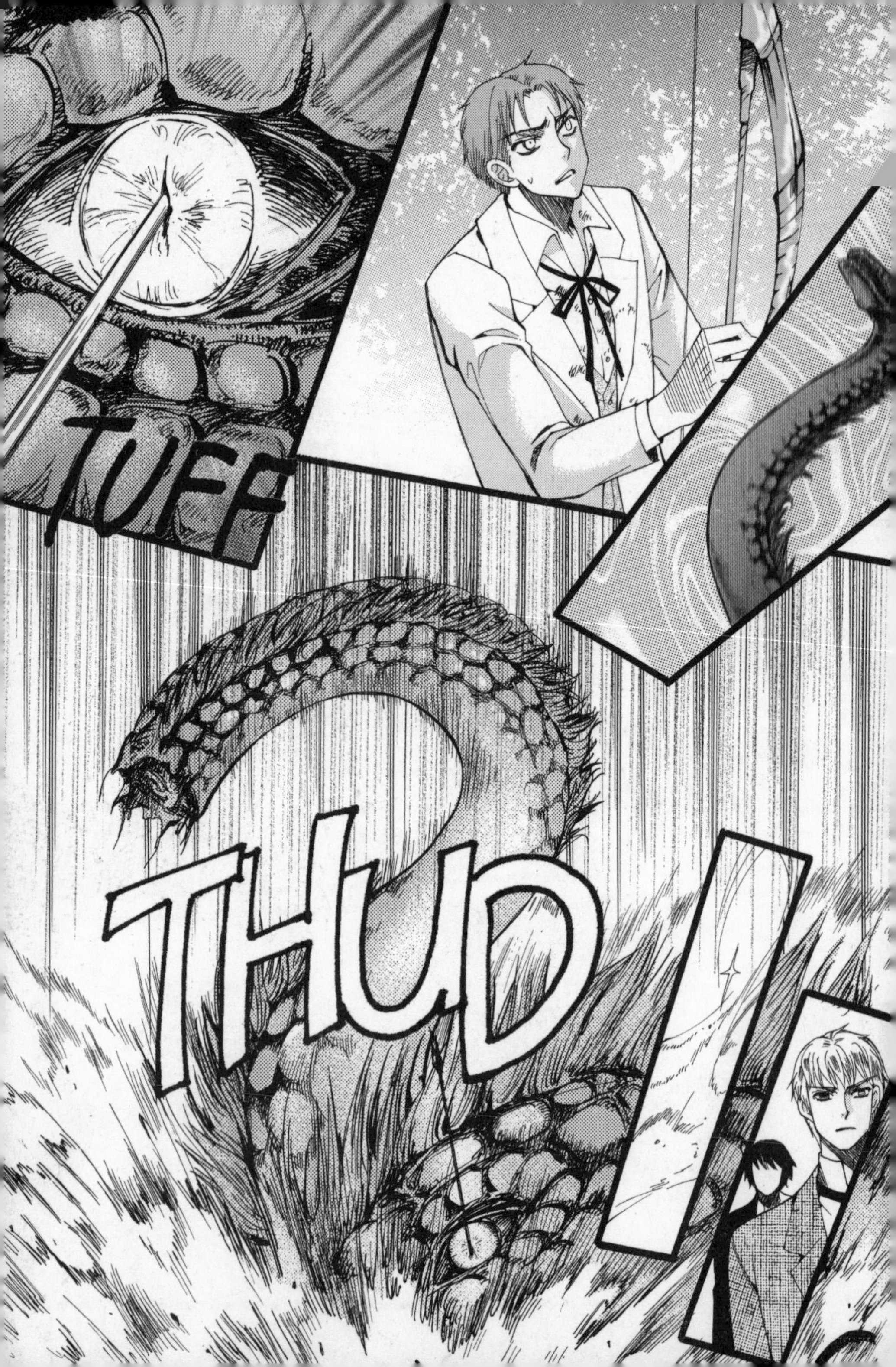
TUFF
THUD!!

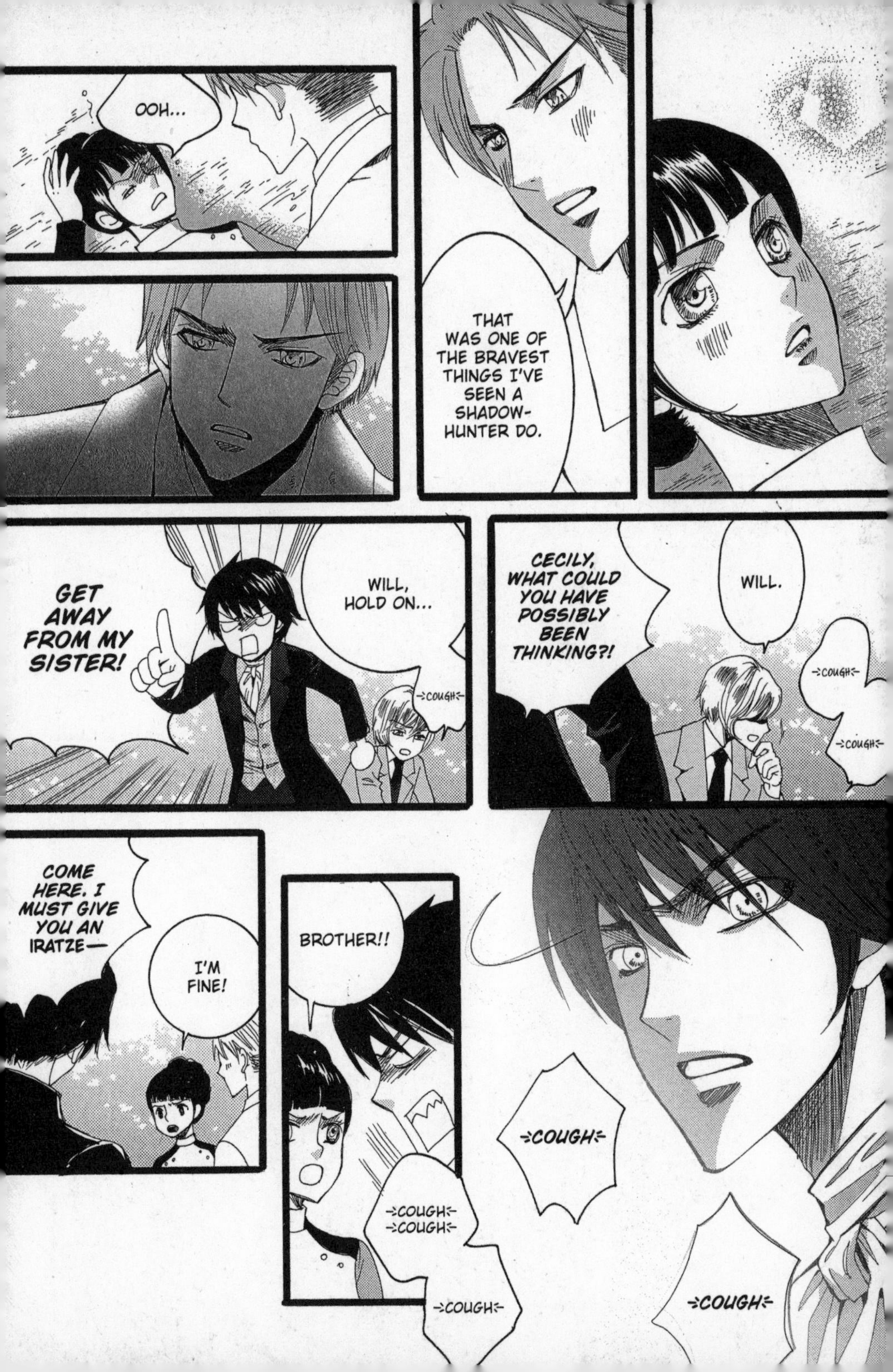
OOH...
THAT WAS ONE OF THE BRAVEST THINGS I'VE SEEN A SHADOW-HUNTER DO.
GET AWAY FROM MY SISTER!
WILL, HOLD ON...
COUGH
CECILY, WHAT COULD YOU HAVE POSSIBLY BEEN THINKING?!
WILL.
COUGH
COUGH
COME HERE. I MUST GIVE YOU AN IRATZE—
I'M FINE!
BROTHER!!
COUGH
COUGH
COUGH
COUGH
COUGH
COUGH

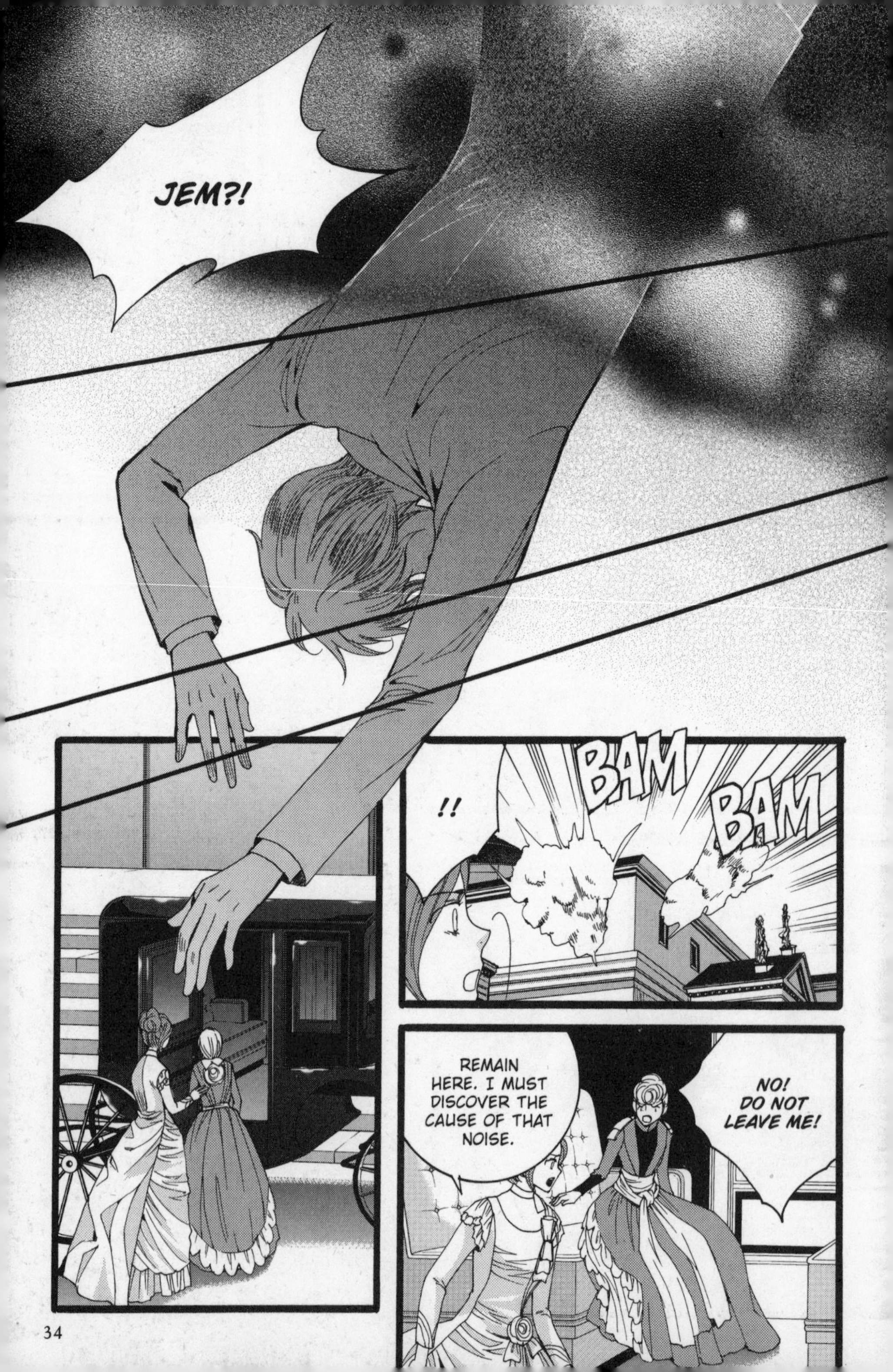
JEM?!
!!
BAM
BAM
NO! DO NOT LEAVE ME!
REMAIN HERE. I MUST DISCOVER THE CAUSE OF THAT NOISE.

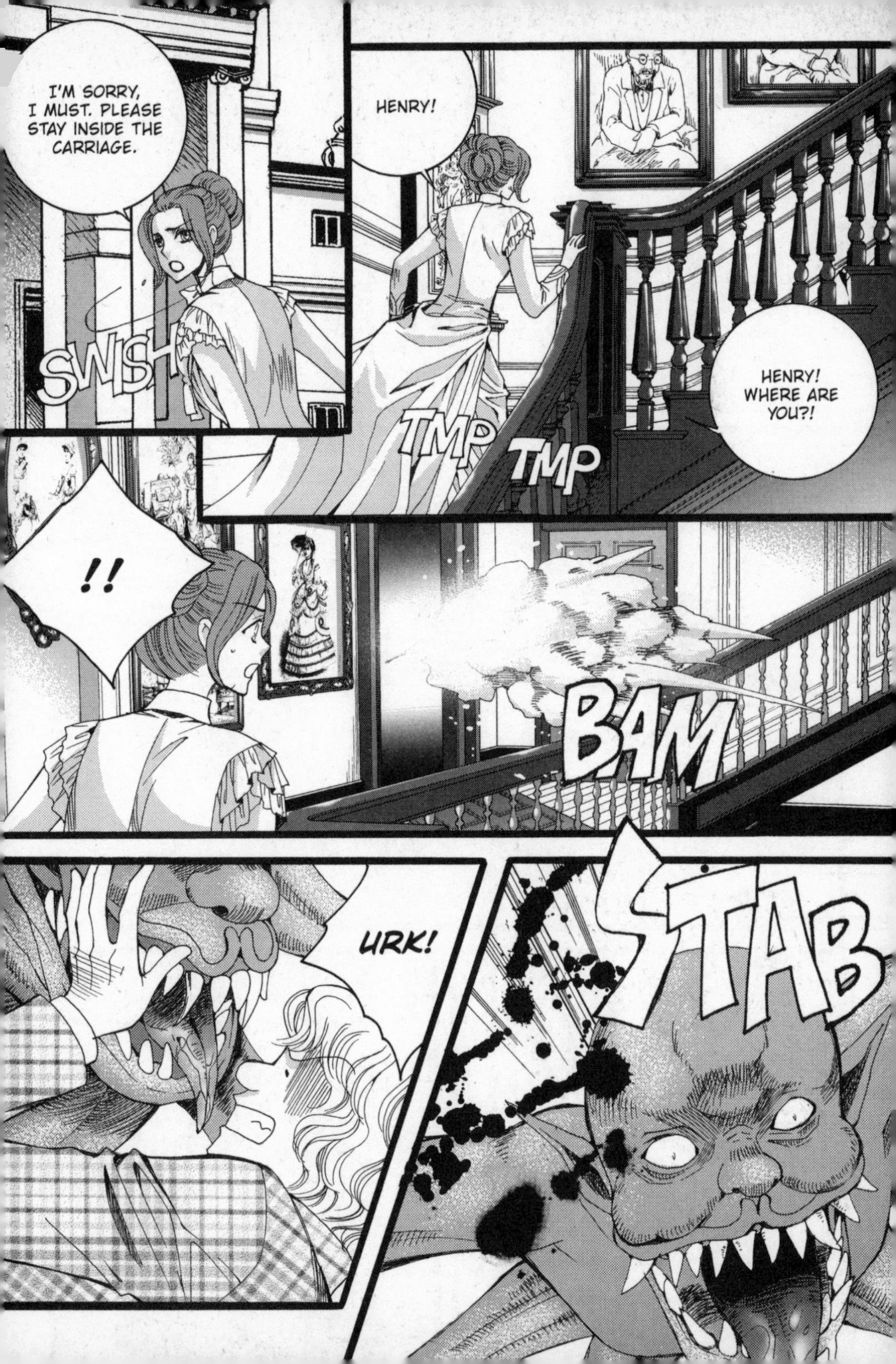
I'M SORRY, I MUST. PLEASE STAY INSIDE THE CARRIAGE.
SWISH
HENRY!
HENRY! WHERE ARE YOU?!
TMP TMP
!!
BAM
URK!
STAB

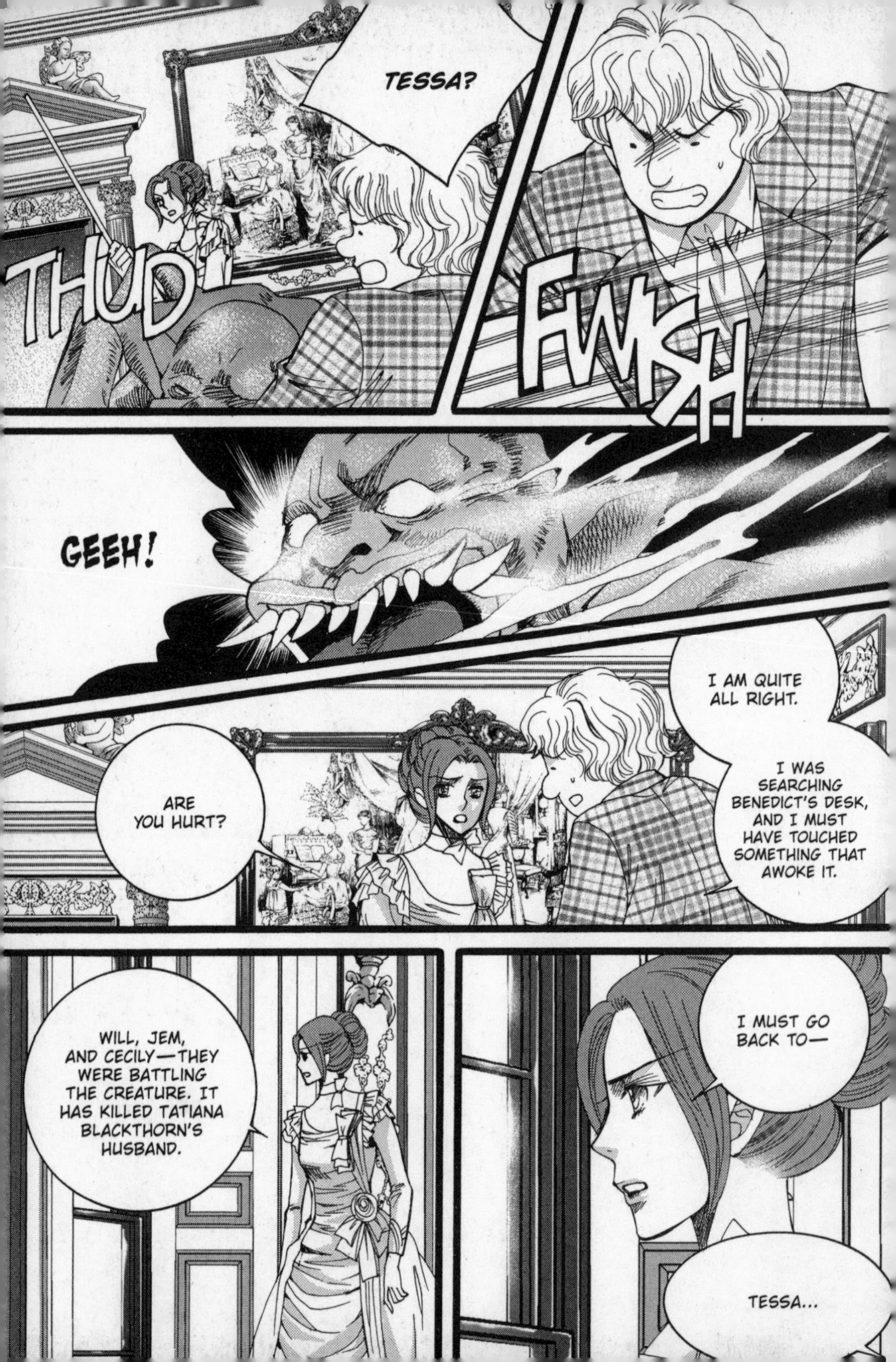
THUD
TESSA?
FWISH
GEEH!
I AM QUITE ALL RIGHT.
I WAS SEARCHING BENEDICT'S DESK, AND I MUST HAVE TOUCHED SOMETHING THAT AWOKE IT.
ARE YOU HURT?
I MUST GO BACK TO—
TESSA...
WILL, JEM, AND CECILY—THEY WERE BATTLING THE CREATURE. IT HAS KILLED TATIANA BLACKTHORN'S HUSBAND.

The Infernal Devices are
without pity.
The Infernal Devices are
Without regret.
The Infernal Devices are
without number.
The Infernal DEvices will
NEVER Stop Coming.
The Infernal DEvices
NEVER Stop Coming.

To: Consul Josiah Wayland
From: The Council

Dear Sir,
As you are doubtless aware, your term of service as Consul, after ten years,
is coming to an end. The time has come to appoint a successor.
As for ourselves, we are giving serious consideration to the appointment of
Charlotte Branwell. She has done good work as the head of the London Institute,
and we believe her to have your stamp of approval, as she was appointed
by you after the death of her father.
As your opinion and esteem are to us of the highest value, we would appreciate
any thoughts that you might have on the matter.
Yours with the hightest regards,
Victor Whitelaw, Inquisitor, on behalf of the Council.

To: Members of the Council
From: Consul Josiah Wayland

Forgive the delay in my reply, gentlemen. I wished to be sure that I was not giving you
my opinions in any spirit of precipitate haste, but rather that my words were the sound
and well-reasoned results of patient thought.
I am afraid I cannot second your recommendation of Charlotte Branwell as my successor.
Though possessed of a good heart, she is altogether too flighty, emotional, passionate,
and disobedient to have the making of a Consul. As we know, the fair sex has its weaknesses
that men are not heir to, and sadly she is prey to all of them. No, I cannot recommend her.
I urge you to consider another—my own nephew, George Penhallow, who will be twenty-five
this November and is a fine Shadowhunter and an upstanding young man. I believe he has
the moral certainty and strength of character to lead the Shadowhunters into a new decade.
In Raziel's name,
Consul Josiah Wayland

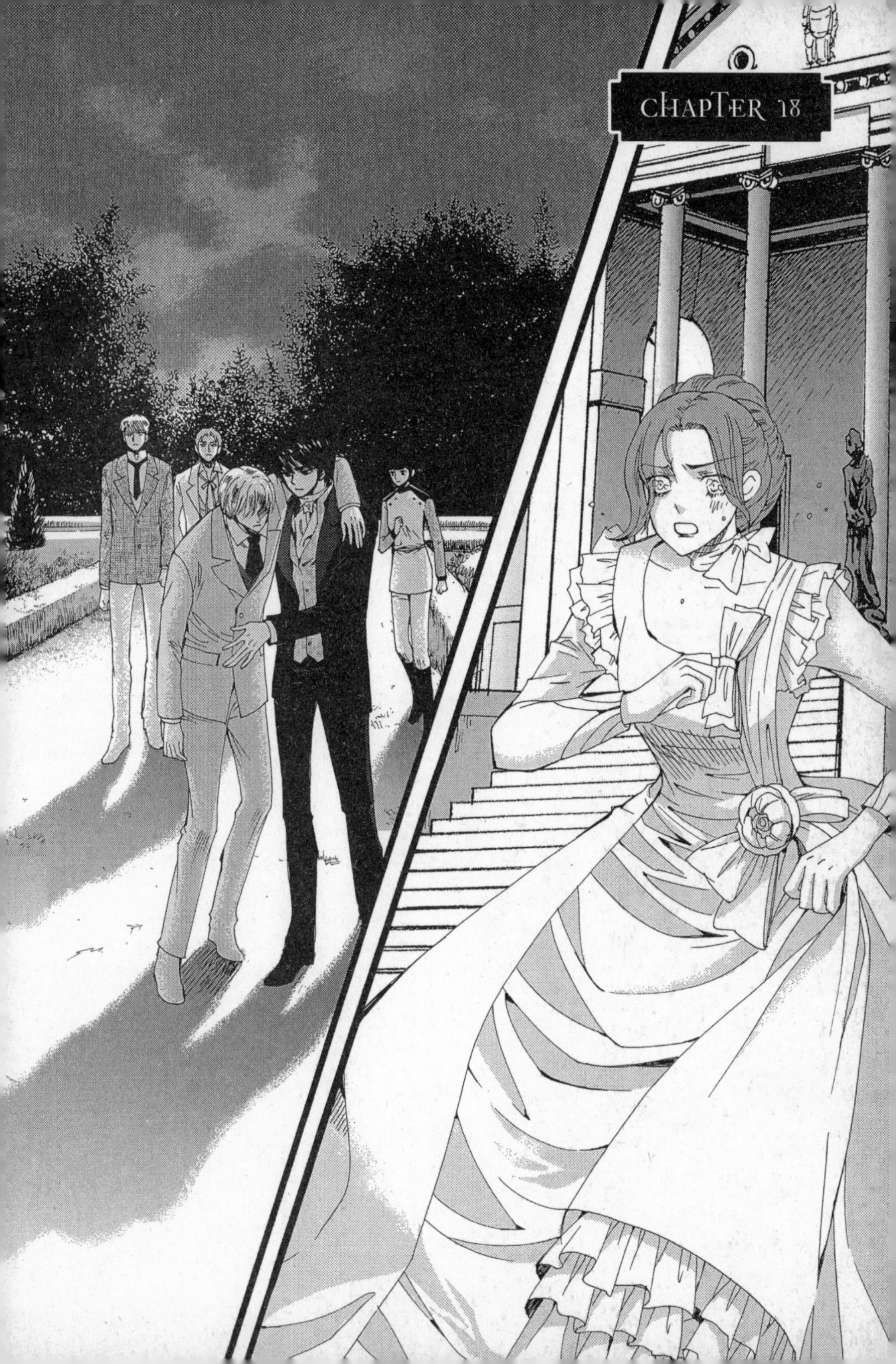
CHAPTER 18

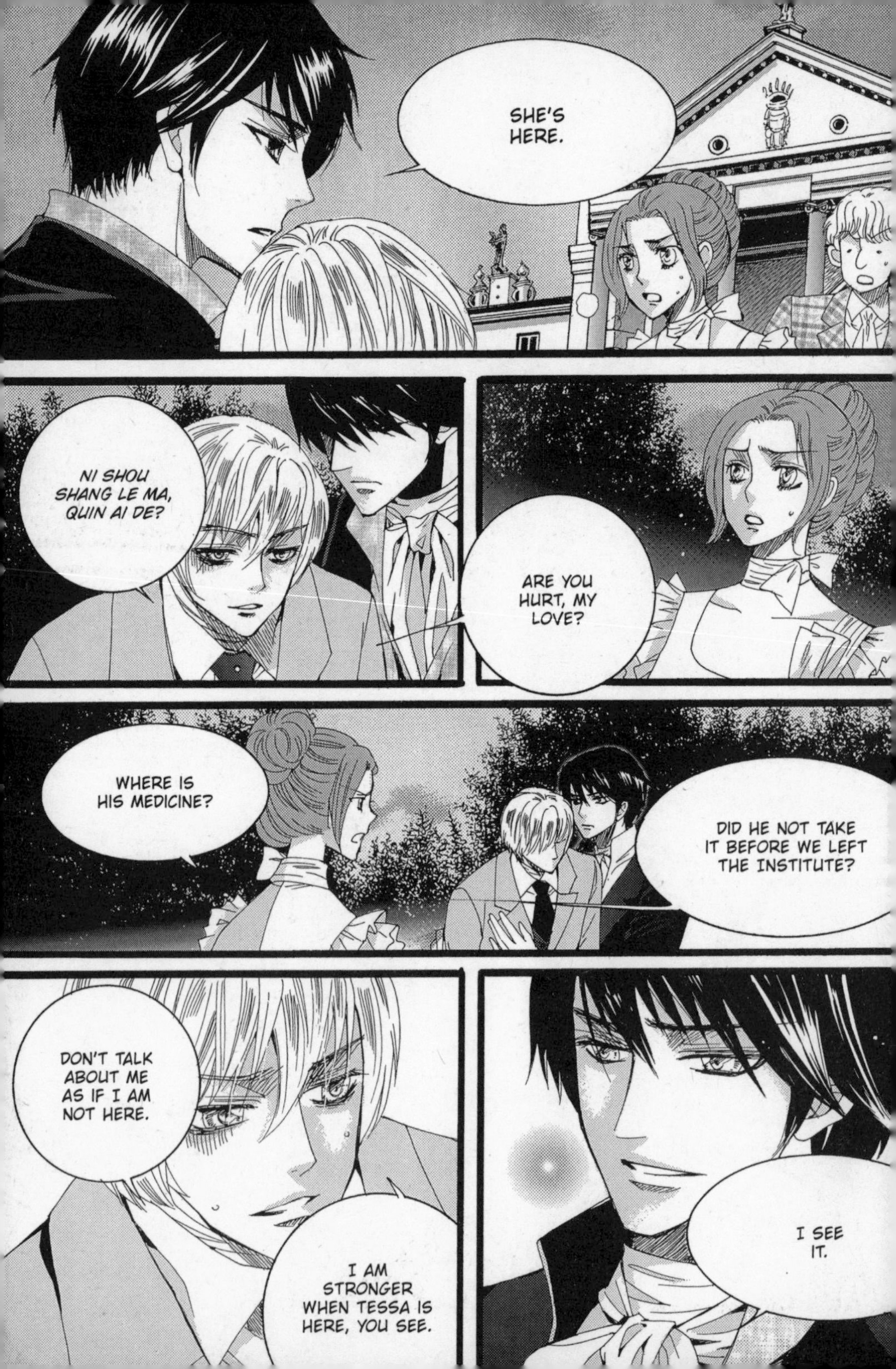
SHE'S HERE.
NI SHOU SHANG LE MA, QUIN AI DE?
ARE YOU HURT, MY LOVE?
WHERE IS HIS MEDICINE?
DID HE NOT TAKE IT BEFORE WE LEFT THE INSTITUTE?
DON'T TALK ABOUT ME AS IF I AM NOT HERE.
I AM STRONGER WHEN TESSA IS HERE, YOU SEE.
I SEE IT.

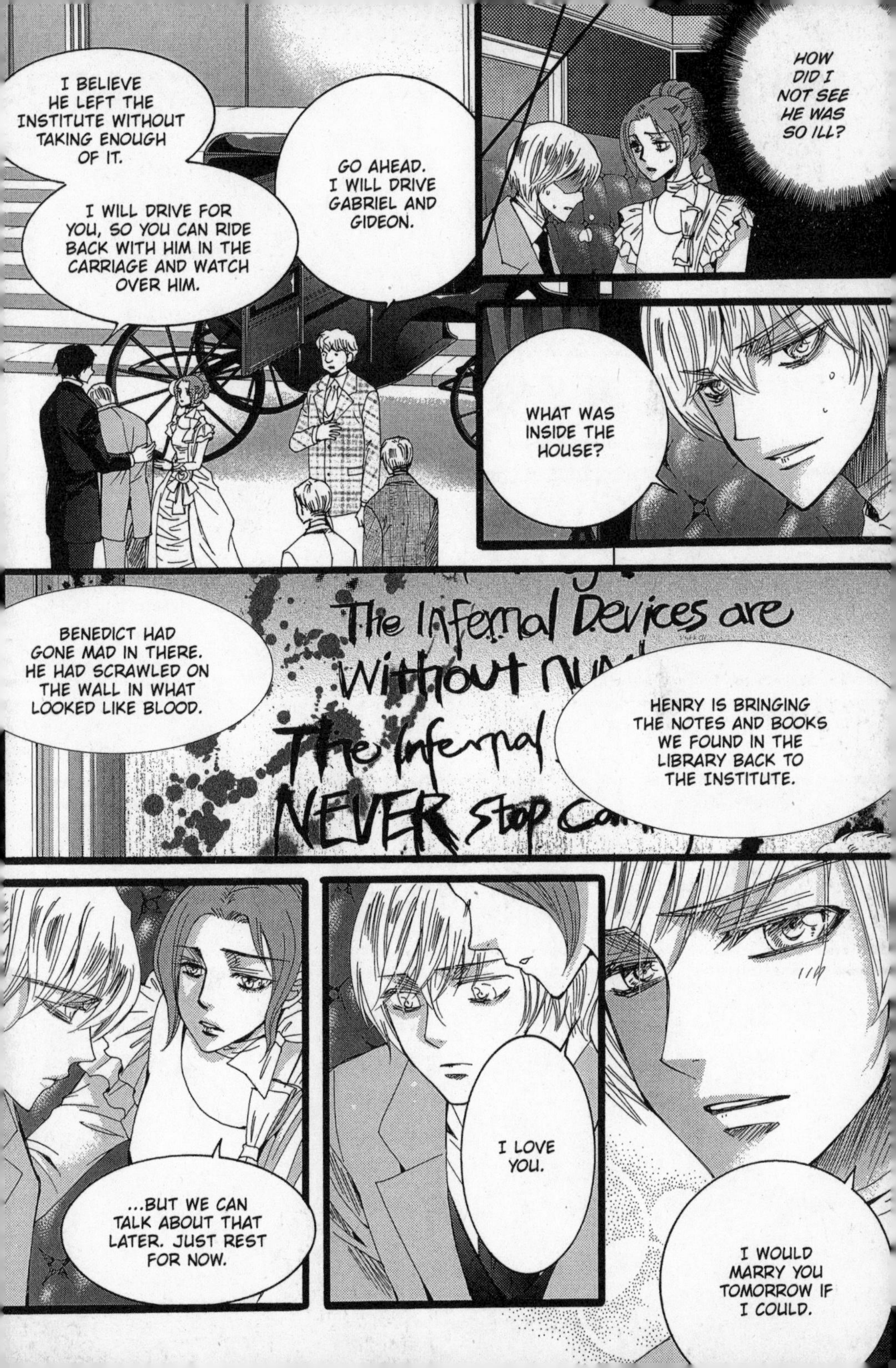
I BELIEVE HE LEFT THE INSTITUTE WITHOUT TAKING ENOUGH OF IT.
I WILL DRIVE FOR YOU, SO YOU CAN RIDE BACK WITH HIM IN THE CARRIAGE AND WATCH OVER HIM.
GO AHEAD. I WILL DRIVE GABRIEL AND GIDEON.
HOW DID I NOT SEE HE WAS SO ILL?
WHAT WAS INSIDE THE HOUSE?
BENEDICT HAD GONE MAD IN THERE. HE HAD SCRAWLED ON THE WALL IN WHAT LOOKED LIKE BLOOD.
The Infernal Devices are
NEVER Stop
HENRY IS BRINGING THE NOTES AND BOOKS WE FOUND IN THE LIBRARY BACK TO THE INSTITUTE.
...BUT WE CAN TALK ABOUT THAT LATER. JUST REST FOR NOW.
I LOVE YOU.
I WOULD MARRY YOU TOMORROW IF I COULD.

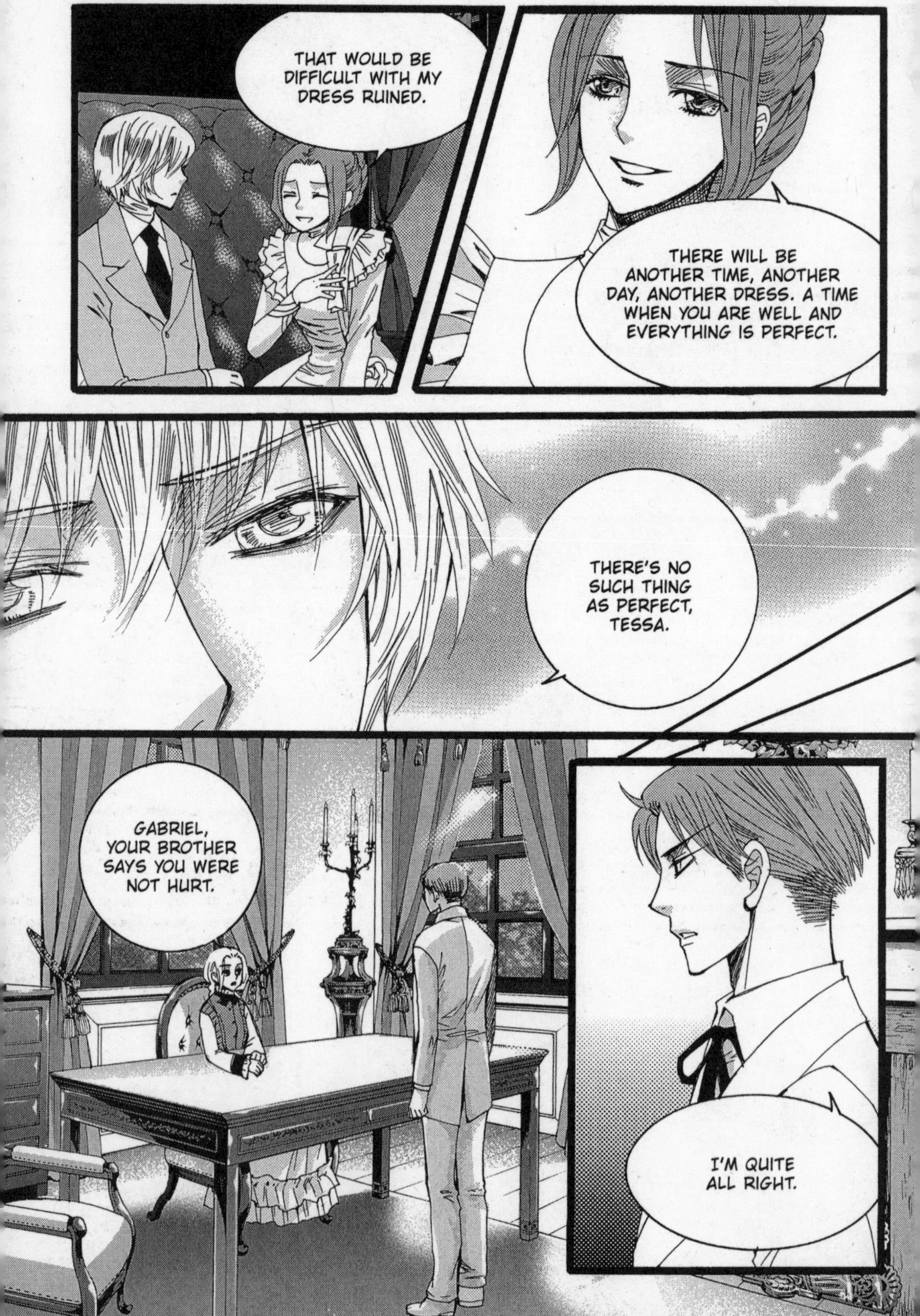
THAT WOULD BE DIFFICULT WITH MY DRESS RUINED.
THERE WILL BE ANOTHER TIME, ANOTHER DAY, ANOTHER DRESS. A TIME WHEN YOU ARE WELL AND EVERYTHING IS PERFECT.
THERE'S NO SUCH THING AS PERFECT, TESSA.
GABRIEL, YOUR BROTHER SAYS YOU WERE NOT HURT.
I'M QUITE ALL RIGHT.

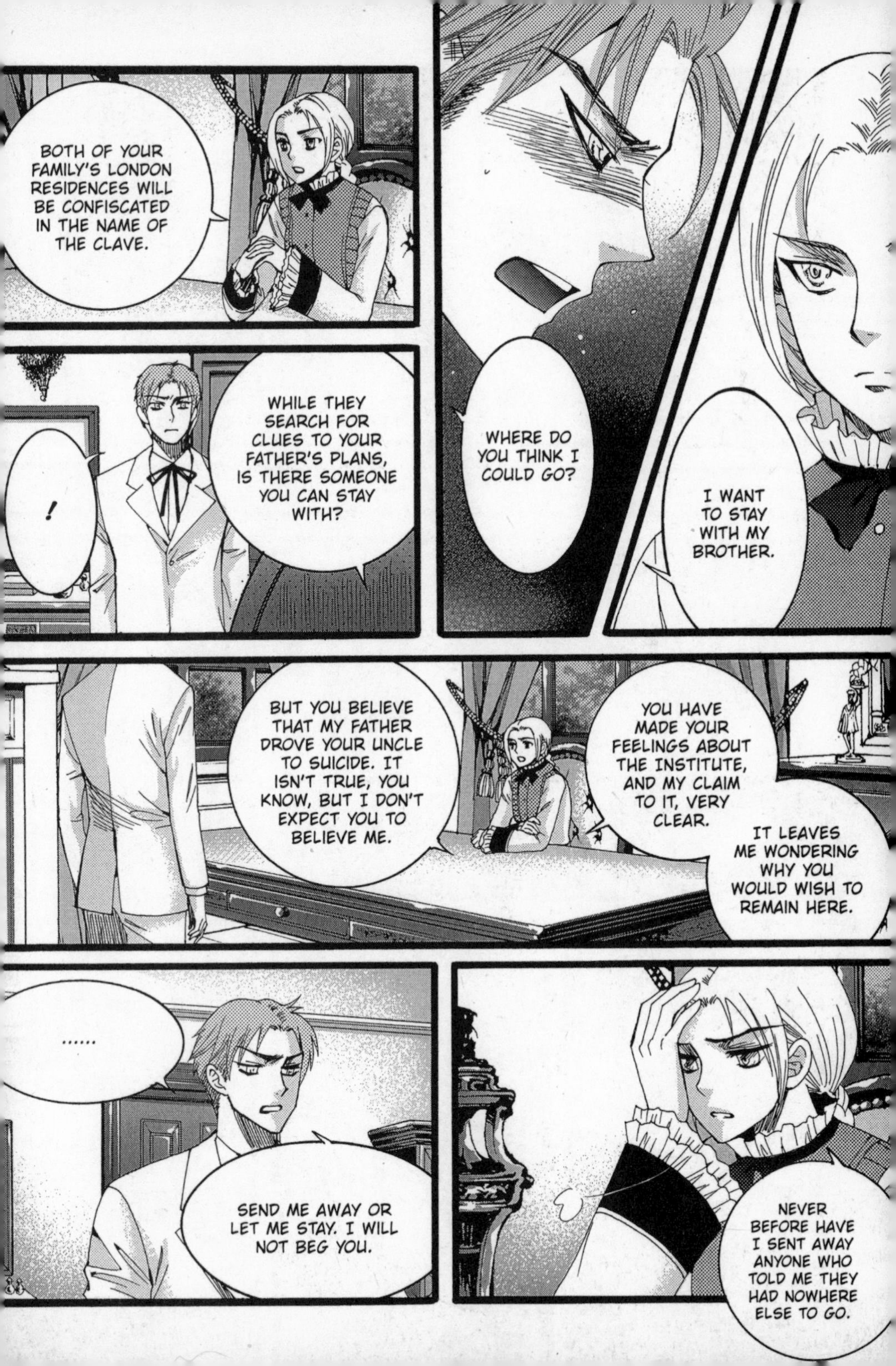
BOTH OF YOUR FAMILY'S LONDON RESIDENCES WILL BE CONFISCATED IN THE NAME OF THE CLAVE.
WHILE THEY SEARCH FOR CLUES TO YOUR FATHER'S PLANS, IS THERE SOMEONE YOU CAN STAY WITH?
!
WHERE DO YOU THINK I COULD GO?
I WANT TO STAY WITH MY BROTHER.
BUT YOU BELIEVE THAT MY FATHER DROVE YOUR UNCLE TO SUICIDE. IT ISN'T TRUE, YOU KNOW, BUT I DON'T EXPECT YOU TO BELIEVE ME.
YOU HAVE MADE YOUR FEELINGS ABOUT THE INSTITUTE, AND MY CLAIM TO IT, VERY CLEAR.
IT LEAVES ME WONDERING WHY YOU WOULD WISH TO REMAIN HERE.
......
SEND ME AWAY OR LET ME STAY. I WILL NOT BEG YOU.
NEVER BEFORE HAVE I SENT AWAY ANYONE WHO TOLD ME THEY HAD NOWHERE ELSE TO GO.

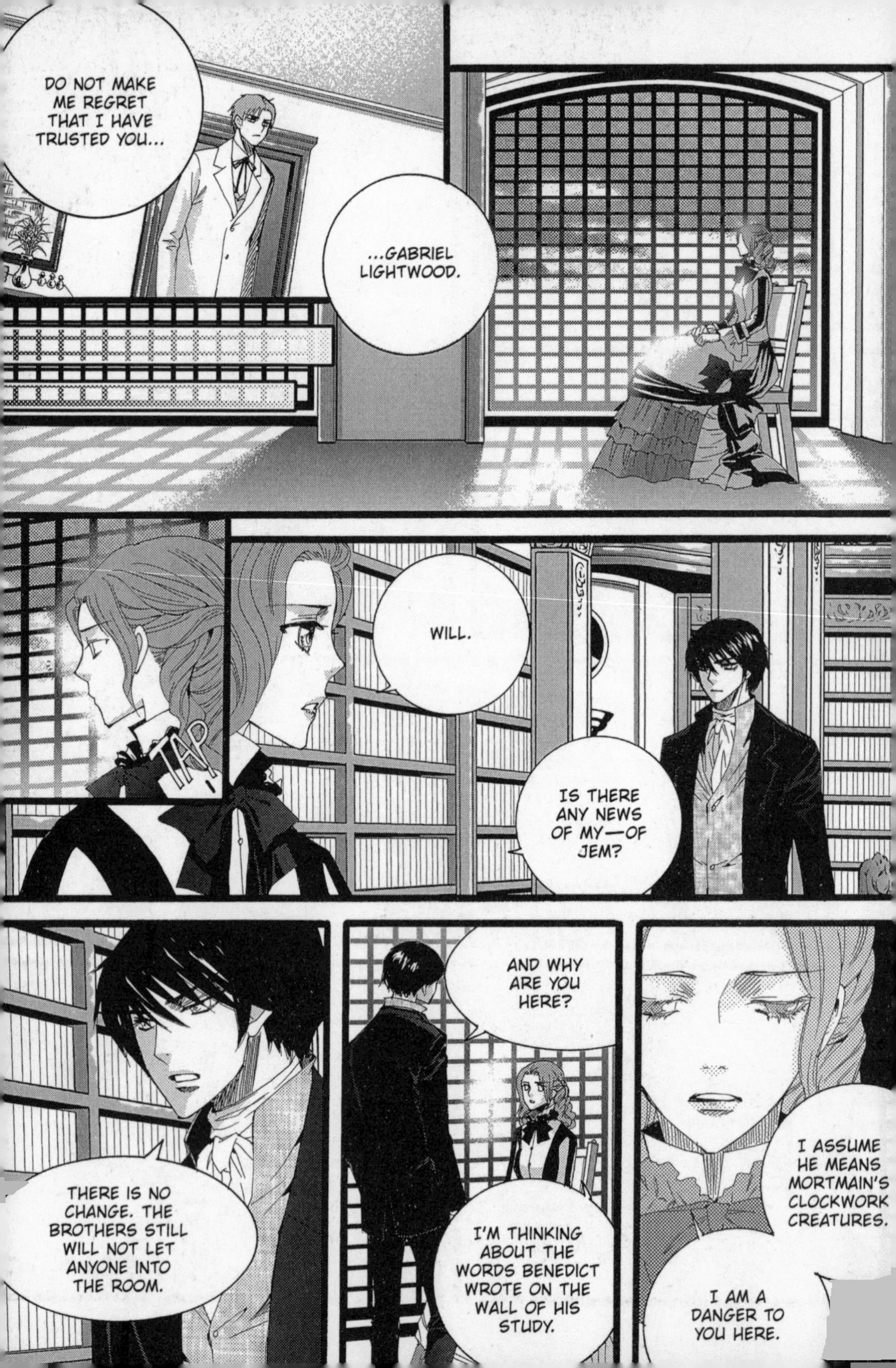
DO NOT MAKE ME REGRET THAT I HAVE TRUSTED YOU...
...GABRIEL LIGHTWOOD.
TAP
WILL.
IS THERE ANY NEWS OF MY—OF JEM?
THERE IS NO CHANGE. THE BROTHERS STILL WILL NOT LET ANYONE INTO THE ROOM.
AND WHY ARE YOU HERE?
I'M THINKING ABOUT THE WORDS BENEDICT WROTE ON THE WALL OF HIS STUDY.
I ASSUME HE MEANS MORTMAIN'S CLOCKWORK CREATURES.
I AM A DANGER TO YOU HERE.

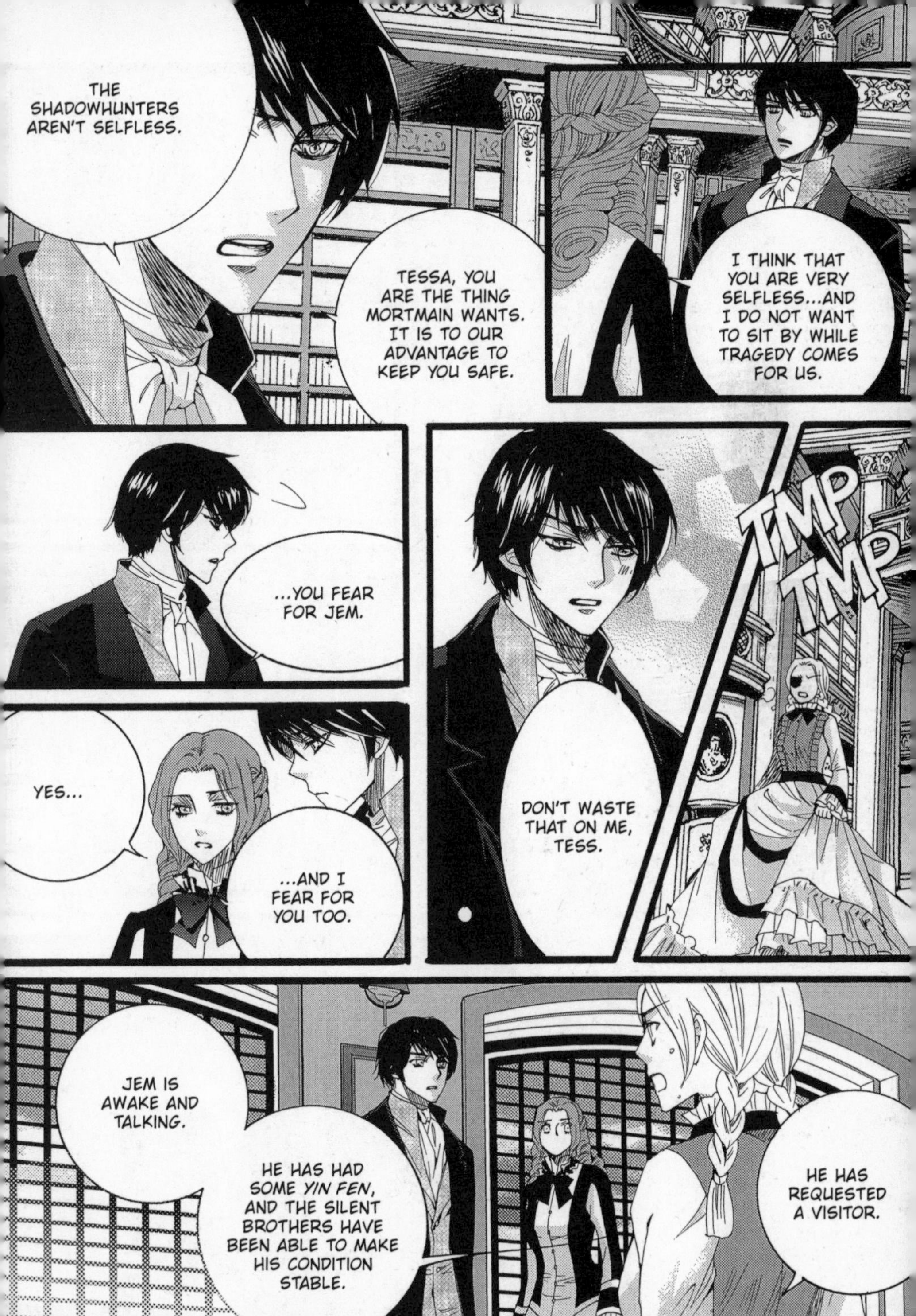
THE SHADOWHUNTERS AREN'T SELFLESS.
TESSA, YOU ARE THE THING MORTMAIN WANTS. IT IS TO OUR ADVANTAGE TO KEEP YOU SAFE.
I THINK THAT YOU ARE VERY SELFLESS...AND I DO NOT WANT TO SIT BY WHILE TRAGEDY COMES FOR US.
...YOU FEAR FOR JEM.
YES...
...AND I FEAR FOR YOU TOO.
DON'T WASTE THAT ON ME, TESS.
TMP TMP
JEM IS AWAKE AND TALKING.
HE HAS HAD SOME *YIN FEN*, AND THE SILENT BROTHERS HAVE BEEN ABLE TO MAKE HIS CONDITION STABLE.
HE HAS REQUESTED A VISITOR.

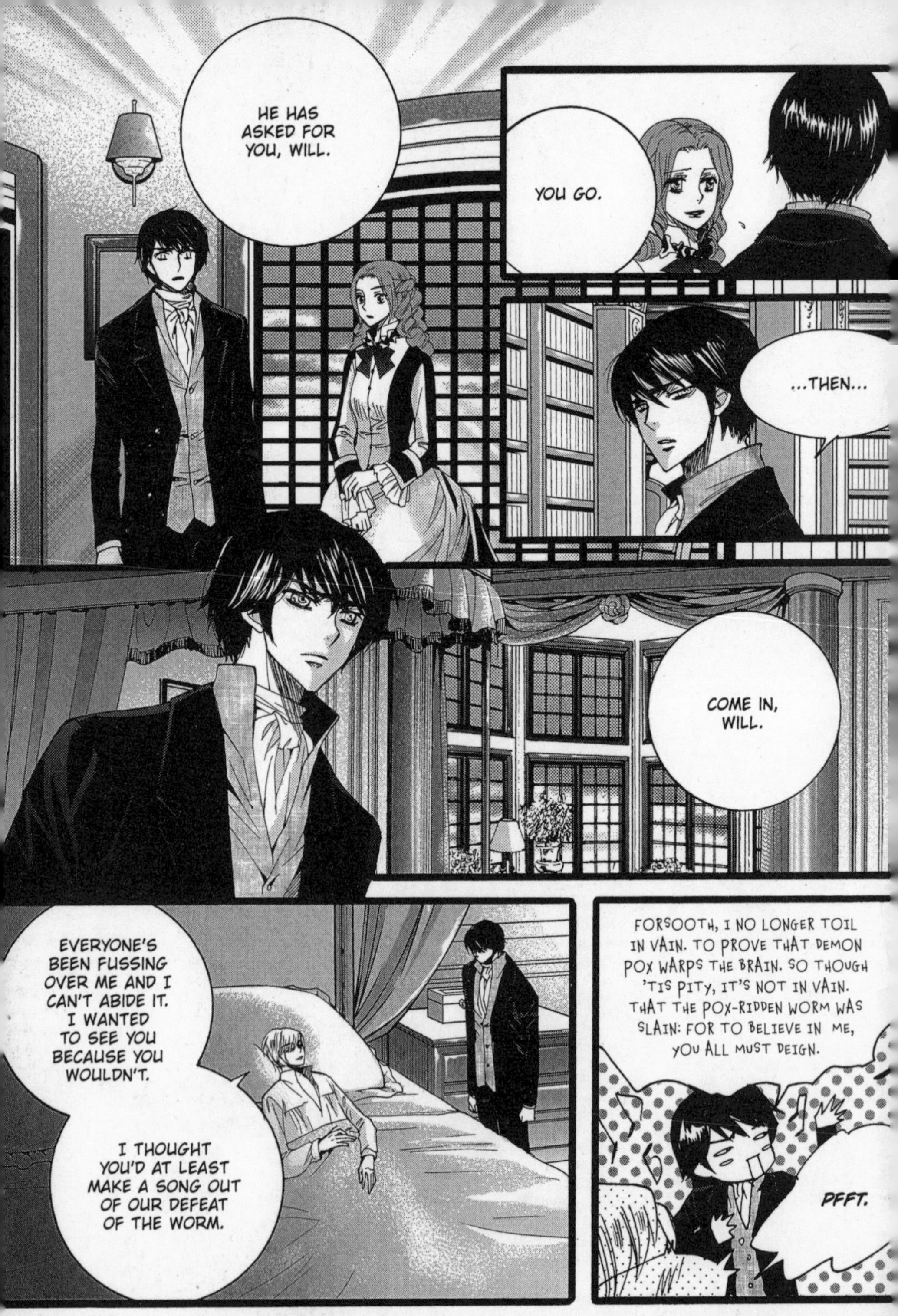
HE HAS ASKED FOR YOU, WILL.
YOU GO.
...THEN...
COME IN, WILL.
EVERYONE'S BEEN FUSSING OVER ME AND I CAN'T ABIDE IT. I WANTED TO SEE YOU BECAUSE YOU WOULDN'T.
I THOUGHT YOU'D AT LEAST MAKE A SONG OUT OF OUR DEFEAT OF THE WORM.
FORSOOTH, I NO LONGER TOIL IN VAIN. TO PROVE THAT DEMON POX WARPS THE BRAIN. SO THOUGH 'TIS PITY, IT'S NOT IN VAIN. THAT THE POX-RIDDEN WORM WAS SLAIN: FOR TO BELIEVE IN ME, YOU ALL MUST DEIGN.
PFFT.

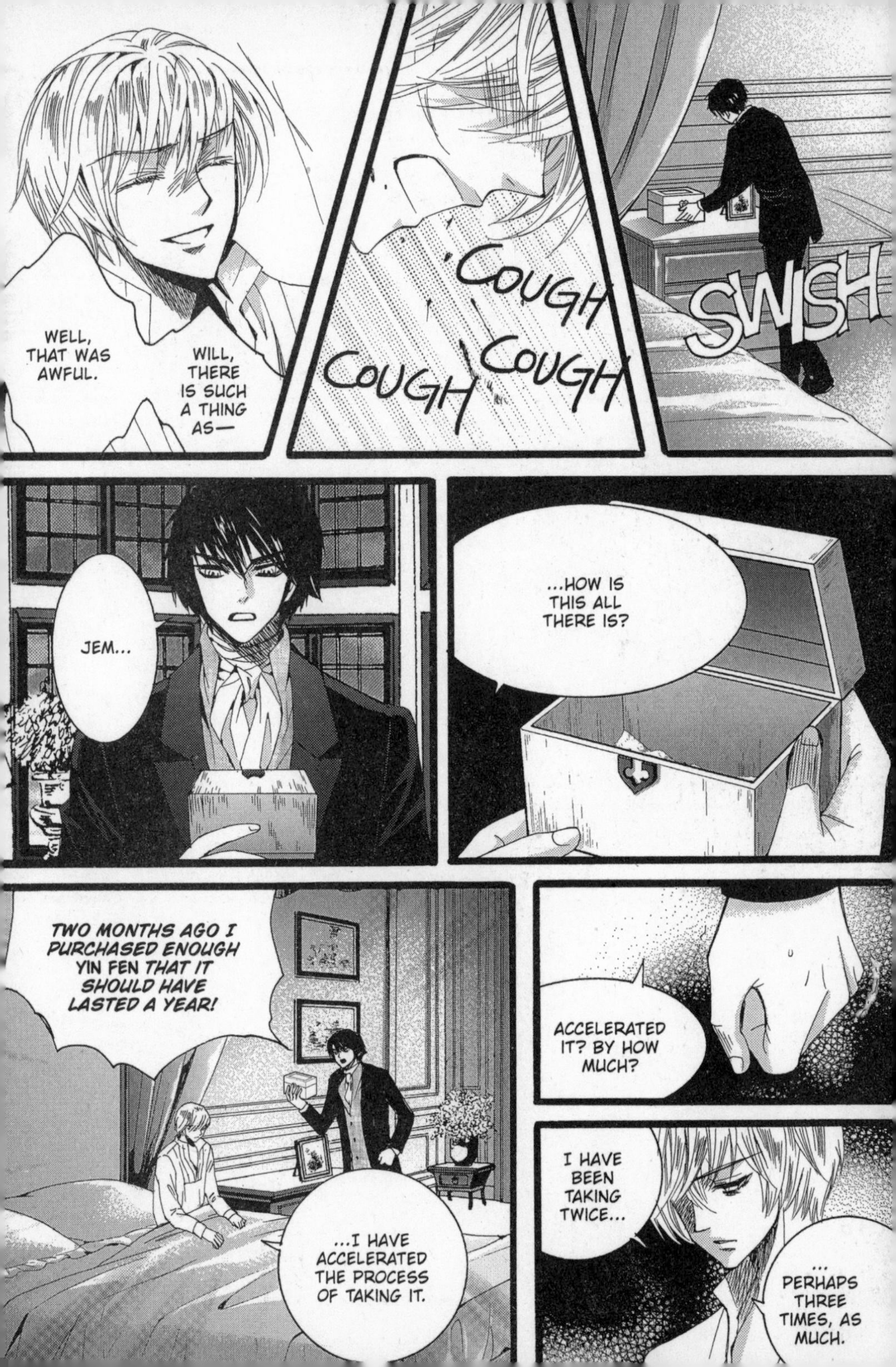
WELL, THAT WAS AWFUL.
WILL, THERE IS SUCH A THING AS—
COUGH COUGH
COUGH
SWISH
JEM...
...HOW IS THIS ALL THERE IS?
TWO MONTHS AGO I PURCHASED ENOUGH YIN FEN THAT IT SHOULD HAVE LASTED A YEAR!
...I HAVE ACCELERATED THE PROCESS OF TAKING IT.
ACCELERATED IT? BY HOW MUCH?
I HAVE BEEN TAKING TWICE...
...PERHAPS THREE TIMES, AS MUCH.

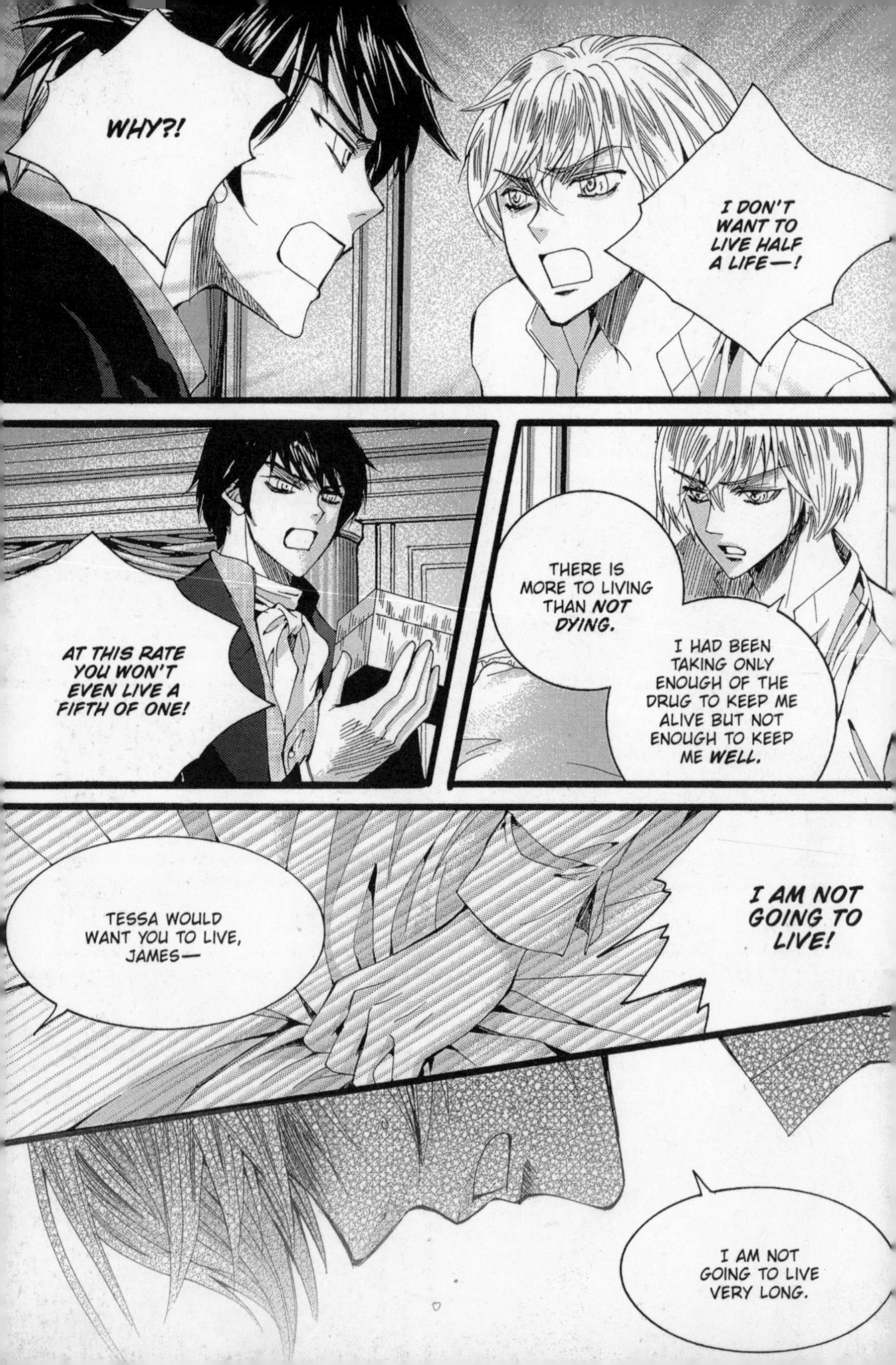
WHY?!
I DON'T WANT TO LIVE HALF A LIFE—!
AT THIS RATE YOU WON'T EVEN LIVE A FIFTH OF ONE!
THERE IS MORE TO LIVING THAN NOT DYING.
I HAD BEEN TAKING ONLY ENOUGH OF THE DRUG TO KEEP ME ALIVE BUT NOT ENOUGH TO KEEP ME WELL.
TESSA WOULD WANT YOU TO LIVE, JAMES—
I AM NOT GOING TO LIVE!
I AM NOT GOING TO LIVE VERY LONG.

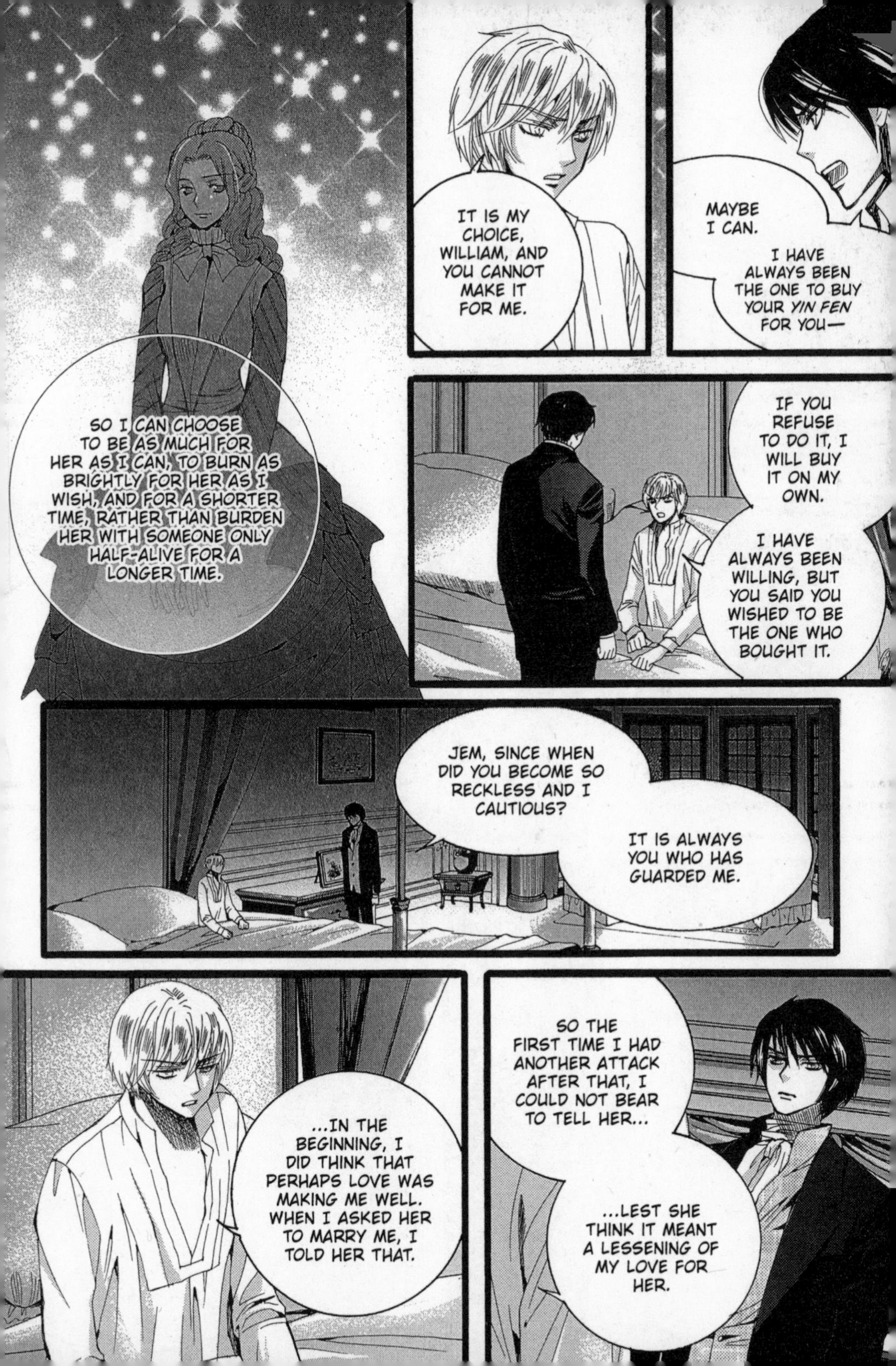
IT IS MY CHOICE, WILLIAM, AND YOU CANNOT MAKE IT FOR ME.
MAYBE I CAN.
I HAVE ALWAYS BEEN THE ONE TO BUY YOUR *YIN FEN* FOR YOU—
SO I CAN CHOOSE TO BE AS MUCH FOR HER AS I CAN, TO BURN AS BRIGHTLY FOR HER AS I WISH, AND FOR A SHORTER TIME, RATHER THAN BURDEN HER WITH SOMEONE ONLY HALF-ALIVE FOR A LONGER TIME.
IF YOU REFUSE TO DO IT, I WILL BUY IT ON MY OWN.
I HAVE ALWAYS BEEN WILLING, BUT YOU SAID YOU WISHED TO BE THE ONE WHO BOUGHT IT.
JEM, SINCE WHEN DID YOU BECOME SO RECKLESS AND I CAUTIOUS?
IT IS ALWAYS YOU WHO HAS GUARDED ME.
...IN THE BEGINNING, I DID THINK THAT PERHAPS LOVE WAS MAKING ME WELL. WHEN I ASKED HER TO MARRY ME, I TOLD HER THAT.
SO THE FIRST TIME I HAD ANOTHER ATTACK AFTER THAT, I COULD NOT BEAR TO TELL HER...
...LEST SHE THINK IT MEANT A LESSENING OF MY LOVE FOR HER.

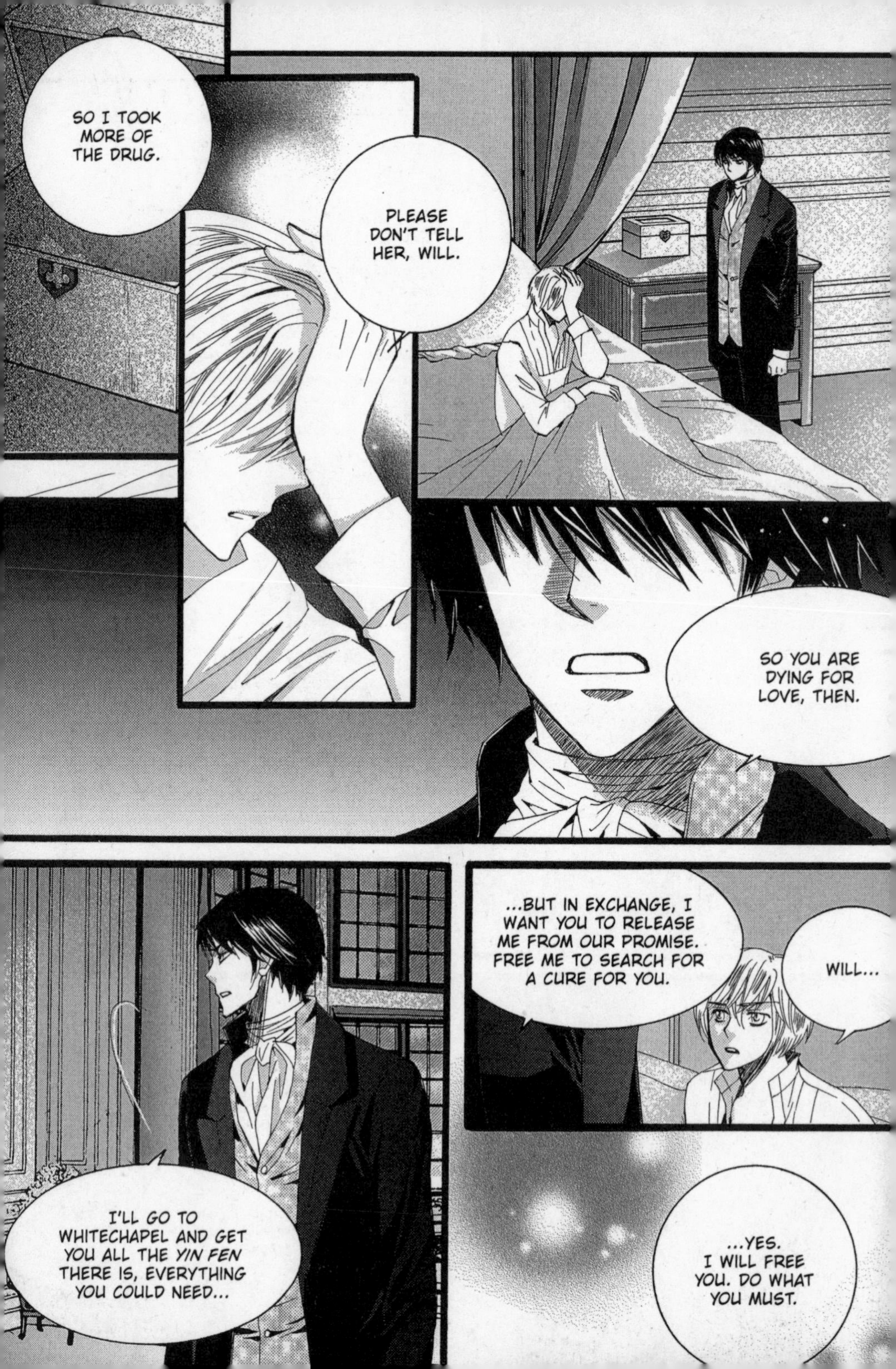
SO I TOOK MORE OF THE DRUG.
PLEASE DON'T TELL HER, WILL.
SO YOU ARE DYING FOR LOVE, THEN.
I'LL GO TO WHITECHAPEL AND GET YOU ALL THE *YIN FEN* THERE IS, EVERYTHING YOU COULD NEED...
...BUT IN EXCHANGE, I WANT YOU TO RELEASE ME FROM OUR PROMISE. FREE ME TO SEARCH FOR A CURE FOR YOU.
WILL...
...YES. I WILL FREE YOU. DO WHAT YOU MUST.

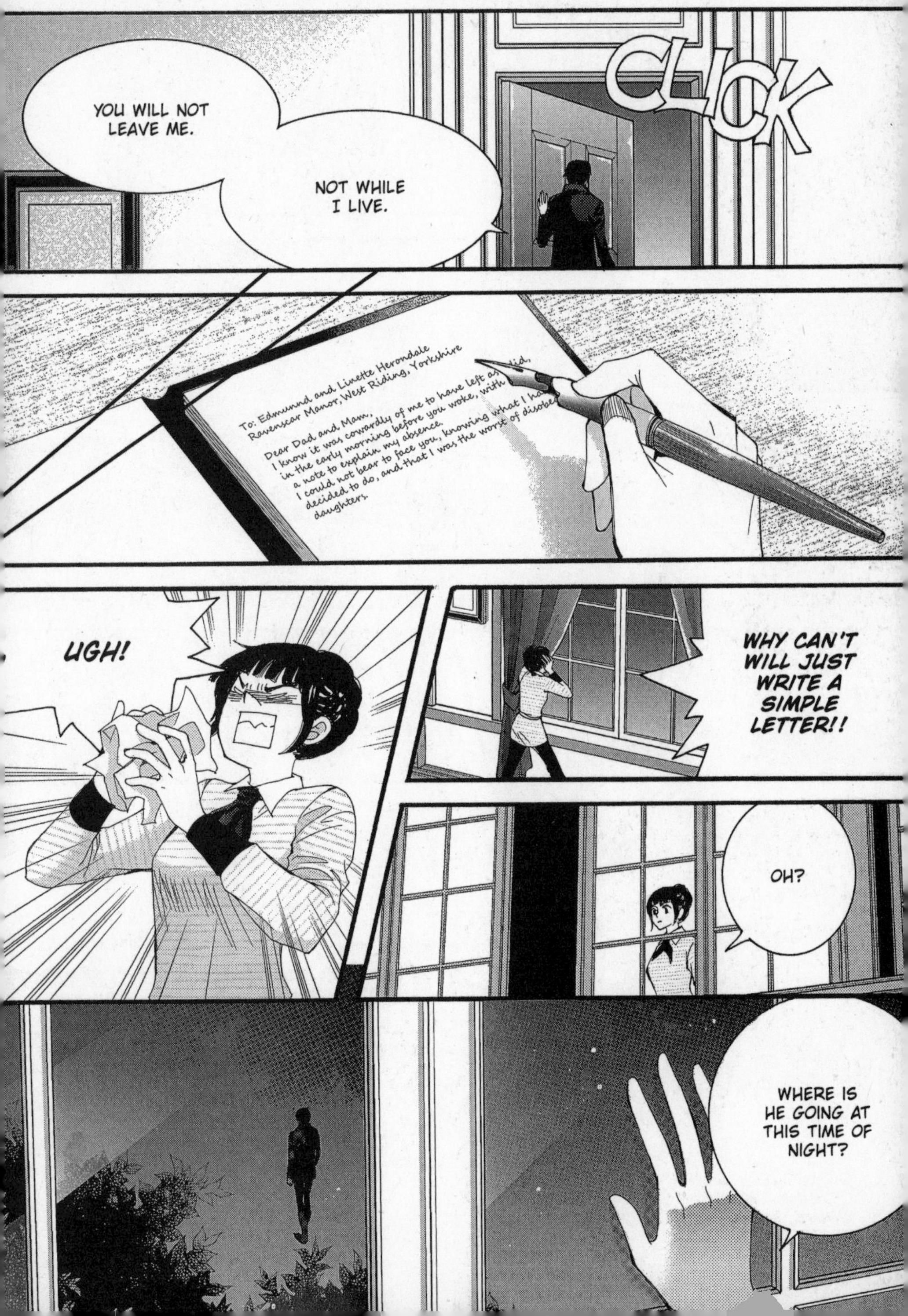
YOU WILL NOT LEAVE ME.
NOT WHILE I LIVE.
CLICK
To: Edmunnd and Linette Herondale
Ravenscar Manor, West Riding, Yorkshire
Dear Dad and Mam,
I know it was cowardly of me to have left as
in the early morning before you woke, with
a note to explain my absence.
I could not bear to face you, knowing what I
decided to do, and that I was the worst of
daughters.
UGH!
WHY CAN'T WILL JUST WRITE A SIMPLE LETTER!!
OH?
WHERE IS HE GOING AT THIS TIME OF NIGHT?

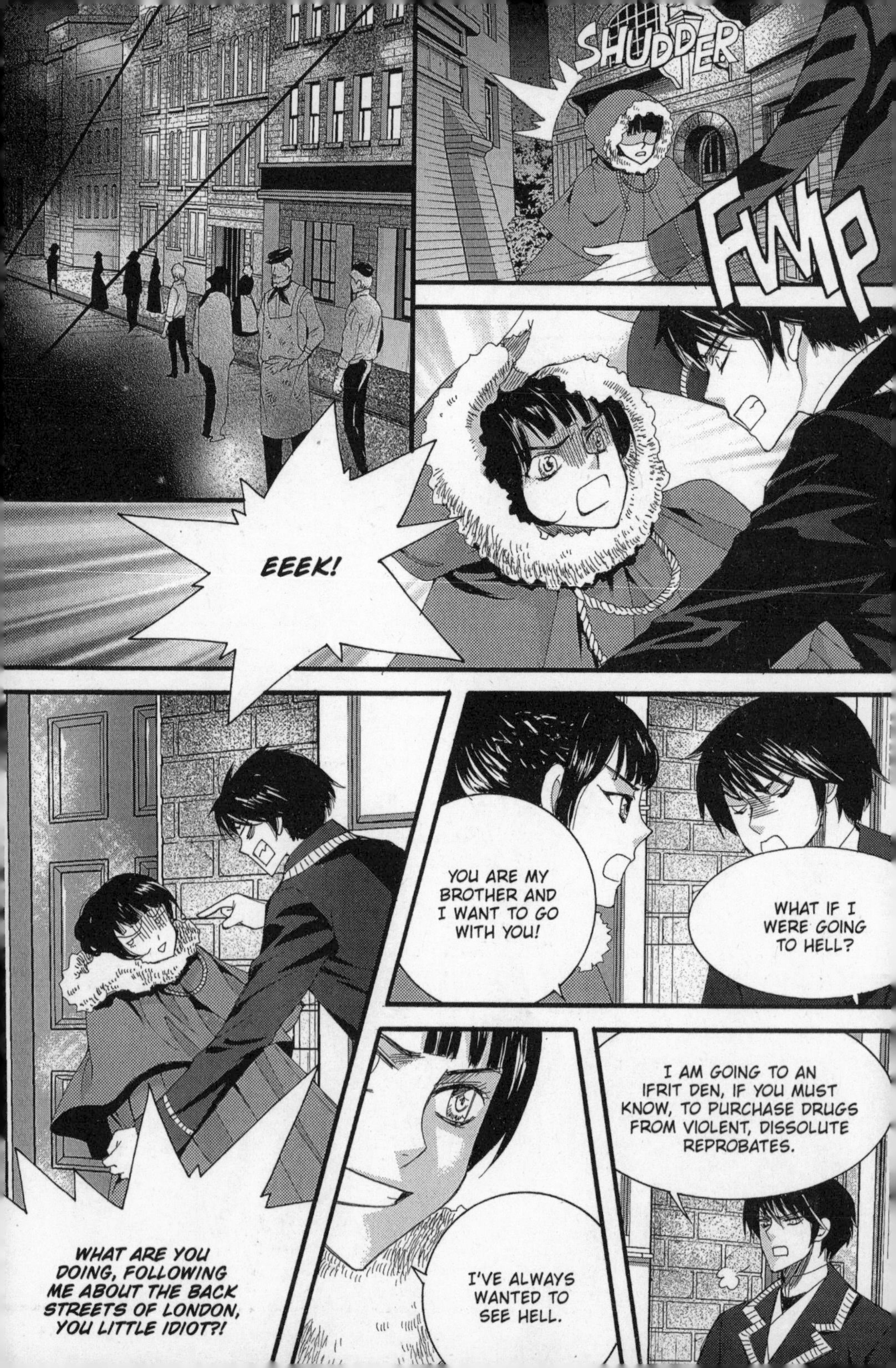
SHUDDER
FWMP
EEEK!
WHAT ARE YOU DOING, FOLLOWING ME ABOUT THE BACK STREETS OF LONDON, YOU LITTLE IDIOT?!
YOU ARE MY BROTHER AND I WANT TO GO WITH YOU!
WHAT IF I WERE GOING TO HELL?
I AM GOING TO AN IFRIT DEN, IF YOU MUST KNOW, TO PURCHASE DRUGS FROM VIOLENT, DISSOLUTE REPROBATES.
I'VE ALWAYS WANTED TO SEE HELL.

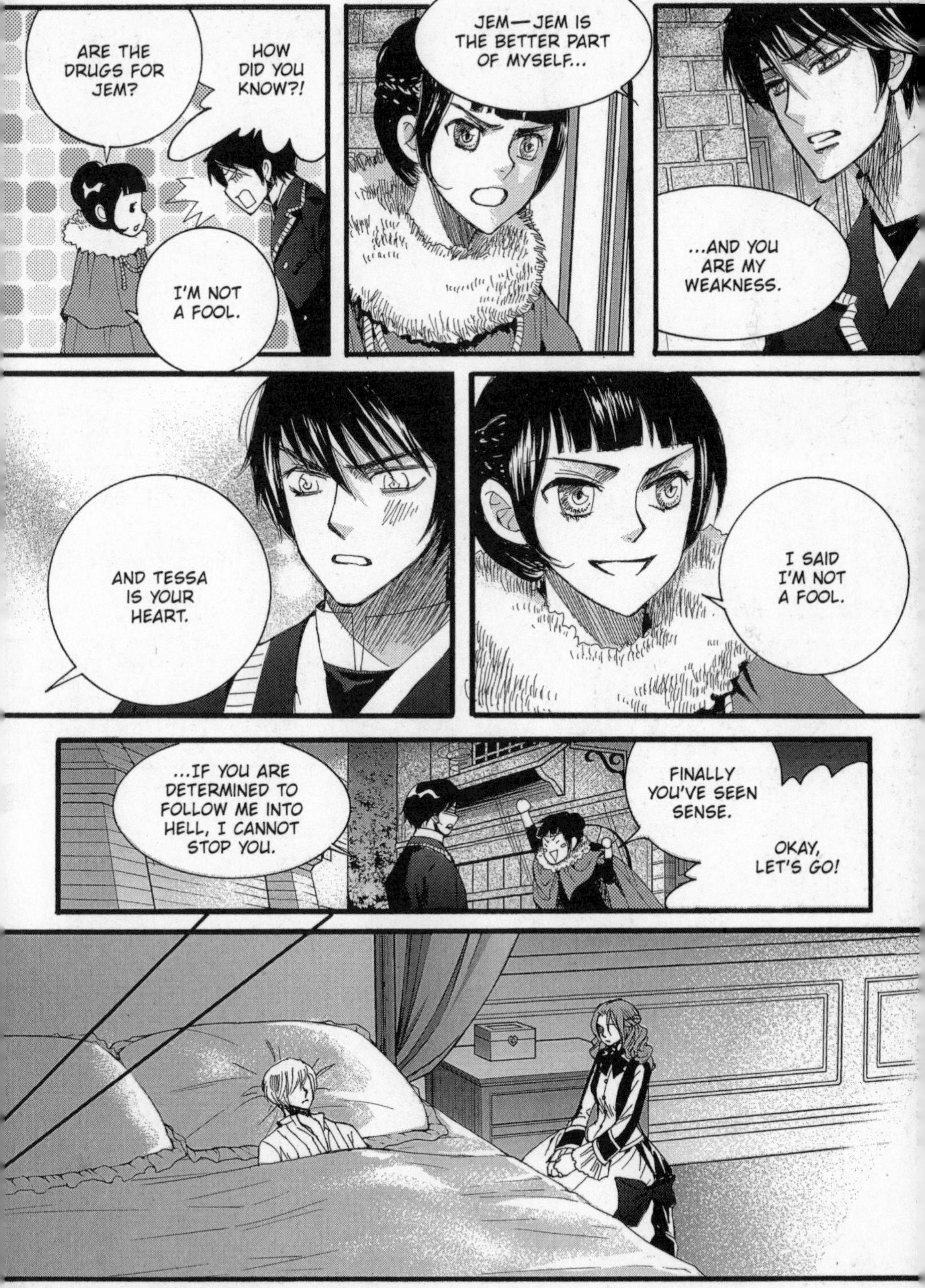
ARE THE DRUGS FOR JEM?
HOW DID YOU KNOW?!
I'M NOT A FOOL.
JEM—JEM IS THE BETTER PART OF MYSELF...
...AND YOU ARE MY WEAKNESS.
AND TESSA IS YOUR HEART.
I SAID I'M NOT A FOOL.
...IF YOU ARE DETERMINED TO FOLLOW ME INTO HELL, I CANNOT STOP YOU.
FINALLY YOU'VE SEEN SENSE.
OKAY, LET'S GO!

......

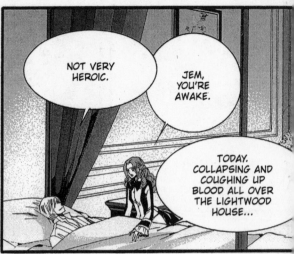

NOT VERY HEROIC.

JEM, YOU'RE AWAKE.

TODAY. COLLAPSING AND COUGHING UP BLOOD ALL OVER THE LIGHTWOOD HOUSE...

JEM... HAVE YOU EVER...

...HAVE YOU EVER THOUGHT OF WAYS TO PROLONG YOUR LIFE THAT ARE NOT A CURE FOR THE DRUG?

WHAT DO YOU MEAN?

TESSA, NO. YOU CAN'T THINK THAT WAY.

IS THE THOUGHT OF BECOMING A DOWNWORLDER TRULY SO HORRIBLE TO YOU?

BECOMING A VAMPIRE...

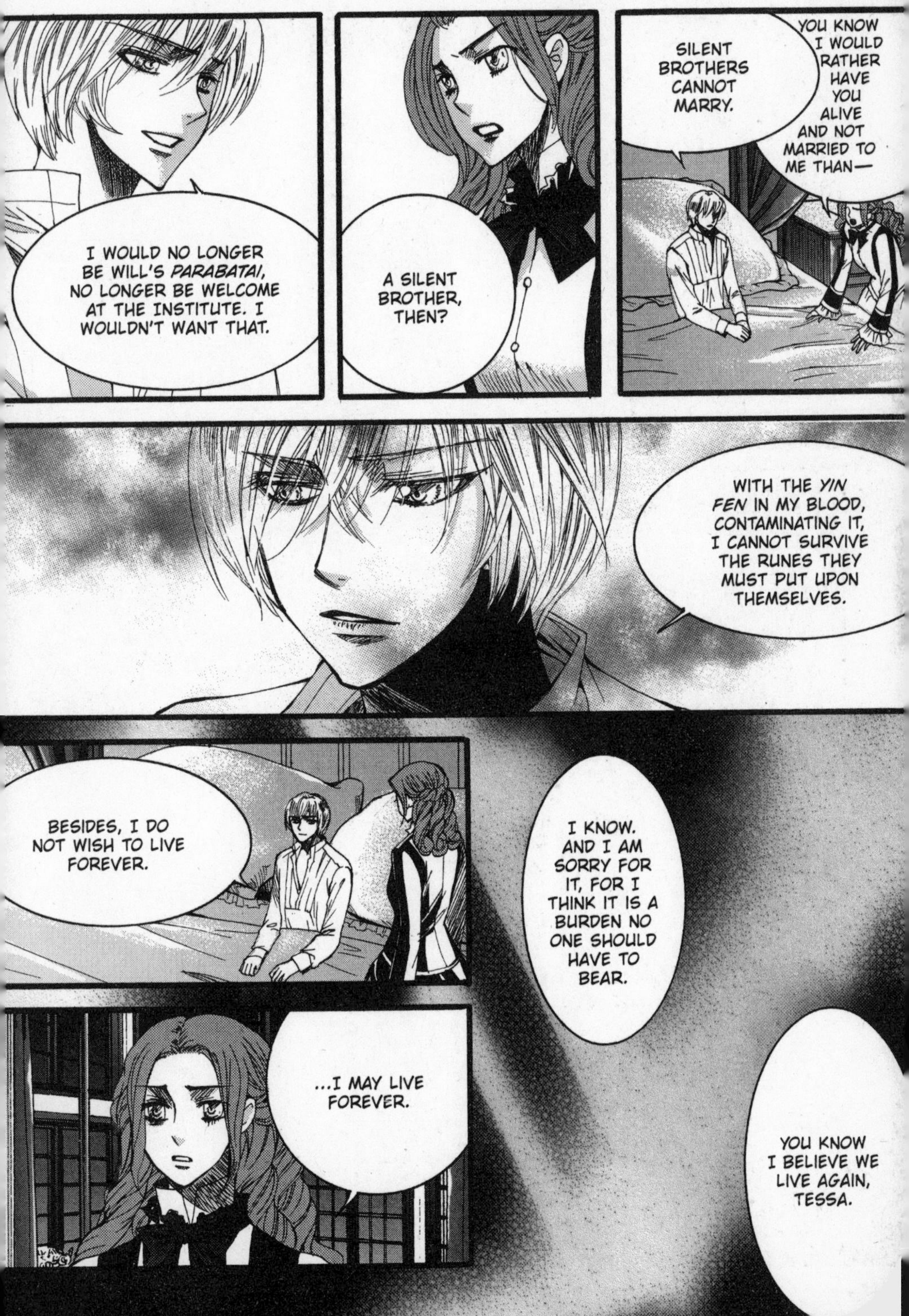

I WOULD NO LONGER BE WILL'S *PARABATAI*, NO LONGER BE WELCOME AT THE INSTITUTE. I WOULDN'T WANT THAT.
A SILENT BROTHER, THEN?
SILENT BROTHERS CANNOT MARRY.
YOU KNOW I WOULD RATHER HAVE YOU ALIVE AND NOT MARRIED TO ME THAN—
WITH THE *YIN FEN* IN MY BLOOD, CONTAMINATING IT, I CANNOT SURVIVE THE RUNES THEY MUST PUT UPON THEMSELVES.
BESIDES, I DO NOT WISH TO LIVE FOREVER.
I KNOW. AND I AM SORRY FOR IT, FOR I THINK IT IS A BURDEN NO ONE SHOULD HAVE TO BEAR.
...I MAY LIVE FOREVER.
YOU KNOW I BELIEVE WE LIVE AGAIN, TESSA.

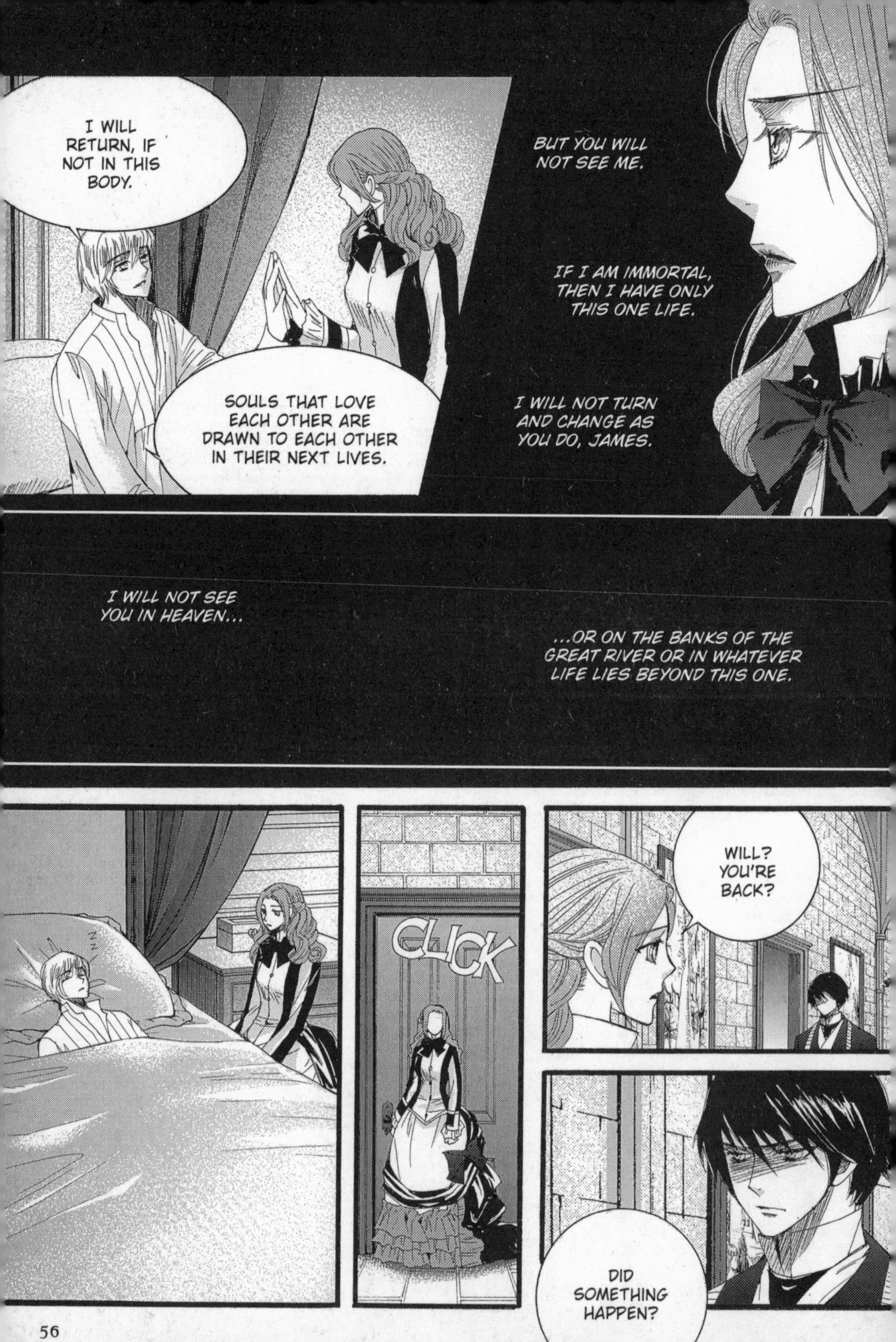
I WILL RETURN, IF NOT IN THIS BODY.
SOULS THAT LOVE EACH OTHER ARE DRAWN TO EACH OTHER IN THEIR NEXT LIVES.
BUT YOU WILL NOT SEE ME.
IF I AM IMMORTAL, THEN I HAVE ONLY THIS ONE LIFE.
I WILL NOT TURN AND CHANGE AS YOU DO, JAMES.
I WILL NOT SEE YOU IN HEAVEN...
...OR ON THE BANKS OF THE GREAT RIVER OR IN WHATEVER LIFE LIES BEYOND THIS ONE.
Z Z
CLICK
WILL? YOU'RE BACK?
DID SOMETHING HAPPEN?

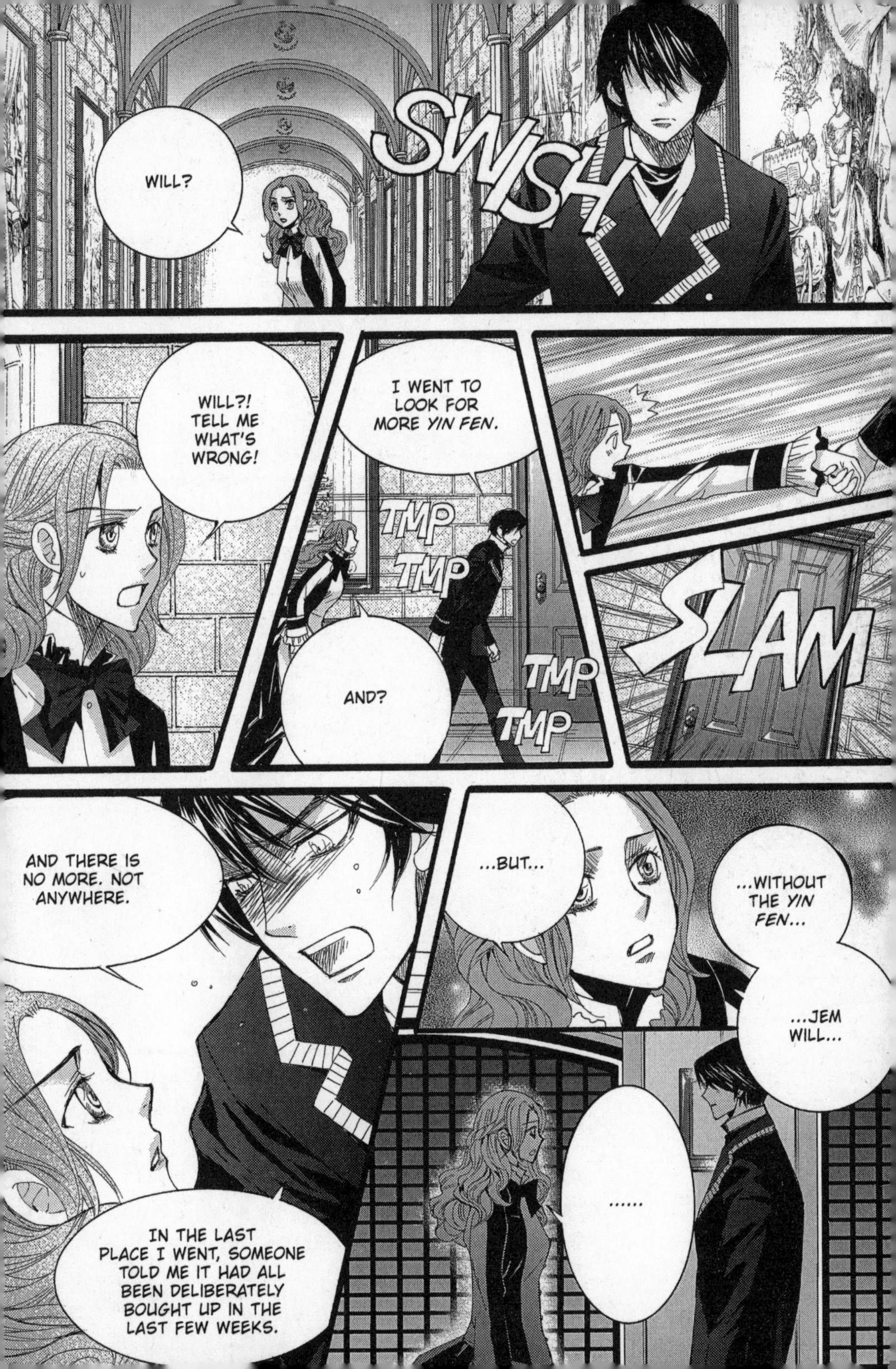

WILL?
SWISH
WILL?! TELL ME WHAT'S WRONG!
I WENT TO LOOK FOR MORE *YIN FEN*.
TMP TMP
AND?
TMP TMP
SLAM
AND THERE IS NO MORE. NOT ANYWHERE.
IN THE LAST PLACE I WENT, SOMEONE TOLD ME IT HAD ALL BEEN DELIBERATELY BOUGHT UP IN THE LAST FEW WEEKS.
...BUT...
...WITHOUT THE *YIN FEN*...
...JEM WILL...
......

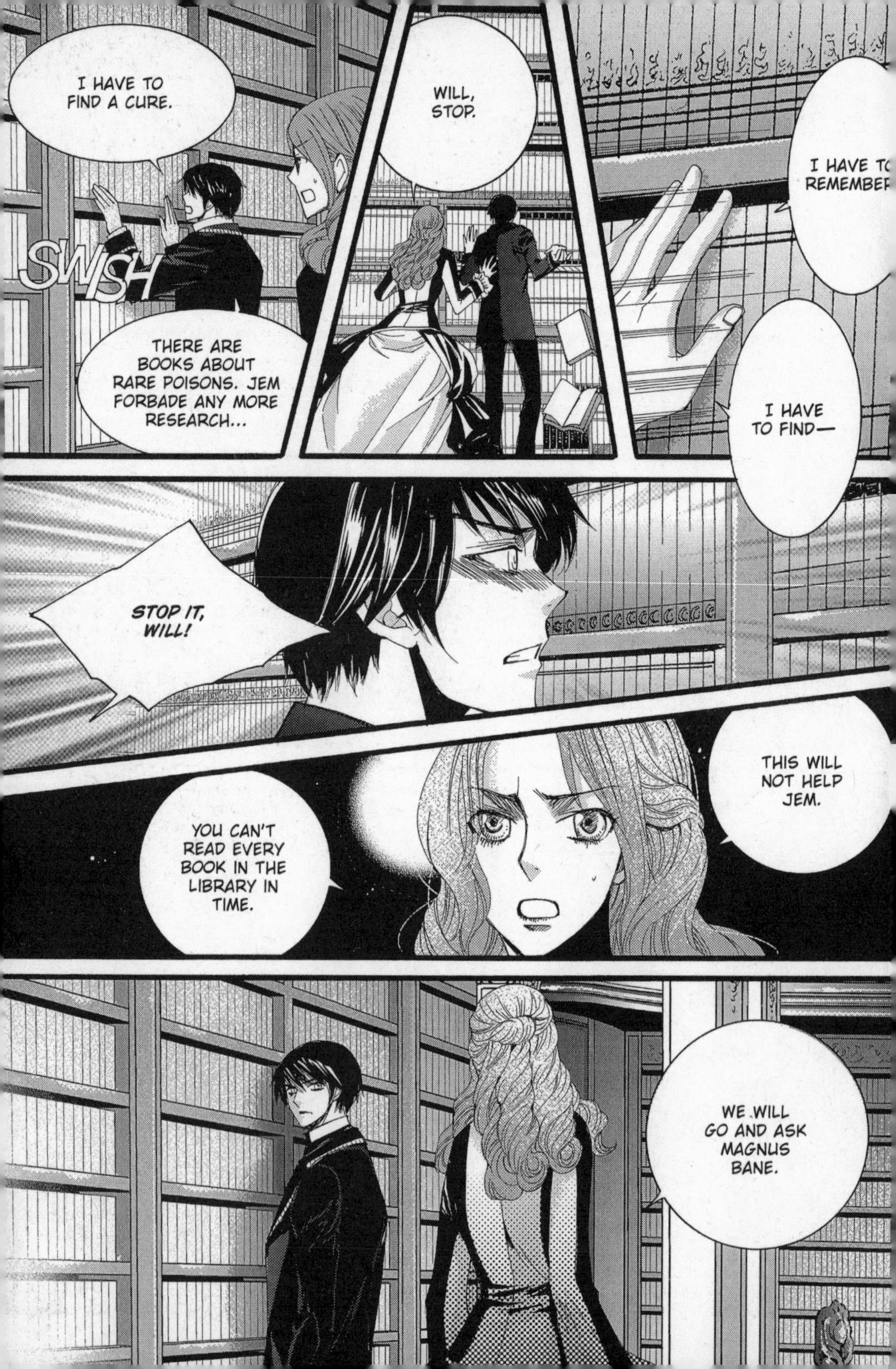
I HAVE TO FIND A CURE.
SWISH
THERE ARE BOOKS ABOUT RARE POISONS. JEM FORBADE ANY MORE RESEARCH...
WILL, STOP.
I HAVE TO REMEMBER
I HAVE TO FIND—
STOP IT, WILL!
YOU CAN'T READ EVERY BOOK IN THE LIBRARY IN TIME.
THIS WILL NOT HELP JEM.
WE WILL GO AND ASK MAGNUS BANE.

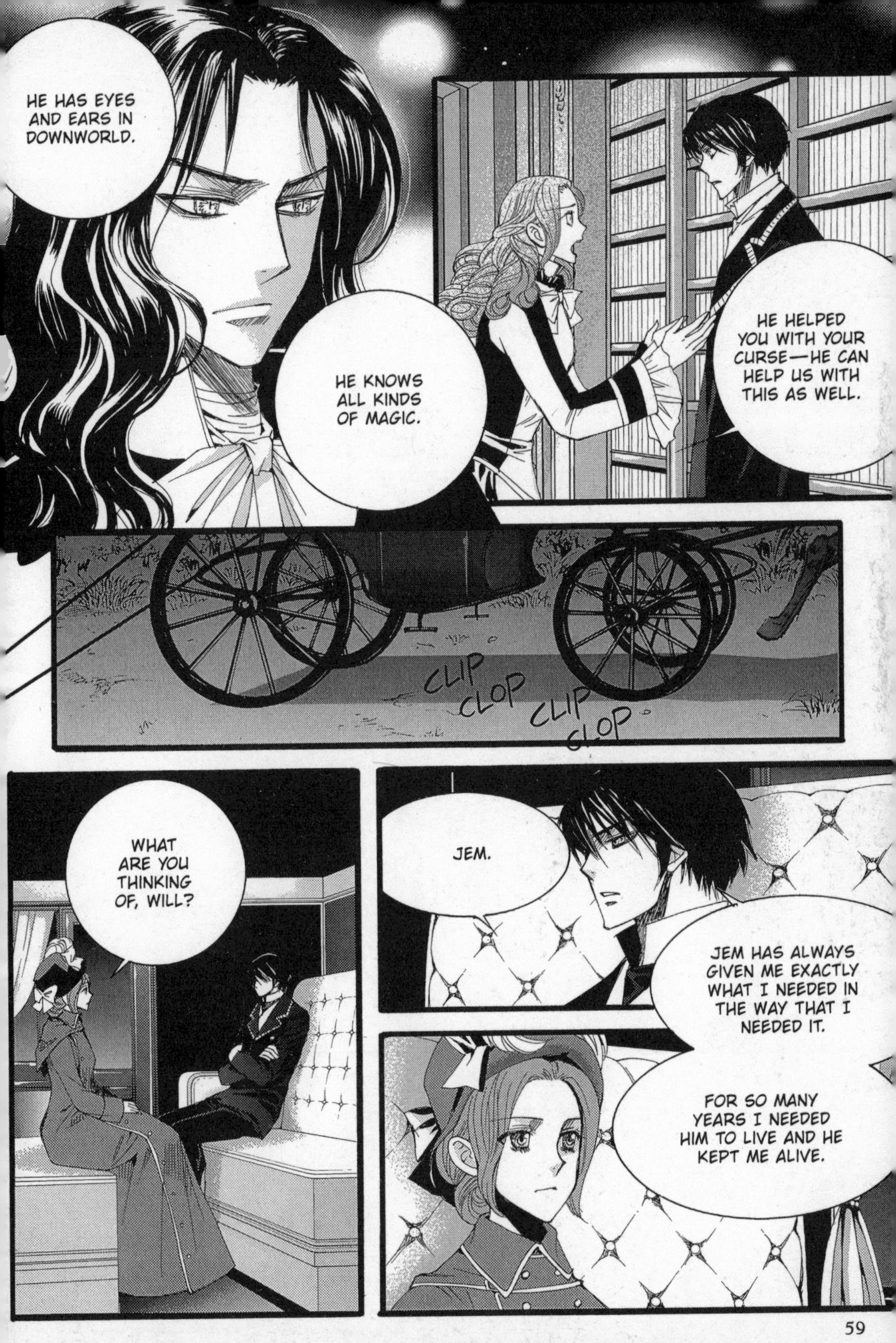
HE HAS EYES AND EARS IN DOWNWORLD.
HE KNOWS ALL KINDS OF MAGIC.
HE HELPED YOU WITH YOUR CURSE—HE CAN HELP US WITH THIS AS WELL.
CLIP CLOP CLIP CLOP
WHAT ARE YOU THINKING OF, WILL?
JEM.
JEM HAS ALWAYS GIVEN ME EXACTLY WHAT I NEEDED IN THE WAY THAT I NEEDED IT.
FOR SO MANY YEARS I NEEDED HIM TO LIVE AND HE KEPT ME ALIVE.

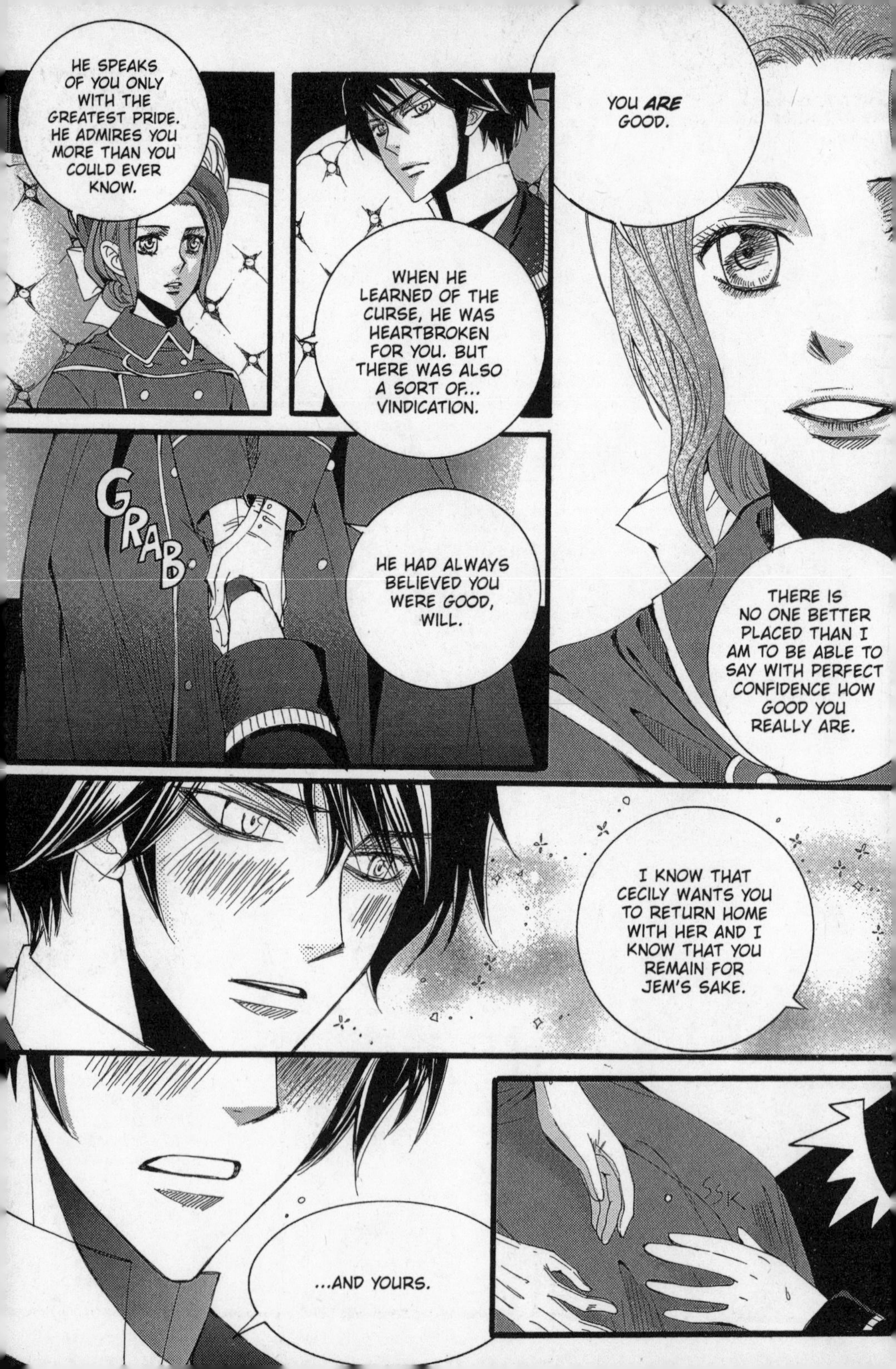

HE SPEAKS OF YOU ONLY WITH THE GREATEST PRIDE. HE ADMIRES YOU MORE THAN YOU COULD EVER KNOW.
WHEN HE LEARNED OF THE CURSE, HE WAS HEARTBROKEN FOR YOU. BUT THERE WAS ALSO A SORT OF... VINDICATION.
GRAB
HE HAD ALWAYS BELIEVED YOU WERE GOOD, WILL.
YOU **ARE** GOOD.
THERE IS NO ONE BETTER PLACED THAN I AM TO BE ABLE TO SAY WITH PERFECT CONFIDENCE HOW GOOD YOU REALLY ARE.
I KNOW THAT CECILY WANTS YOU TO RETURN HOME WITH HER AND I KNOW THAT YOU REMAIN FOR JEM'S SAKE.
...AND YOURS.
SSK.

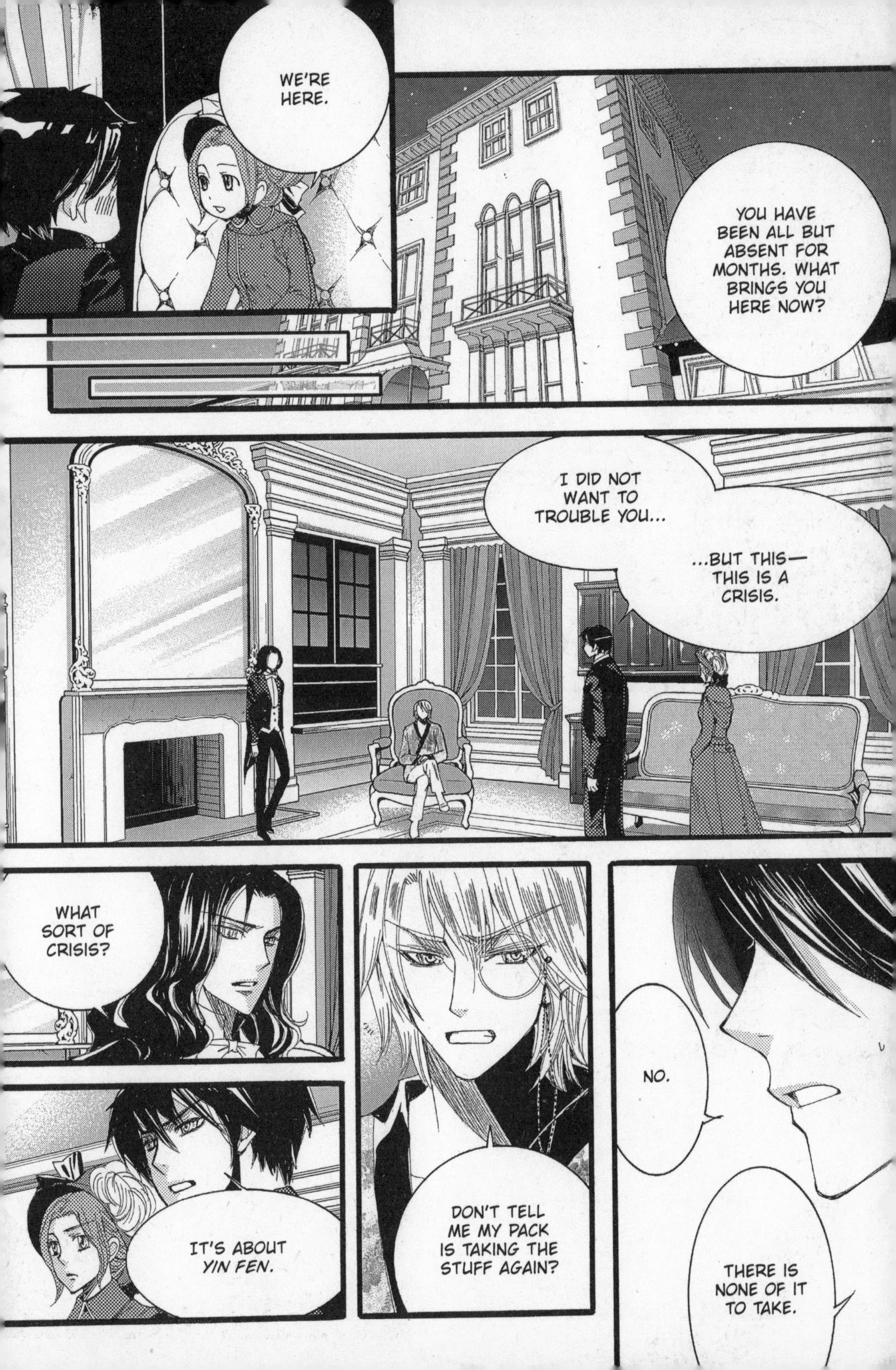
WE'RE HERE.
YOU HAVE BEEN ALL BUT ABSENT FOR MONTHS. WHAT BRINGS YOU HERE NOW?
I DID NOT WANT TO TROUBLE YOU...
...BUT THIS—THIS IS A CRISIS.
WHAT SORT OF CRISIS?
IT'S ABOUT *YIN FEN.*
DON'T TELL ME MY PACK IS TAKING THE STUFF AGAIN?
NO.
THERE IS NONE OF IT TO TAKE.

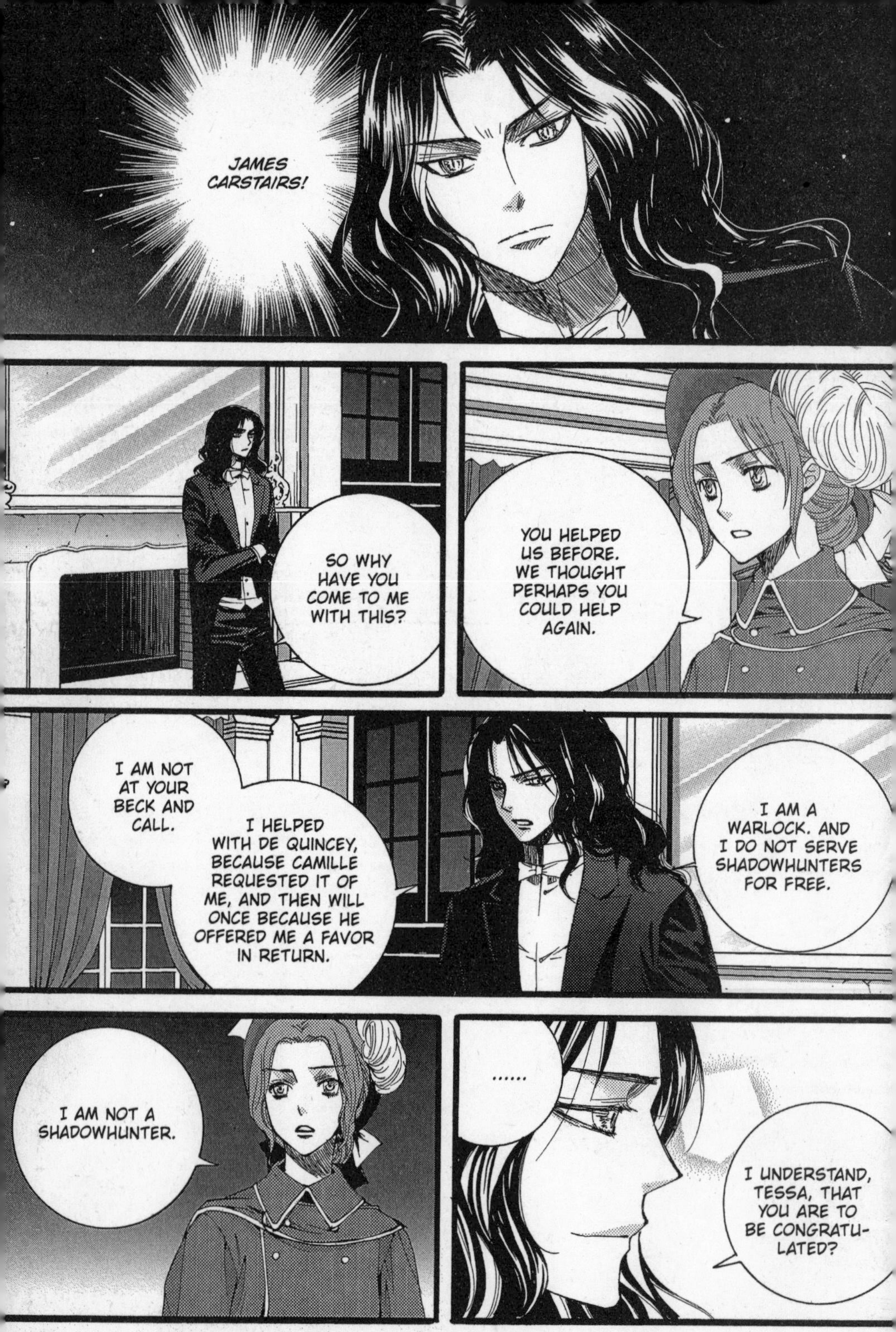
JAMES CARSTAIRS!
SO WHY HAVE YOU COME TO ME WITH THIS?
YOU HELPED US BEFORE. WE THOUGHT PERHAPS YOU COULD HELP AGAIN.
I AM NOT AT YOUR BECK AND CALL.
I HELPED WITH DE QUINCEY, BECAUSE CAMILLE REQUESTED IT OF ME, AND THEN WILL ONCE BECAUSE HE OFFERED ME A FAVOR IN RETURN.
I AM A WARLOCK. AND I DO NOT SERVE SHADOWHUNTERS FOR FREE.
I AM NOT A SHADOWHUNTER.
......
I UNDERSTAND, TESSA, THAT YOU ARE TO BE CONGRATU-LATED?

ON YOUR ENGAGEMENT TO JAMES CARSTAIRS.

OH.

YES, THANK YOU.

IF SOMEONE IS BUYING UP ALL THE *YIN FEN* IN THE COUNTRY, THERE'S NO ONE ELSE WITH A REASON BUT MORTMAIN.

YOU DON'T WANT TO HELP US.

YOU DO NOT WANT TO POSITION YOURSELF AS AN ENEMY OF MORTMAIN'S.

WELL, CAN YOU BLAME HIM?

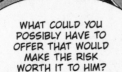

WHAT COULD YOU POSSIBLY HAVE TO OFFER THAT WOULD MAKE THE RISK WORTH IT TO HIM?

I WILL GIVE YOU ANYTHING.

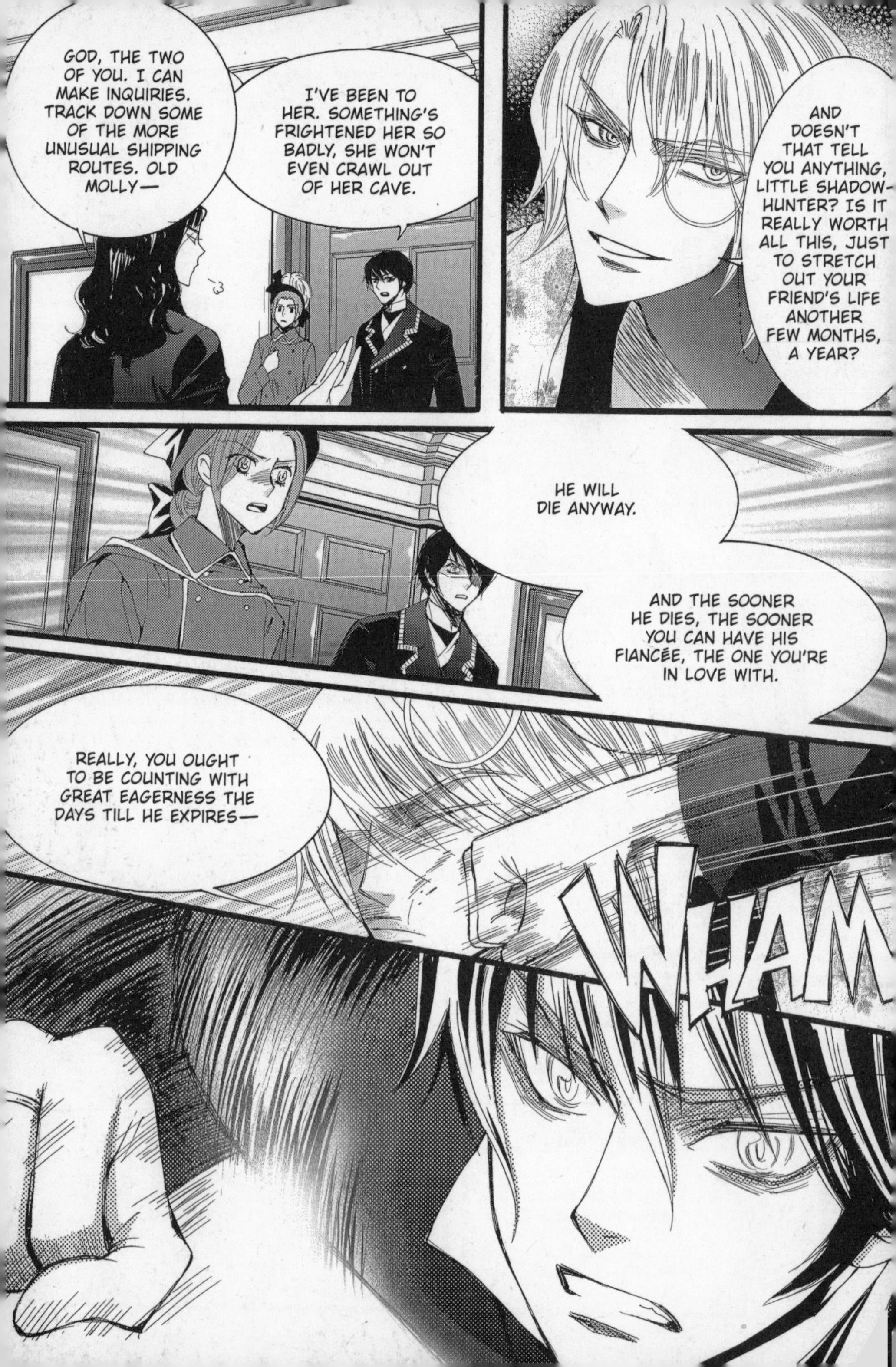
GOD, THE TWO OF YOU. I CAN MAKE INQUIRIES. TRACK DOWN SOME OF THE MORE UNUSUAL SHIPPING ROUTES. OLD MOLLY—
I'VE BEEN TO HER. SOMETHING'S FRIGHTENED HER SO BADLY, SHE WON'T EVEN CRAWL OUT OF HER CAVE.
AND DOESN'T THAT TELL YOU ANYTHING, LITTLE SHADOW-HUNTER? IS IT REALLY WORTH ALL THIS, JUST TO STRETCH OUT YOUR FRIEND'S LIFE ANOTHER FEW MONTHS, A YEAR?
HE WILL DIE ANYWAY.
AND THE SOONER HE DIES, THE SOONER YOU CAN HAVE HIS FIANCÉE, THE ONE YOU'RE IN LOVE WITH.
REALLY, YOU OUGHT TO BE COUNTING WITH GREAT EAGERNESS THE DAYS TILL HE EXPIRES—
WHAM

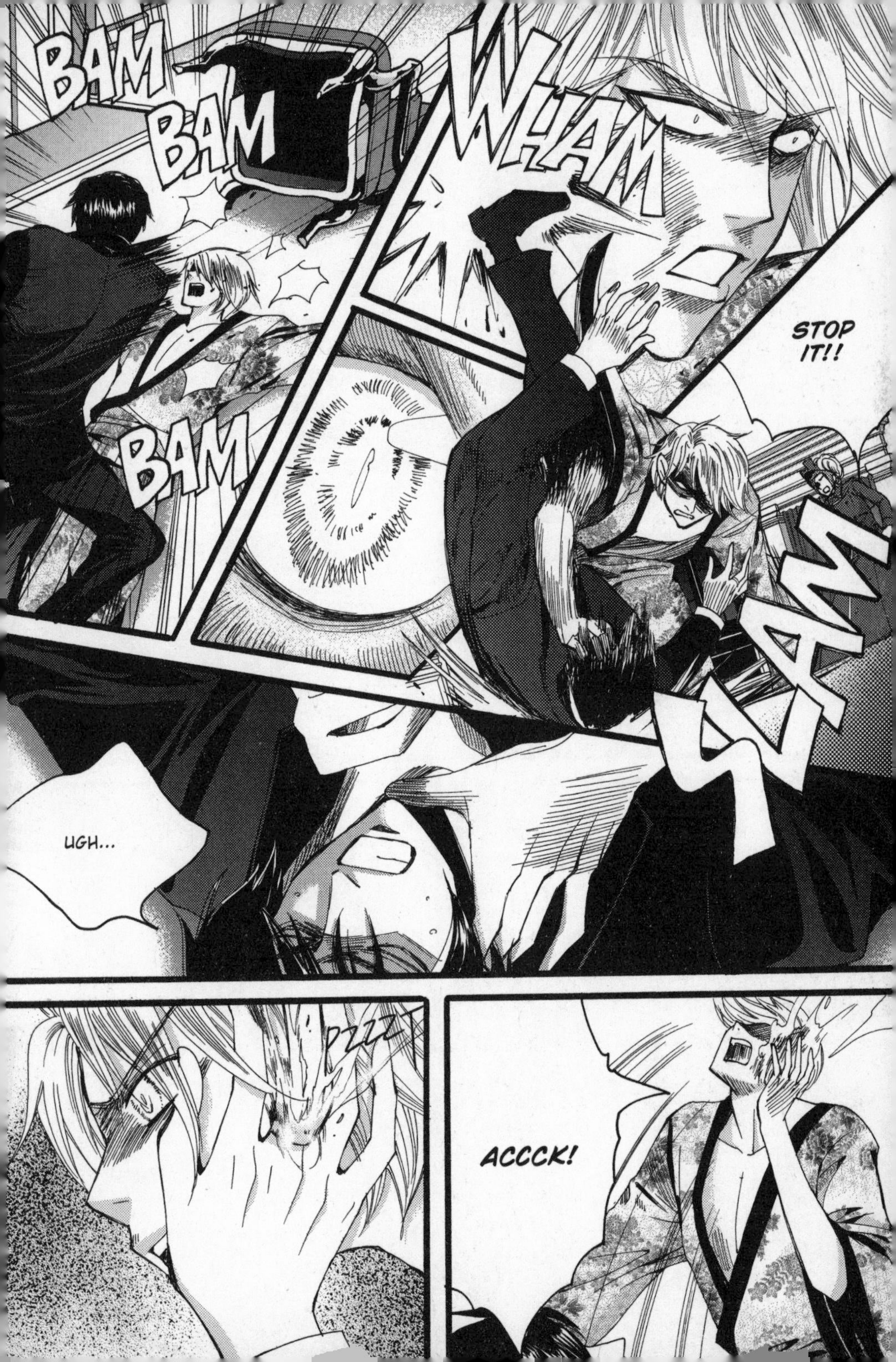
WHAM
BAM
BAM
BAM
STOP IT!!
SLAM
UGH...
PZZZT
ACCCK!

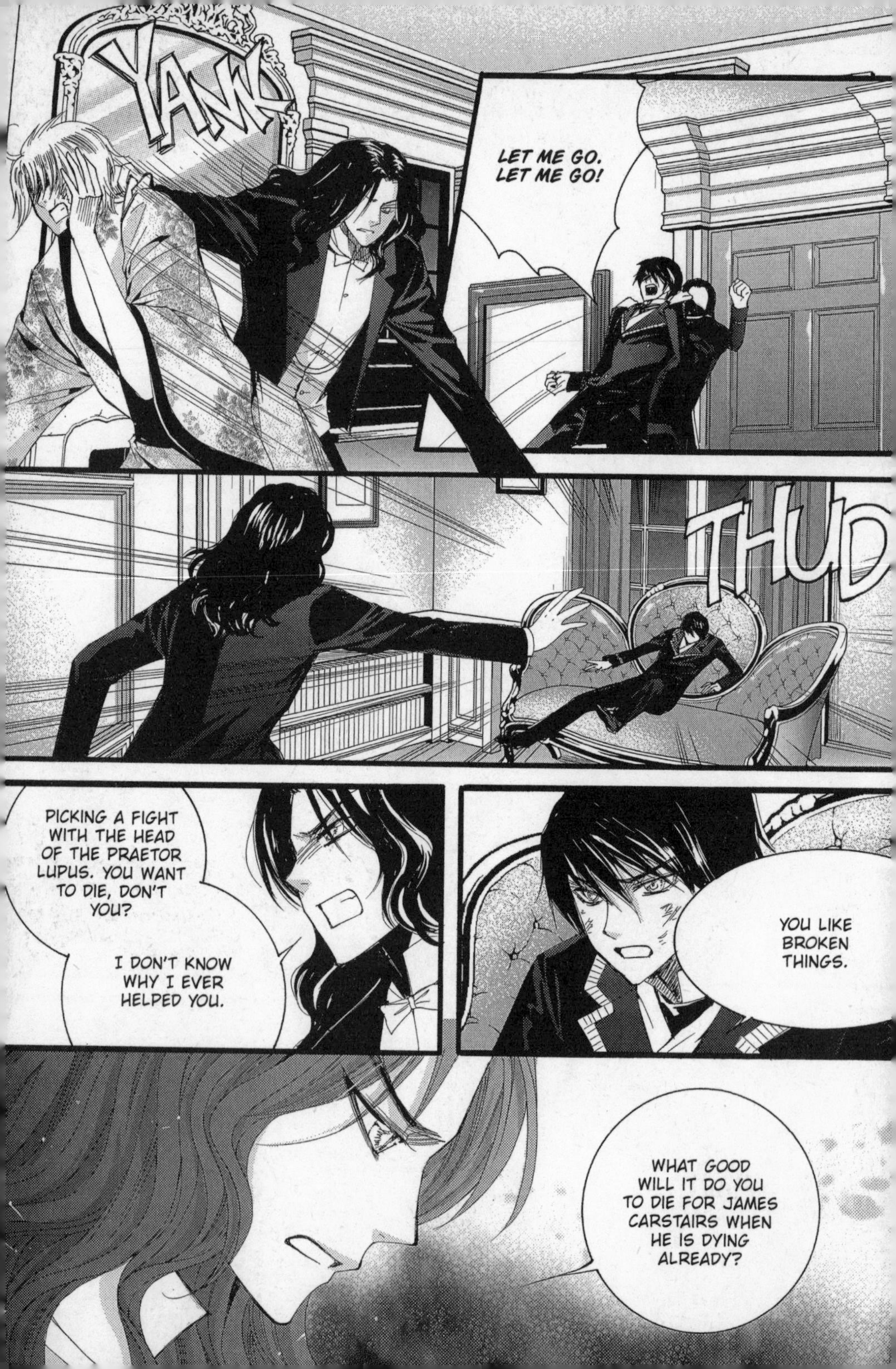
YANK
LET ME GO. LET ME GO!
THUD
PICKING A FIGHT WITH THE HEAD OF THE PRAETOR LUPUS. YOU WANT TO DIE, DON'T YOU?
I DON'T KNOW WHY I EVER HELPED YOU.
YOU LIKE BROKEN THINGS.
WHAT GOOD WILL IT DO YOU TO DIE FOR JAMES CARSTAIRS WHEN HE IS DYING ALREADY?

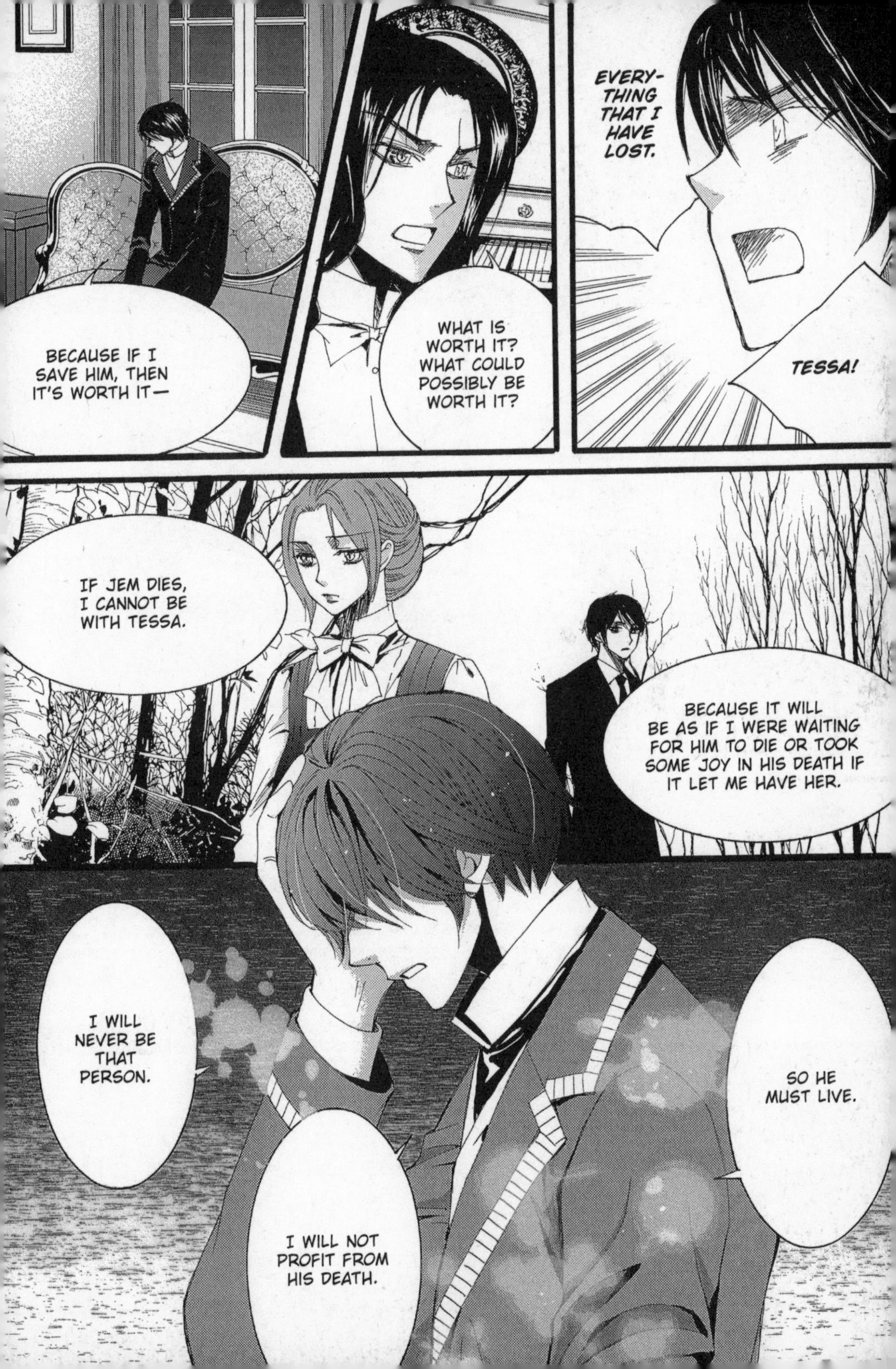
BECAUSE IF I SAVE HIM, THEN IT'S WORTH IT—
WHAT IS WORTH IT? WHAT COULD POSSIBLY BE WORTH IT?
EVERY-THING THAT I HAVE LOST.
TESSA!
IF JEM DIES, I CANNOT BE WITH TESSA.
BECAUSE IT WILL BE AS IF I WERE WAITING FOR HIM TO DIE OR TOOK SOME JOY IN HIS DEATH IF IT LET ME HAVE HER.
I WILL NEVER BE THAT PERSON.
I WILL NOT PROFIT FROM HIS DEATH.
SO HE MUST LIVE.

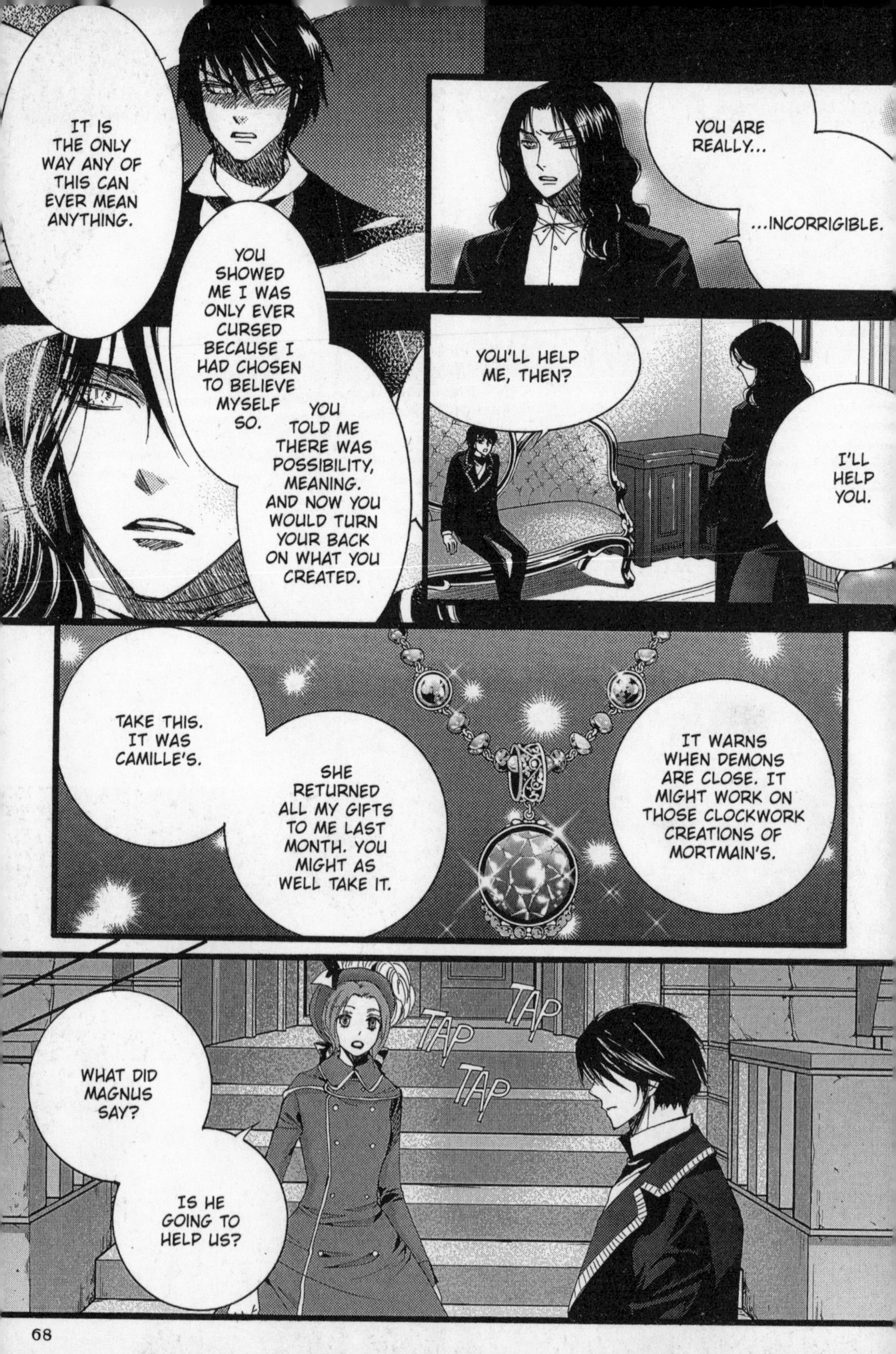
IT IS THE ONLY WAY ANY OF THIS CAN EVER MEAN ANYTHING.
YOU ARE REALLY...
...INCORRIGIBLE.
YOU SHOWED ME I WAS ONLY EVER CURSED BECAUSE I HAD CHOSEN TO BELIEVE MYSELF SO.
YOU TOLD ME THERE WAS POSSIBILITY, MEANING. AND NOW YOU WOULD TURN YOUR BACK ON WHAT YOU CREATED.
YOU'LL HELP ME, THEN?
I'LL HELP YOU.
TAKE THIS. IT WAS CAMILLE'S.
SHE RETURNED ALL MY GIFTS TO ME LAST MONTH. YOU MIGHT AS WELL TAKE IT.
IT WARNS WHEN DEMONS ARE CLOSE. IT MIGHT WORK ON THOSE CLOCKWORK CREATIONS OF MORTMAIN'S.
TAP TAP TAP
WHAT DID MAGNUS SAY?
IS HE GOING TO HELP US?

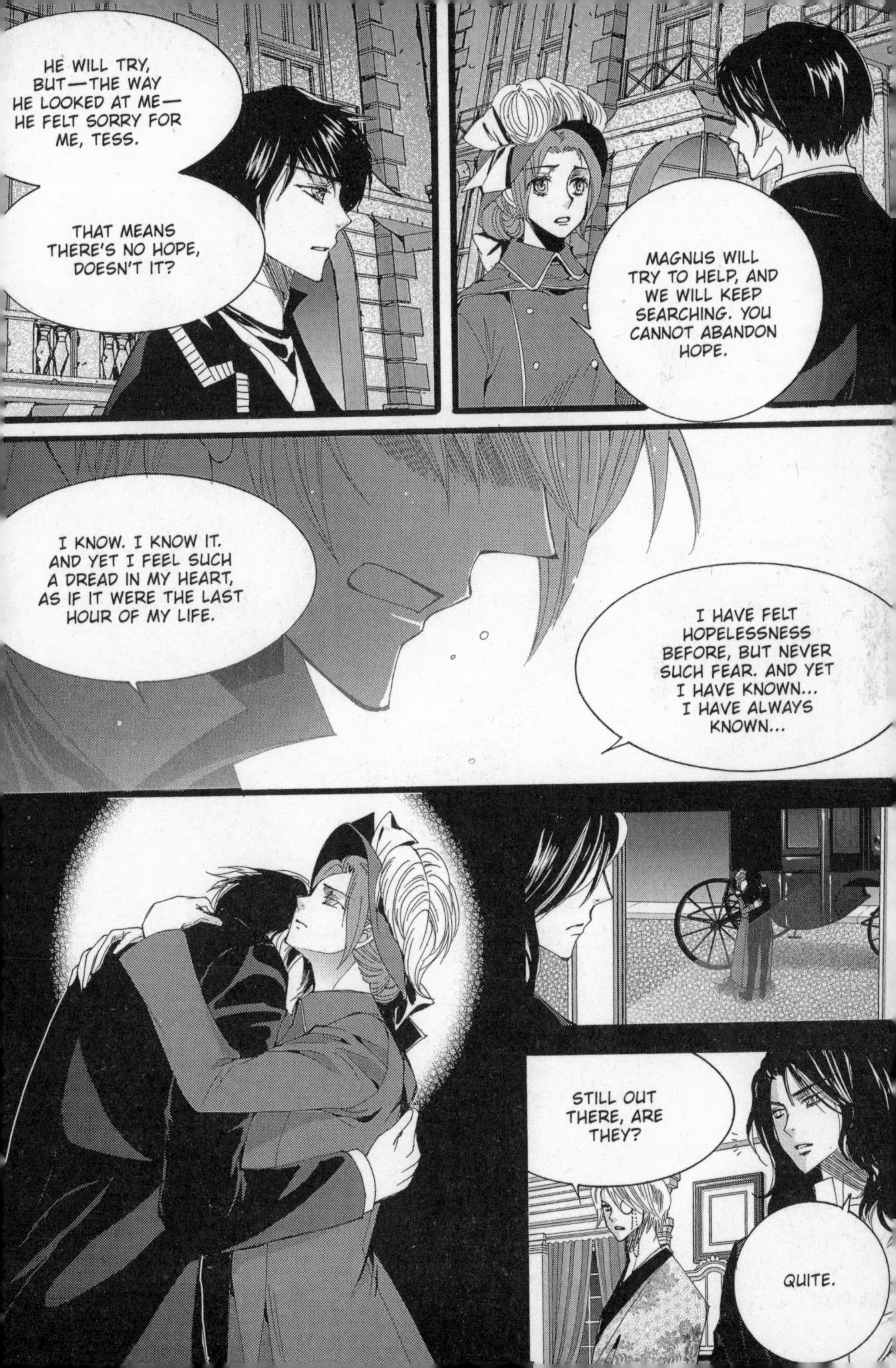
HE WILL TRY, BUT—THE WAY HE LOOKED AT ME—HE FELT SORRY FOR ME, TESS.
THAT MEANS THERE'S NO HOPE, DOESN'T IT?
MAGNUS WILL TRY TO HELP, AND WE WILL KEEP SEARCHING. YOU CANNOT ABANDON HOPE.
I KNOW. I KNOW IT. AND YET I FEEL SUCH A DREAD IN MY HEART, AS IF IT WERE THE LAST HOUR OF MY LIFE.
I HAVE FELT HOPELESSNESS BEFORE, BUT NEVER SUCH FEAR. AND YET I HAVE KNOWN... I HAVE ALWAYS KNOWN...
STILL OUT THERE, ARE THEY?
QUITE.

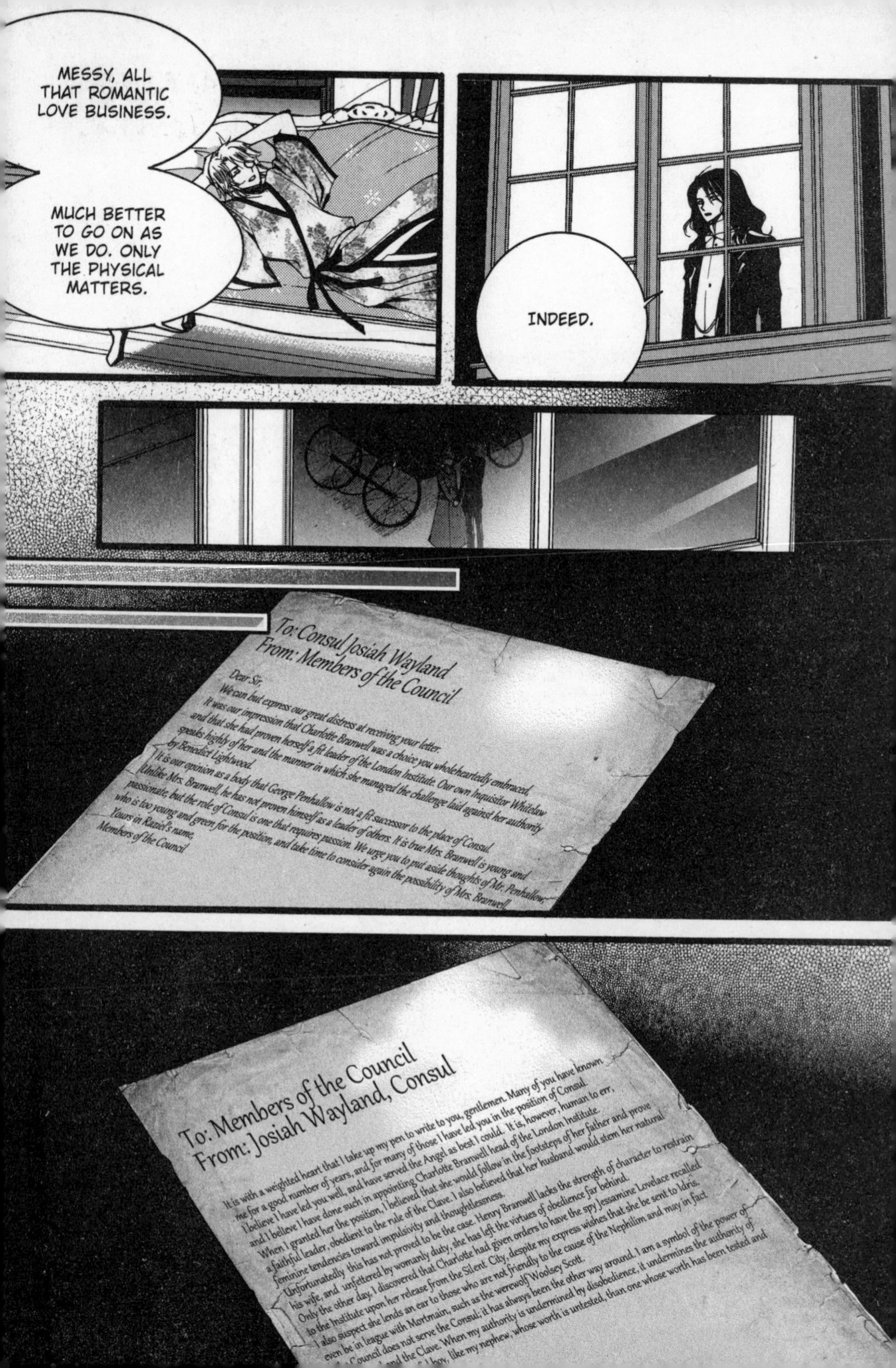
MESSY, ALL THAT ROMANTIC LOVE BUSINESS.
MUCH BETTER TO GO ON AS WE DO. ONLY THE PHYSICAL MATTERS.
INDEED.
To: Consul Josiah Wayland
From: Members of the Council
Dear Sir,
We can but express our great distress at receiving your letter.
It was our impression that Charlotte Branwell was a choice you wholeheartedly embraced,
and that she had proven herself a fit leader of the London Institute. Our own Inquisitor Whitelaw
speaks highly of her and the manner in which she managed the challenge laid against her authority
by Benedict Lightwood.
It is our opinion as a body that George Penhallow is not a fit successor to the place of Consul.
Unlike Mrs. Branwell, he has not proven himself as a leader of others. It is true Mrs. Branwell is young and
passionate, but the role of Consul is one that requires passion. We urge you to put aside thoughts of Mr. Penhallow,
who is too young and green for the position, and take time to consider again the possibility of Mrs. Branwell.
Yours in Raziel's name,
Members of the Council
To: Members of the Council
From: Josiah Wayland, Consul
It is with a weighted heart that I take up my pen to write to you, gentlemen. Many of you have known
me for a good number of years, and for many of those I have led you in the position of Consul.
I believe I have led you well, and have served the Angel as best I could. It is, however, human to err,
and I believe I have done such in appointing Charlotte Branwell head of the London Institute.
When I granted her the position, I believed that she would follow in the footsteps of her father and prove
a faithful leader, obedient to the rule of the Clave. I also believed that her husband would stem her natural
feminine tendencies toward impulsivity and thoughtlessness.
Unfortunatedly this has not proved to be the case. Henry Branwell lacks the strength of character to restrain
his wife, and unfettered by womanly duty, she has left the virtues of obedience far behind.
Only the other day, I discovered that Charlotte had given orders to have the spy Jessamine Lovelace recalled
to the Institute upon her release from the Silent City, despite my express wishes that she be sent to Idris.
I also suspect she lends an ear to those who are not friendly to the cause of the Nephilim and may in fact
even be in league with Mortmain, such as the werewolf Woolsey Scott.
Council does not serve the Consul; it has always been the other way around. I am a symbol of the power of
and the Clave. When my authority is undermined by disobedience, it undermines the authority of
boy, like my nephew, whose worth is untested, than one whose worth has been tested and

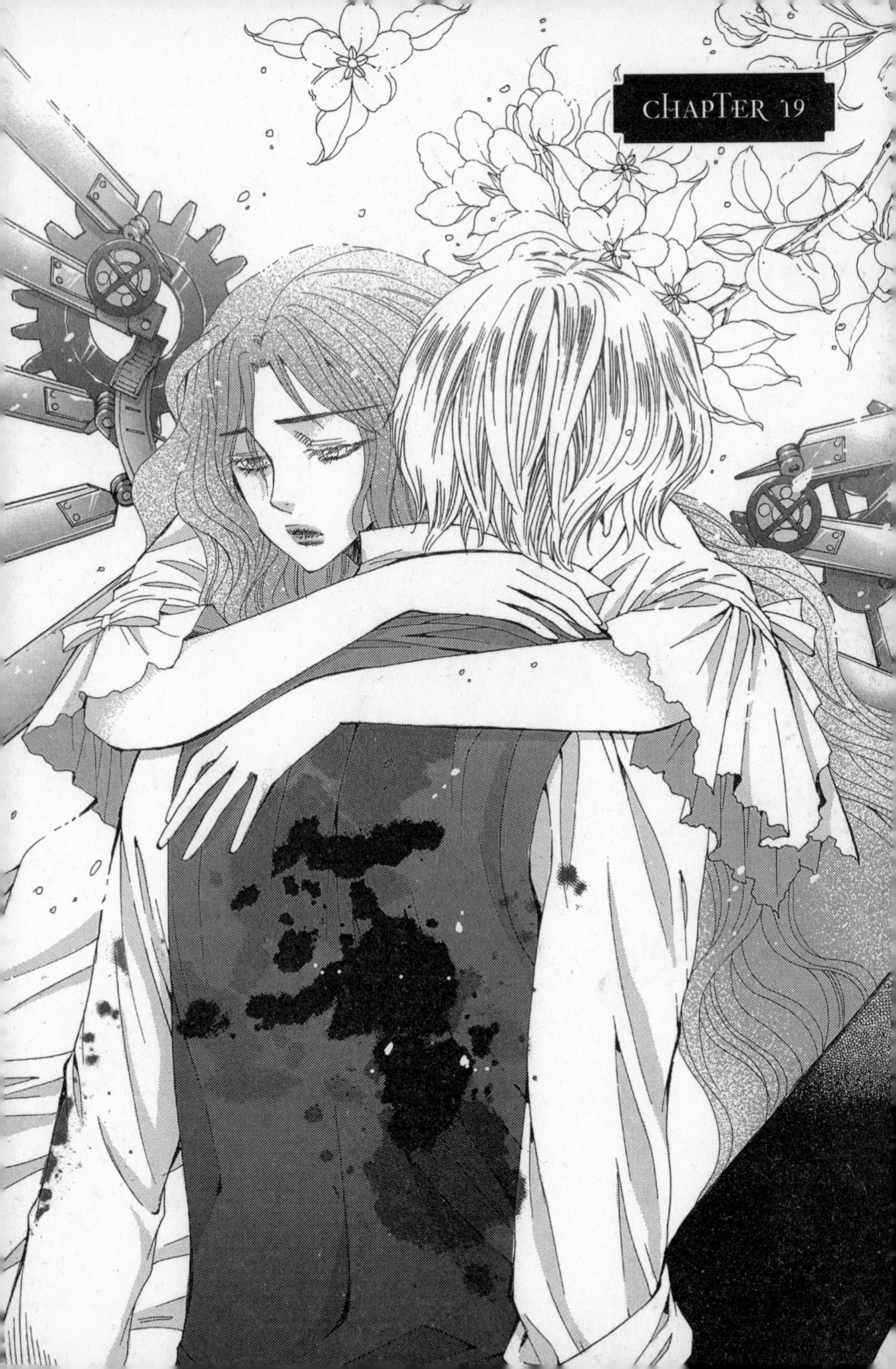
CHAPTER 19

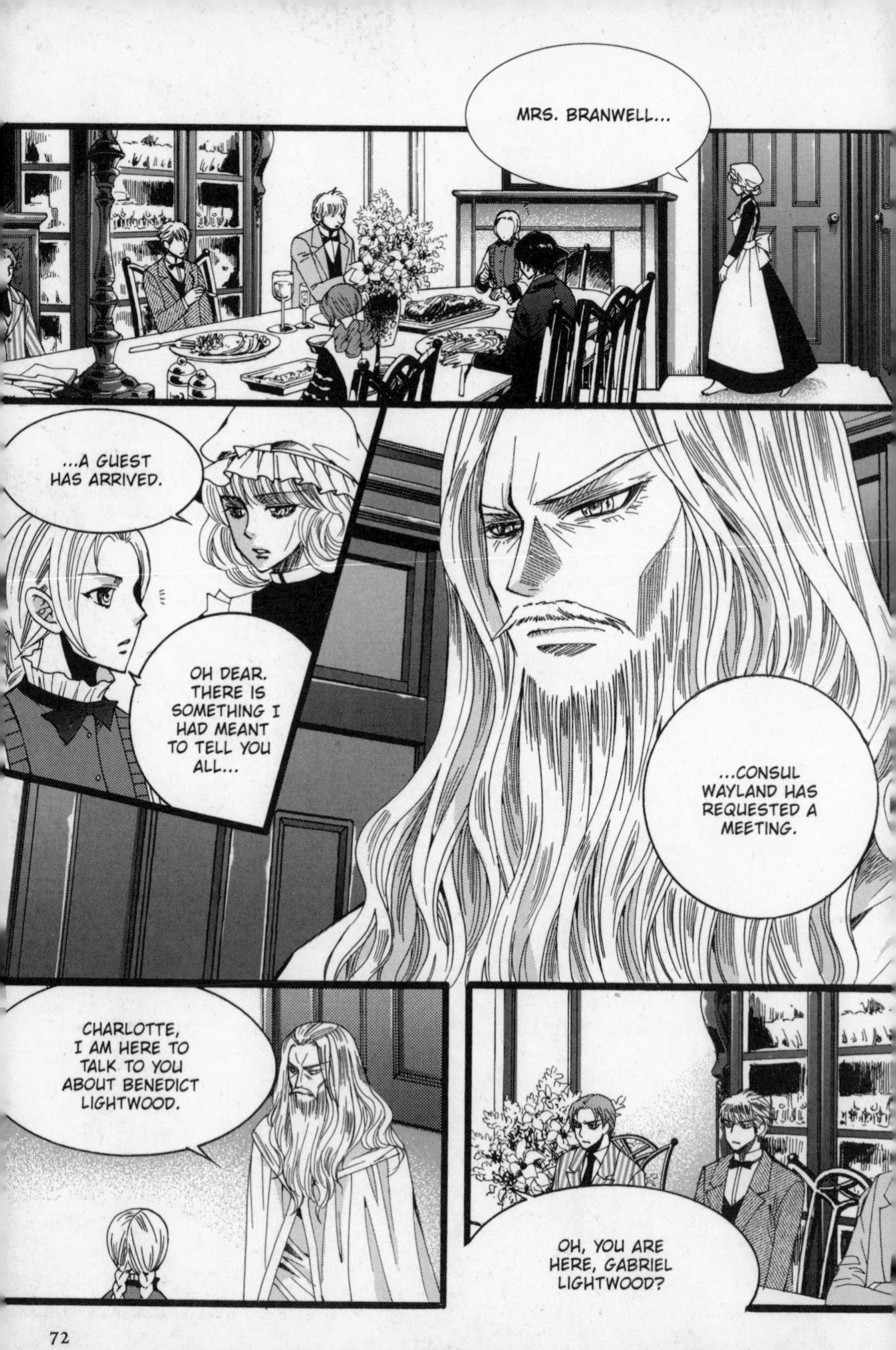
MRS. BRANWELL...
...A GUEST HAS ARRIVED.
OH DEAR. THERE IS SOMETHING I HAD MEANT TO TELL YOU ALL...
...CONSUL WAYLAND HAS REQUESTED A MEETING.
CHARLOTTE, I AM HERE TO TALK TO YOU ABOUT BENEDICT LIGHTWOOD.
OH, YOU ARE HERE, GABRIEL LIGHTWOOD?

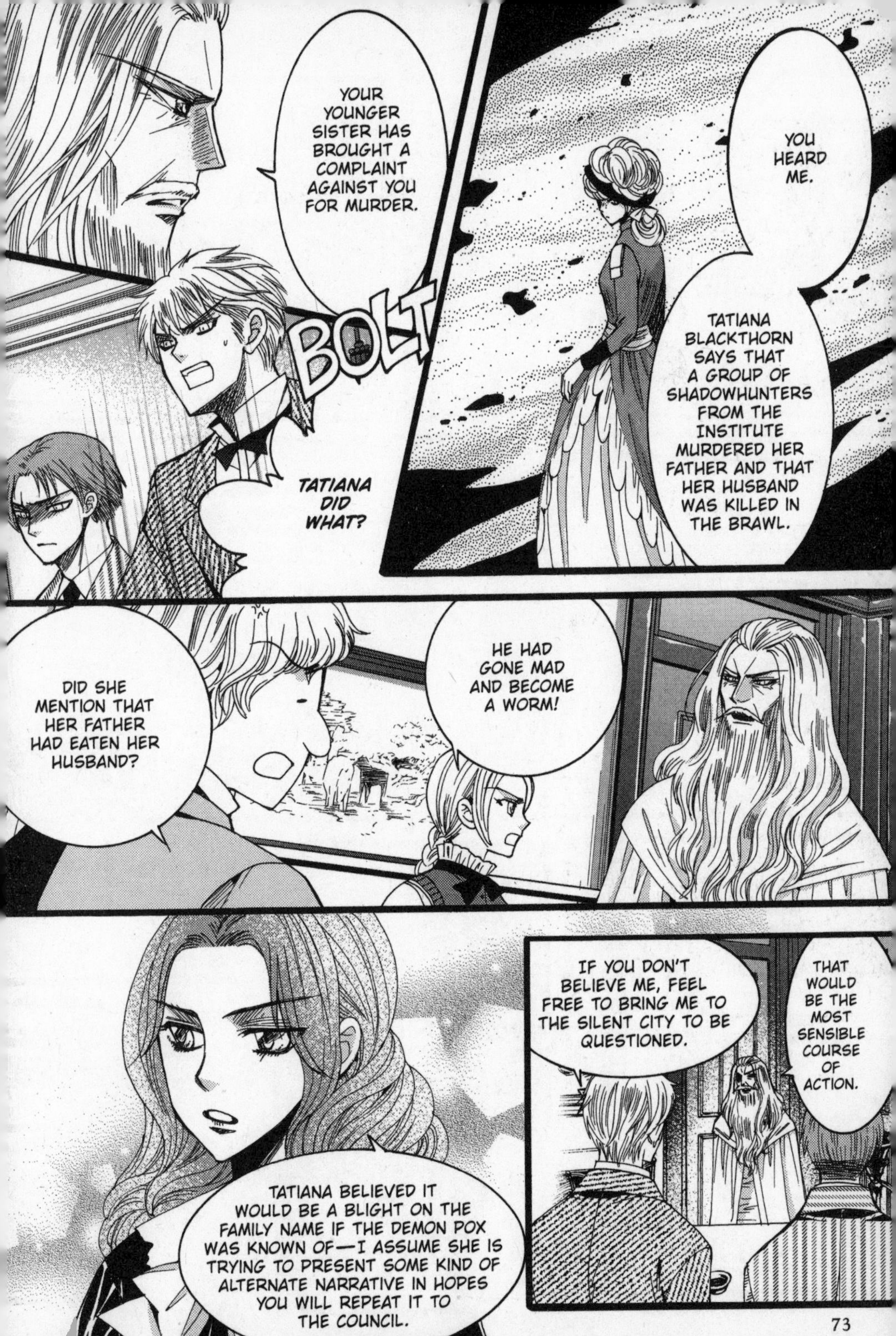

YOUR YOUNGER SISTER HAS BROUGHT A COMPLAINT AGAINST YOU FOR MURDER.
BOLT
TATIANA DID WHAT?
YOU HEARD ME.
TATIANA BLACKTHORN SAYS THAT A GROUP OF SHADOWHUNTERS FROM THE INSTITUTE MURDERED HER FATHER AND THAT HER HUSBAND WAS KILLED IN THE BRAWL.
DID SHE MENTION THAT HER FATHER HAD EATEN HER HUSBAND?
HE HAD GONE MAD AND BECOME A WORM!
TATIANA BELIEVED IT WOULD BE A BLIGHT ON THE FAMILY NAME IF THE DEMON POX WAS KNOWN OF—I ASSUME SHE IS TRYING TO PRESENT SOME KIND OF ALTERNATE NARRATIVE IN HOPES YOU WILL REPEAT IT TO THE COUNCIL.
IF YOU DON'T BELIEVE ME, FEEL FREE TO BRING ME TO THE SILENT CITY TO BE QUESTIONED.
THAT WOULD BE THE MOST SENSIBLE COURSE OF ACTION.

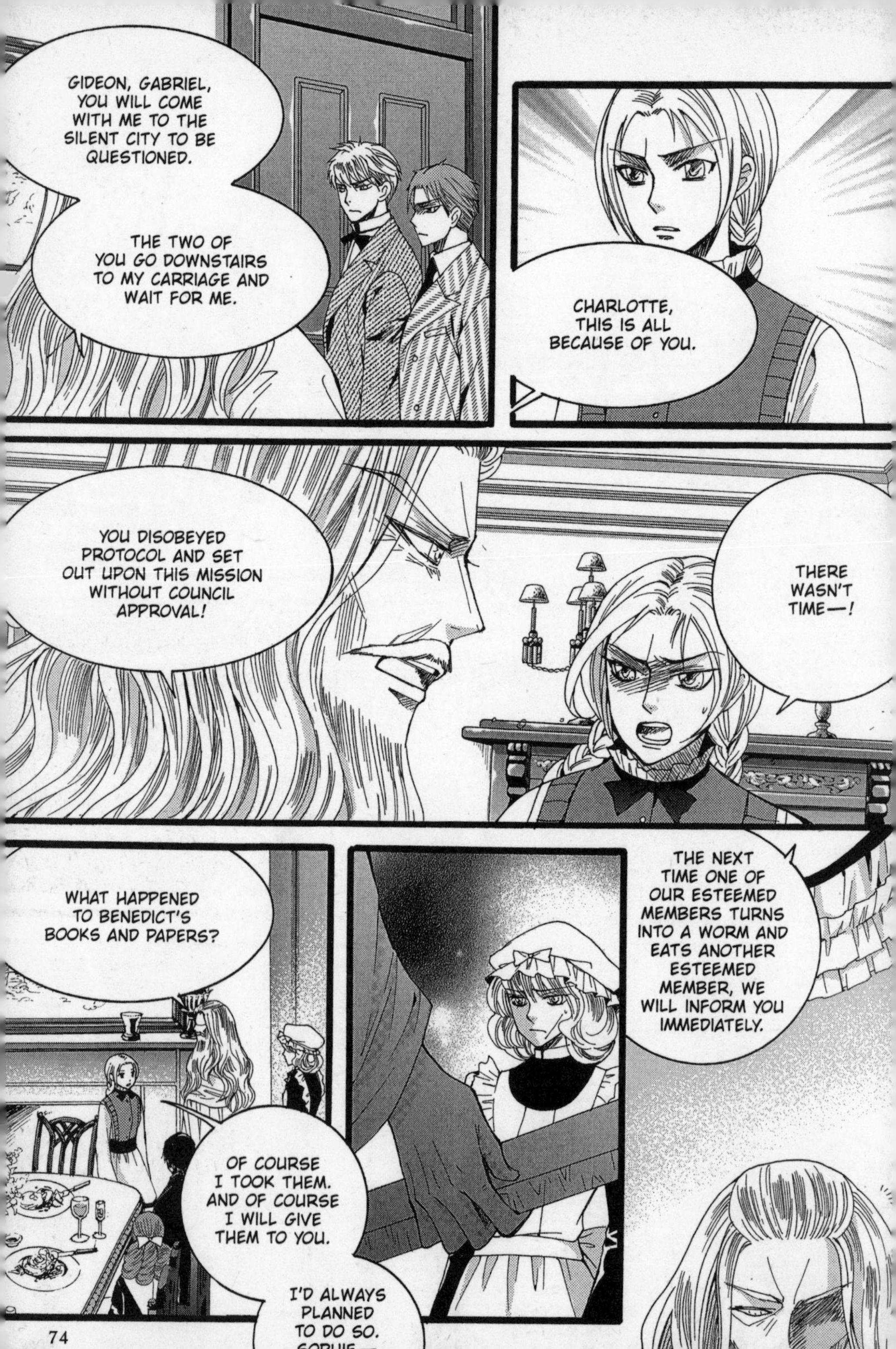
GIDEON, GABRIEL, YOU WILL COME WITH ME TO THE SILENT CITY TO BE QUESTIONED.
THE TWO OF YOU GO DOWNSTAIRS TO MY CARRIAGE AND WAIT FOR ME.
CHARLOTTE, THIS IS ALL BECAUSE OF YOU.
YOU DISOBEYED PROTOCOL AND SET OUT UPON THIS MISSION WITHOUT COUNCIL APPROVAL!
THERE WASN'T TIME—!
WHAT HAPPENED TO BENEDICT'S BOOKS AND PAPERS?
THE NEXT TIME ONE OF OUR ESTEEMED MEMBERS TURNS INTO A WORM AND EATS ANOTHER ESTEEMED MEMBER, WE WILL INFORM YOU IMMEDIATELY.
OF COURSE I TOOK THEM. AND OF COURSE I WILL GIVE THEM TO YOU.
I'D ALWAYS PLANNED TO DO SO. SOPHIE—

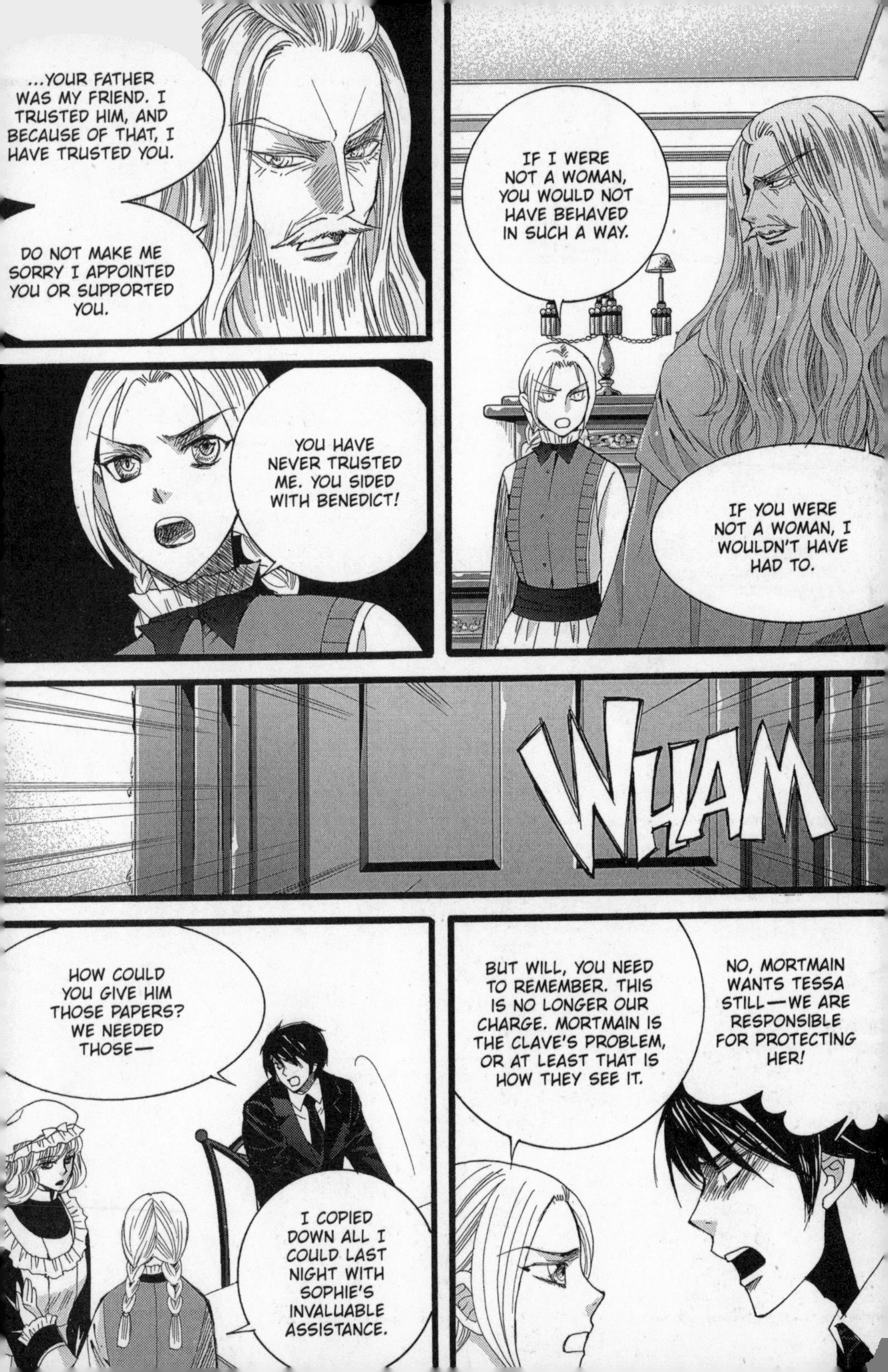

...YOUR FATHER WAS MY FRIEND. I TRUSTED HIM, AND BECAUSE OF THAT, I HAVE TRUSTED YOU.
DO NOT MAKE ME SORRY I APPOINTED YOU OR SUPPORTED YOU.
IF I WERE NOT A WOMAN, YOU WOULD NOT HAVE BEHAVED IN SUCH A WAY.
YOU HAVE NEVER TRUSTED ME. YOU SIDED WITH BENEDICT!
IF YOU WERE NOT A WOMAN, I WOULDN'T HAVE HAD TO.
WHAM
HOW COULD YOU GIVE HIM THOSE PAPERS? WE NEEDED THOSE—
I COPIED DOWN ALL I COULD LAST NIGHT WITH SOPHIE'S INVALUABLE ASSISTANCE.
BUT WILL, YOU NEED TO REMEMBER. THIS IS NO LONGER OUR CHARGE. MORTMAIN IS THE CLAVE'S PROBLEM, OR AT LEAST THAT IS HOW THEY SEE IT.
NO, MORTMAIN WANTS TESSA STILL—WE ARE RESPONSIBLE FOR PROTECTING HER!

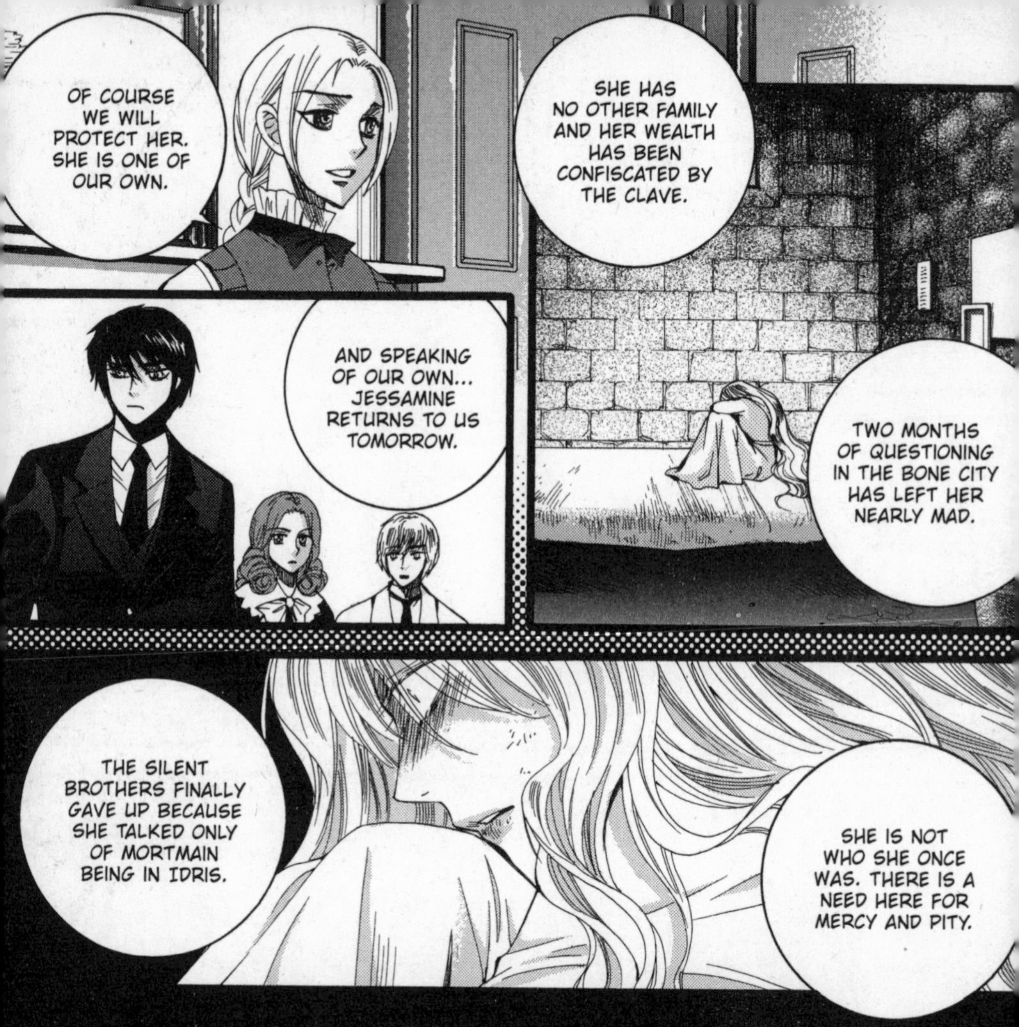

OF COURSE WE WILL PROTECT HER. SHE IS ONE OF OUR OWN.
SHE HAS NO OTHER FAMILY AND HER WEALTH HAS BEEN CONFISCATED BY THE CLAVE.
AND SPEAKING OF OUR OWN... JESSAMINE RETURNS TO US TOMORROW.
TWO MONTHS OF QUESTIONING IN THE BONE CITY HAS LEFT HER NEARLY MAD.
THE SILENT BROTHERS FINALLY GAVE UP BECAUSE SHE TALKED ONLY OF MORTMAIN BEING IN IDRIS.
SHE IS NOT WHO SHE ONCE WAS. THERE IS A NEED HERE FOR MERCY AND PITY.

To: Consul Wayland
From: The Council

Dear Sir,

Until our receipt of your last letter, we had thought our difference in thought on the topic of Charlotte Branwell to be a matter of simple opinion. Though you may not have given express permission for the removal of Jessamine Lovelace to the Institute, the approval was granted by the Brotherhood, who are in charge of such things. It seemed to us the action of a generous heart to allow the girl back into the only home she has ever known, despite her wrongdoing. As for Woolsey Scott, he heads the Praetor Lupus, an organization we have long considered allies.

Your suggestion that Mrs. Branwell may have given her ear to those who do not have the Clave's best interests at heart is deeply troubling. Without proof, however, we are reluctant to move forward with this as a basis of information.

In Raziel's name,
The Members of the Nephilim Council

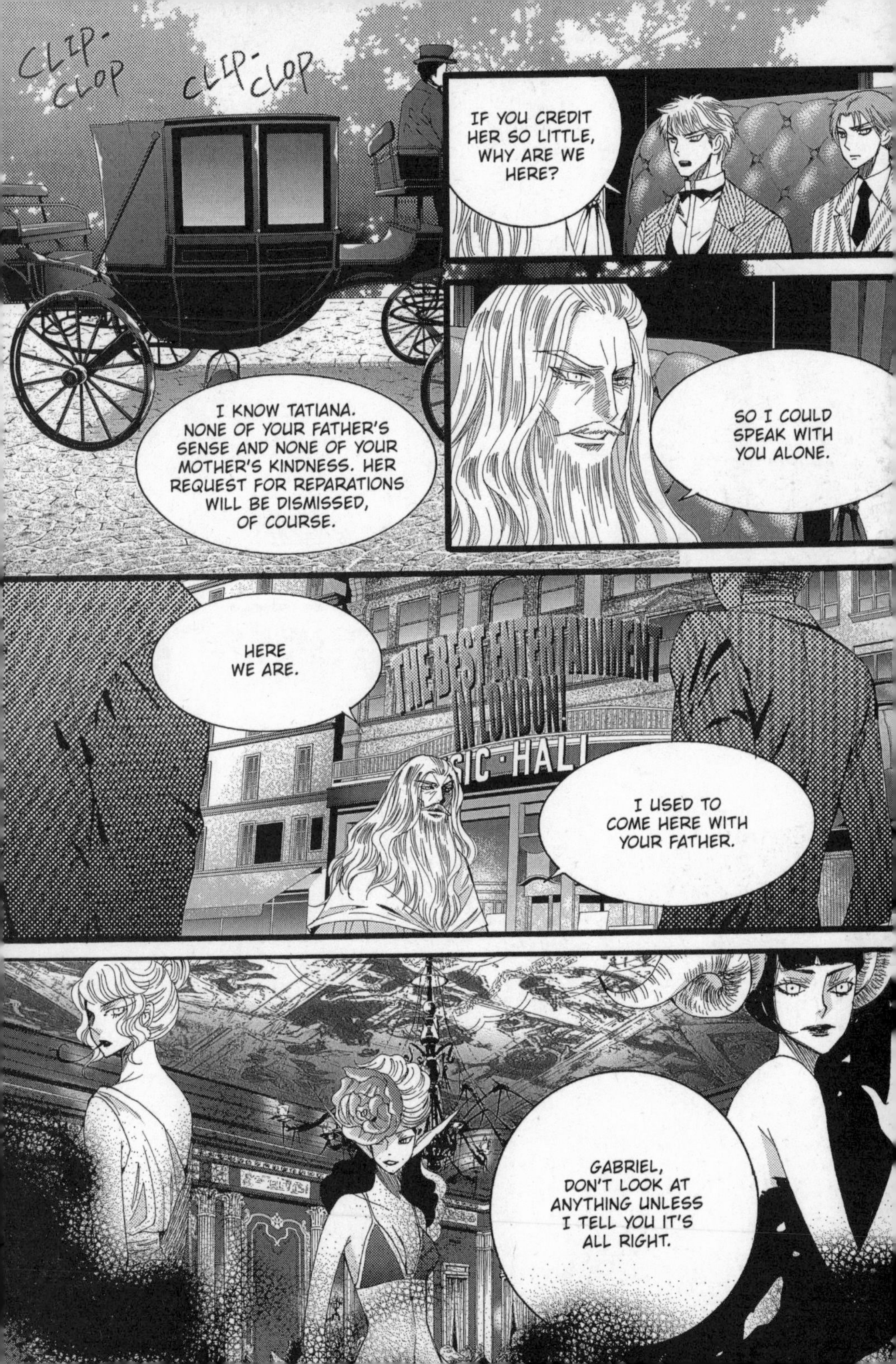
CLIP-CLOP
CLIP-CLOP
IF YOU CREDIT HER SO LITTLE, WHY ARE WE HERE?
I KNOW TATIANA. NONE OF YOUR FATHER'S SENSE AND NONE OF YOUR MOTHER'S KINDNESS. HER REQUEST FOR REPARATIONS WILL BE DISMISSED, OF COURSE.
SO I COULD SPEAK WITH YOU ALONE.
HERE WE ARE.
THE BEST ENTERTAINMENT IN LONDON!
SIC · HALL
I USED TO COME HERE WITH YOUR FATHER.
GABRIEL, DON'T LOOK AT ANYTHING UNLESS I TELL YOU IT'S ALL RIGHT.

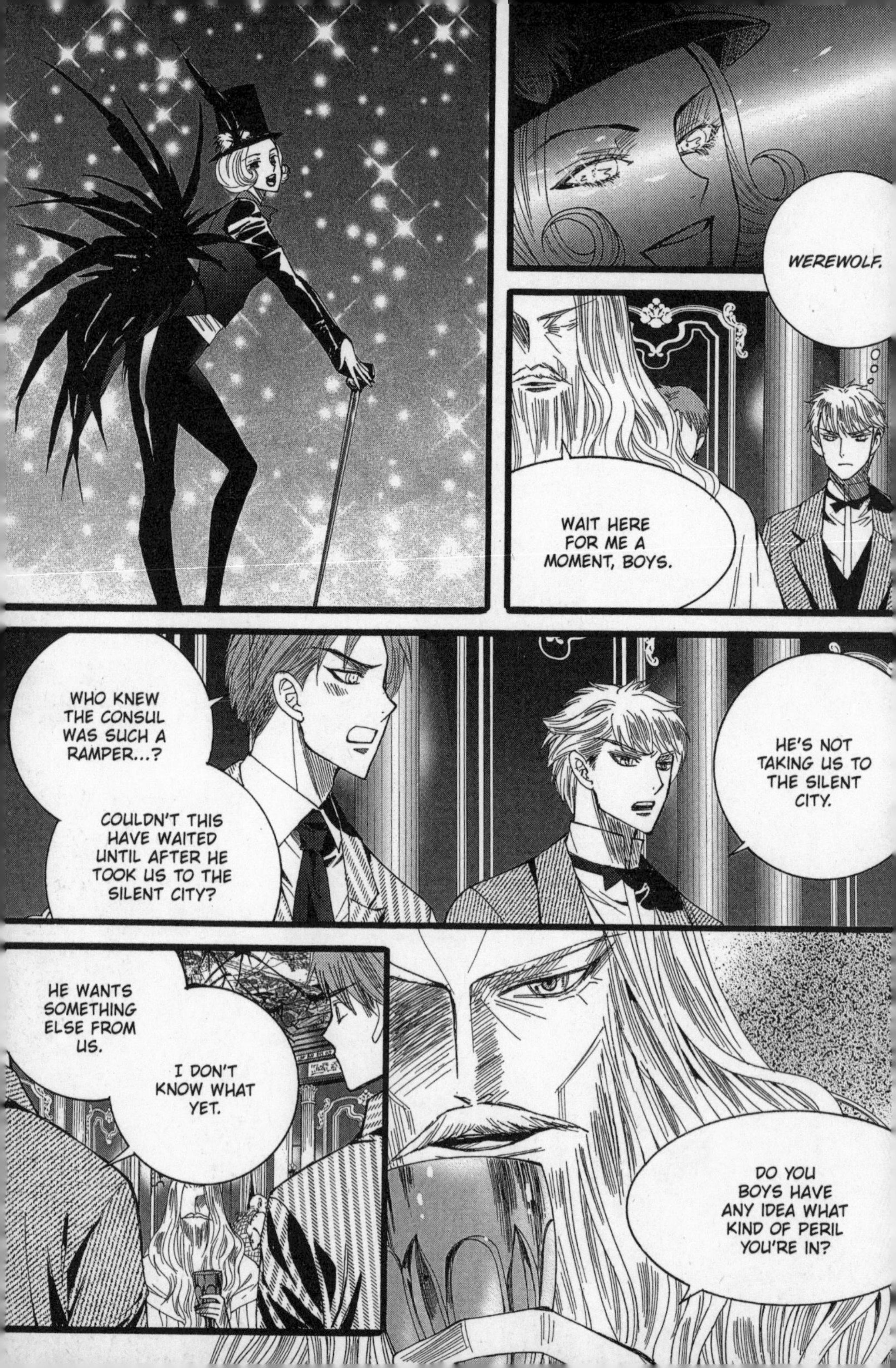
WEREWOLF.
WAIT HERE FOR ME A MOMENT, BOYS.
WHO KNEW THE CONSUL WAS SUCH A RAMPER...?
COULDN'T THIS HAVE WAITED UNTIL AFTER HE TOOK US TO THE SILENT CITY?
HE'S NOT TAKING US TO THE SILENT CITY.
HE WANTS SOMETHING ELSE FROM US.
I DON'T KNOW WHAT YET.
DO YOU BOYS HAVE ANY IDEA WHAT KIND OF PERIL YOU'RE IN?

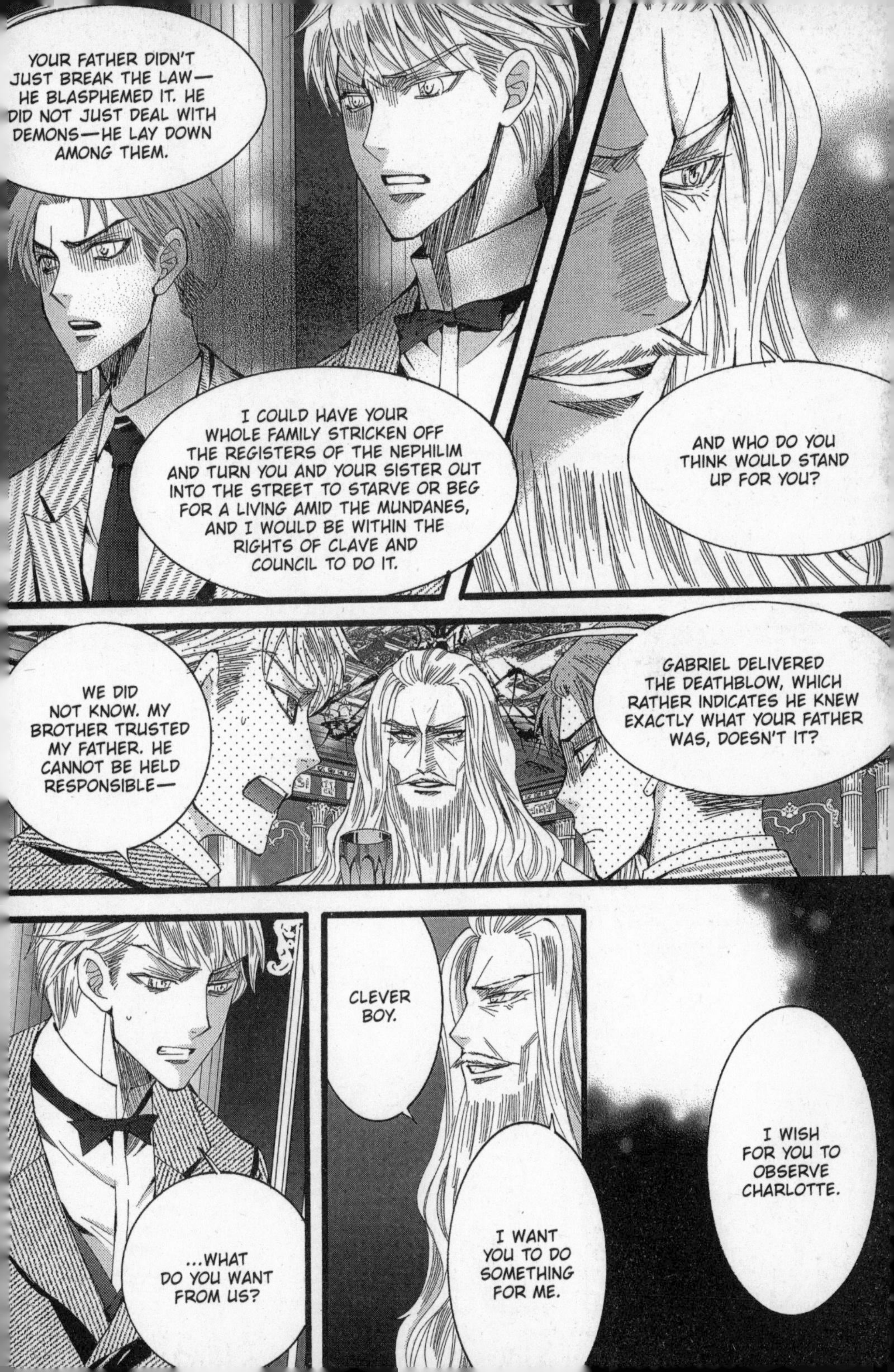
YOUR FATHER DIDN'T JUST BREAK THE LAW— HE BLASPHEMED IT. HE DID NOT JUST DEAL WITH DEMONS—HE LAY DOWN AMONG THEM.
I COULD HAVE YOUR WHOLE FAMILY STRICKEN OFF THE REGISTERS OF THE NEPHILIM AND TURN YOU AND YOUR SISTER OUT INTO THE STREET TO STARVE OR BEG FOR A LIVING AMID THE MUNDANES, AND I WOULD BE WITHIN THE RIGHTS OF CLAVE AND COUNCIL TO DO IT.
AND WHO DO YOU THINK WOULD STAND UP FOR YOU?
WE DID NOT KNOW. MY BROTHER TRUSTED MY FATHER. HE CANNOT BE HELD RESPONSIBLE—
GABRIEL DELIVERED THE DEATHBLOW, WHICH RATHER INDICATES HE KNEW EXACTLY WHAT YOUR FATHER WAS, DOESN'T IT?
...WHAT DO YOU WANT FROM US?
CLEVER BOY.
I WANT YOU TO DO SOMETHING FOR ME.
I WISH FOR YOU TO OBSERVE CHARLOTTE.

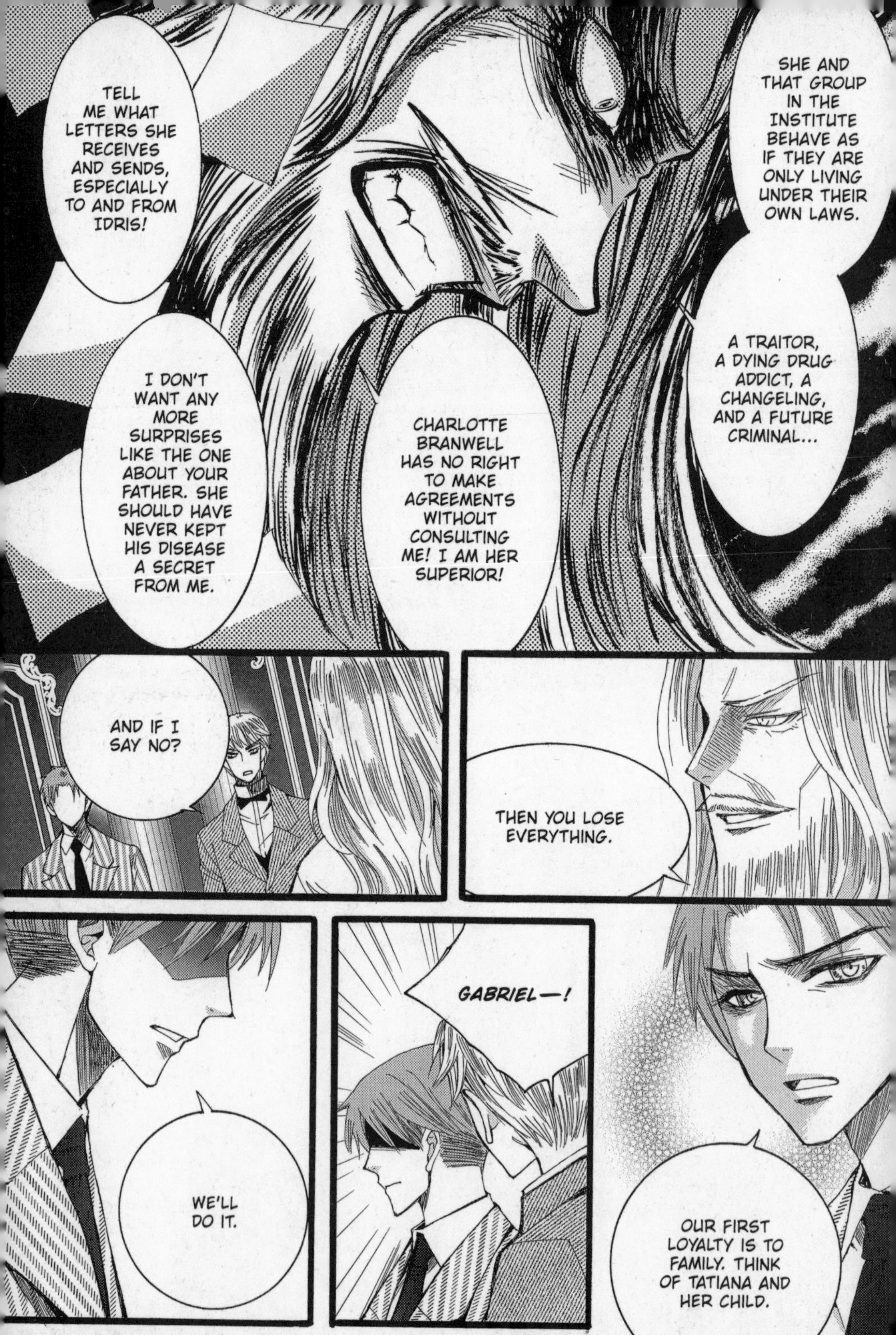
SHE AND THAT GROUP IN THE INSTITUTE BEHAVE AS IF THEY ARE ONLY LIVING UNDER THEIR OWN LAWS.
A TRAITOR, A DYING DRUG ADDICT, A CHANGELING, AND A FUTURE CRIMINAL...
CHARLOTTE BRANWELL HAS NO RIGHT TO MAKE AGREEMENTS WITHOUT CONSULTING ME! I AM HER SUPERIOR!
I DON'T WANT ANY MORE SURPRISES LIKE THE ONE ABOUT YOUR FATHER. SHE SHOULD HAVE NEVER KEPT HIS DISEASE A SECRET FROM ME.
TELL ME WHAT LETTERS SHE RECEIVES AND SENDS, ESPECIALLY TO AND FROM IDRIS!
AND IF I SAY NO?
THEN YOU LOSE EVERYTHING.
OUR FIRST LOYALTY IS TO FAMILY. THINK OF TATIANA AND HER CHILD.
GABRIEL—!
WE'LL DO IT.

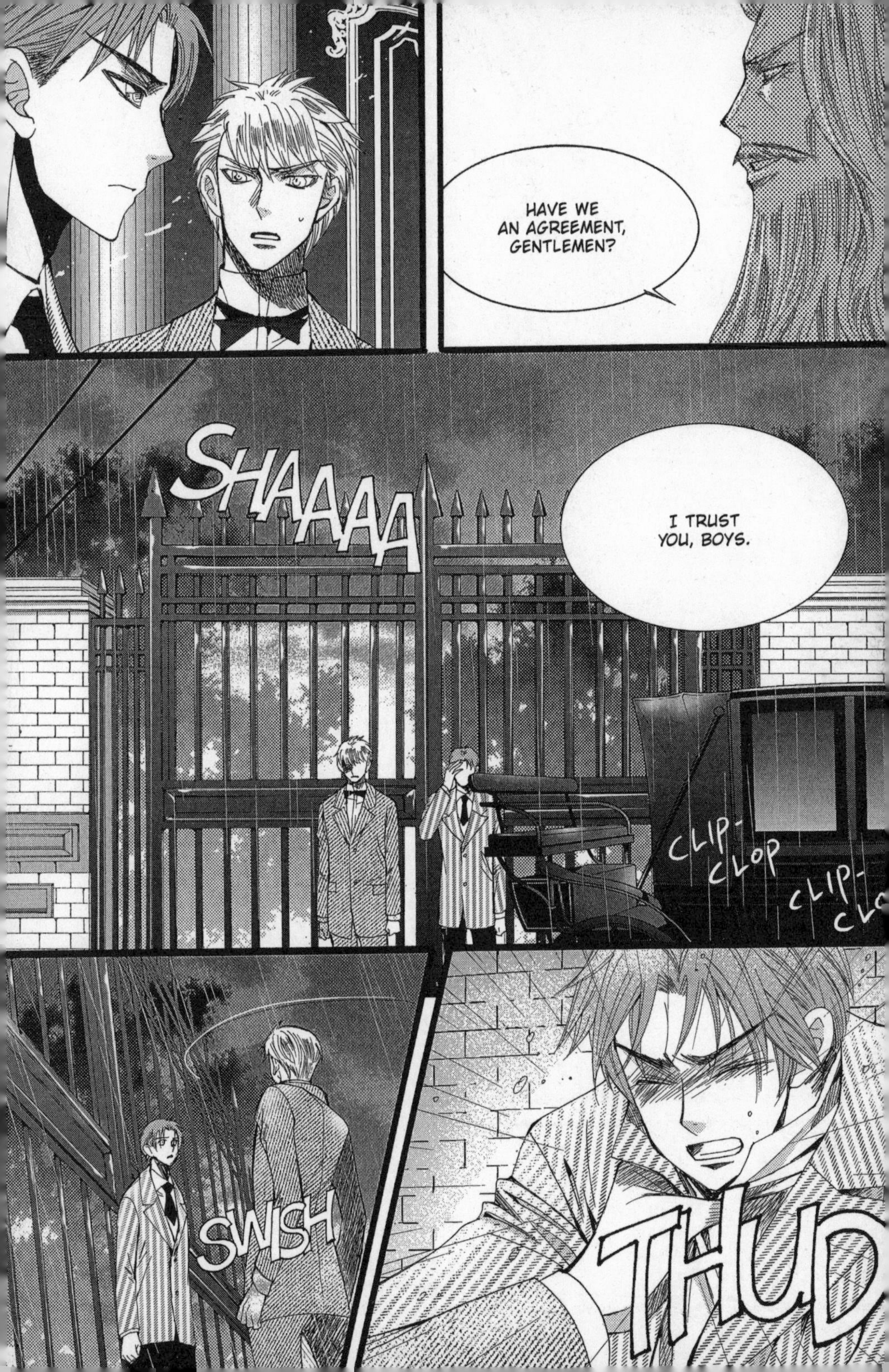
HAVE WE AN AGREEMENT, GENTLEMEN?
SHAAAAA
I TRUST YOU, BOYS.
CLIP-CLOP
CLIP-CLO
SWISH
THUD

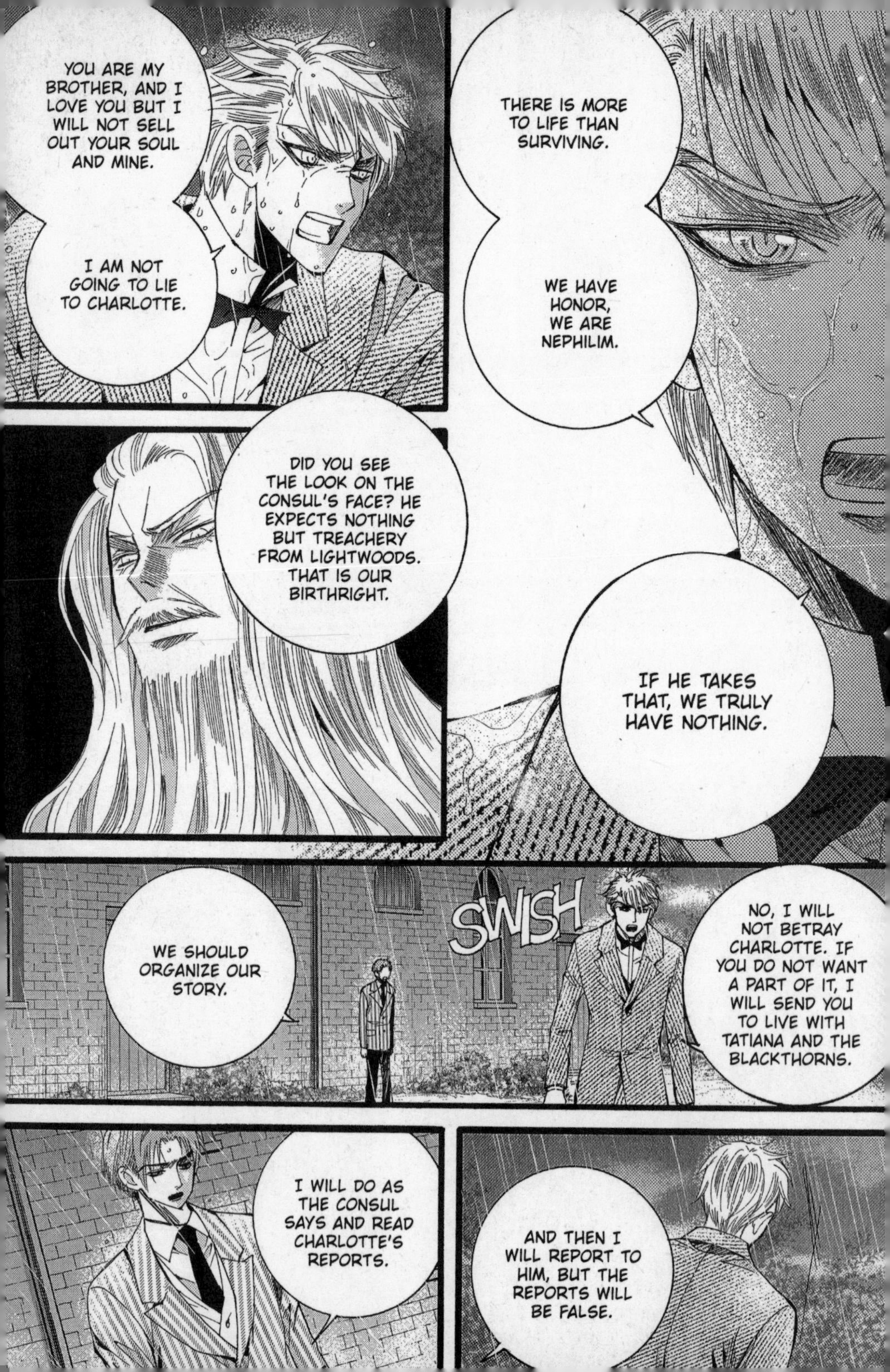
YOU ARE MY BROTHER, AND I LOVE YOU BUT I WILL NOT SELL OUT YOUR SOUL AND MINE.
I AM NOT GOING TO LIE TO CHARLOTTE.
THERE IS MORE TO LIFE THAN SURVIVING.
WE HAVE HONOR, WE ARE NEPHILIM.
DID YOU SEE THE LOOK ON THE CONSUL'S FACE? HE EXPECTS NOTHING BUT TREACHERY FROM LIGHTWOODS. THAT IS OUR BIRTHRIGHT.
IF HE TAKES THAT, WE TRULY HAVE NOTHING.
WE SHOULD ORGANIZE OUR STORY.
SWISH
NO, I WILL NOT BETRAY CHARLOTTE. IF YOU DO NOT WANT A PART OF IT, I WILL SEND YOU TO LIVE WITH TATIANA AND THE BLACKTHORNS.
I WILL DO AS THE CONSUL SAYS AND READ CHARLOTTE'S REPORTS.
AND THEN I WILL REPORT TO HIM, BUT THE REPORTS WILL BE FALSE.

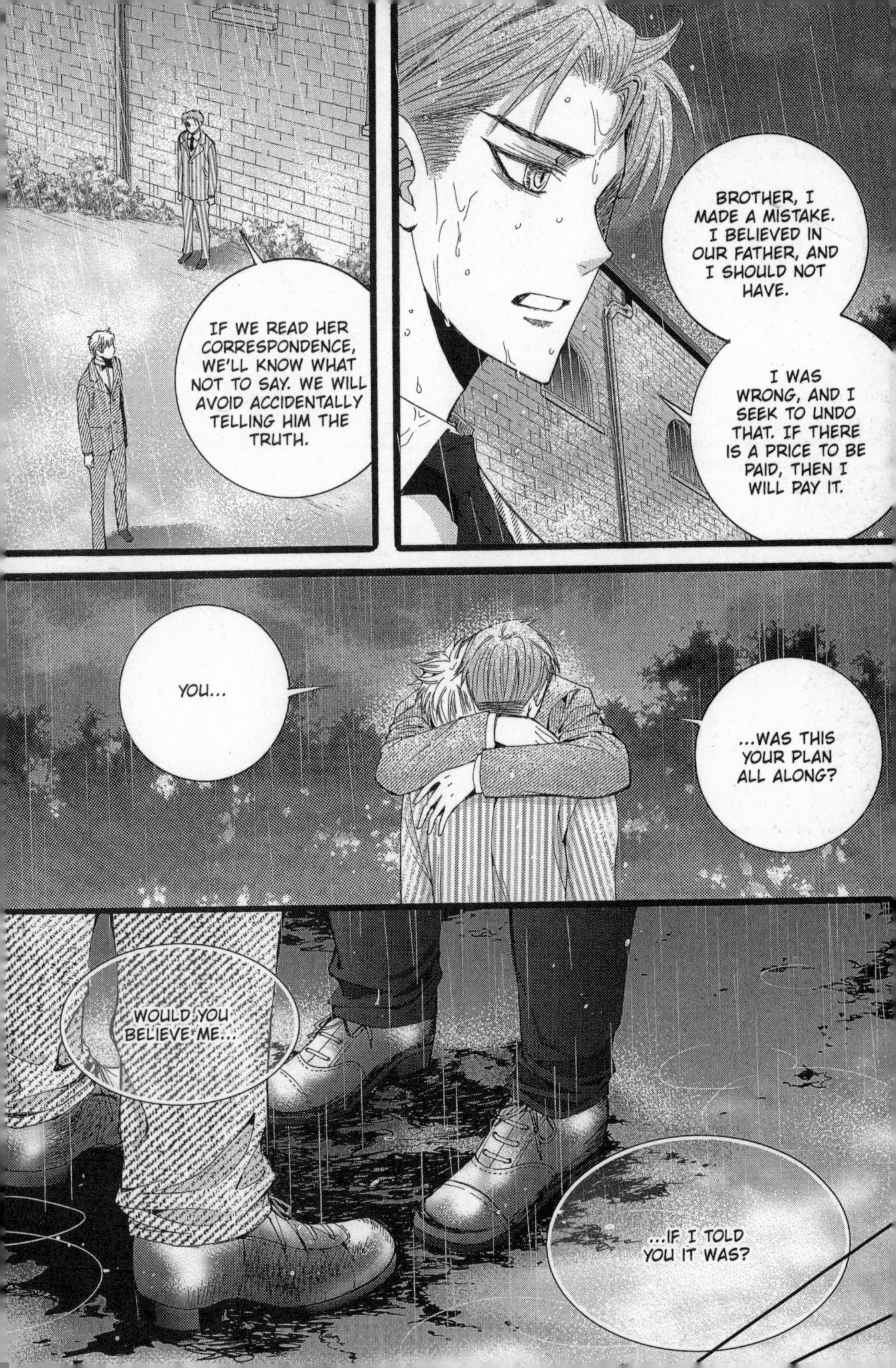
IF WE READ HER CORRESPONDENCE, WE'LL KNOW WHAT NOT TO SAY. WE WILL AVOID ACCIDENTALLY TELLING HIM THE TRUTH.
BROTHER, I MADE A MISTAKE. I BELIEVED IN OUR FATHER, AND I SHOULD NOT HAVE.
I WAS WRONG, AND I SEEK TO UNDO THAT. IF THERE IS A PRICE TO BE PAID, THEN I WILL PAY IT.
YOU...
...WAS THIS YOUR PLAN ALL ALONG?
WOULD YOU BELIEVE ME...
...IF I TOLD YOU IT WAS?

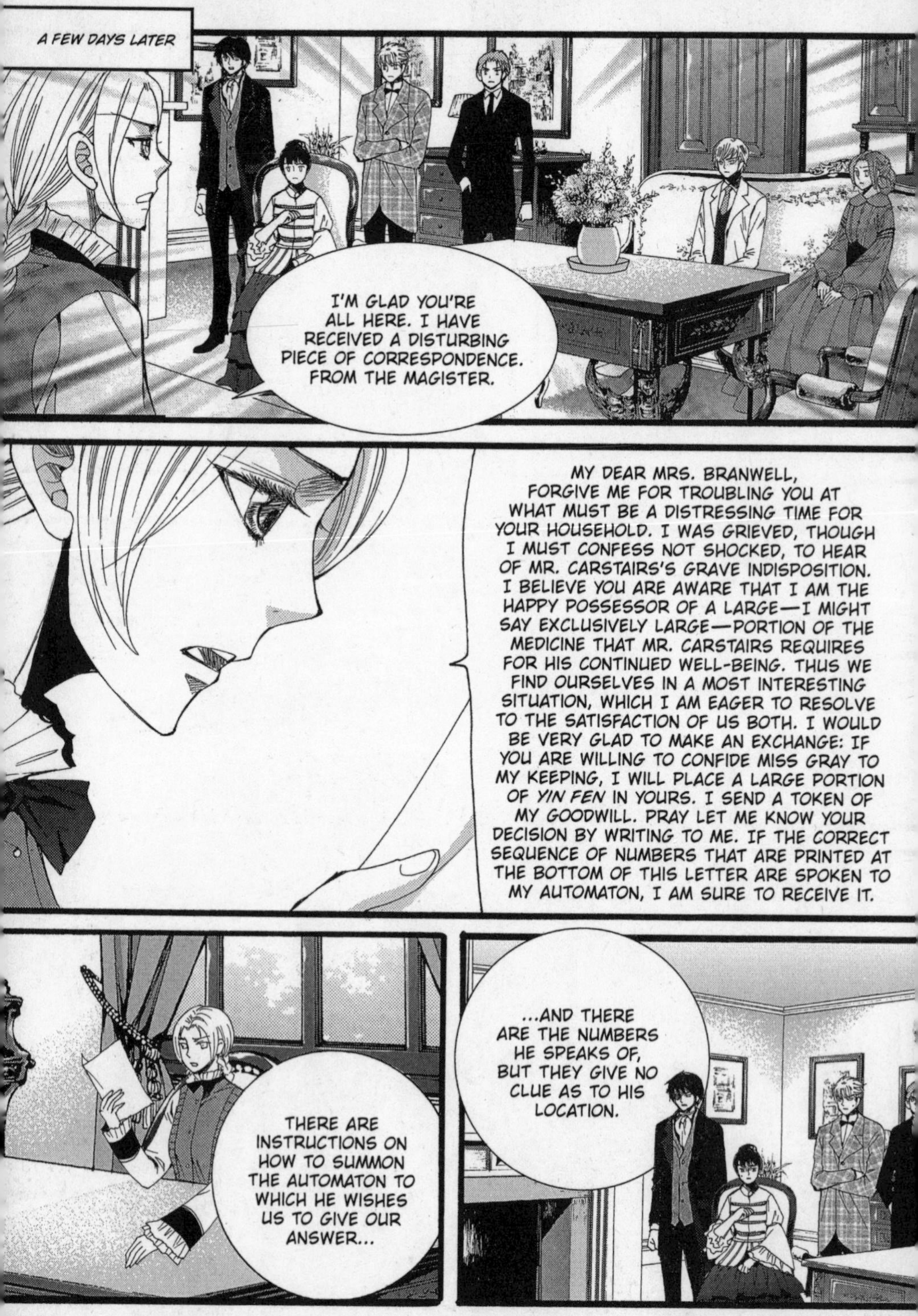
A FEW DAYS LATER
I'M GLAD YOU'RE ALL HERE. I HAVE RECEIVED A DISTURBING PIECE OF CORRESPONDENCE. FROM THE MAGISTER.
MY DEAR MRS. BRANWELL, FORGIVE ME FOR TROUBLING YOU AT WHAT MUST BE A DISTRESSING TIME FOR YOUR HOUSEHOLD. I WAS GRIEVED, THOUGH I MUST CONFESS NOT SHOCKED, TO HEAR OF MR. CARSTAIRS'S GRAVE INDISPOSITION. I BELIEVE YOU ARE AWARE THAT I AM THE HAPPY POSSESSOR OF A LARGE—I MIGHT SAY EXCLUSIVELY LARGE—PORTION OF THE MEDICINE THAT MR. CARSTAIRS REQUIRES FOR HIS CONTINUED WELL-BEING. THUS WE FIND OURSELVES IN A MOST INTERESTING SITUATION, WHICH I AM EAGER TO RESOLVE TO THE SATISFACTION OF US BOTH. I WOULD BE VERY GLAD TO MAKE AN EXCHANGE: IF YOU ARE WILLING TO CONFIDE MISS GRAY TO MY KEEPING, I WILL PLACE A LARGE PORTION OF *YIN FEN* IN YOURS. I SEND A TOKEN OF MY GOODWILL. PRAY LET ME KNOW YOUR DECISION BY WRITING TO ME. IF THE CORRECT SEQUENCE OF NUMBERS THAT ARE PRINTED AT THE BOTTOM OF THIS LETTER ARE SPOKEN TO MY AUTOMATON, I AM SURE TO RECEIVE IT.
THERE ARE INSTRUCTIONS ON HOW TO SUMMON THE AUTOMATON TO WHICH HE WISHES US TO GIVE OUR ANSWER...
...AND THERE ARE THE NUMBERS HE SPEAKS OF, BUT THEY GIVE NO CLUE AS TO HIS LOCATION.

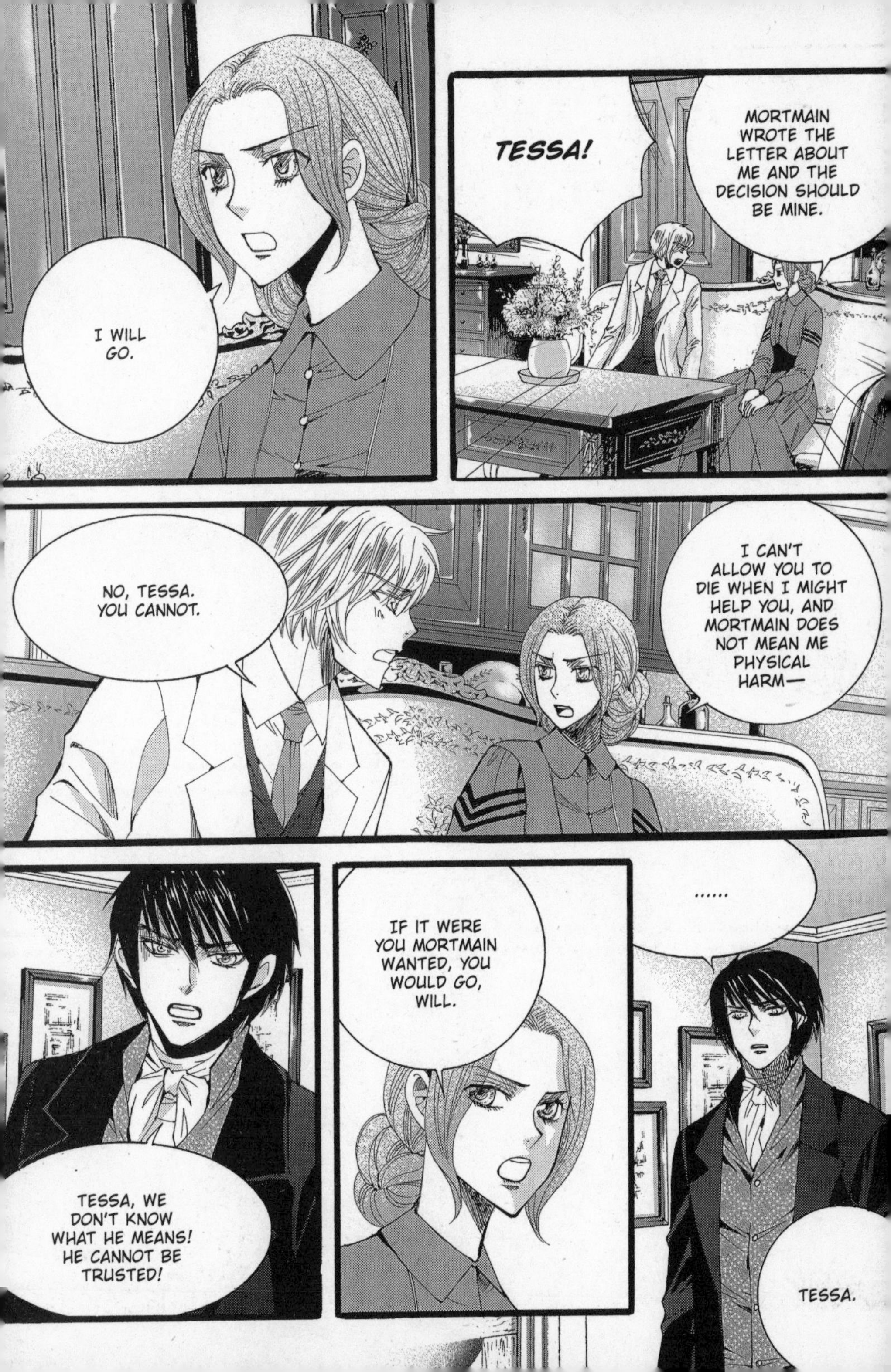
I WILL GO.
TESSA!
MORTMAIN WROTE THE LETTER ABOUT ME AND THE DECISION SHOULD BE MINE.
NO, TESSA. YOU CANNOT.
I CAN'T ALLOW YOU TO DIE WHEN I MIGHT HELP YOU, AND MORTMAIN DOES NOT MEAN ME PHYSICAL HARM—
TESSA, WE DON'T KNOW WHAT HE MEANS! HE CANNOT BE TRUSTED!
IF IT WERE YOU MORTMAIN WANTED, YOU WOULD GO, WILL.
......
TESSA.

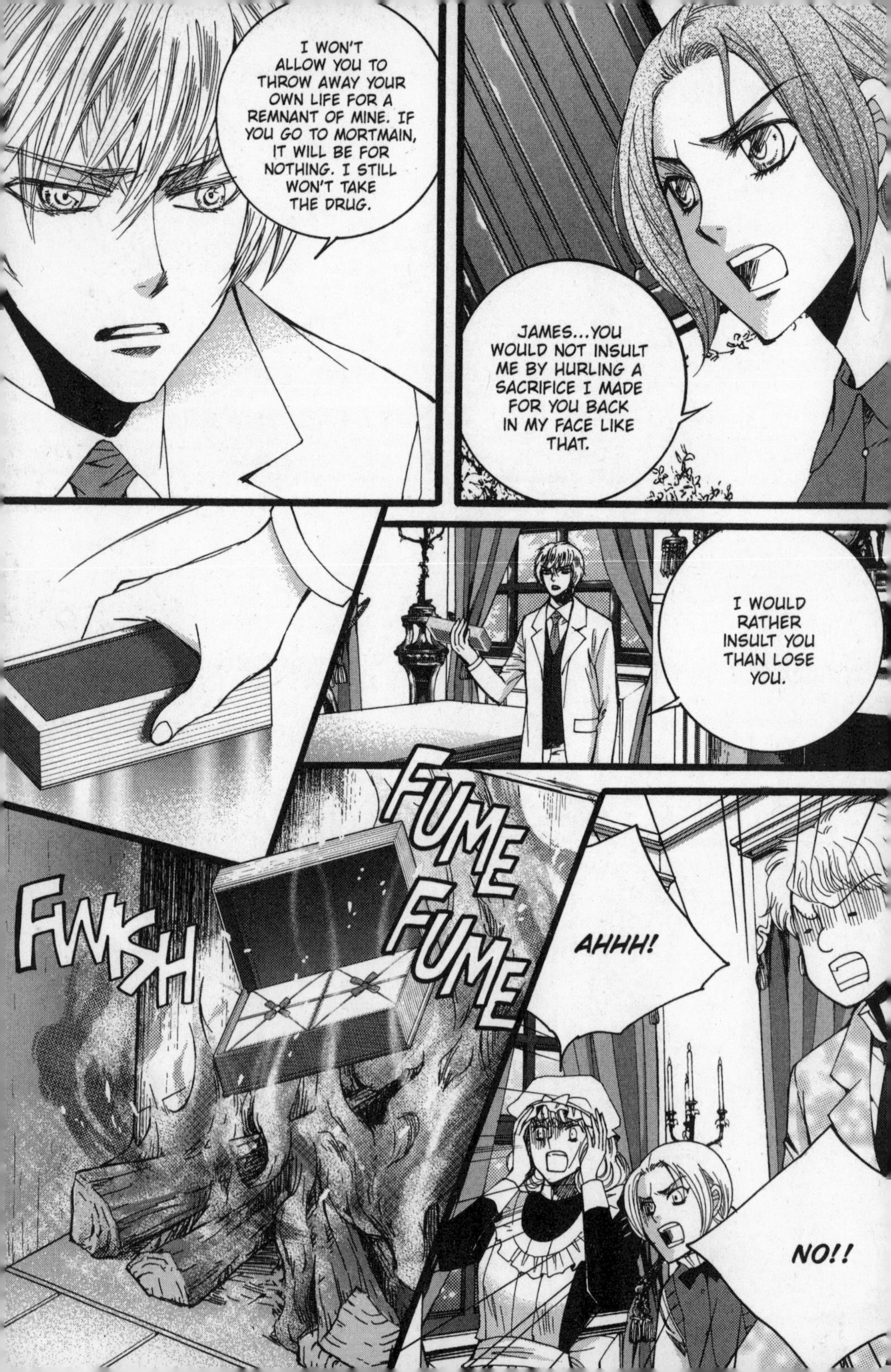

I WON'T ALLOW YOU TO THROW AWAY YOUR OWN LIFE FOR A REMNANT OF MINE. IF YOU GO TO MORTMAIN, IT WILL BE FOR NOTHING. I STILL WON'T TAKE THE DRUG.
JAMES...YOU WOULD NOT INSULT ME BY HURLING A SACRIFICE I MADE FOR YOU BACK IN MY FACE LIKE THAT.
I WOULD RATHER INSULT YOU THAN LOSE YOU.
FWISH
FUME FUME
AHHH!
NO!!

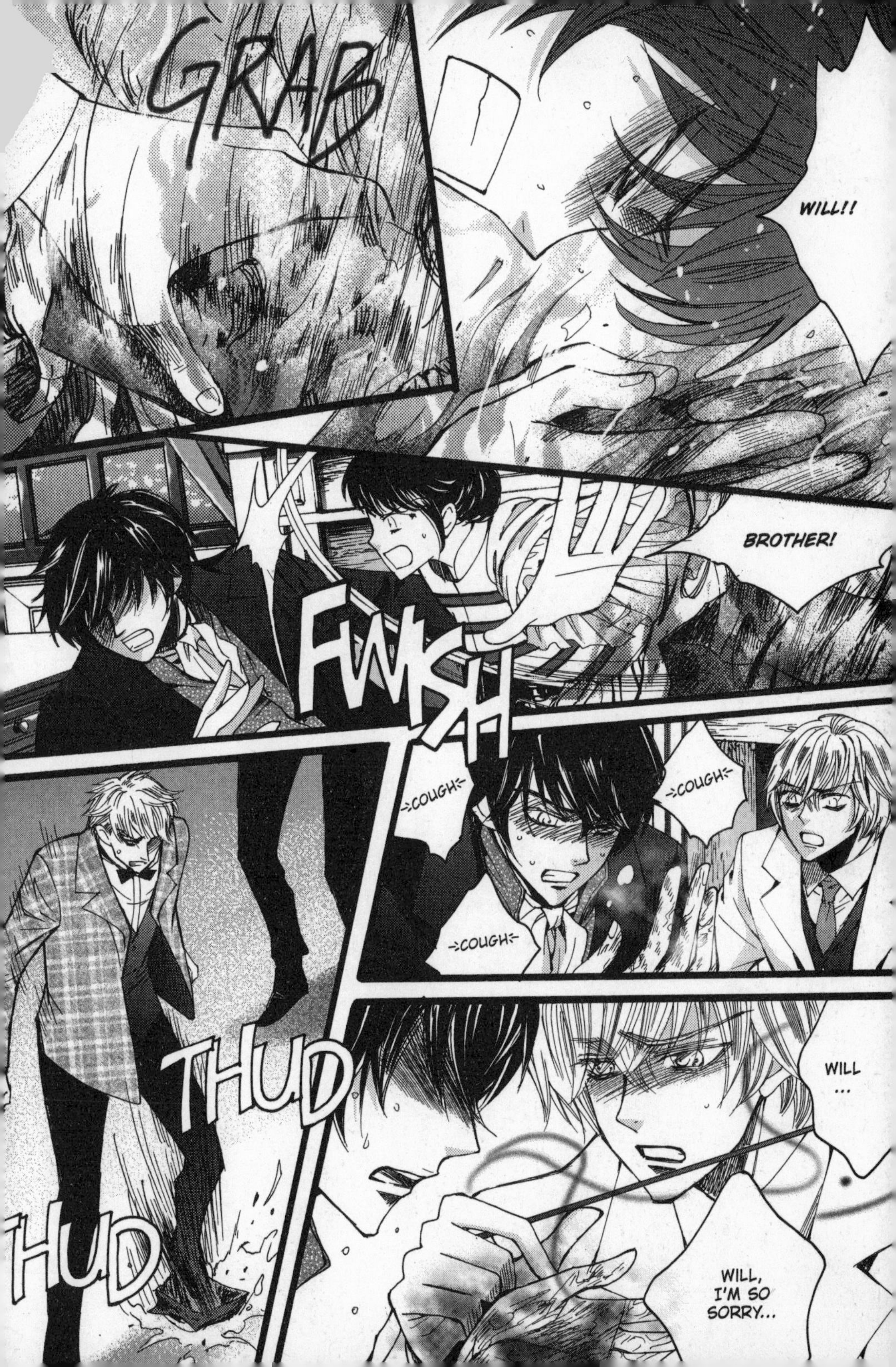
WILL!!
GRAB
BROTHER!
FWISH
COUGH
COUGH
COUGH
THUD
THUD
WILL
...
WILL, I'M SO SORRY...

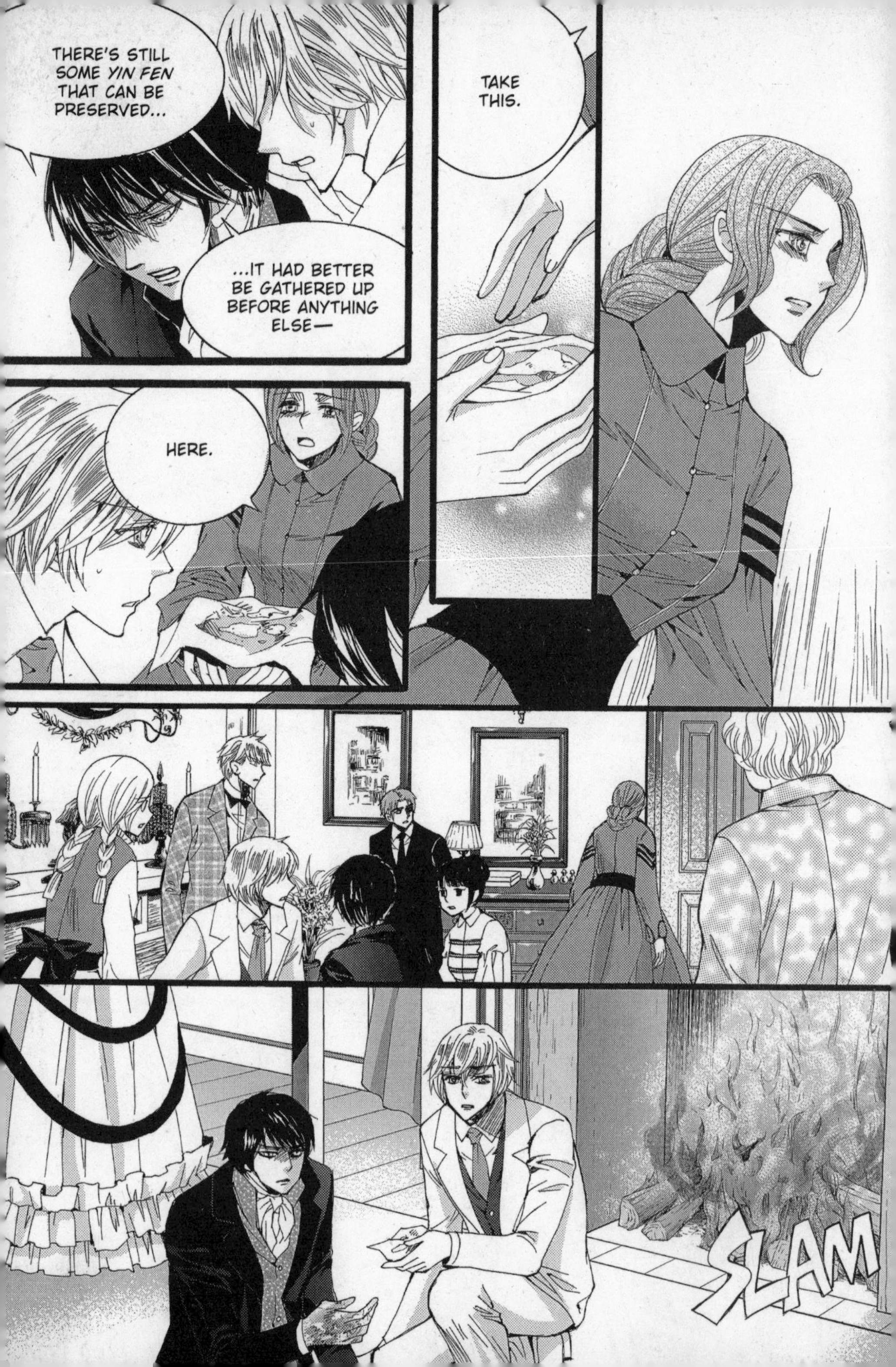
TAKE THIS.
THERE'S STILL SOME *YIN FEN* THAT CAN BE PRESERVED...
...IT HAD BETTER BE GATHERED UP BEFORE ANYTHING ELSE—
HERE.
SLAM

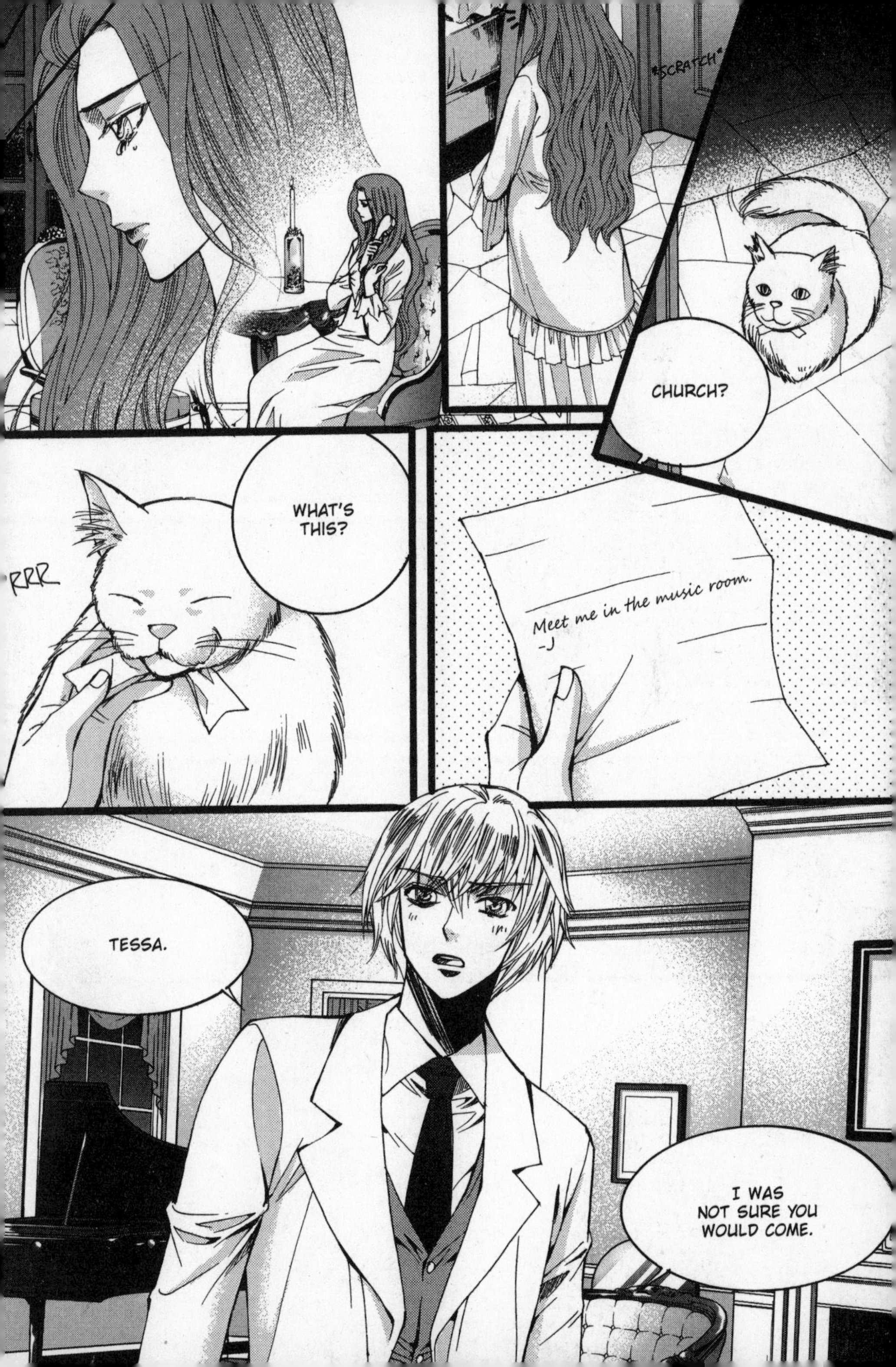
SCRATCH
CHURCH?
WHAT'S THIS?
RRR
Meet me in the music room.
-J
TESSA.
I WAS NOT SURE YOU WOULD COME.

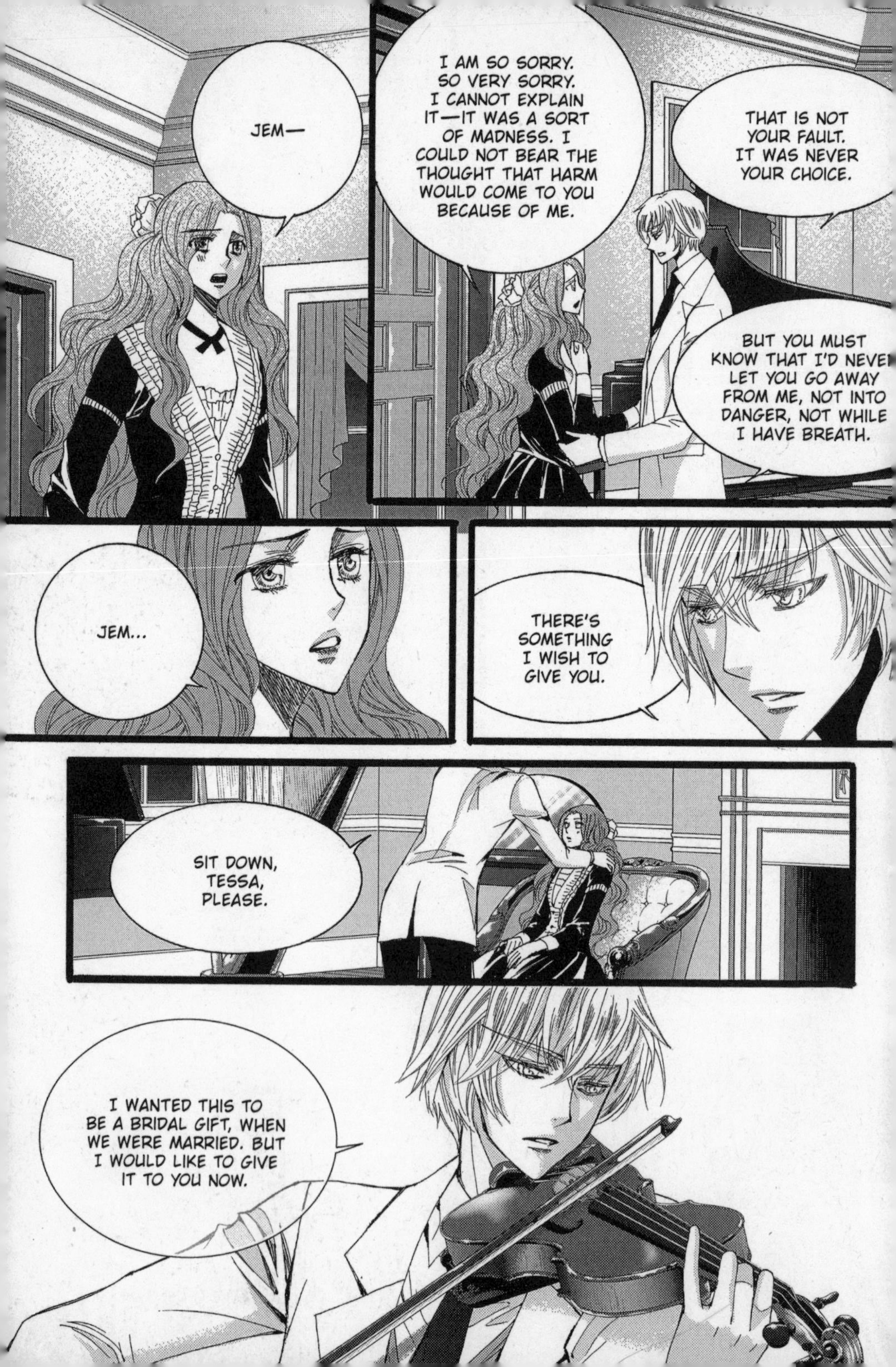
JEM—
I AM SO SORRY. SO VERY SORRY. I CANNOT EXPLAIN IT—IT WAS A SORT OF MADNESS. I COULD NOT BEAR THE THOUGHT THAT HARM WOULD COME TO YOU BECAUSE OF ME.
THAT IS NOT YOUR FAULT. IT WAS NEVER YOUR CHOICE.
BUT YOU MUST KNOW THAT I'D NEVER LET YOU GO AWAY FROM ME, NOT INTO DANGER, NOT WHILE I HAVE BREATH.
JEM...
THERE'S SOMETHING I WISH TO GIVE YOU.
SIT DOWN, TESSA, PLEASE.
I WANTED THIS TO BE A BRIDAL GIFT, WHEN WE WERE MARRIED. BUT I WOULD LIKE TO GIVE IT TO YOU NOW.

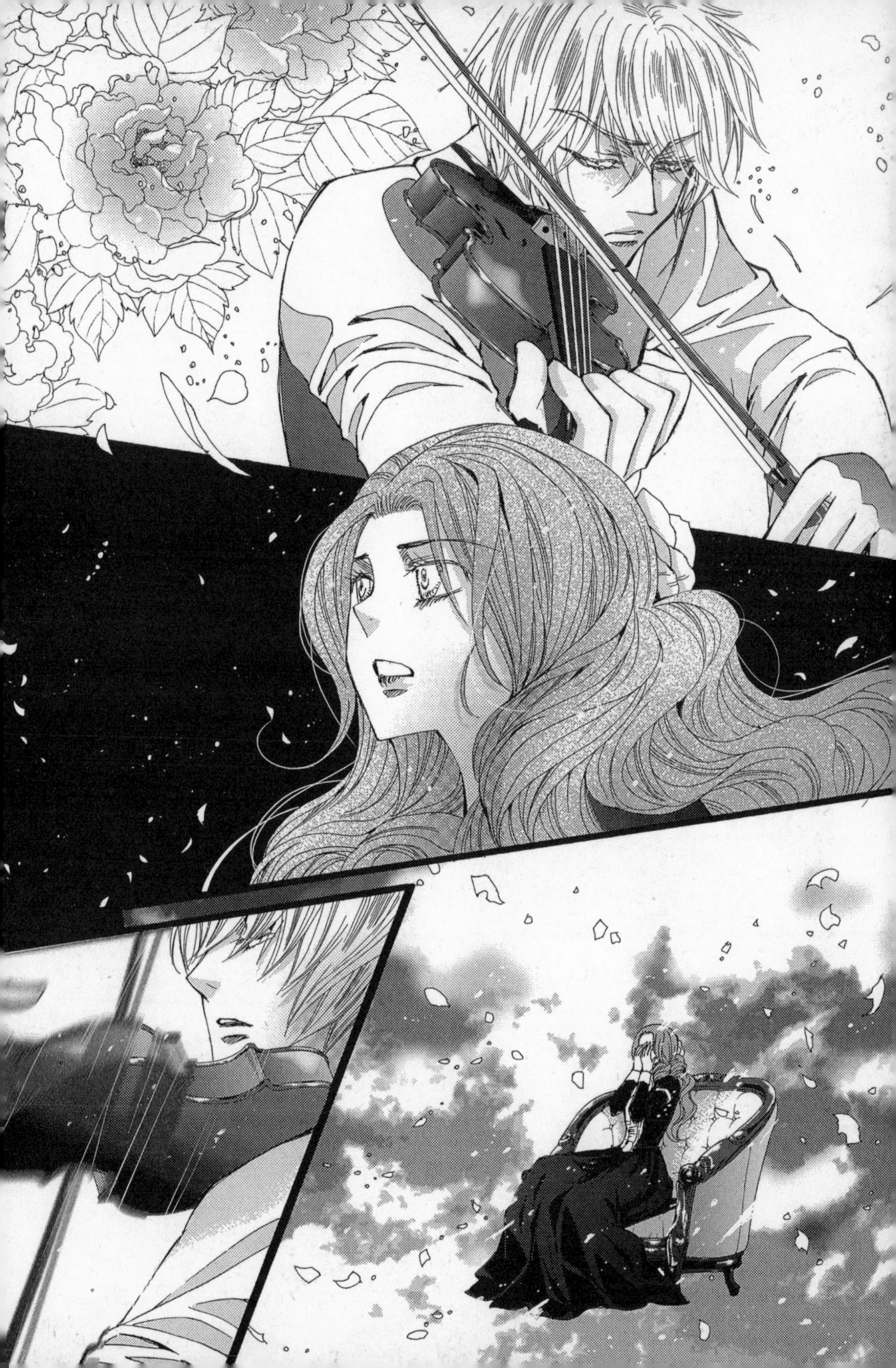

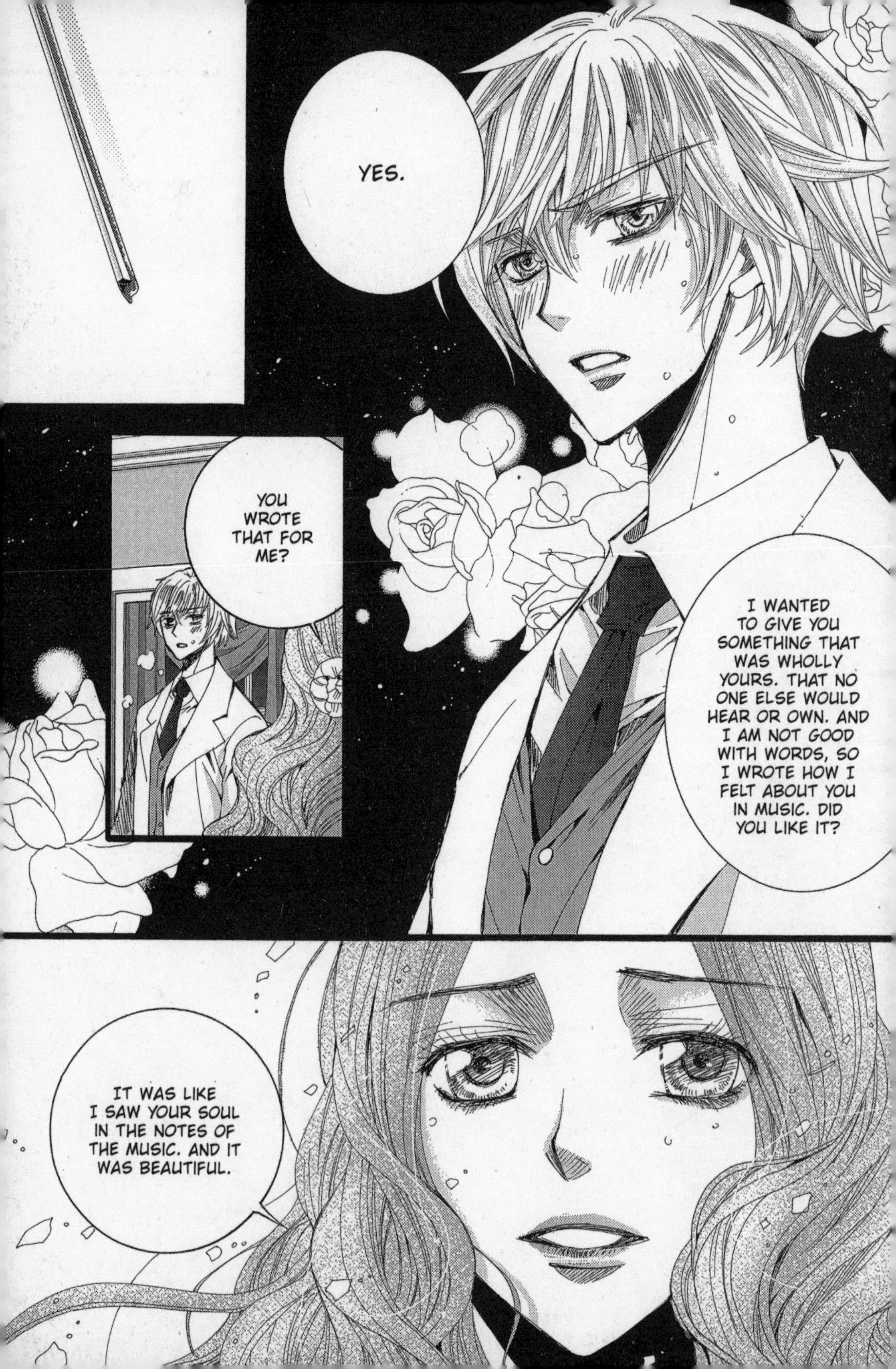
YES.
YOU WROTE THAT FOR ME?
I WANTED TO GIVE YOU SOMETHING THAT WAS WHOLLY YOURS. THAT NO ONE ELSE WOULD HEAR OR OWN. AND I AM NOT GOOD WITH WORDS, SO I WROTE HOW I FELT ABOUT YOU IN MUSIC. DID YOU LIKE IT?
IT WAS LIKE I SAW YOUR SOUL IN THE NOTES OF THE MUSIC. AND IT WAS BEAUTIFUL.

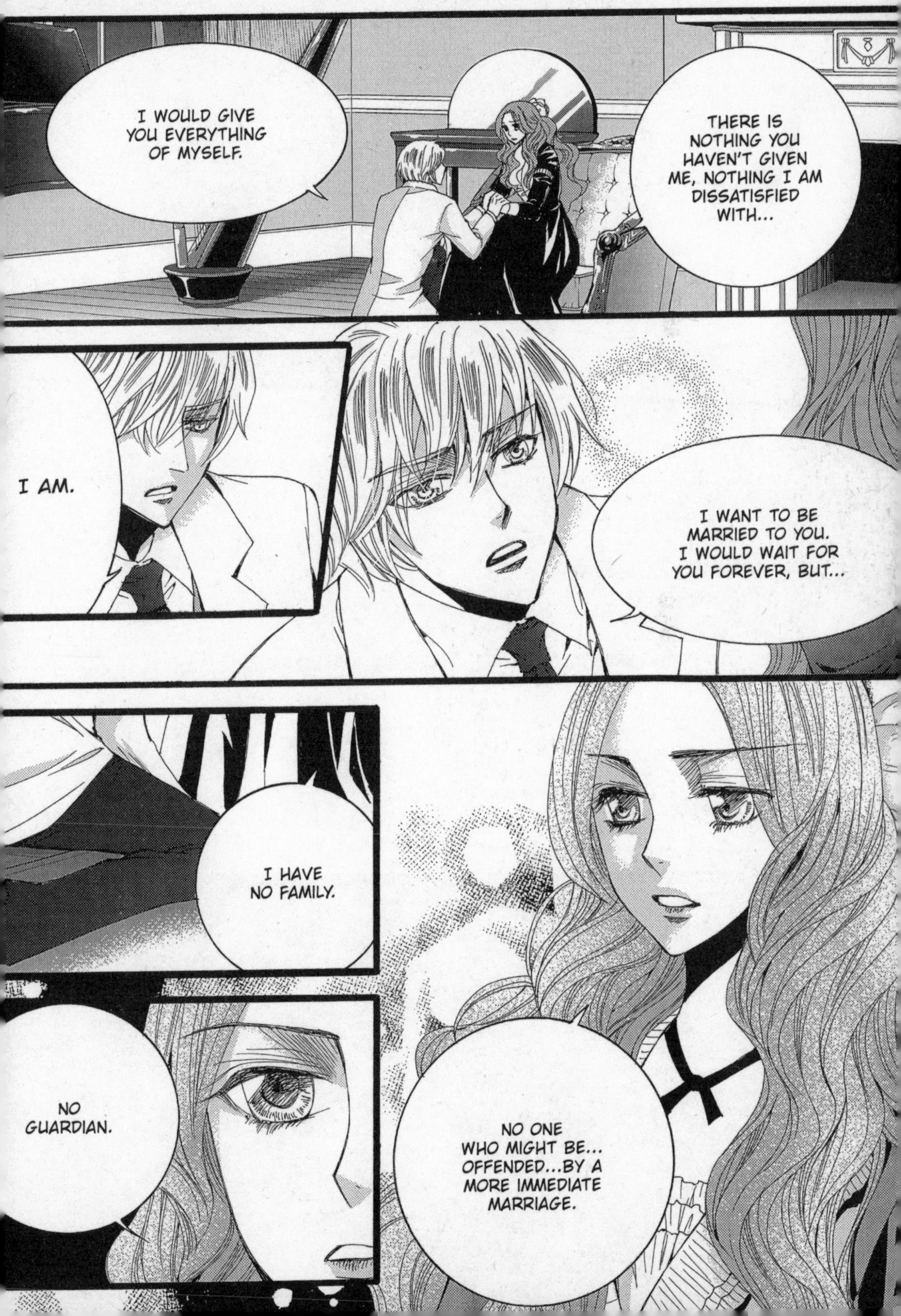
I WOULD GIVE YOU EVERYTHING OF MYSELF.
THERE IS NOTHING YOU HAVEN'T GIVEN ME, NOTHING I AM DISSATISFIED WITH...
I AM.
I WANT TO BE MARRIED TO YOU. I WOULD WAIT FOR YOU FOREVER, BUT...
I HAVE NO FAMILY.
NO GUARDIAN.
NO ONE WHO MIGHT BE... OFFENDED...BY A MORE IMMEDIATE MARRIAGE.

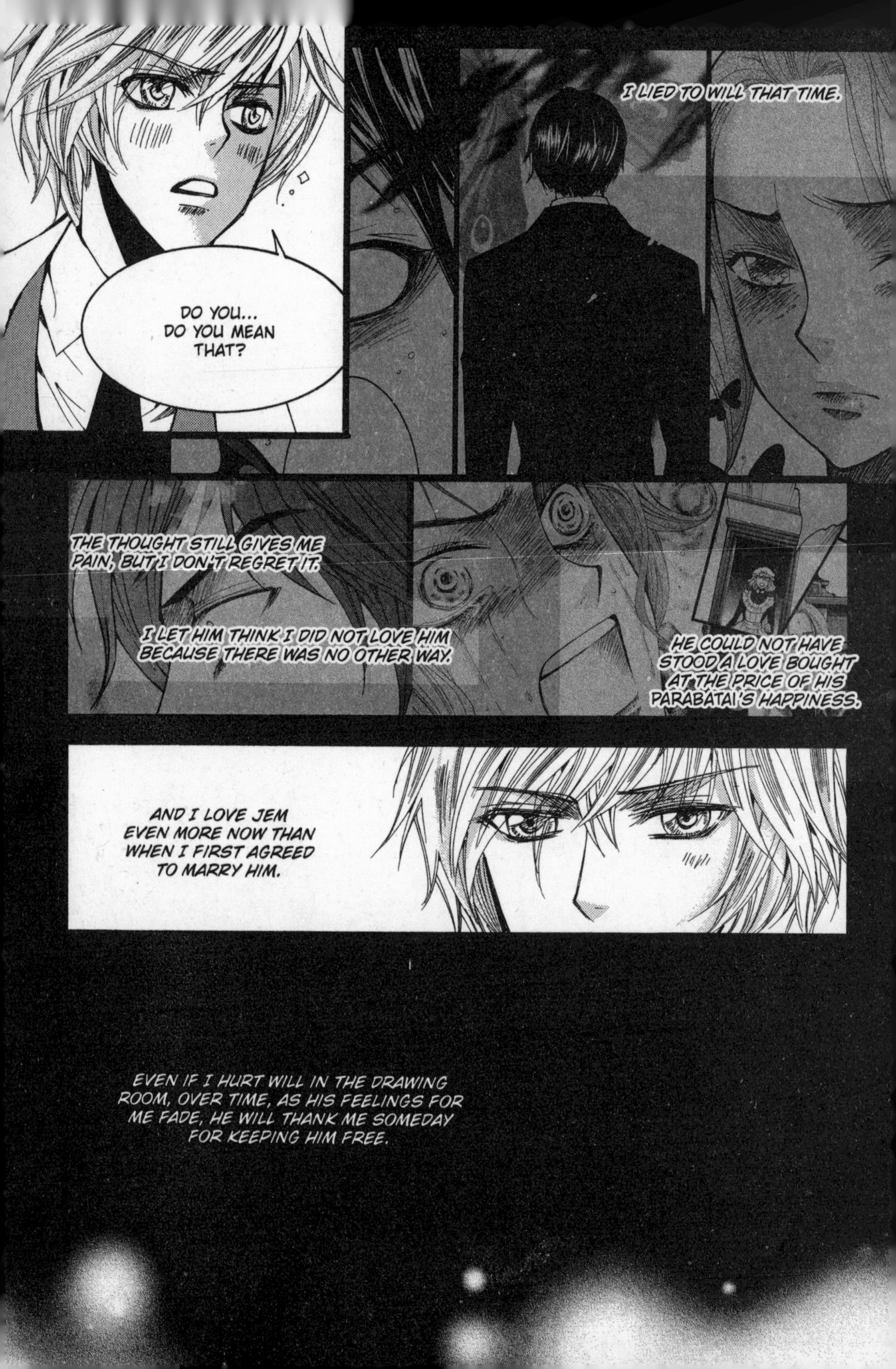
DO YOU...
DO YOU MEAN THAT?
I LIED TO WILL THAT TIME.
THE THOUGHT STILL GIVES ME PAIN, BUT I DON'T REGRET IT.
I LET HIM THINK I DID NOT LOVE HIM BECAUSE THERE WAS NO OTHER WAY.
HE COULD NOT HAVE STOOD A LOVE BOUGHT AT THE PRICE OF HIS PARABATAI'S HAPPINESS.
AND I LOVE JEM EVEN MORE NOW THAN WHEN I FIRST AGREED TO MARRY HIM.
EVEN IF I HURT WILL IN THE DRAWING ROOM, OVER TIME, AS HIS FEELINGS FOR ME FADE, HE WILL THANK ME SOMEDAY FOR KEEPING HIM FREE.

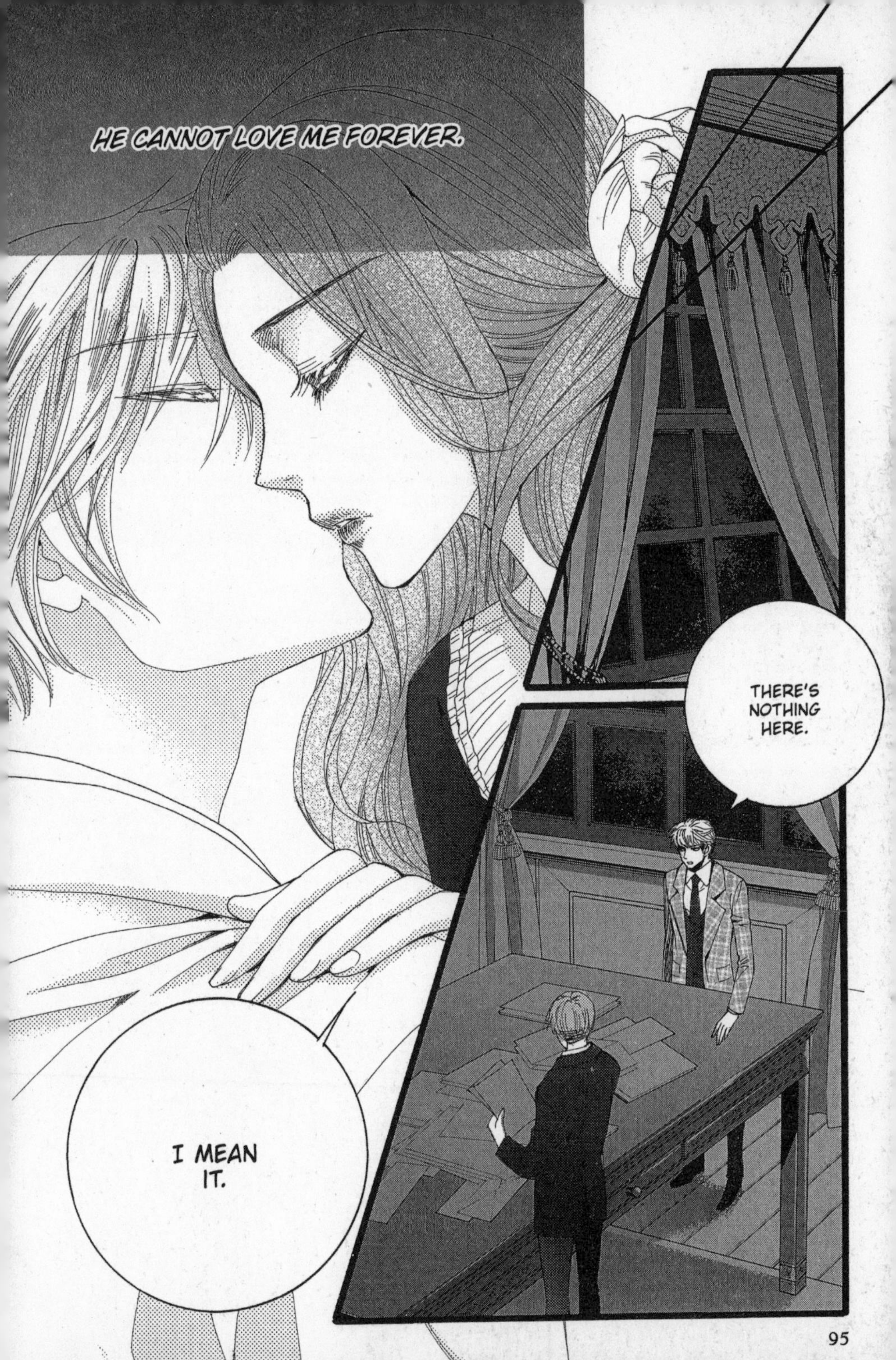
HE CANNOT LOVE ME FOREVER.
THERE'S NOTHING HERE.
I MEAN IT.

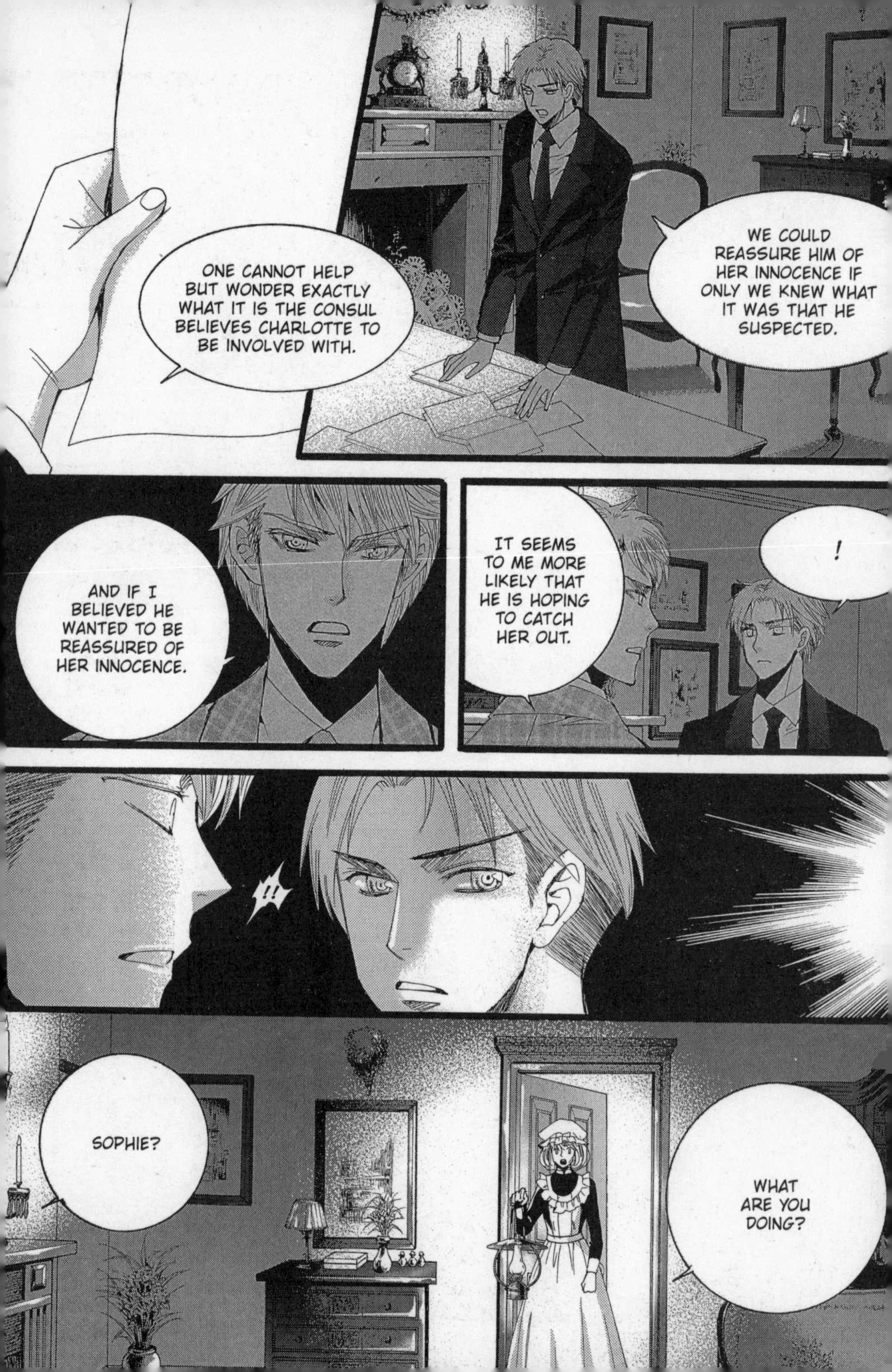
ONE CANNOT HELP BUT WONDER EXACTLY WHAT IT IS THE CONSUL BELIEVES CHARLOTTE TO BE INVOLVED WITH.
WE COULD REASSURE HIM OF HER INNOCENCE IF ONLY WE KNEW WHAT IT WAS THAT HE SUSPECTED.
AND IF I BELIEVED HE WANTED TO BE REASSURED OF HER INNOCENCE.
IT SEEMS TO ME MORE LIKELY THAT HE IS HOPING TO CATCH HER OUT.
!
!!
SOPHIE?
WHAT ARE YOU DOING?

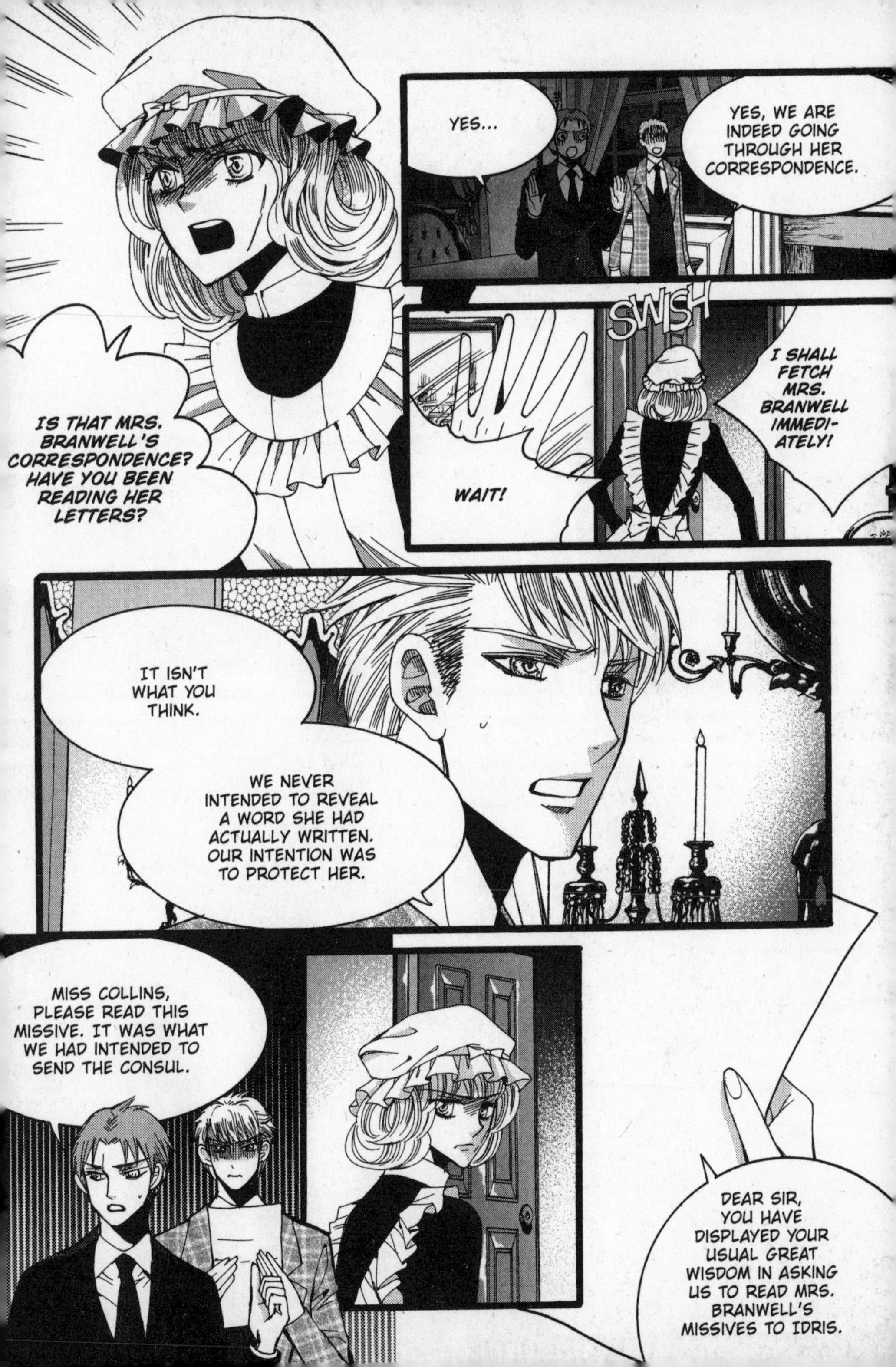

IS THAT MRS. BRANWELL'S CORRESPONDENCE? HAVE YOU BEEN READING HER LETTERS?
YES...
YES, WE ARE INDEED GOING THROUGH HER CORRESPONDENCE.
SWISH
I SHALL FETCH MRS. BRANWELL IMMEDI-ATELY!
WAIT!
IT ISN'T WHAT YOU THINK.
WE NEVER INTENDED TO REVEAL A WORD SHE HAD ACTUALLY WRITTEN. OUR INTENTION WAS TO PROTECT HER.
MISS COLLINS, PLEASE READ THIS MISSIVE. IT WAS WHAT WE HAD INTENDED TO SEND THE CONSUL.
DEAR SIR, YOU HAVE DISPLAYED YOUR USUAL GREAT WISDOM IN ASKING US TO READ MRS. BRANWELL'S MISSIVES TO IDRIS.

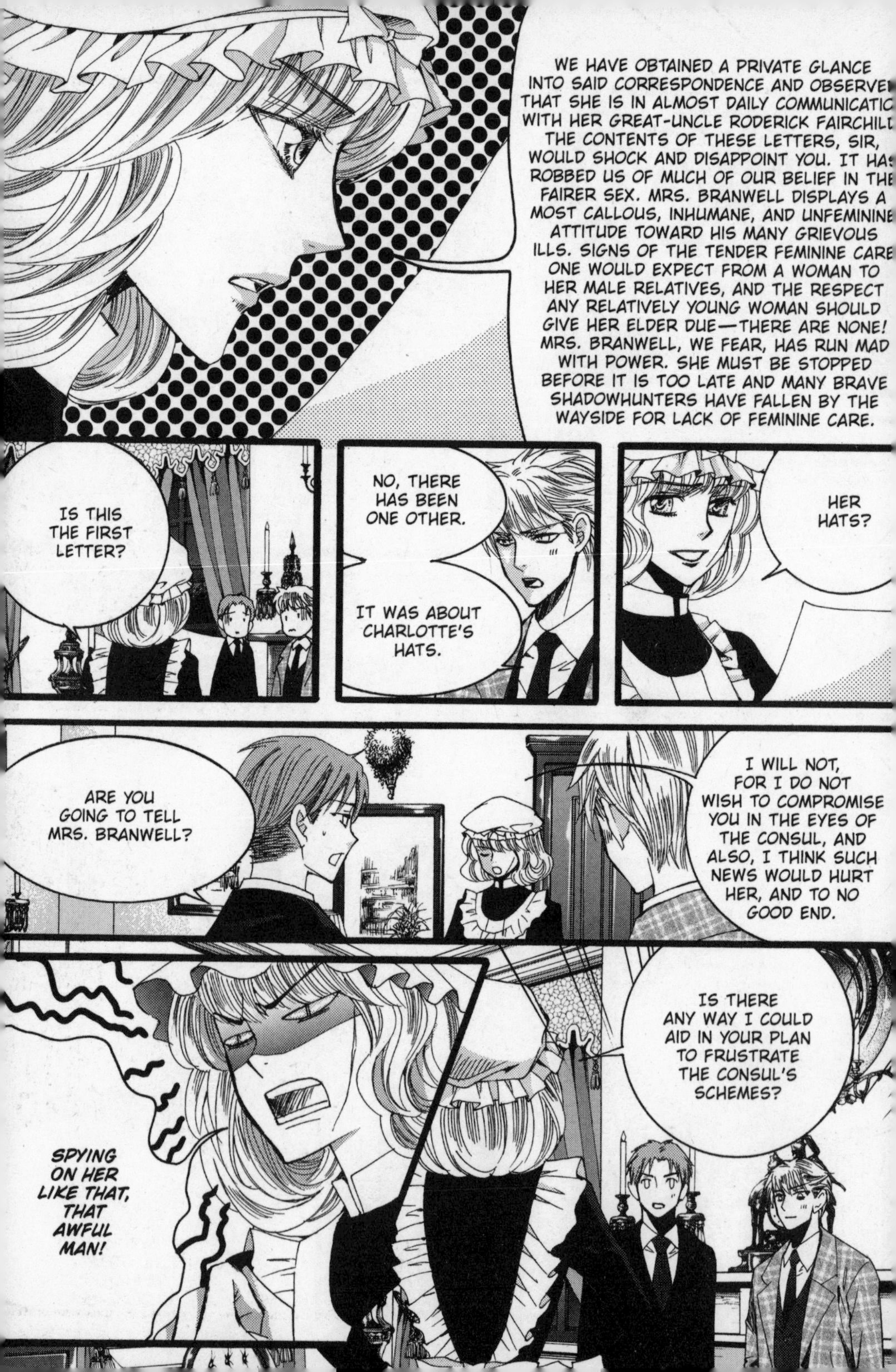
WE HAVE OBTAINED A PRIVATE GLANCE INTO SAID CORRESPONDENCE AND OBSERVE THAT SHE IS IN ALMOST DAILY COMMUNICATI WITH HER GREAT-UNCLE RODERICK FAIRCHIL THE CONTENTS OF THESE LETTERS, SIR, WOULD SHOCK AND DISAPPOINT YOU. IT HA ROBBED US OF MUCH OF OUR BELIEF IN THE FAIRER SEX. MRS. BRANWELL DISPLAYS A MOST CALLOUS, INHUMANE, AND UNFEMININE ATTITUDE TOWARD HIS MANY GRIEVOUS ILLS. SIGNS OF THE TENDER FEMININE CARE ONE WOULD EXPECT FROM A WOMAN TO HER MALE RELATIVES, AND THE RESPECT ANY RELATIVELY YOUNG WOMAN SHOULD GIVE HER ELDER DUE—THERE ARE NONE! MRS. BRANWELL, WE FEAR, HAS RUN MAD WITH POWER. SHE MUST BE STOPPED BEFORE IT IS TOO LATE AND MANY BRAVE SHADOWHUNTERS HAVE FALLEN BY THE WAYSIDE FOR LACK OF FEMININE CARE.
IS THIS THE FIRST LETTER?
NO, THERE HAS BEEN ONE OTHER.
IT WAS ABOUT CHARLOTTE'S HATS.
HER HATS?
ARE YOU GOING TO TELL MRS. BRANWELL?
I WILL NOT, FOR I DO NOT WISH TO COMPROMISE YOU IN THE EYES OF THE CONSUL, AND ALSO, I THINK SUCH NEWS WOULD HURT HER, AND TO NO GOOD END.
SPYING ON HER LIKE THAT, THAT AWFUL MAN!
IS THERE ANY WAY I COULD AID IN YOUR PLAN TO FRUSTRATE THE CONSUL'S SCHEMES?

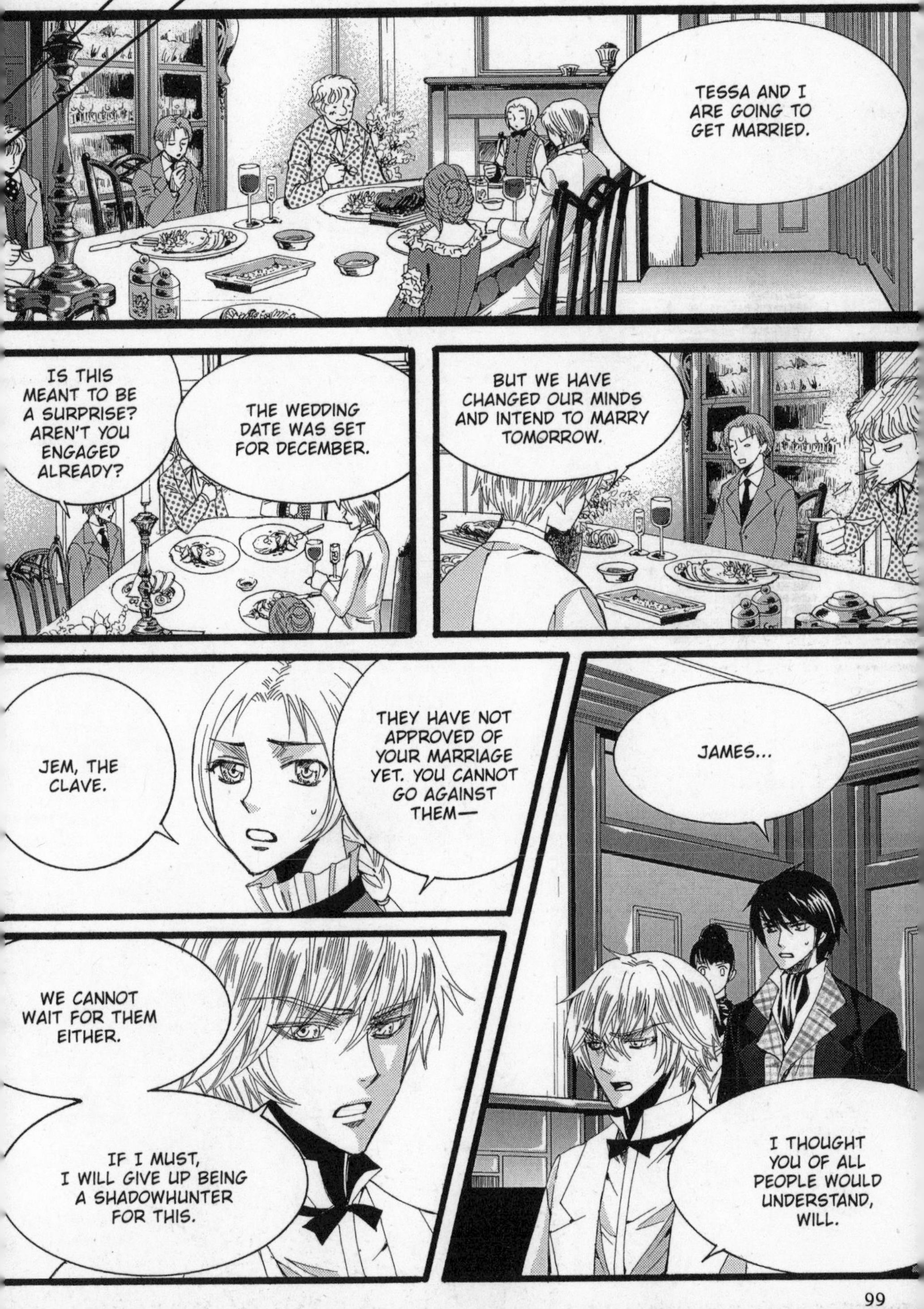
TESSA AND I ARE GOING TO GET MARRIED.
IS THIS MEANT TO BE A SURPRISE? AREN'T YOU ENGAGED ALREADY?
THE WEDDING DATE WAS SET FOR DECEMBER.
BUT WE HAVE CHANGED OUR MINDS AND INTEND TO MARRY TOMORROW.
JEM, THE CLAVE.
THEY HAVE NOT APPROVED OF YOUR MARRIAGE YET. YOU CANNOT GO AGAINST THEM—
JAMES...
WE CANNOT WAIT FOR THEM EITHER.
IF I MUST, I WILL GIVE UP BEING A SHADOWHUNTER FOR THIS.
I THOUGHT YOU OF ALL PEOPLE WOULD UNDERSTAND, WILL.

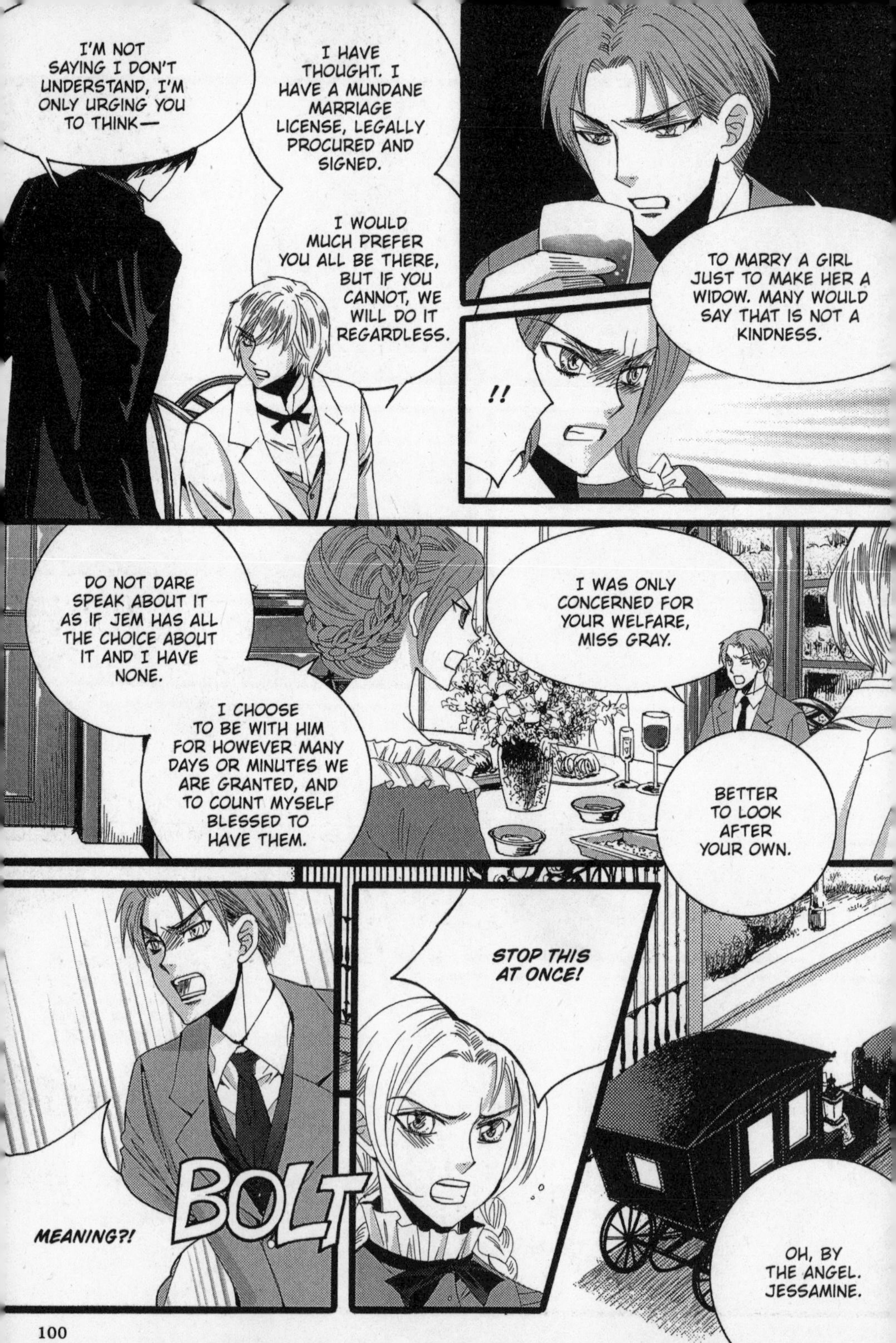
I'M NOT SAYING I DON'T UNDERSTAND, I'M ONLY URGING YOU TO THINK—
I HAVE THOUGHT. I HAVE A MUNDANE MARRIAGE LICENSE, LEGALLY PROCURED AND SIGNED.
I WOULD MUCH PREFER YOU ALL BE THERE, BUT IF YOU CANNOT, WE WILL DO IT REGARDLESS.
TO MARRY A GIRL JUST TO MAKE HER A WIDOW. MANY WOULD SAY THAT IS NOT A KINDNESS.
!!
DO NOT DARE SPEAK ABOUT IT AS IF JEM HAS ALL THE CHOICE ABOUT IT AND I HAVE NONE.
I CHOOSE TO BE WITH HIM FOR HOWEVER MANY DAYS OR MINUTES WE ARE GRANTED, AND TO COUNT MYSELF BLESSED TO HAVE THEM.
I WAS ONLY CONCERNED FOR YOUR WELFARE, MISS GRAY.
BETTER TO LOOK AFTER YOUR OWN.
MEANING?!
BOLT
STOP THIS AT ONCE!
OH, BY THE ANGEL. JESSAMINE.

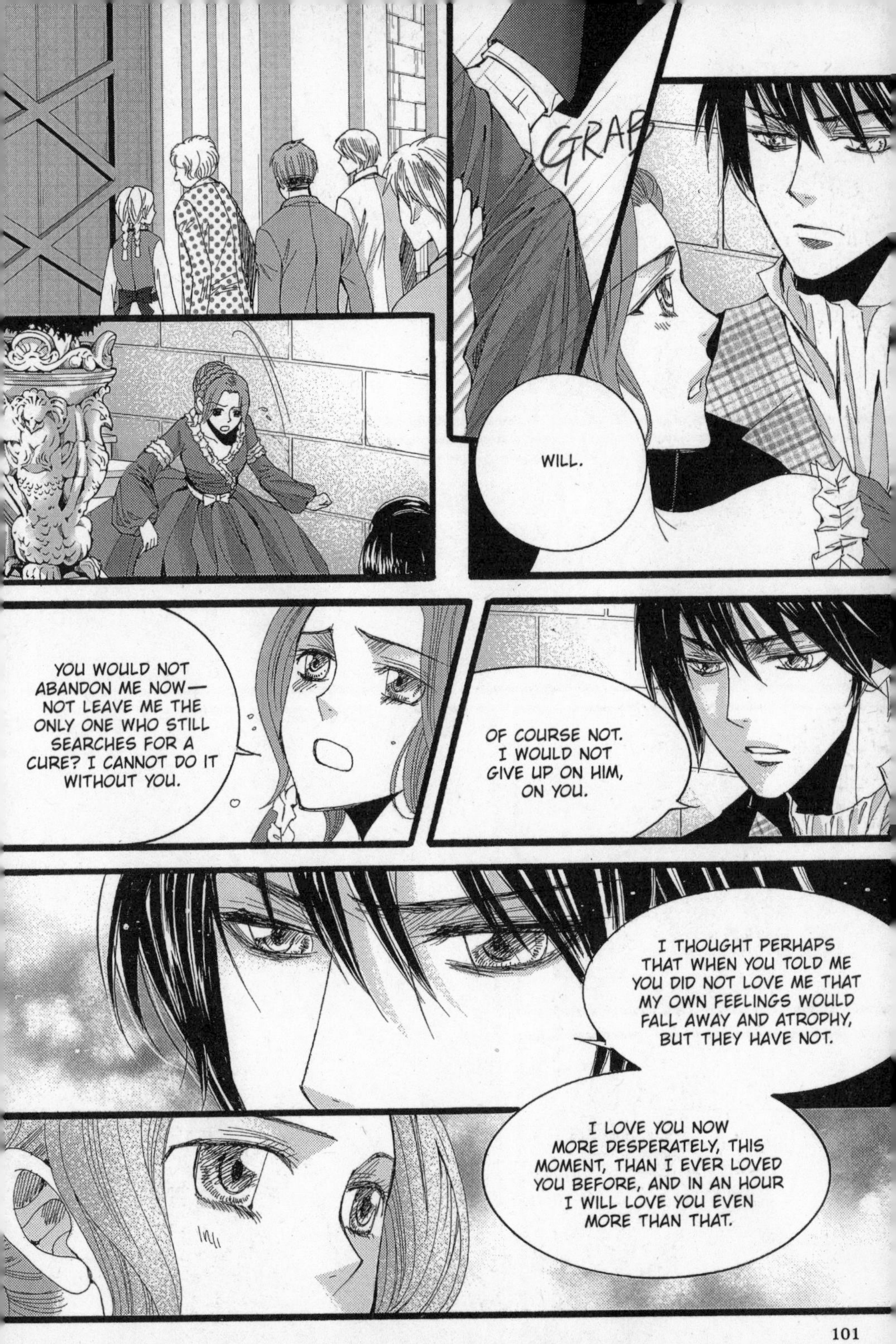
GRAB
WILL.
YOU WOULD NOT ABANDON ME NOW— NOT LEAVE ME THE ONLY ONE WHO STILL SEARCHES FOR A CURE? I CANNOT DO IT WITHOUT YOU.
OF COURSE NOT. I WOULD NOT GIVE UP ON HIM, ON YOU.
I THOUGHT PERHAPS THAT WHEN YOU TOLD ME YOU DID NOT LOVE ME THAT MY OWN FEELINGS WOULD FALL AWAY AND ATROPHY, BUT THEY HAVE NOT.
I LOVE YOU NOW MORE DESPERATELY, THIS MOMENT, THAN I EVER LOVED YOU BEFORE, AND IN AN HOUR I WILL LOVE YOU EVEN MORE THAN THAT.

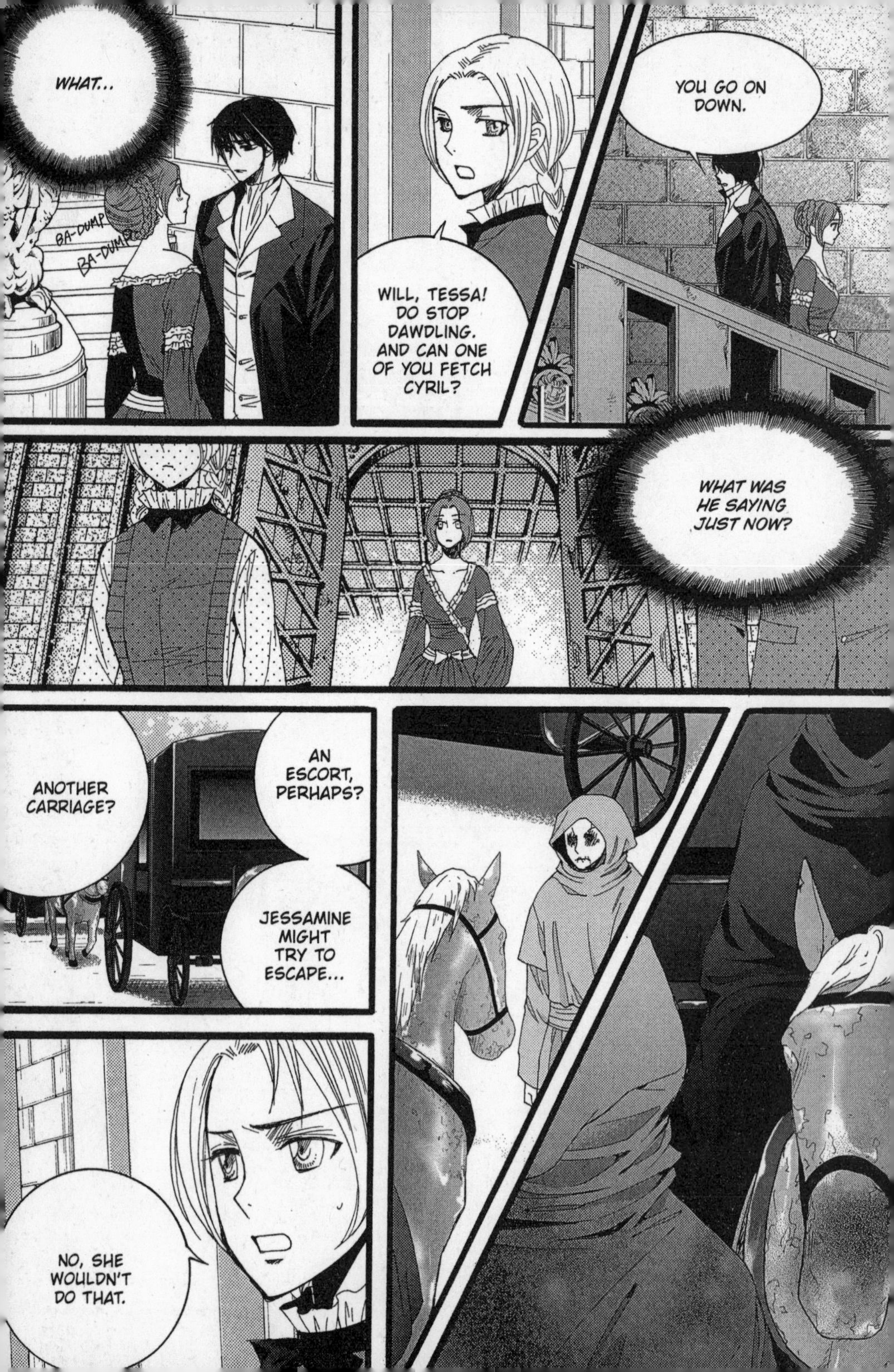
WHAT...
BA-DUMP
BA-DUMP
WILL, TESSA! DO STOP DAWDLING. AND CAN ONE OF YOU FETCH CYRIL?
YOU GO ON DOWN.
WHAT WAS HE SAYING JUST NOW?
ANOTHER CARRIAGE?
AN ESCORT, PERHAPS?
JESSAMINE MIGHT TRY TO ESCAPE...
NO, SHE WOULDN'T DO THAT.

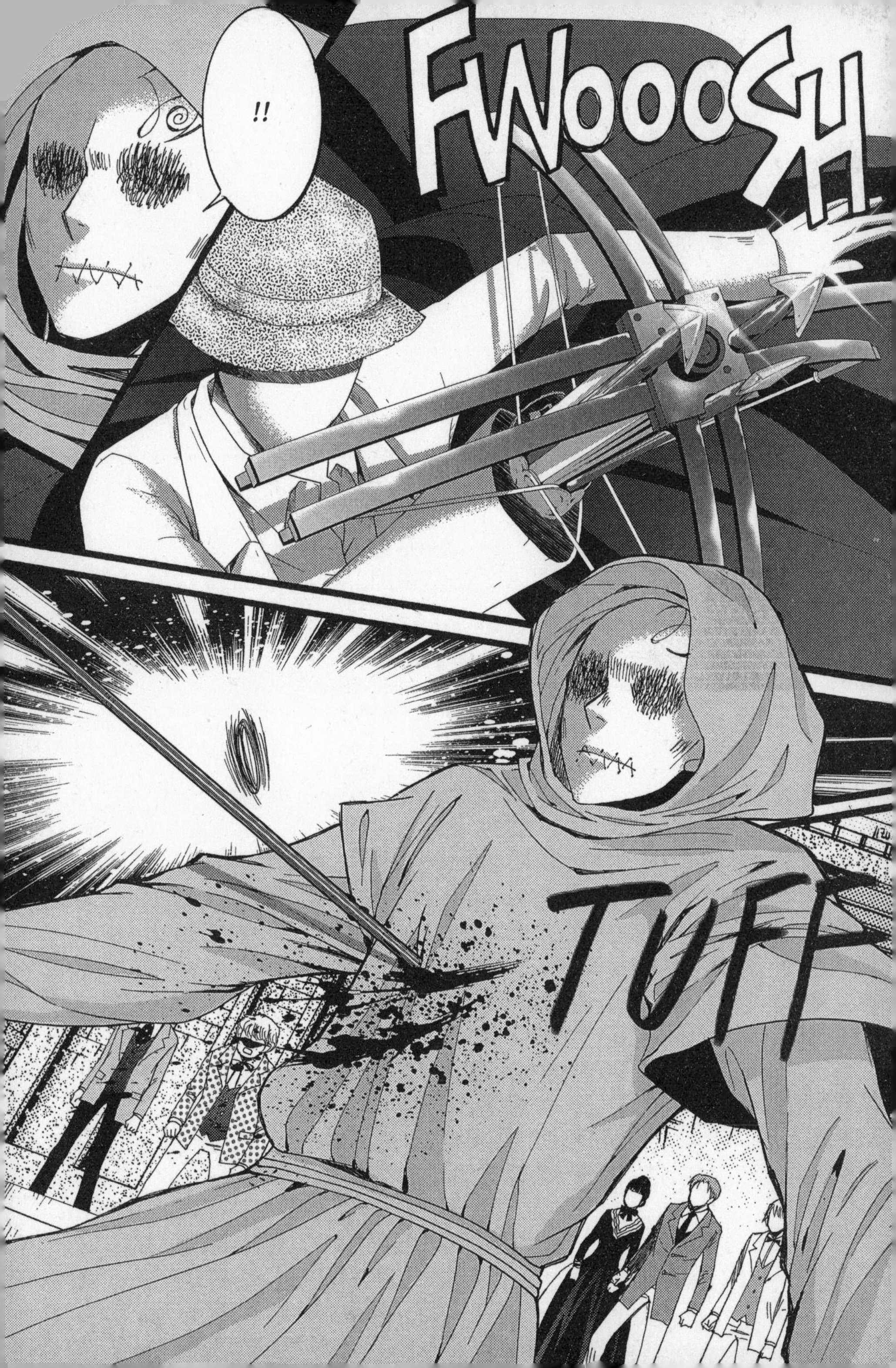
FWOOOSH
!!
TUFF

THE INFERNAL DEVICES
CLOCKWORK PRINCESS

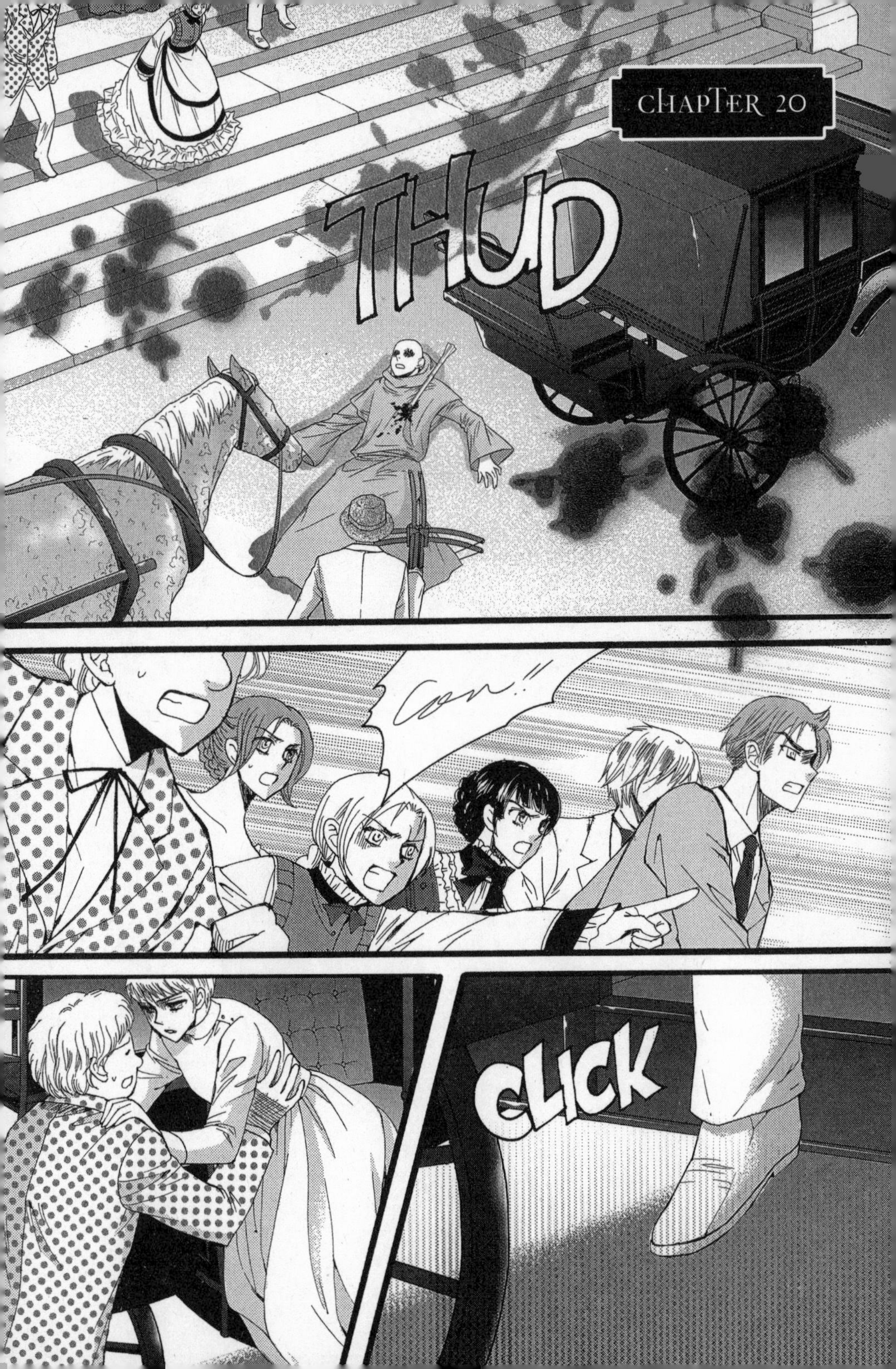
Chapter 20
THUD
Con!!
CLICK

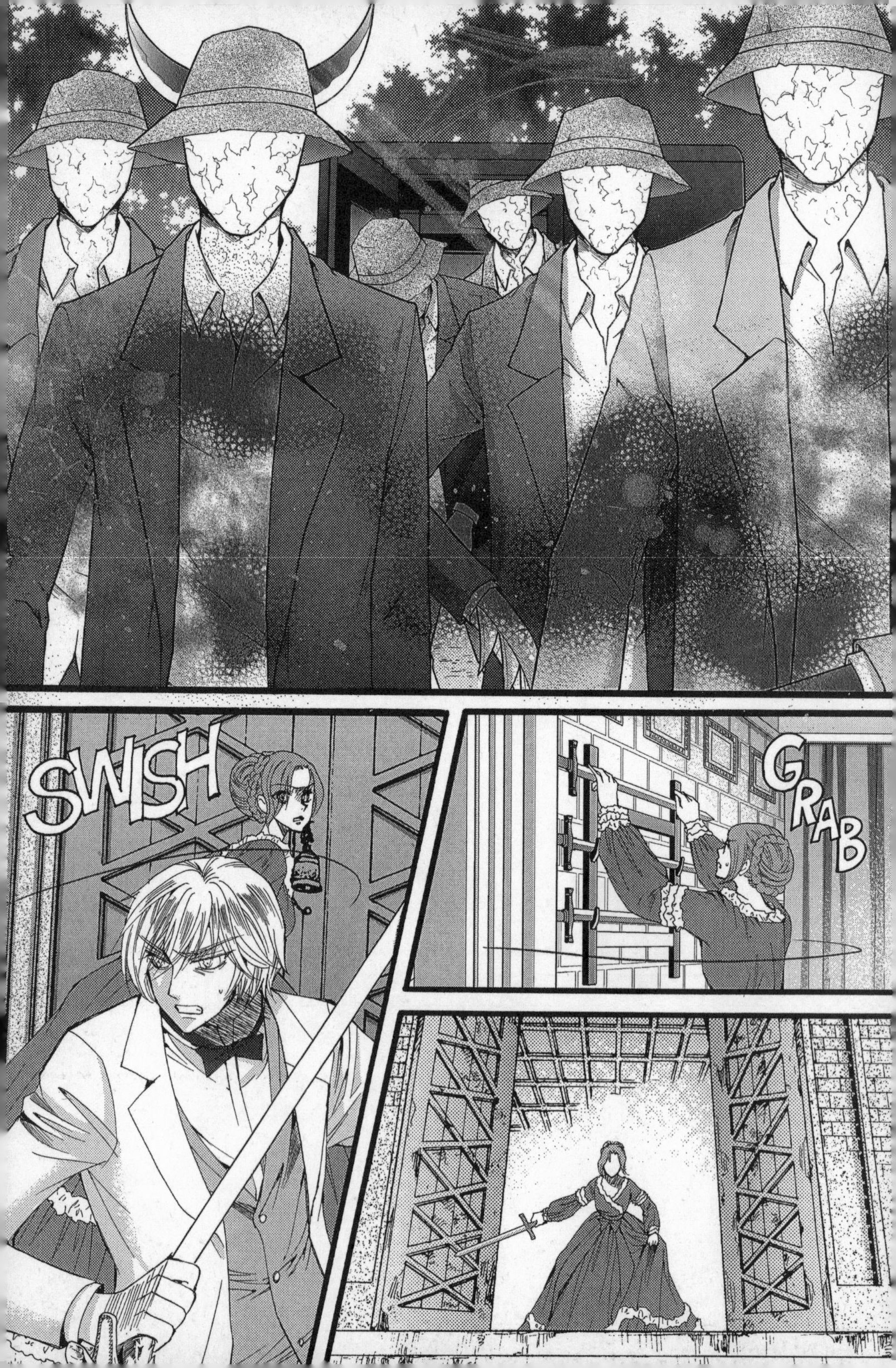
GRAB
SWISH

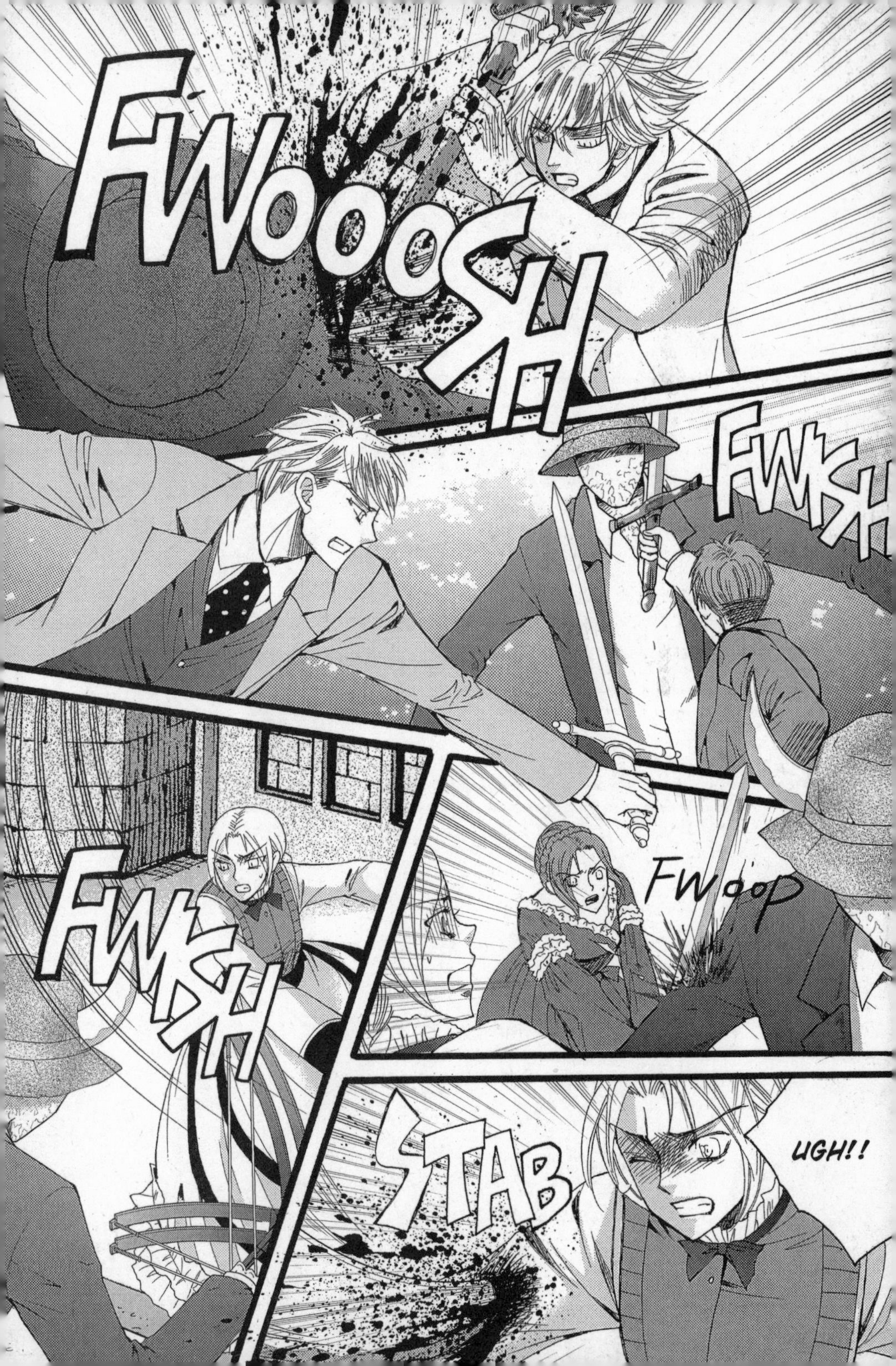
FWOOOSH
FWISH
FWOOP
FWISH
UGH!!
STAB

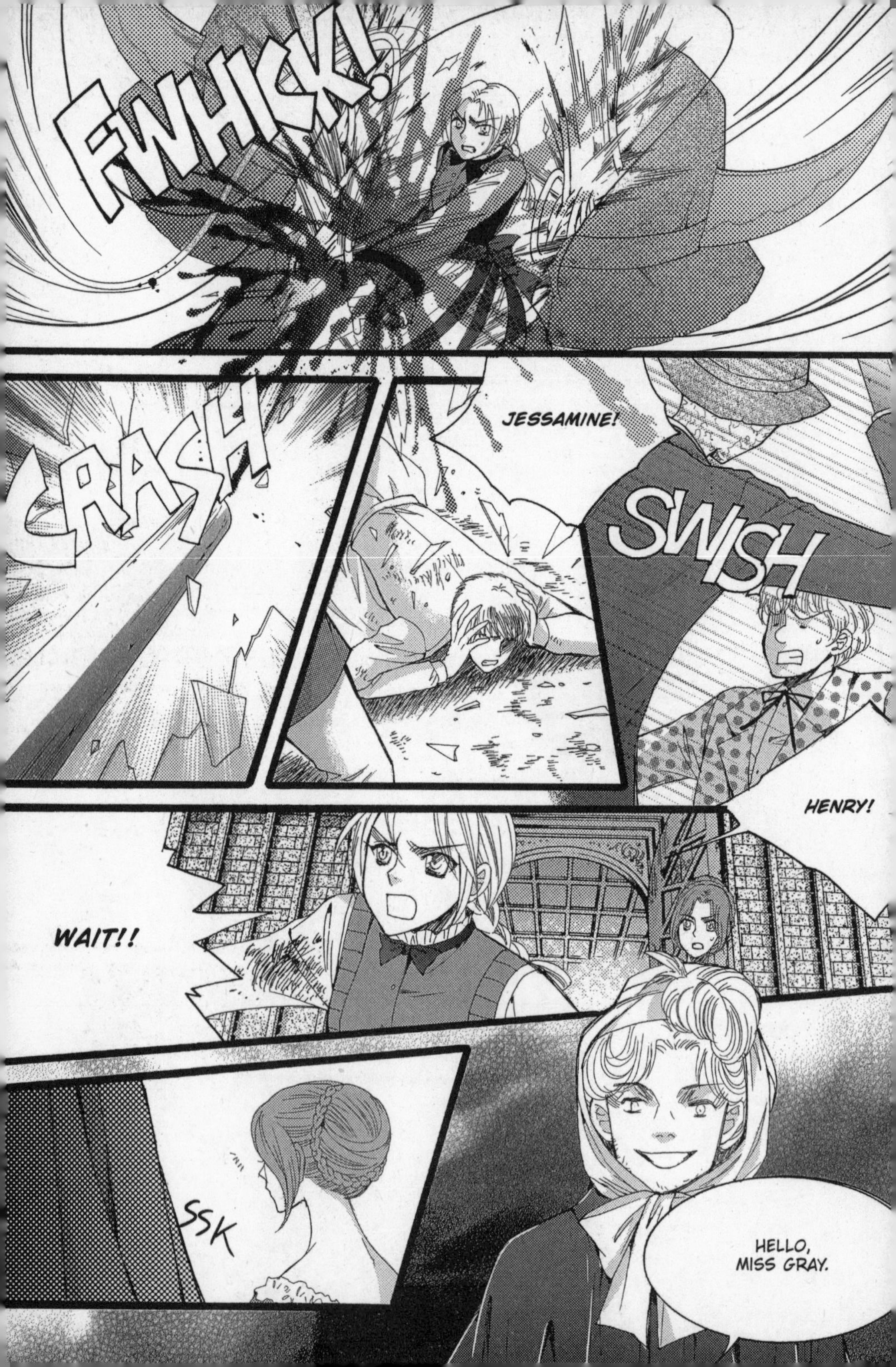
FWHICK!
CRASH
JESSAMINE!
SWISH
HENRY!
WAIT!!
SSK
HELLO, MISS GRAY.

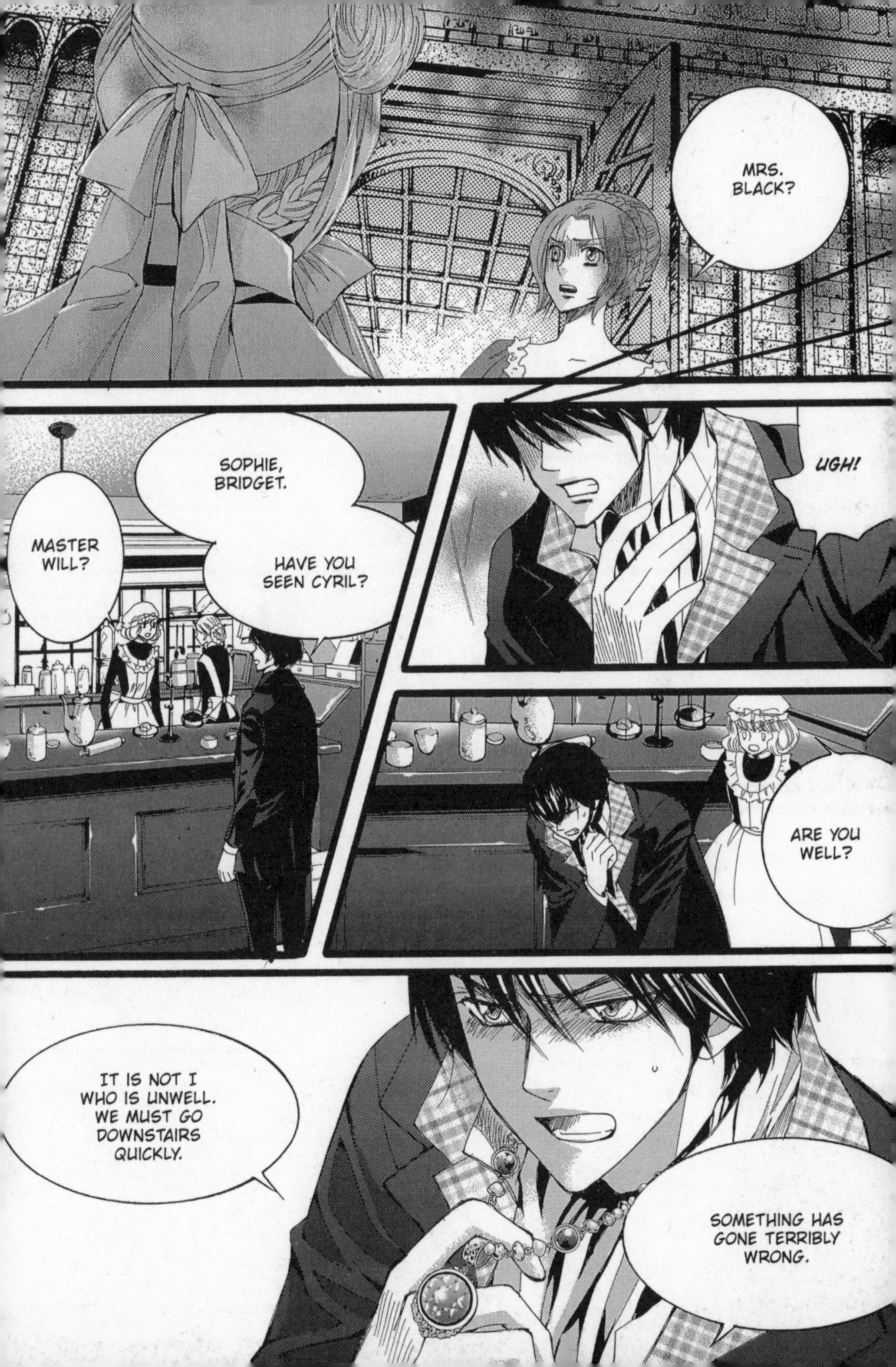
MRS. BLACK?
SOPHIE, BRIDGET.
HAVE YOU SEEN CYRIL?
MASTER WILL?
UGH!
ARE YOU WELL?
IT IS NOT I WHO IS UNWELL. WE MUST GO DOWNSTAIRS QUICKLY.
SOMETHING HAS GONE TERRIBLY WRONG.

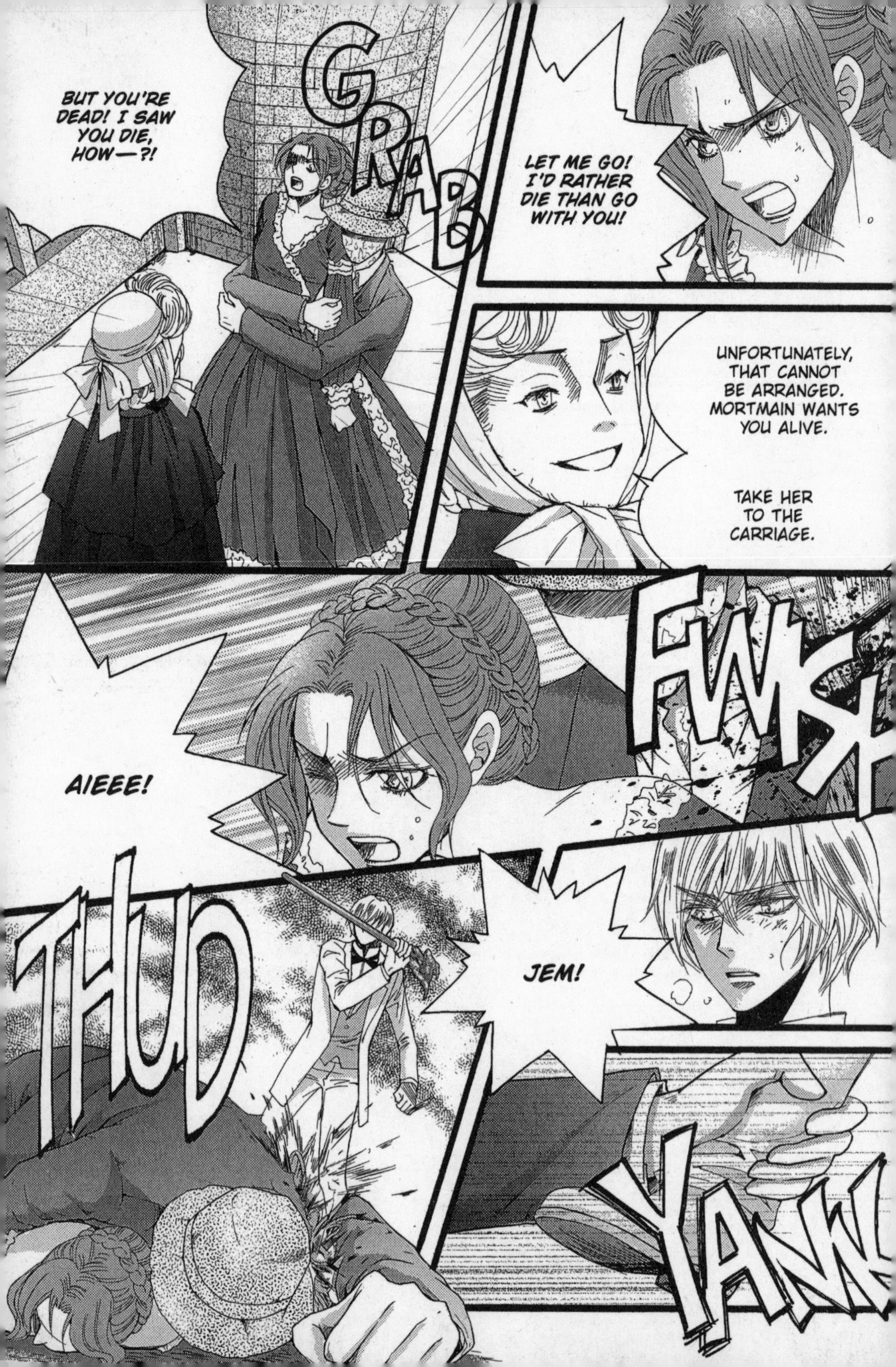
BUT YOU'RE DEAD! I SAW YOU DIE, HOW—?!
GRAB
LET ME GO! I'D RATHER DIE THAN GO WITH YOU!
UNFORTUNATELY, THAT CANNOT BE ARRANGED. MORTMAIN WANTS YOU ALIVE.
TAKE HER TO THE CARRIAGE.
AIEEE!
FWX
THUD
JEM!
YANK

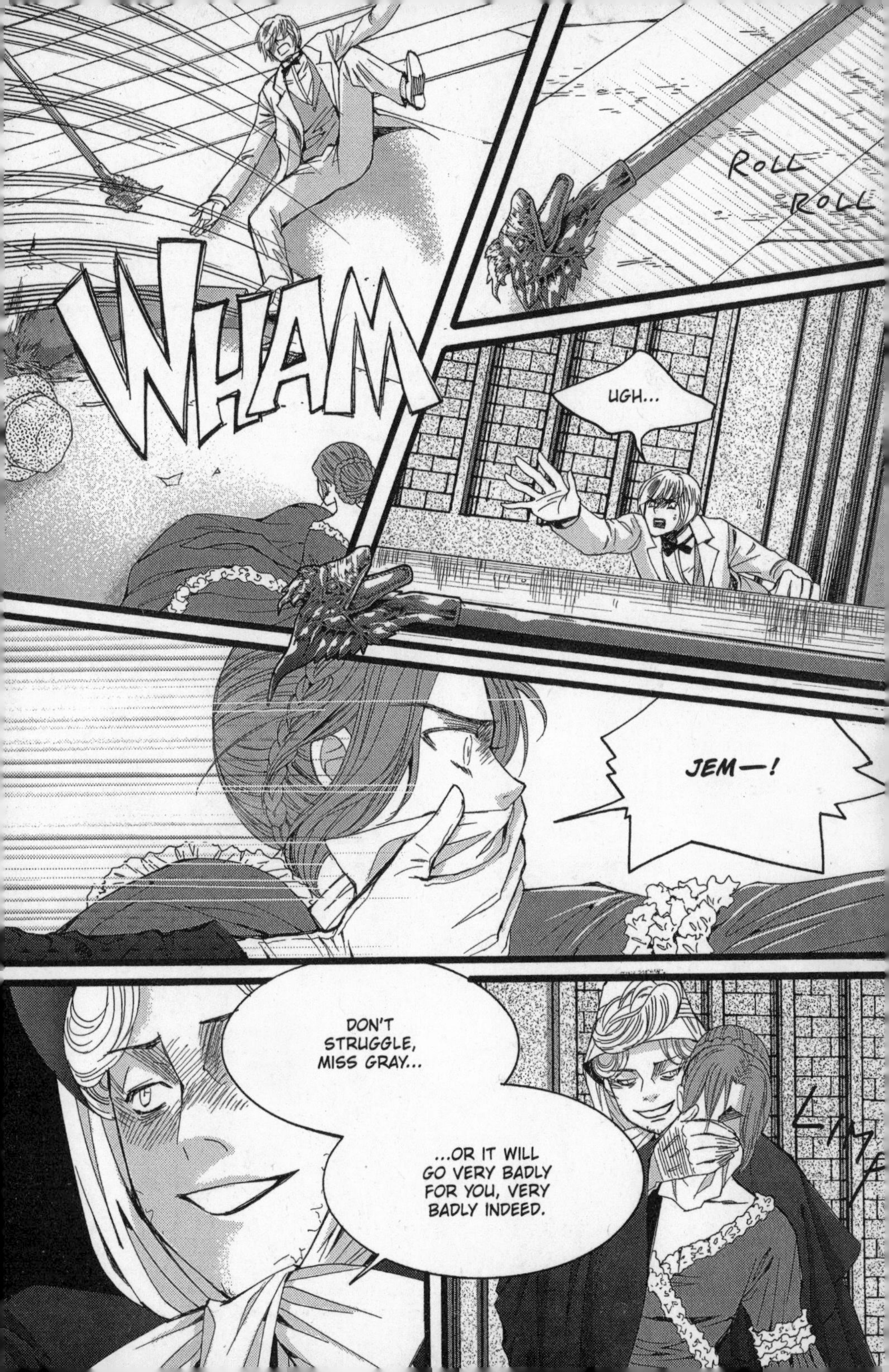
WHAM
ROLL
ROLL
UGH...
JEM—!
DON'T STRUGGLE, MISS GRAY...
...OR IT WILL GO VERY BADLY FOR YOU, VERY BADLY INDEED.

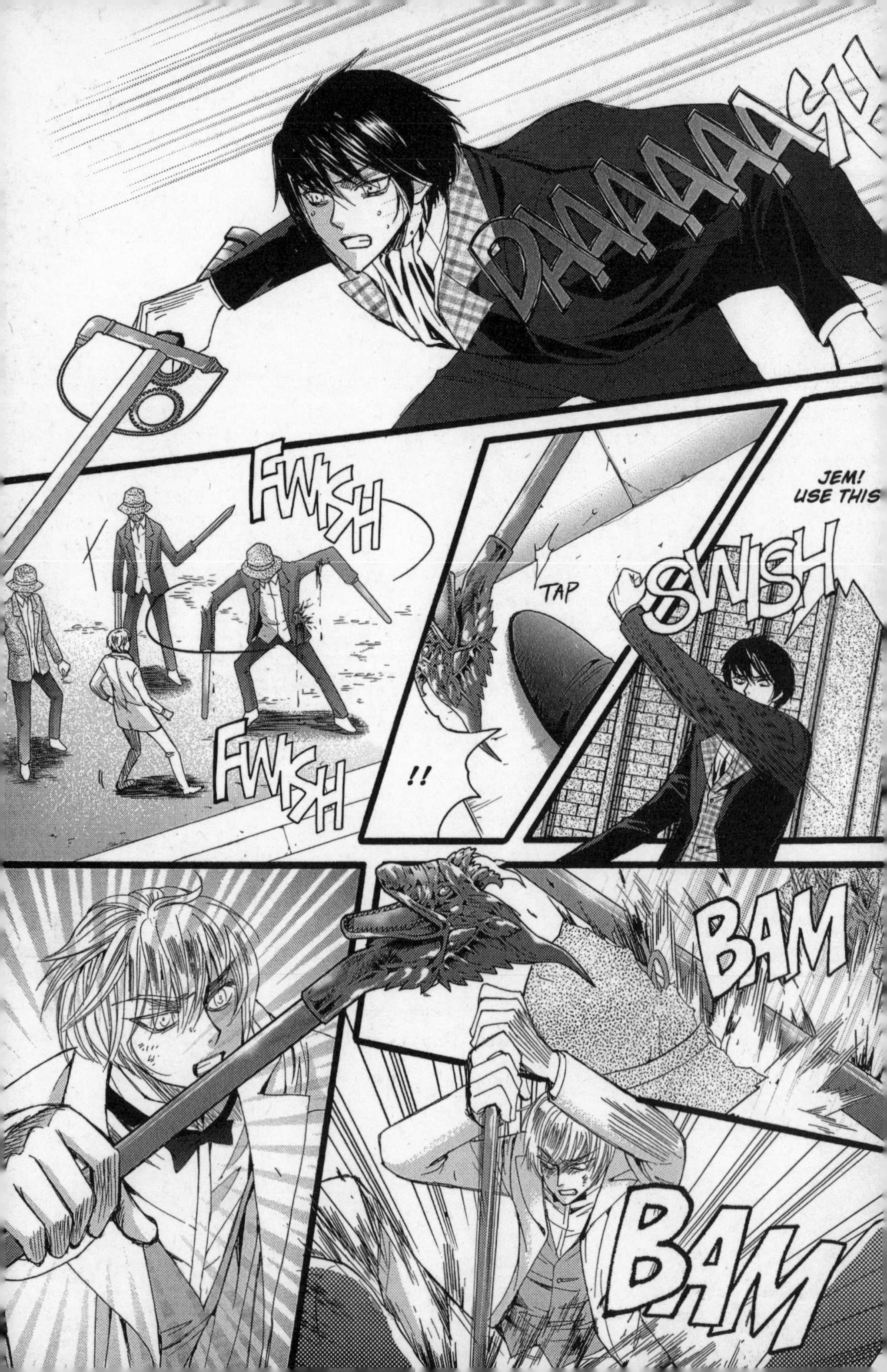
DAAAAASH!
JEM!
USE THIS
SWISH
TAP
!!
FWISH
FWISH
BAM
BAM

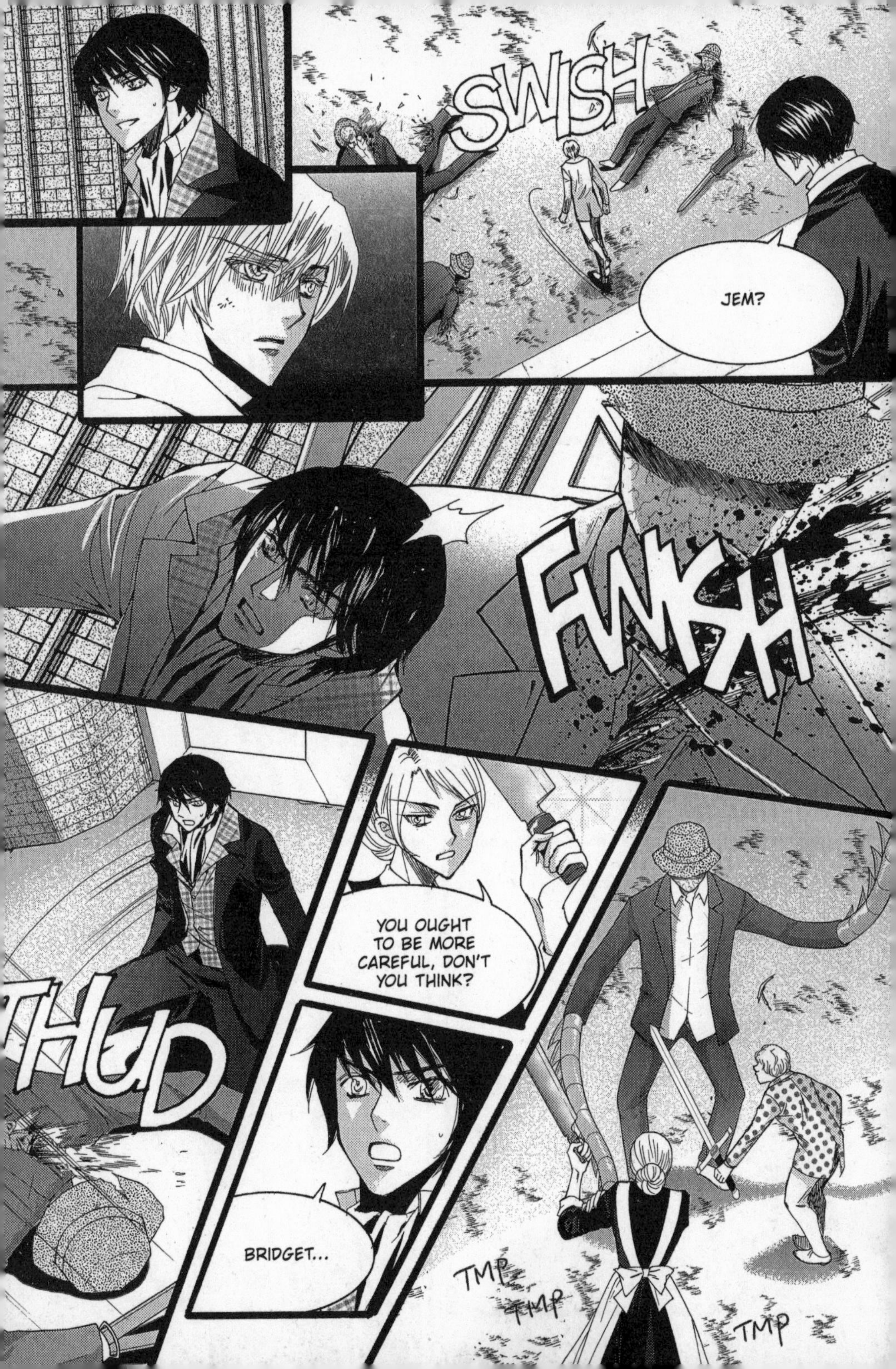
SWISH
JEM?
FWISH
YOU OUGHT TO BE MORE CAREFUL, DON'T YOU THINK?
THUD
BRIDGET...
TMP
TMP
TMP

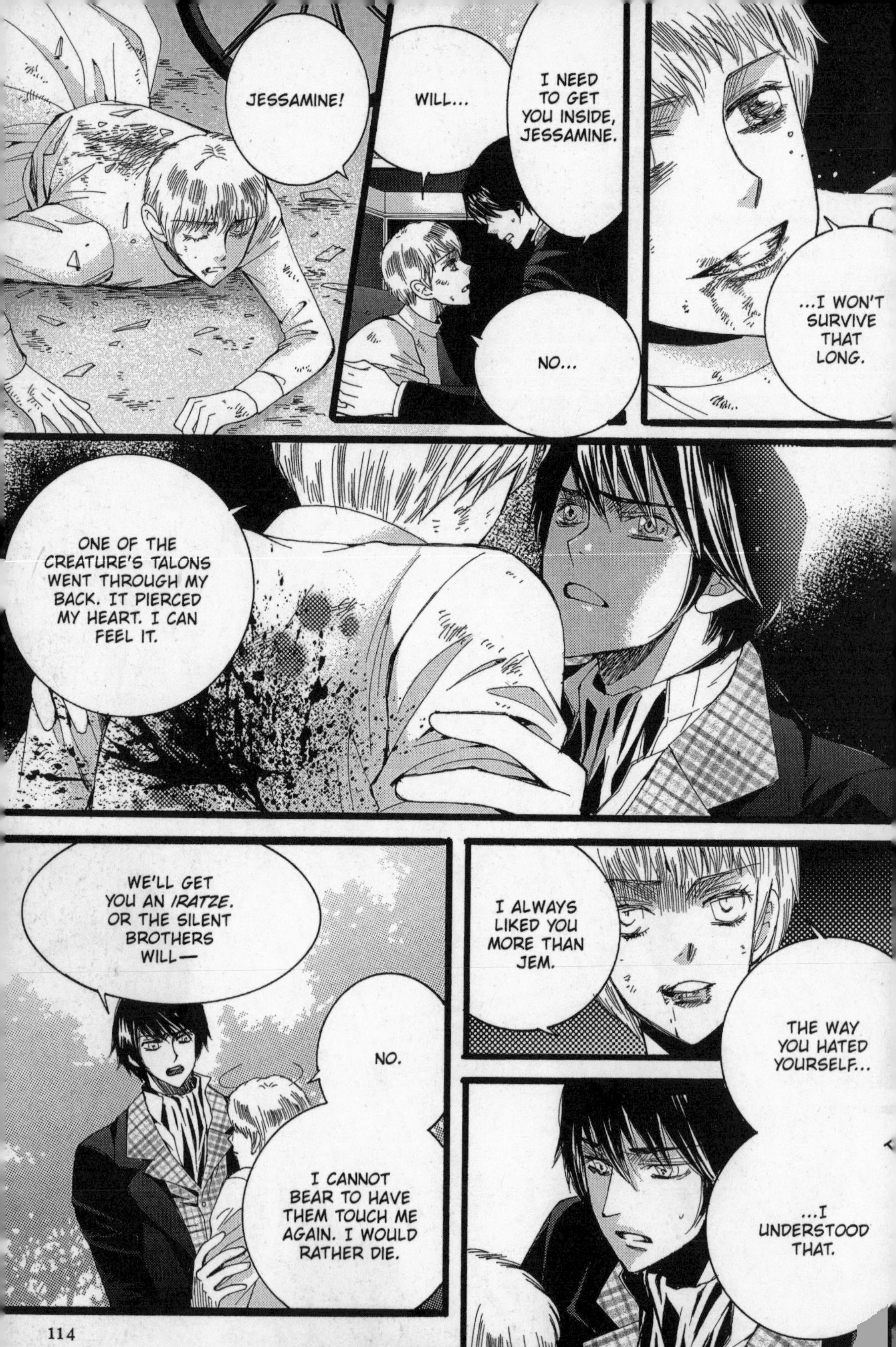
JESSAMINE!
WILL...
I NEED TO GET YOU INSIDE, JESSAMINE.
NO...
...I WON'T SURVIVE THAT LONG.
ONE OF THE CREATURE'S TALONS WENT THROUGH MY BACK. IT PIERCED MY HEART. I CAN FEEL IT.
WE'LL GET YOU AN *IRATZE*. OR THE SILENT BROTHERS WILL—
NO.
I CANNOT BEAR TO HAVE THEM TOUCH ME AGAIN. I WOULD RATHER DIE.
I ALWAYS LIKED YOU MORE THAN JEM.
THE WAY YOU HATED YOURSELF...
...I UNDERSTOOD THAT.

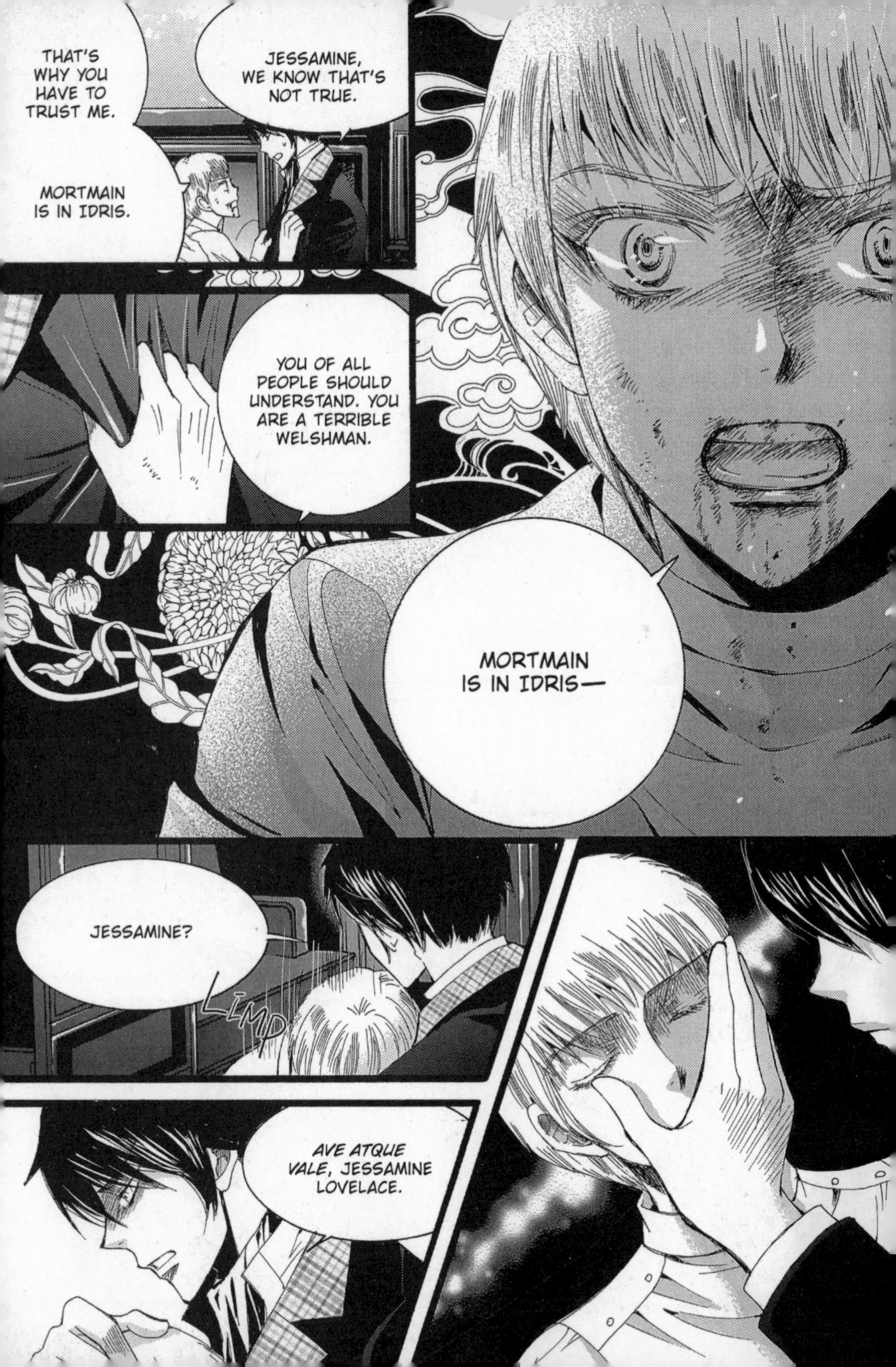
JESSAMINE, WE KNOW THAT'S NOT TRUE.
THAT'S WHY YOU HAVE TO TRUST ME.
MORTMAIN IS IN IDRIS.
YOU OF ALL PEOPLE SHOULD UNDERSTAND. YOU ARE A TERRIBLE WELSHMAN.
MORTMAIN IS IN IDRIS—
JESSAMINE?
LIMP
AVE ATQUE VALE, JESSAMINE LOVELACE.

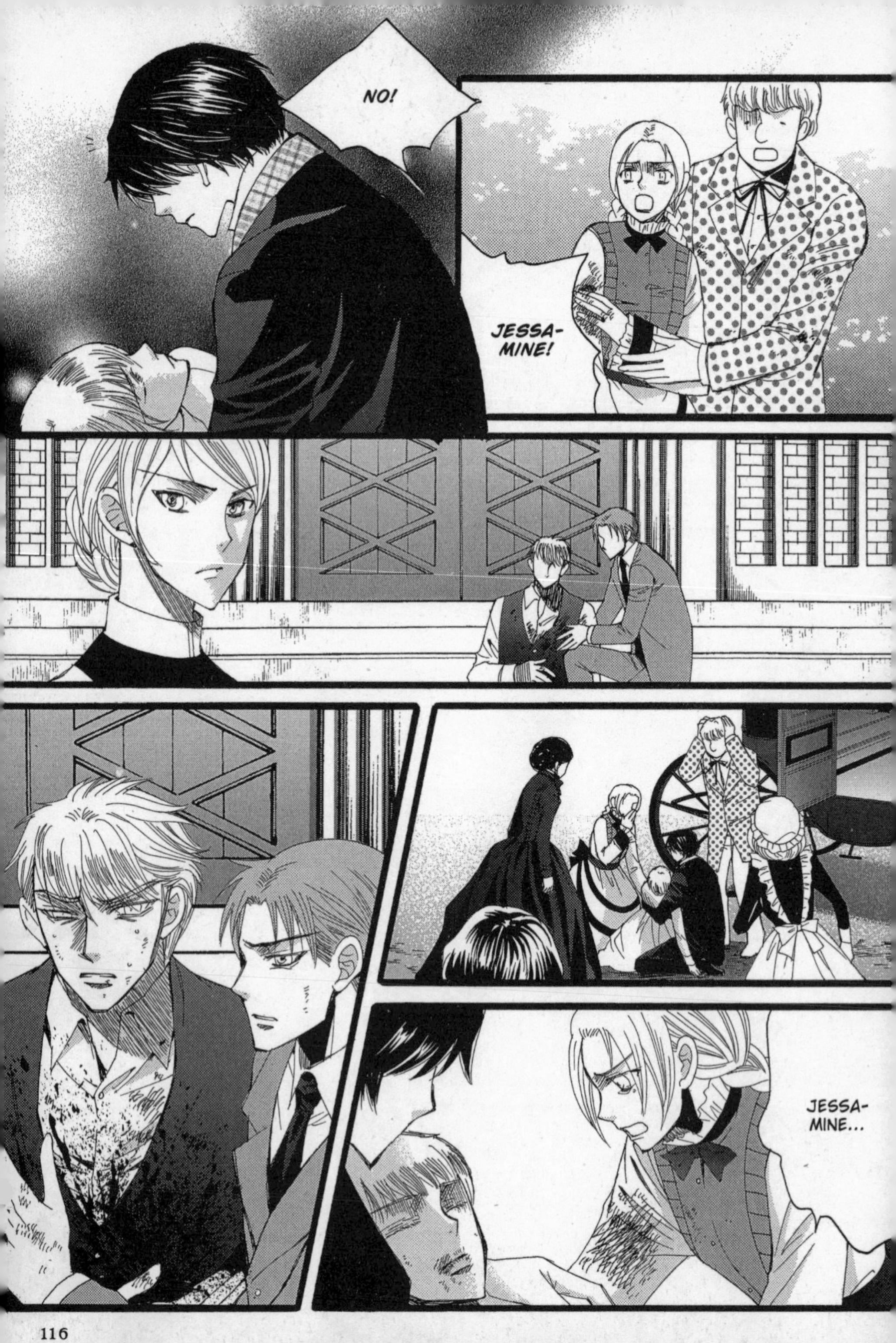
NO!
JESSA-
MINE!
JESSA-
MINE...

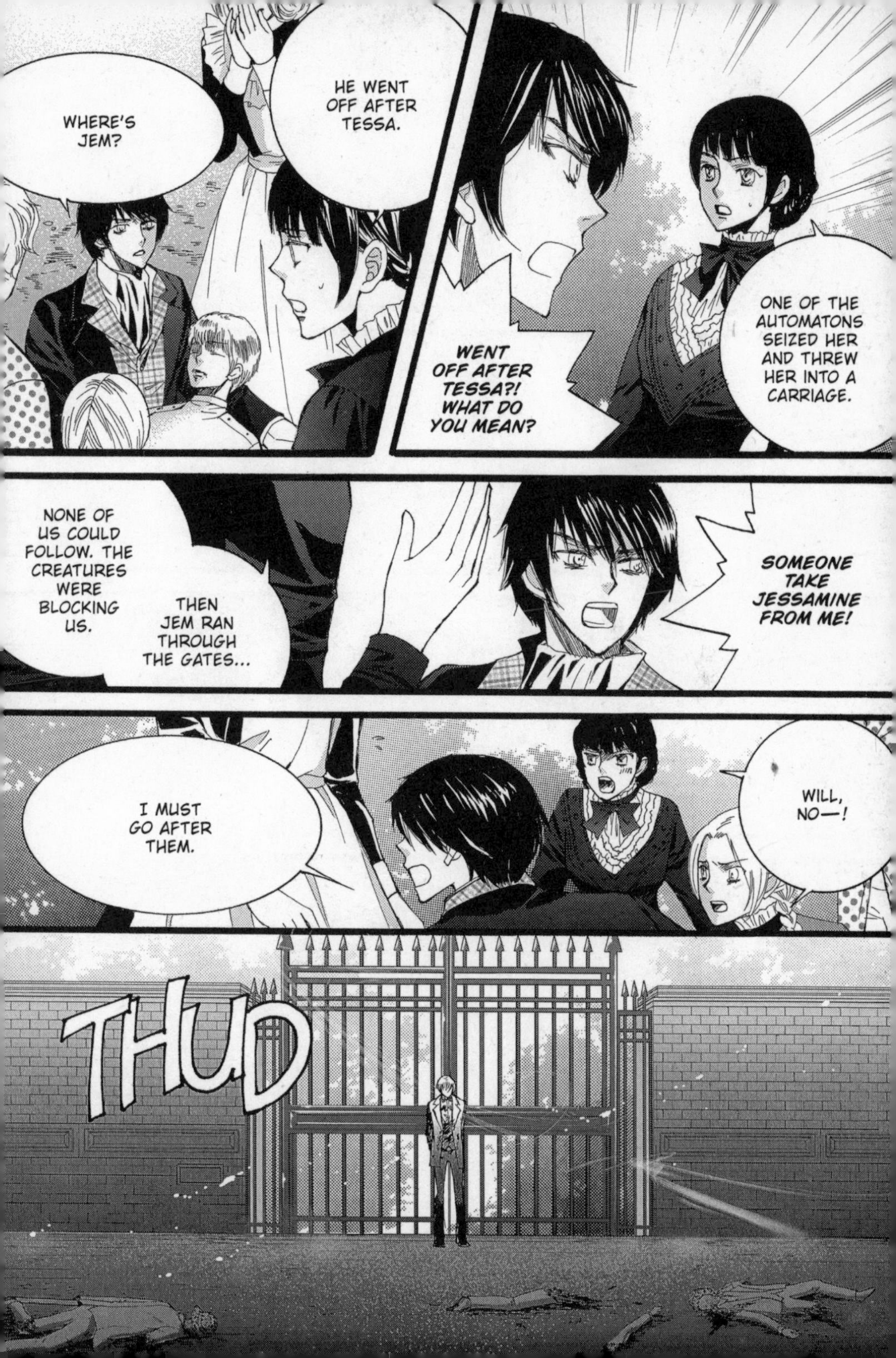
WHERE'S JEM?
HE WENT OFF AFTER TESSA.
WENT OFF AFTER TESSA?! WHAT DO YOU MEAN?
ONE OF THE AUTOMATONS SEIZED HER AND THREW HER INTO A CARRIAGE.
NONE OF US COULD FOLLOW. THE CREATURES WERE BLOCKING US.
THEN JEM RAN THROUGH THE GATES...
SOMEONE TAKE JESSAMINE FROM ME!
I MUST GO AFTER THEM.
WILL, NO—!
THUD

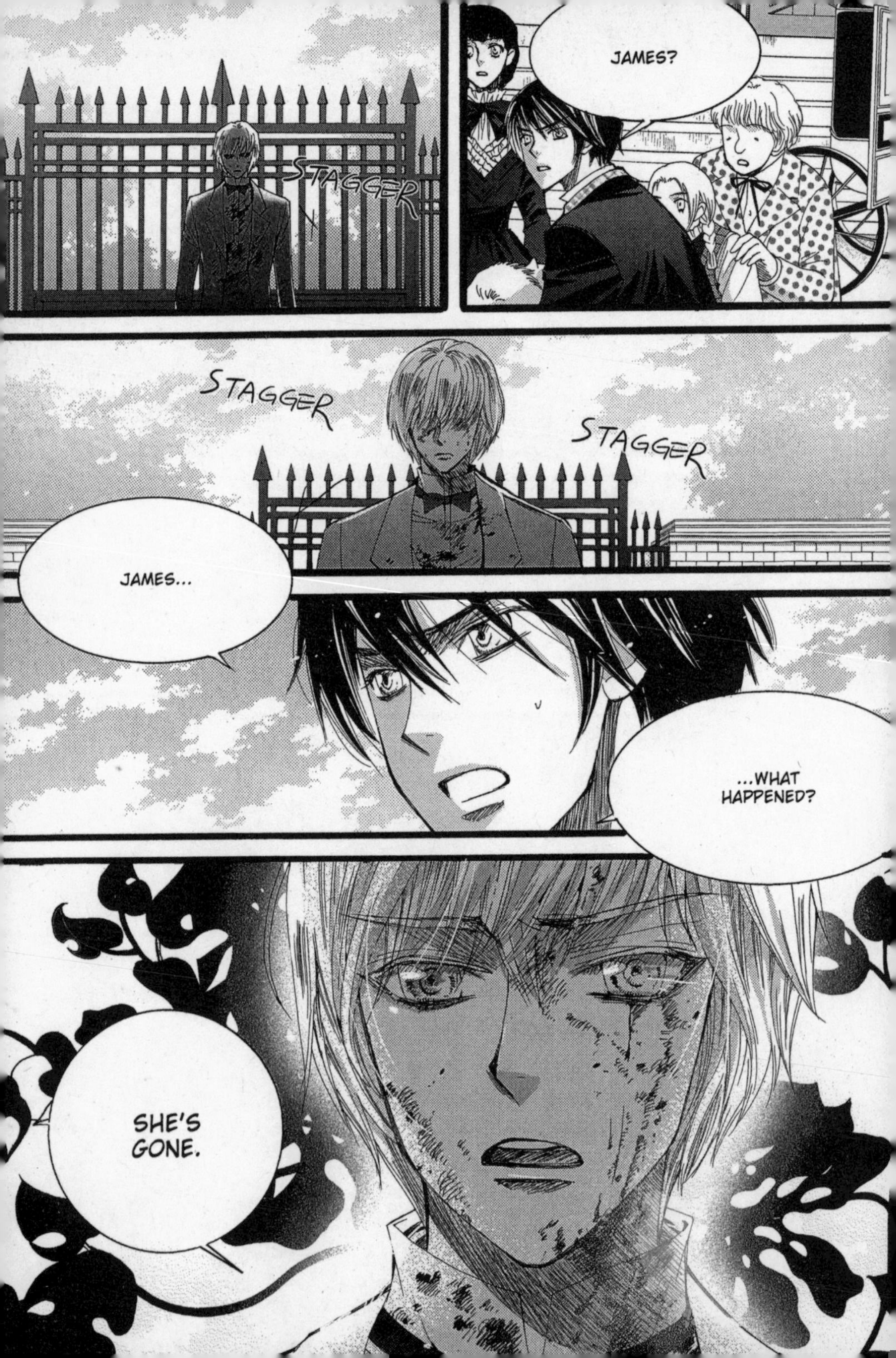
STAGGER
JAMES?
STAGGER
STAGGER
JAMES...
...WHAT HAPPENED?
SHE'S GONE.

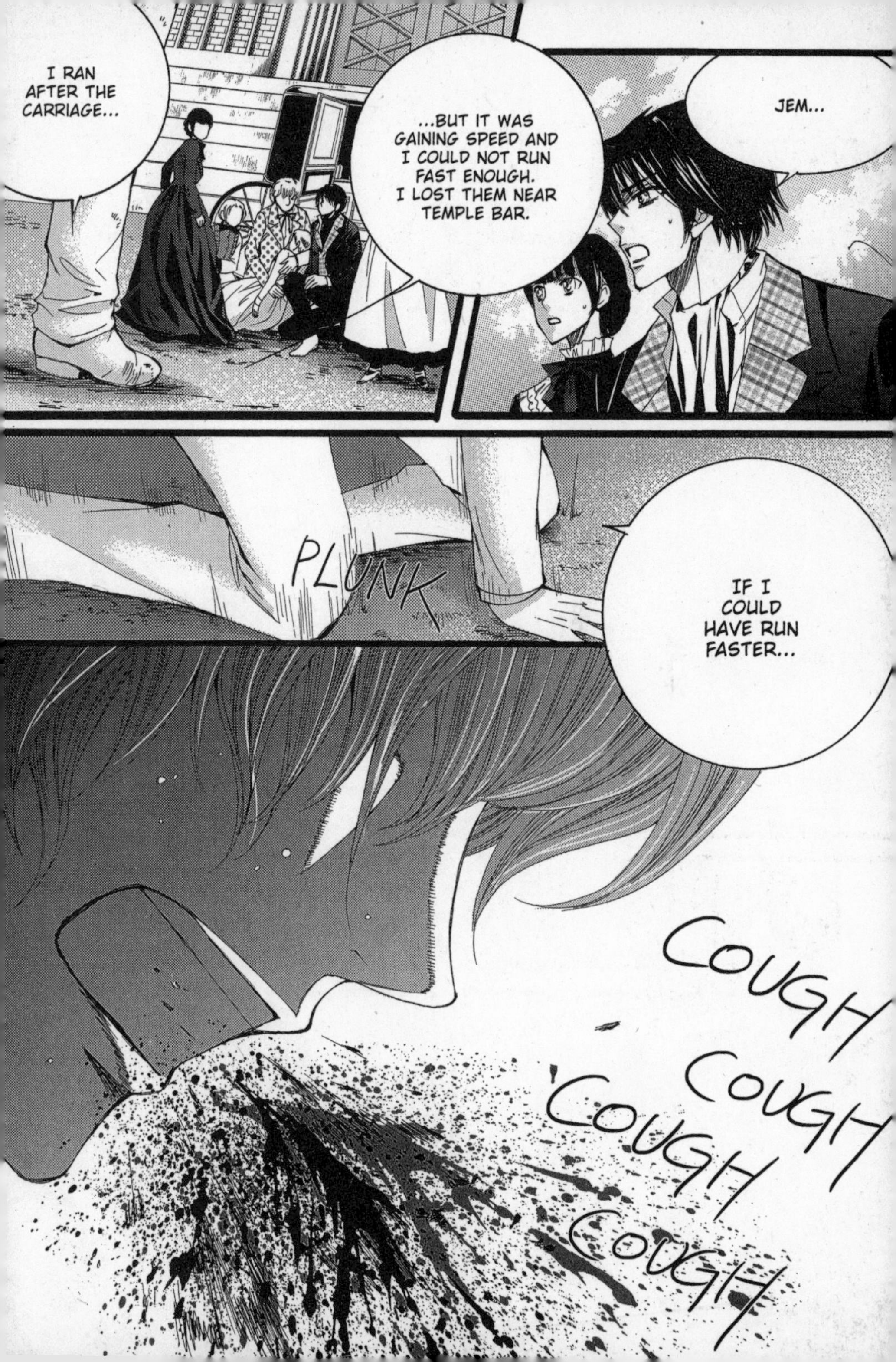
I RAN AFTER THE CARRIAGE...
...BUT IT WAS GAINING SPEED AND I COULD NOT RUN FAST ENOUGH. I LOST THEM NEAR TEMPLE BAR.
JEM...
PLUNK
IF I COULD HAVE RUN FASTER...
COUGH
COUGH
COUGH
COUGH

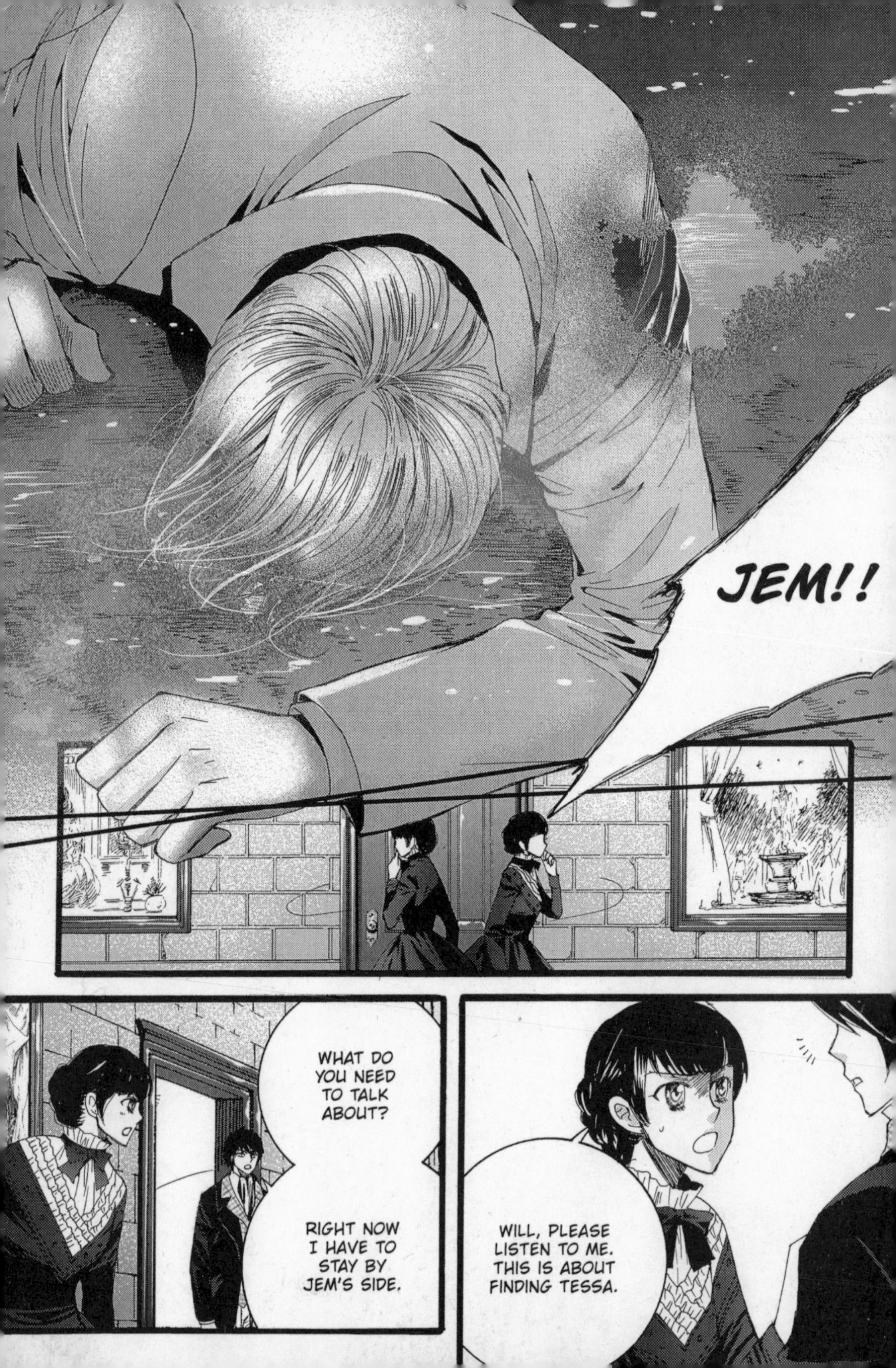
JEM!!
WHAT DO YOU NEED TO TALK ABOUT?
RIGHT NOW I HAVE TO STAY BY JEM'S SIDE.
WILL, PLEASE LISTEN TO ME. THIS IS ABOUT FINDING TESSA.

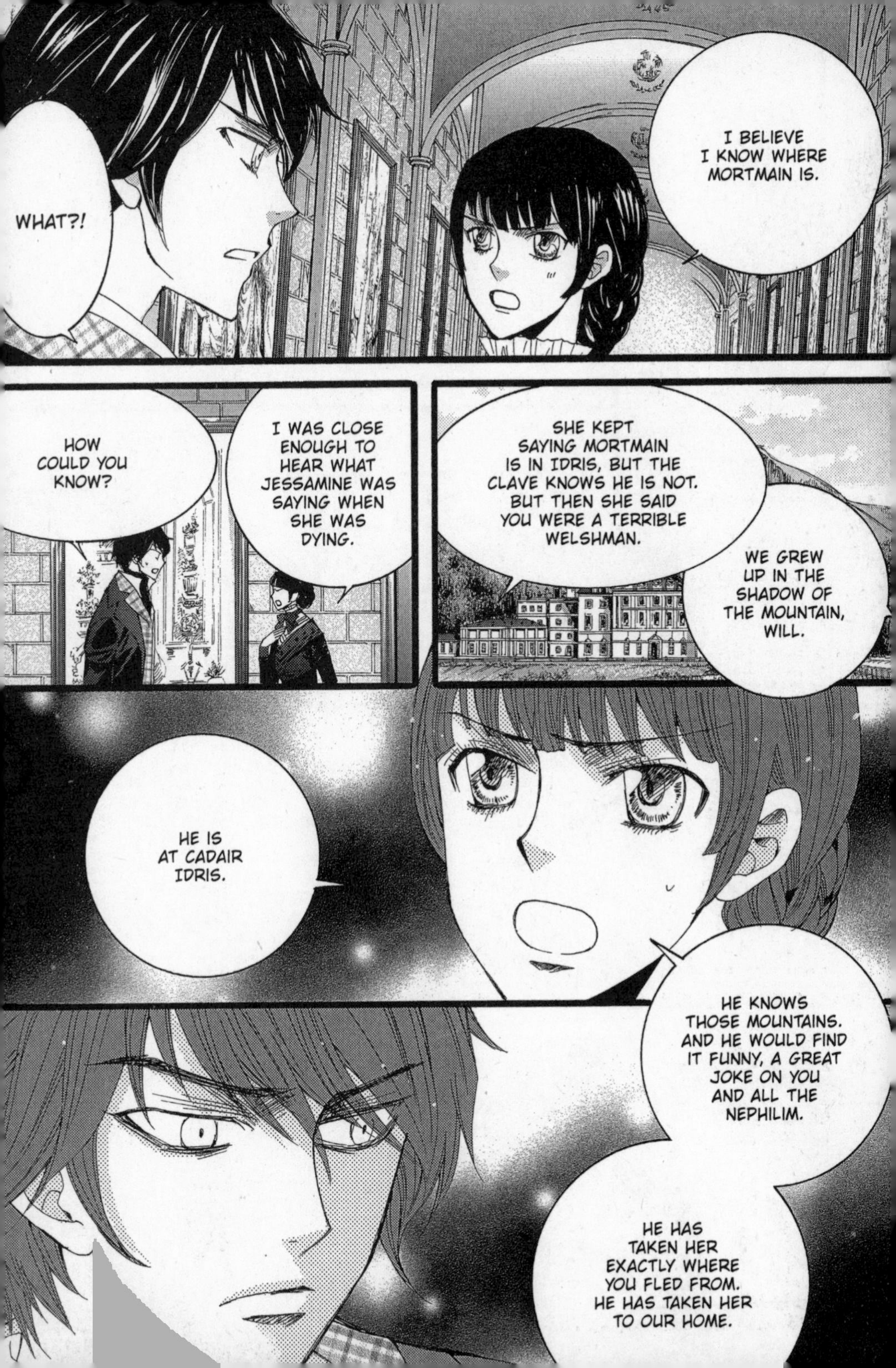
WHAT?!
I BELIEVE I KNOW WHERE MORTMAIN IS.
HOW COULD YOU KNOW?
I WAS CLOSE ENOUGH TO HEAR WHAT JESSAMINE WAS SAYING WHEN SHE WAS DYING.
SHE KEPT SAYING MORTMAIN IS IN IDRIS, BUT THE CLAVE KNOWS HE IS NOT. BUT THEN SHE SAID YOU WERE A TERRIBLE WELSHMAN.
WE GREW UP IN THE SHADOW OF THE MOUNTAIN, WILL.
HE IS AT CADAIR IDRIS.
HE KNOWS THOSE MOUNTAINS. AND HE WOULD FIND IT FUNNY, A GREAT JOKE ON YOU AND ALL THE NEPHILIM.
HE HAS TAKEN HER EXACTLY WHERE YOU FLED FROM. HE HAS TAKEN HER TO OUR HOME.

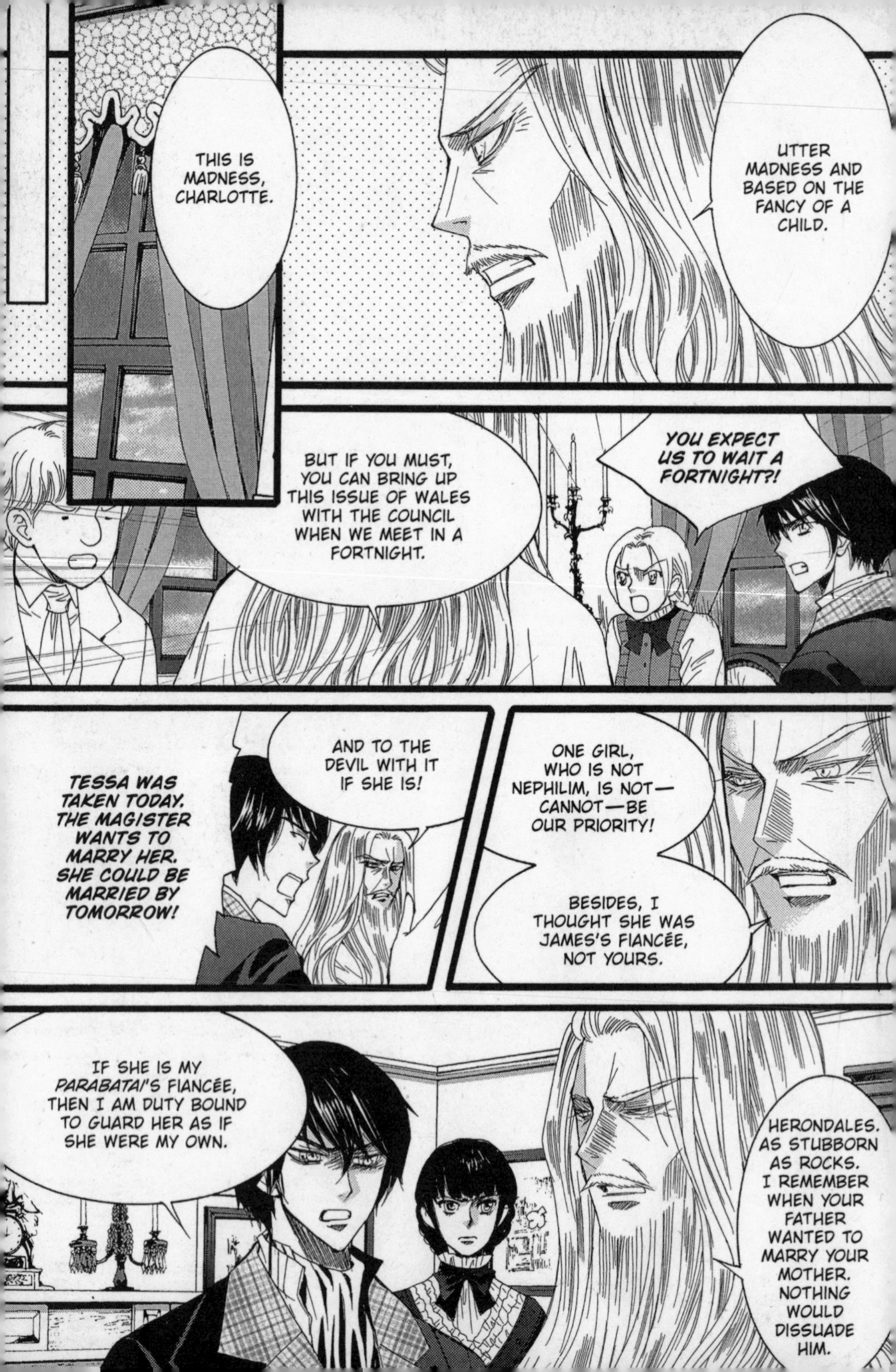
THIS IS MADNESS, CHARLOTTE.
UTTER MADNESS AND BASED ON THE FANCY OF A CHILD.
BUT IF YOU MUST, YOU CAN BRING UP THIS ISSUE OF WALES WITH THE COUNCIL WHEN WE MEET IN A FORTNIGHT.
YOU EXPECT US TO WAIT A FORTNIGHT?!
TESSA WAS TAKEN TODAY. THE MAGISTER WANTS TO MARRY HER. SHE COULD BE MARRIED BY TOMORROW!
AND TO THE DEVIL WITH IT IF SHE IS!
ONE GIRL, WHO IS NOT NEPHILIM, IS NOT—CANNOT—BE OUR PRIORITY!
BESIDES, I THOUGHT SHE WAS JAMES'S FIANCÉE, NOT YOURS.
IF SHE IS MY *PARABATAI*'S FIANCÉE, THEN I AM DUTY BOUND TO GUARD HER AS IF SHE WERE MY OWN.
HERONDALES. AS STUBBORN AS ROCKS. I REMEMBER WHEN YOUR FATHER WANTED TO MARRY YOUR MOTHER. NOTHING WOULD DISSUADE HIM.

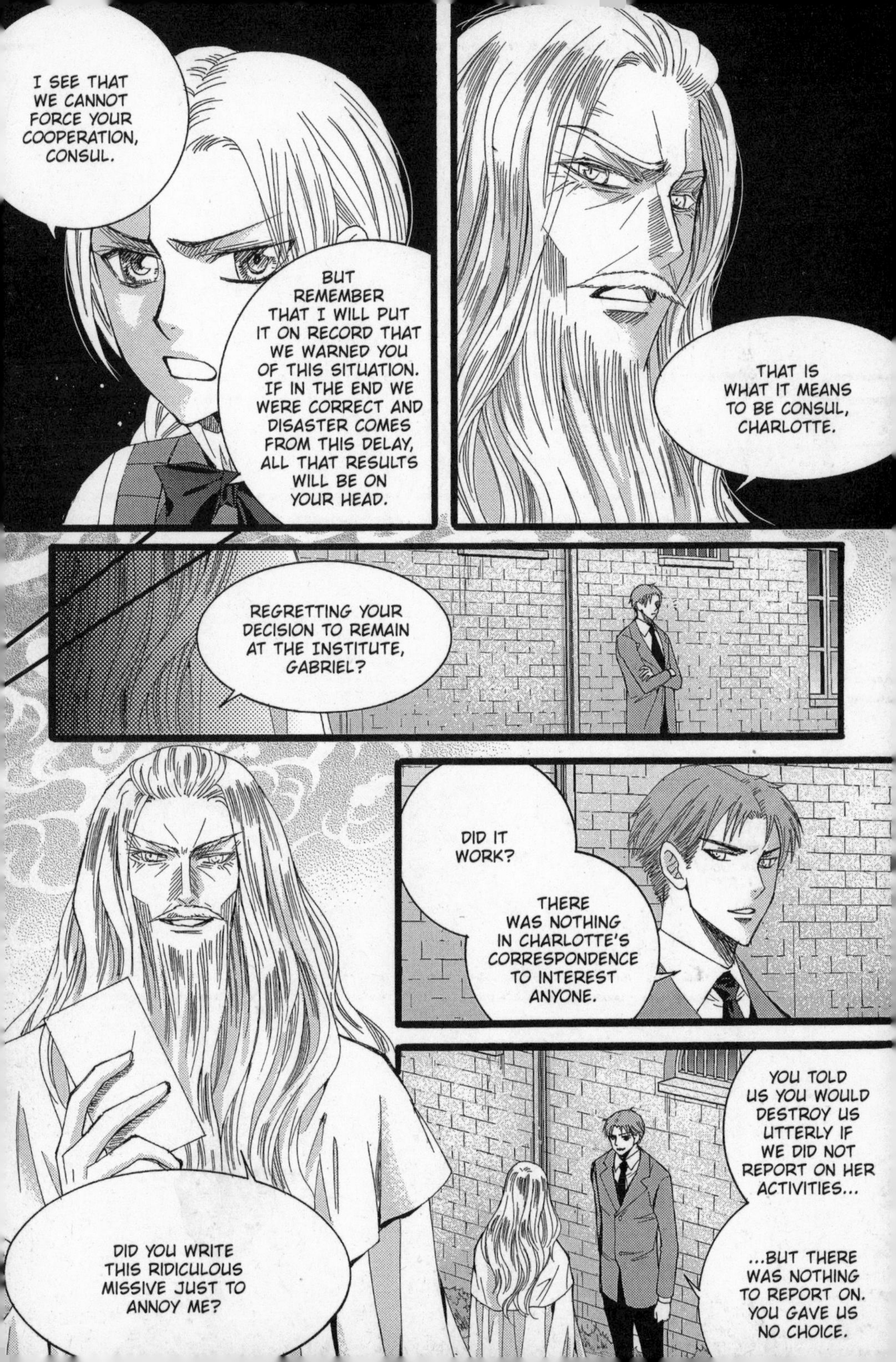
I SEE THAT WE CANNOT FORCE YOUR COOPERATION, CONSUL.
BUT REMEMBER THAT I WILL PUT IT ON RECORD THAT WE WARNED YOU OF THIS SITUATION. IF IN THE END WE WERE CORRECT AND DISASTER COMES FROM THIS DELAY, ALL THAT RESULTS WILL BE ON YOUR HEAD.
THAT IS WHAT IT MEANS TO BE CONSUL, CHARLOTTE.
REGRETTING YOUR DECISION TO REMAIN AT THE INSTITUTE, GABRIEL?
DID IT WORK?
THERE WAS NOTHING IN CHARLOTTE'S CORRESPONDENCE TO INTEREST ANYONE.
DID YOU WRITE THIS RIDICULOUS MISSIVE JUST TO ANNOY ME?
YOU TOLD US YOU WOULD DESTROY US UTTERLY IF WE DID NOT REPORT ON HER ACTIVITIES...
...BUT THERE WAS NOTHING TO REPORT ON. YOU GAVE US NO CHOICE.

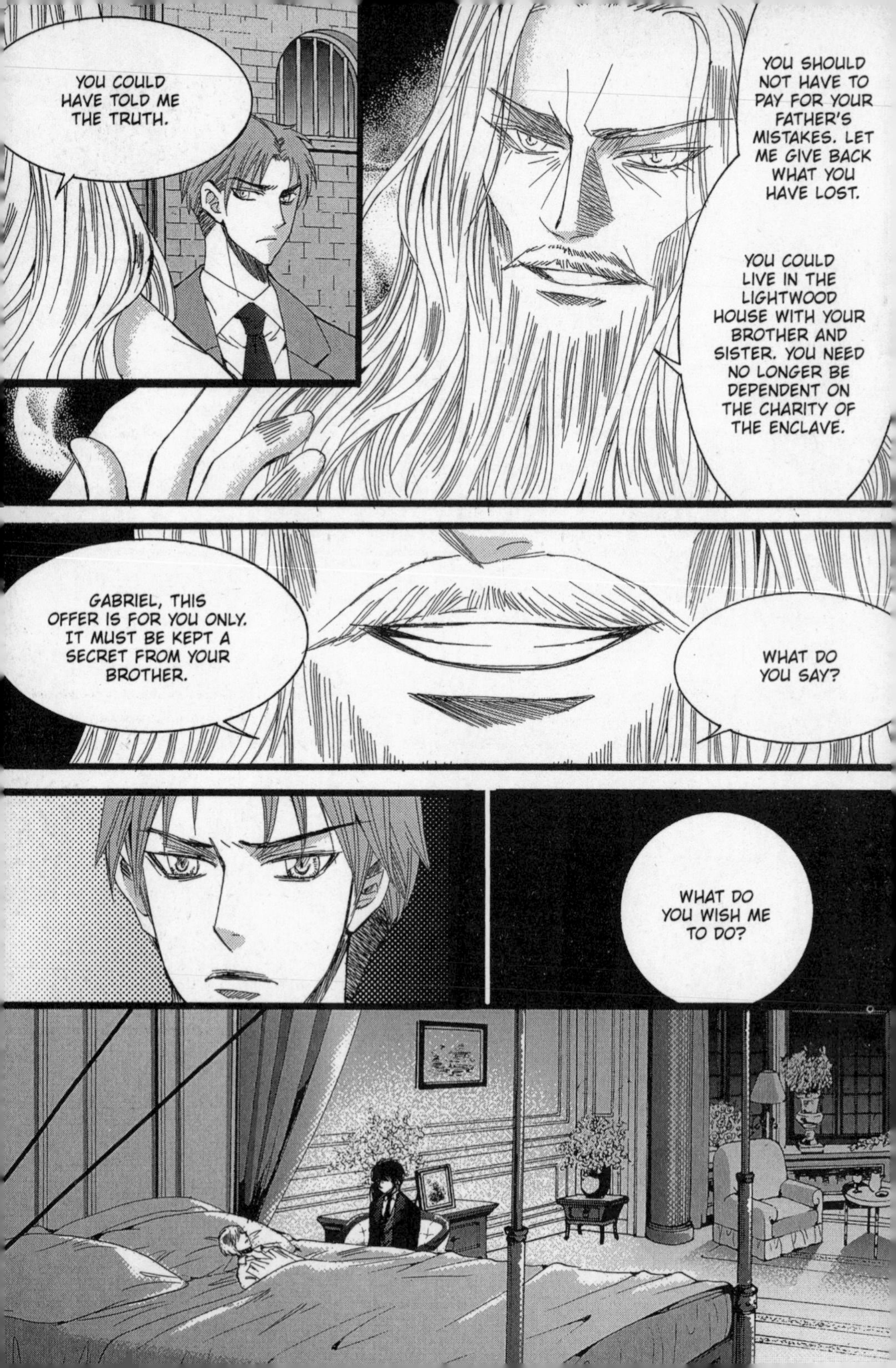
YOU COULD HAVE TOLD ME THE TRUTH.
YOU SHOULD NOT HAVE TO PAY FOR YOUR FATHER'S MISTAKES. LET ME GIVE BACK WHAT YOU HAVE LOST.
YOU COULD LIVE IN THE LIGHTWOOD HOUSE WITH YOUR BROTHER AND SISTER. YOU NEED NO LONGER BE DEPENDENT ON THE CHARITY OF THE ENCLAVE.
GABRIEL, THIS OFFER IS FOR YOU ONLY. IT MUST BE KEPT A SECRET FROM YOUR BROTHER.
WHAT DO YOU SAY?
WHAT DO YOU WISH ME TO DO?

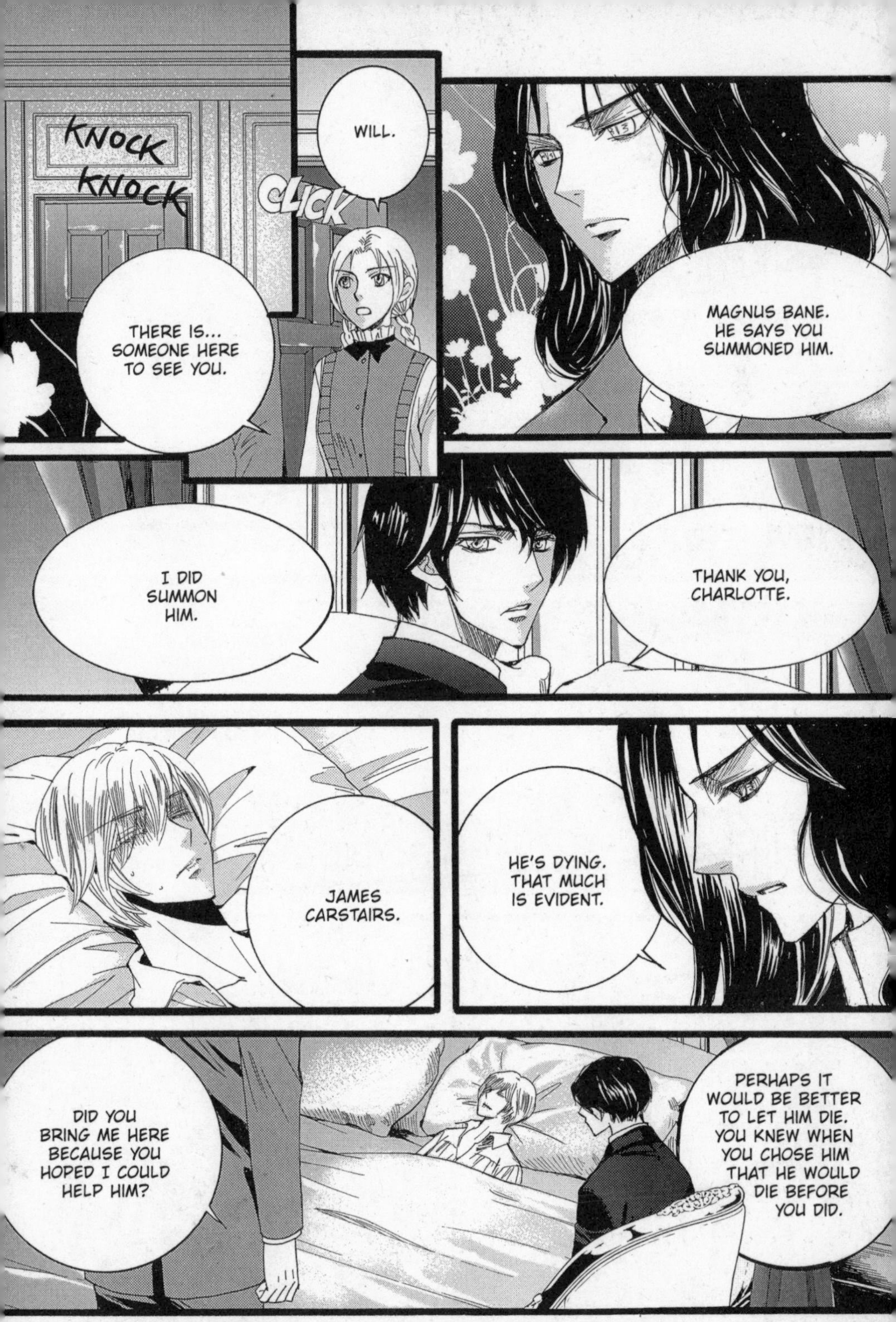
KNOCK KNOCK
CLICK
WILL.
THERE IS... SOMEONE HERE TO SEE YOU.
MAGNUS BANE. HE SAYS YOU SUMMONED HIM.
I DID SUMMON HIM.
THANK YOU, CHARLOTTE.
JAMES CARSTAIRS.
HE'S DYING. THAT MUCH IS EVIDENT.
DID YOU BRING ME HERE BECAUSE YOU HOPED I COULD HELP HIM?
PERHAPS IT WOULD BE BETTER TO LET HIM DIE. YOU KNEW WHEN YOU CHOSE HIM THAT HE WOULD DIE BEFORE YOU DID.

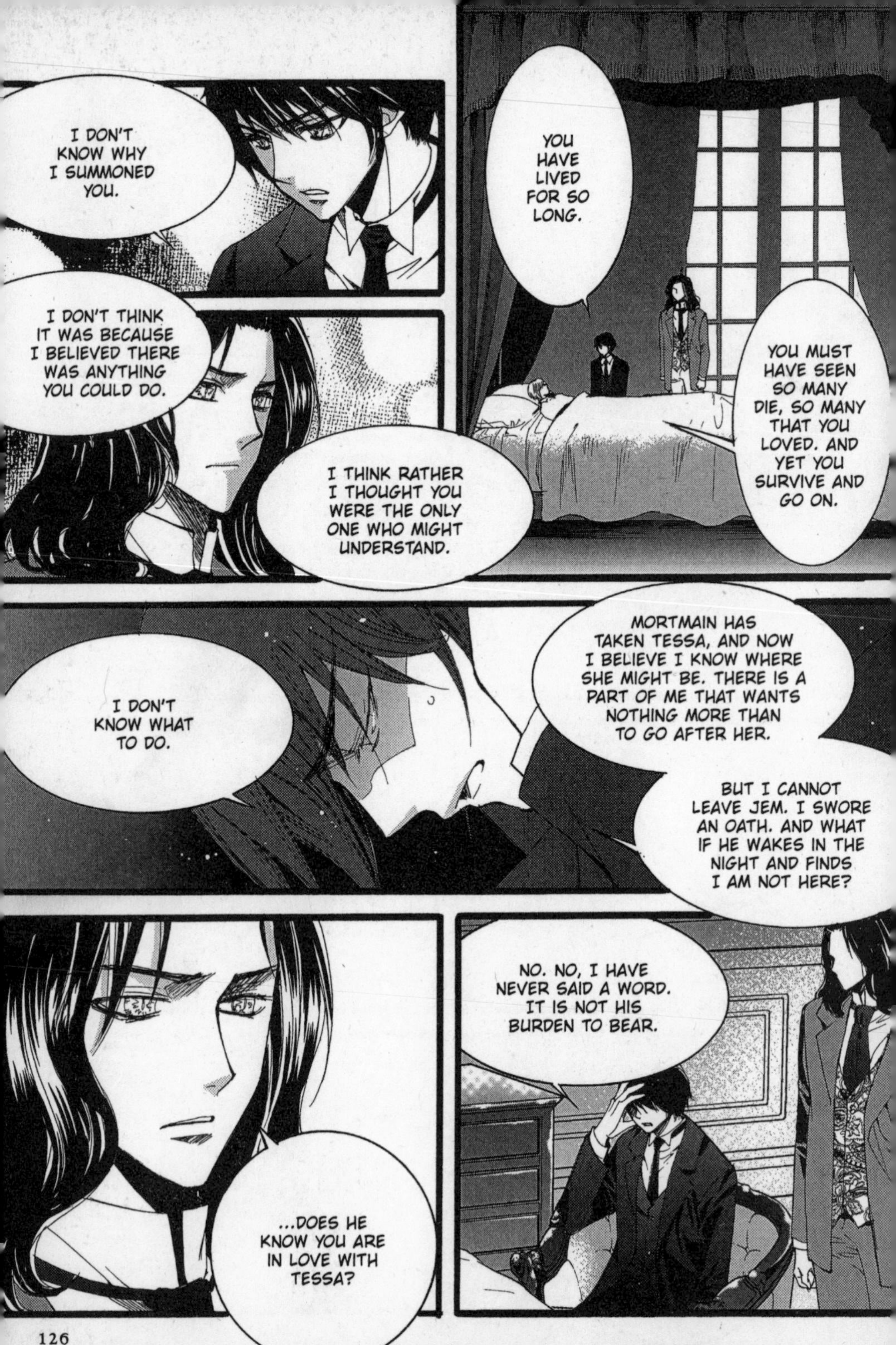
I DON'T KNOW WHY I SUMMONED YOU.
I DON'T THINK IT WAS BECAUSE I BELIEVED THERE WAS ANYTHING YOU COULD DO.
I THINK RATHER I THOUGHT YOU WERE THE ONLY ONE WHO MIGHT UNDERSTAND.
YOU HAVE LIVED FOR SO LONG.
YOU MUST HAVE SEEN SO MANY DIE, SO MANY THAT YOU LOVED. AND YET YOU SURVIVE AND GO ON.
I DON'T KNOW WHAT TO DO.
MORTMAIN HAS TAKEN TESSA, AND NOW I BELIEVE I KNOW WHERE SHE MIGHT BE. THERE IS A PART OF ME THAT WANTS NOTHING MORE THAN TO GO AFTER HER.
BUT I CANNOT LEAVE JEM. I SWORE AN OATH. AND WHAT IF HE WAKES IN THE NIGHT AND FINDS I AM NOT HERE?
...DOES HE KNOW YOU ARE IN LOVE WITH TESSA?
NO. NO, I HAVE NEVER SAID A WORD. IT IS NOT HIS BURDEN TO BEAR.

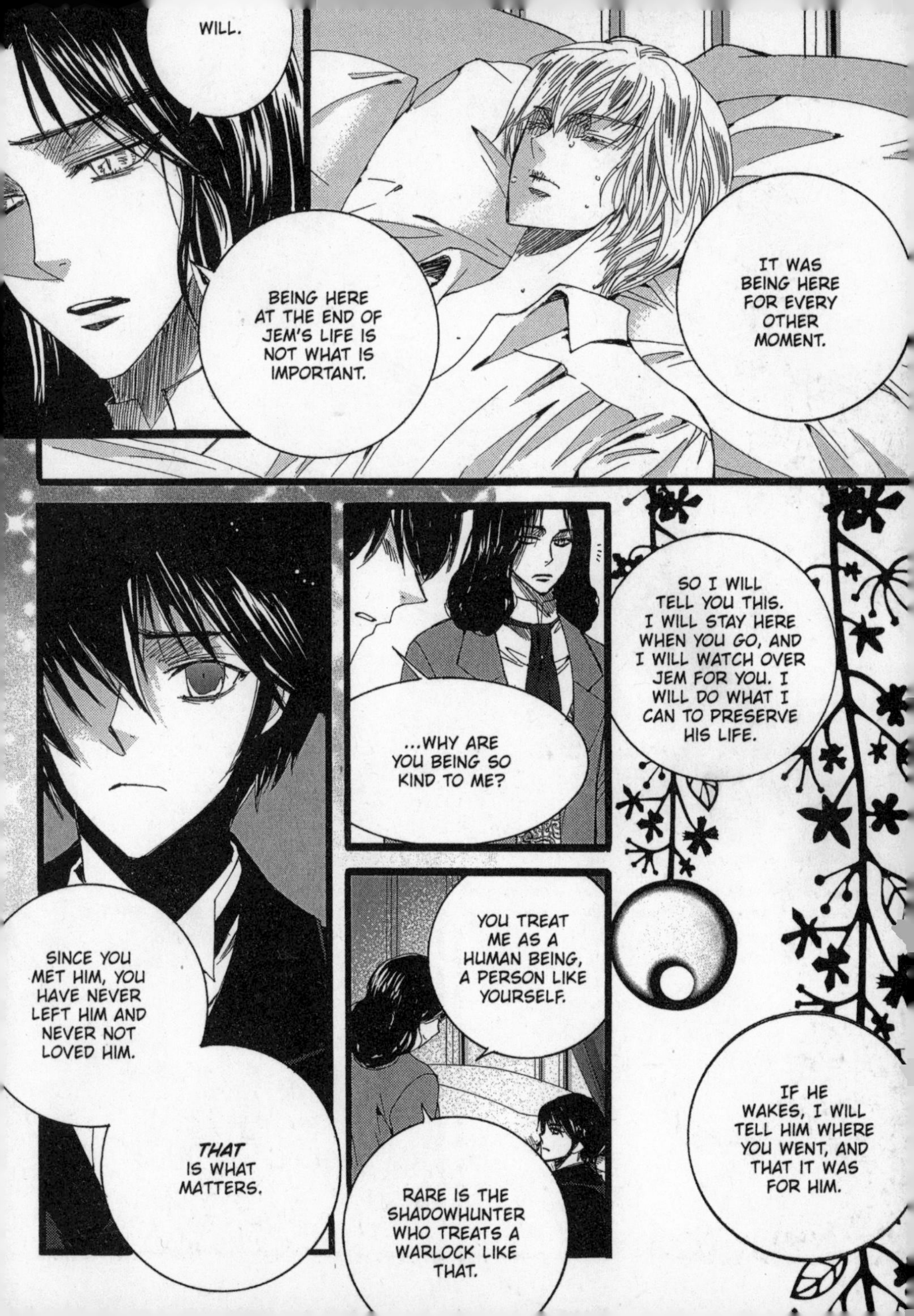
WILL.
BEING HERE AT THE END OF JEM'S LIFE IS NOT WHAT IS IMPORTANT.
IT WAS BEING HERE FOR EVERY OTHER MOMENT.
SINCE YOU MET HIM, YOU HAVE NEVER LEFT HIM AND NEVER NOT LOVED HIM.
THAT IS WHAT MATTERS.
SO I WILL TELL YOU THIS. I WILL STAY HERE WHEN YOU GO, AND I WILL WATCH OVER JEM FOR YOU. I WILL DO WHAT I CAN TO PRESERVE HIS LIFE.
...WHY ARE YOU BEING SO KIND TO ME?
YOU TREAT ME AS A HUMAN BEING, A PERSON LIKE YOURSELF.
RARE IS THE SHADOWHUNTER WHO TREATS A WARLOCK LIKE THAT.
IF HE WAKES, I WILL TELL HIM WHERE YOU WENT, AND THAT IT WAS FOR HIM.

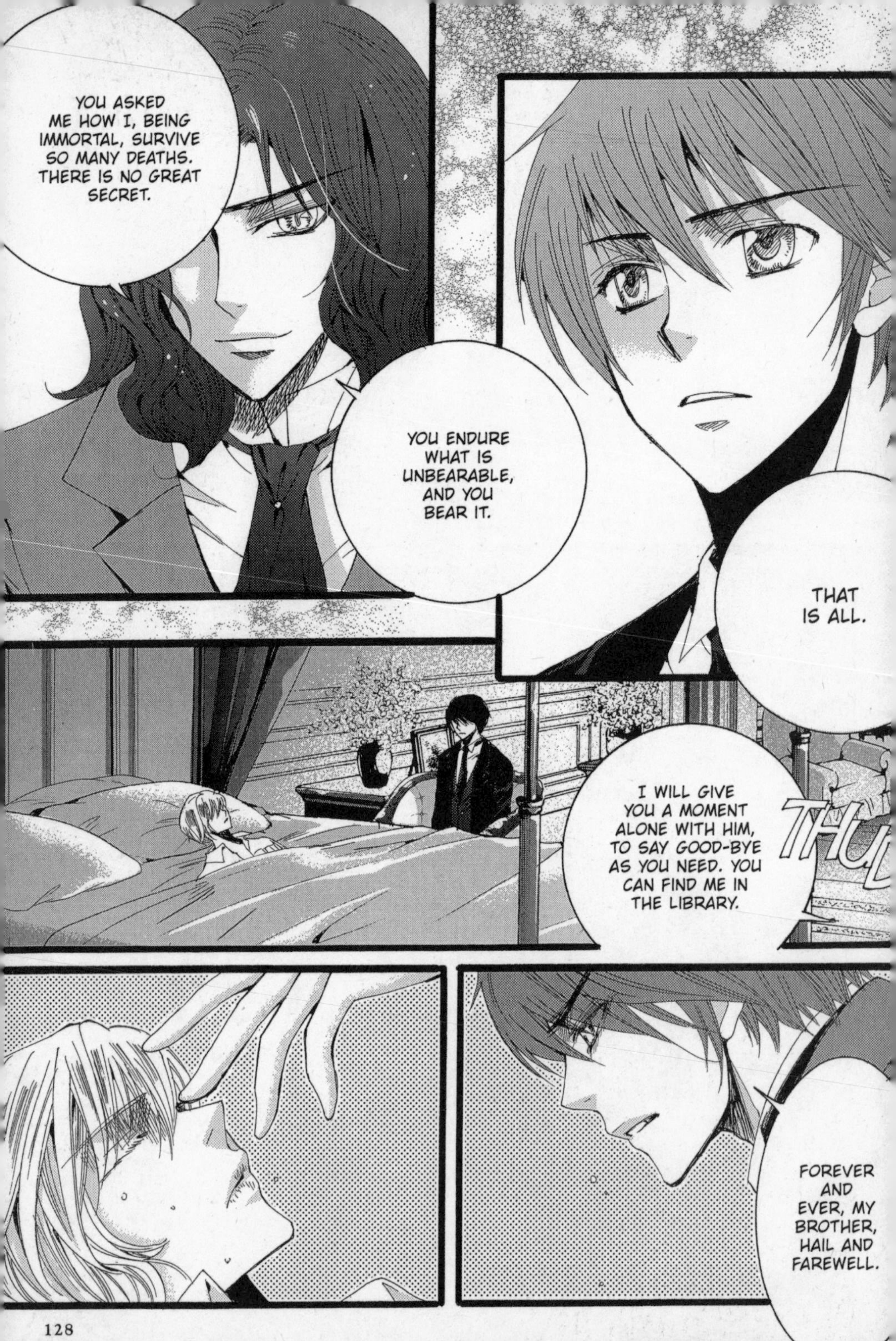
YOU ASKED ME HOW I, BEING IMMORTAL, SURVIVE SO MANY DEATHS. THERE IS NO GREAT SECRET.
YOU ENDURE WHAT IS UNBEARABLE, AND YOU BEAR IT.
THAT IS ALL.
I WILL GIVE YOU A MOMENT ALONE WITH HIM, TO SAY GOOD-BYE AS YOU NEED. YOU CAN FIND ME IN THE LIBRARY.
FOREVER AND EVER, MY BROTHER, HAIL AND FAREWELL.

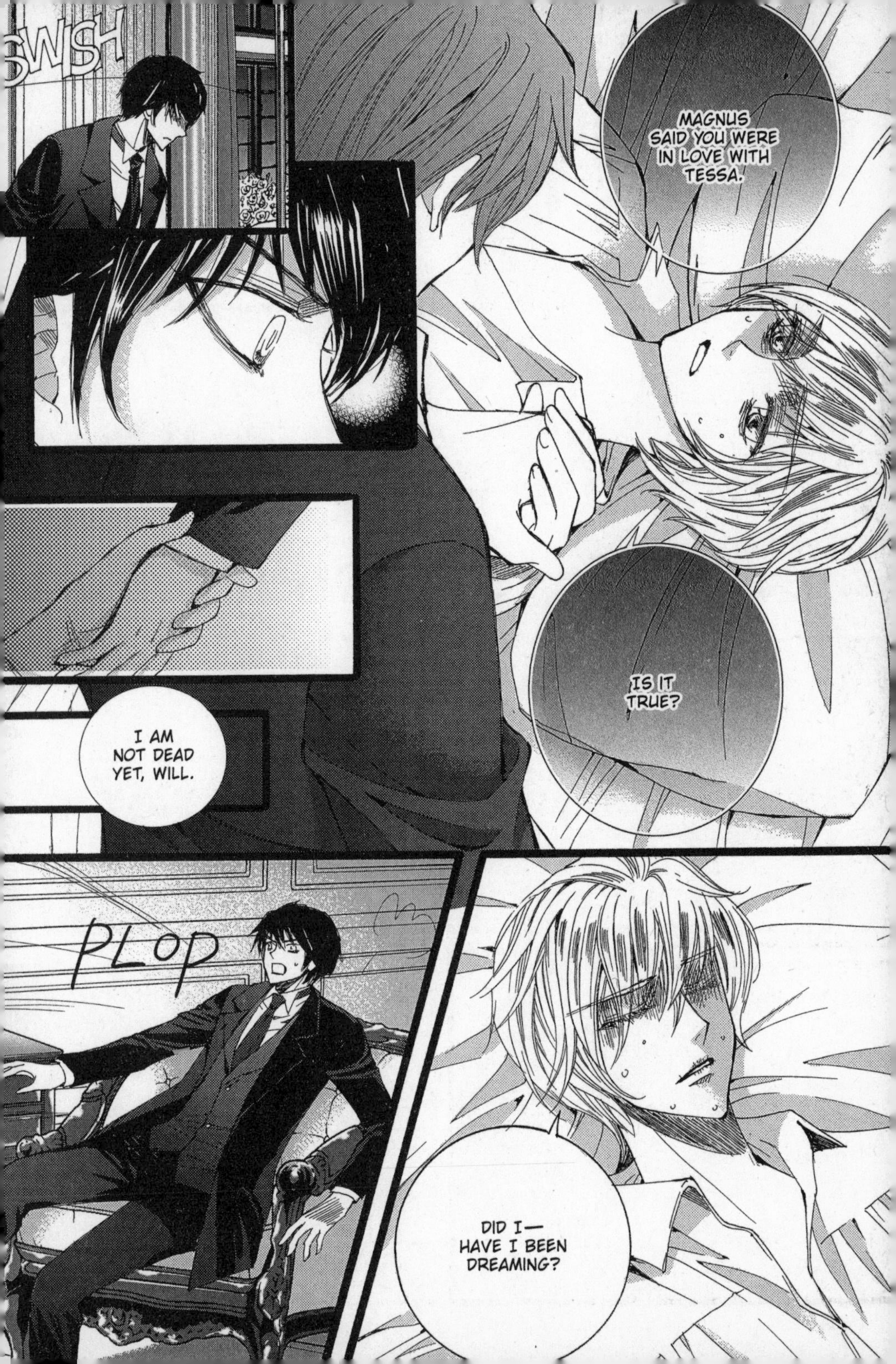
MAGNUS SAID YOU WERE IN LOVE WITH TESSA.
IS IT TRUE?
SWISH
I AM NOT DEAD YET, WILL.
DID I— HAVE I BEEN DREAMING?
PLOP

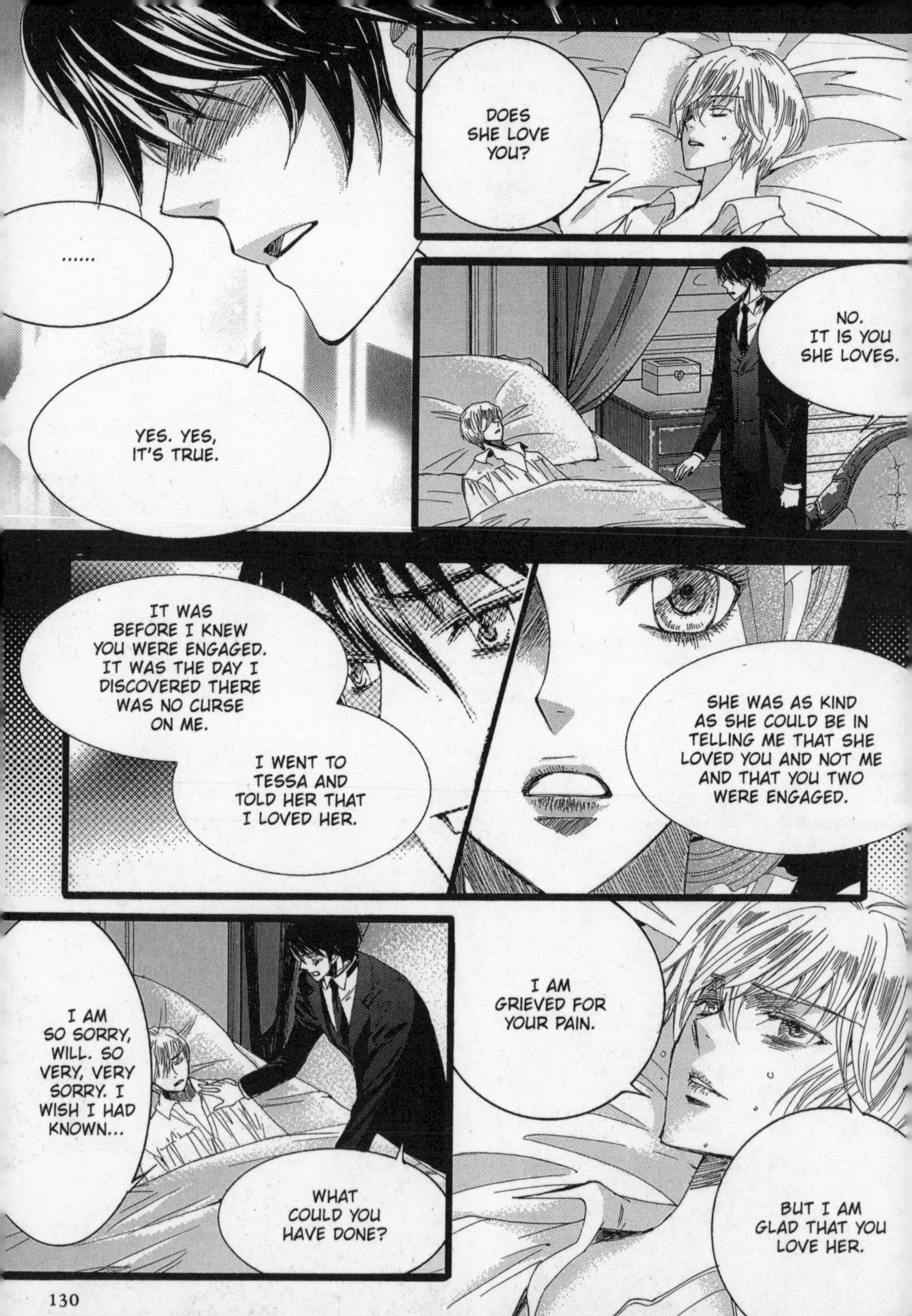
DOES SHE LOVE YOU?
......
YES. YES, IT'S TRUE.
NO. IT IS YOU SHE LOVES.
IT WAS BEFORE I KNEW YOU WERE ENGAGED. IT WAS THE DAY I DISCOVERED THERE WAS NO CURSE ON ME.
I WENT TO TESSA AND TOLD HER THAT I LOVED HER.
SHE WAS AS KIND AS SHE COULD BE IN TELLING ME THAT SHE LOVED YOU AND NOT ME AND THAT YOU TWO WERE ENGAGED.
I AM SO SORRY, WILL. SO VERY, VERY SORRY. I WISH I HAD KNOWN...
WHAT COULD YOU HAVE DONE?
I AM GRIEVED FOR YOUR PAIN.
BUT I AM GLAD THAT YOU LOVE HER.

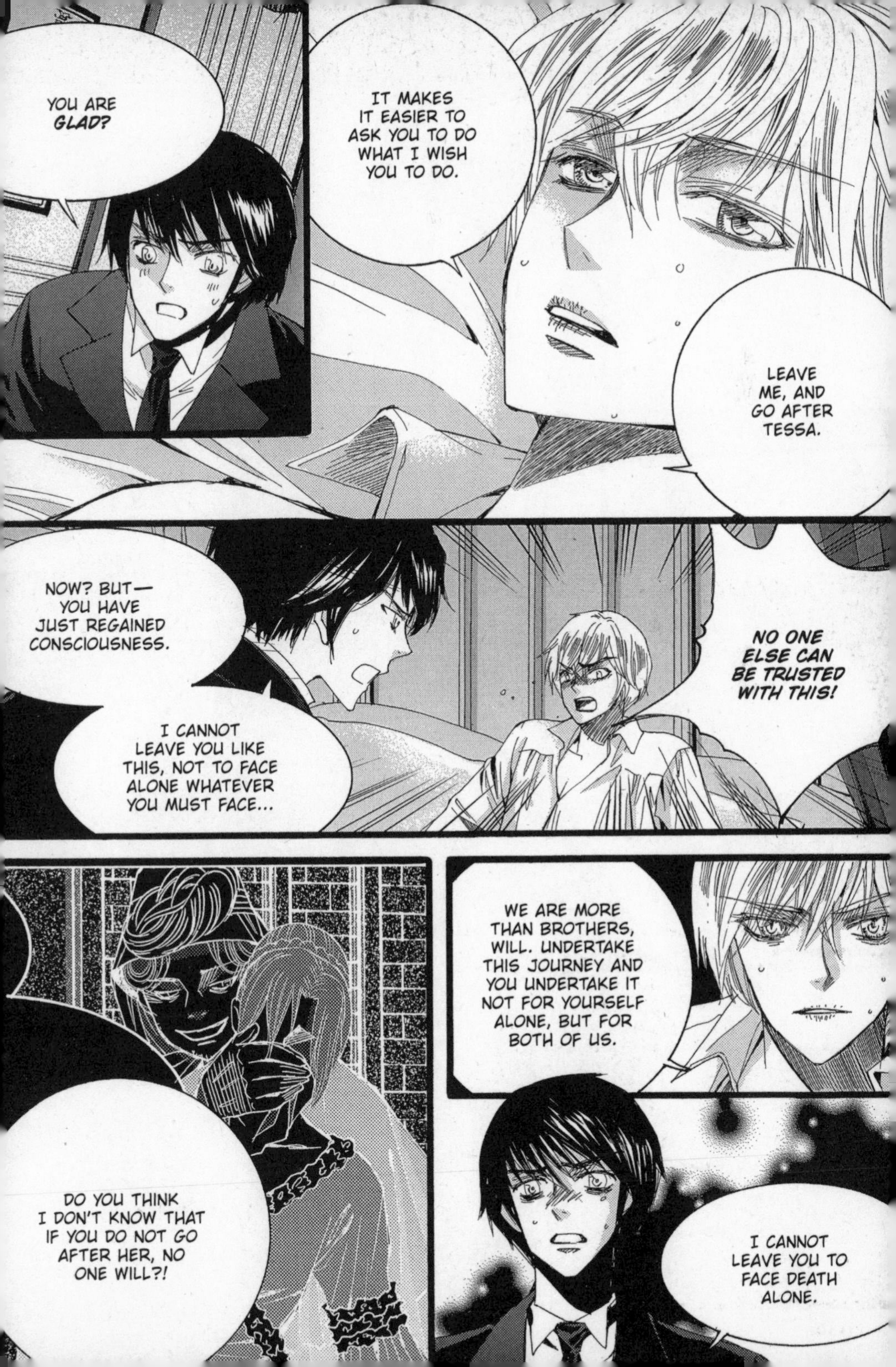
YOU ARE GLAD?
IT MAKES IT EASIER TO ASK YOU TO DO WHAT I WISH YOU TO DO.
LEAVE ME, AND GO AFTER TESSA.
NOW? BUT— YOU HAVE JUST REGAINED CONSCIOUSNESS.
I CANNOT LEAVE YOU LIKE THIS, NOT TO FACE ALONE WHATEVER YOU MUST FACE...
NO ONE ELSE CAN BE TRUSTED WITH THIS!
WE ARE MORE THAN BROTHERS, WILL. UNDERTAKE THIS JOURNEY AND YOU UNDERTAKE IT NOT FOR YOURSELF ALONE, BUT FOR BOTH OF US.
DO YOU THINK I DON'T KNOW THAT IF YOU DO NOT GO AFTER HER, NO ONE WILL?!
I CANNOT LEAVE YOU TO FACE DEATH ALONE.

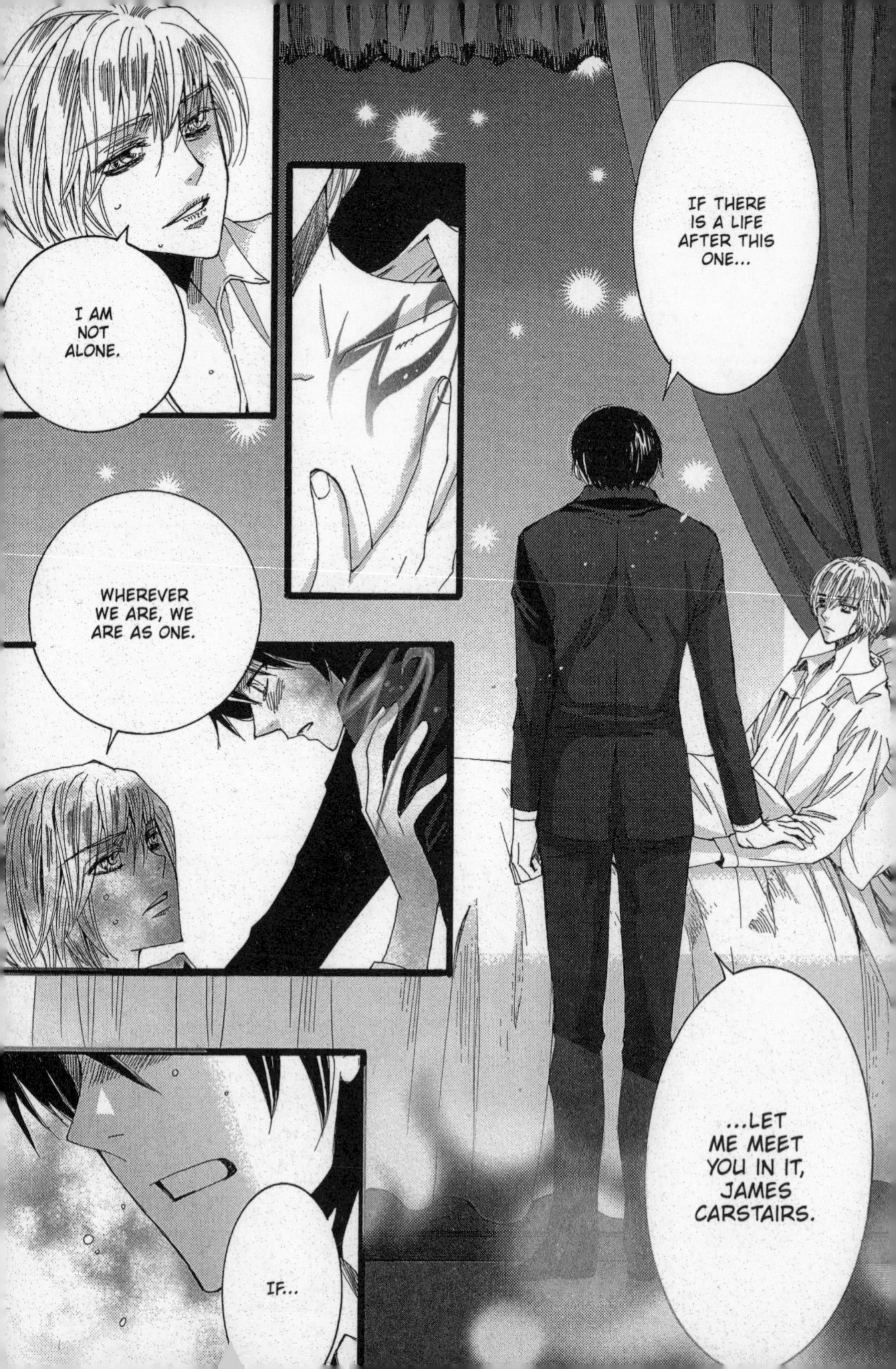
I AM NOT ALONE.
WHEREVER WE ARE, WE ARE AS ONE.
IF...
IF THERE IS A LIFE AFTER THIS ONE...
...LET ME MEET YOU IN IT, JAMES CARSTAIRS.

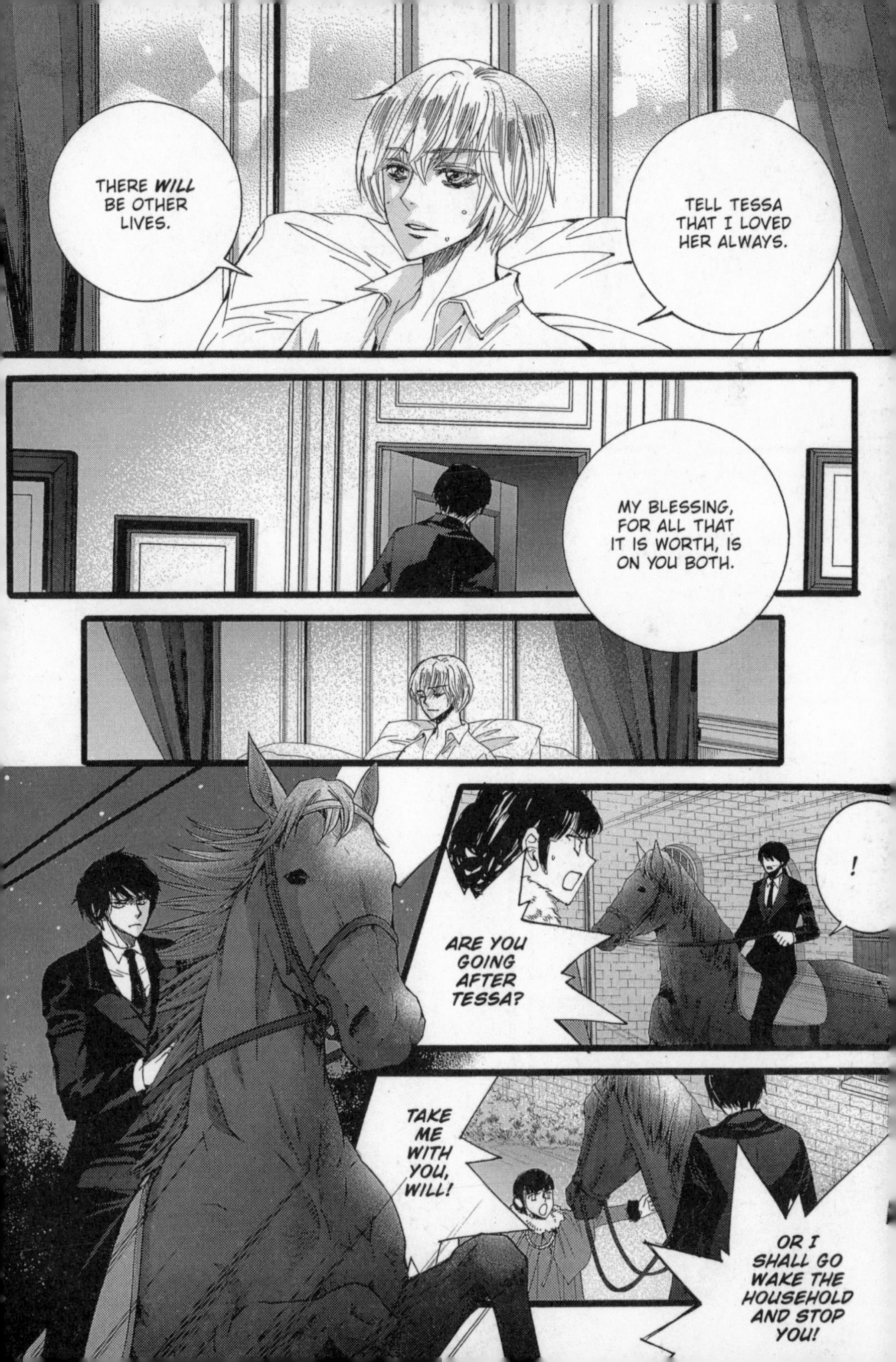

TELL TESSA THAT I LOVED HER ALWAYS.
THERE WILL BE OTHER LIVES.
MY BLESSING, FOR ALL THAT IT IS WORTH, IS ON YOU BOTH.
!
ARE YOU GOING AFTER TESSA?
TAKE ME WITH YOU, WILL!
OR I SHALL GO WAKE THE HOUSEHOLD AND STOP YOU!

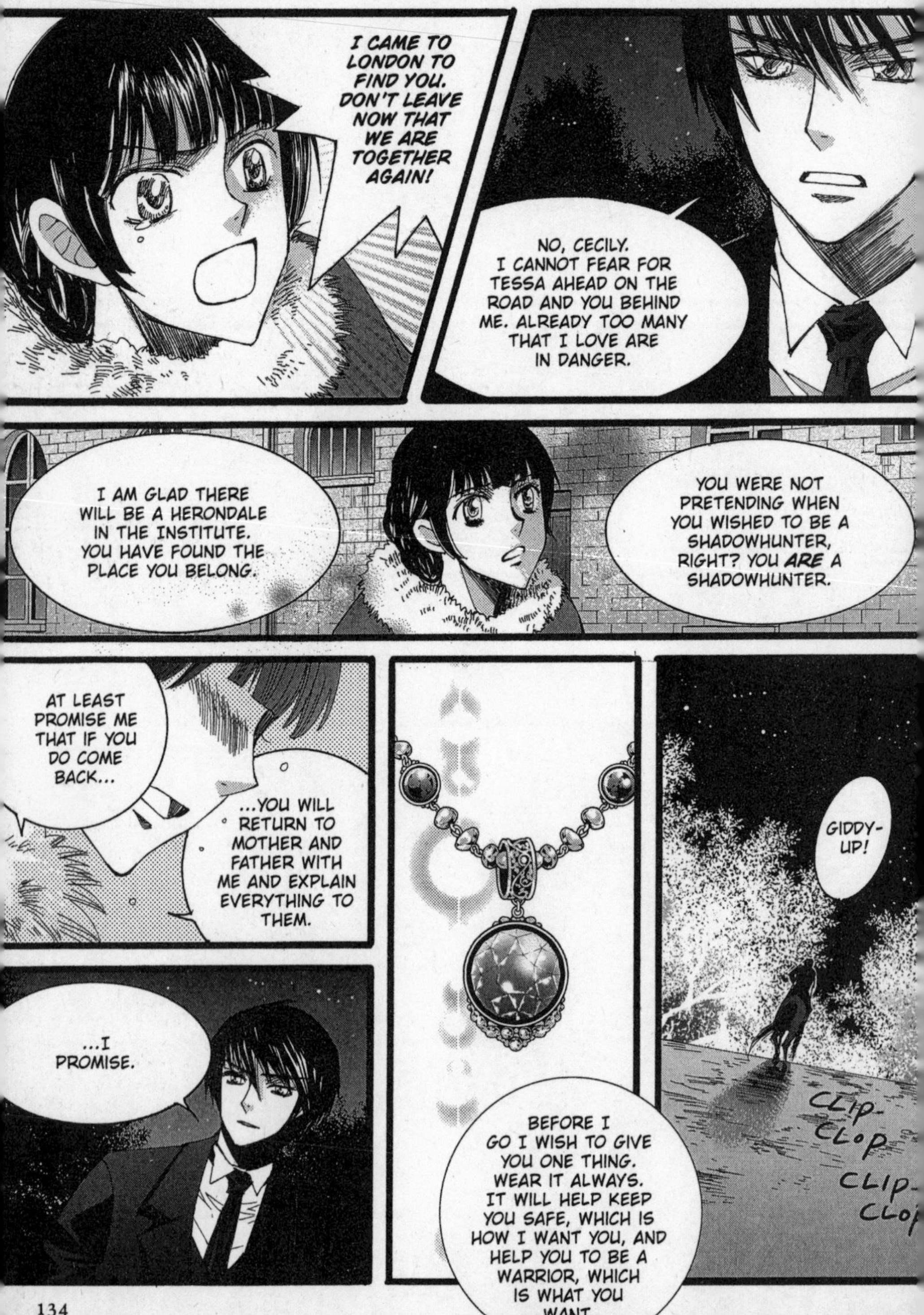
I CAME TO LONDON TO FIND YOU. DON'T LEAVE NOW THAT WE ARE TOGETHER AGAIN!
NO, CECILY. I CANNOT FEAR FOR TESSA AHEAD ON THE ROAD AND YOU BEHIND ME. ALREADY TOO MANY THAT I LOVE ARE IN DANGER.
I AM GLAD THERE WILL BE A HERONDALE IN THE INSTITUTE. YOU HAVE FOUND THE PLACE YOU BELONG.
YOU WERE NOT PRETENDING WHEN YOU WISHED TO BE A SHADOWHUNTER, RIGHT? YOU *ARE* A SHADOWHUNTER.
AT LEAST PROMISE ME THAT IF YOU DO COME BACK...
...YOU WILL RETURN TO MOTHER AND FATHER WITH ME AND EXPLAIN EVERYTHING TO THEM.
...I PROMISE.
BEFORE I GO I WISH TO GIVE YOU ONE THING. WEAR IT ALWAYS. IT WILL HELP KEEP YOU SAFE, WHICH IS HOW I WANT YOU, AND HELP YOU TO BE A WARRIOR, WHICH IS WHAT YOU WANT.
GIDDY-UP!
CLIP-CLOP
CLIP-CLOP

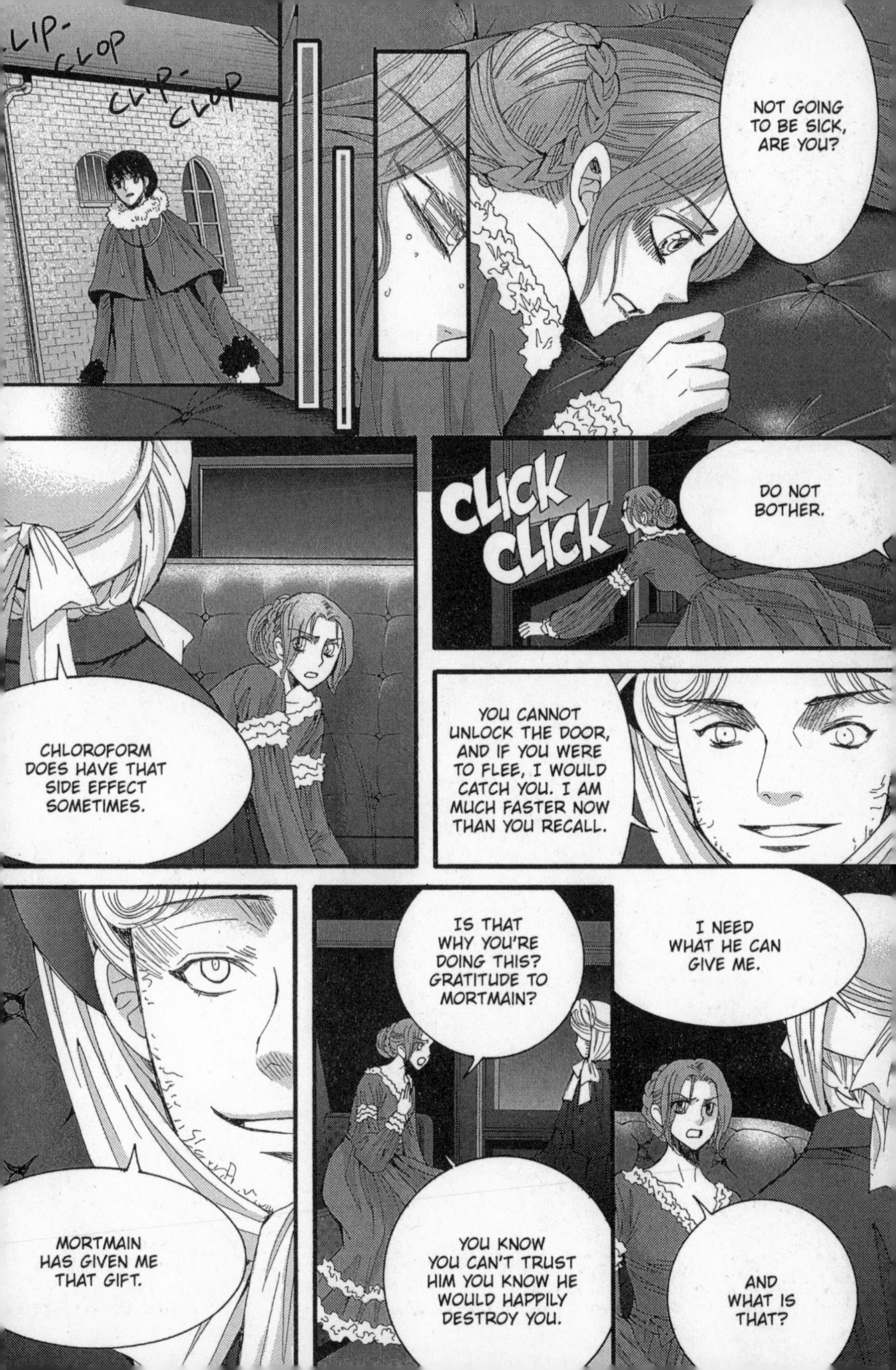
CLIP-CLOP CLIP-CLOP
NOT GOING TO BE SICK, ARE YOU?
CHLOROFORM DOES HAVE THAT SIDE EFFECT SOMETIMES.
CLICK CLICK
DO NOT BOTHER.
YOU CANNOT UNLOCK THE DOOR, AND IF YOU WERE TO FLEE, I WOULD CATCH YOU. I AM MUCH FASTER NOW THAN YOU RECALL.
MORTMAIN HAS GIVEN ME THAT GIFT.
IS THAT WHY YOU'RE DOING THIS? GRATITUDE TO MORTMAIN?
YOU KNOW YOU CAN'T TRUST HIM YOU KNOW HE WOULD HAPPILY DESTROY YOU.
I NEED WHAT HE CAN GIVE ME.
AND WHAT IS THAT?

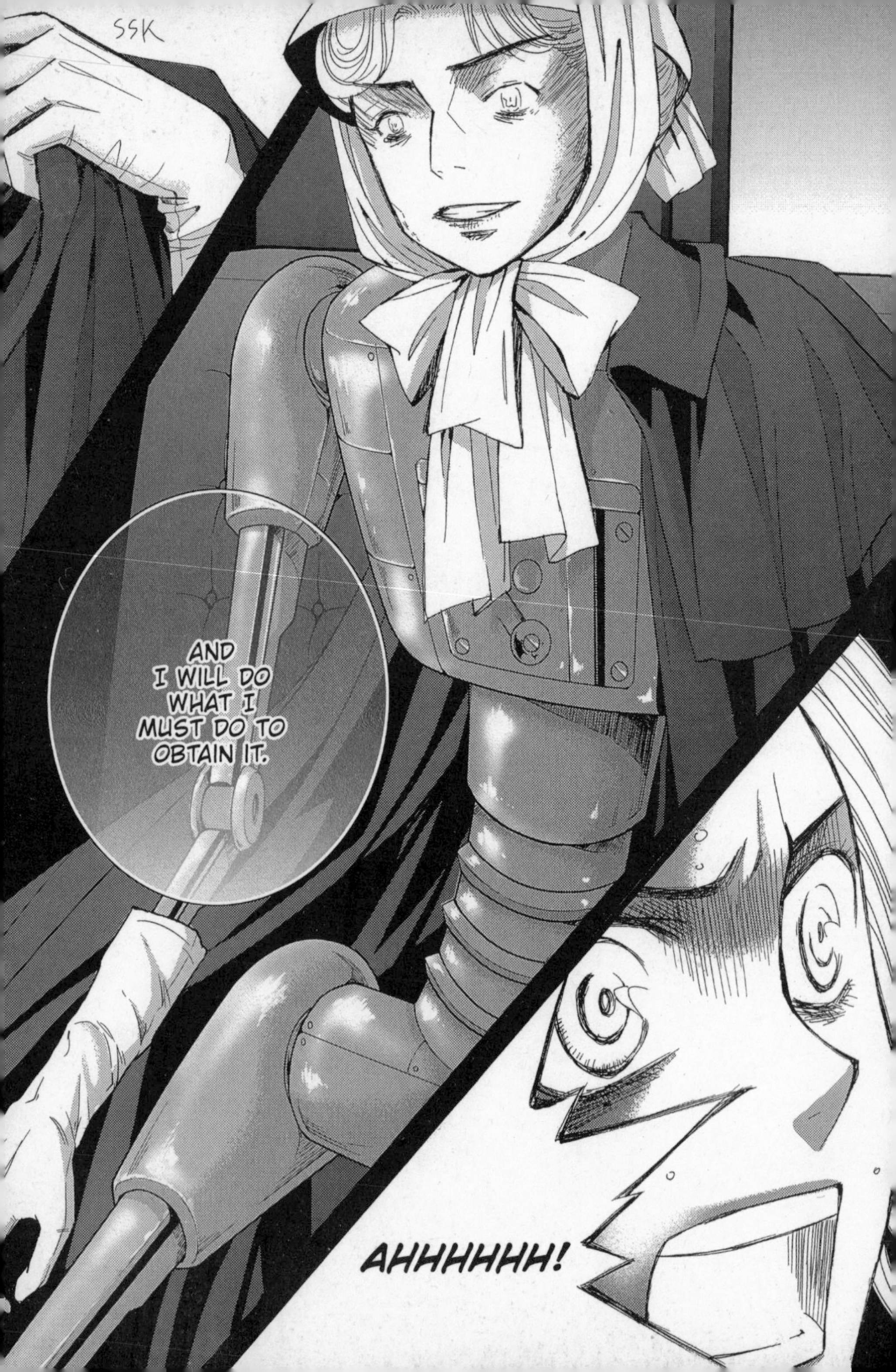
SSK
AND I WILL DO WHAT I MUST DO TO OBTAIN IT.
AHHHHHH!

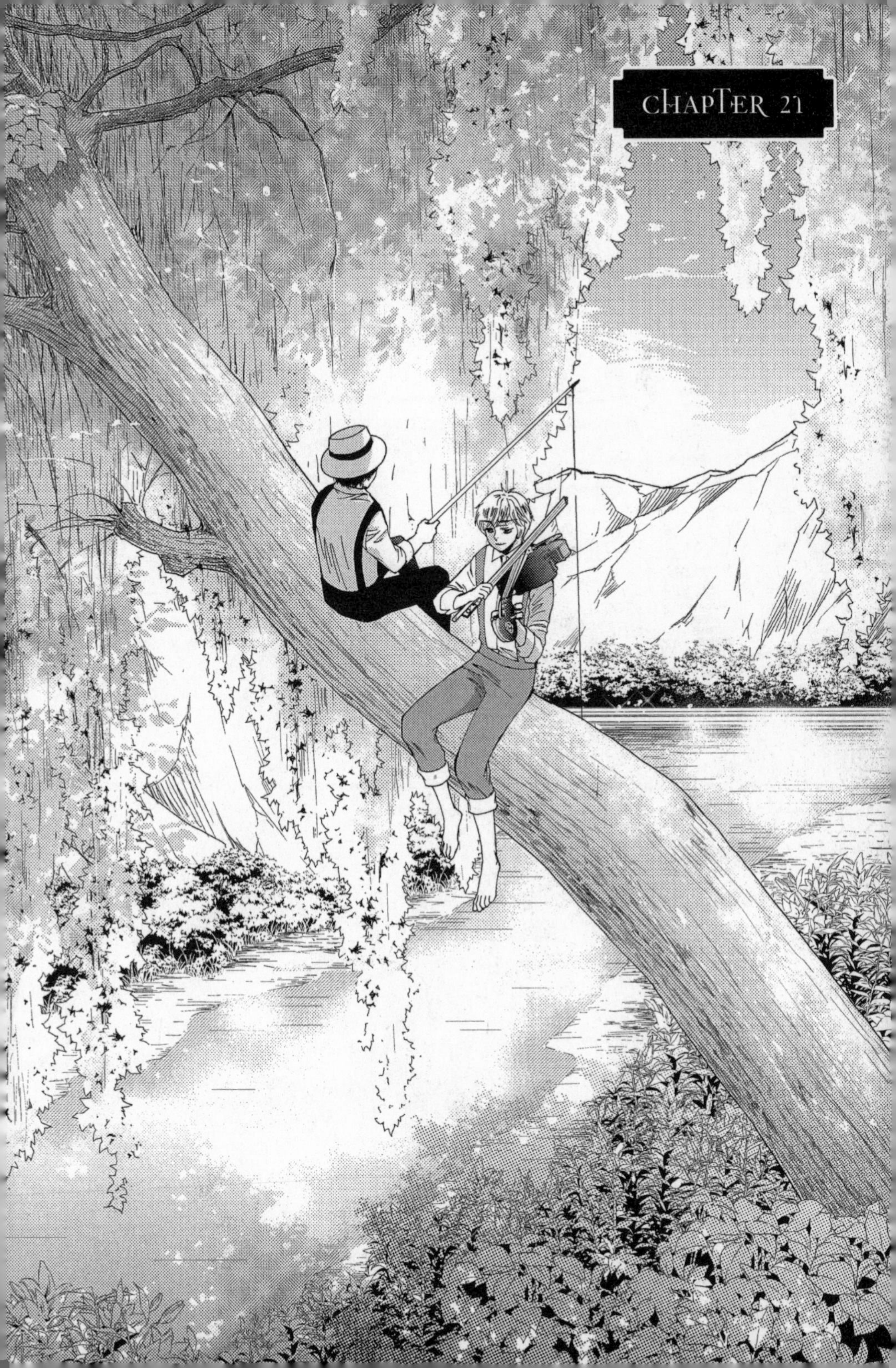
CHAPTER 21

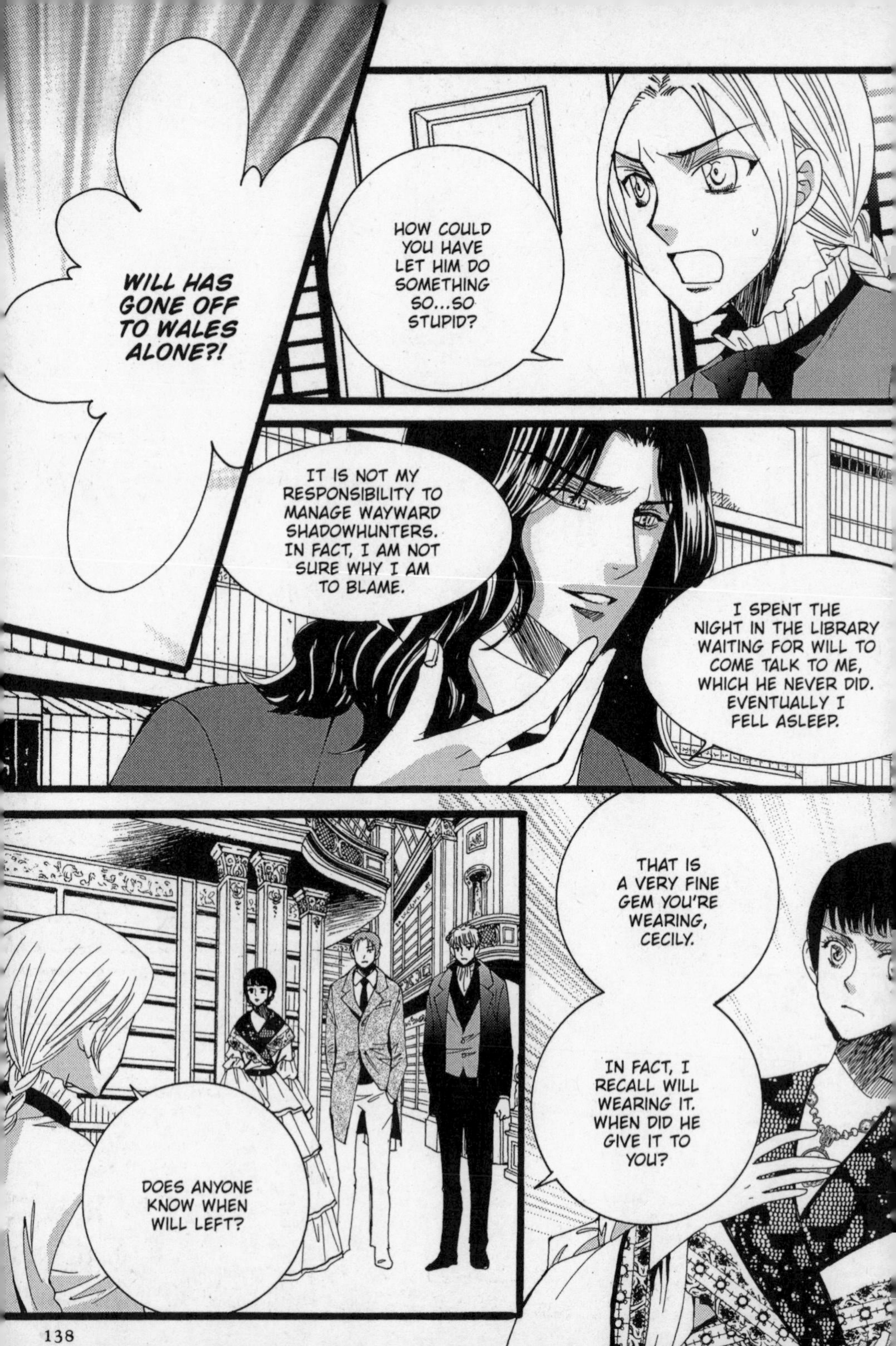
WILL HAS GONE OFF TO WALES ALONE?!
HOW COULD YOU HAVE LET HIM DO SOMETHING SO...SO STUPID?
IT IS NOT MY RESPONSIBILITY TO MANAGE WAYWARD SHADOWHUNTERS. IN FACT, I AM NOT SURE WHY I AM TO BLAME.
I SPENT THE NIGHT IN THE LIBRARY WAITING FOR WILL TO COME TALK TO ME, WHICH HE NEVER DID. EVENTUALLY I FELL ASLEEP.
THAT IS A VERY FINE GEM YOU'RE WEARING, CECILY.
IN FACT, I RECALL WILL WEARING IT. WHEN DID HE GIVE IT TO YOU?
DOES ANYONE KNOW WHEN WILL LEFT?

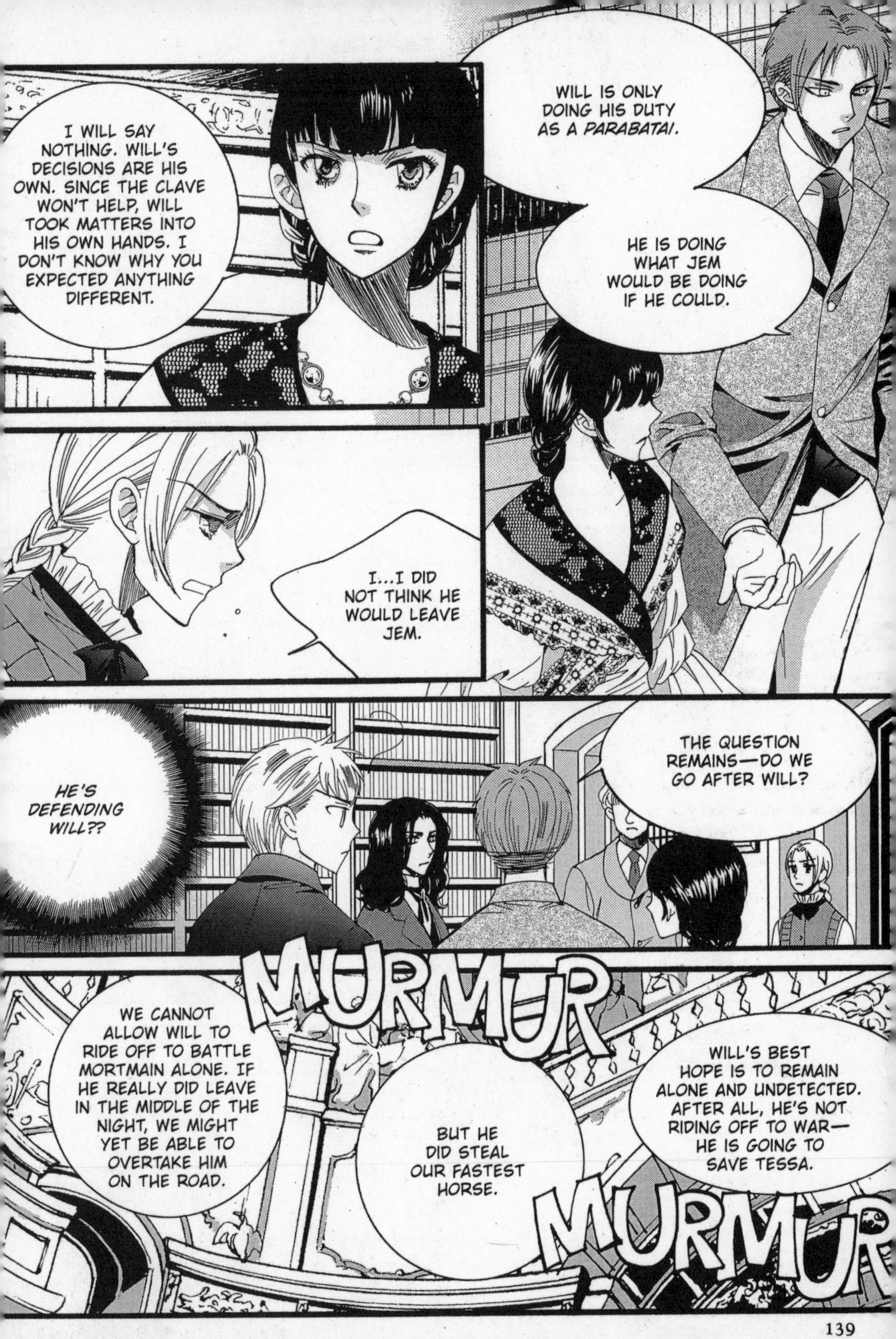
I WILL SAY NOTHING. WILL'S DECISIONS ARE HIS OWN. SINCE THE CLAVE WON'T HELP, WILL TOOK MATTERS INTO HIS OWN HANDS. I DON'T KNOW WHY YOU EXPECTED ANYTHING DIFFERENT.
WILL IS ONLY DOING HIS DUTY AS A *PARABATAI*.
HE IS DOING WHAT JEM WOULD BE DOING IF HE COULD.
I...I DID NOT THINK HE WOULD LEAVE JEM.
HE'S DEFENDING WILL??
THE QUESTION REMAINS—DO WE GO AFTER WILL?
MURMUR
WE CANNOT ALLOW WILL TO RIDE OFF TO BATTLE MORTMAIN ALONE. IF HE REALLY DID LEAVE IN THE MIDDLE OF THE NIGHT, WE MIGHT YET BE ABLE TO OVERTAKE HIM ON THE ROAD.
BUT HE DID STEAL OUR FASTEST HORSE.
WILL'S BEST HOPE IS TO REMAIN ALONE AND UNDETECTED. AFTER ALL, HE'S NOT RIDING OFF TO WAR—HE IS GOING TO SAVE TESSA.
MURMUR

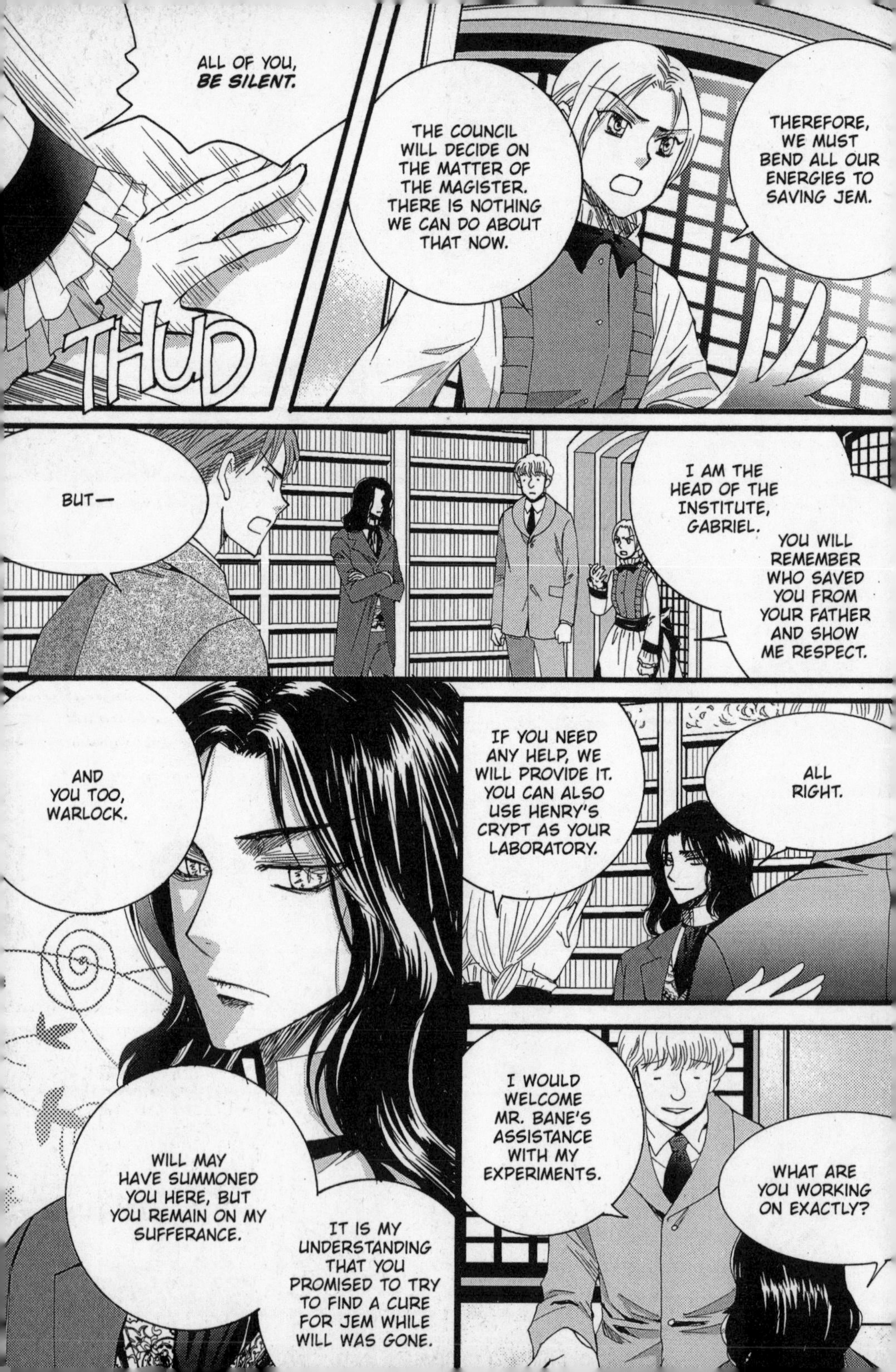

ALL OF YOU, *BE SILENT.*
THUD
THE COUNCIL WILL DECIDE ON THE MATTER OF THE MAGISTER. THERE IS NOTHING WE CAN DO ABOUT THAT NOW.
THEREFORE, WE MUST BEND ALL OUR ENERGIES TO SAVING JEM.
BUT—
I AM THE HEAD OF THE INSTITUTE, GABRIEL.
YOU WILL REMEMBER WHO SAVED YOU FROM YOUR FATHER AND SHOW ME RESPECT.
AND YOU TOO, WARLOCK.
WILL MAY HAVE SUMMONED YOU HERE, BUT YOU REMAIN ON MY SUFFERANCE.
IT IS MY UNDERSTANDING THAT YOU PROMISED TO TRY TO FIND A CURE FOR JEM WHILE WILL WAS GONE.
IF YOU NEED ANY HELP, WE WILL PROVIDE IT. YOU CAN ALSO USE HENRY'S CRYPT AS YOUR LABORATORY.
ALL RIGHT.
I WOULD WELCOME MR. BANE'S ASSISTANCE WITH MY EXPERIMENTS.
WHAT ARE YOU WORKING ON EXACTLY?

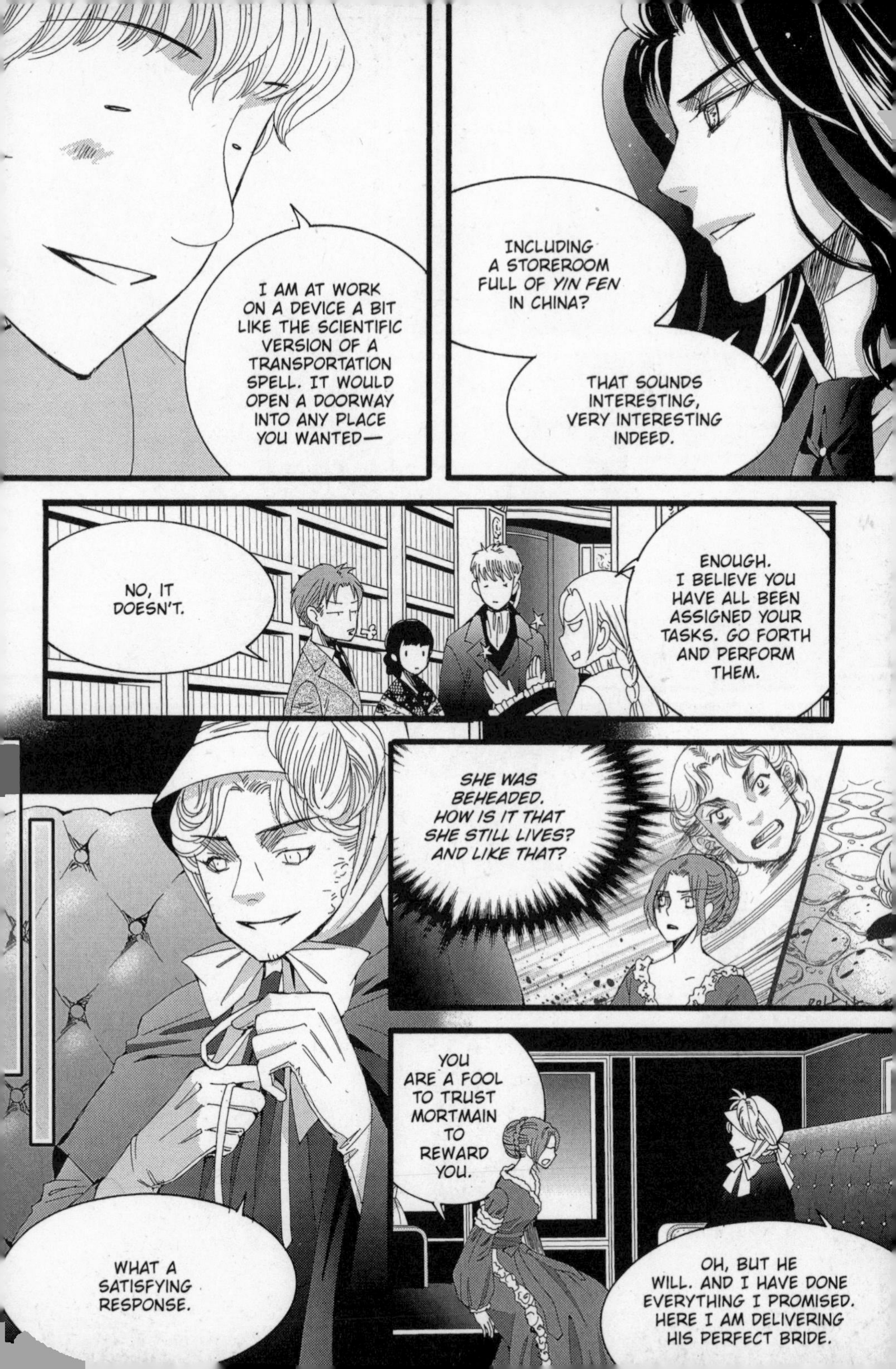
I AM AT WORK ON A DEVICE A BIT LIKE THE SCIENTIFIC VERSION OF A TRANSPORTATION SPELL. IT WOULD OPEN A DOORWAY INTO ANY PLACE YOU WANTED—
INCLUDING A STOREROOM FULL OF *YIN FEN* IN CHINA?
THAT SOUNDS INTERESTING, VERY INTERESTING INDEED.
NO, IT DOESN'T.
ENOUGH. I BELIEVE YOU HAVE ALL BEEN ASSIGNED YOUR TASKS. GO FORTH AND PERFORM THEM.
SHE WAS BEHEADED. HOW IS IT THAT SHE STILL LIVES? AND LIKE THAT?
YOU ARE A FOOL TO TRUST MORTMAIN TO REWARD YOU.
WHAT A SATISFYING RESPONSE.
OH, BUT HE WILL. AND I HAVE DONE EVERYTHING I PROMISED. HERE I AM DELIVERING HIS PERFECT BRIDE.

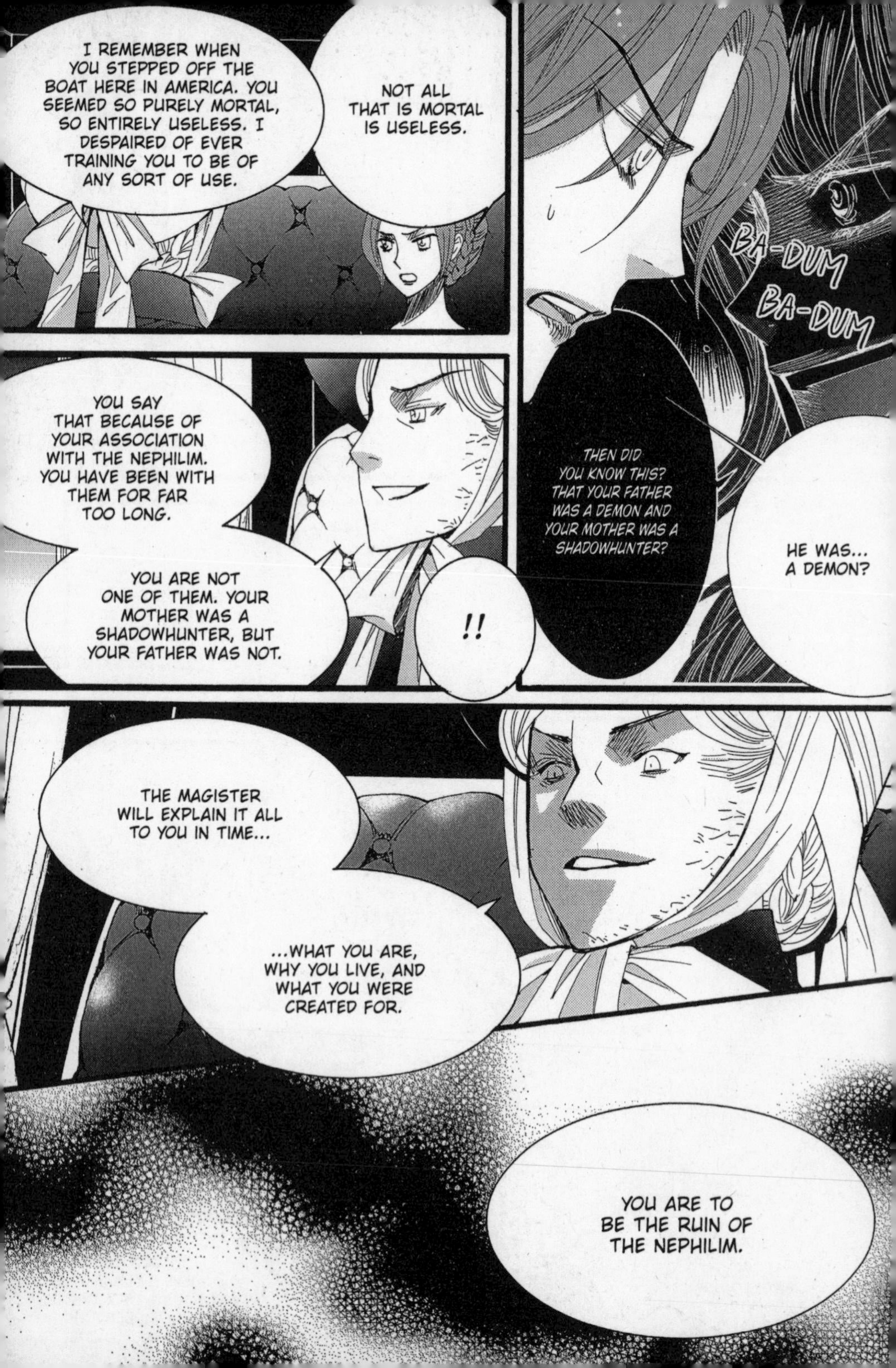
I REMEMBER WHEN YOU STEPPED OFF THE BOAT HERE IN AMERICA. YOU SEEMED SO PURELY MORTAL, SO ENTIRELY USELESS. I DESPAIRED OF EVER TRAINING YOU TO BE OF ANY SORT OF USE.
NOT ALL THAT IS MORTAL IS USELESS.
BA-DUM
BA-DUM
YOU SAY THAT BECAUSE OF YOUR ASSOCIATION WITH THE NEPHILIM. YOU HAVE BEEN WITH THEM FOR FAR TOO LONG.
YOU ARE NOT ONE OF THEM. YOUR MOTHER WAS A SHADOWHUNTER, BUT YOUR FATHER WAS NOT.
!!
THEN DID YOU KNOW THIS? THAT YOUR FATHER WAS A DEMON AND YOUR MOTHER WAS A SHADOWHUNTER?
HE WAS... A DEMON?
THE MAGISTER WILL EXPLAIN IT ALL TO YOU IN TIME...
...WHAT YOU ARE, WHY YOU LIVE, AND WHAT YOU WERE CREATED FOR.
YOU ARE TO BE THE RUIN OF THE NEPHILIM.

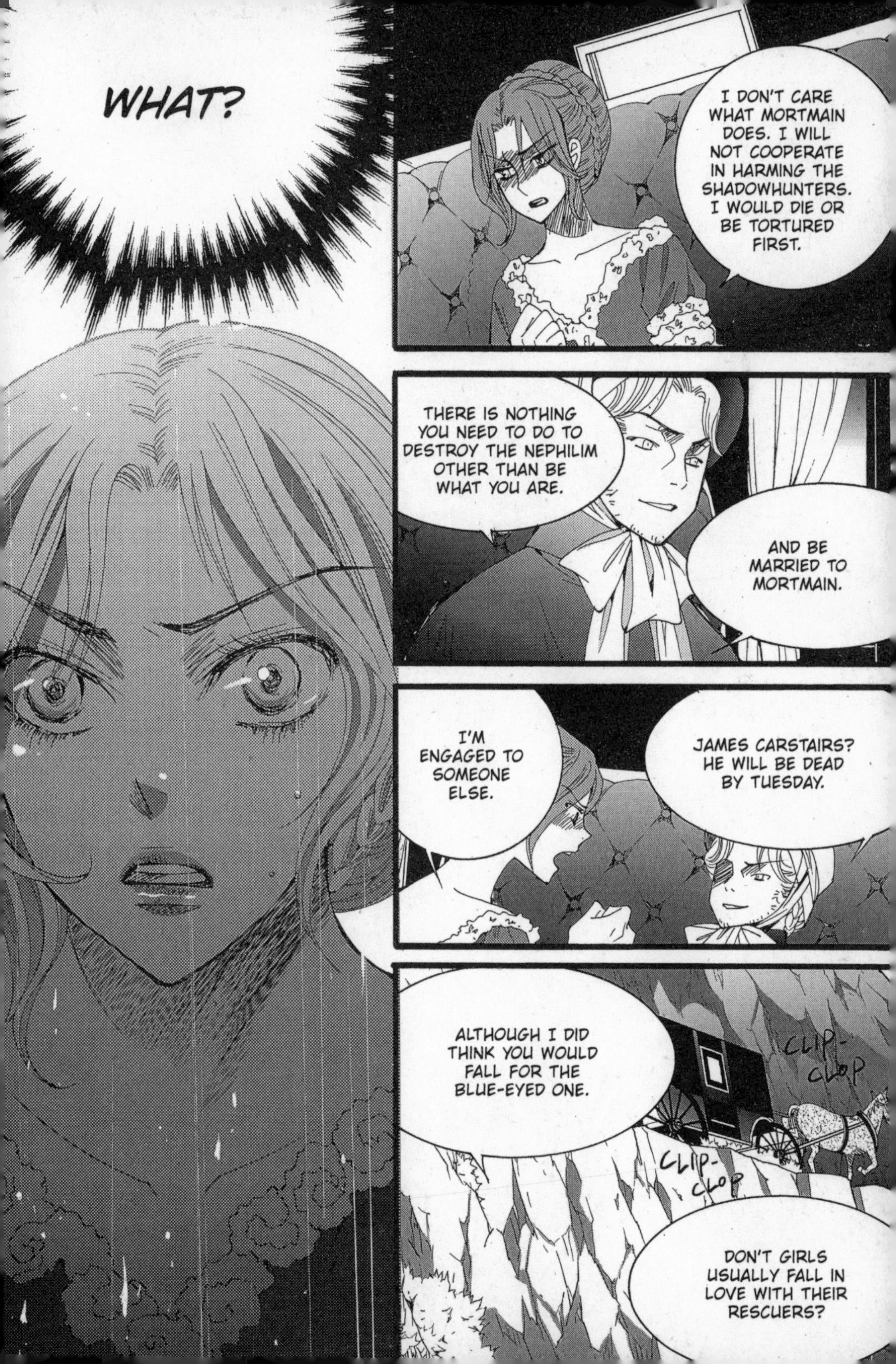
WHAT?
I DON'T CARE WHAT MORTMAIN DOES. I WILL NOT COOPERATE IN HARMING THE SHADOWHUNTERS. I WOULD DIE OR BE TORTURED FIRST.
THERE IS NOTHING YOU NEED TO DO TO DESTROY THE NEPHILIM OTHER THAN BE WHAT YOU ARE.
AND BE MARRIED TO MORTMAIN.
I'M ENGAGED TO SOMEONE ELSE.
JAMES CARSTAIRS? HE WILL BE DEAD BY TUESDAY.
ALTHOUGH I DID THINK YOU WOULD FALL FOR THE BLUE-EYED ONE.
CLIP-CLOP
CLIP-CLOP
DON'T GIRLS USUALLY FALL IN LOVE WITH THEIR RESCUERS?

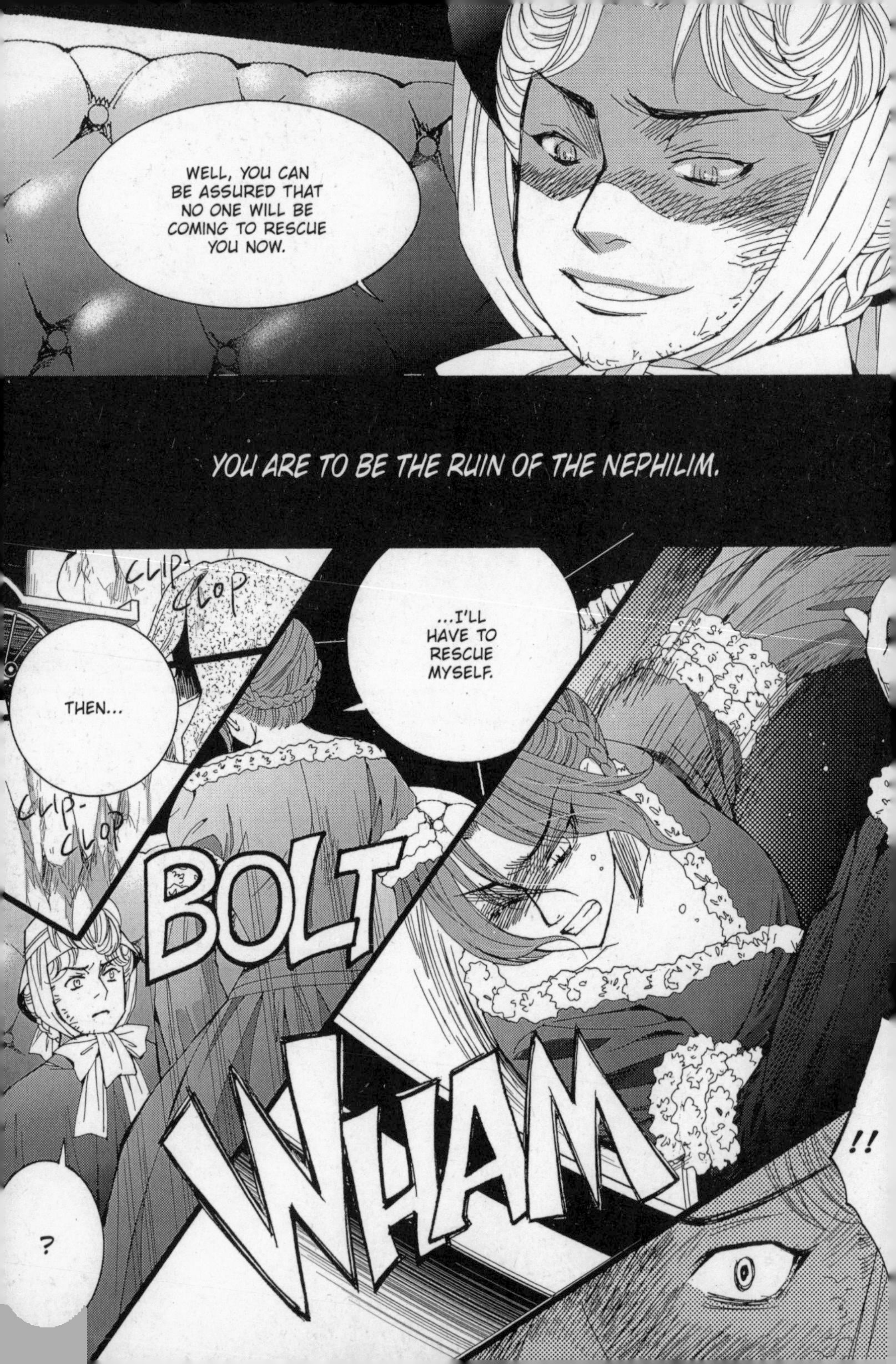
WELL, YOU CAN BE ASSURED THAT NO ONE WILL BE COMING TO RESCUE YOU NOW.
YOU ARE TO BE THE RUIN OF THE NEPHILIM.
CLIP-CLOP
...I'LL HAVE TO RESCUE MYSELF.
THEN...
CLIP-CLOP
BOLT
WHAM
!!
?

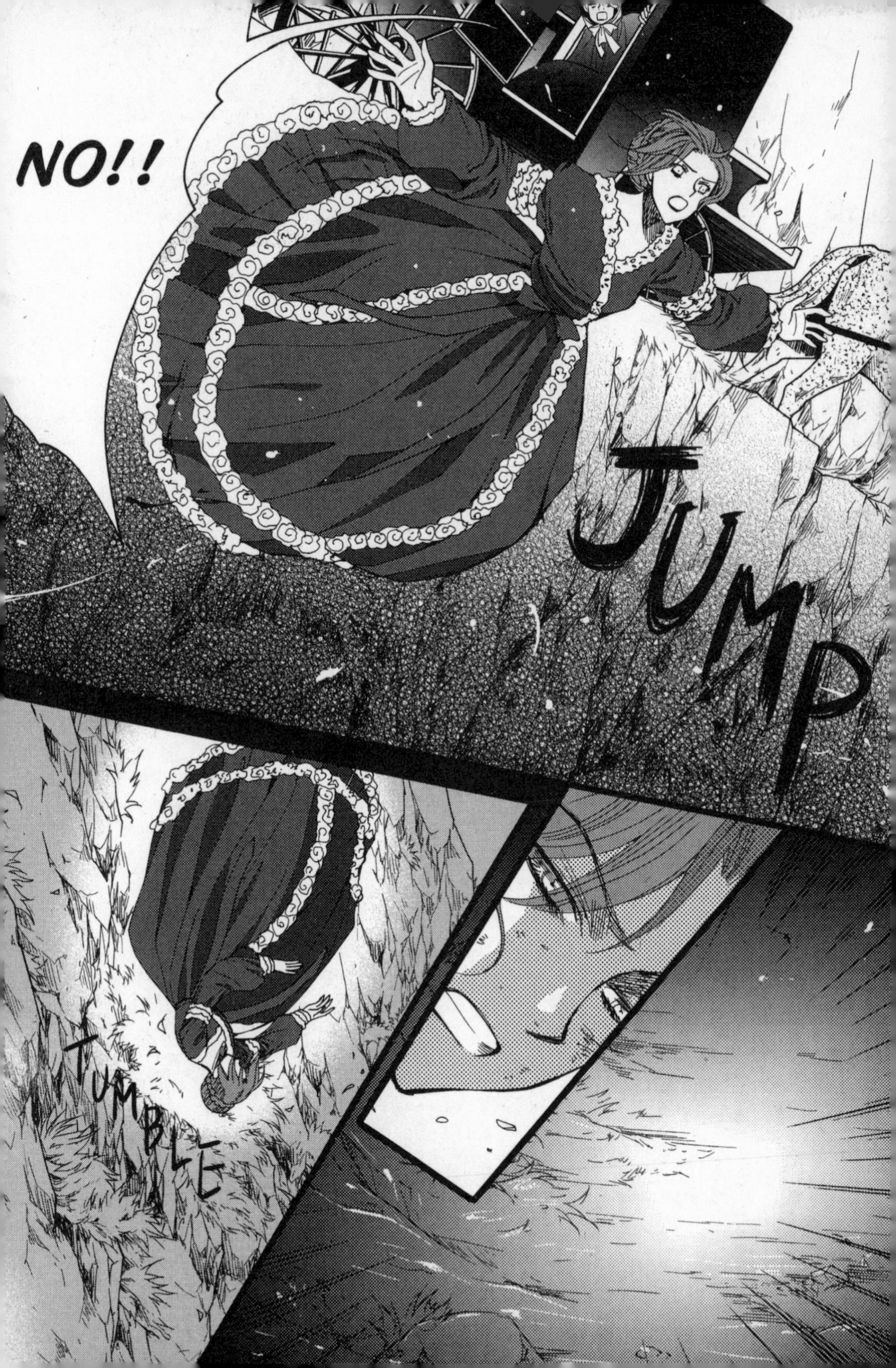

NO!!
JUMP
TUMBLE

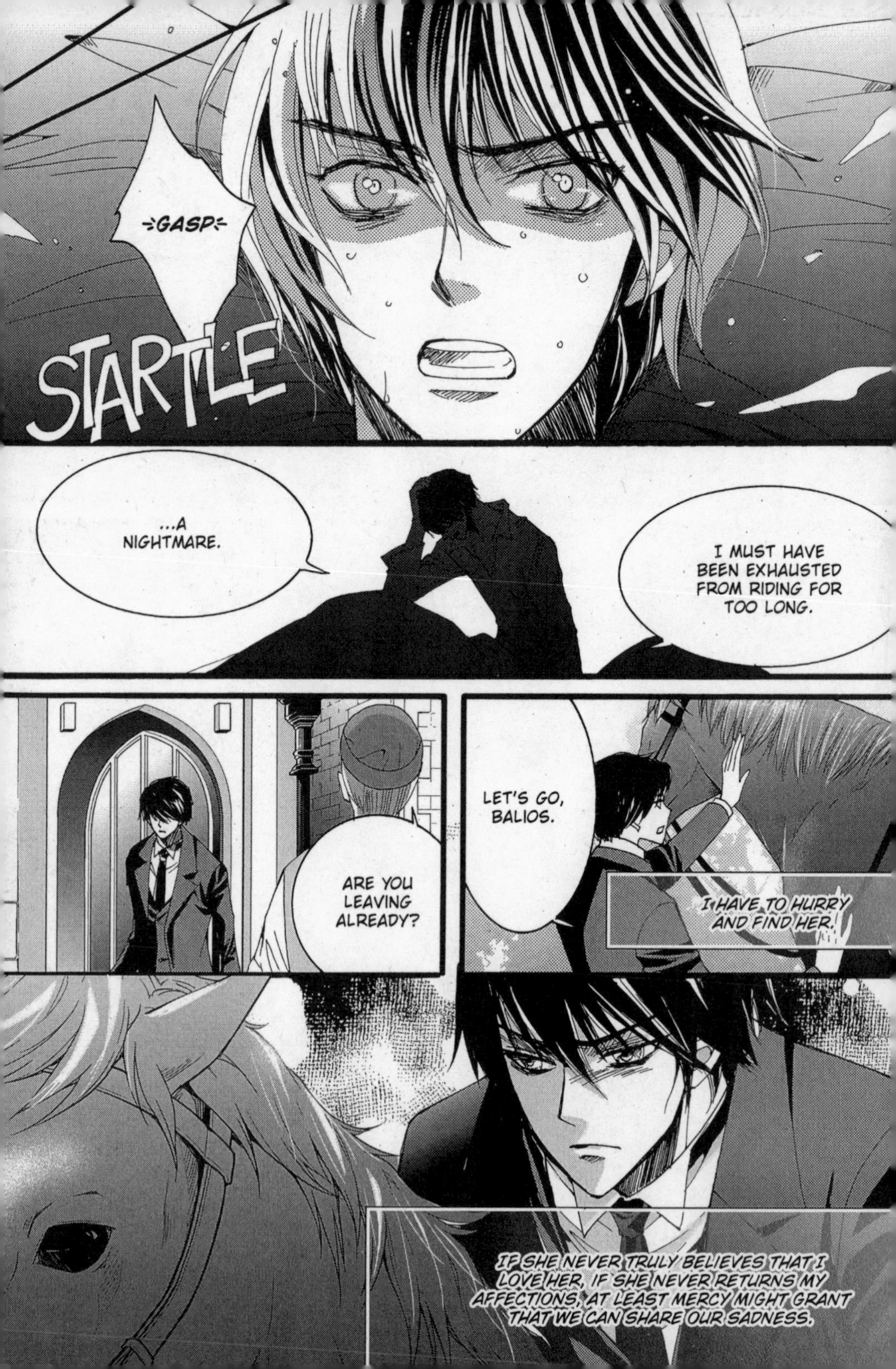

GASP
STARTLE
...A NIGHTMARE.
I MUST HAVE BEEN EXHAUSTED FROM RIDING FOR TOO LONG.
ARE YOU LEAVING ALREADY?
LET'S GO, BALIOS.
I HAVE TO HURRY AND FIND HER.
IF SHE NEVER TRULY BELIEVES THAT I LOVE HER, IF SHE NEVER RETURNS MY AFFECTIONS, AT LEAST MERCY MIGHT GRANT THAT WE CAN SHARE OUR SADNESS.

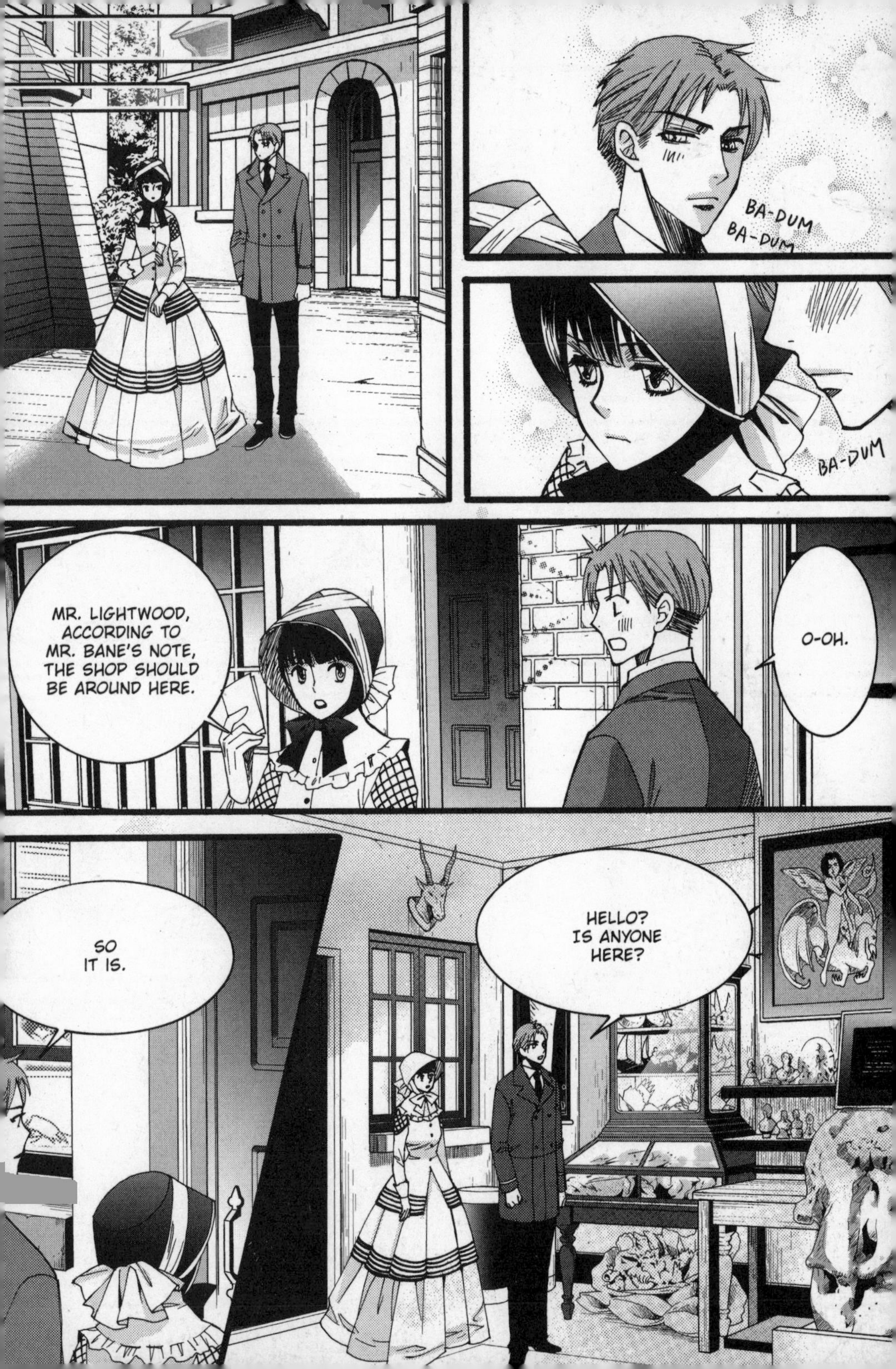
BA-DUM
BA-DUM
BA-DUM
MR. LIGHTWOOD, ACCORDING TO MR. BANE'S NOTE, THE SHOP SHOULD BE AROUND HERE.
O-OH.
HELLO? IS ANYONE HERE?
SO IT IS.

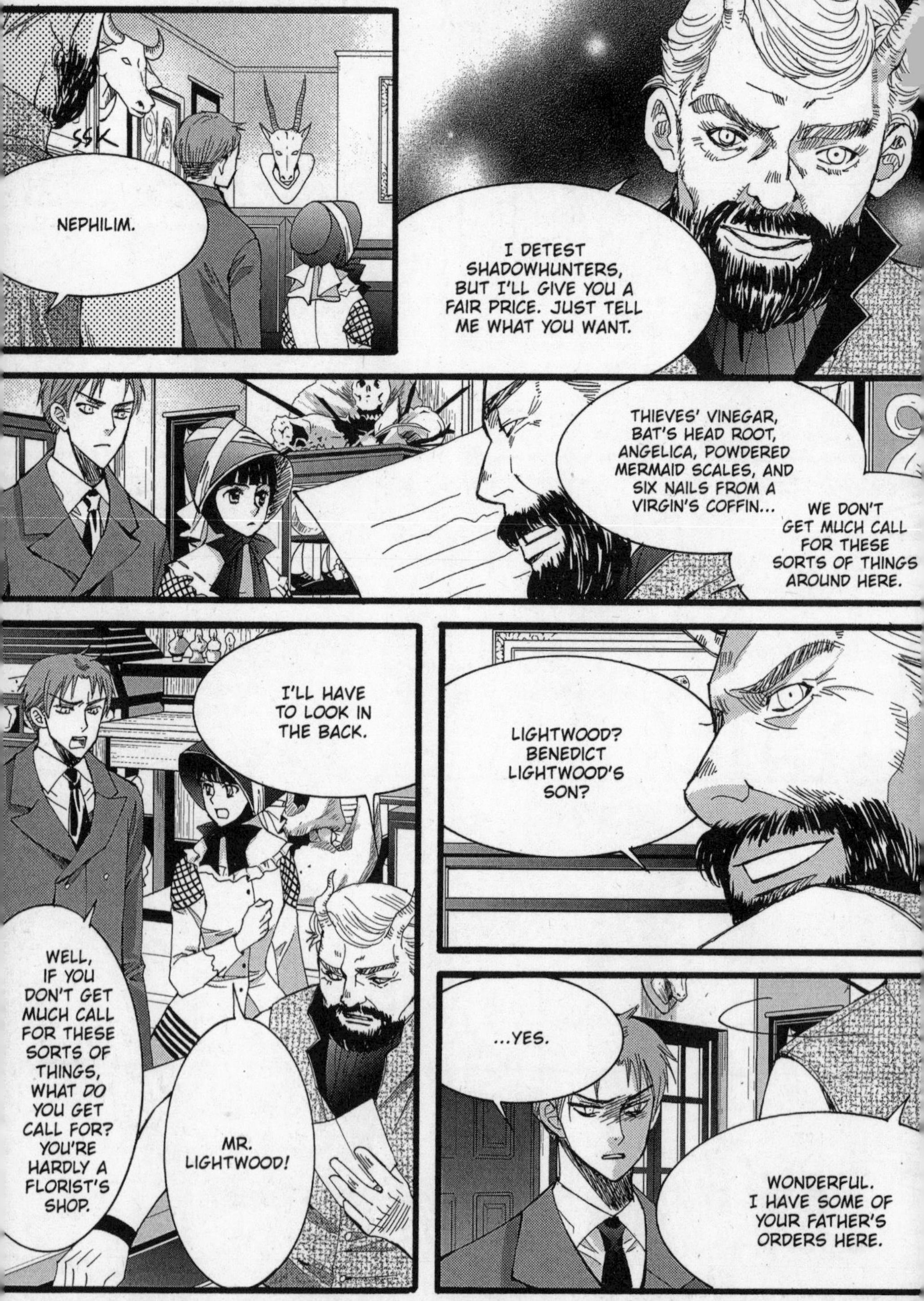
SSK
NEPHILIM.
I DETEST SHADOWHUNTERS, BUT I'LL GIVE YOU A FAIR PRICE. JUST TELL ME WHAT YOU WANT.
THIEVES' VINEGAR, BAT'S HEAD ROOT, ANGELICA, POWDERED MERMAID SCALES, AND SIX NAILS FROM A VIRGIN'S COFFIN...
WE DON'T GET MUCH CALL FOR THESE SORTS OF THINGS AROUND HERE.
I'LL HAVE TO LOOK IN THE BACK.
WELL, IF YOU DON'T GET MUCH CALL FOR THESE SORTS OF THINGS, WHAT DO YOU GET CALL FOR? YOU'RE HARDLY A FLORIST'S SHOP.
MR. LIGHTWOOD!
LIGHTWOOD? BENEDICT LIGHTWOOD'S SON?
...YES.
WONDERFUL. I HAVE SOME OF YOUR FATHER'S ORDERS HERE.

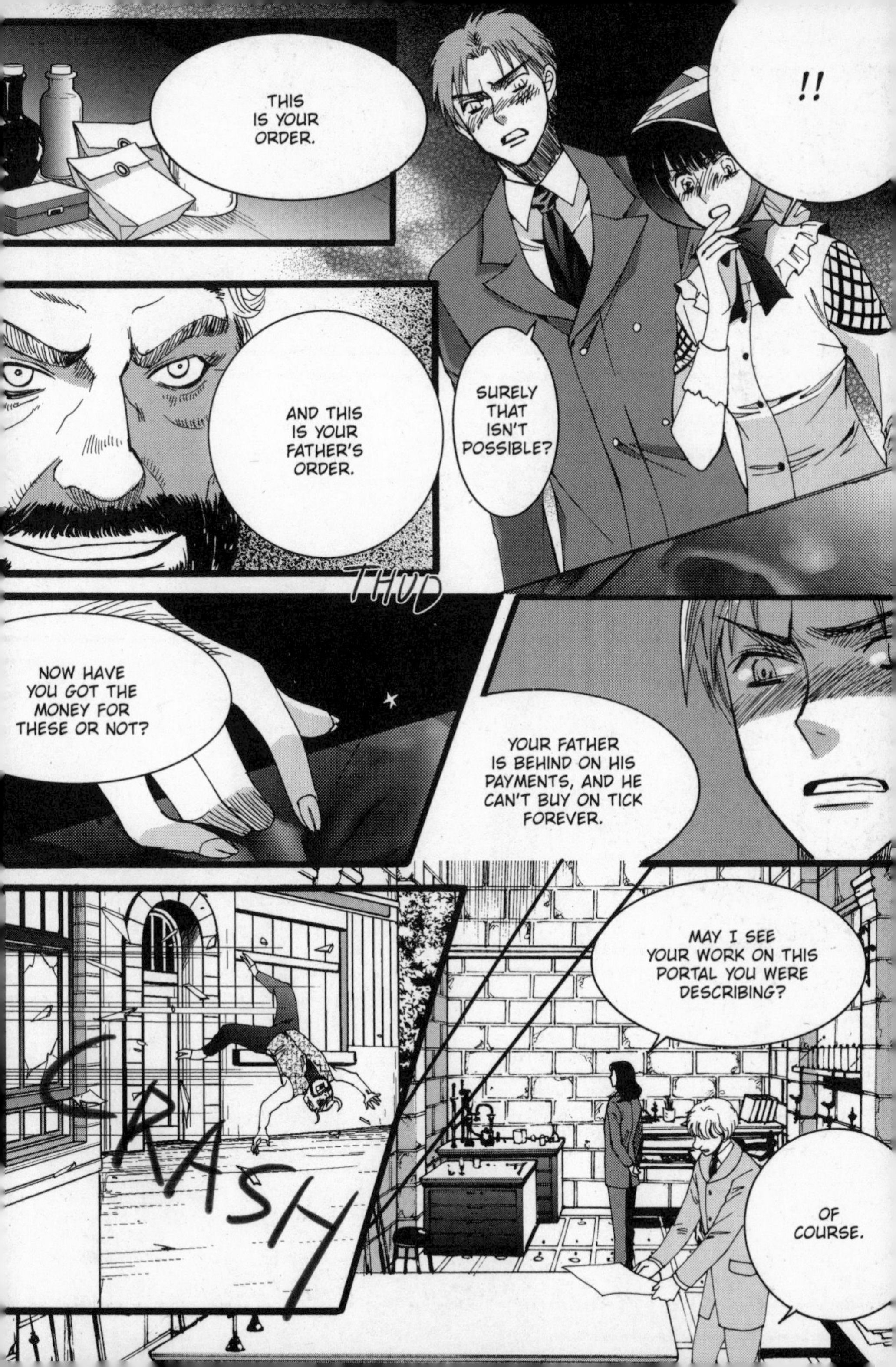
THIS IS YOUR ORDER.
!!
AND THIS IS YOUR FATHER'S ORDER.
SURELY THAT ISN'T POSSIBLE?
THUD
NOW HAVE YOU GOT THE MONEY FOR THESE OR NOT?
YOUR FATHER IS BEHIND ON HIS PAYMENTS, AND HE CAN'T BUY ON TICK FOREVER.
CRASH
MAY I SEE YOUR WORK ON THIS PORTAL YOU WERE DESCRIBING?
OF COURSE.

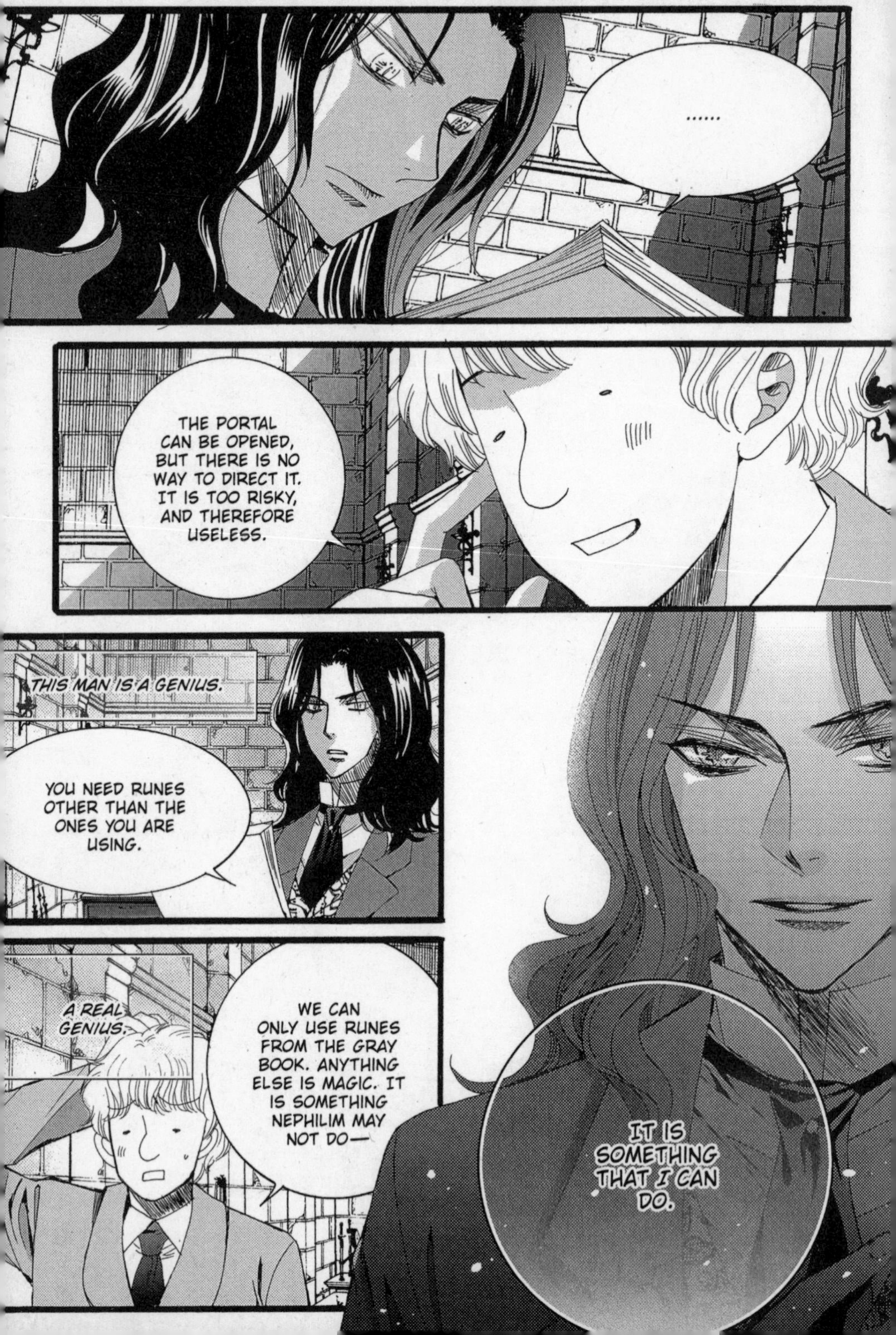
......
THE PORTAL CAN BE OPENED, BUT THERE IS NO WAY TO DIRECT IT. IT IS TOO RISKY, AND THEREFORE USELESS.
THIS MAN IS A GENIUS.
YOU NEED RUNES OTHER THAN THE ONES YOU ARE USING.
A REAL GENIUS.
WE CAN ONLY USE RUNES FROM THE GRAY BOOK. ANYTHING ELSE IS MAGIC. IT IS SOMETHING NEPHILIM MAY NOT DO—
IT IS SOMETHING THAT I CAN DO.

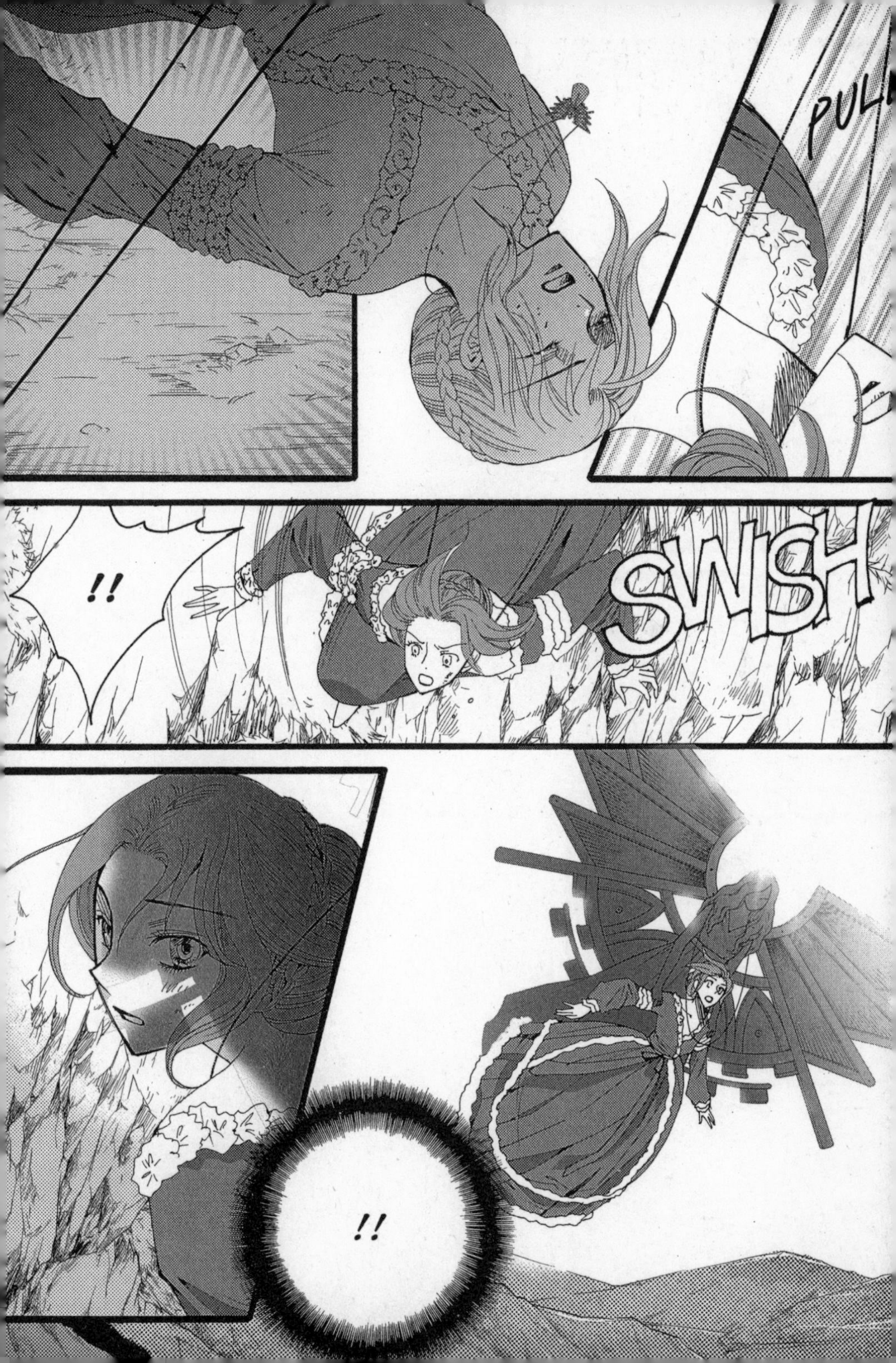
PULL
SWISH
!!
!!

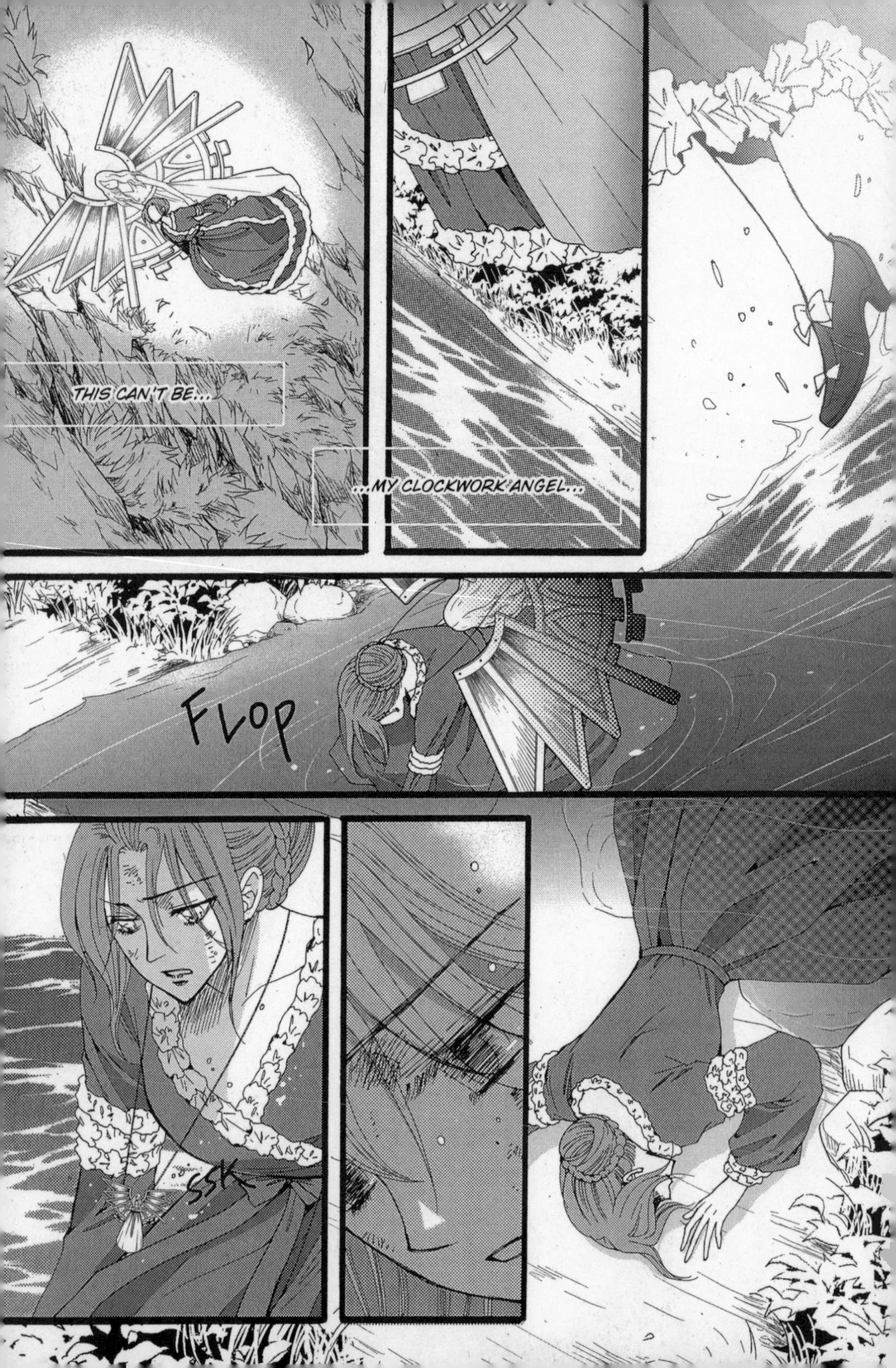
THIS CAN'T BE...
...MY CLOCKWORK ANGEL...
FLOP
SSK

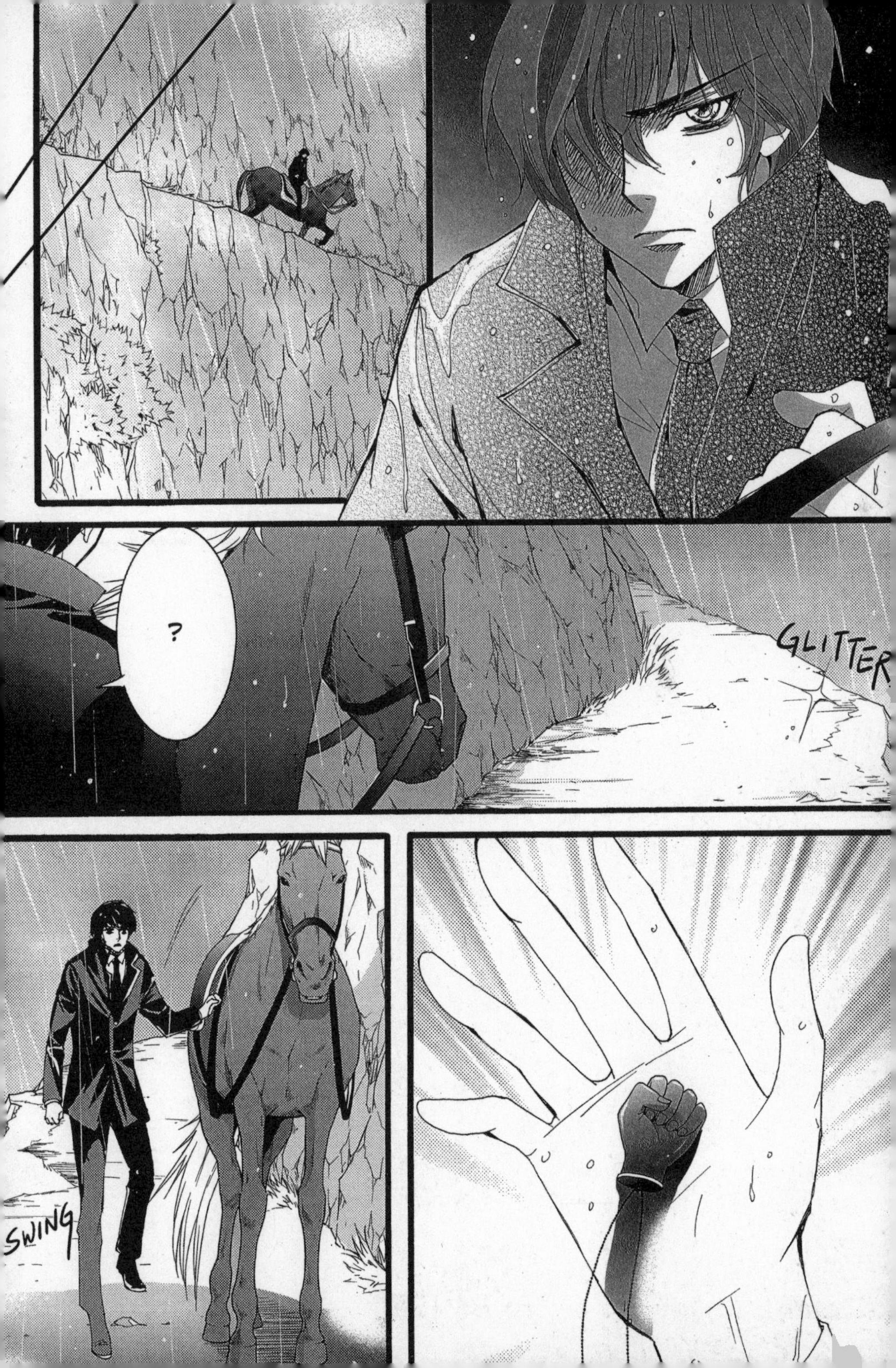

GLITTER
?
SWING

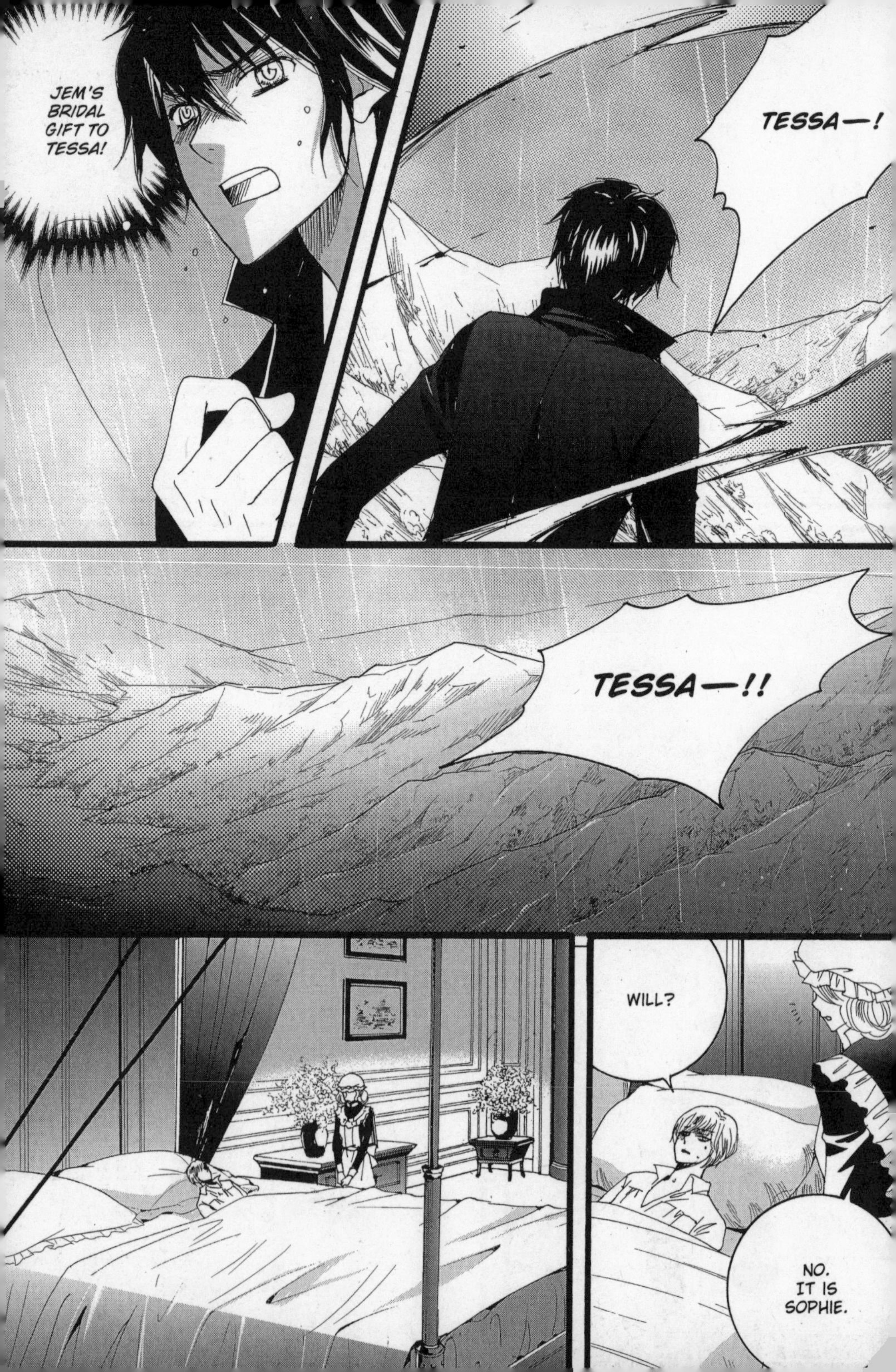

TESSA—!
JEM'S BRIDAL GIFT TO TESSA!
TESSA—!!
WILL?
NO. IT IS SOPHIE.

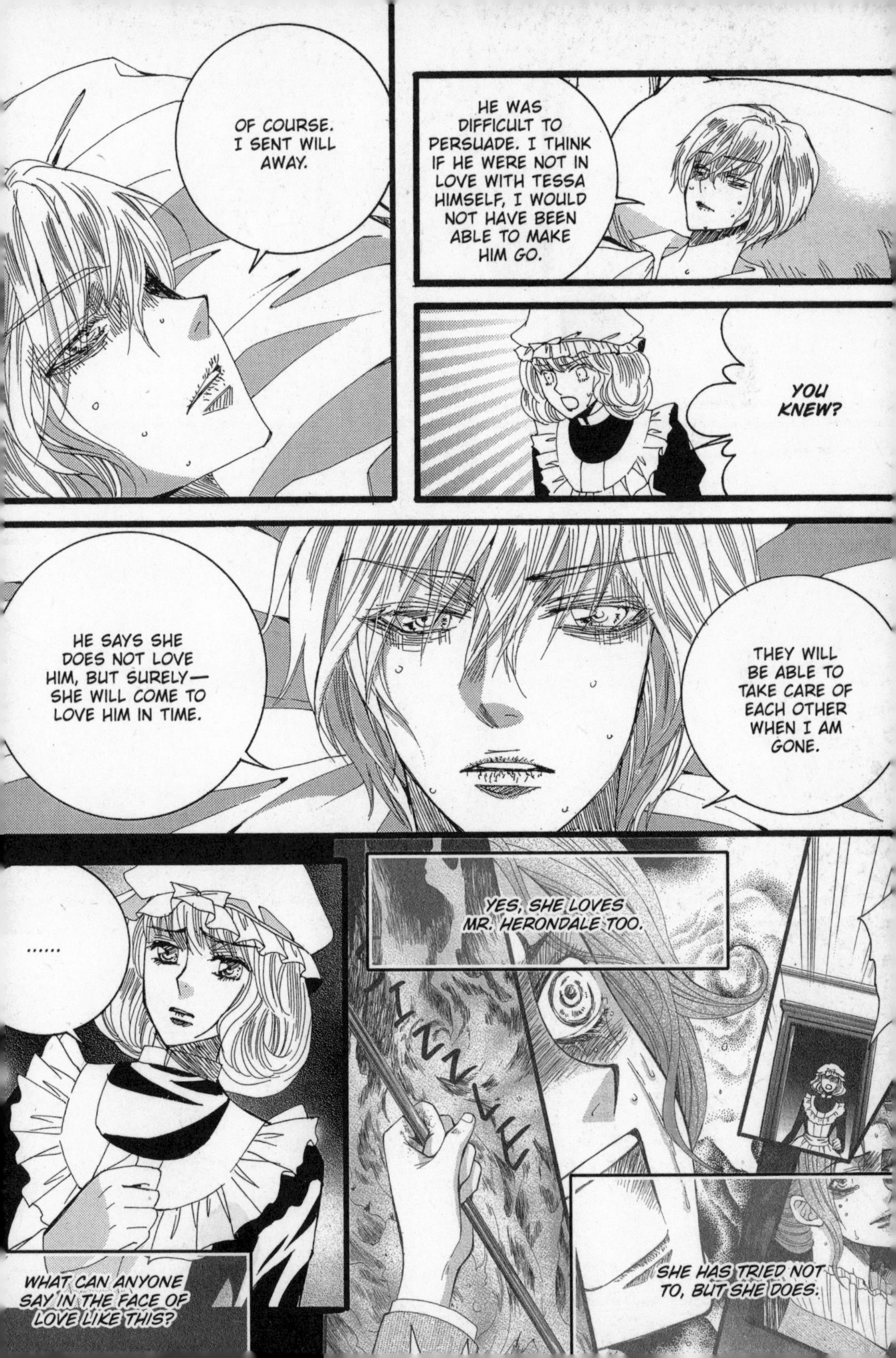
OF COURSE. I SENT WILL AWAY.
HE WAS DIFFICULT TO PERSUADE. I THINK IF HE WERE NOT IN LOVE WITH TESSA HIMSELF, I WOULD NOT HAVE BEEN ABLE TO MAKE HIM GO.
YOU KNEW?
HE SAYS SHE DOES NOT LOVE HIM, BUT SURELY— SHE WILL COME TO LOVE HIM IN TIME.
THEY WILL BE ABLE TO TAKE CARE OF EACH OTHER WHEN I AM GONE.
......
YES, SHE LOVES MR. HERONDALE TOO.
WHAT CAN ANYONE SAY IN THE FACE OF LOVE LIKE THIS?
SHE HAS TRIED NOT TO, BUT SHE DOES.

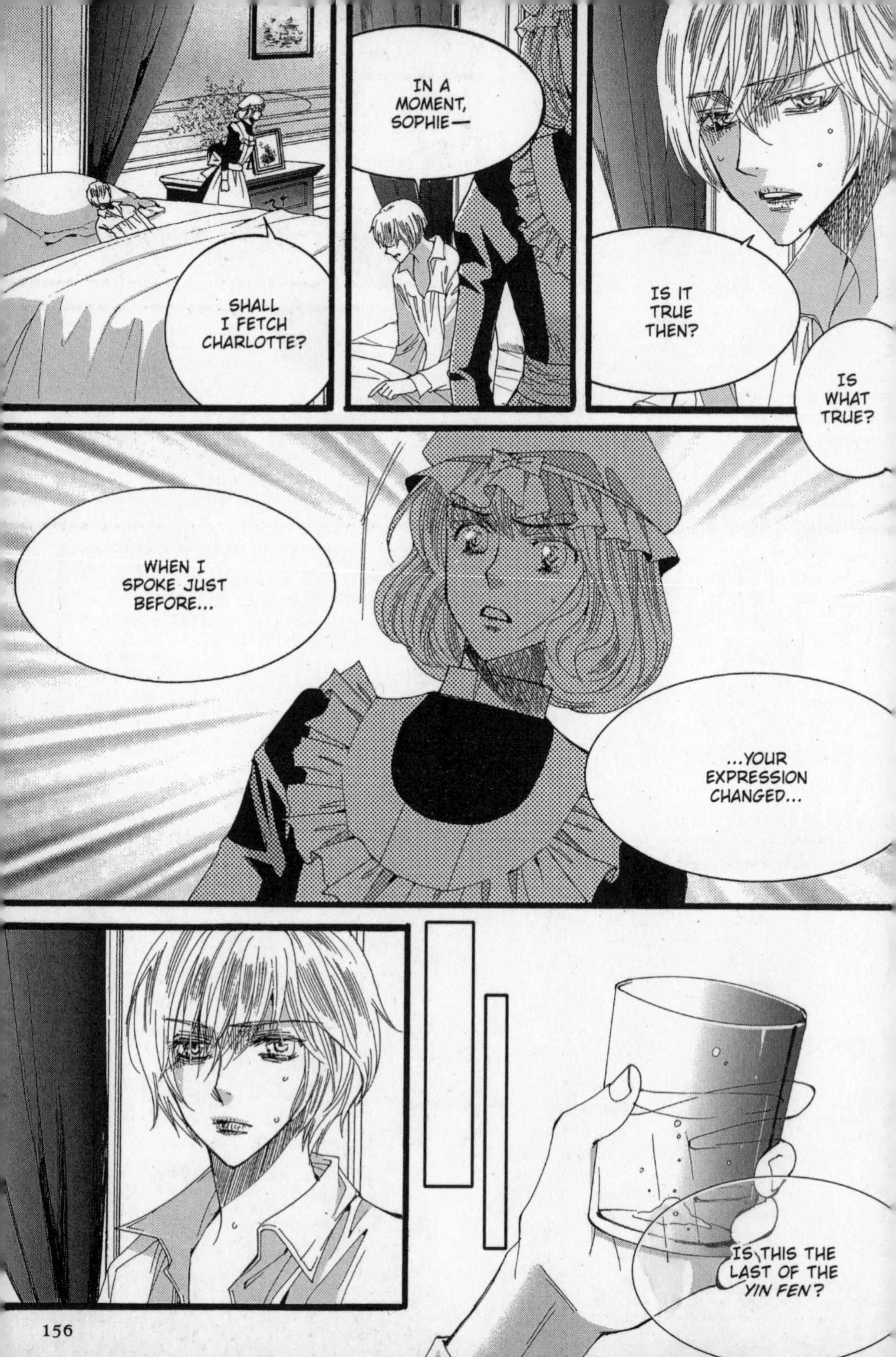
SHALL I FETCH CHARLOTTE?
IN A MOMENT, SOPHIE—
IS IT TRUE THEN?
IS WHAT TRUE?
WHEN I SPOKE JUST BEFORE...
...YOUR EXPRESSION CHANGED...
IS THIS THE LAST OF THE *YIN FEN*?

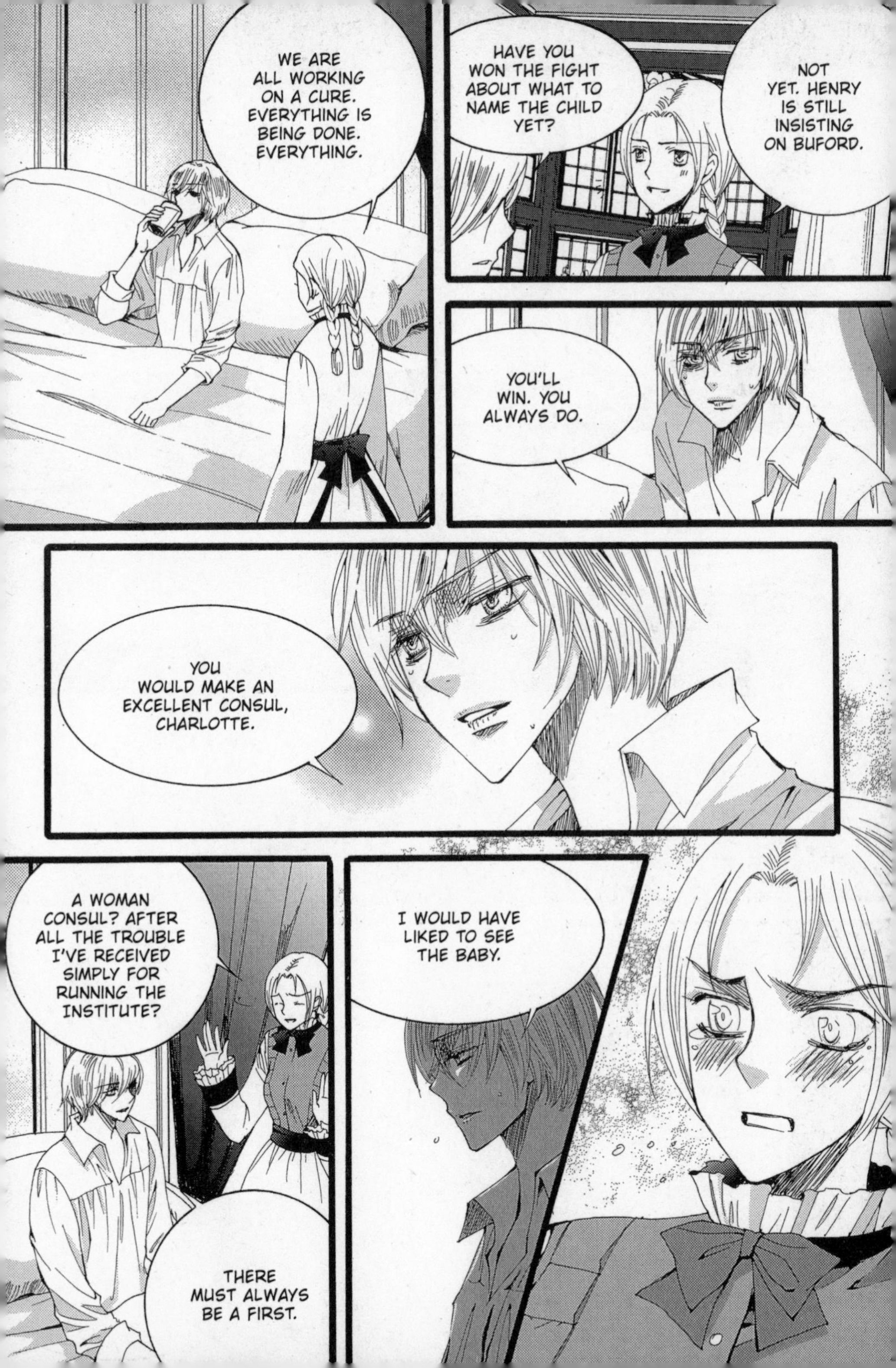
WE ARE ALL WORKING ON A CURE. EVERYTHING IS BEING DONE. EVERYTHING.
HAVE YOU WON THE FIGHT ABOUT WHAT TO NAME THE CHILD YET?
NOT YET. HENRY IS STILL INSISTING ON BUFORD.
YOU'LL WIN. YOU ALWAYS DO.
YOU WOULD MAKE AN EXCELLENT CONSUL, CHARLOTTE.
A WOMAN CONSUL? AFTER ALL THE TROUBLE I'VE RECEIVED SIMPLY FOR RUNNING THE INSTITUTE?
THERE MUST ALWAYS BE A FIRST.
I WOULD HAVE LIKED TO SEE THE BABY.

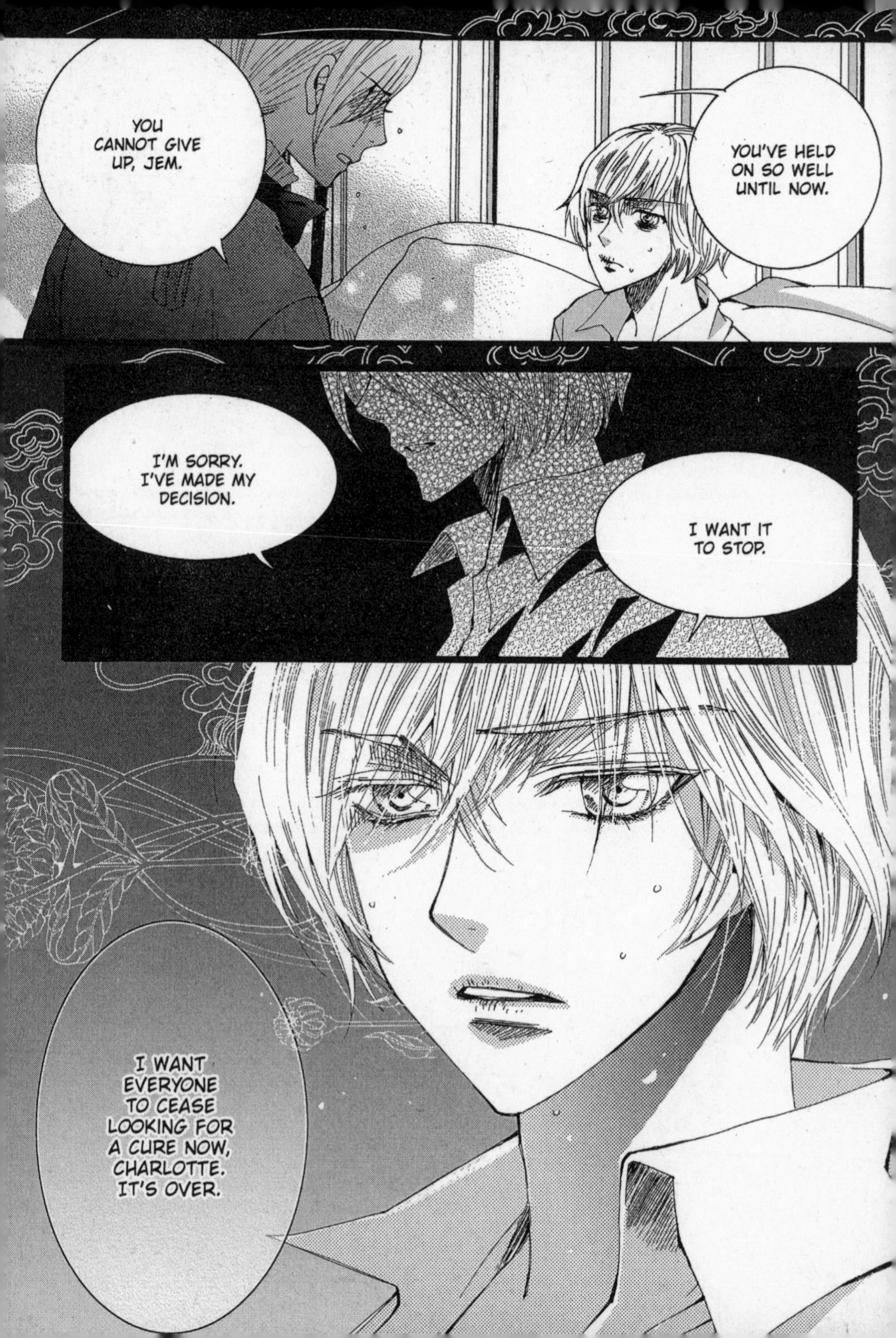
YOU'VE HELD ON SO WELL UNTIL NOW.
YOU CANNOT GIVE UP, JEM.
I WANT IT TO STOP.
I'M SORRY. I'VE MADE MY DECISION.
I WANT EVERYONE TO CEASE LOOKING FOR A CURE NOW, CHARLOTTE. IT'S OVER.

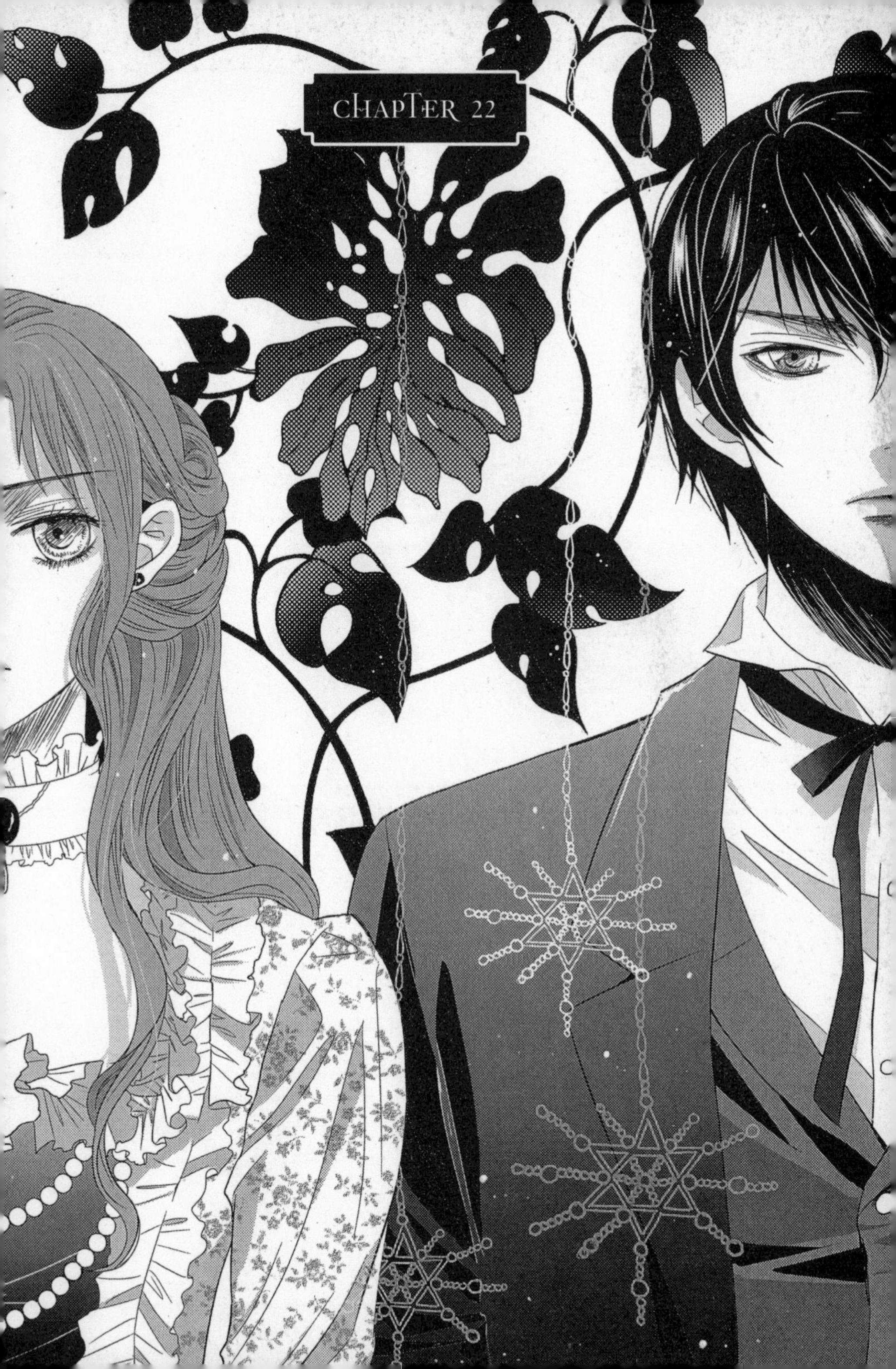
CHAPTER 22

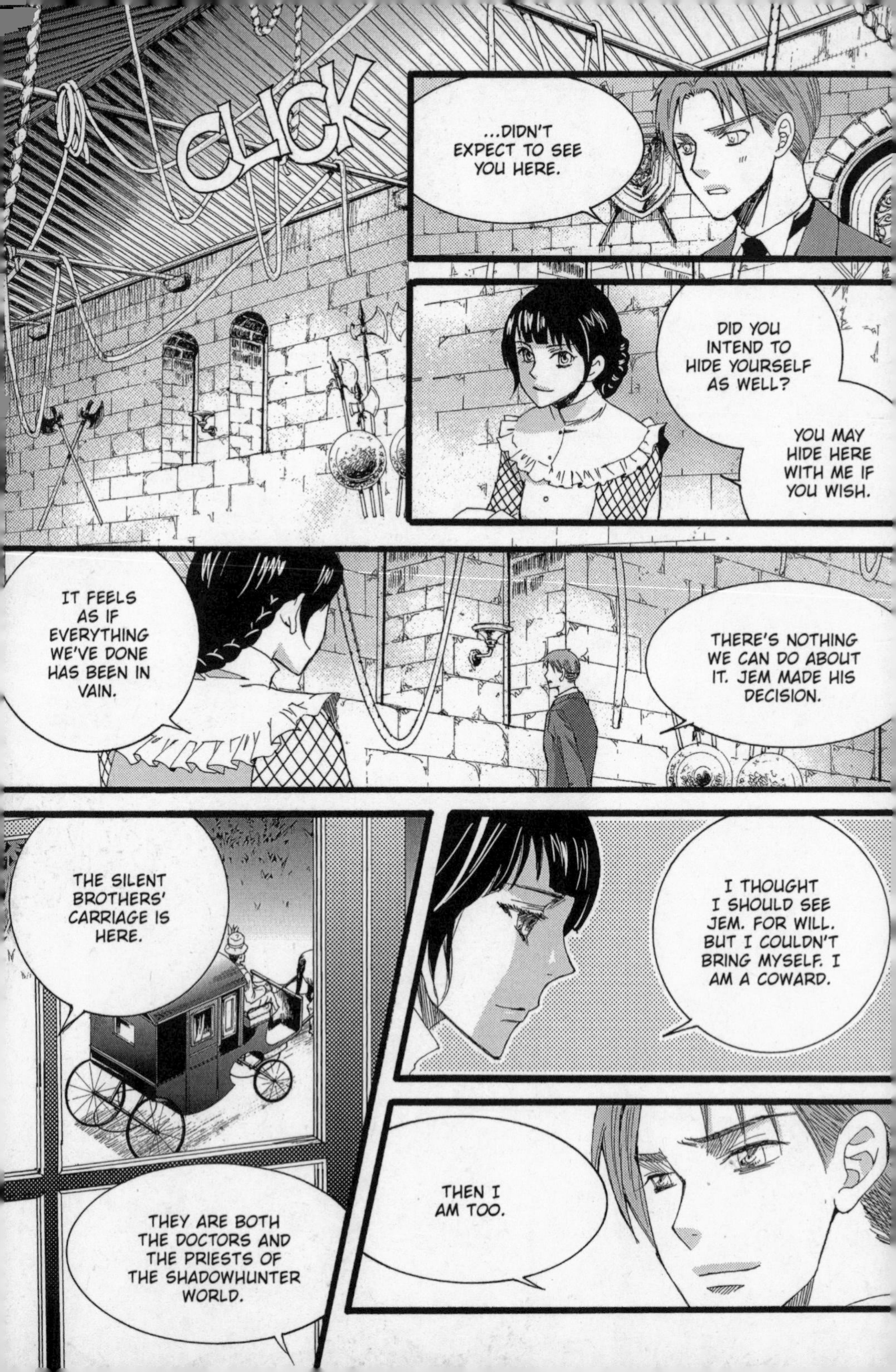
CLICK
...DIDN'T EXPECT TO SEE YOU HERE.
DID YOU INTEND TO HIDE YOURSELF AS WELL?
YOU MAY HIDE HERE WITH ME IF YOU WISH.
IT FEELS AS IF EVERYTHING WE'VE DONE HAS BEEN IN VAIN.
THERE'S NOTHING WE CAN DO ABOUT IT. JEM MADE HIS DECISION.
THE SILENT BROTHERS' CARRIAGE IS HERE.
THEY ARE BOTH THE DOCTORS AND THE PRIESTS OF THE SHADOWHUNTER WORLD.
I THOUGHT I SHOULD SEE JEM. FOR WILL. BUT I COULDN'T BRING MYSELF. I AM A COWARD.
THEN I AM TOO.

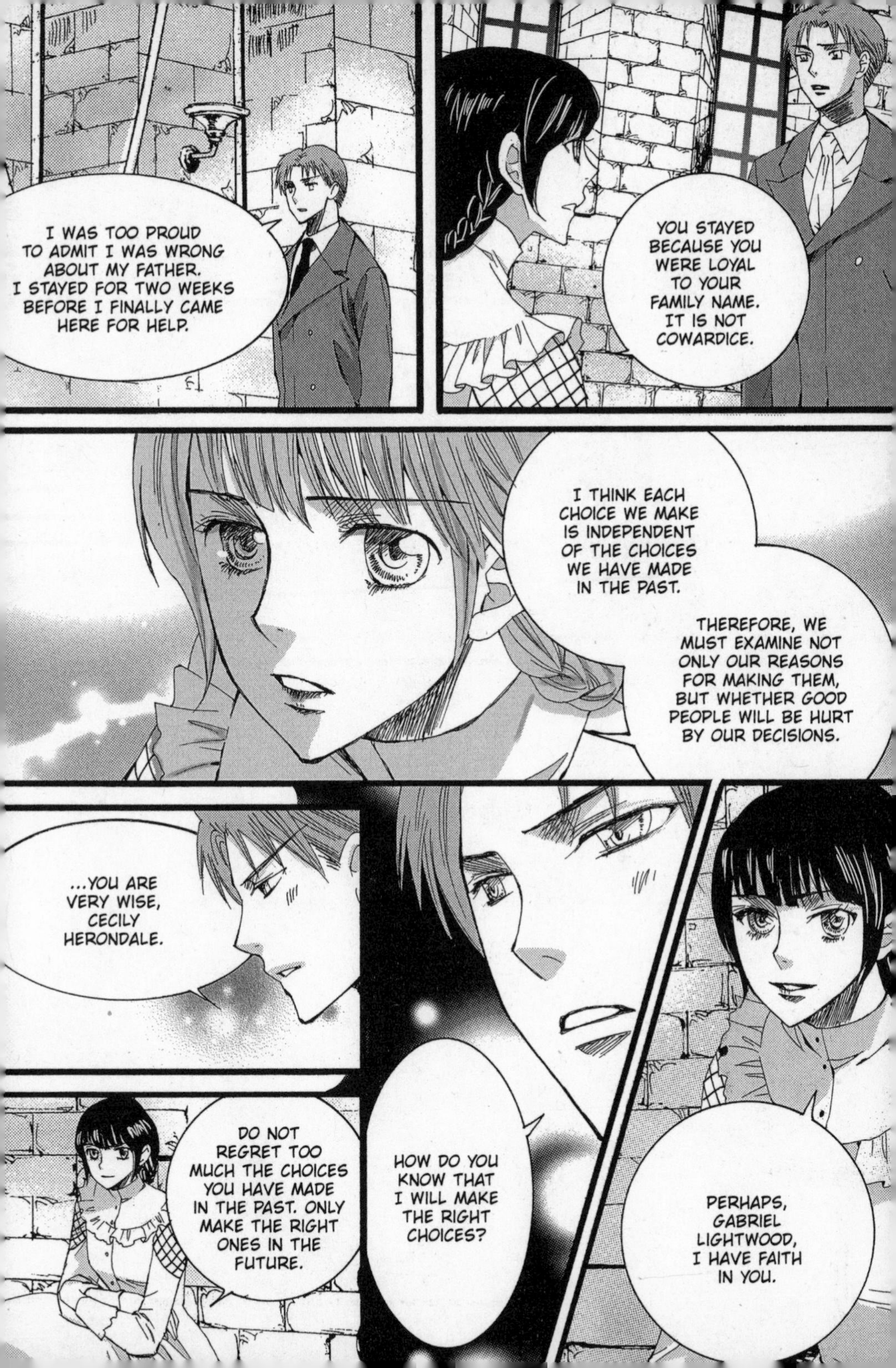
I WAS TOO PROUD TO ADMIT I WAS WRONG ABOUT MY FATHER. I STAYED FOR TWO WEEKS BEFORE I FINALLY CAME HERE FOR HELP.
YOU STAYED BECAUSE YOU WERE LOYAL TO YOUR FAMILY NAME. IT IS NOT COWARDICE.
I THINK EACH CHOICE WE MAKE IS INDEPENDENT OF THE CHOICES WE HAVE MADE IN THE PAST.
THEREFORE, WE MUST EXAMINE NOT ONLY OUR REASONS FOR MAKING THEM, BUT WHETHER GOOD PEOPLE WILL BE HURT BY OUR DECISIONS.
...YOU ARE VERY WISE, CECILY HERONDALE.
DO NOT REGRET TOO MUCH THE CHOICES YOU HAVE MADE IN THE PAST. ONLY MAKE THE RIGHT ONES IN THE FUTURE.
HOW DO YOU KNOW THAT I WILL MAKE THE RIGHT CHOICES?
PERHAPS, GABRIEL LIGHTWOOD, I HAVE FAITH IN YOU.

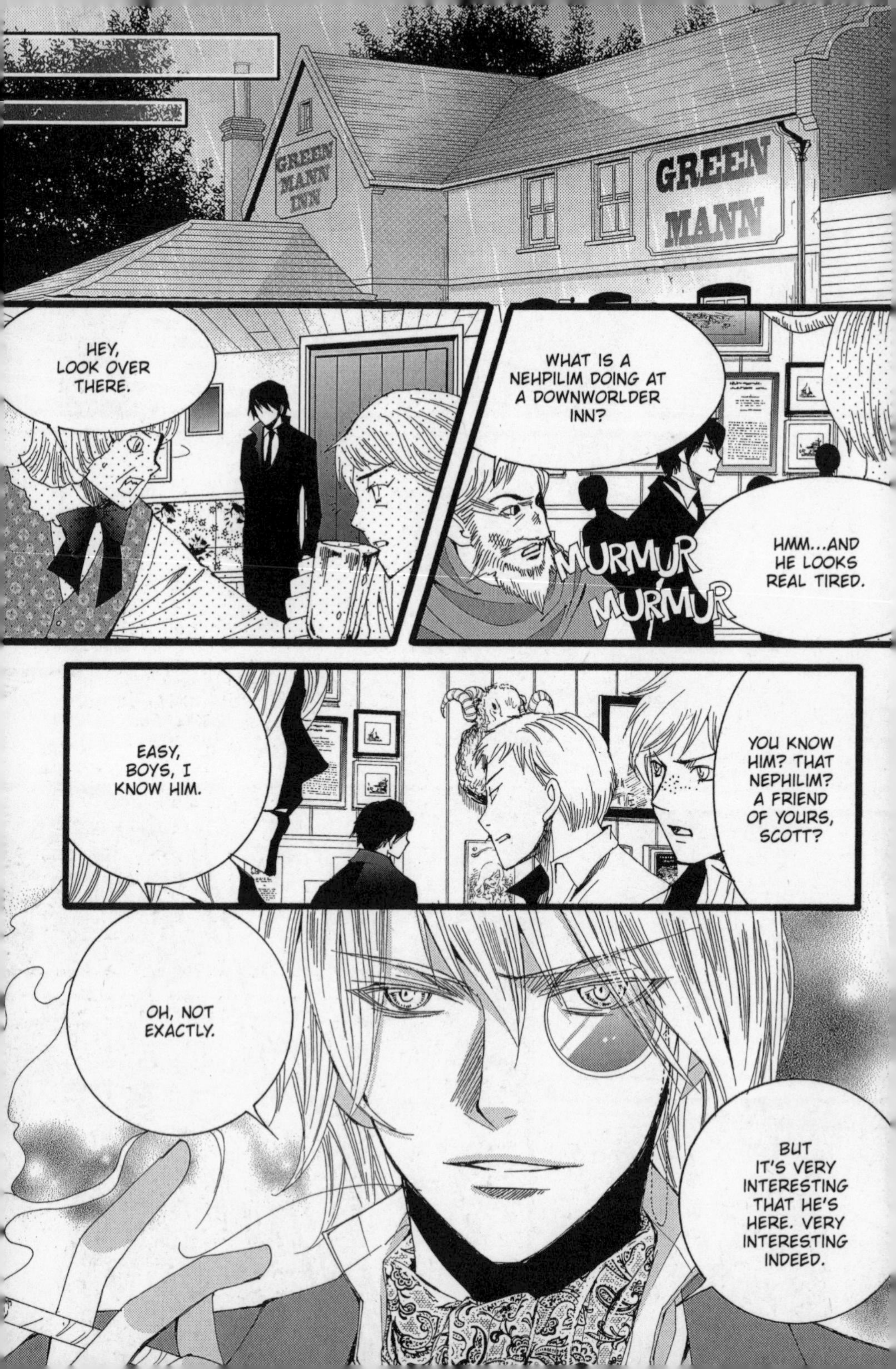
GREEN MANN INN
GREEN MANN
HEY, LOOK OVER THERE.
WHAT IS A NEHPILIM DOING AT A DOWNWORLDER INN?
MURMUR MURMUR
HMM...AND HE LOOKS REAL TIRED.
EASY, BOYS, I KNOW HIM.
YOU KNOW HIM? THAT NEPHILIM? A FRIEND OF YOURS, SCOTT?
OH, NOT EXACTLY.
BUT IT'S VERY INTERESTING THAT HE'S HERE. VERY INTERESTING INDEED.

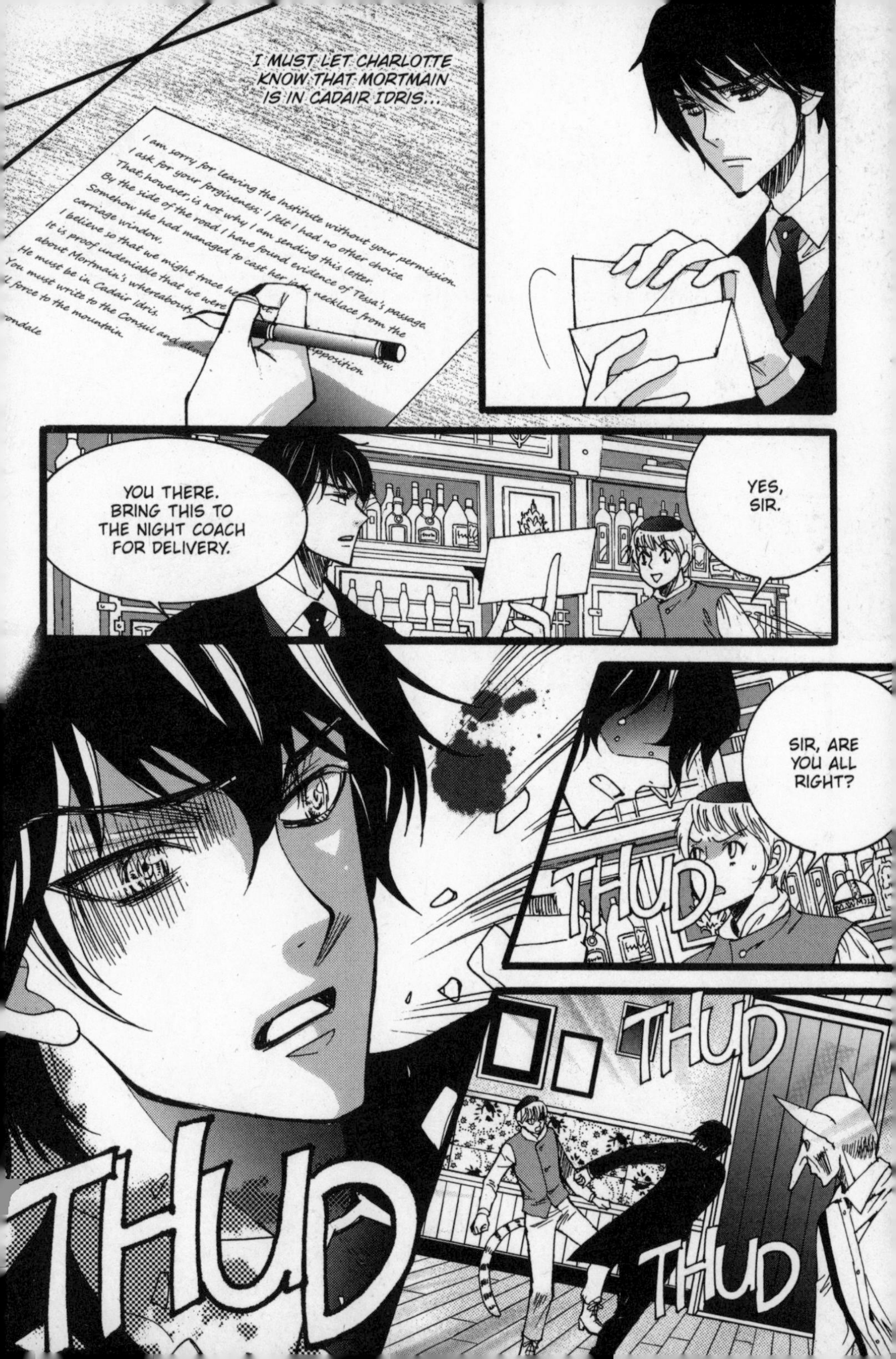
I MUST LET CHARLOTTE KNOW THAT MORTMAIN IS IN CADAIR IDRIS...
I am sorry for leaving the Institute without your permission
I ask for your forgiveness; I felt I had no other choice.
That, however, is not why I am sending this letter.
By the side of the road I have found evidence of Tessa's passage.
Somehow she had managed to cast her
necklace from the
carriage window,
I believe so that we might trace he
It is proof undeniable that we were
about Mortmain's whereabouts.
He must be in Cadair Idris.
You must write to the Consul and
force to the mountain
opposition
ondale
YOU THERE. BRING THIS TO THE NIGHT COACH FOR DELIVERY.
YES, SIR.
SIR, ARE YOU ALL RIGHT?
THUD
THUD
THUD
THUD

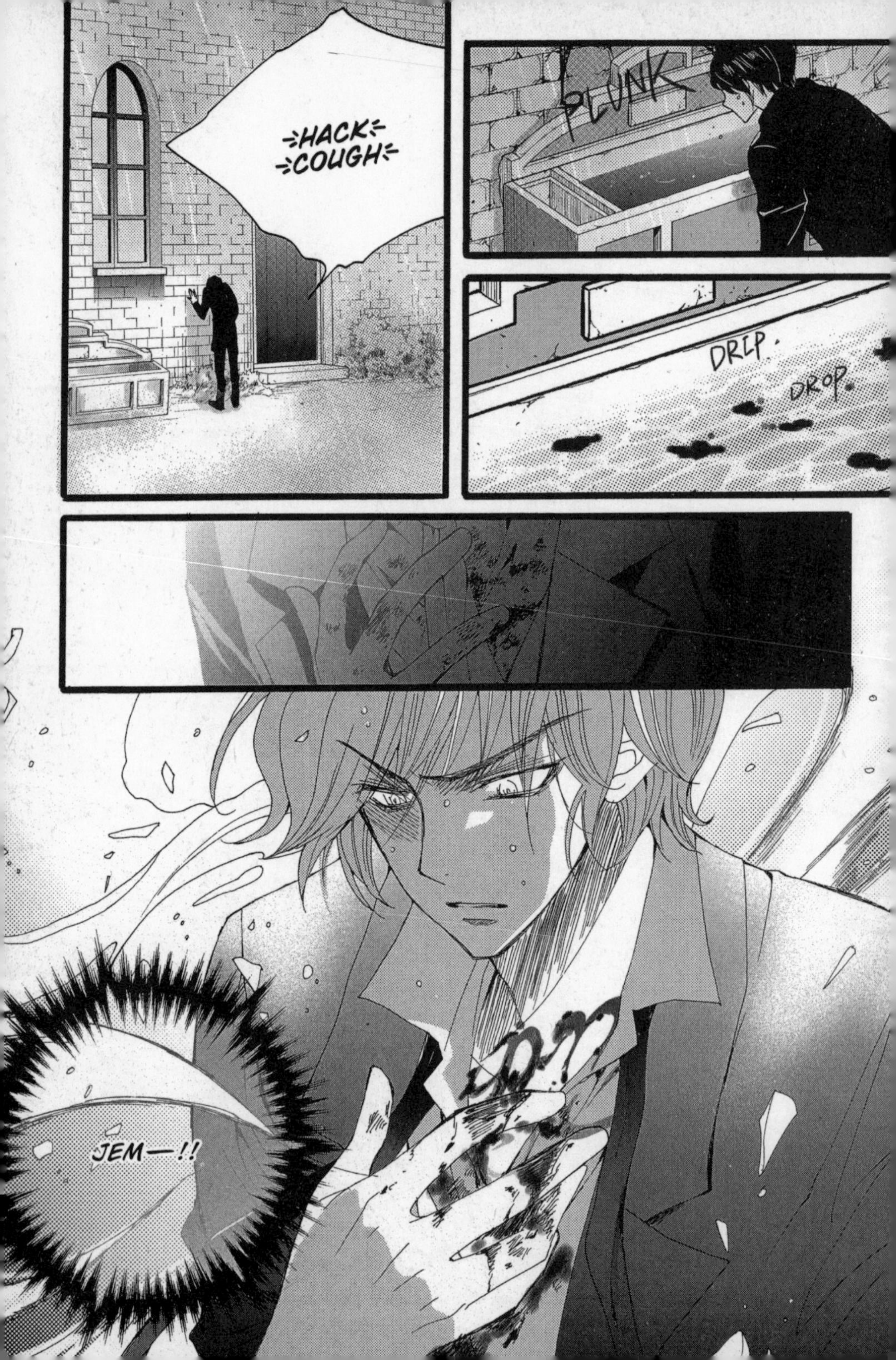
HACK COUGH
PLUNK
DRIP.
DROP.
JEM—!!

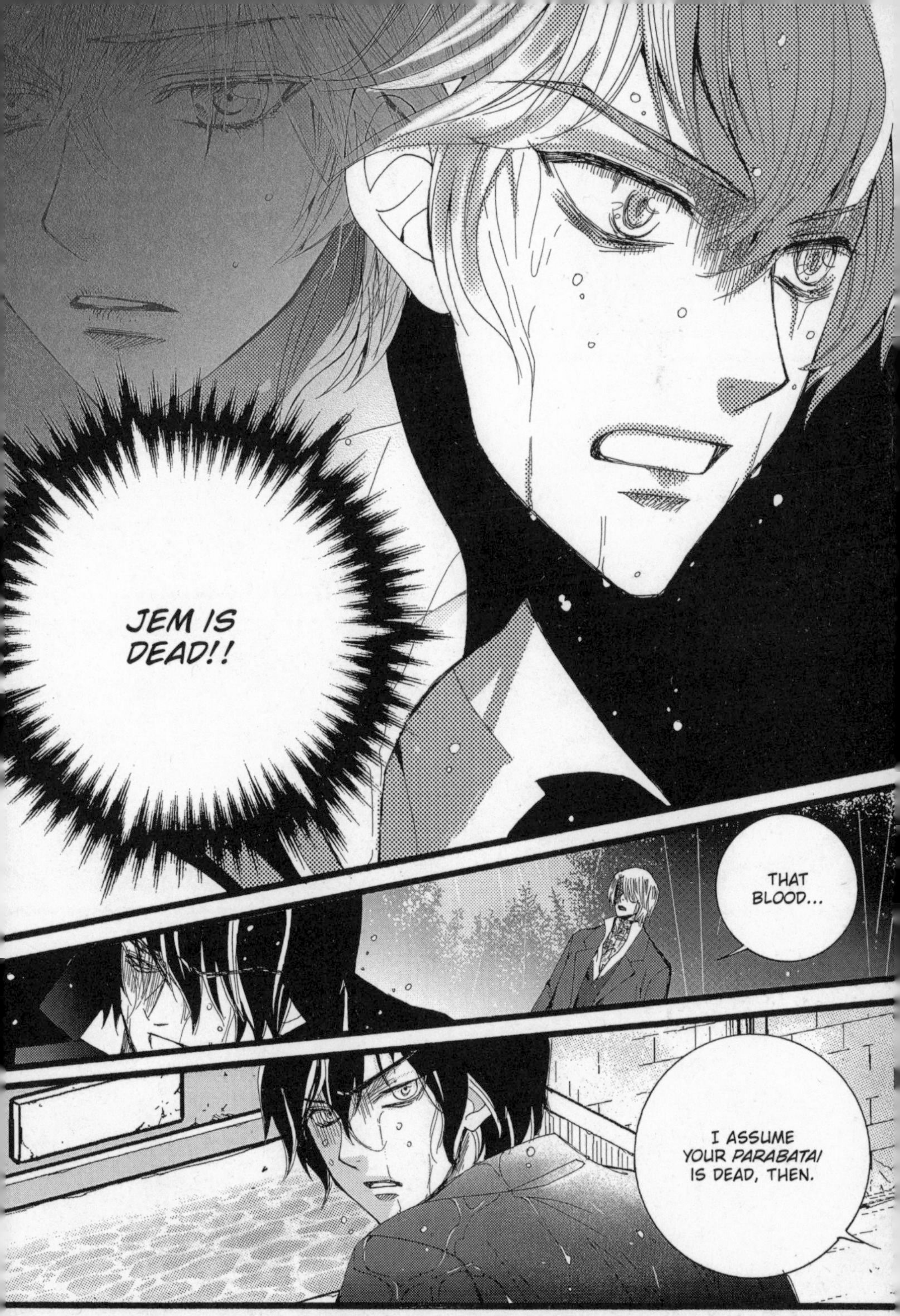
JEM IS DEAD!!
THAT BLOOD...
I ASSUME YOUR *PARABATAI* IS DEAD, THEN.

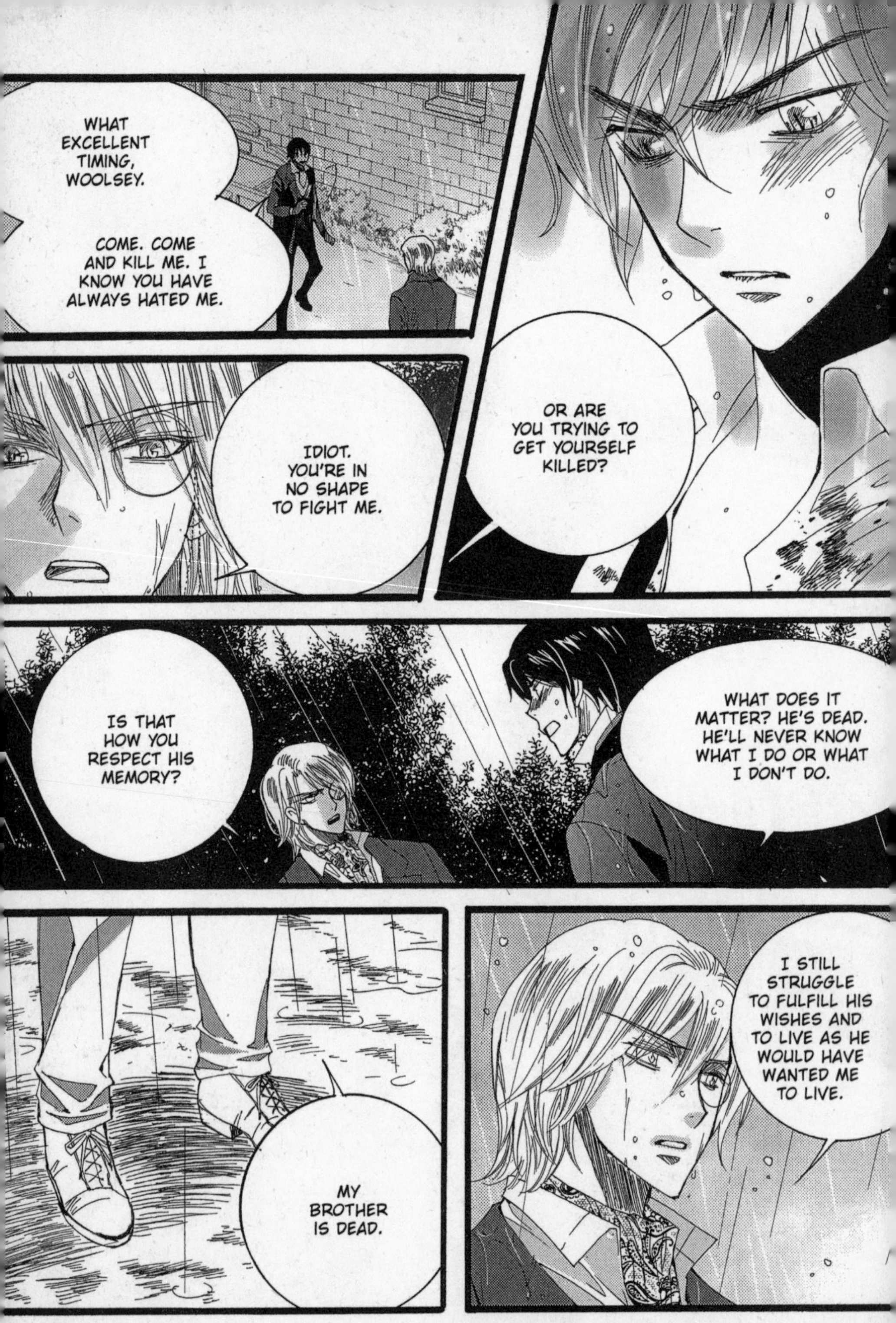
WHAT EXCELLENT TIMING, WOOLSEY.
COME. COME AND KILL ME. I KNOW YOU HAVE ALWAYS HATED ME.
IDIOT. YOU'RE IN NO SHAPE TO FIGHT ME.
OR ARE YOU TRYING TO GET YOURSELF KILLED?
IS THAT HOW YOU RESPECT HIS MEMORY?
WHAT DOES IT MATTER? HE'S DEAD. HE'LL NEVER KNOW WHAT I DO OR WHAT I DON'T DO.
MY BROTHER IS DEAD.
I STILL STRUGGLE TO FULFILL HIS WISHES AND TO LIVE AS HE WOULD HAVE WANTED ME TO LIVE.

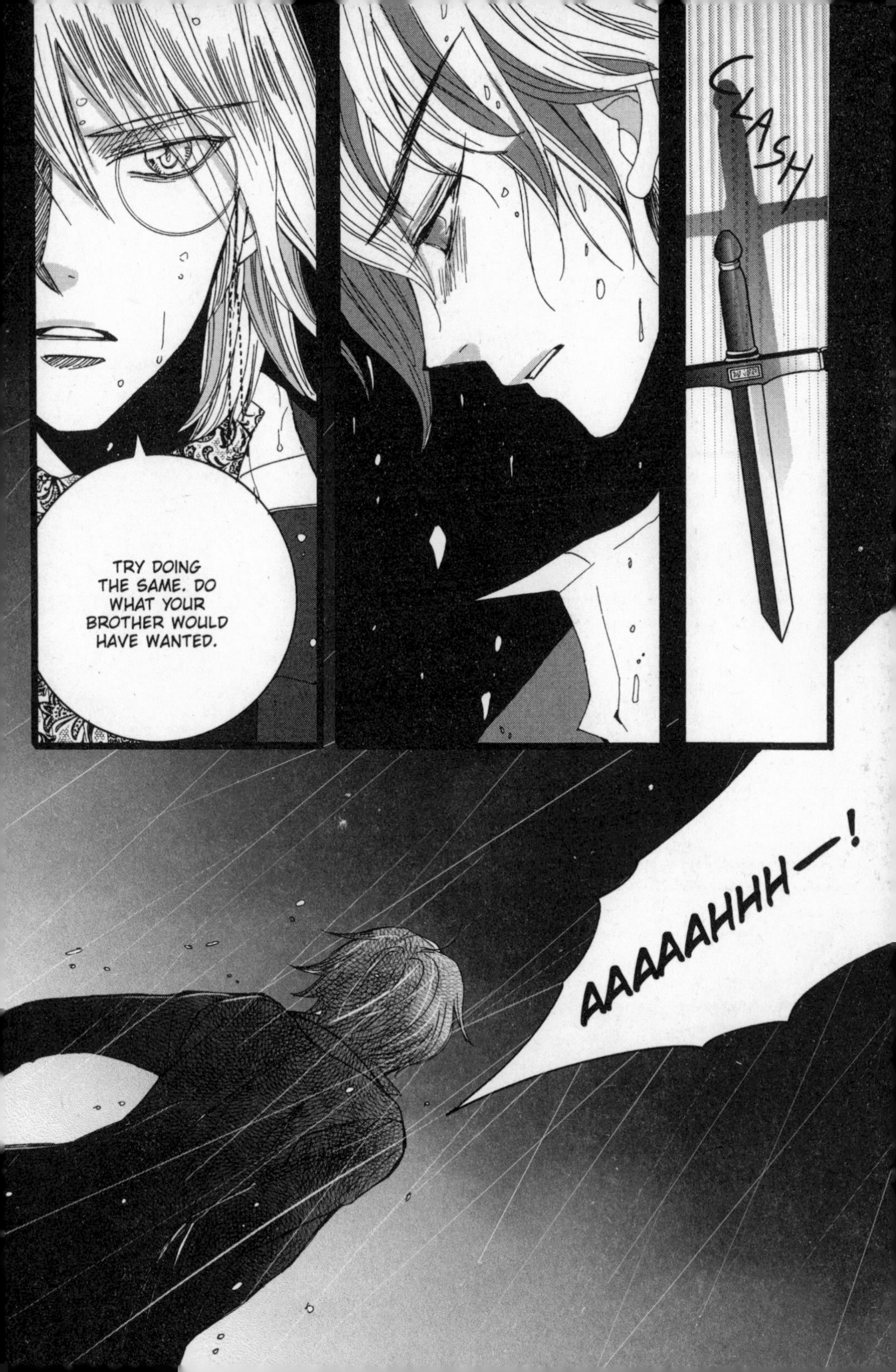
CLASH
TRY DOING THE SAME. DO WHAT YOUR BROTHER WOULD HAVE WANTED.
AAAAAHHH—!

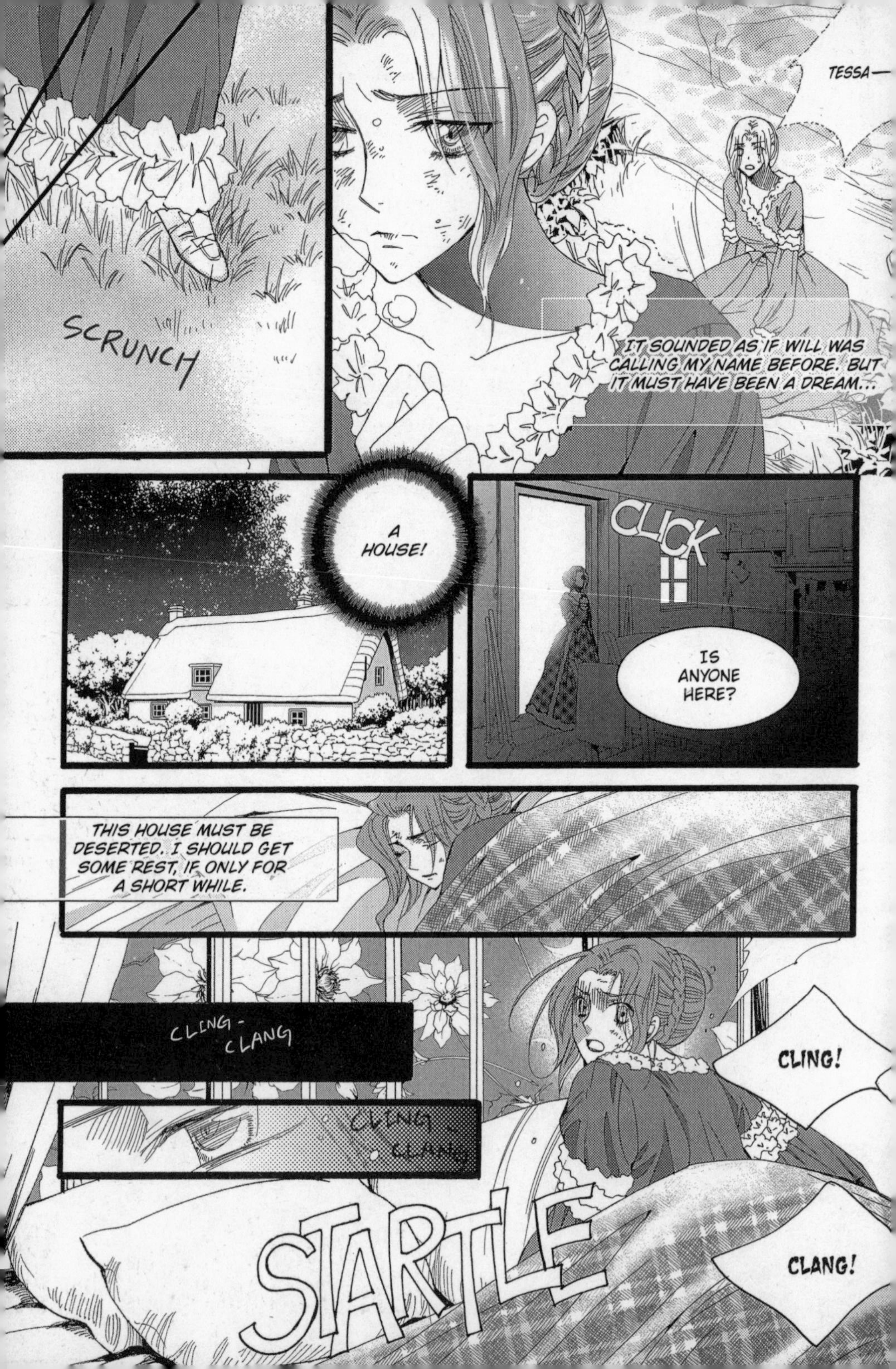
TESSA—
SCRUNCH
IT SOUNDED AS IF WILL WAS CALLING MY NAME BEFORE. BUT IT MUST HAVE BEEN A DREAM...
A HOUSE!
CLICK
IS ANYONE HERE?
THIS HOUSE MUST BE DESERTED. I SHOULD GET SOME REST, IF ONLY FOR A SHORT WHILE.
CLING-CLANG
CLING!
CLING CLANG
STARTLE
CLANG!

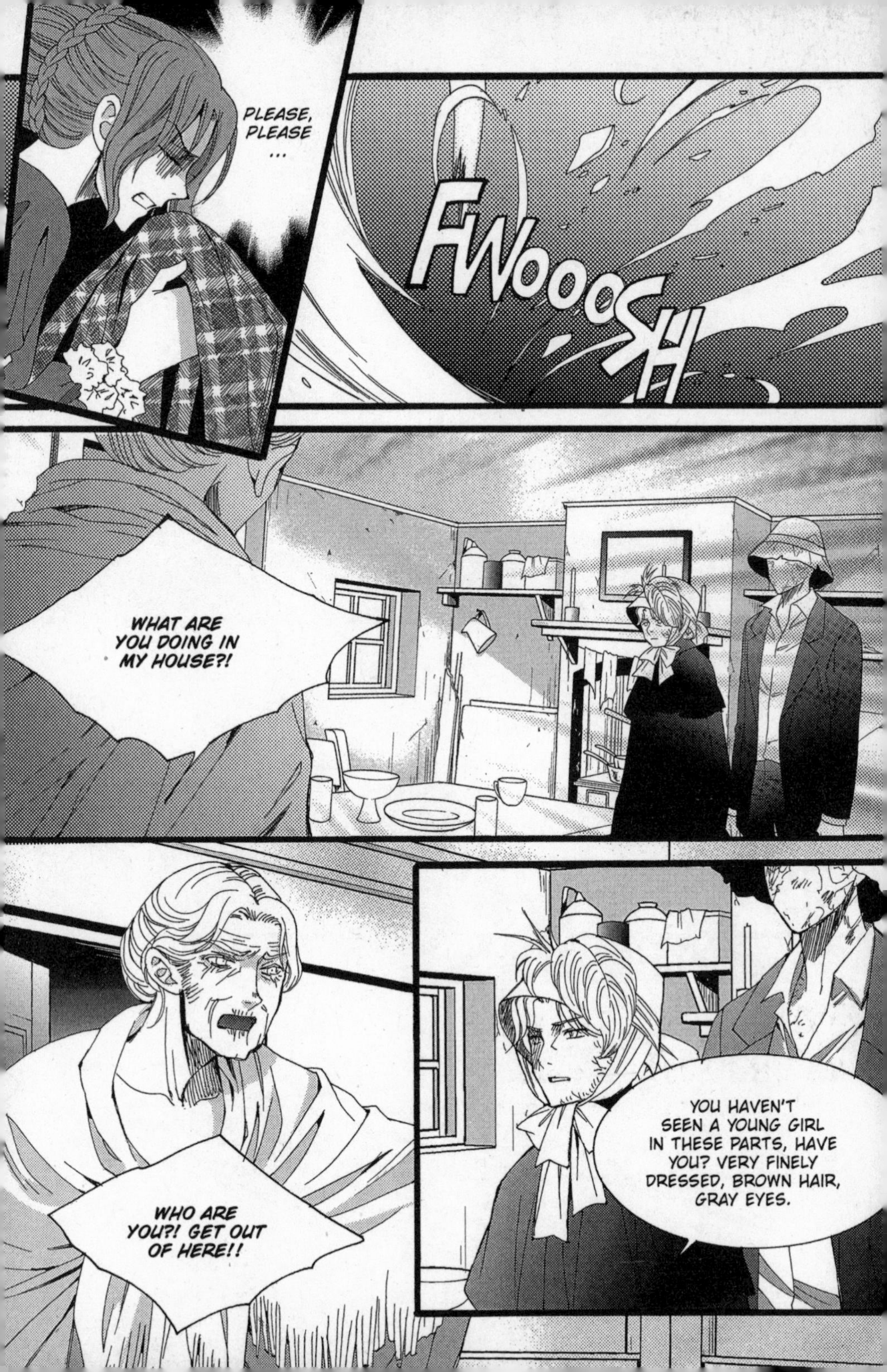
PLEASE, PLEASE ...
FWOOOSH
WHAT ARE YOU DOING IN MY HOUSE?!
WHO ARE YOU?! GET OUT OF HERE!!
YOU HAVEN'T SEEN A YOUNG GIRL IN THESE PARTS, HAVE YOU? VERY FINELY DRESSED, BROWN HAIR, GRAY EYES.

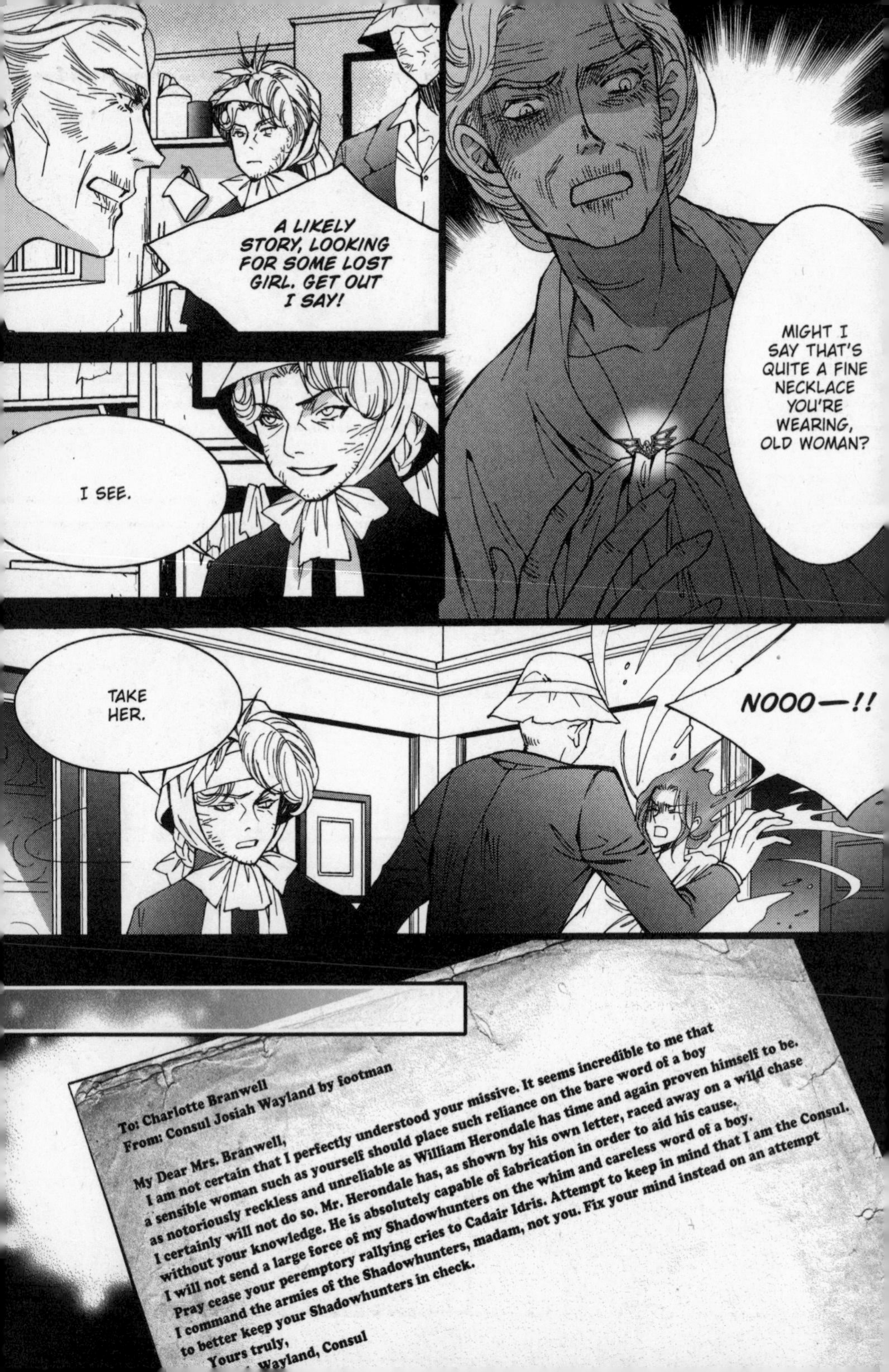
A LIKELY STORY, LOOKING FOR SOME LOST GIRL. GET OUT I SAY!
I SEE.
MIGHT I SAY THAT'S QUITE A FINE NECKLACE YOU'RE WEARING, OLD WOMAN?
TAKE HER.
NOOO—!!
To: Charlotte Branwell
From: Consul Josiah Wayland by footman
My Dear Mrs. Branwell,
I am not certain that I perfectly understood your missive. It seems incredible to me that
a sensible woman such as yourself should place such reliance on the bare word of a boy
as notoriously reckless and unreliable as William Herondale has time and again proven himself to be.
I certainly will not do so. Mr. Herondale has, as shown by his own letter, raced away on a wild chase
without your knowledge. He is absolutely capable of fabrication in order to aid his cause.
I will not send a large force of my Shadowhunters on the whim and careless word of a boy.
Pray cease your peremptory rallying cries to Cadair Idris. Attempt to keep in mind that I am the Consul.
I command the armies of the Shadowhunters, madam, not you. Fix your mind instead on an attempt
to better keep your Shadowhunters in check.
Yours truly,
Wayland, Consul

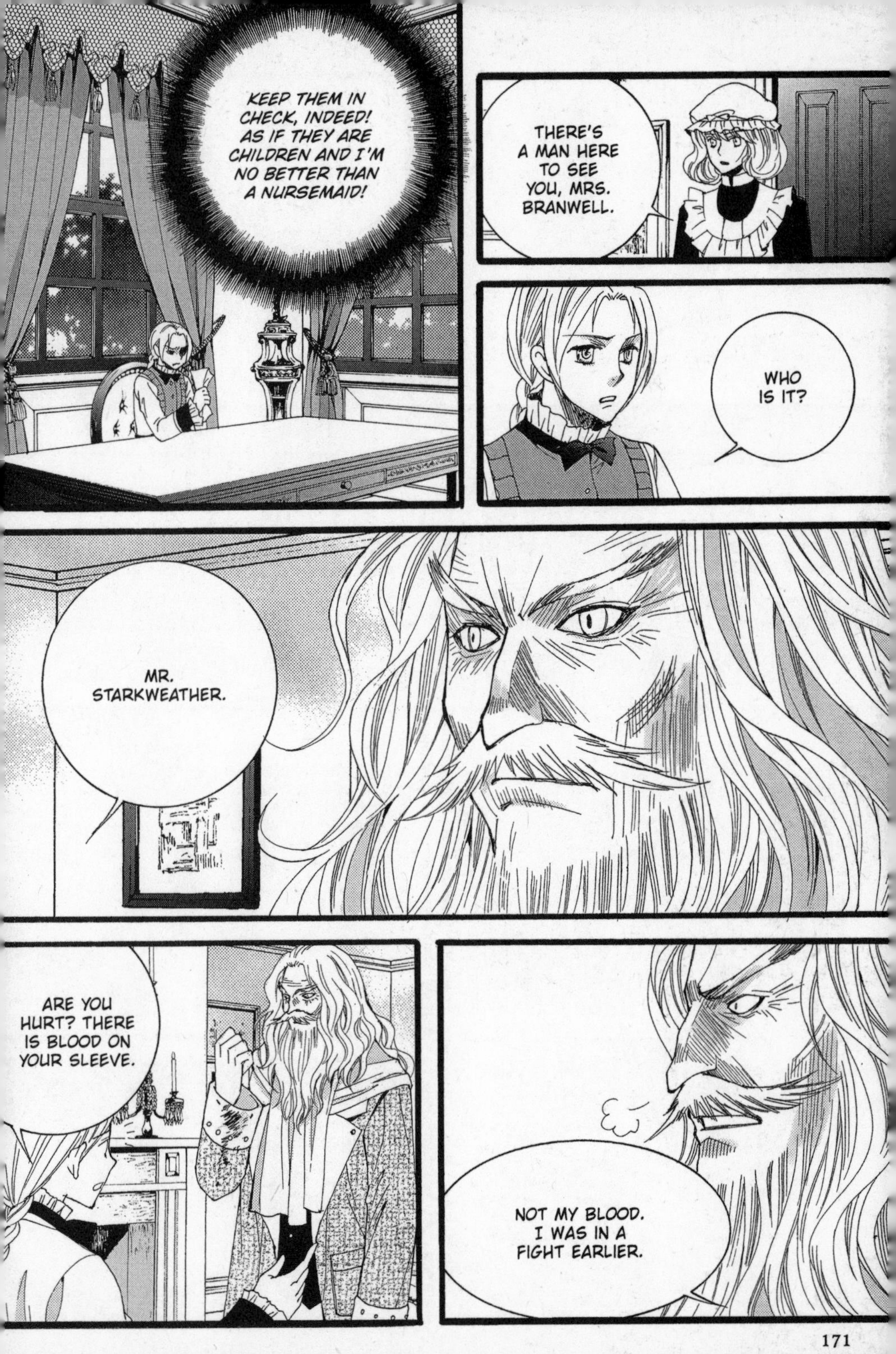
KEEP THEM IN CHECK, INDEED! AS IF THEY ARE CHILDREN AND I'M NO BETTER THAN A NURSEMAID!
THERE'S A MAN HERE TO SEE YOU, MRS. BRANWELL.
WHO IS IT?
MR. STARKWEATHER.
ARE YOU HURT? THERE IS BLOOD ON YOUR SLEEVE.
NOT MY BLOOD. I WAS IN A FIGHT EARLIER.

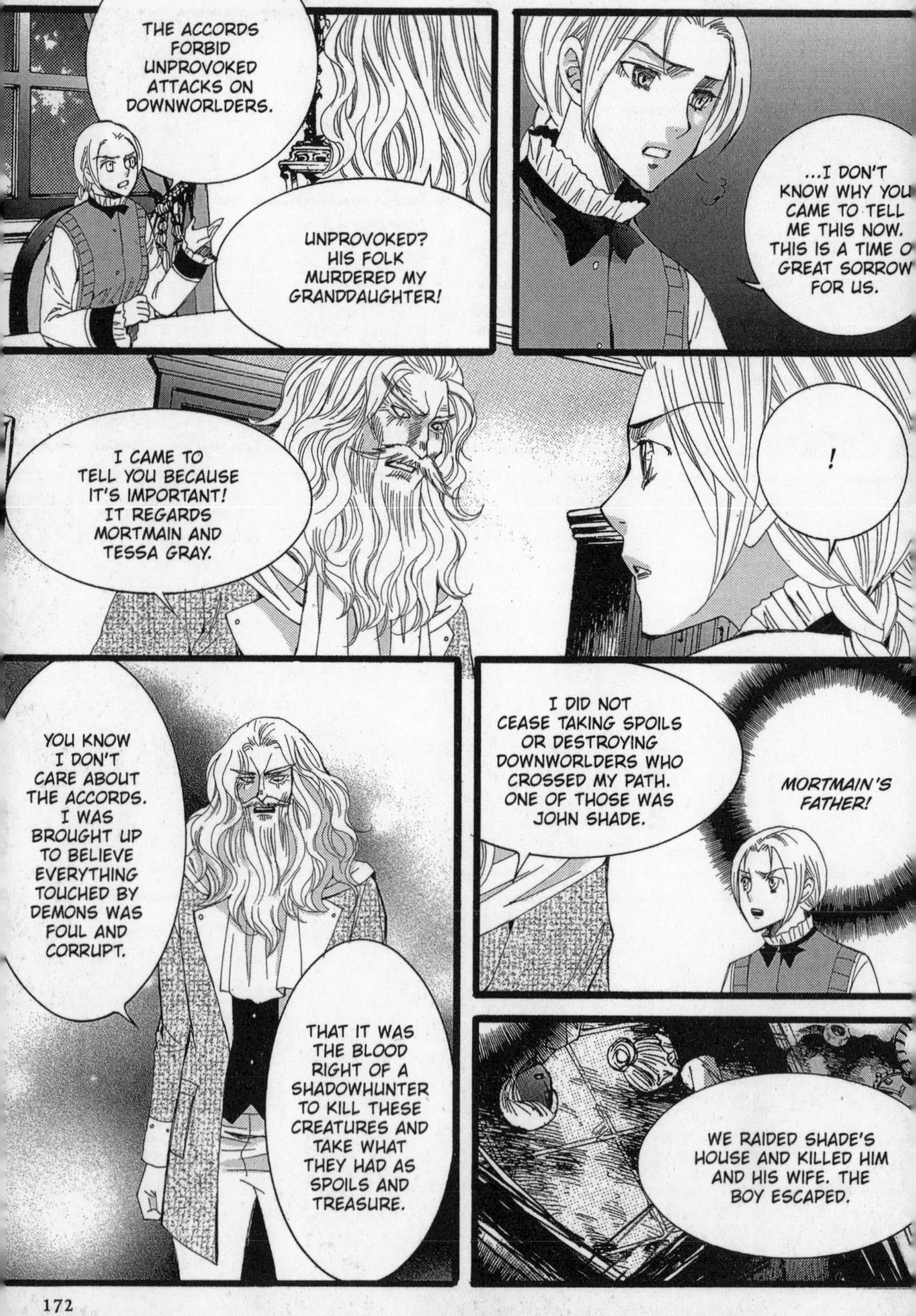
THE ACCORDS FORBID UNPROVOKED ATTACKS ON DOWNWORLDERS.
UNPROVOKED? HIS FOLK MURDERED MY GRANDDAUGHTER!
...I DON'T KNOW WHY YOU CAME TO TELL ME THIS NOW. THIS IS A TIME OF GREAT SORROW FOR US.
I CAME TO TELL YOU BECAUSE IT'S IMPORTANT! IT REGARDS MORTMAIN AND TESSA GRAY.
!
YOU KNOW I DON'T CARE ABOUT THE ACCORDS. I WAS BROUGHT UP TO BELIEVE EVERYTHING TOUCHED BY DEMONS WAS FOUL AND CORRUPT.
THAT IT WAS THE BLOOD RIGHT OF A SHADOWHUNTER TO KILL THESE CREATURES AND TAKE WHAT THEY HAD AS SPOILS AND TREASURE.
I DID NOT CEASE TAKING SPOILS OR DESTROYING DOWNWORLDERS WHO CROSSED MY PATH. ONE OF THOSE WAS JOHN SHADE.
MORTMAIN'S FATHER!
WE RAIDED SHADE'S HOUSE AND KILLED HIM AND HIS WIFE. THE BOY ESCAPED.

IT WAS A ROUTINE RAID. EVERYTHING WENT ACCORDING TO PLAN. THAT IS, UNTIL MY GRANDDAUGHTER, ADELE, WAS BORN.

MY DAUGHTER-IN-LAW INSISTED THAT THE CHILD IN HER CRADLE WAS NOT HER DAUGHTER, THOUGH SHE LOOKED EXACTLY LIKE ADELE.

IT WASN'T UNTIL ADELE PASSED AWAY FROM HER FIRST RUNE CEREMONY THAT I BEGAN TO SUSPECT.

AND THEN I HEARD STRANGE RUMORS OF FAERIES AND OTHER DOWNWORLDERS WHO BOASTED ...

MY DAUGHTER-IN-LAW HAD BEEN RIGHT.

...THAT THEY HAD HAD THEIR REVENGE ON THE STARKWEATHERS, HAD TAKEN ONE OF THEIR CHILDREN FROM THEM AND REPLACED HER WITH A SICKLY HUMAN.

A GRAY, SIR. NDANE GIRL, HE BETROTHED AN ASCENDANT.

I HAD NEARLY GIVEN UP ON FINDING WHERE MY GRANDDAUGHTER HAD GONE WHEN TESSA GRAY CAME TO MY INSTITUTE.

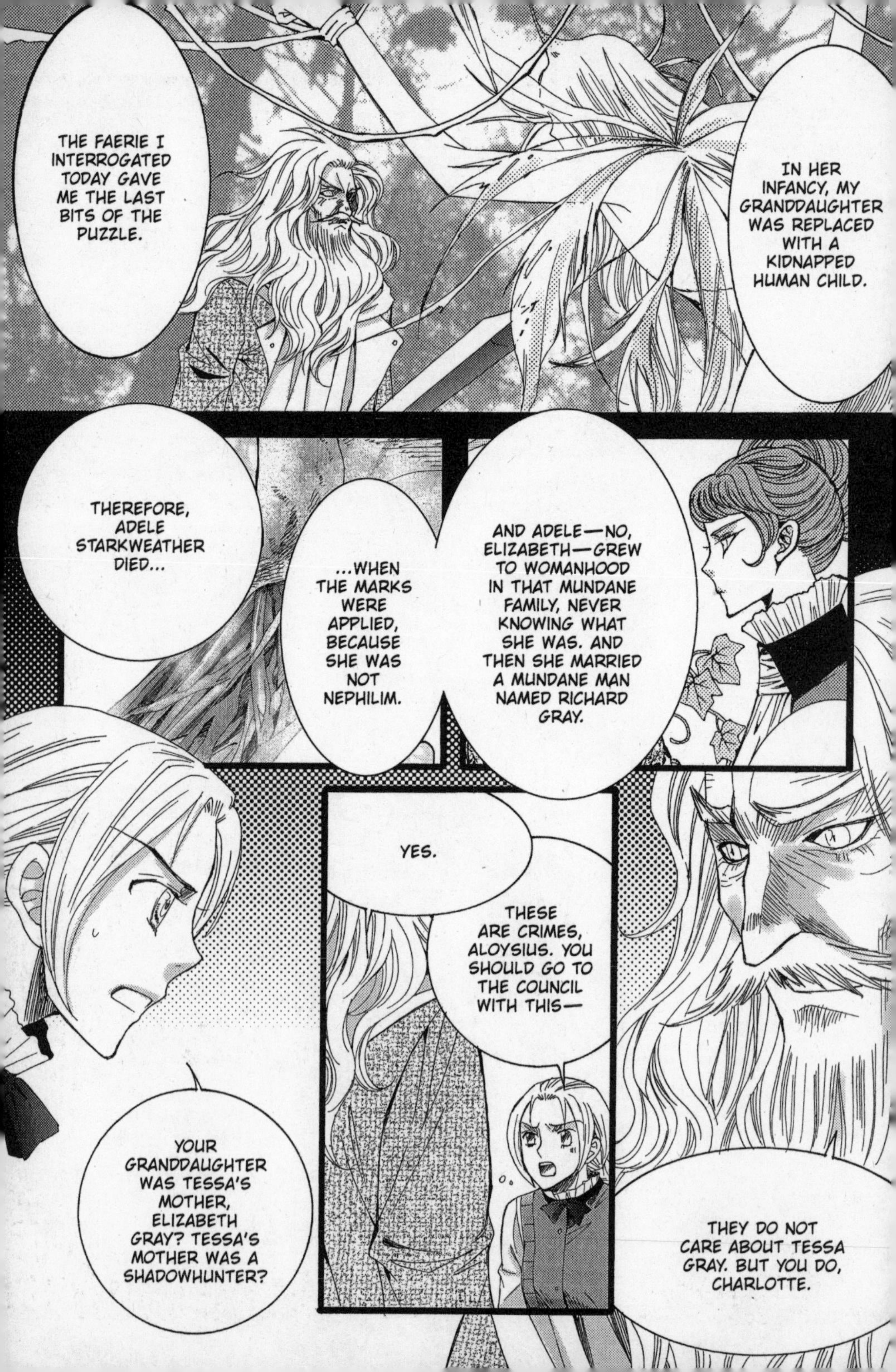
THE FAERIE I INTERROGATED TODAY GAVE ME THE LAST BITS OF THE PUZZLE.
IN HER INFANCY, MY GRANDDAUGHTER WAS REPLACED WITH A KIDNAPPED HUMAN CHILD.
THEREFORE, ADELE STARKWEATHER DIED...
...WHEN THE MARKS WERE APPLIED, BECAUSE SHE WAS NOT NEPHILIM.
AND ADELE—NO, ELIZABETH—GREW TO WOMANHOOD IN THAT MUNDANE FAMILY, NEVER KNOWING WHAT SHE WAS. AND THEN SHE MARRIED A MUNDANE MAN NAMED RICHARD GRAY.
YOUR GRANDDAUGHTER WAS TESSA'S MOTHER, ELIZABETH GRAY? TESSA'S MOTHER WAS A SHADOWHUNTER?
YES.
THESE ARE CRIMES, ALOYSIUS. YOU SHOULD GO TO THE COUNCIL WITH THIS—
THEY DO NOT CARE ABOUT TESSA GRAY. BUT YOU DO, CHARLOTTE.

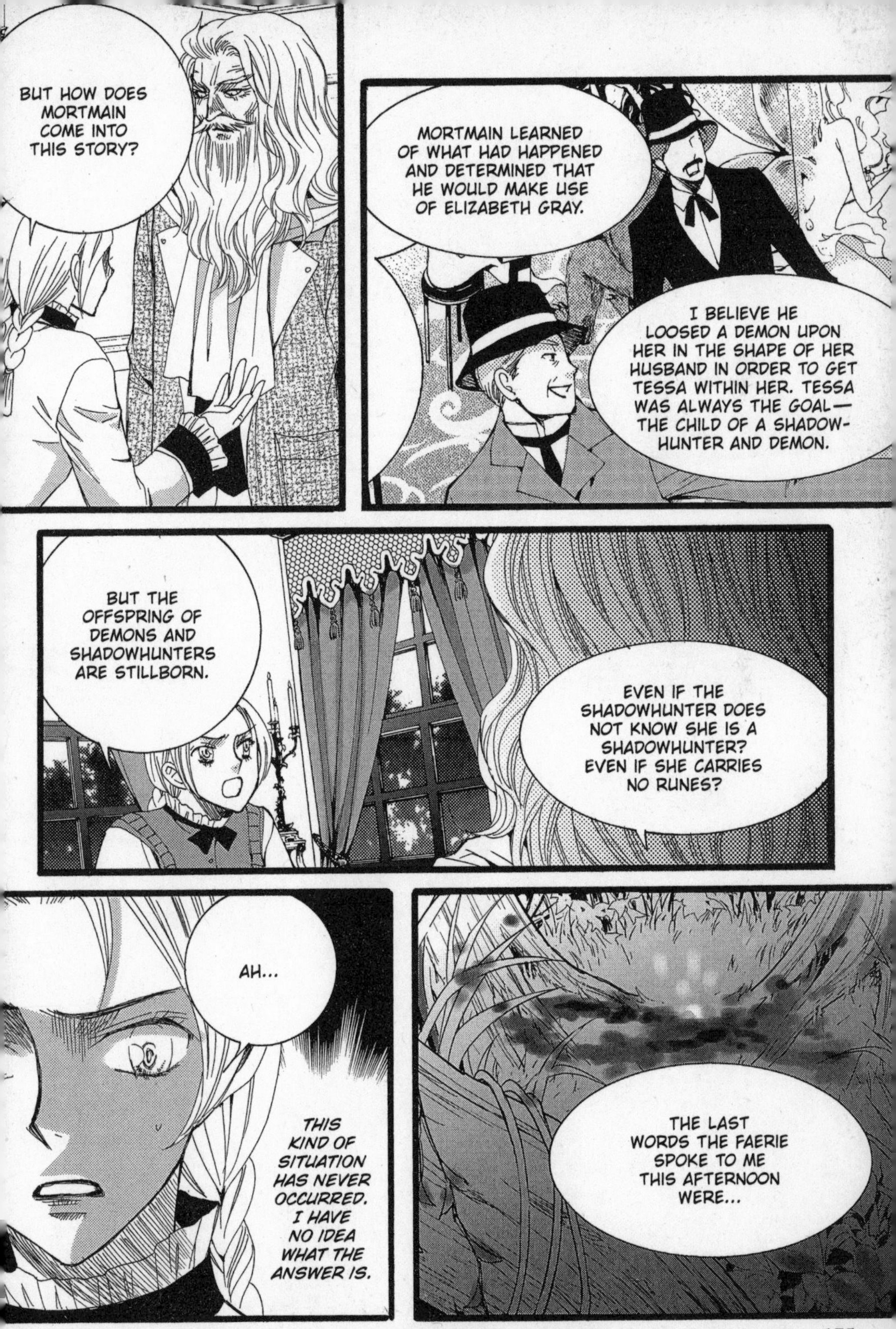

BUT HOW DOES MORTMAIN COME INTO THIS STORY?
MORTMAIN LEARNED OF WHAT HAD HAPPENED AND DETERMINED THAT HE WOULD MAKE USE OF ELIZABETH GRAY.
I BELIEVE HE LOOSED A DEMON UPON HER IN THE SHAPE OF HER HUSBAND IN ORDER TO GET TESSA WITHIN HER. TESSA WAS ALWAYS THE GOAL— THE CHILD OF A SHADOW-HUNTER AND DEMON.
BUT THE OFFSPRING OF DEMONS AND SHADOWHUNTERS ARE STILLBORN.
EVEN IF THE SHADOWHUNTER DOES NOT KNOW SHE IS A SHADOWHUNTER? EVEN IF SHE CARRIES NO RUNES?
AH...
THIS KIND OF SITUATION HAS NEVER OCCURRED. I HAVE NO IDEA WHAT THE ANSWER IS.
THE LAST WORDS THE FAERIE SPOKE TO ME THIS AFTERNOON WERE...

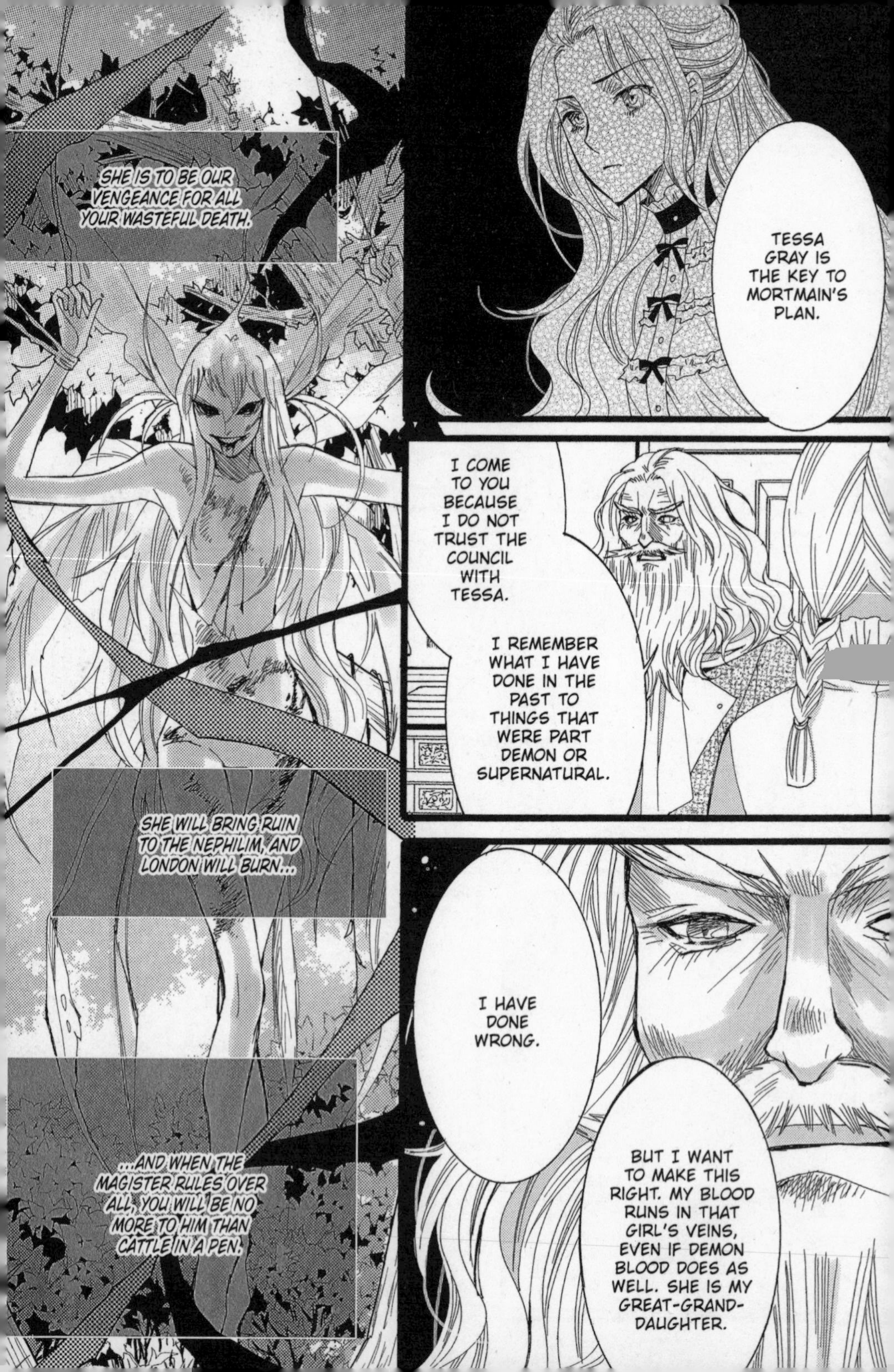
SHE IS TO BE OUR VENGEANCE FOR ALL YOUR WASTEFUL DEATH.
SHE WILL BRING RUIN TO THE NEPHILIM, AND LONDON WILL BURN...
...AND WHEN THE MAGISTER RULES OVER ALL, YOU WILL BE NO MORE TO HIM THAN CATTLE IN A PEN.
TESSA GRAY IS THE KEY TO MORTMAIN'S PLAN.
I COME TO YOU BECAUSE I DO NOT TRUST THE COUNCIL WITH TESSA.
I REMEMBER WHAT I HAVE DONE IN THE PAST TO THINGS THAT WERE PART DEMON OR SUPERNATURAL.
I HAVE DONE WRONG.
BUT I WANT TO MAKE THIS RIGHT. MY BLOOD RUNS IN THAT GIRL'S VEINS, EVEN IF DEMON BLOOD DOES AS WELL. SHE IS MY GREAT-GRAND-DAUGHTER.

I ASK ONLY ONE THING OF YOU, CHARLOTTE.

WHEN YOU FIND TESSA GRAY, AND YOU WILL FIND HER, TELL HER SHE IS WELCOME TO THE NAME OF STARKWEATHER.

To: Consul Josiah Wayland
From: Gabriel Lightwood

Most Honored Consul,
I write to you today at last with the news that you requested of me. I had expected it to come from Idris, but as chance would have it, it's source is much closer to home. Today Aloysius Starkweather, head of the York Institute, came to call upon Mrs. Branwell.
He is an old man gone mad with grief, and as such, he has created an elaborate set of fabrications with which he explains to himself his great loss. He is certainly to be pitied, but not to be taken seriously, nor should he explains the policy of the Council rest upon the words of the untrustworthy and the mad.
I regret to report this, but they spoke together of both Council and Consul with great disrespect.
It is clear that Mrs. Branwell resents what she sees as unnecessary interference in her plans.
She met Mr. Starkweather's wild claims, such as that Mortmain has bred demons and Shadowhunters together, a clear impossibility, with sheer credulousness. It appears that you were correct, and she is far too headstrong and easily influenced to head an Institute properly.
Though Mrs. Branwell exhorts you to send a force of Shadowhunters to Cadair Idris, anyone who takes the opinions of madmen and hysterics the cornerstone of their policies lacks the objectivity necessary, I shall swear by the Mortal Sword that all this is true.
Yours in Raziel's name,
Gabriel Lightwood

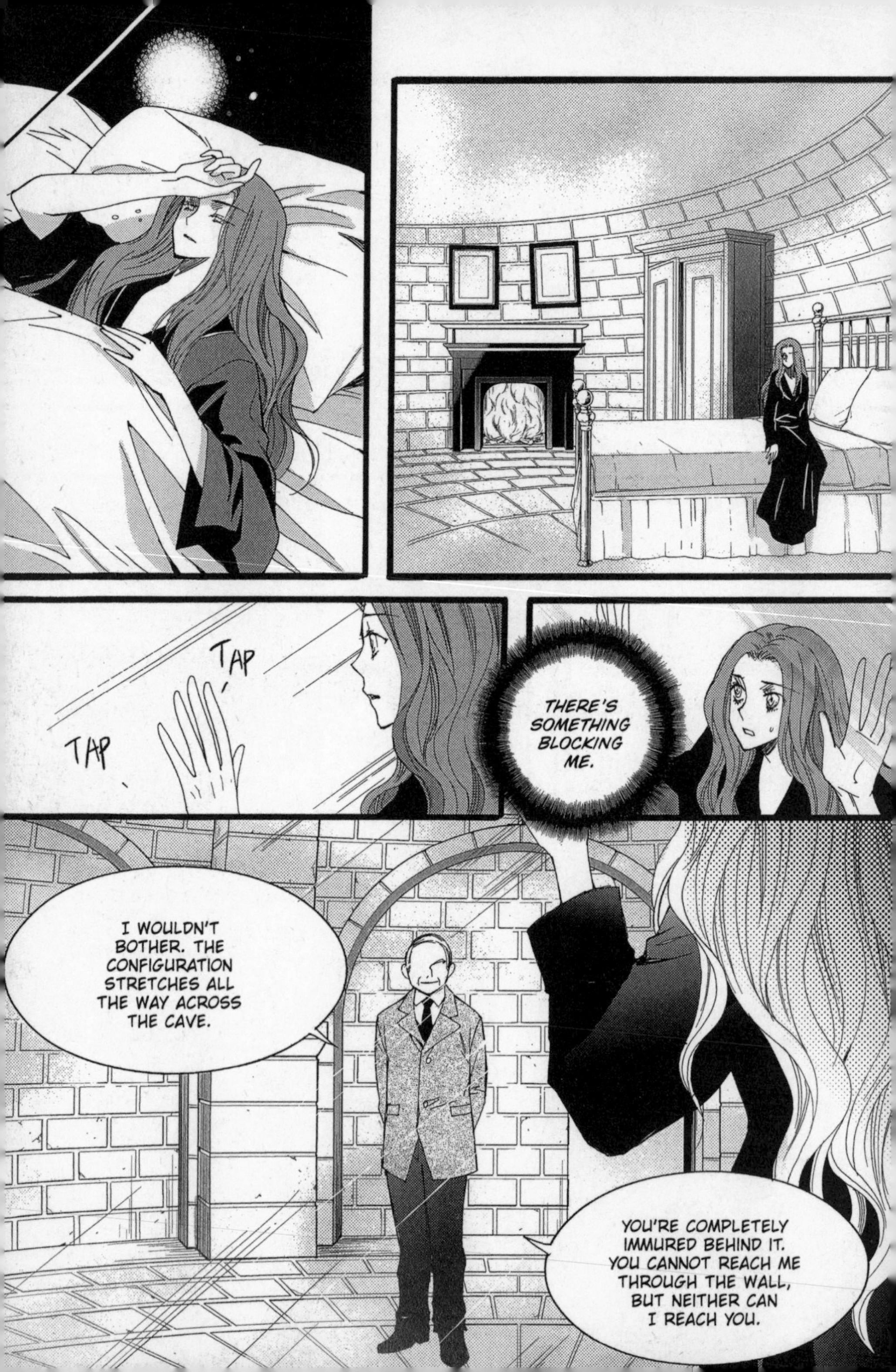
TAP
TAP
THERE'S SOMETHING BLOCKING ME.
I WOULDN'T BOTHER. THE CONFIGURATION STRETCHES ALL THE WAY ACROSS THE CAVE.
YOU'RE COMPLETELY IMMURED BEHIND IT. YOU CANNOT REACH ME THROUGH THE WALL, BUT NEITHER CAN I REACH YOU.

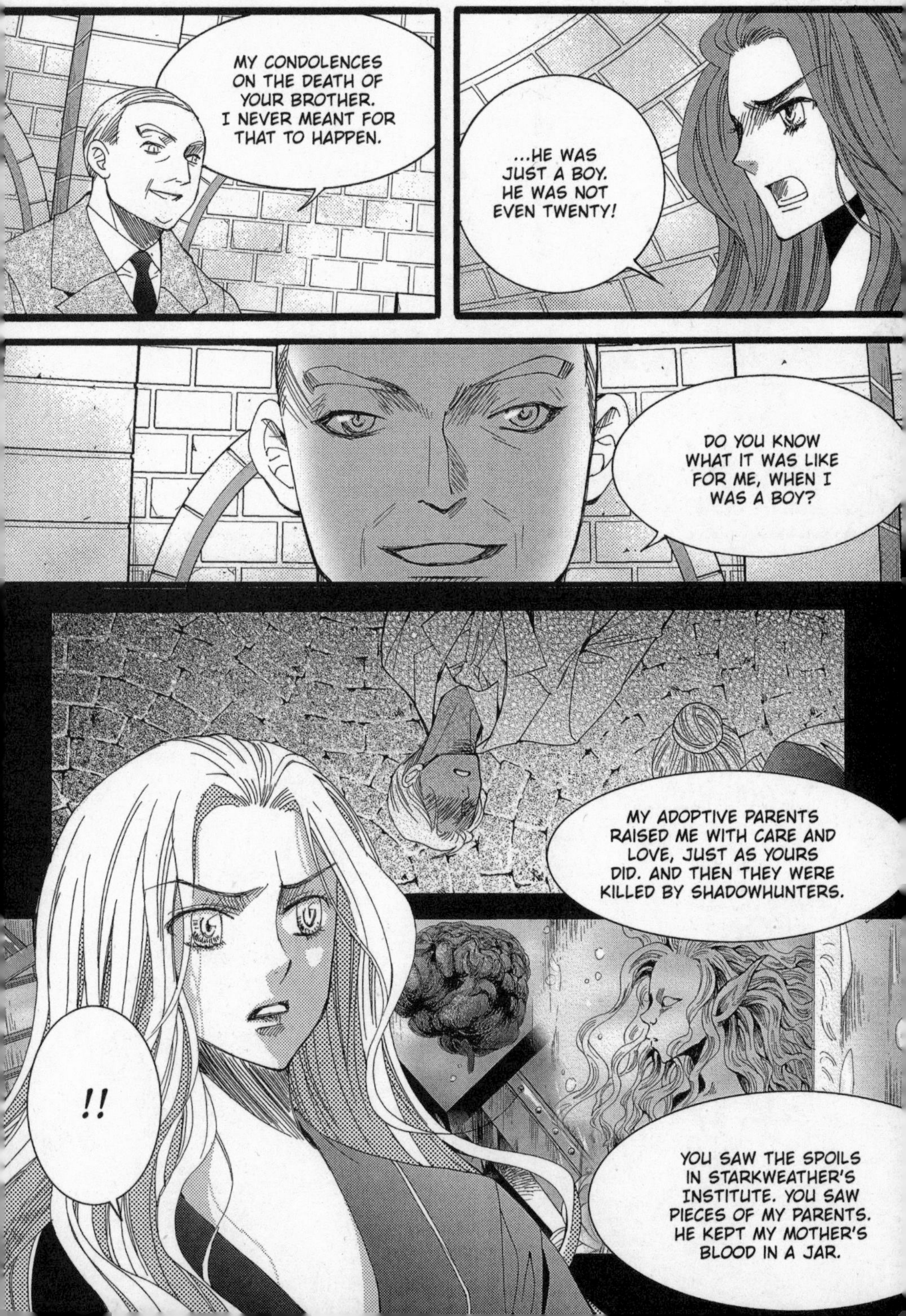
MY CONDOLENCES ON THE DEATH OF YOUR BROTHER. I NEVER MEANT FOR THAT TO HAPPEN.
...HE WAS JUST A BOY. HE WAS NOT EVEN TWENTY!
DO YOU KNOW WHAT IT WAS LIKE FOR ME, WHEN I WAS A BOY?
MY ADOPTIVE PARENTS RAISED ME WITH CARE AND LOVE, JUST AS YOURS DID. AND THEN THEY WERE KILLED BY SHADOWHUNTERS.
!!
YOU SAW THE SPOILS IN STARKWEATHER'S INSTITUTE. YOU SAW PIECES OF MY PARENTS. HE KEPT MY MOTHER'S BLOOD IN A JAR.

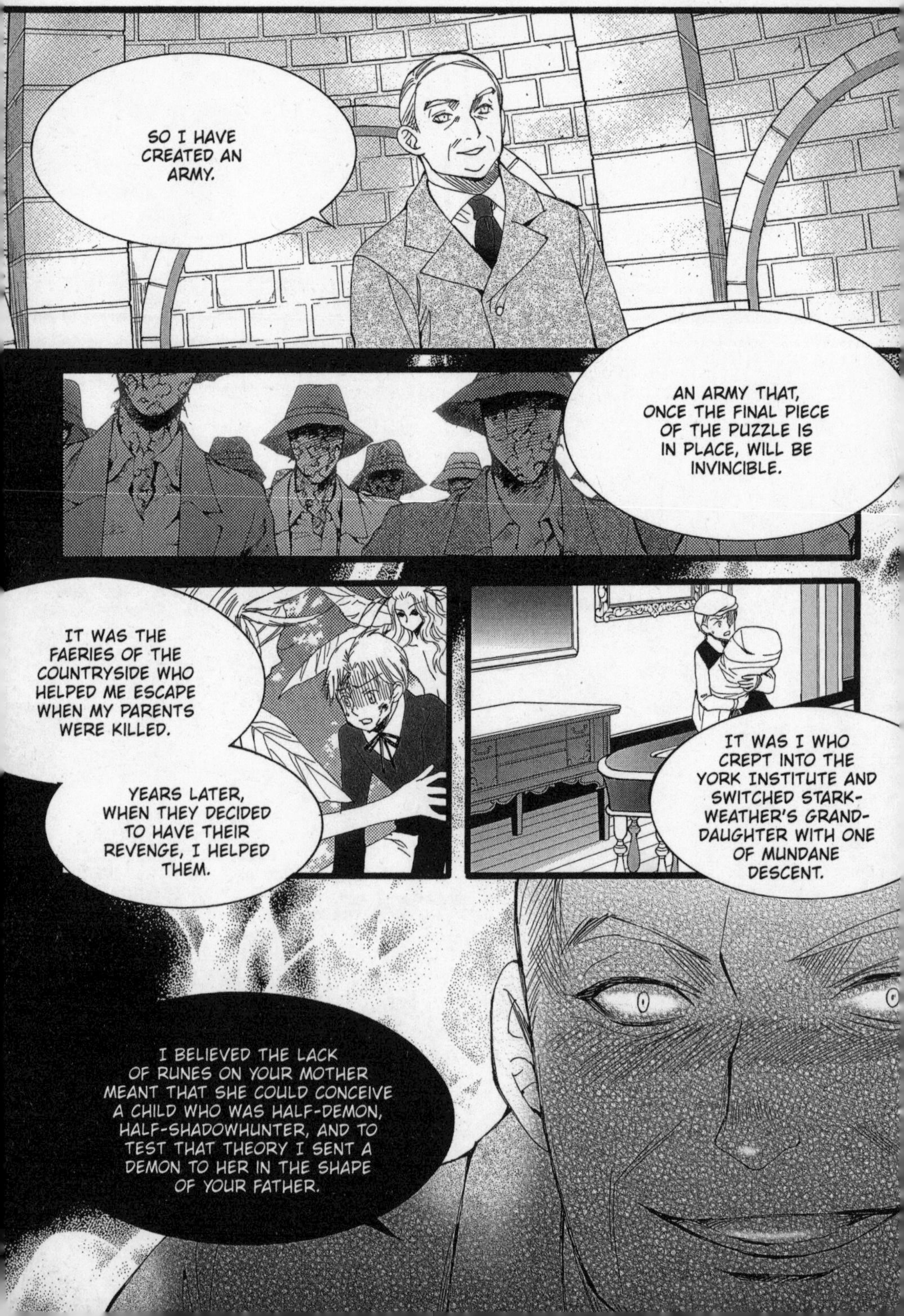
SO I HAVE CREATED AN ARMY.
AN ARMY THAT, ONCE THE FINAL PIECE OF THE PUZZLE IS IN PLACE, WILL BE INVINCIBLE.
IT WAS THE FAERIES OF THE COUNTRYSIDE WHO HELPED ME ESCAPE WHEN MY PARENTS WERE KILLED.
YEARS LATER, WHEN THEY DECIDED TO HAVE THEIR REVENGE, I HELPED THEM.
IT WAS I WHO CREPT INTO THE YORK INSTITUTE AND SWITCHED STARK-WEATHER'S GRAND-DAUGHTER WITH ONE OF MUNDANE DESCENT.
I BELIEVED THE LACK OF RUNES ON YOUR MOTHER MEANT THAT SHE COULD CONCEIVE A CHILD WHO WAS HALF-DEMON, HALF-SHADOWHUNTER, AND TO TEST THAT THEORY I SENT A DEMON TO HER IN THE SHAPE OF YOUR FATHER.

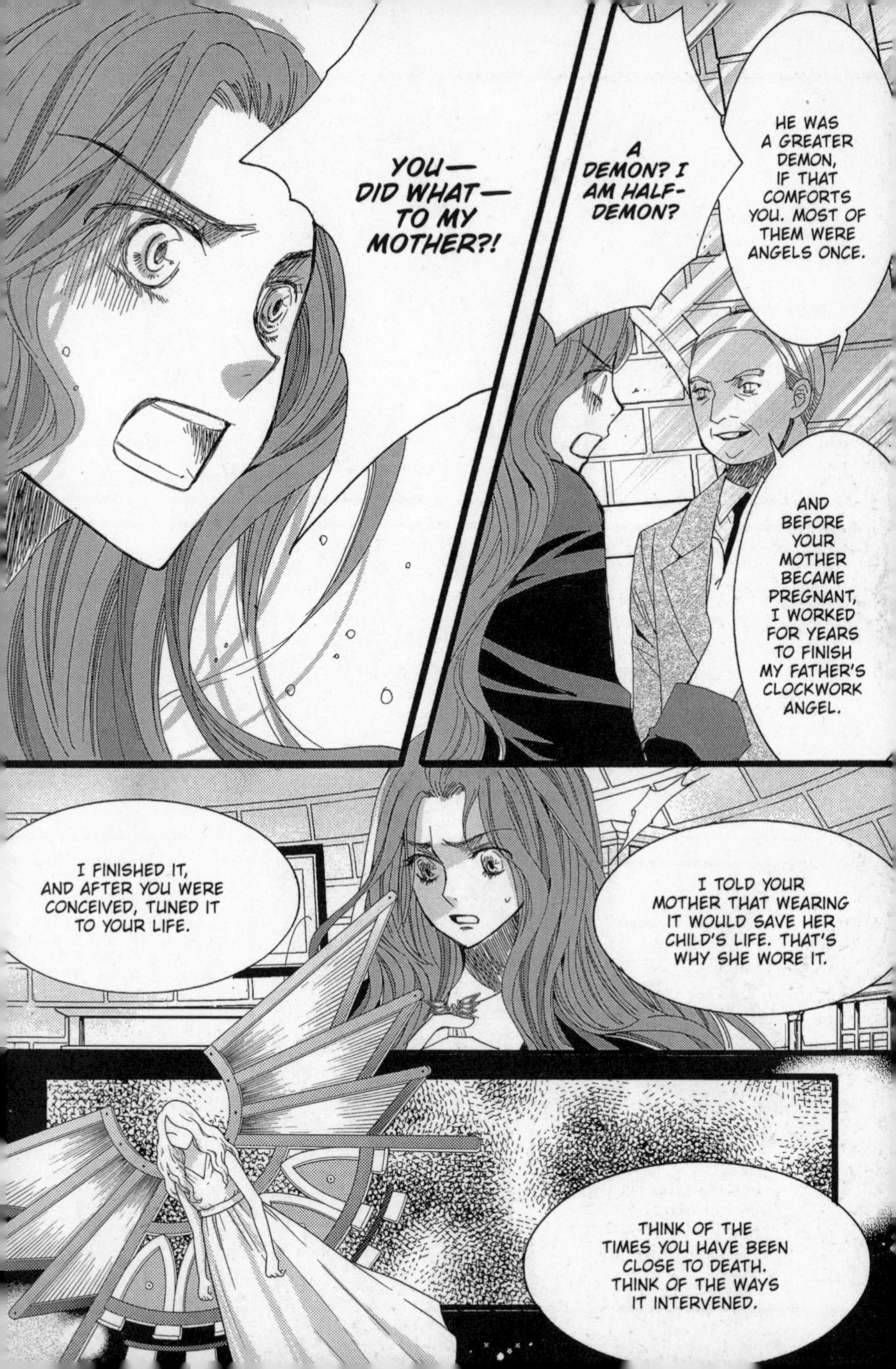
YOU—
DID WHAT—
TO MY
MOTHER?!
A
DEMON? I
AM HALF-
DEMON?
HE WAS A GREATER DEMON, IF THAT COMFORTS YOU. MOST OF THEM WERE ANGELS ONCE.
AND BEFORE YOUR MOTHER BECAME PREGNANT, I WORKED FOR YEARS TO FINISH MY FATHER'S CLOCKWORK ANGEL.
I FINISHED IT, AND AFTER YOU WERE CONCEIVED, TUNED IT TO YOUR LIFE.
I TOLD YOUR MOTHER THAT WEARING IT WOULD SAVE HER CHILD'S LIFE. THAT'S WHY SHE WORE IT.
THINK OF THE TIMES YOU HAVE BEEN CLOSE TO DEATH. THINK OF THE WAYS IT INTERVENED.

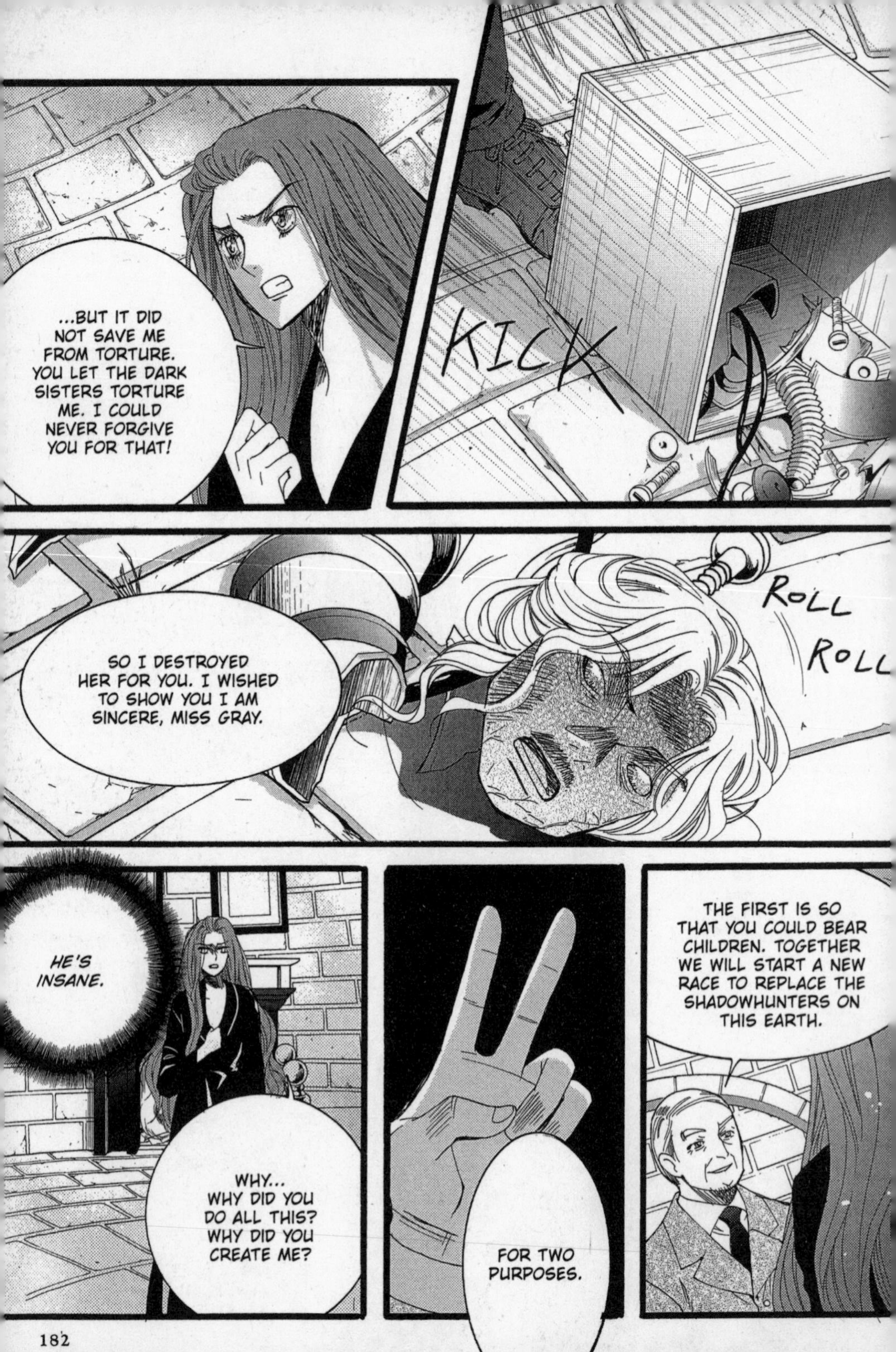
...BUT IT DID NOT SAVE ME FROM TORTURE. YOU LET THE DARK SISTERS TORTURE ME. I COULD NEVER FORGIVE YOU FOR THAT!
KICK
SO I DESTROYED HER FOR YOU. I WISHED TO SHOW YOU I AM SINCERE, MISS GRAY.
ROLL ROLL
HE'S INSANE.
WHY... WHY DID YOU DO ALL THIS? WHY DID YOU CREATE ME?
FOR TWO PURPOSES.
THE FIRST IS SO THAT YOU COULD BEAR CHILDREN. TOGETHER WE WILL START A NEW RACE TO REPLACE THE SHADOWHUNTERS ON THIS EARTH.

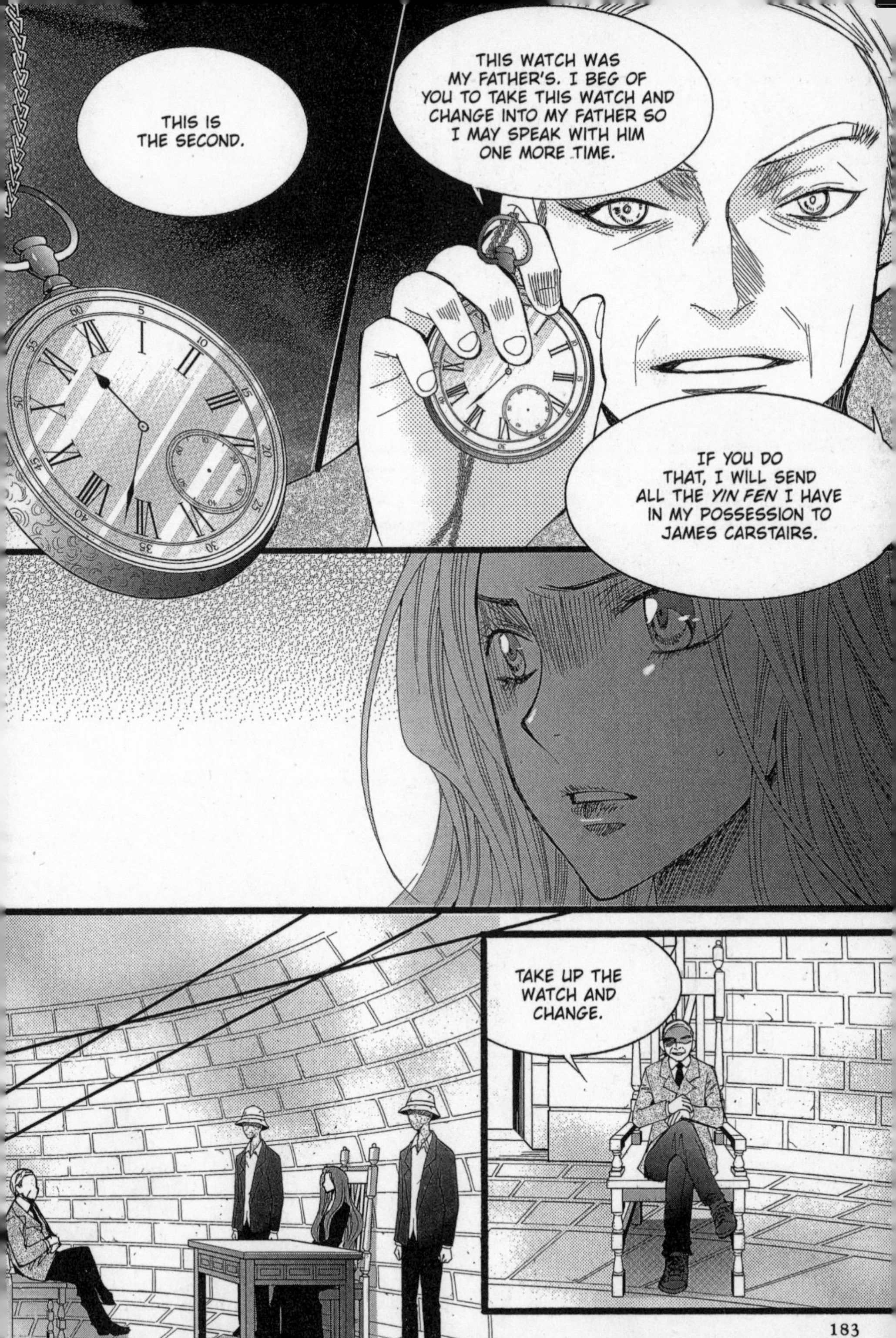
THIS IS
THE SECOND.
THIS WATCH WAS MY FATHER'S. I BEG OF YOU TO TAKE THIS WATCH AND CHANGE INTO MY FATHER SO I MAY SPEAK WITH HIM ONE MORE TIME.
IF YOU DO THAT, I WILL SEND ALL THE *YIN FEN* I HAVE IN MY POSSESSION TO JAMES CARSTAIRS.
TAKE UP THE WATCH AND CHANGE.

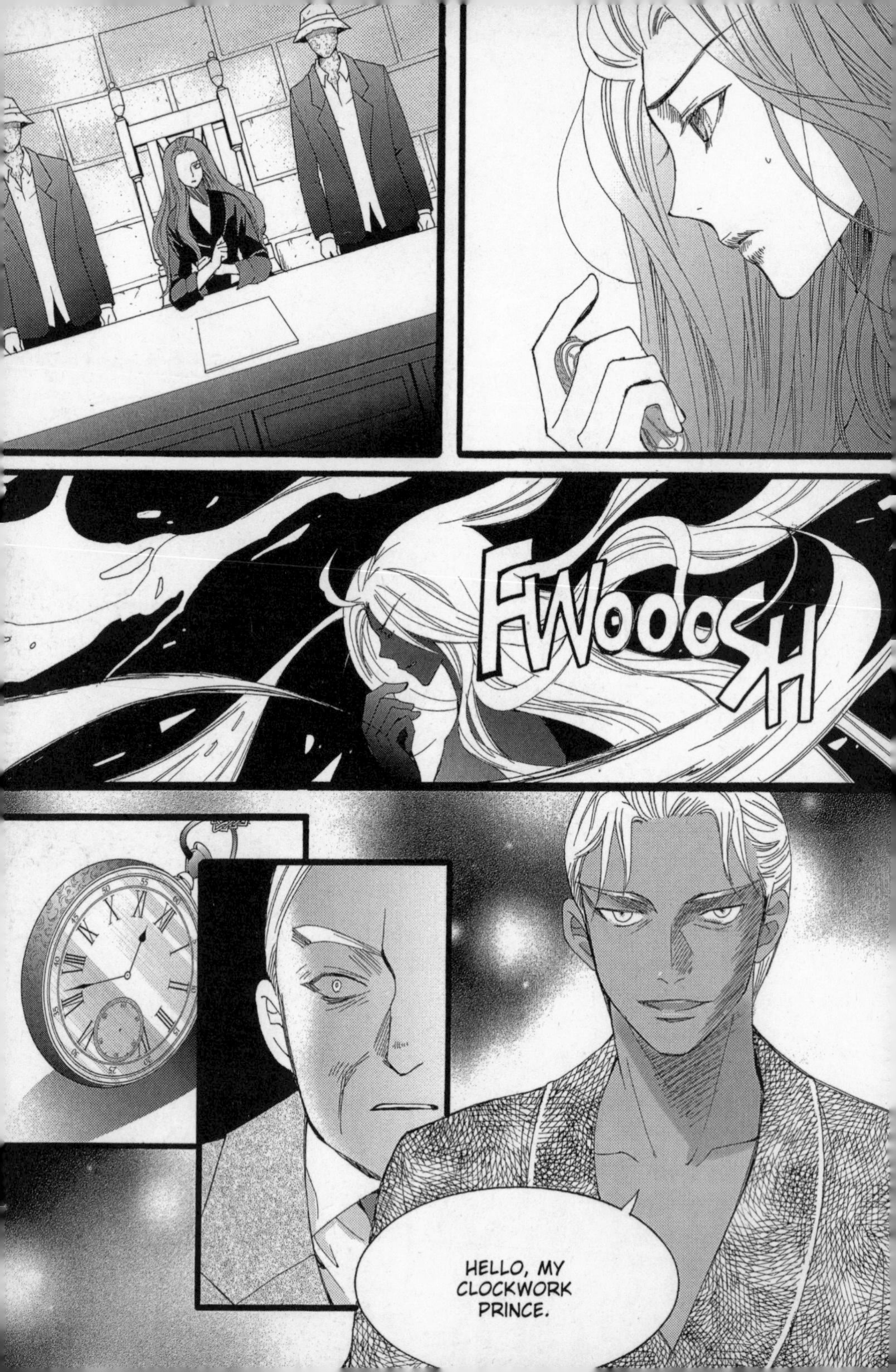
FWOOOSH
HELLO, MY CLOCKWORK PRINCE.

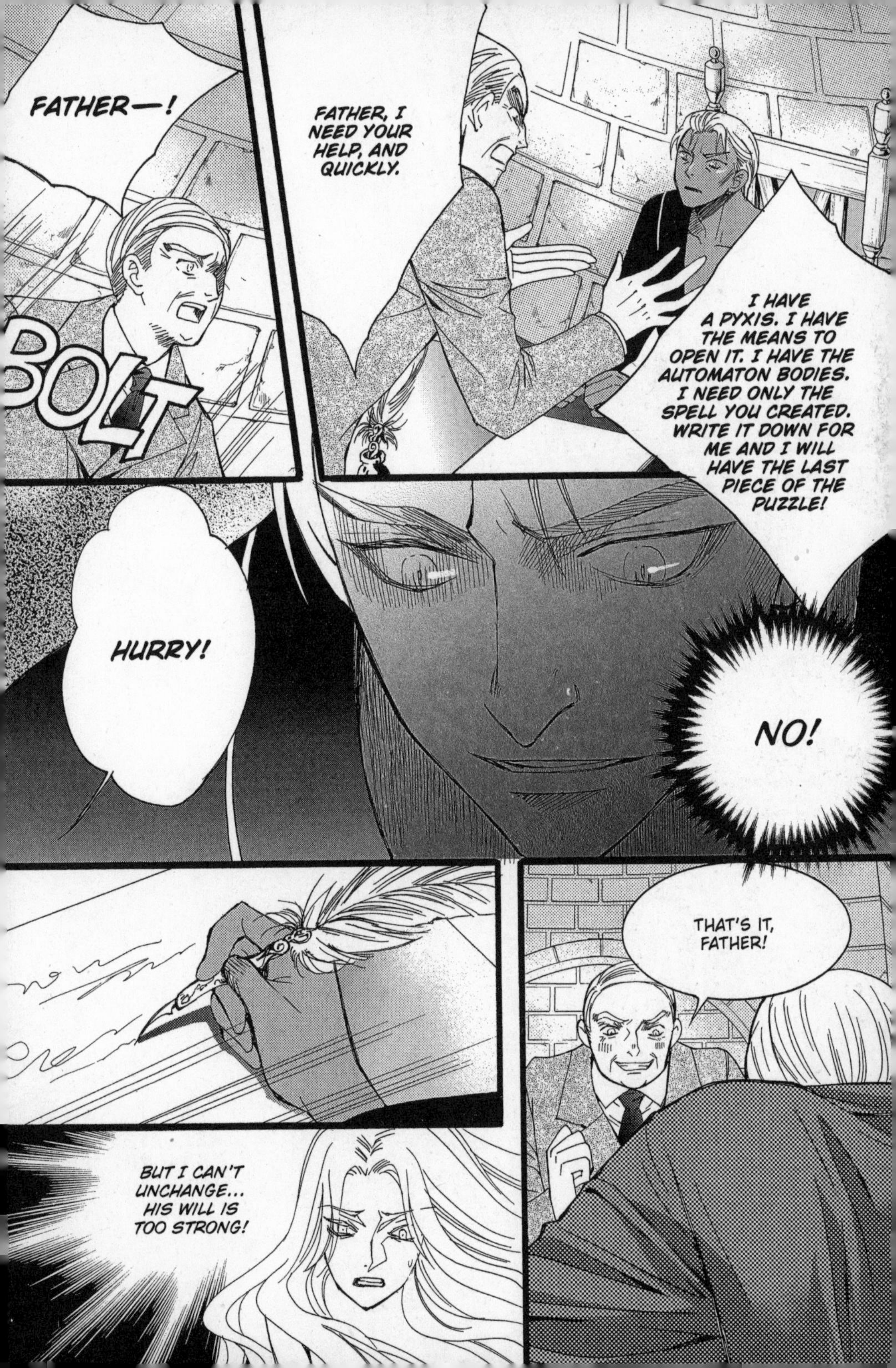
FATHER—!
BOLT
FATHER, I NEED YOUR HELP, AND QUICKLY.
I HAVE A PYXIS. I HAVE THE MEANS TO OPEN IT. I HAVE THE AUTOMATON BODIES. I NEED ONLY THE SPELL YOU CREATED. WRITE IT DOWN FOR ME AND I WILL HAVE THE LAST PIECE OF THE PUZZLE!
NO!
HURRY!
THAT'S IT, FATHER!
BUT I CAN'T UNCHANGE... HIS WILL IS TOO STRONG!

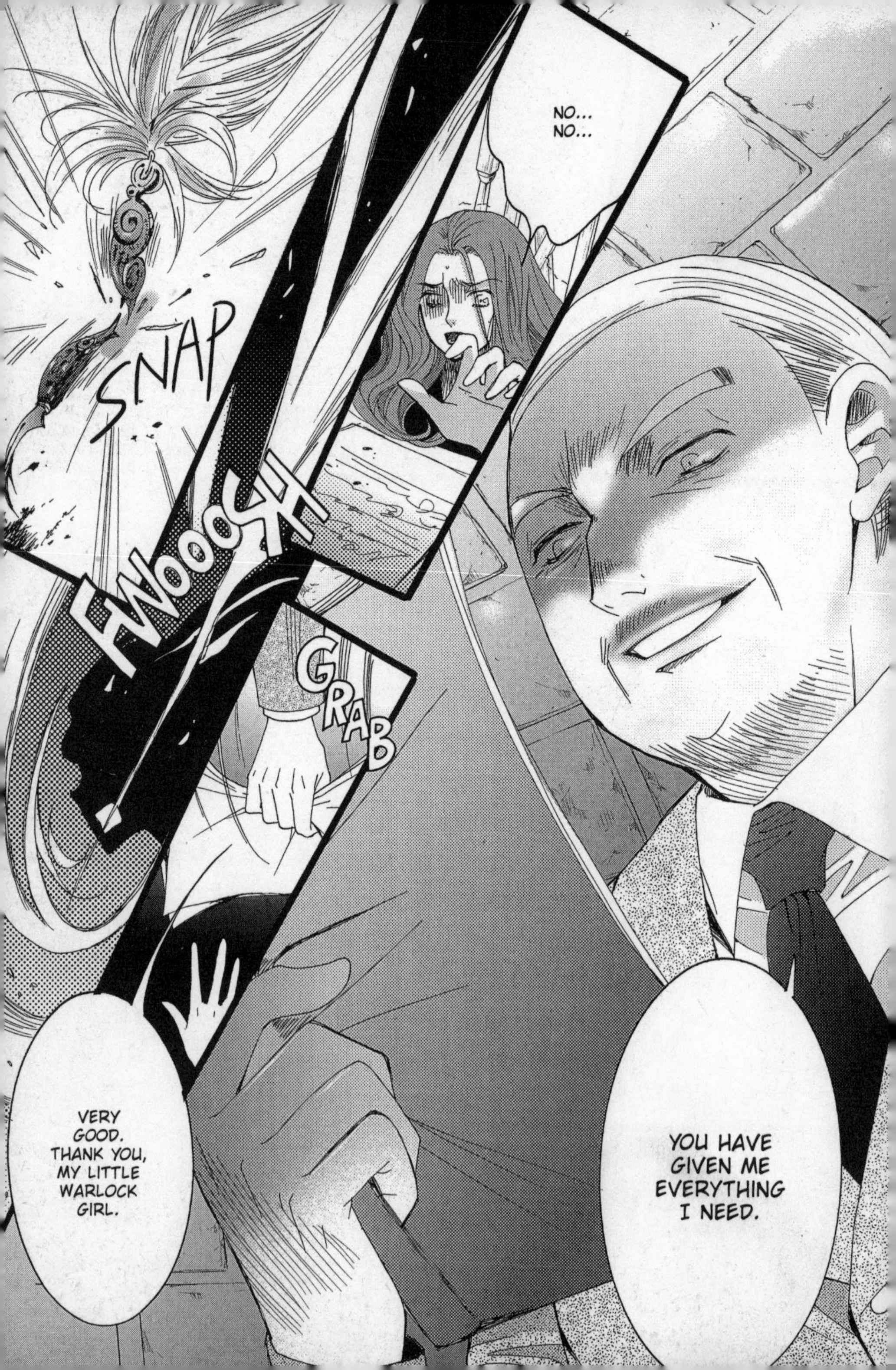
NO... NO...
SNAP
FWOOSH
GRAB
YOU HAVE GIVEN ME EVERYTHING I NEED.
VERY GOOD. THANK YOU, MY LITTLE WARLOCK GIRL.

CHAPTER 23

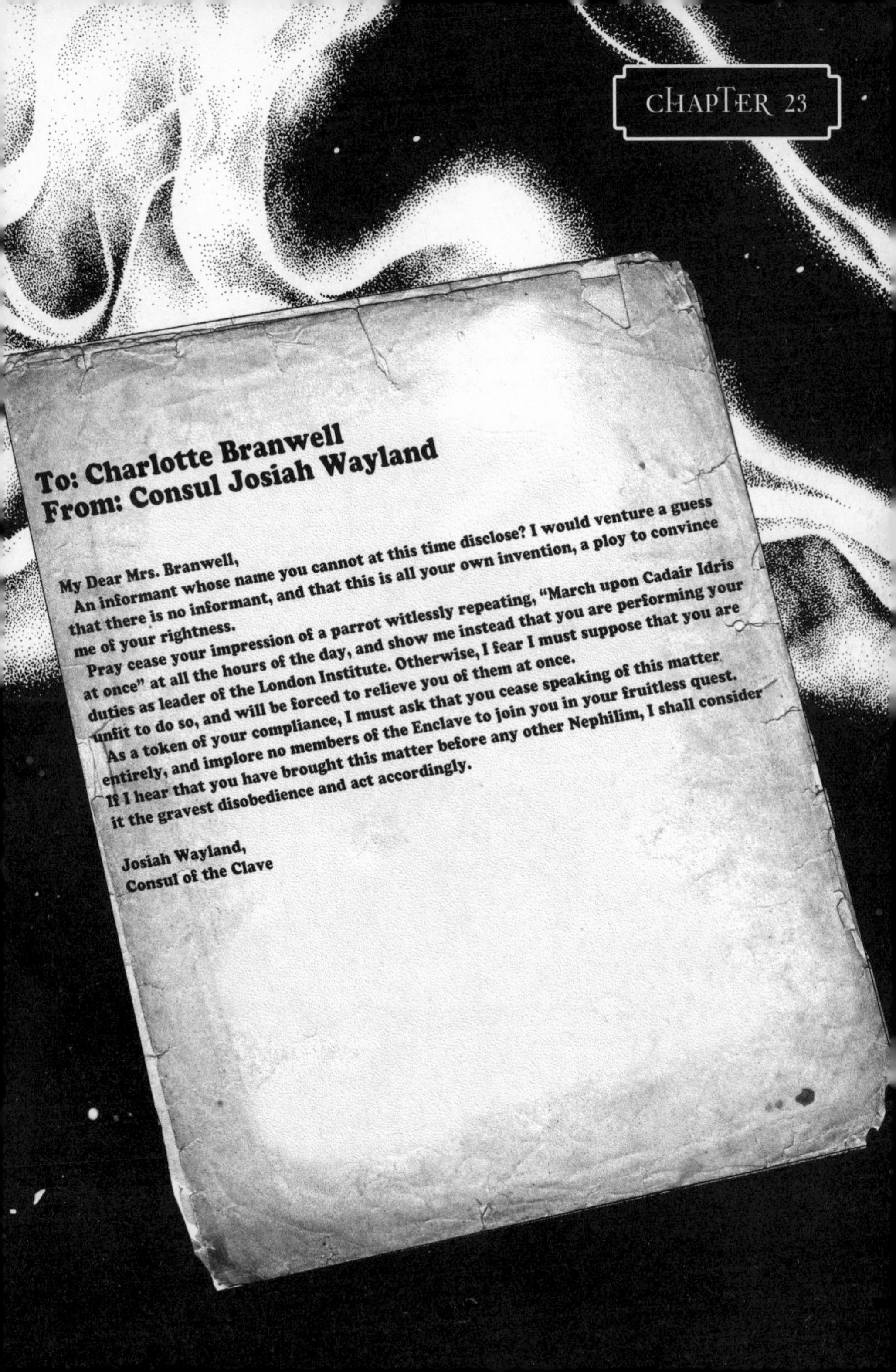

To: Charlotte Branwell
From: Consul Josiah Wayland

My Dear Mrs. Branwell,

An informant whose name you cannot at this time disclose? I would venture a guess that there is no informant, and that this is all your own invention, a ploy to convince me of your rightness.

Pray cease your impression of a parrot witlessly repeating, "March upon Cadair Idris at once" at all the hours of the day, and show me instead that you are performing your duties as leader of the London Institute. Otherwise, I fear I must suppose that you are unfit to do so, and will be forced to relieve you of them at once.

As a token of your compliance, I must ask that you cease speaking of this matter entirely, and implore no members of the Enclave to join you in your fruitless quest. If I hear that you have brought this matter before any other Nephilim, I shall consider it the gravest disobedience and act accordingly.

Josiah Wayland,
Consul of the Clave

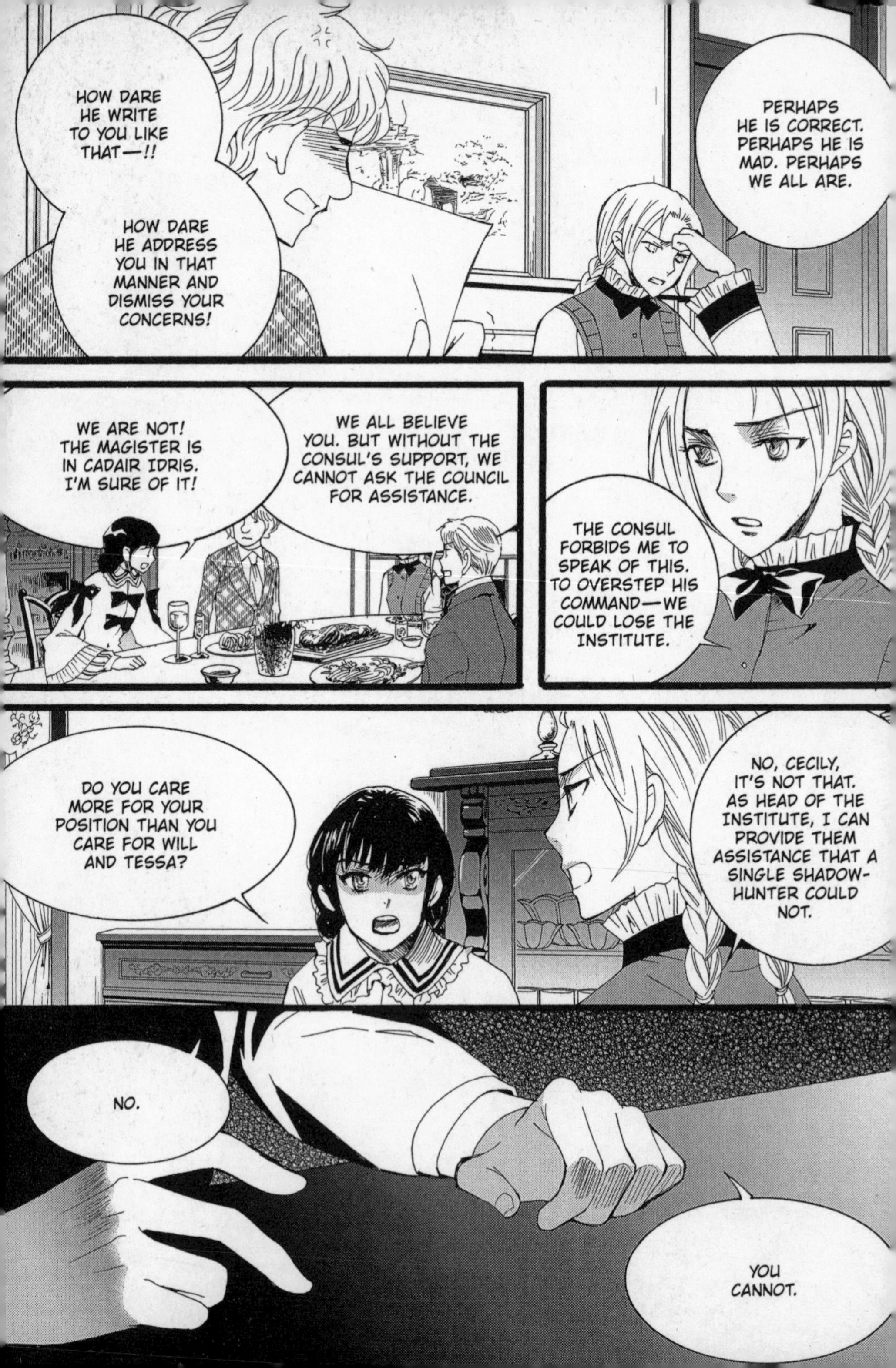
HOW DARE HE WRITE TO YOU LIKE THAT—!!
HOW DARE HE ADDRESS YOU IN THAT MANNER AND DISMISS YOUR CONCERNS!
PERHAPS HE IS CORRECT. PERHAPS HE IS MAD. PERHAPS WE ALL ARE.
WE ARE NOT! THE MAGISTER IS IN CADAIR IDRIS. I'M SURE OF IT!
WE ALL BELIEVE YOU. BUT WITHOUT THE CONSUL'S SUPPORT, WE CANNOT ASK THE COUNCIL FOR ASSISTANCE.
THE CONSUL FORBIDS ME TO SPEAK OF THIS. TO OVERSTEP HIS COMMAND—WE COULD LOSE THE INSTITUTE.
DO YOU CARE MORE FOR YOUR POSITION THAN YOU CARE FOR WILL AND TESSA?
NO, CECILY, IT'S NOT THAT. AS HEAD OF THE INSTITUTE, I CAN PROVIDE THEM ASSISTANCE THAT A SINGLE SHADOW-HUNTER COULD NOT.
NO.
YOU CANNOT.

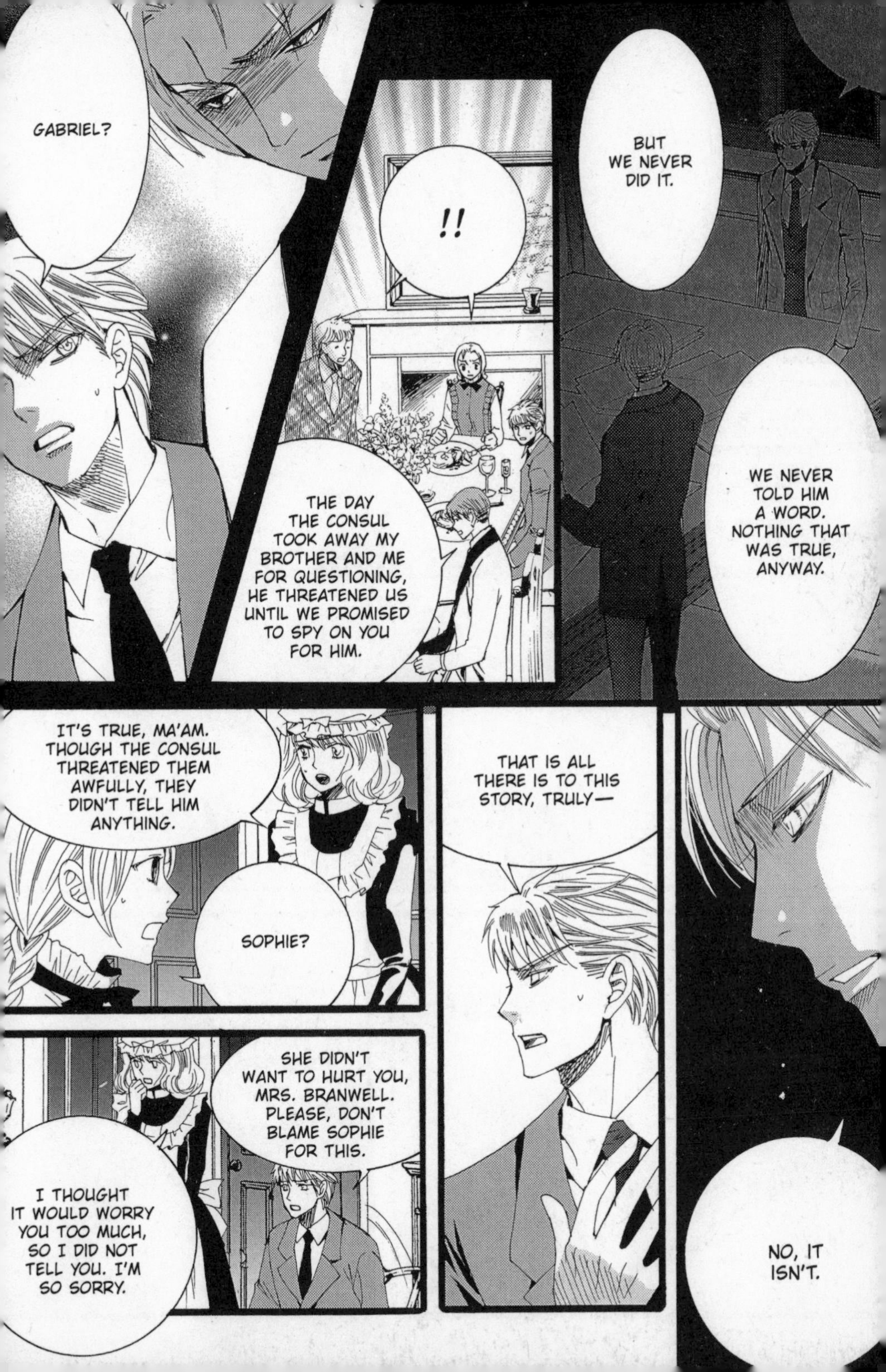
GABRIEL?
!!
THE DAY THE CONSUL TOOK AWAY MY BROTHER AND ME FOR QUESTIONING, HE THREATENED US UNTIL WE PROMISED TO SPY ON YOU FOR HIM.
BUT WE NEVER DID IT.
WE NEVER TOLD HIM A WORD. NOTHING THAT WAS TRUE, ANYWAY.
IT'S TRUE, MA'AM. THOUGH THE CONSUL THREATENED THEM AWFULLY, THEY DIDN'T TELL HIM ANYTHING.
SOPHIE?
I THOUGHT IT WOULD WORRY YOU TOO MUCH, SO I DID NOT TELL YOU. I'M SO SORRY.
SHE DIDN'T WANT TO HURT YOU, MRS. BRANWELL. PLEASE, DON'T BLAME SOPHIE FOR THIS.
THAT IS ALL THERE IS TO THIS STORY, TRULY—
NO, IT ISN'T.

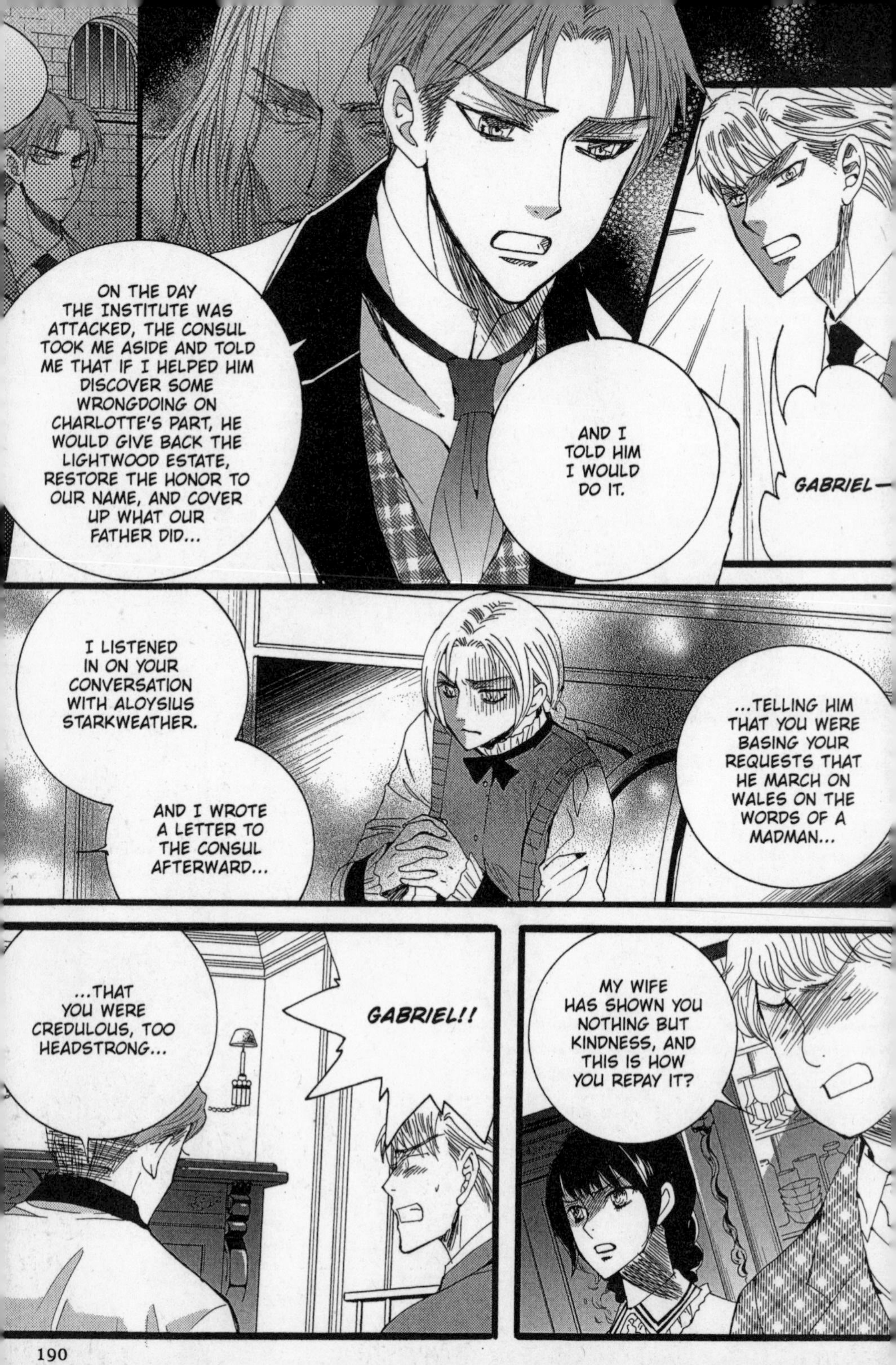
ON THE DAY THE INSTITUTE WAS ATTACKED, THE CONSUL TOOK ME ASIDE AND TOLD ME THAT IF I HELPED HIM DISCOVER SOME WRONGDOING ON CHARLOTTE'S PART, HE WOULD GIVE BACK THE LIGHTWOOD ESTATE, RESTORE THE HONOR TO OUR NAME, AND COVER UP WHAT OUR FATHER DID...
AND I TOLD HIM I WOULD DO IT.
GABRIEL—
I LISTENED IN ON YOUR CONVERSATION WITH ALOYSIUS STARKWEATHER.
AND I WROTE A LETTER TO THE CONSUL AFTERWARD...
...TELLING HIM THAT YOU WERE BASING YOUR REQUESTS THAT HE MARCH ON WALES ON THE WORDS OF A MADMAN...
...THAT YOU WERE CREDULOUS, TOO HEADSTRONG...
GABRIEL!!
MY WIFE HAS SHOWN YOU NOTHING BUT KINDNESS, AND THIS IS HOW YOU REPAY IT?

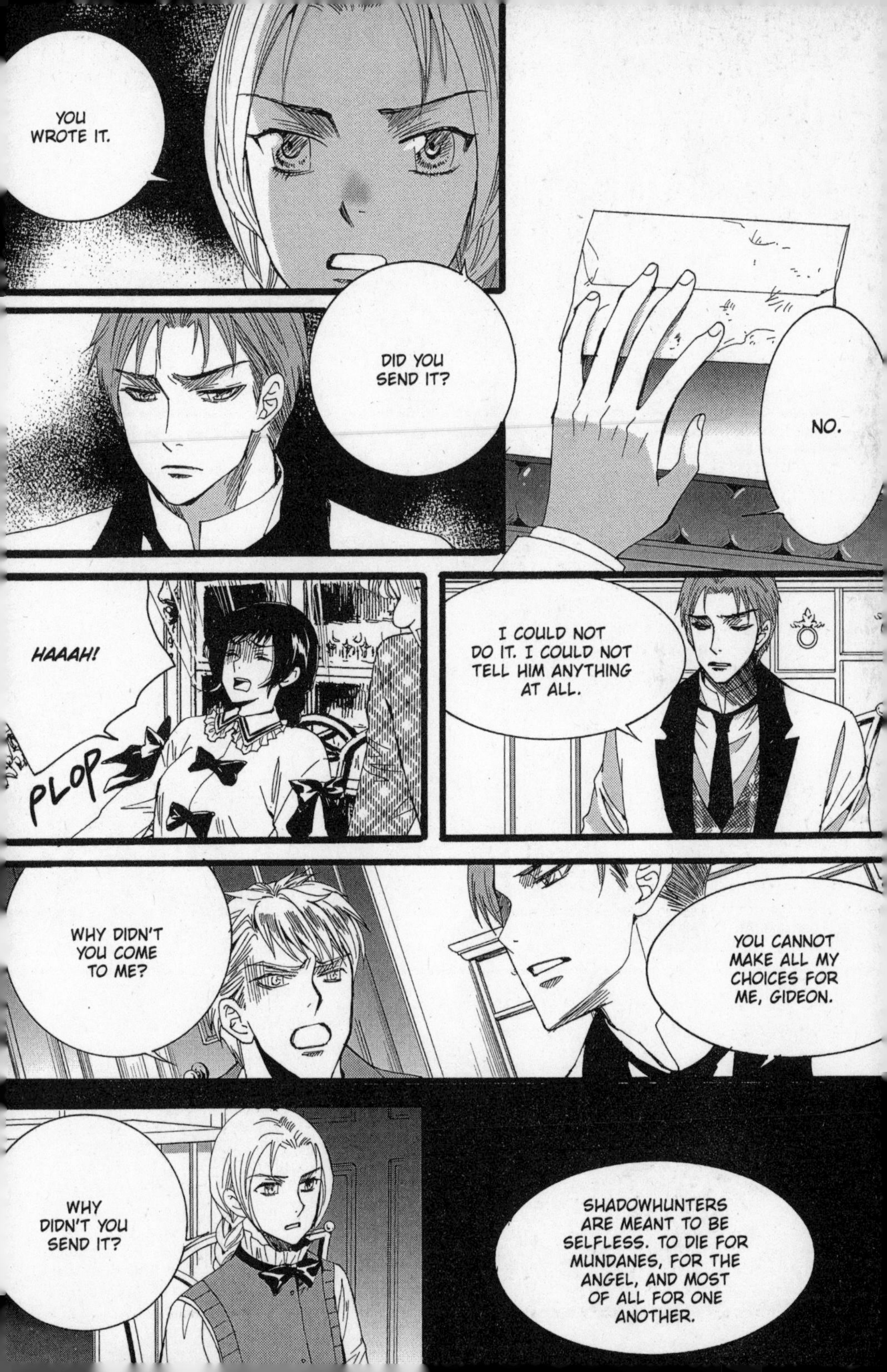
YOU WROTE IT.
DID YOU SEND IT?
NO.
HAAAH!
PLOP
I COULD NOT DO IT. I COULD NOT TELL HIM ANYTHING AT ALL.
WHY DIDN'T YOU COME TO ME?
YOU CANNOT MAKE ALL MY CHOICES FOR ME, GIDEON.
WHY DIDN'T YOU SEND IT?
SHADOWHUNTERS ARE MEANT TO BE SELFLESS. TO DIE FOR MUNDANES, FOR THE ANGEL, AND MOST OF ALL FOR ONE ANOTHER.

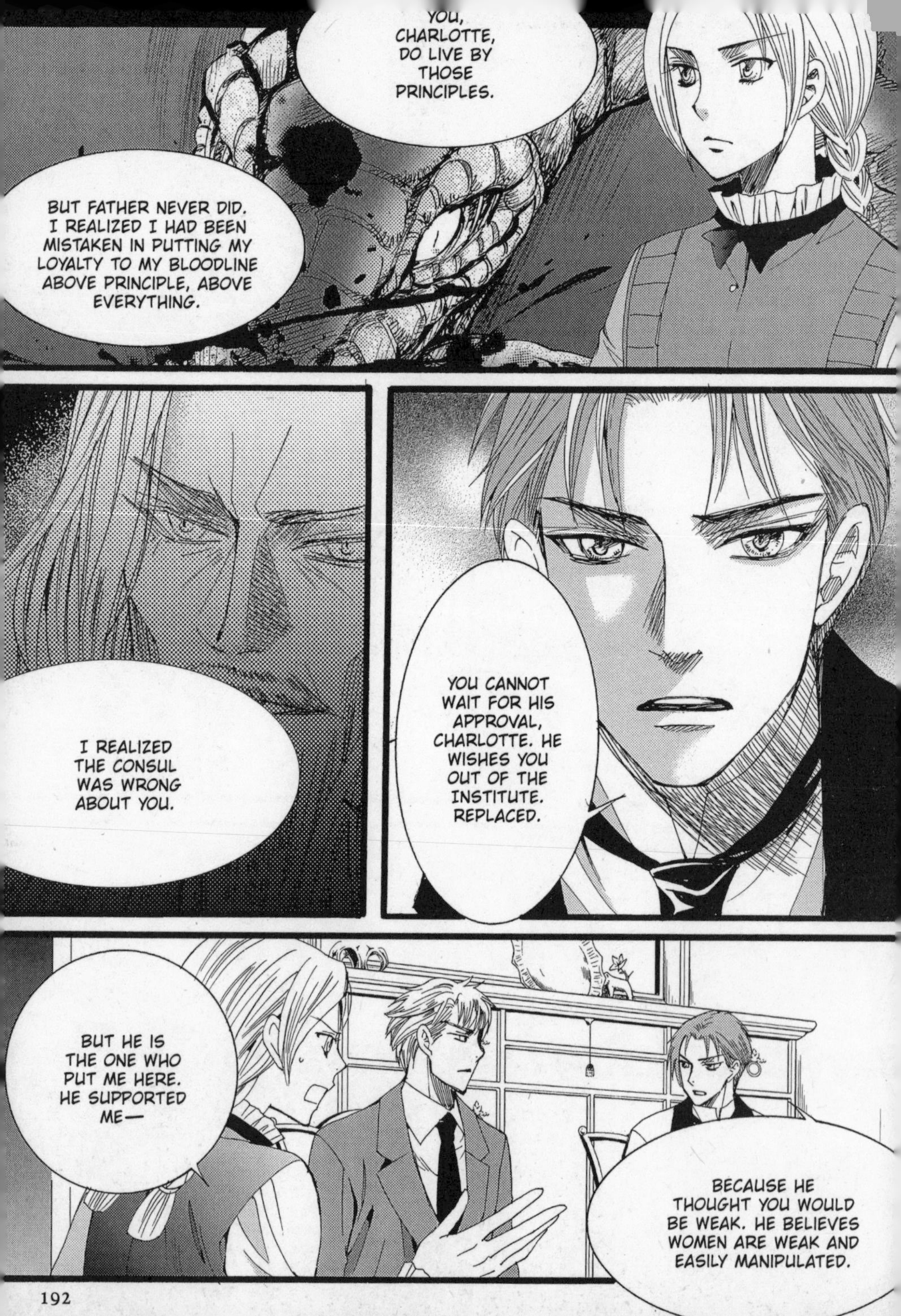
YOU, CHARLOTTE, DO LIVE BY THOSE PRINCIPLES.
BUT FATHER NEVER DID. I REALIZED I HAD BEEN MISTAKEN IN PUTTING MY LOYALTY TO MY BLOODLINE ABOVE PRINCIPLE, ABOVE EVERYTHING.
YOU CANNOT WAIT FOR HIS APPROVAL, CHARLOTTE. HE WISHES YOU OUT OF THE INSTITUTE. REPLACED.
I REALIZED THE CONSUL WAS WRONG ABOUT YOU.
BUT HE IS THE ONE WHO PUT ME HERE. HE SUPPORTED ME—
BECAUSE HE THOUGHT YOU WOULD BE WEAK. HE BELIEVES WOMEN ARE WEAK AND EASILY MANIPULATED.

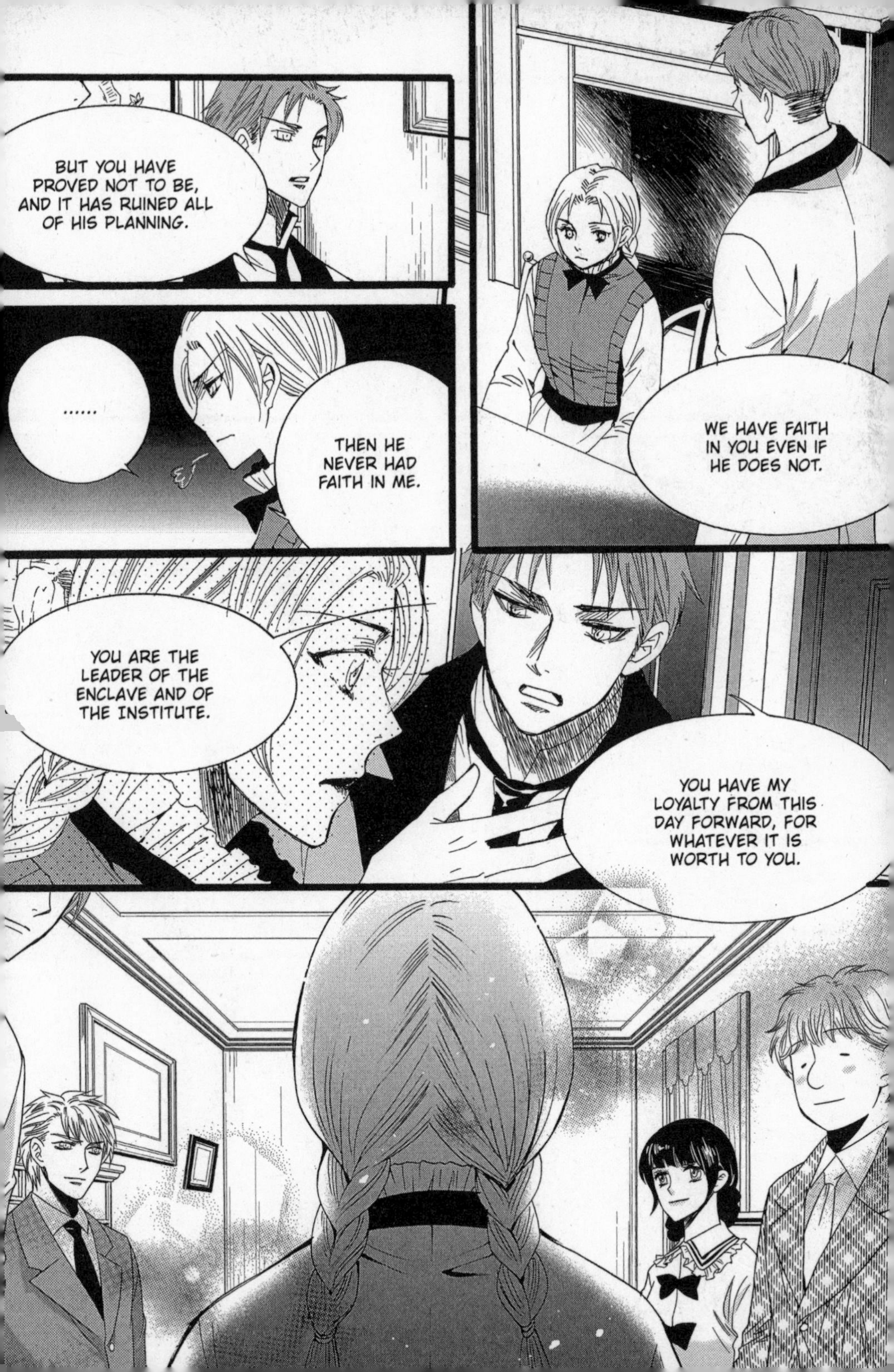
BUT YOU HAVE PROVED NOT TO BE, AND IT HAS RUINED ALL OF HIS PLANNING.
......
THEN HE NEVER HAD FAITH IN ME.
WE HAVE FAITH IN YOU EVEN IF HE DOES NOT.
YOU ARE THE LEADER OF THE ENCLAVE AND OF THE INSTITUTE.
YOU HAVE MY LOYALTY FROM THIS DAY FORWARD, FOR WHATEVER IT IS WORTH TO YOU.

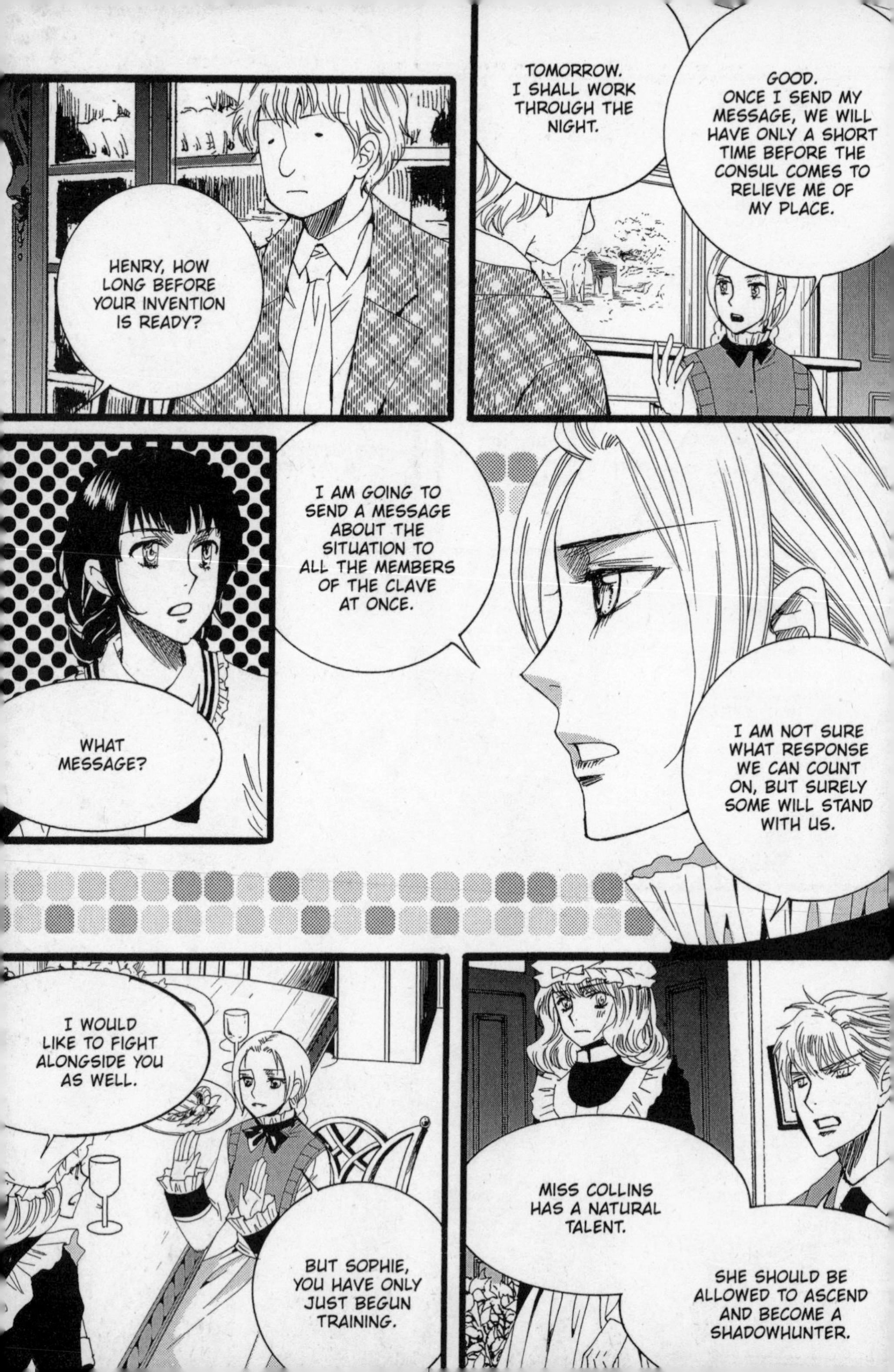
HENRY, HOW LONG BEFORE YOUR INVENTION IS READY?
TOMORROW. I SHALL WORK THROUGH THE NIGHT.
GOOD. ONCE I SEND MY MESSAGE, WE WILL HAVE ONLY A SHORT TIME BEFORE THE CONSUL COMES TO RELIEVE ME OF MY PLACE.
WHAT MESSAGE?
I AM GOING TO SEND A MESSAGE ABOUT THE SITUATION TO ALL THE MEMBERS OF THE CLAVE AT ONCE.
I AM NOT SURE WHAT RESPONSE WE CAN COUNT ON, BUT SURELY SOME WILL STAND WITH US.
I WOULD LIKE TO FIGHT ALONGSIDE YOU AS WELL.
BUT SOPHIE, YOU HAVE ONLY JUST BEGUN TRAINING.
MISS COLLINS HAS A NATURAL TALENT.
SHE SHOULD BE ALLOWED TO ASCEND AND BECOME A SHADOWHUNTER.

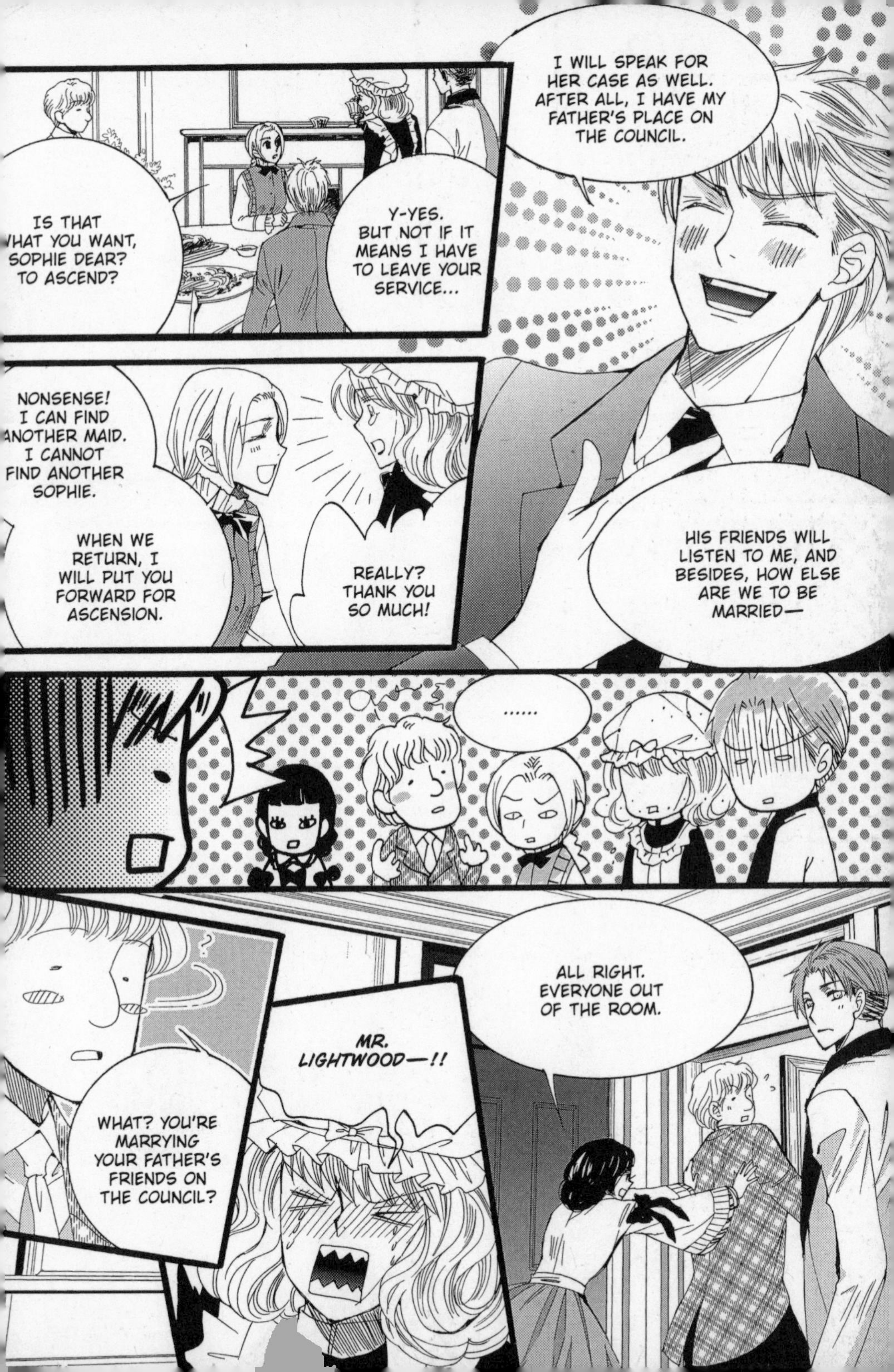
IS THAT WHAT YOU WANT, SOPHIE DEAR? TO ASCEND?
Y-YES. BUT NOT IF IT MEANS I HAVE TO LEAVE YOUR SERVICE...
NONSENSE! I CAN FIND ANOTHER MAID. I CANNOT FIND ANOTHER SOPHIE.
WHEN WE RETURN, I WILL PUT YOU FORWARD FOR ASCENSION.
REALLY? THANK YOU SO MUCH!
I WILL SPEAK FOR HER CASE AS WELL. AFTER ALL, I HAVE MY FATHER'S PLACE ON THE COUNCIL.
HIS FRIENDS WILL LISTEN TO ME, AND BESIDES, HOW ELSE ARE WE TO BE MARRIED—
......
WHAT? YOU'RE MARRYING YOUR FATHER'S FRIENDS ON THE COUNCIL?
MR. LIGHTWOOD—!!
ALL RIGHT. EVERYONE OUT OF THE ROOM.

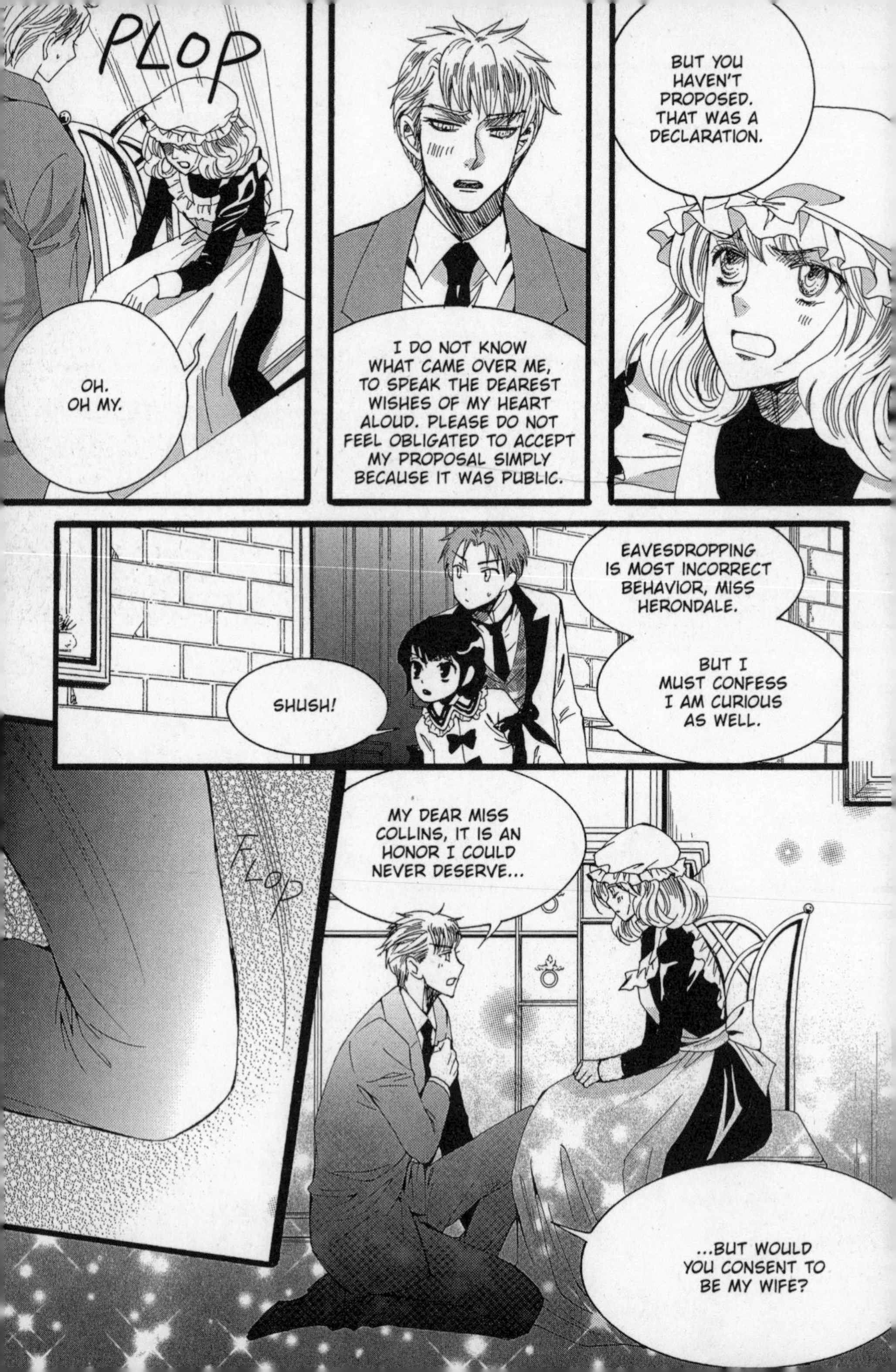
PLOP
OH. OH MY.
I DO NOT KNOW WHAT CAME OVER ME, TO SPEAK THE DEAREST WISHES OF MY HEART ALOUD. PLEASE DO NOT FEEL OBLIGATED TO ACCEPT MY PROPOSAL SIMPLY BECAUSE IT WAS PUBLIC.
BUT YOU HAVEN'T PROPOSED. THAT WAS A DECLARATION.
EAVESDROPPING IS MOST INCORRECT BEHAVIOR, MISS HERONDALE.
BUT I MUST CONFESS I AM CURIOUS AS WELL.
SHUSH!
FLOP
MY DEAR MISS COLLINS, IT IS AN HONOR I COULD NEVER DESERVE...
...BUT WOULD YOU CONSENT TO BE MY WIFE?

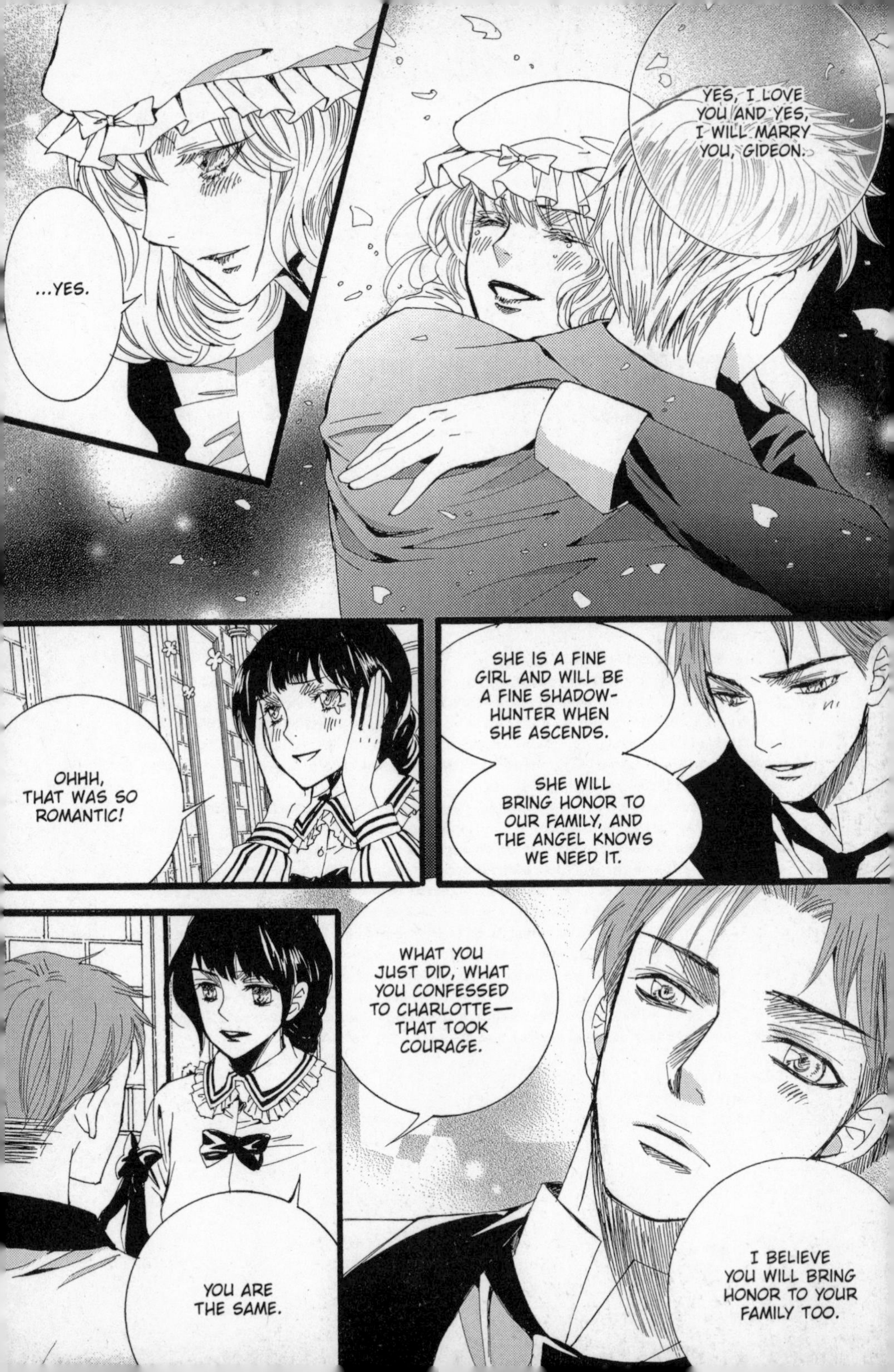
...YES.
YES, I LOVE YOU AND YES, I WILL MARRY YOU, GIDEON.
OHHH, THAT WAS SO ROMANTIC!
SHE IS A FINE GIRL AND WILL BE A FINE SHADOW-HUNTER WHEN SHE ASCENDS.
SHE WILL BRING HONOR TO OUR FAMILY, AND THE ANGEL KNOWS WE NEED IT.
WHAT YOU JUST DID, WHAT YOU CONFESSED TO CHARLOTTE—THAT TOOK COURAGE.
YOU ARE THE SAME.
I BELIEVE YOU WILL BRING HONOR TO YOUR FAMILY TOO.

To: Members of the Clave of the Nephilim
From: Charlotte Branwell

My Dear Brothers and Sisters in Arms,
  It is my sad duty to relate to you all that despite the fact that I have presented Consul
Wayland with incontrovertible proof provided by one of my Shadowhunters that Mortmain,
the gravest threat the Nephilim has faced in our times, is resident at Cadair Idris in Wales,
our esteemed Consul has mysteriously decided to ignore this information. I myself regard
knowledge of the location of our enemy and the opportunity to defeat his plans for our
destruction as of the deepest importance.
  By means provided to me by my husband, the renowned inventor Henry Branwell,
the Shadowhunters at my disposal in the London Institute will be proceeding with utmost
dispatch to Cadair Idris, there to lay down our lives in an attempt to stop Mortmain. I am
most grieved to leave the Institute undefended, but if Consul Wayland can be roused to
any action at all, he is most welcome to send guards to defend a deserted building. There are
but nine of our number, three of them not even Shadowhunters, but brave mundanes trained
by us at the Institute who have volunteered to fight beside us. I cannot say that our hopes
at this time are high, but I believe the attempt must be made.
  Obviously I cannot compel any of you. As Consul Wayland has reminded me, I am not in a
position to command the forces of the Shadowhunters, but I would be most obliged if any
of you who agree with me that Mortmain must be fought and fought now will come to the
London Institute tomorrow at midday and render us your assistance.

 Yours truly,
 Charlotte Branwell,
 head of the London Intitute

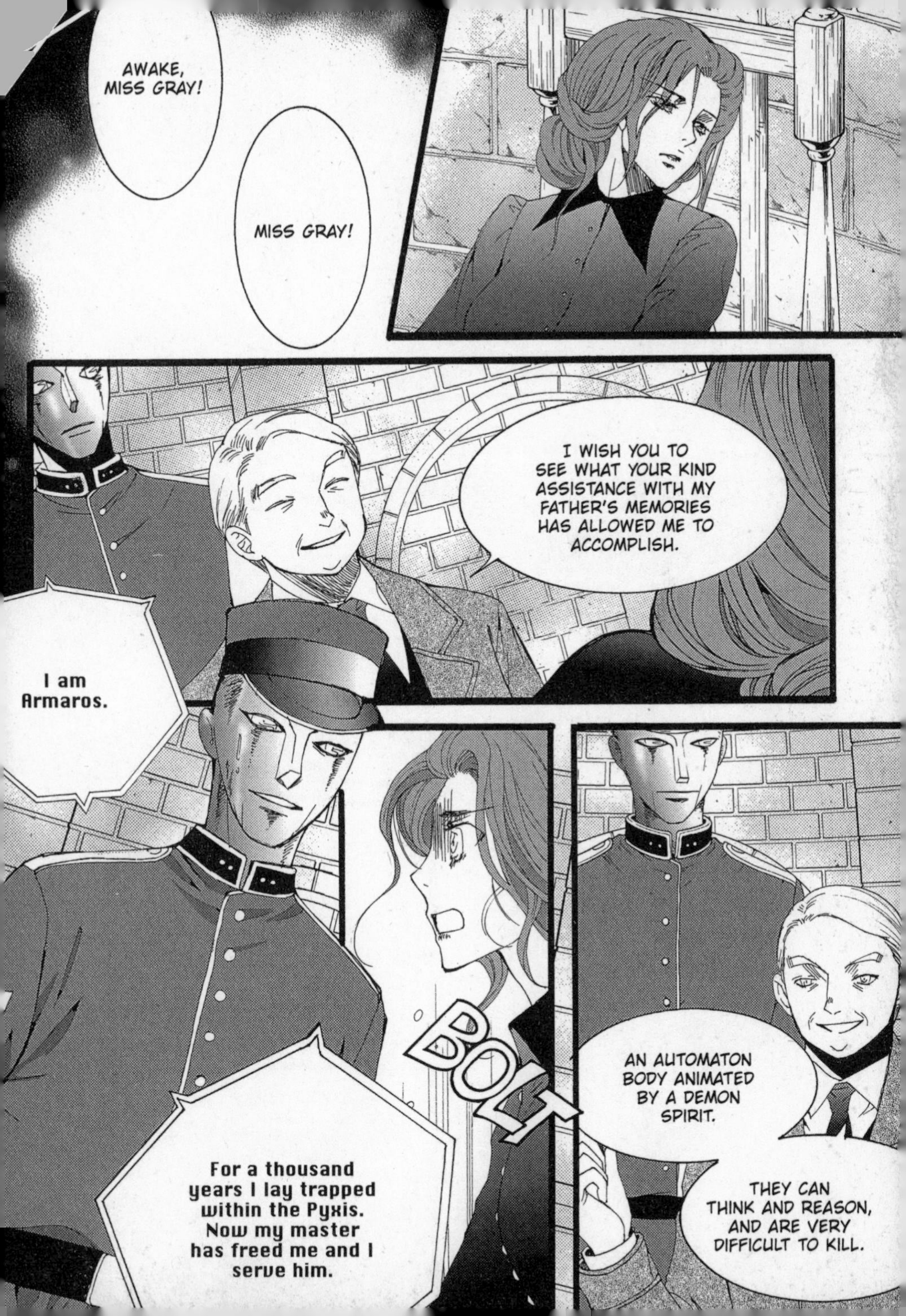
AWAKE, MISS GRAY!
MISS GRAY!
I WISH YOU TO SEE WHAT YOUR KIND ASSISTANCE WITH MY FATHER'S MEMORIES HAS ALLOWED ME TO ACCOMPLISH.
I am Armaros.
For a thousand years I lay trapped within the Pyxis. Now my master has freed me and I serve him.
BOLT
AN AUTOMATON BODY ANIMATED BY A DEMON SPIRIT.
THEY CAN THINK AND REASON, AND ARE VERY DIFFICULT TO KILL.

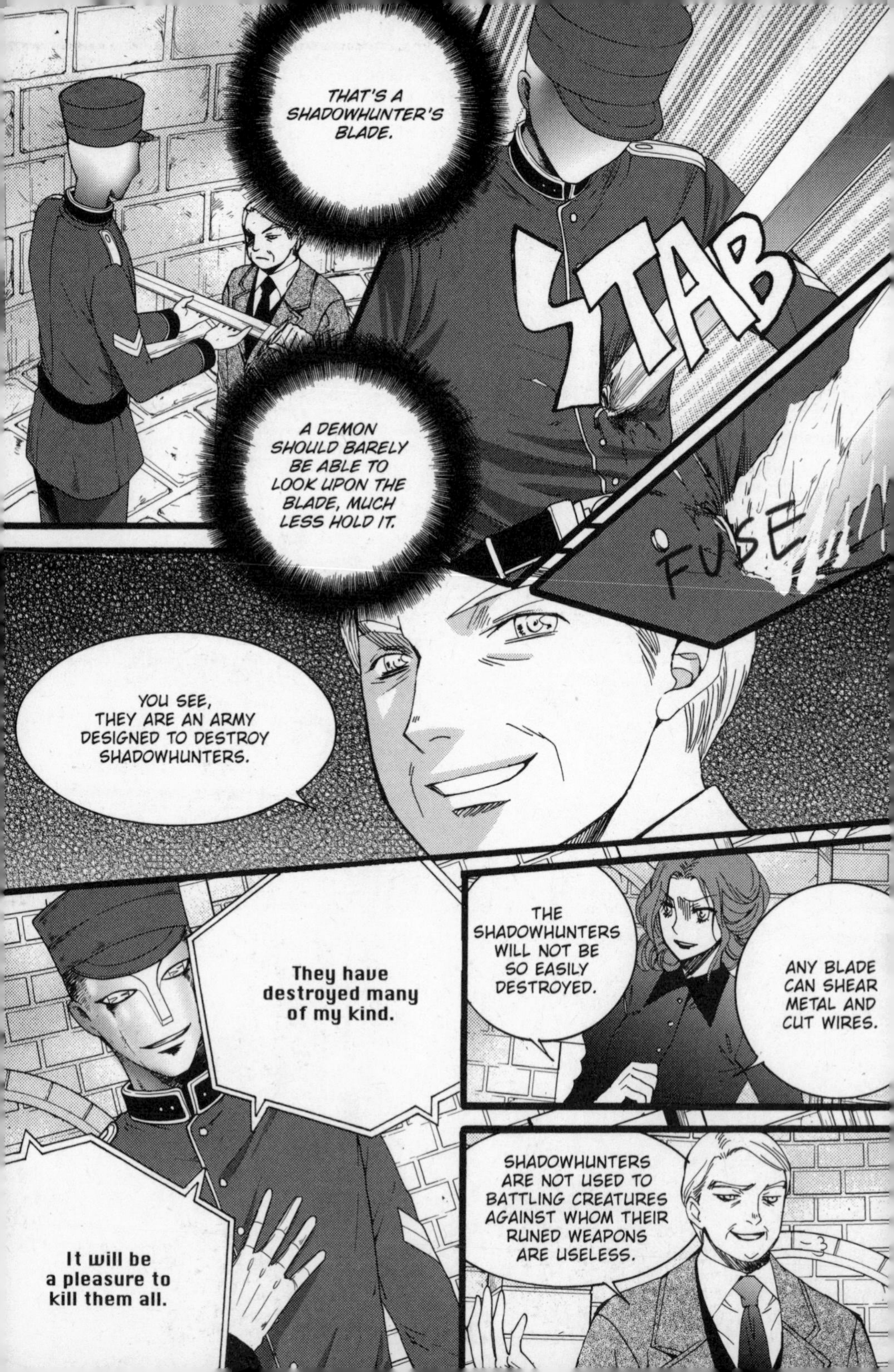
THAT'S A SHADOWHUNTER'S BLADE.
STAB
A DEMON SHOULD BARELY BE ABLE TO LOOK UPON THE BLADE, MUCH LESS HOLD IT.
FUSE
YOU SEE, THEY ARE AN ARMY DESIGNED TO DESTROY SHADOWHUNTERS.
They have destroyed many of my kind.
It will be a pleasure to kill them all.
THE SHADOWHUNTERS WILL NOT BE SO EASILY DESTROYED.
ANY BLADE CAN SHEAR METAL AND CUT WIRES.
SHADOWHUNTERS ARE NOT USED TO BATTLING CREATURES AGAINST WHOM THEIR RUNED WEAPONS ARE USELESS.

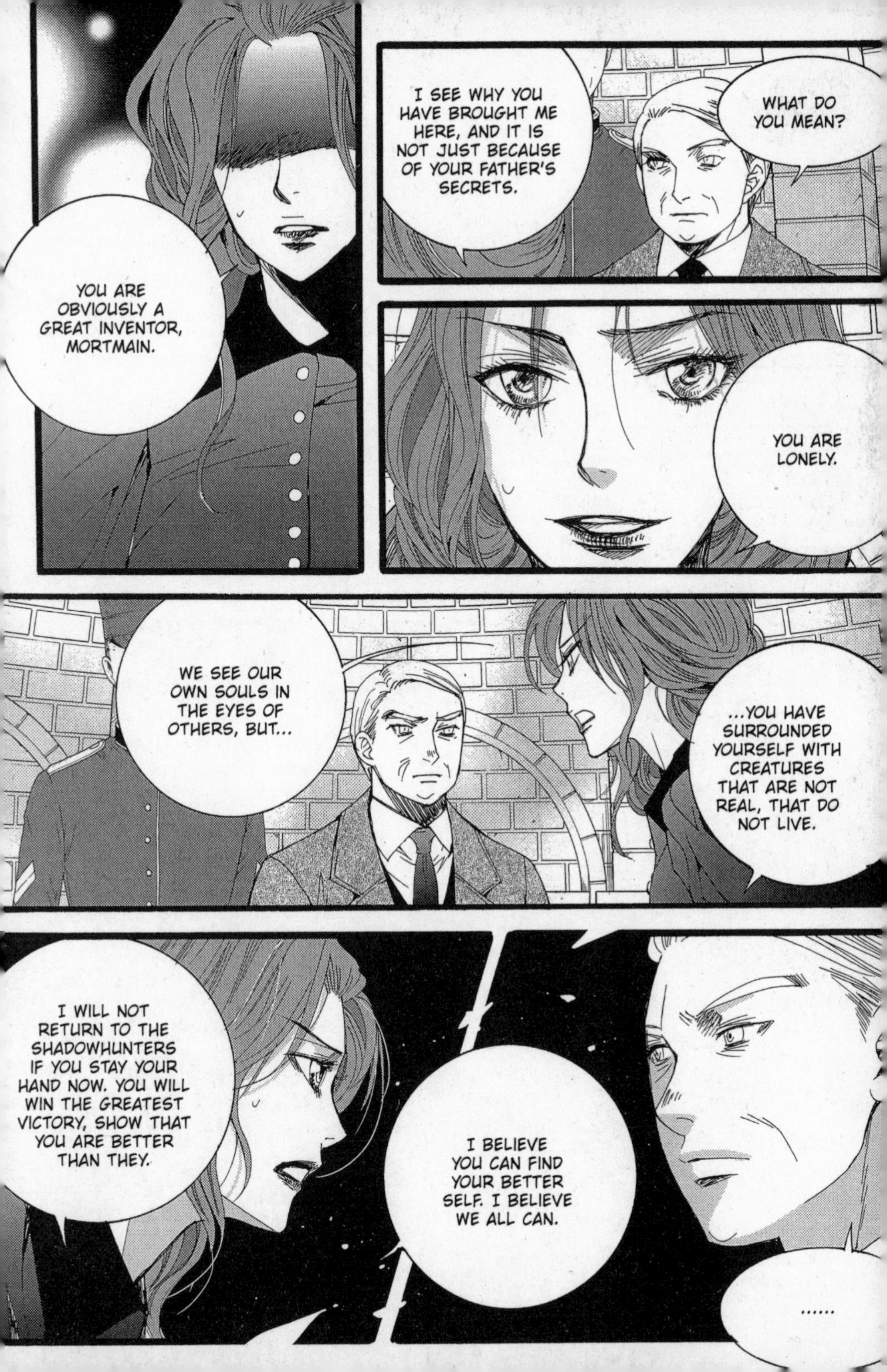
YOU ARE OBVIOUSLY A GREAT INVENTOR, MORTMAIN.
I SEE WHY YOU HAVE BROUGHT ME HERE, AND IT IS NOT JUST BECAUSE OF YOUR FATHER'S SECRETS.
WHAT DO YOU MEAN?
YOU ARE LONELY.
WE SEE OUR OWN SOULS IN THE EYES OF OTHERS, BUT...
...YOU HAVE SURROUNDED YOURSELF WITH CREATURES THAT ARE NOT REAL, THAT DO NOT LIVE.
I WILL NOT RETURN TO THE SHADOWHUNTERS IF YOU STAY YOUR HAND NOW. YOU WILL WIN THE GREATEST VICTORY, SHOW THAT YOU ARE BETTER THAN THEY.
I BELIEVE YOU CAN FIND YOUR BETTER SELF. I BELIEVE WE ALL CAN.
......

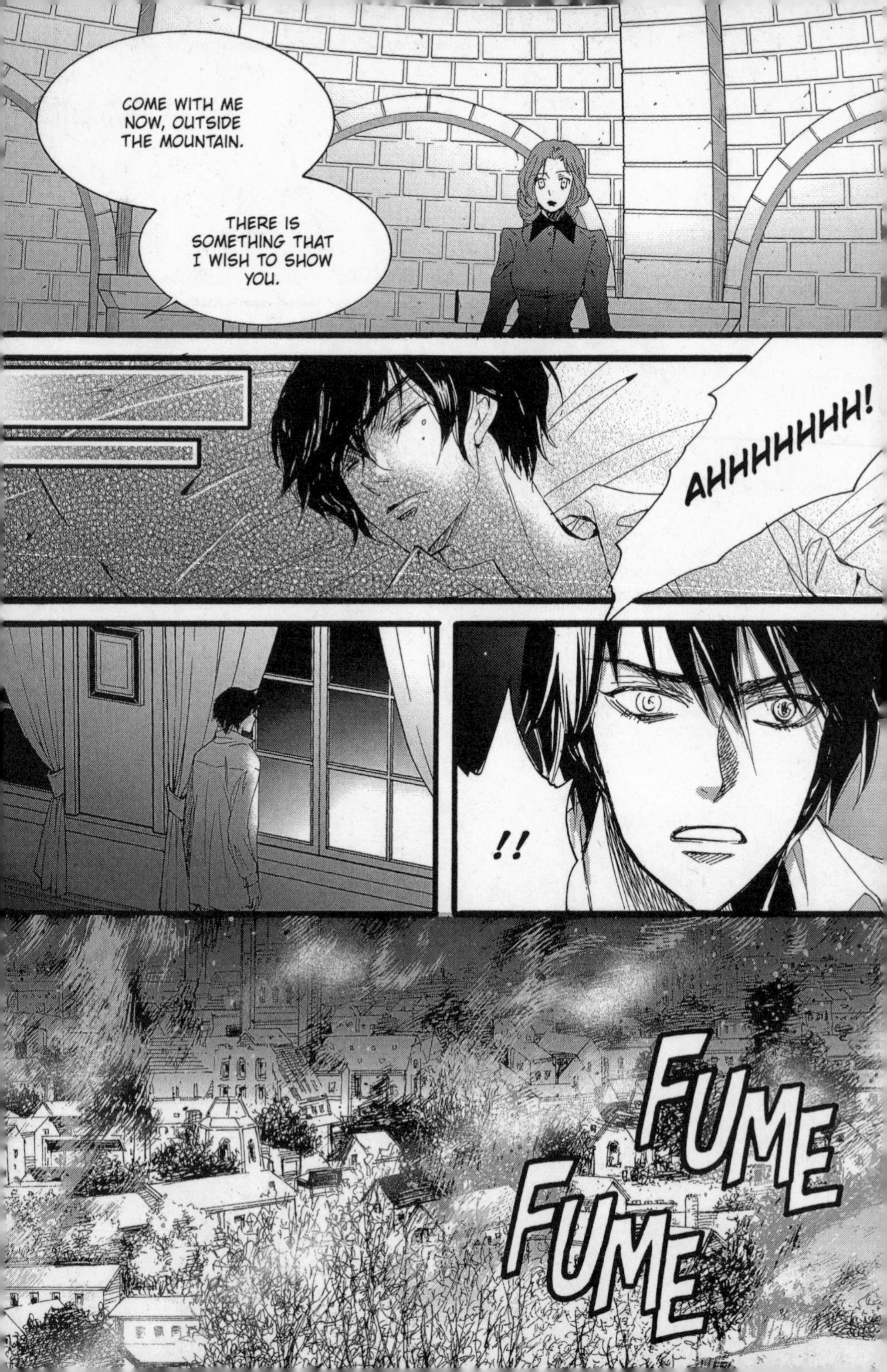
COME WITH ME NOW, OUTSIDE THE MOUNTAIN.
THERE IS SOMETHING THAT I WISH TO SHOW YOU.
AHHHHHHH!
!!
FUME
FUME

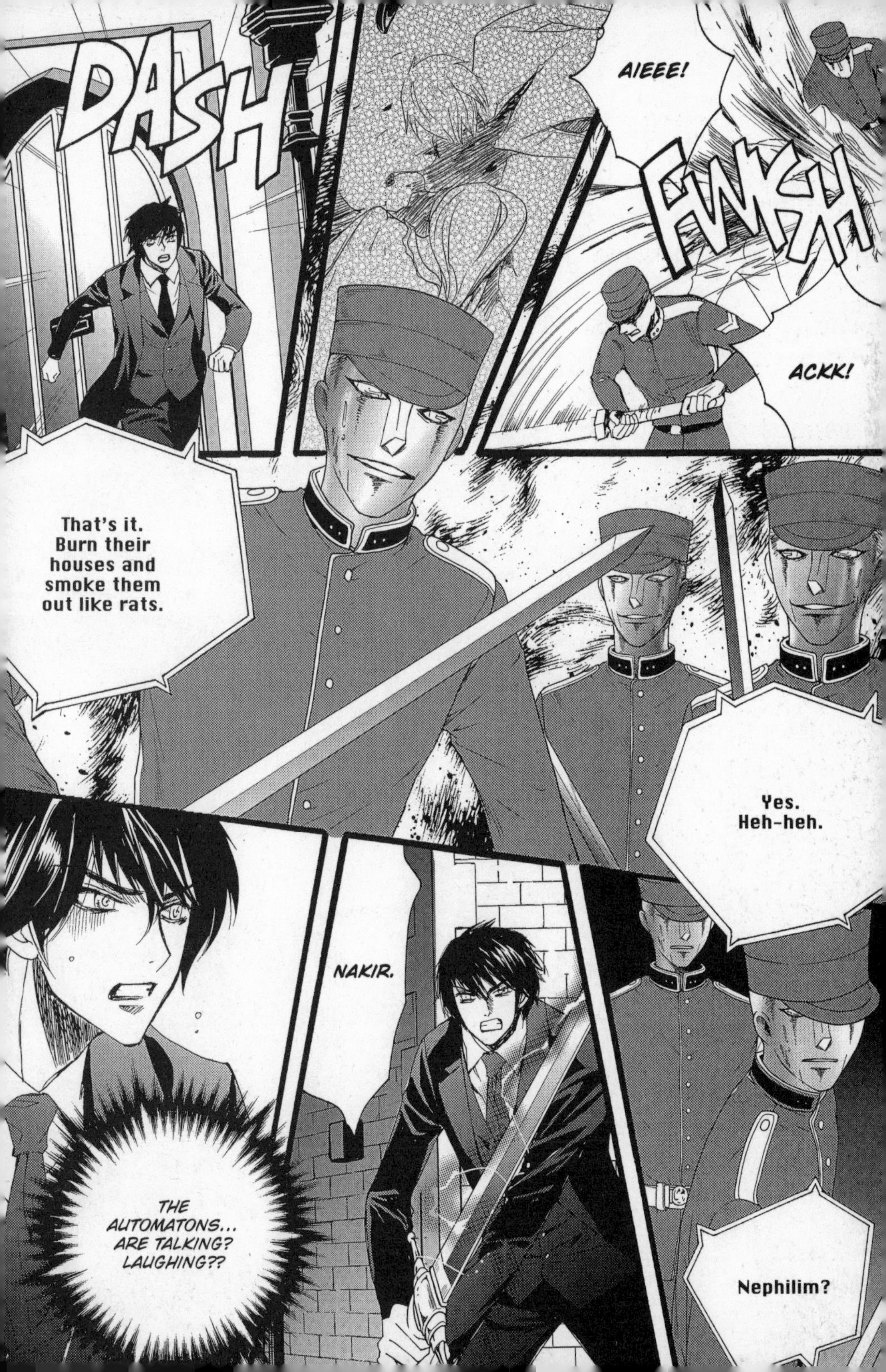
DASH
AIEEE!
FWUSH
ACKK!
That's it. Burn their houses and smoke them out like rats.
Yes. Heh-heh.
NAKIR.
THE AUTOMATONS... ARE TALKING? LAUGHING??
Nephilim?

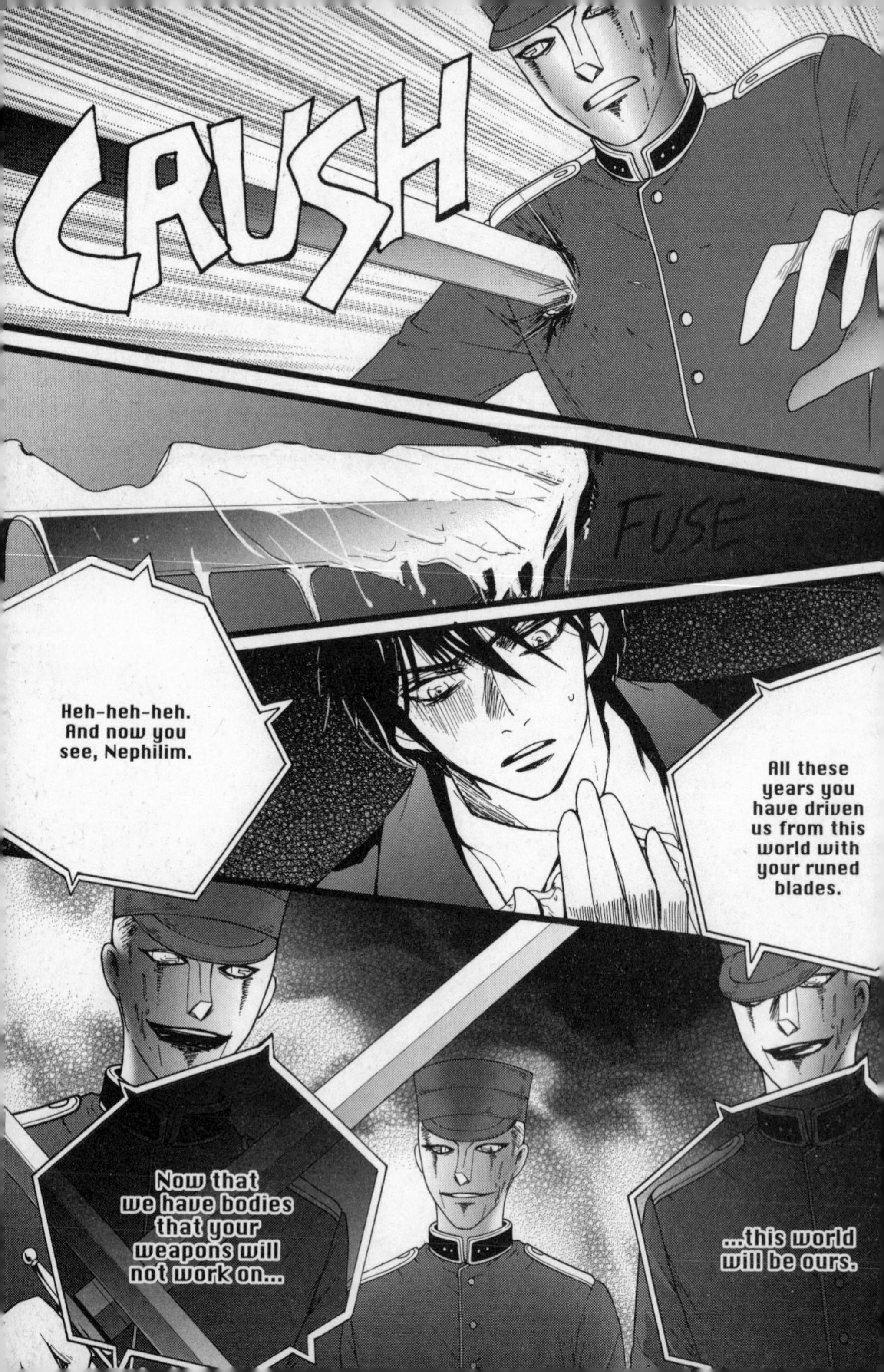
CRUSH
FUSE
Heh-heh-heh. And now you see, Nephilim.
All these years you have driven us from this world with your runed blades.
Now that we have bodies that your weapons will not work on...
...this world will be ours.

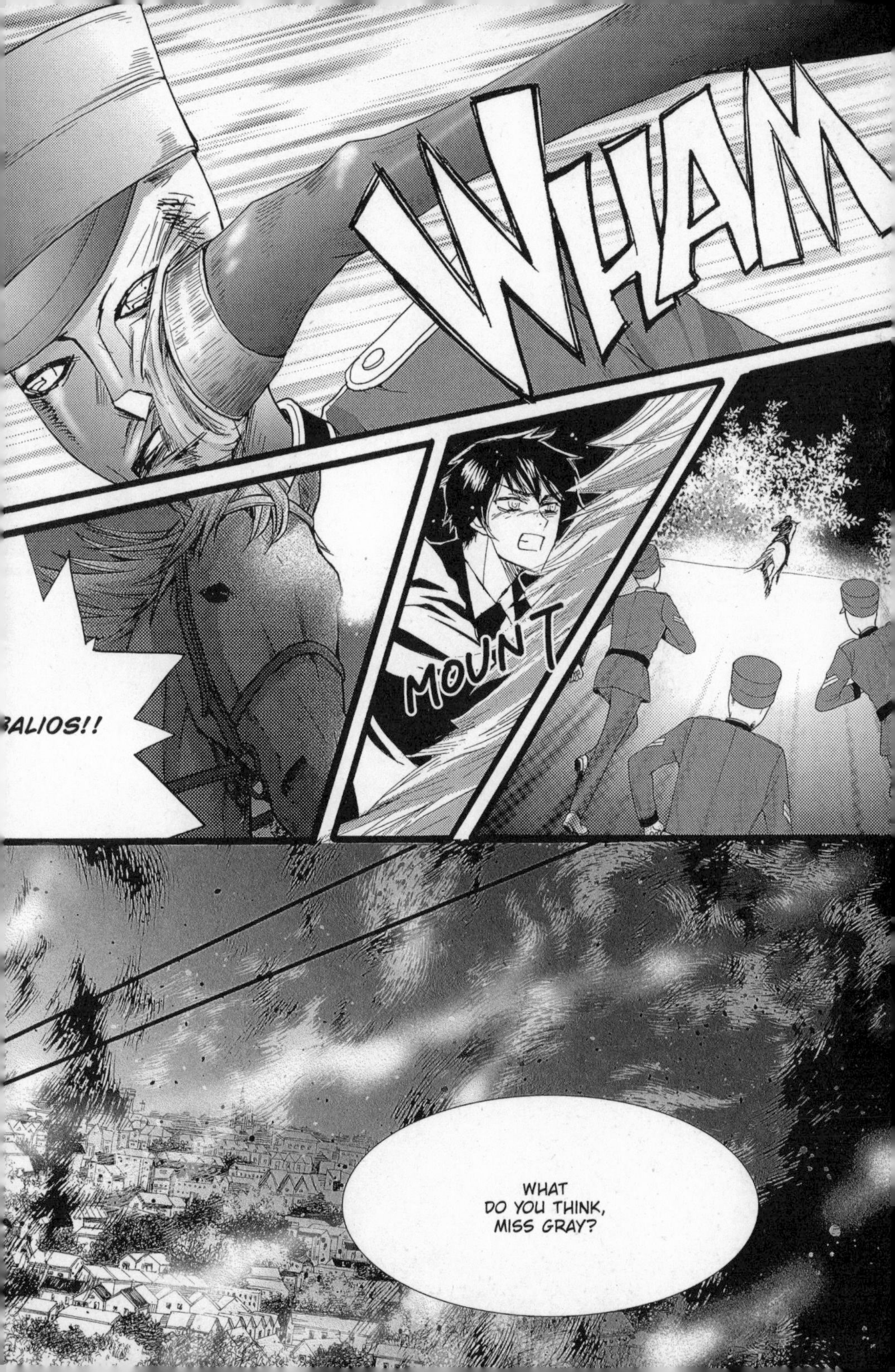
WHAM
MOUNT
BALIOS!!
WHAT DO YOU THINK, MISS GRAY?

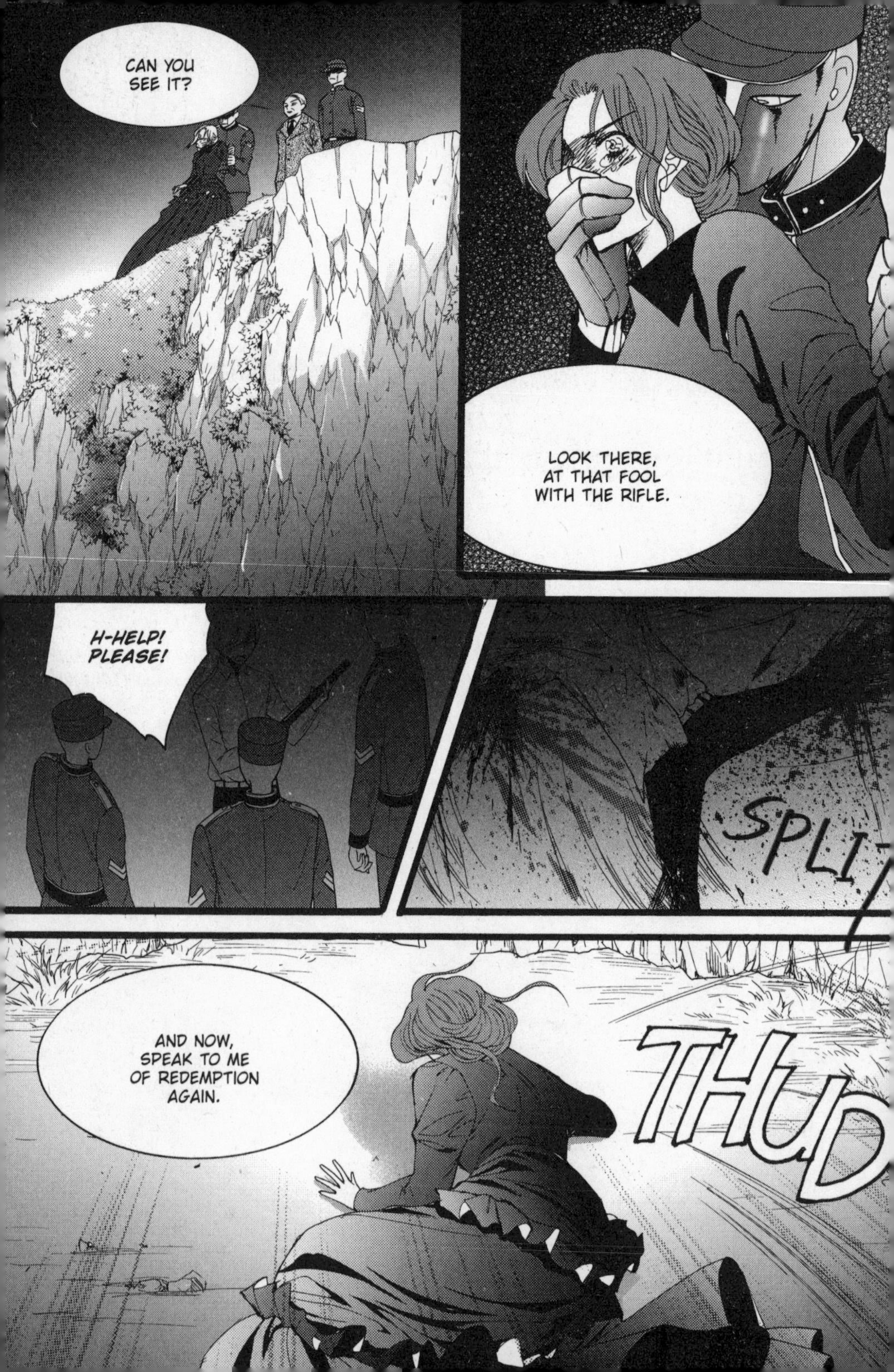
CAN YOU SEE IT?
LOOK THERE, AT THAT FOOL WITH THE RIFLE.
H-HELP! PLEASE!
SPLIT
AND NOW, SPEAK TO ME OF REDEMPTION AGAIN.
THUD

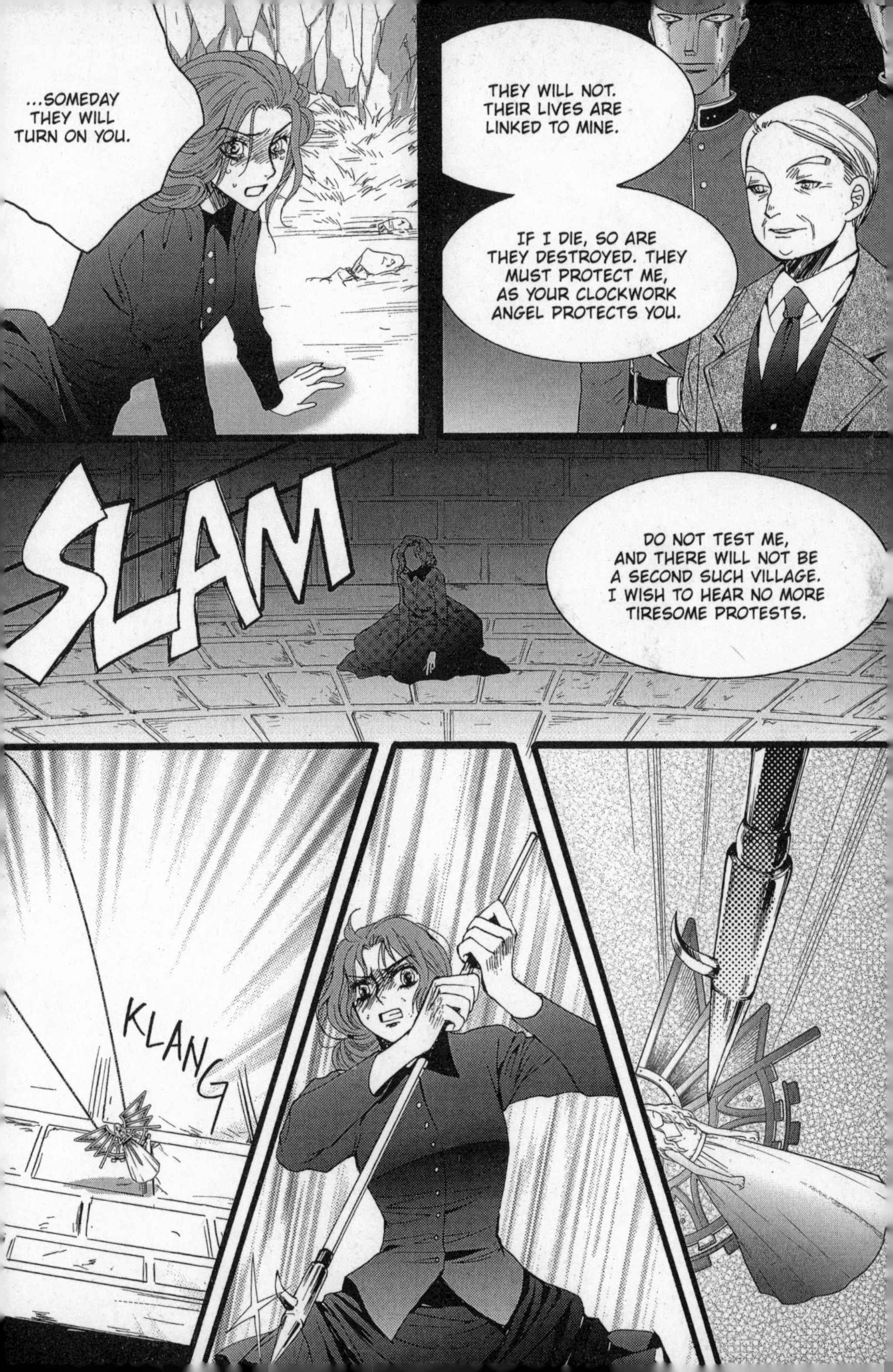
...SOMEDAY THEY WILL TURN ON YOU.
THEY WILL NOT. THEIR LIVES ARE LINKED TO MINE.
IF I DIE, SO ARE THEY DESTROYED. THEY MUST PROTECT ME, AS YOUR CLOCKWORK ANGEL PROTECTS YOU.
SLAM
DO NOT TEST ME, AND THERE WILL NOT BE A SECOND SUCH VILLAGE. I WISH TO HEAR NO MORE TIRESOME PROTESTS.
KLANG

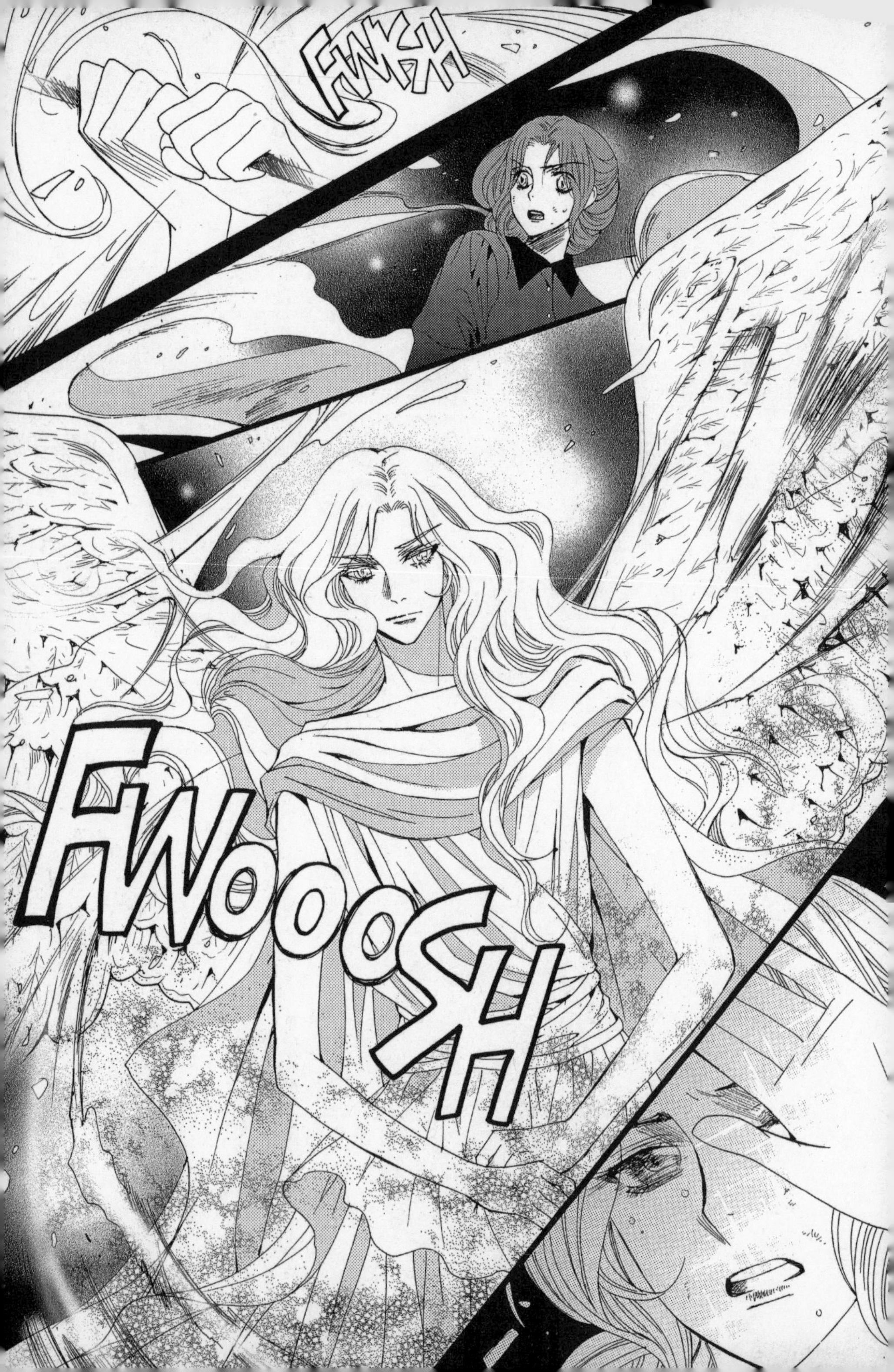

FWSH
FWOOOSH

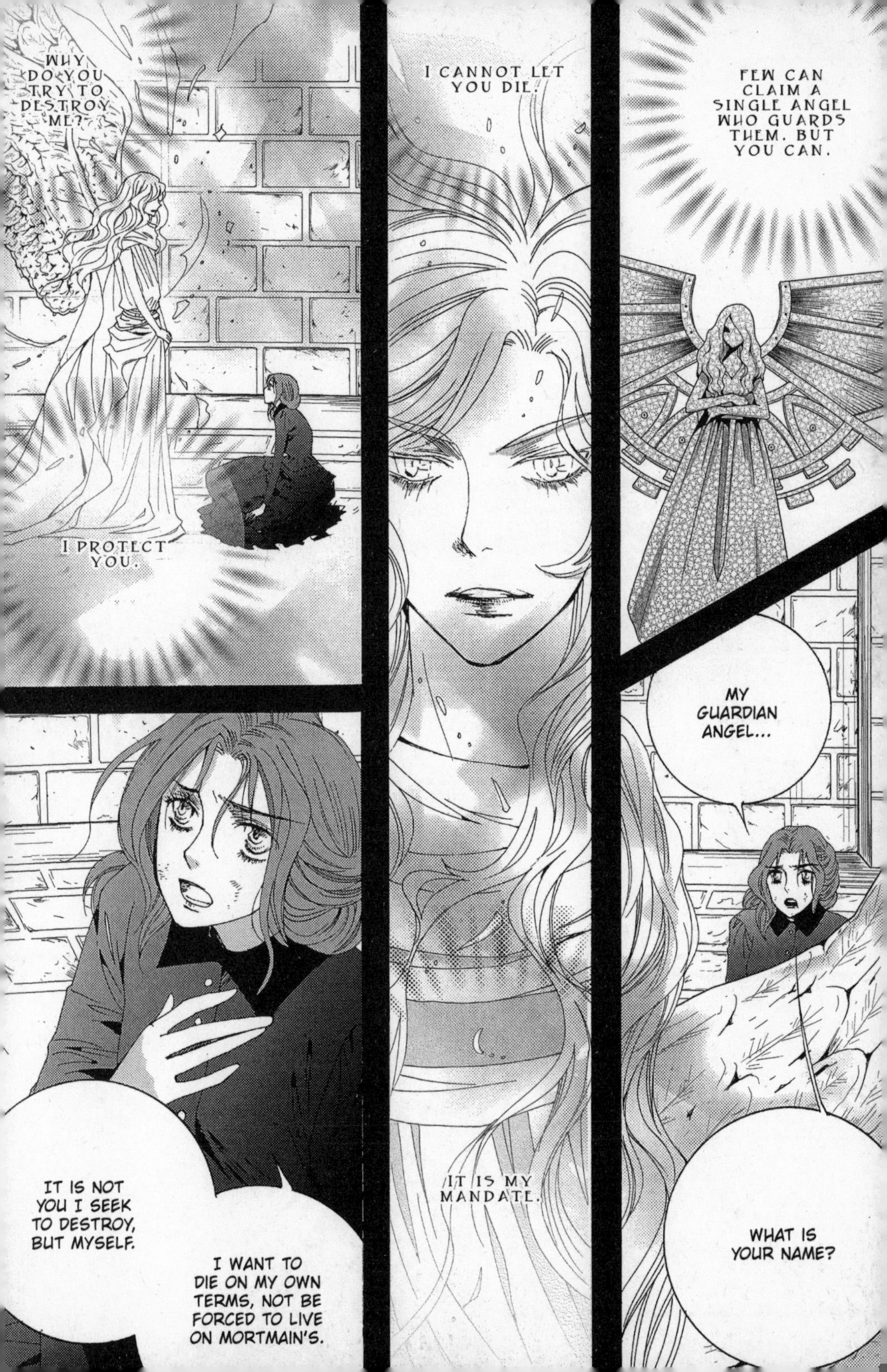
WHY DO YOU TRY TO DESTROY ME?
I PROTECT YOU.
IT IS NOT YOU I SEEK TO DESTROY, BUT MYSELF.
I WANT TO DIE ON MY OWN TERMS, NOT BE FORCED TO LIVE ON MORTMAIN'S.
I CANNOT LET YOU DIE.
IT IS MY MANDATE.
FEW CAN CLAIM A SINGLE ANGEL WHO GUARDS THEM. BUT YOU CAN.
MY GUARDIAN ANGEL...
WHAT IS YOUR NAME?

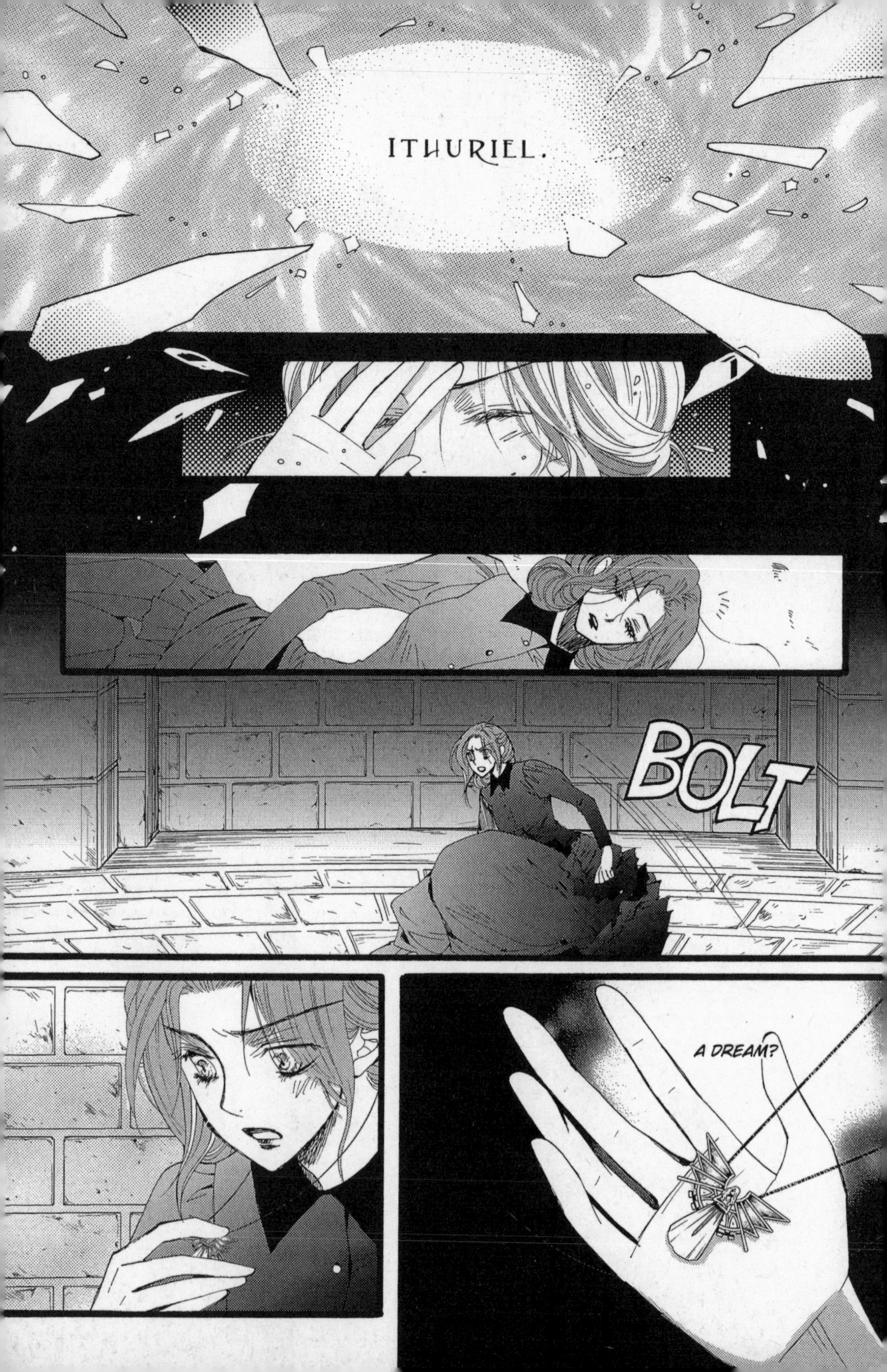
ITHURIEL.
BOLT
A DREAM?

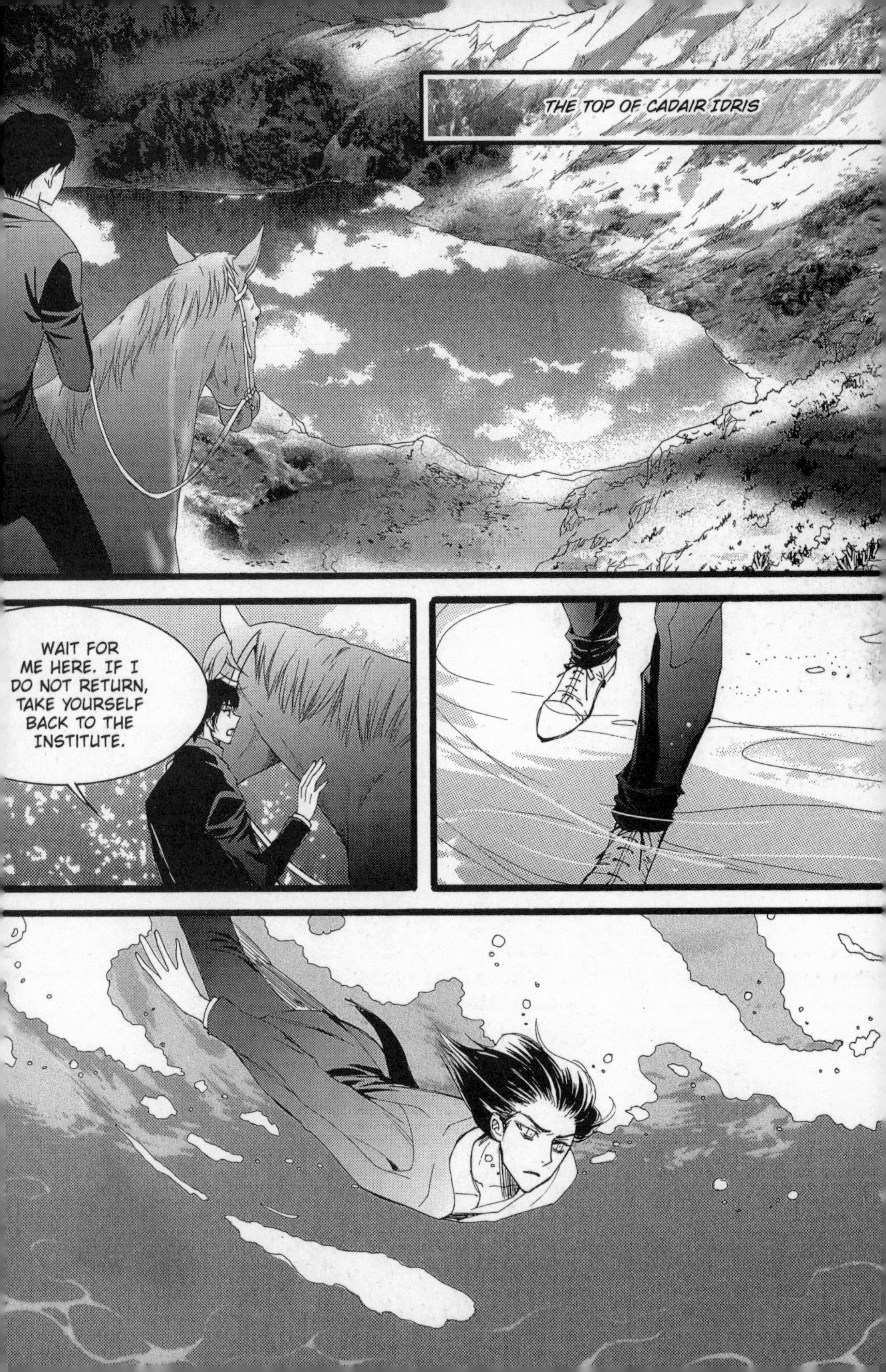
THE TOP OF CADAIR IDRIS
WAIT FOR ME HERE. IF I DO NOT RETURN, TAKE YOURSELF BACK TO THE INSTITUTE.

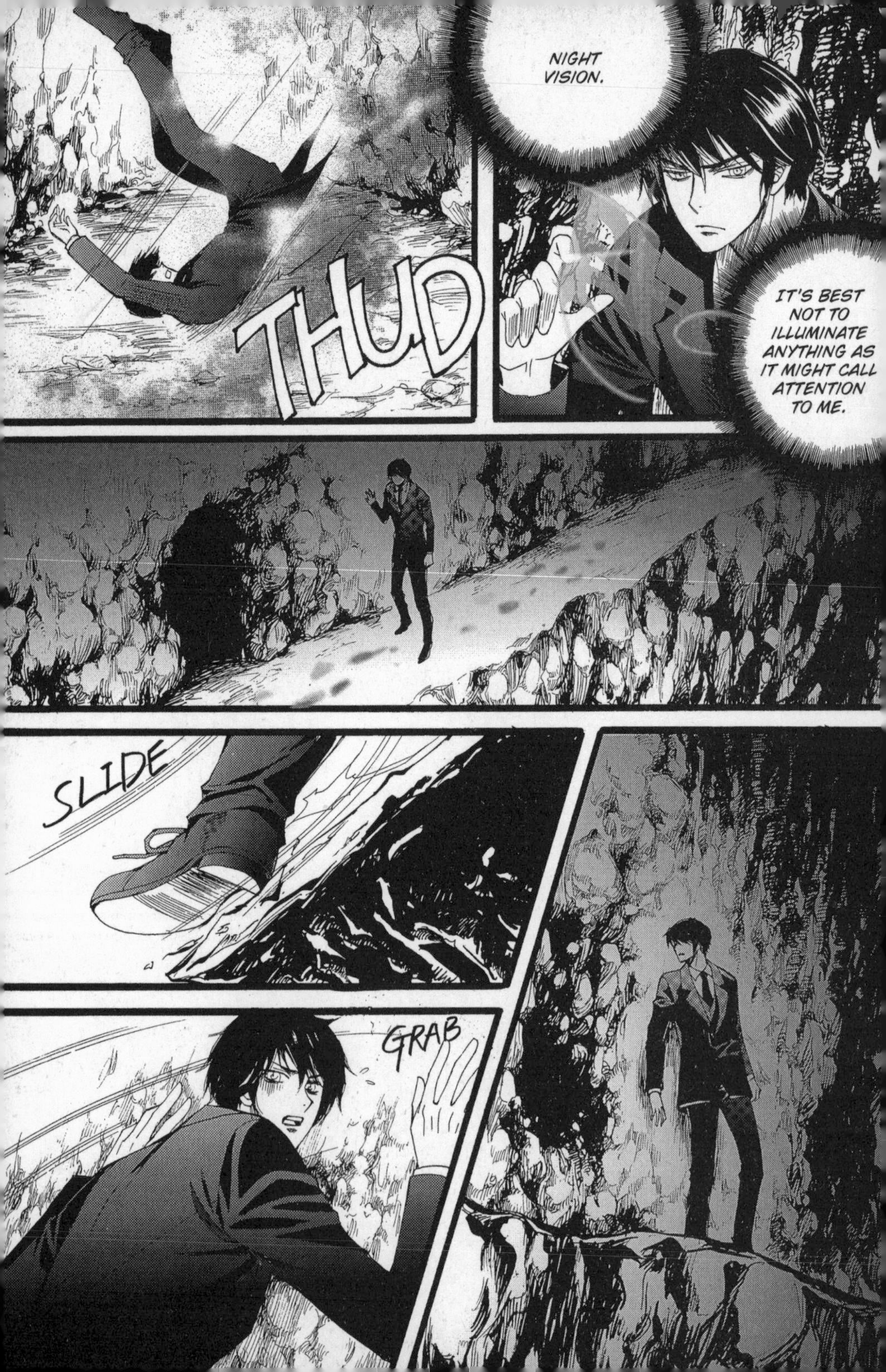
NIGHT VISION.
IT'S BEST NOT TO ILLUMINATE ANYTHING AS IT MIGHT CALL ATTENTION TO ME.
THUD
SLIDE
GRAB

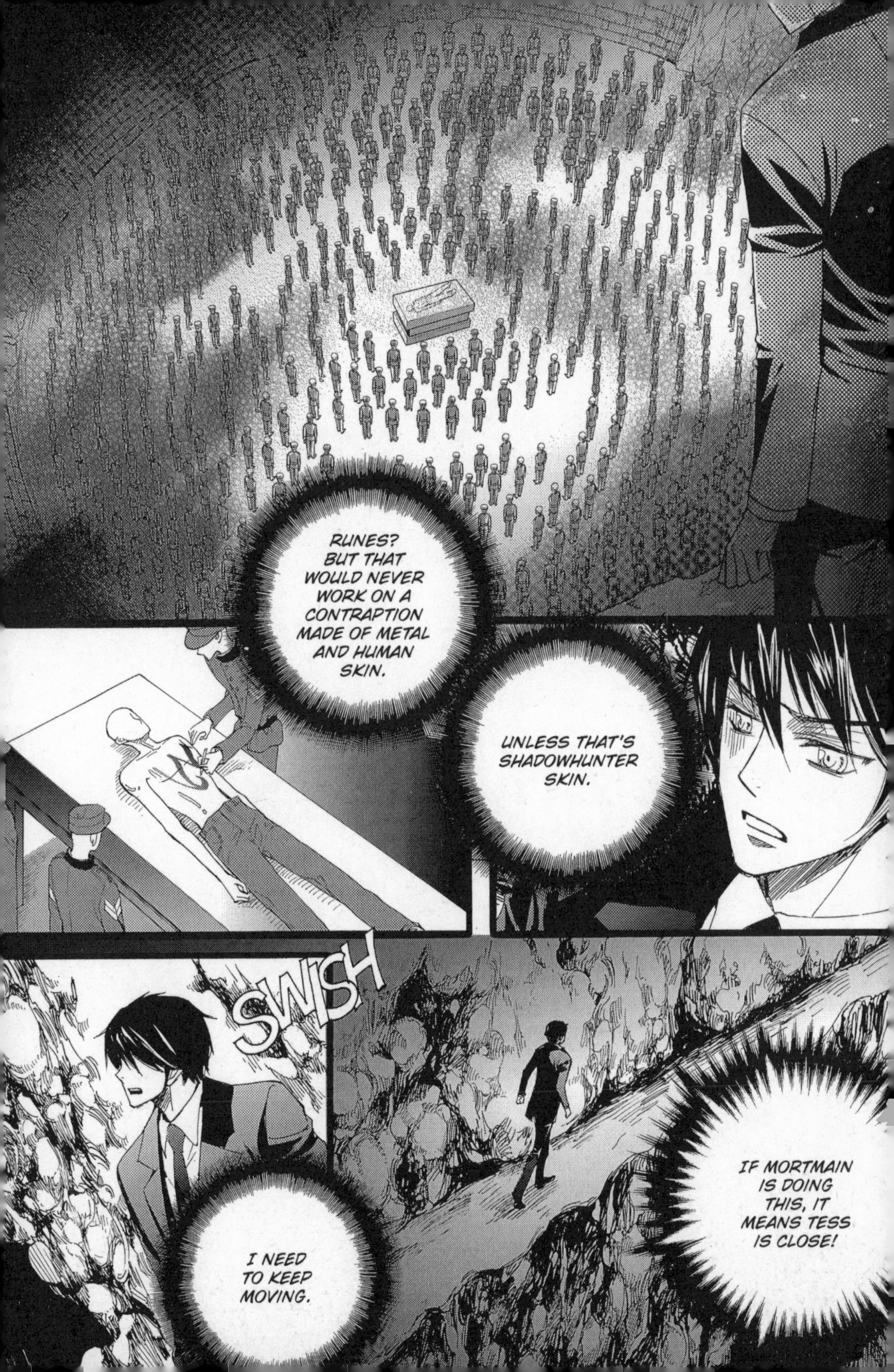
RUNES? BUT THAT WOULD NEVER WORK ON A CONTRAPTION MADE OF METAL AND HUMAN SKIN.
UNLESS THAT'S SHADOWHUNTER SKIN.
SWISH
IF MORTMAIN IS DOING THIS, IT MEANS TESS IS CLOSE!
I NEED TO KEEP MOVING.

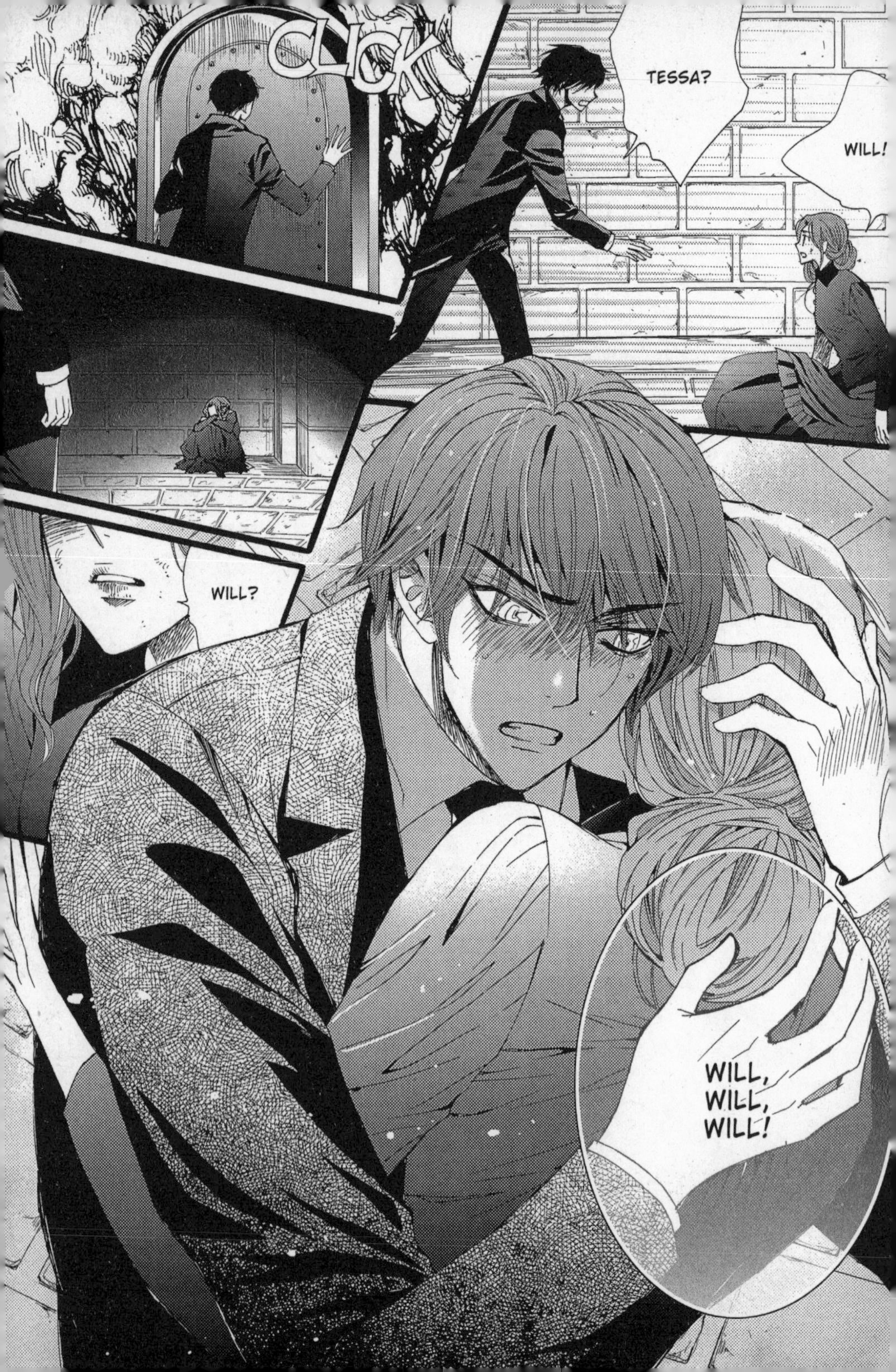
CLICK
TESSA?
WILL!
WILL?
WILL, WILL, WILL!

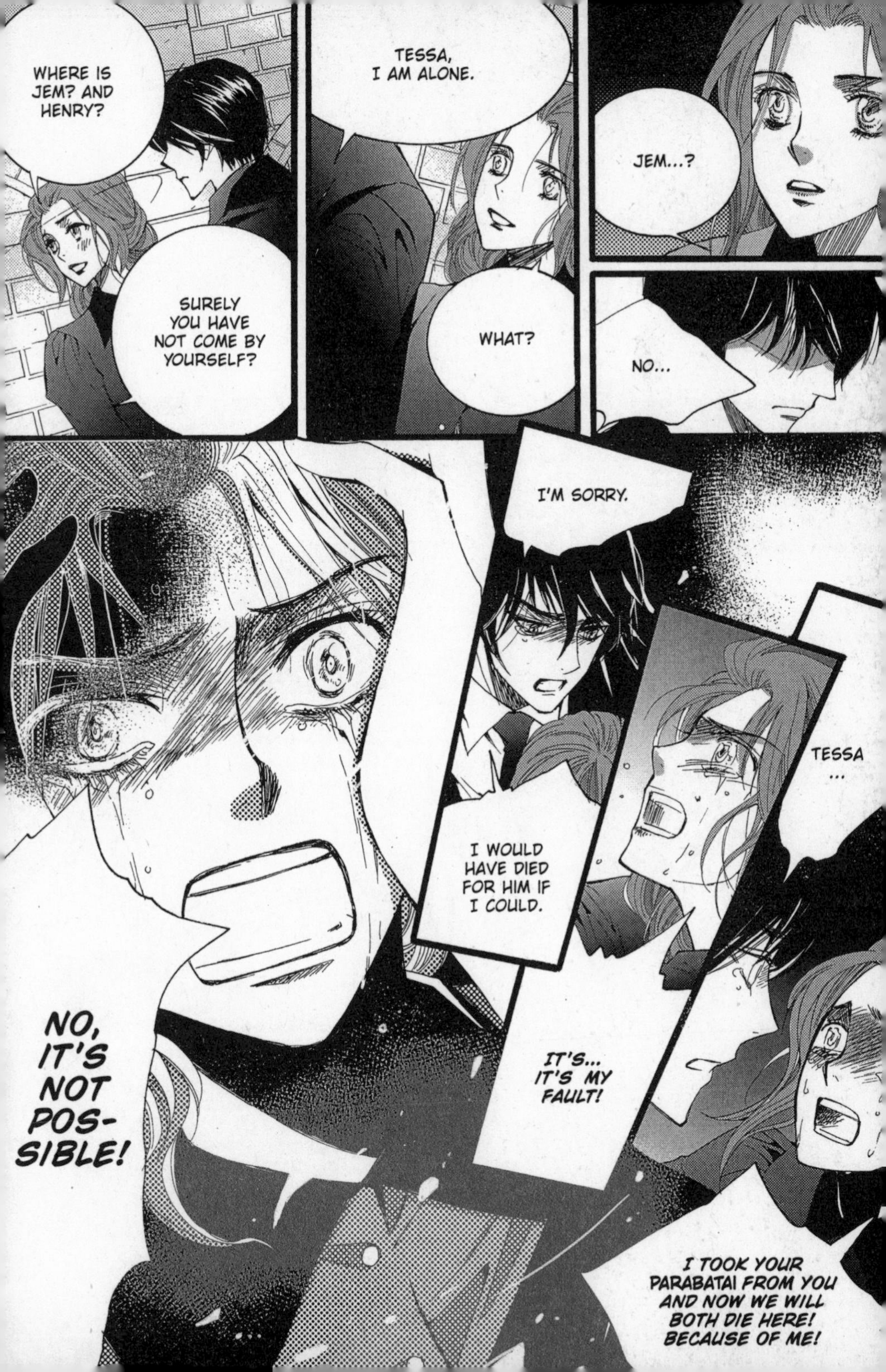
WHERE IS JEM? AND HENRY?
SURELY YOU HAVE NOT COME BY YOURSELF?
TESSA, I AM ALONE.
WHAT?
JEM...?
NO...
I'M SORRY.
I WOULD HAVE DIED FOR HIM IF I COULD.
NO, IT'S NOT POS-SIBLE!
TESSA ...
IT'S... IT'S MY FAULT!
I TOOK YOUR PARABATAI FROM YOU AND NOW WE WILL BOTH DIE HERE! BECAUSE OF ME!

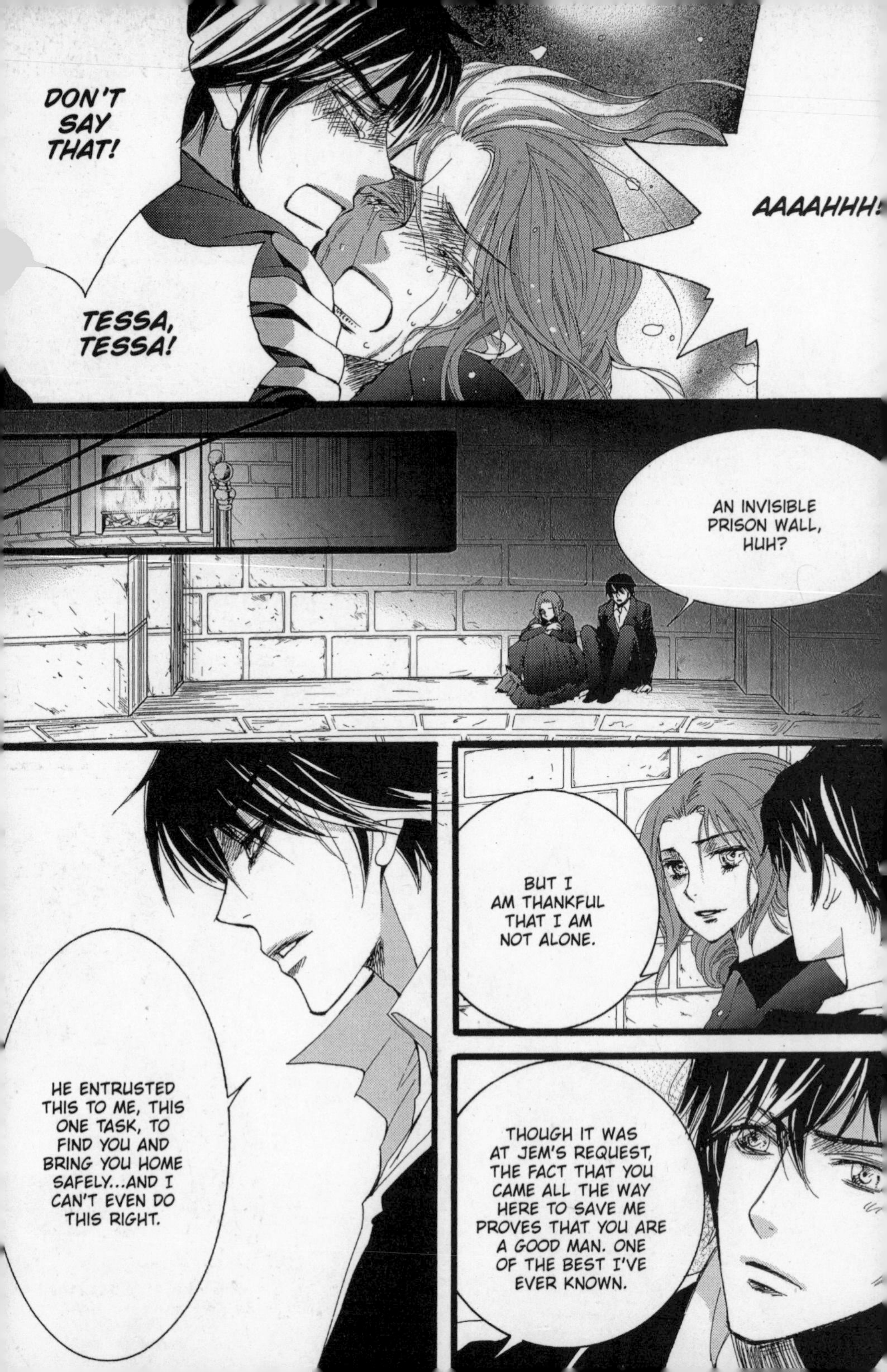
DON'T SAY THAT!
AAAAHHH!
TESSA, TESSA!
AN INVISIBLE PRISON WALL, HUH?
HE ENTRUSTED THIS TO ME, THIS ONE TASK, TO FIND YOU AND BRING YOU HOME SAFELY...AND I CAN'T EVEN DO THIS RIGHT.
BUT I AM THANKFUL THAT I AM NOT ALONE.
THOUGH IT WAS AT JEM'S REQUEST, THE FACT THAT YOU CAME ALL THE WAY HERE TO SAVE ME PROVES THAT YOU ARE A GOOD MAN. ONE OF THE BEST I'VE EVER KNOWN.

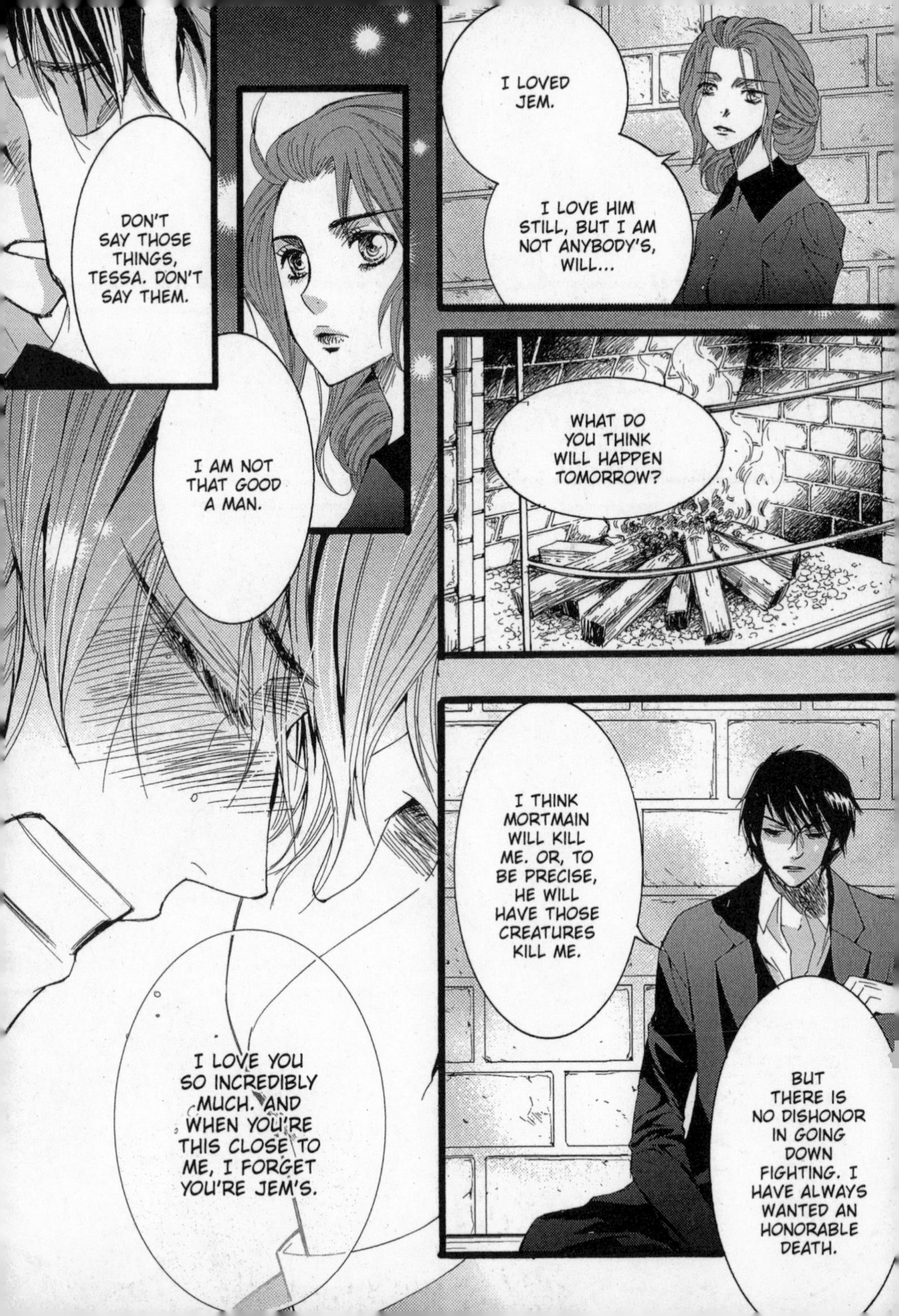
DON'T SAY THOSE THINGS, TESSA. DON'T SAY THEM.
I AM NOT THAT GOOD A MAN.
I LOVE YOU SO INCREDIBLY MUCH. AND WHEN YOU'RE THIS CLOSE TO ME, I FORGET YOU'RE JEM'S.
I LOVED JEM.
I LOVE HIM STILL, BUT I AM NOT ANYBODY'S, WILL...
WHAT DO YOU THINK WILL HAPPEN TOMORROW?
I THINK MORTMAIN WILL KILL ME. OR, TO BE PRECISE, HE WILL HAVE THOSE CREATURES KILL ME.
BUT THERE IS NO DISHONOR IN GOING DOWN FIGHTING. I HAVE ALWAYS WANTED AN HONORABLE DEATH.

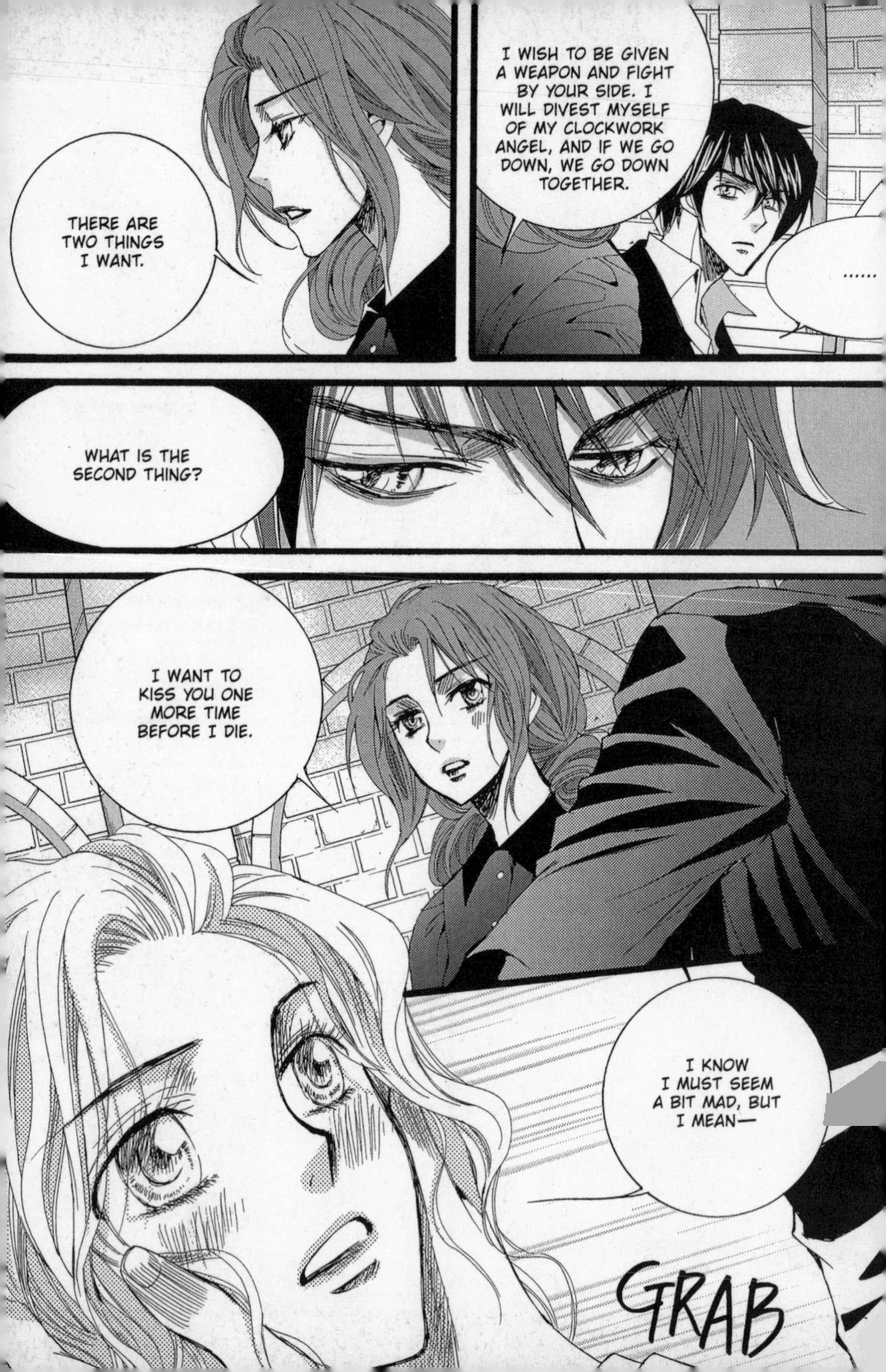
THERE ARE TWO THINGS I WANT.
I WISH TO BE GIVEN A WEAPON AND FIGHT BY YOUR SIDE. I WILL DIVEST MYSELF OF MY CLOCKWORK ANGEL, AND IF WE GO DOWN, WE GO DOWN TOGETHER.
......
WHAT IS THE SECOND THING?
I WANT TO KISS YOU ONE MORE TIME BEFORE I DIE.
I KNOW I MUST SEEM A BIT MAD, BUT I MEAN—
GRAB

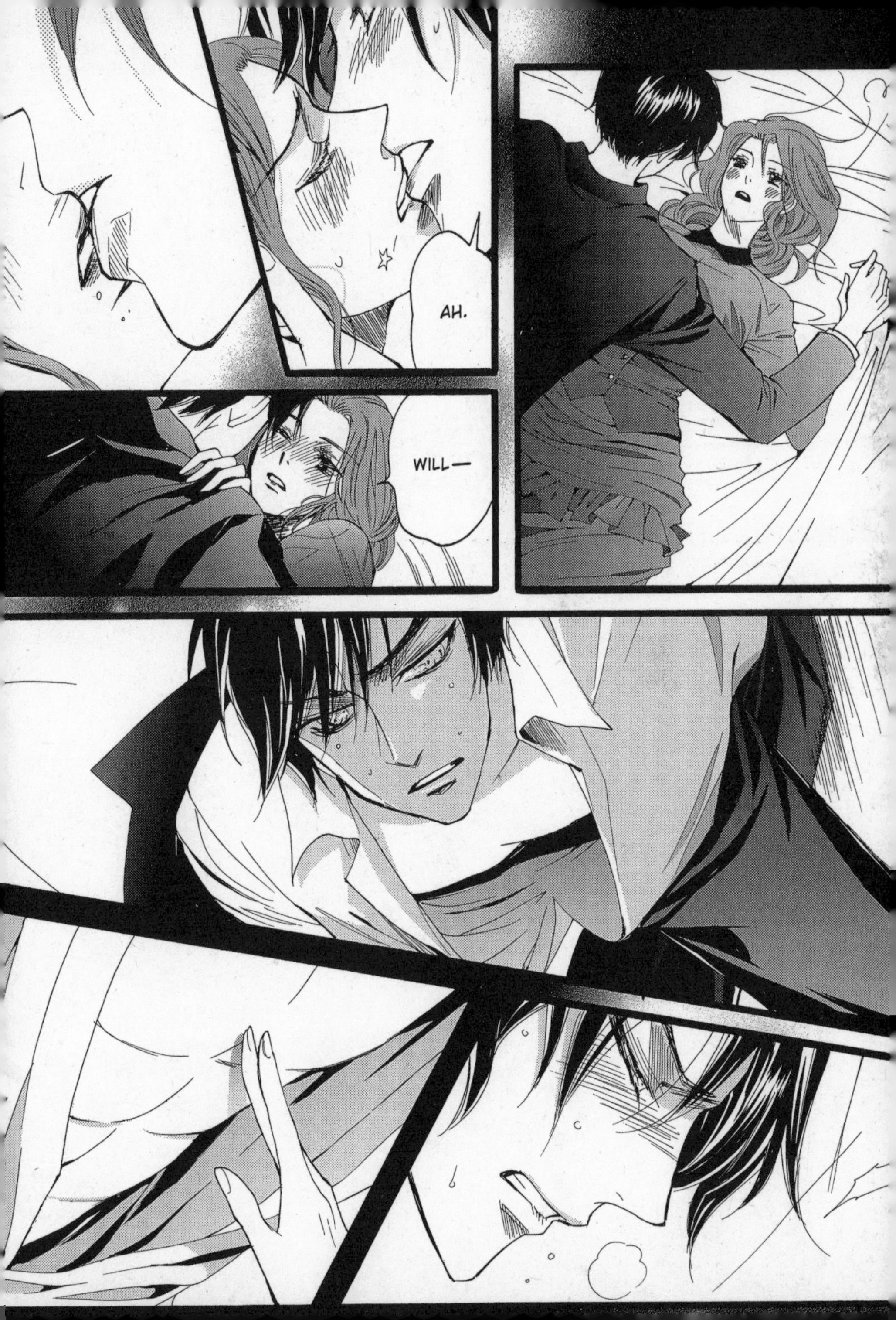
AH.
WILL—

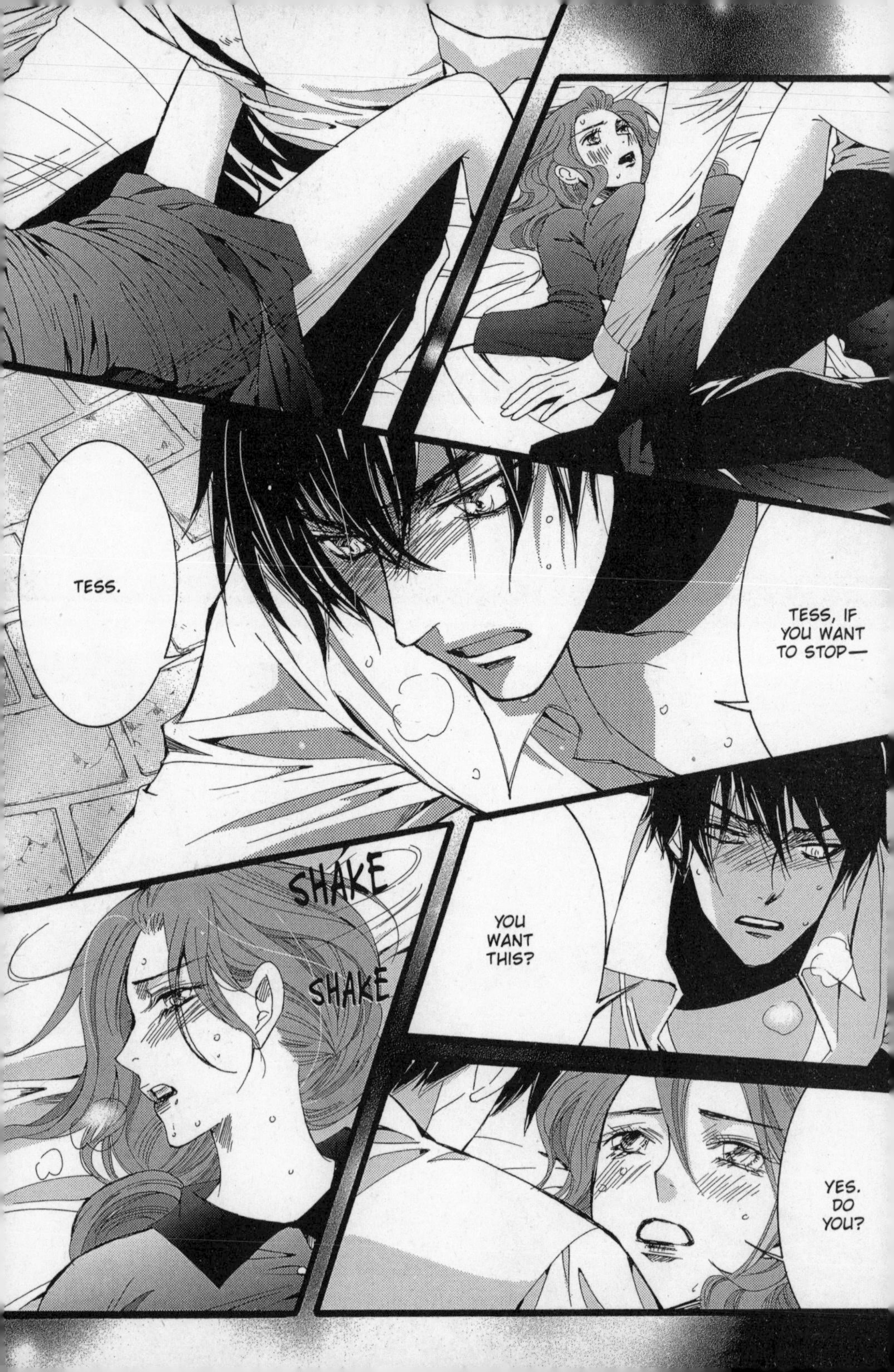

TESS, IF YOU WANT TO STOP—
TESS.
YOU WANT THIS?
SHAKE
SHAKE
YES. DO YOU?

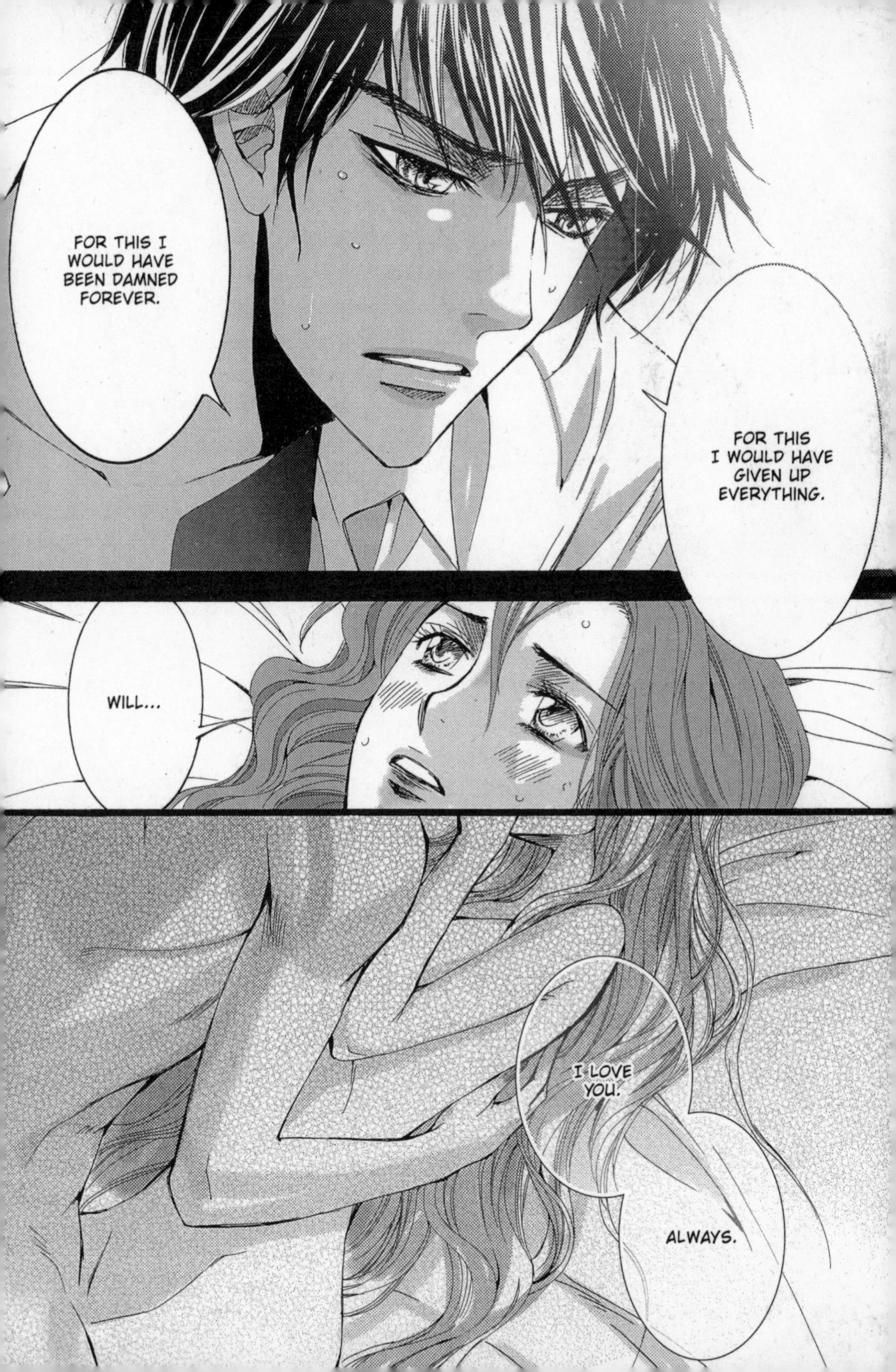
FOR THIS I WOULD HAVE GIVEN UP EVERYTHING.
FOR THIS I WOULD HAVE BEEN DAMNED FOREVER.
WILL...
I LOVE YOU.
ALWAYS.

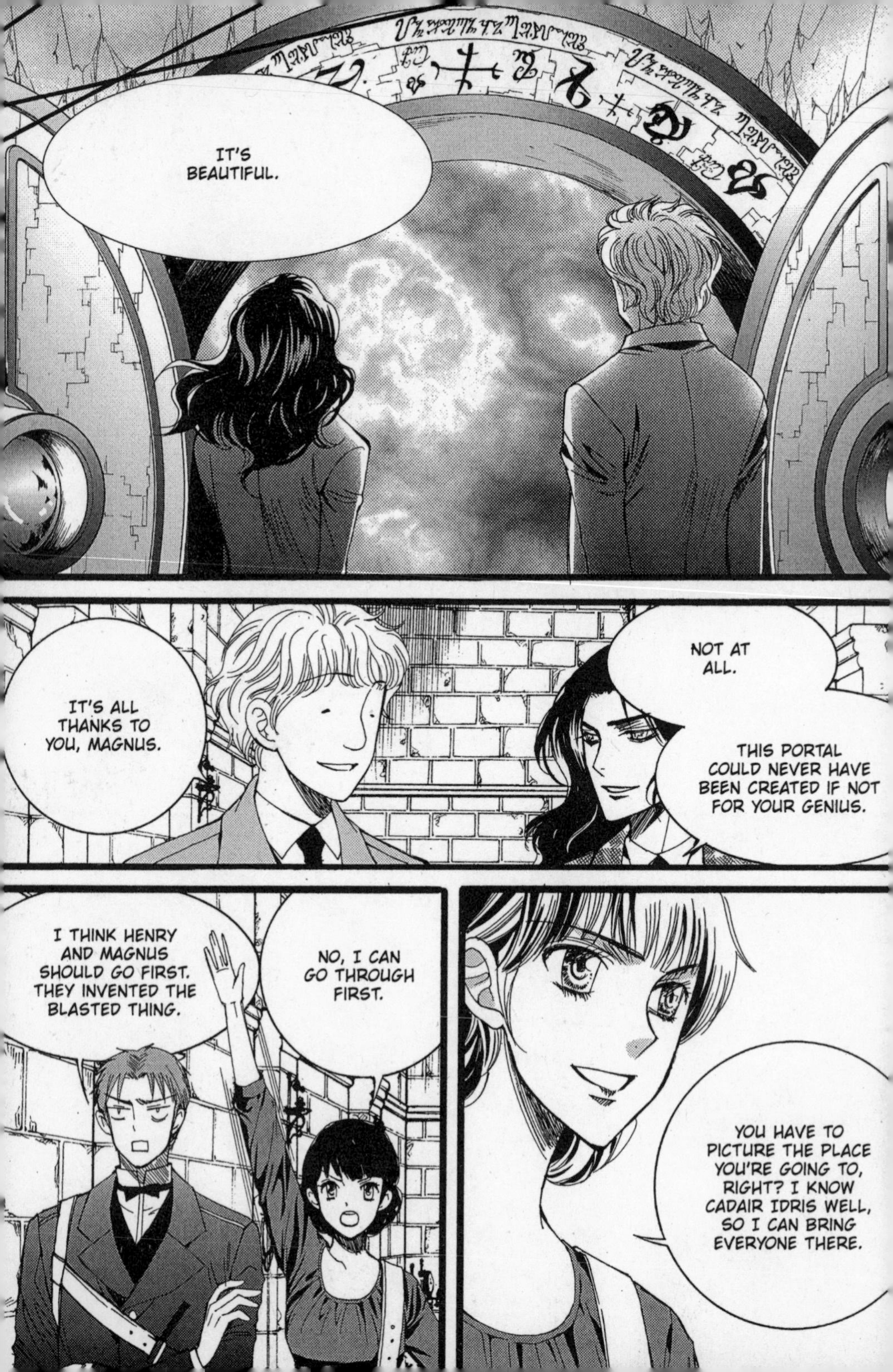
IT'S BEAUTIFUL.
IT'S ALL THANKS TO YOU, MAGNUS.
NOT AT ALL.
THIS PORTAL COULD NEVER HAVE BEEN CREATED IF NOT FOR YOUR GENIUS.
I THINK HENRY AND MAGNUS SHOULD GO FIRST. THEY INVENTED THE BLASTED THING.
NO, I CAN GO THROUGH FIRST.
YOU HAVE TO PICTURE THE PLACE YOU'RE GOING TO, RIGHT? I KNOW CADAIR IDRIS WELL, SO I CAN BRING EVERYONE THERE.

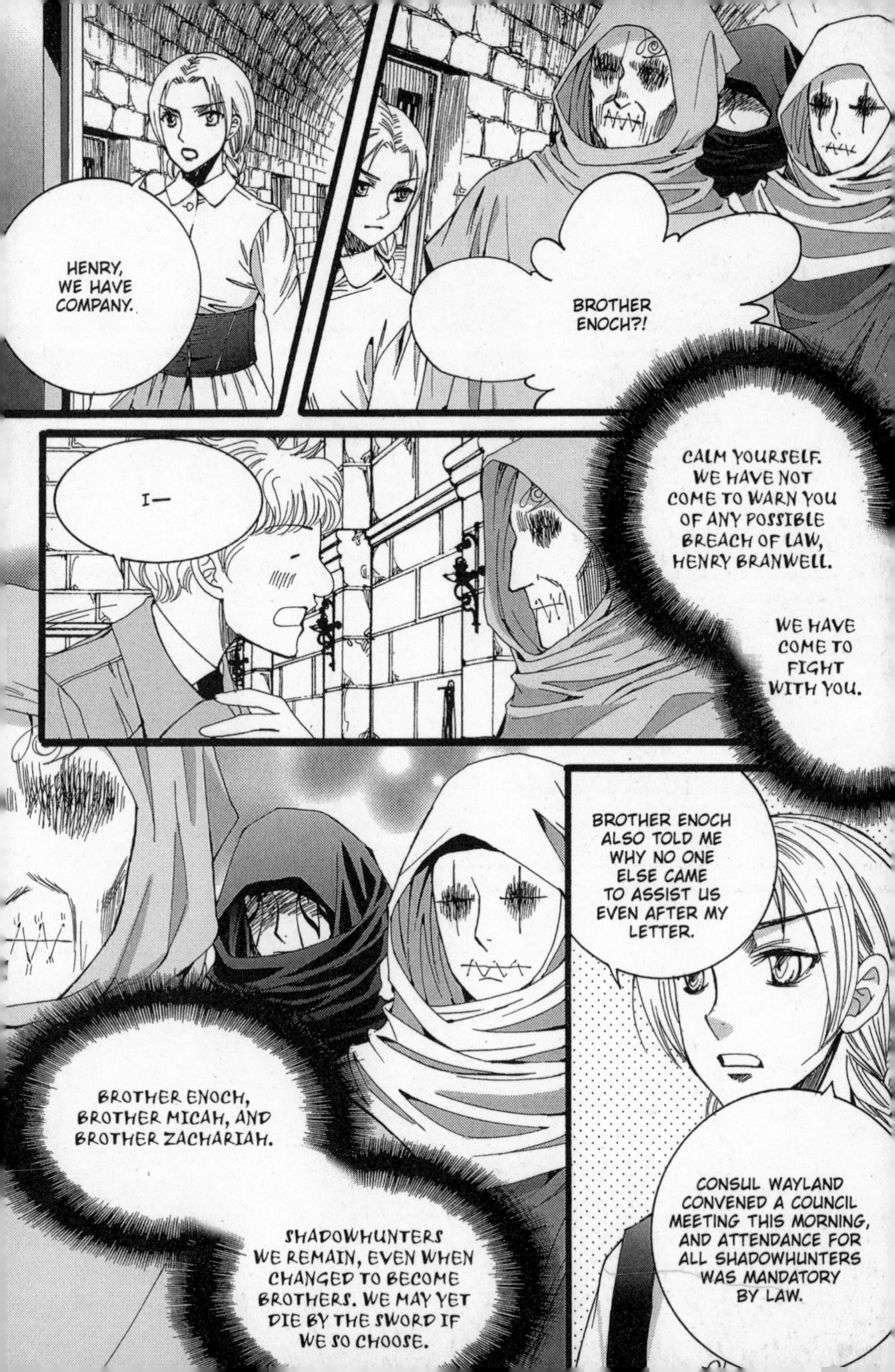
HENRY, WE HAVE COMPANY.
BROTHER ENOCH?!
I—
CALM YOURSELF. WE HAVE NOT COME TO WARN YOU OF ANY POSSIBLE BREACH OF LAW, HENRY BRANWELL.
WE HAVE COME TO FIGHT WITH YOU.
BROTHER ENOCH ALSO TOLD ME WHY NO ONE ELSE CAME TO ASSIST US EVEN AFTER MY LETTER.
BROTHER ENOCH, BROTHER MICAH, AND BROTHER ZACHARIAH.
CONSUL WAYLAND CONVENED A COUNCIL MEETING THIS MORNING, AND ATTENDANCE FOR ALL SHADOWHUNTERS WAS MANDATORY BY LAW.
SHADOWHUNTERS WE REMAIN, EVEN WHEN CHANGED TO BECOME BROTHERS. WE MAY YET DIE BY THE SWORD IF WE SO CHOOSE.

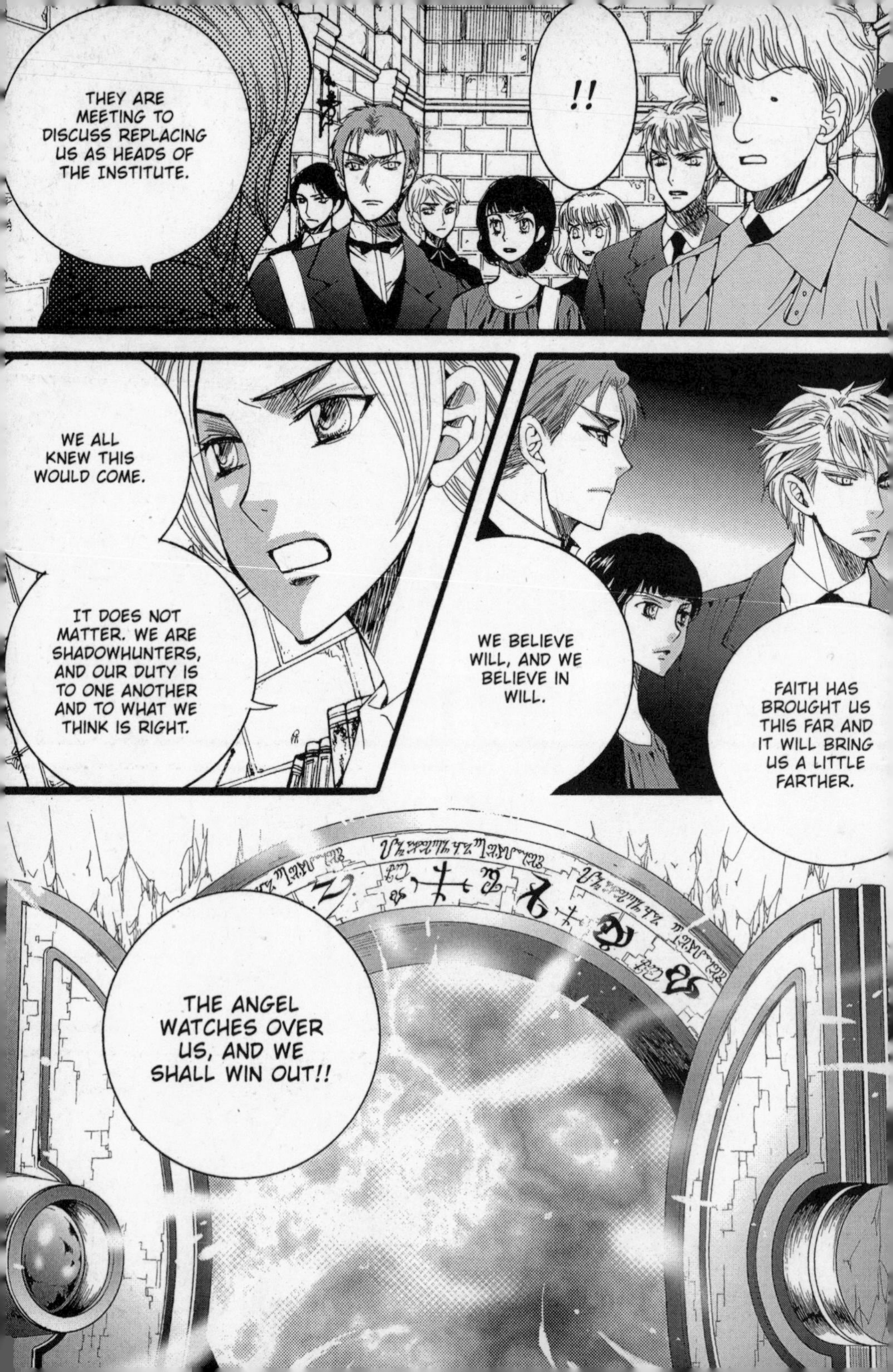
THEY ARE MEETING TO DISCUSS REPLACING US AS HEADS OF THE INSTITUTE.
!!
WE ALL KNEW THIS WOULD COME.
IT DOES NOT MATTER. WE ARE SHADOWHUNTERS, AND OUR DUTY IS TO ONE ANOTHER AND TO WHAT WE THINK IS RIGHT.
WE BELIEVE WILL, AND WE BELIEVE IN WILL.
FAITH HAS BROUGHT US THIS FAR AND IT WILL BRING US A LITTLE FARTHER.
THE ANGEL WATCHES OVER US, AND WE SHALL WIN OUT!!

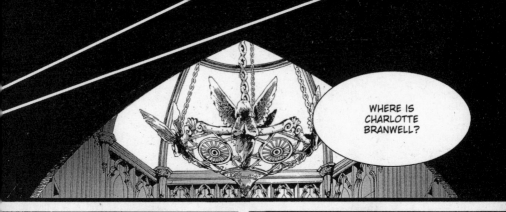

WHERE IS CHARLOTTE BRANWELL?

IT WAS UNDERSTOOD FROM THE MESSAGE YOU SENT THAT SHE WOULD BE HERE TO EXPLAIN THE CONTENTS OF HER LETTER.

CHARLOTTE BRANWELL IS OVERREACTING AND HAS BEEN RELIEVED OF HER POSITION.

I WILL EXPLAIN THE CONTENTS OF HER LETTER.

SHE DOES NOT STRIKE ME AS SOMEONE WHO WOULD EASILY OVERREACT.

SHE IS IN A DELICATE WAY, AND I BELIEVE SHE HAS BECOME... OVERSET.

ARE YOU SUGGESTING THAT MY NIECE IS MAKING UNREASONABLE DECISIONS BECAUSE SHE IS WITH CHILD?

THERE IS NO EVIDENCE TO SUBSTANTIATE HER CLAIMS THAT MORTMAIN IS IN WALES.

ALL EVIDENCE, INCLUDING THE JOURNALS OF BENEDICT LIGHTWOOD, POINT TO AN ATTACK ON LONDON!

AN ATTACK ON LONDON?

MURMUR

MURMUR

THUS WE REQUIRE A NEW LEADER OF THE LONDON ENCLAVE!

I AM GOING TO THROW THE FLOOR OPEN— DOES ANYONE WISH TO STEP FORWARD AS HER REPLACEMENT?

THIS IS RIDICULOUS, JOSIAH. THERE IS NO PROOF YET THAT MORTMAIN IS NOT WHERE CHARLOTTE SAYS HE WILL BE.

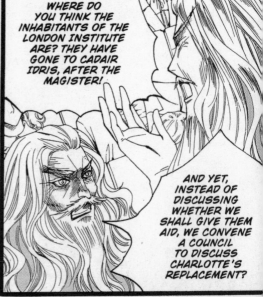

WHERE DO YOU THINK THE INHABITANTS OF THE LONDON INSTITUTE ARE? THEY HAVE GONE TO CADAIR IDRIS, AFTER THE MAGISTER!

AND YET, INSTEAD OF DISCUSSING WHETHER WE SHALL GIVE THEM AID, WE CONVENE A COUNCIL TO DISCUSS CHARLOTTE'S REPLACEMENT?

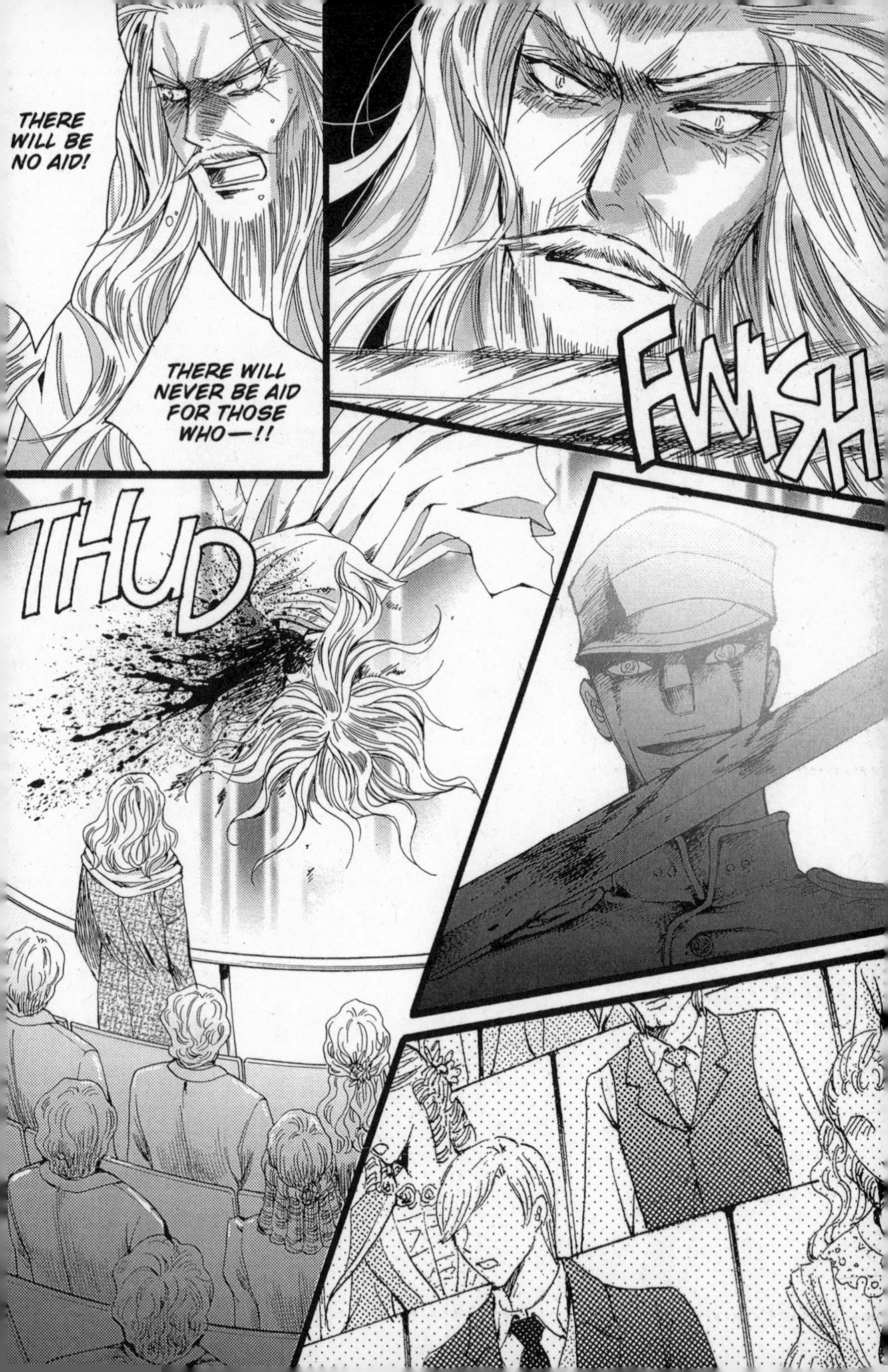
THERE WILL BE NO AID!
THERE WILL NEVER BE AID FOR THOSE WHO—!!
FWISH
THUD

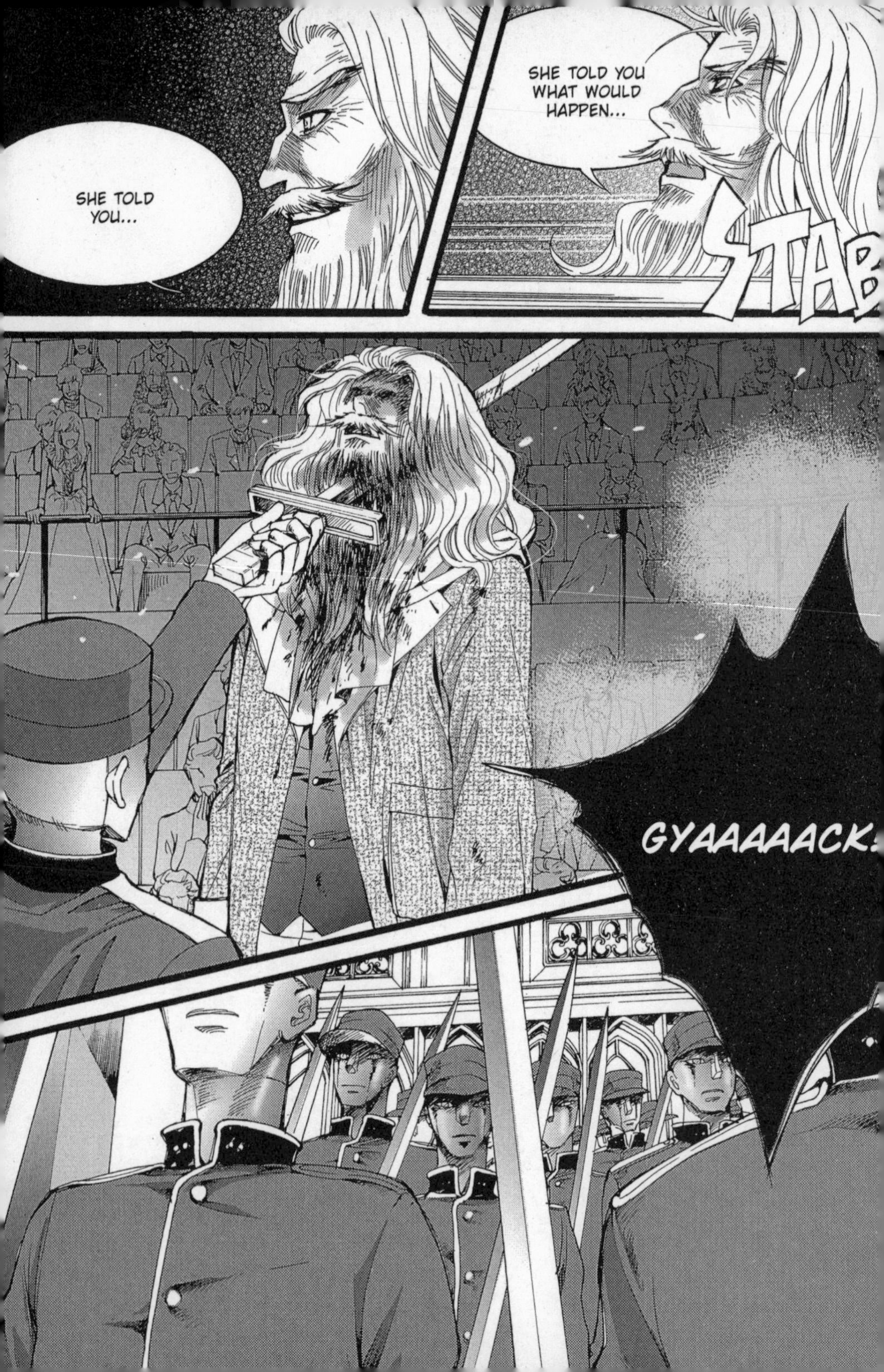
SHE TOLD YOU...
SHE TOLD YOU WHAT WOULD HAPPEN...
STAB
GYAAAAACK!

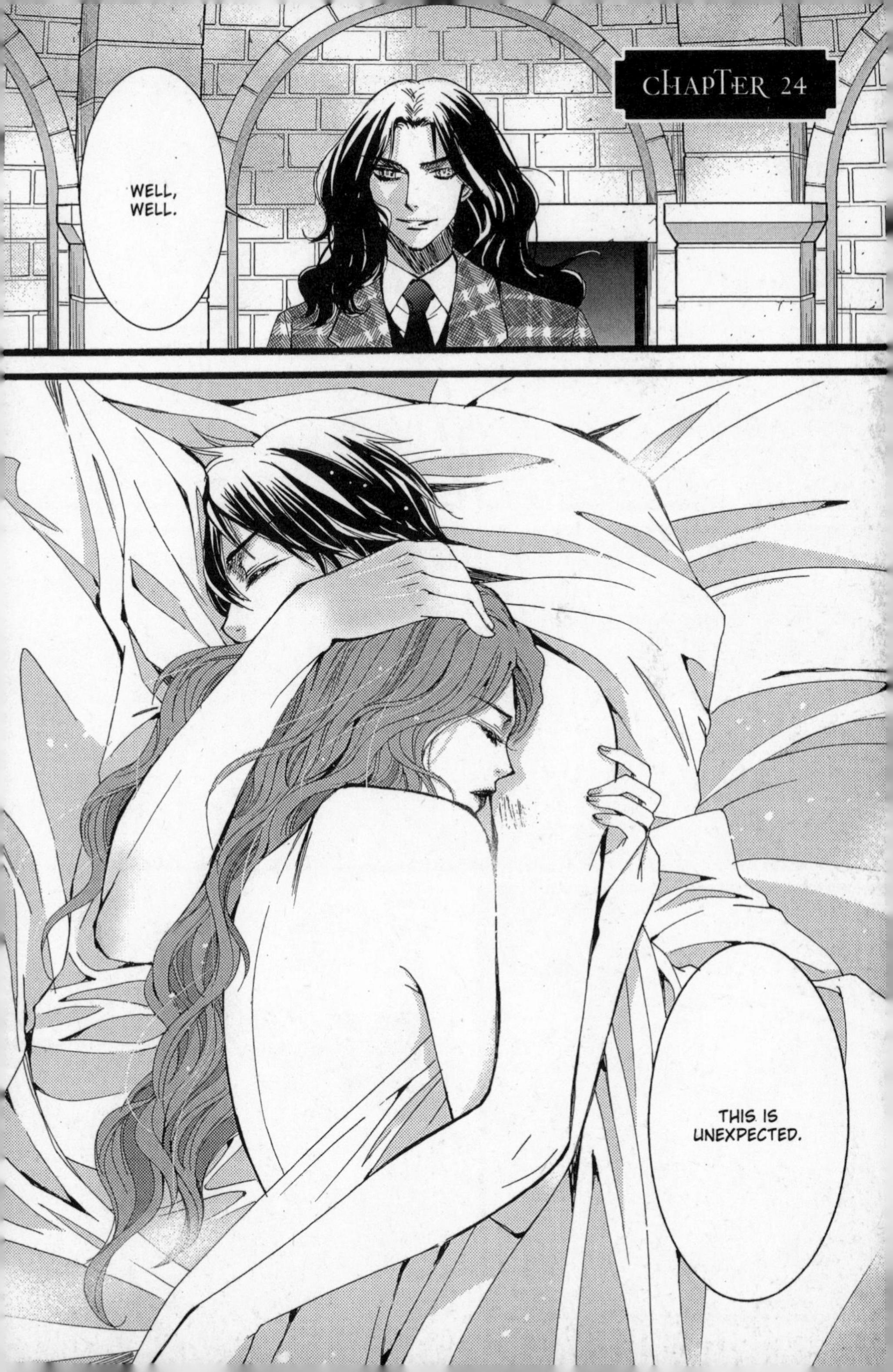
CHAPTER 24
WELL, WELL.
THIS IS UNEXPECTED.

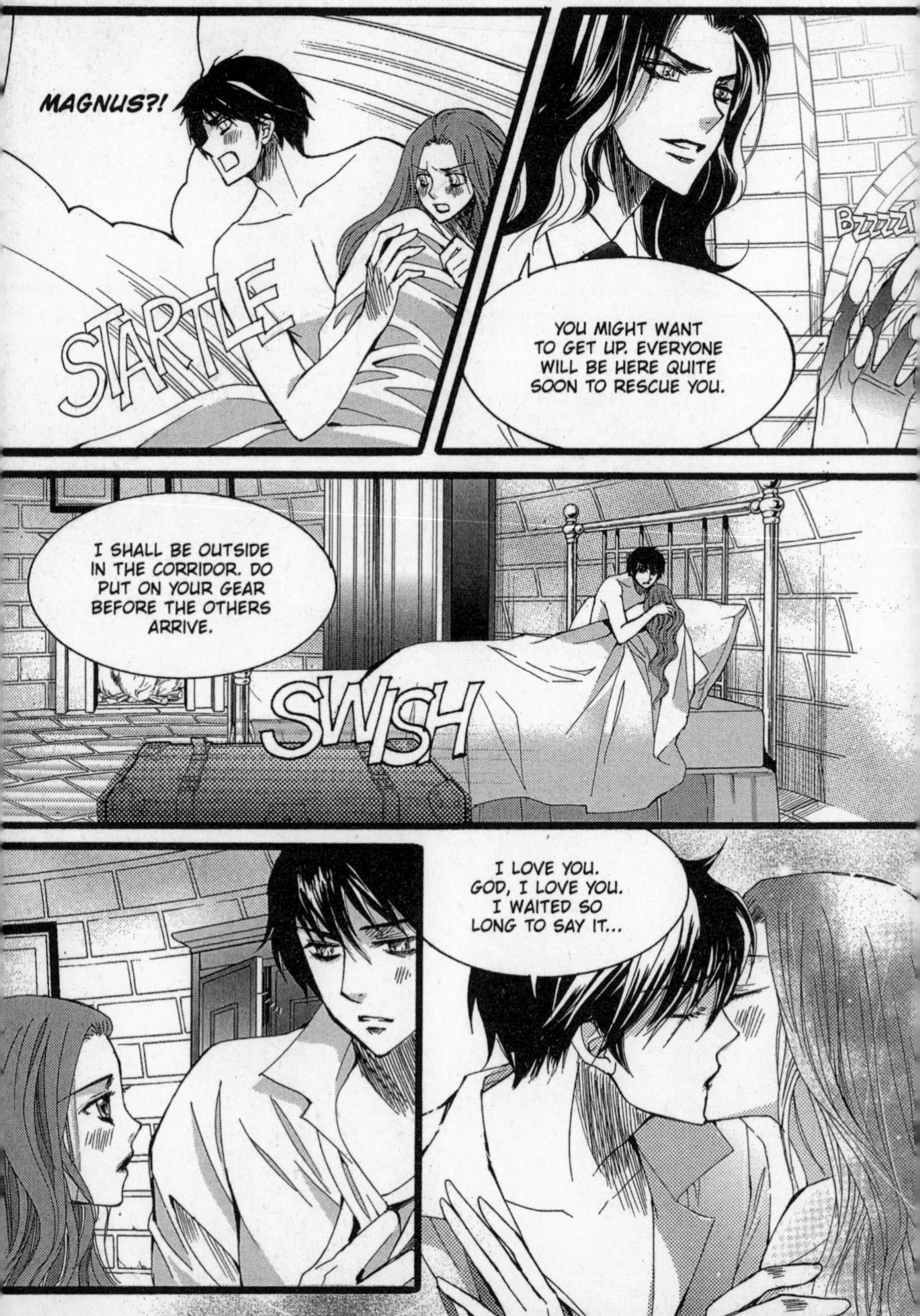
MAGNUS?!
STARTLE
YOU MIGHT WANT TO GET UP. EVERYONE WILL BE HERE QUITE SOON TO RESCUE YOU.
I SHALL BE OUTSIDE IN THE CORRIDOR. DO PUT ON YOUR GEAR BEFORE THE OTHERS ARRIVE.
SWISH
I LOVE YOU. GOD, I LOVE YOU. I WAITED SO LONG TO SAY IT...

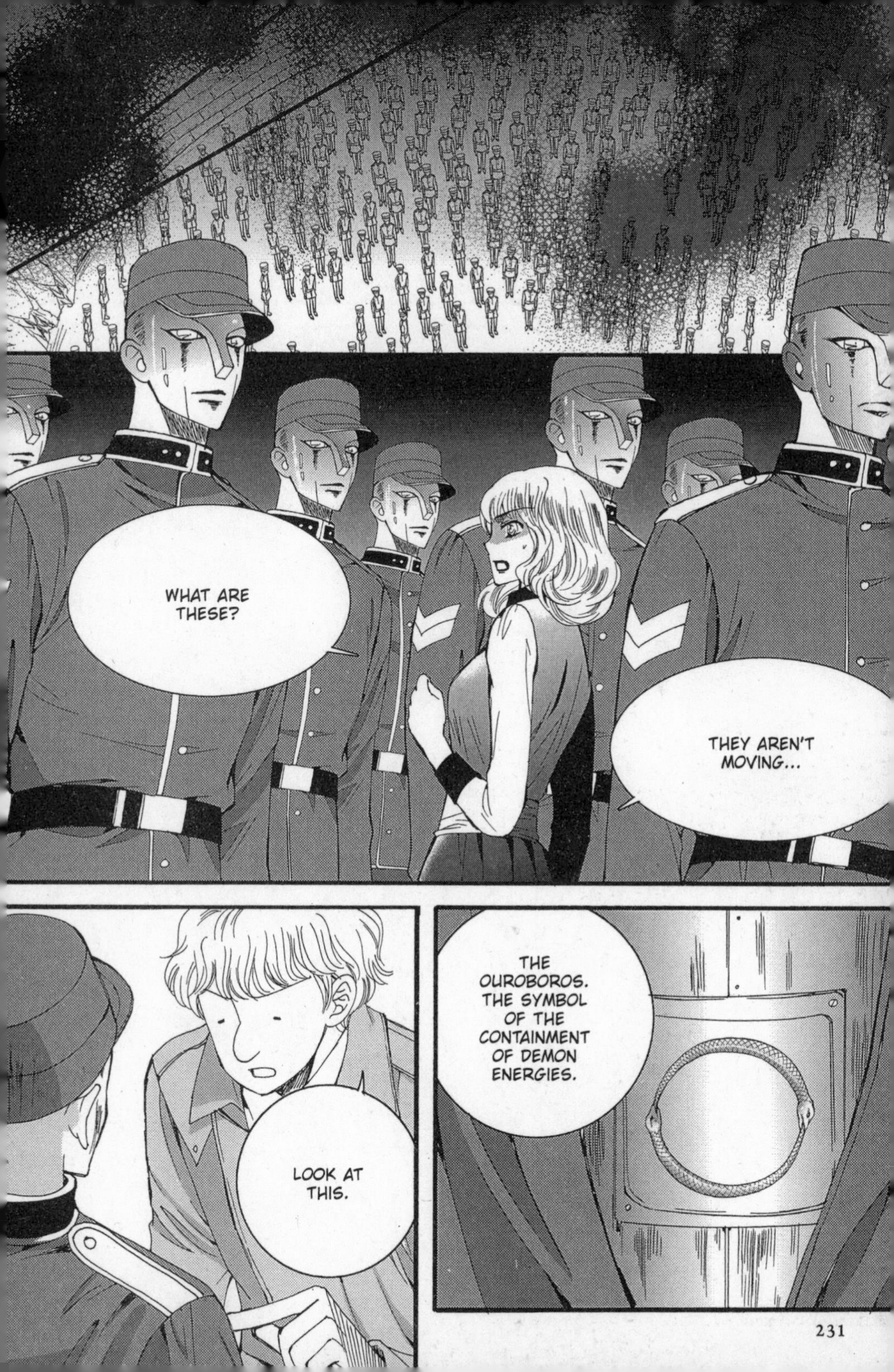
WHAT ARE THESE?
THEY AREN'T MOVING...
LOOK AT THIS.
THE OUROBOROS. THE SYMBOL OF THE CONTAINMENT OF DEMON ENERGIES.

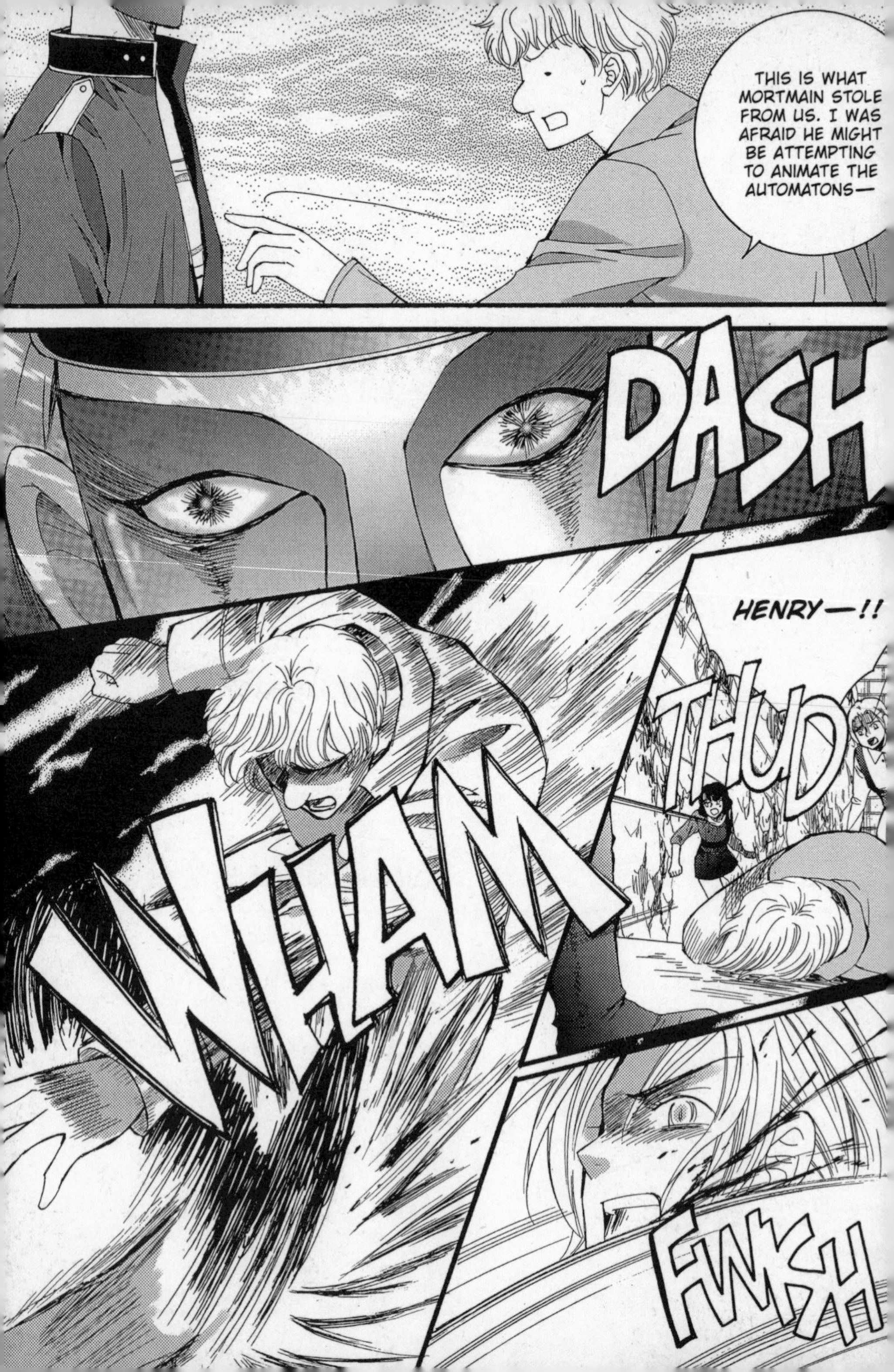
THIS IS WHAT MORTMAIN STOLE FROM US. I WAS AFRAID HE MIGHT BE ATTEMPTING TO ANIMATE THE AUTOMATONS—
DASH
HENRY—!!
THUD
WHAM
FWISH

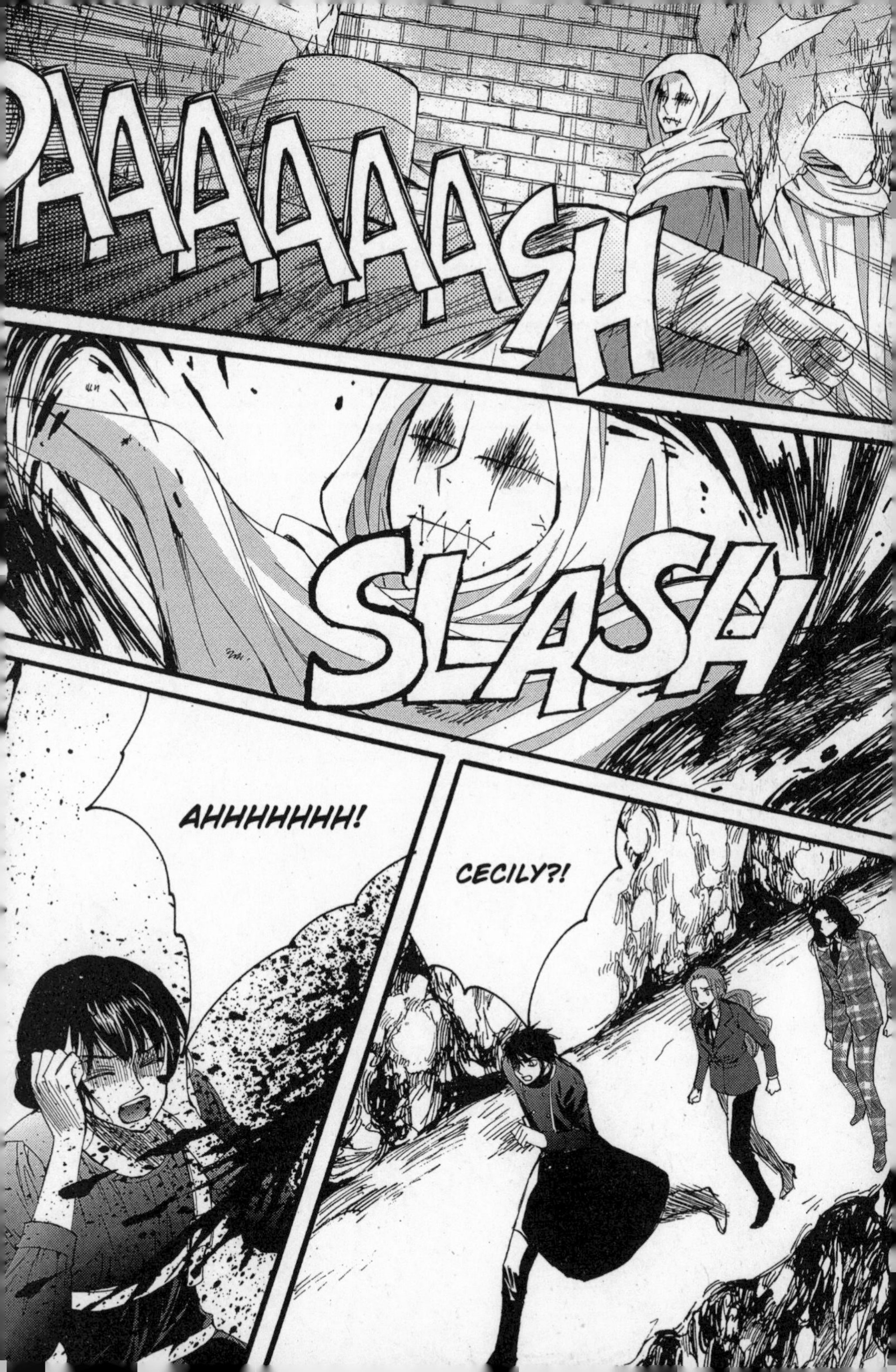

PAAAAAASH
SLASH
CECILY?!
AHHHHHHH!

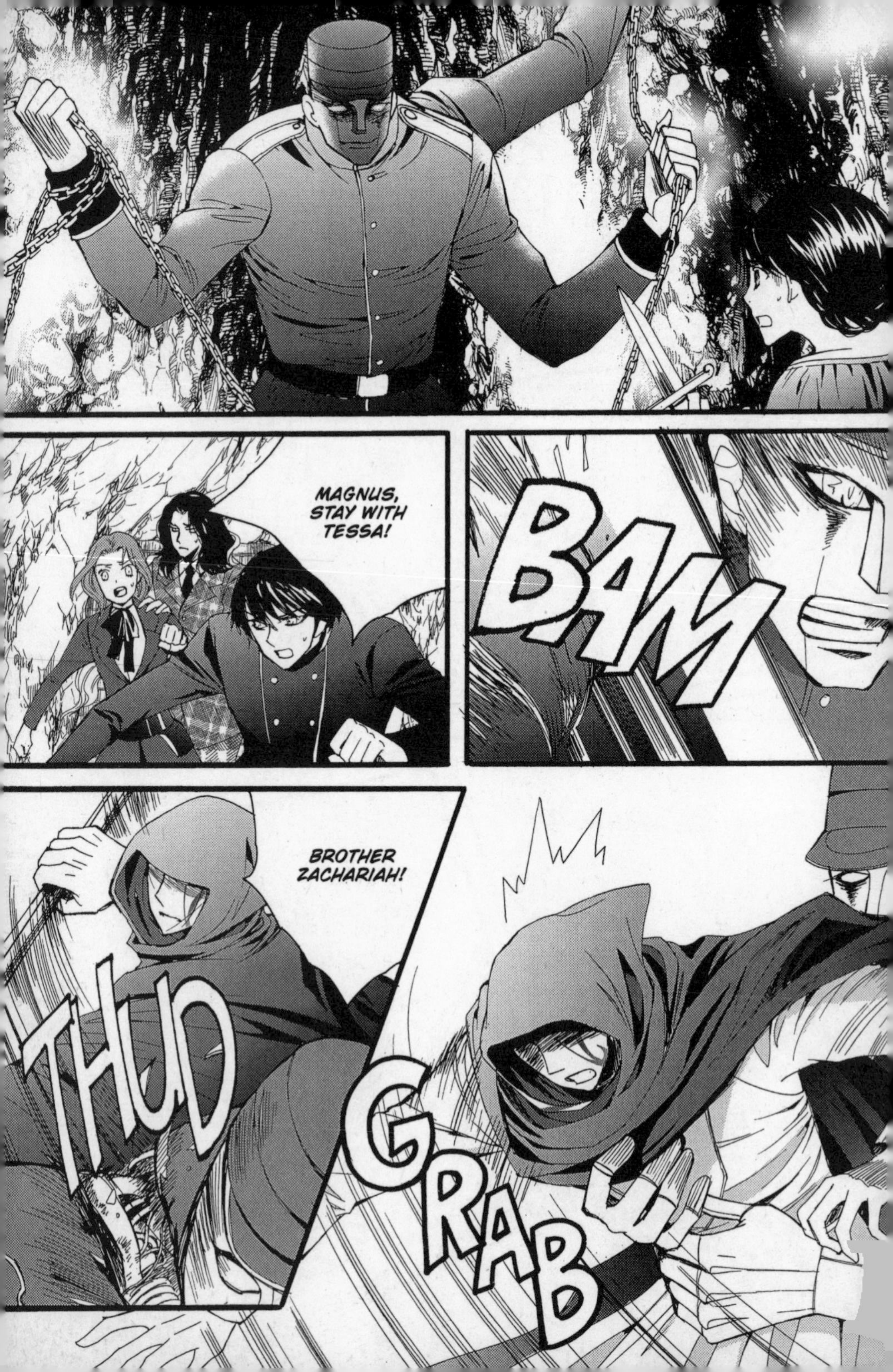
BAM
MAGNUS, STAY WITH TESSA!
BROTHER ZACHARIAH!
GRAB
THUD

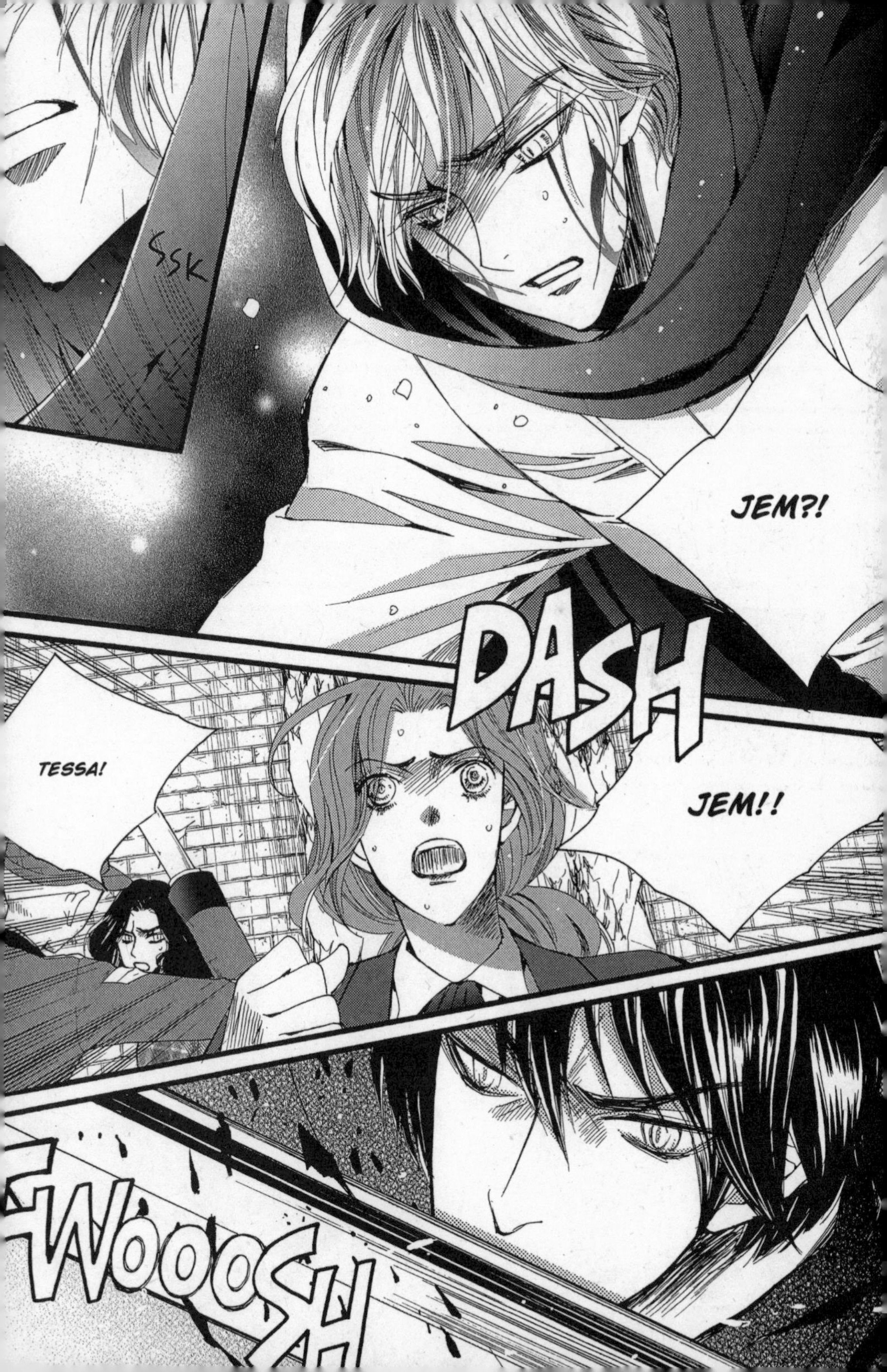
SSK
JEM?!
DASH
JEM!!
TESSA!
FWOOOSH

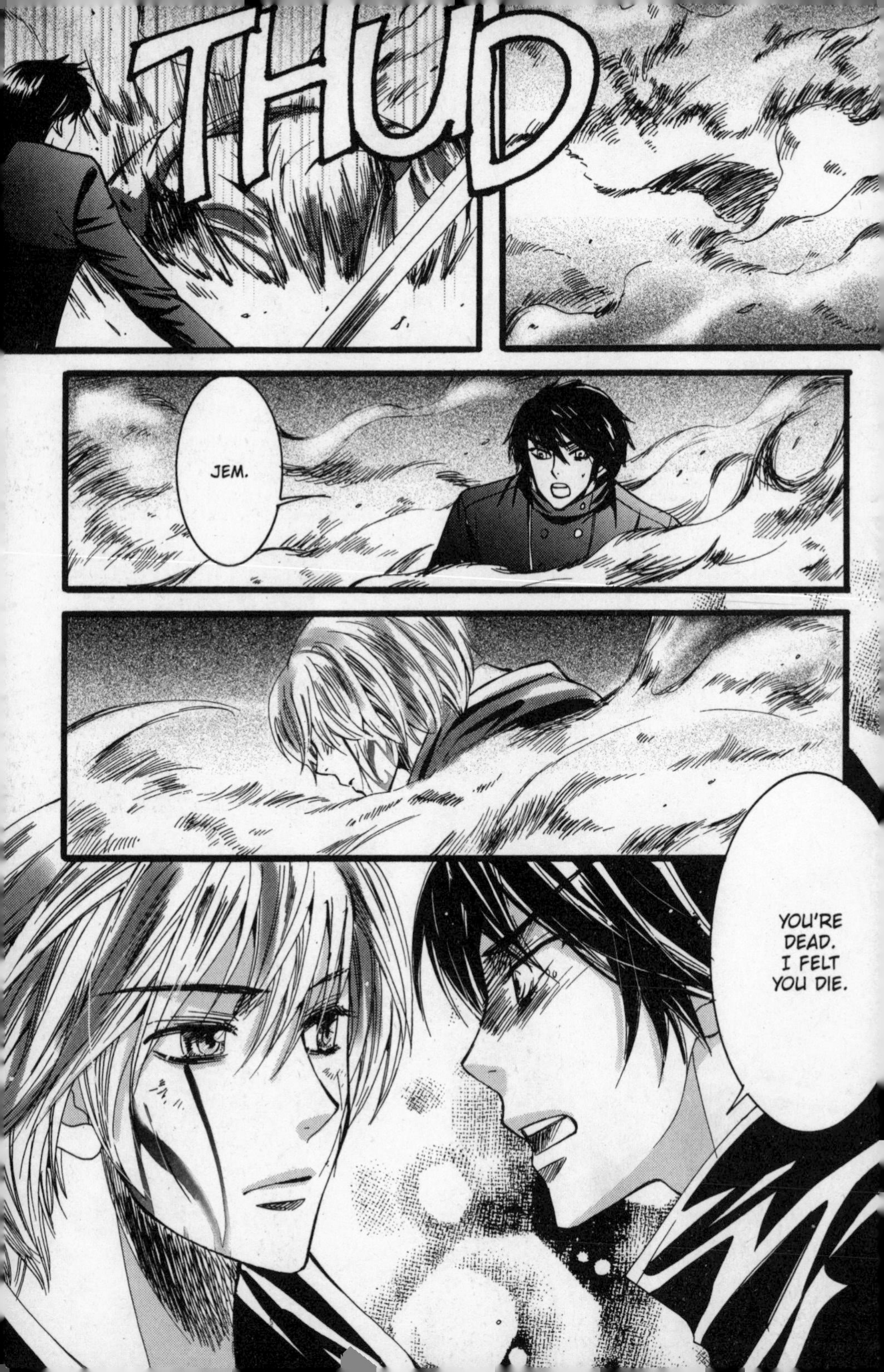
THUD
JEM.
YOU'RE DEAD. I FELT YOU DIE.

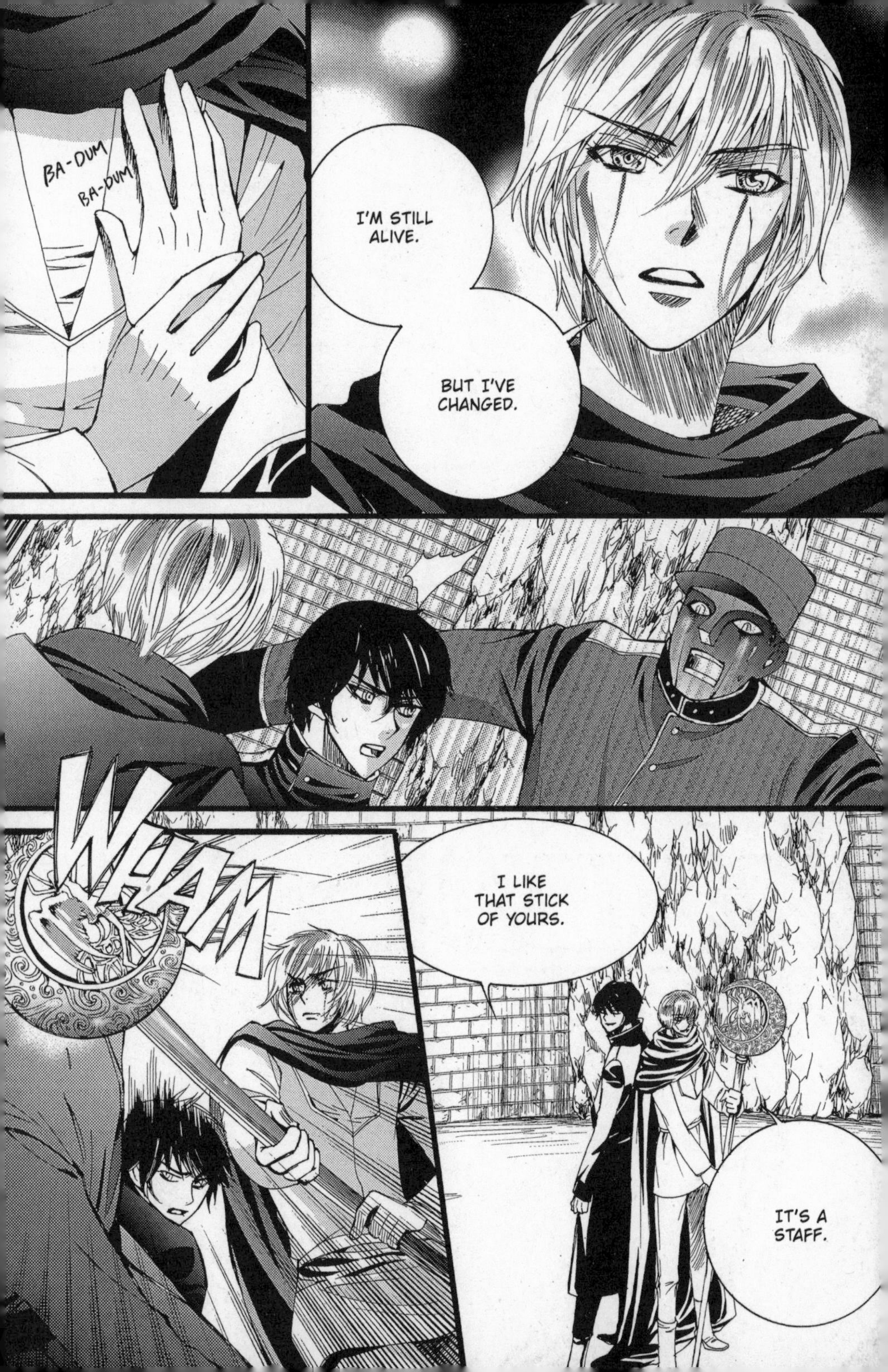
BA-DUM
BA-DUM
I'M STILL ALIVE.
BUT I'VE CHANGED.
WHAM
I LIKE THAT STICK OF YOURS.
IT'S A STAFF.

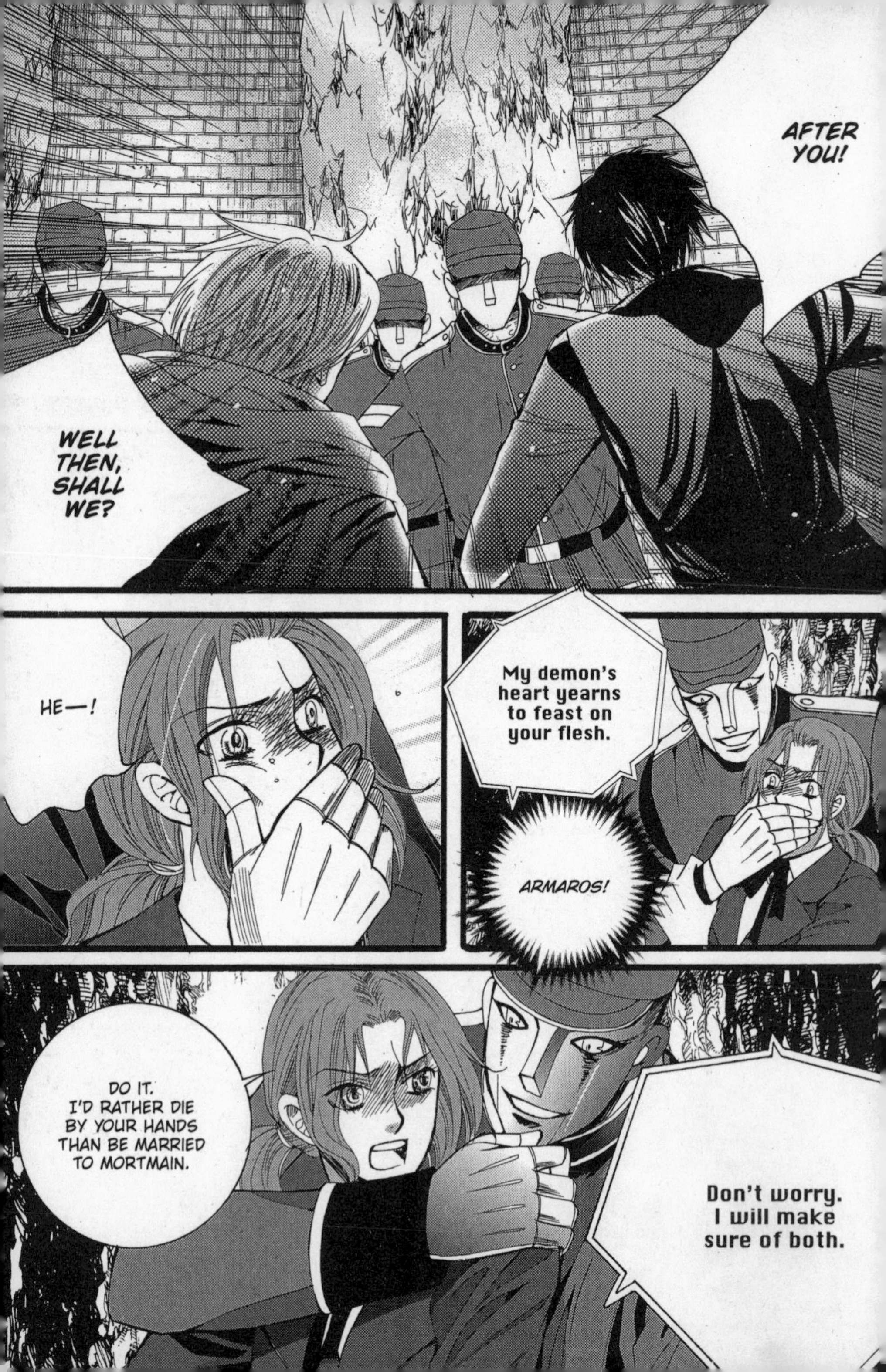
AFTER YOU!
WELL THEN, SHALL WE?
My demon's heart yearns to feast on your flesh.
ARMAROS!
HE—!
DO IT. I'D RATHER DIE BY YOUR HANDS THAN BE MARRIED TO MORTMAIN.
Don't worry. I will make sure of both.

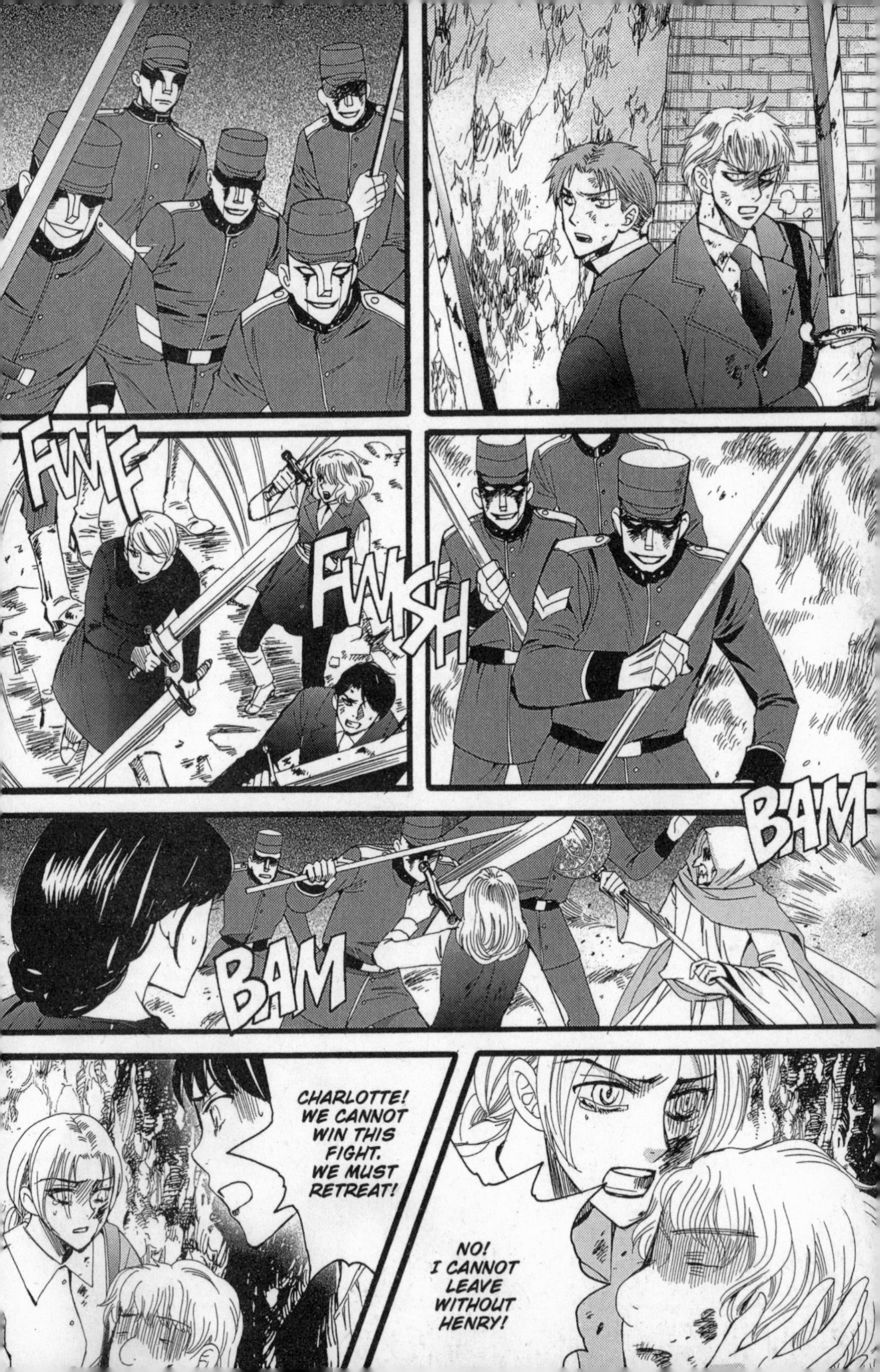
FWF
FWISH
BAM
BAM
CHARLOTTE! WE CANNOT WIN THIS FIGHT. WE MUST RETREAT!
NO! I CANNOT LEAVE WITHOUT HENRY!

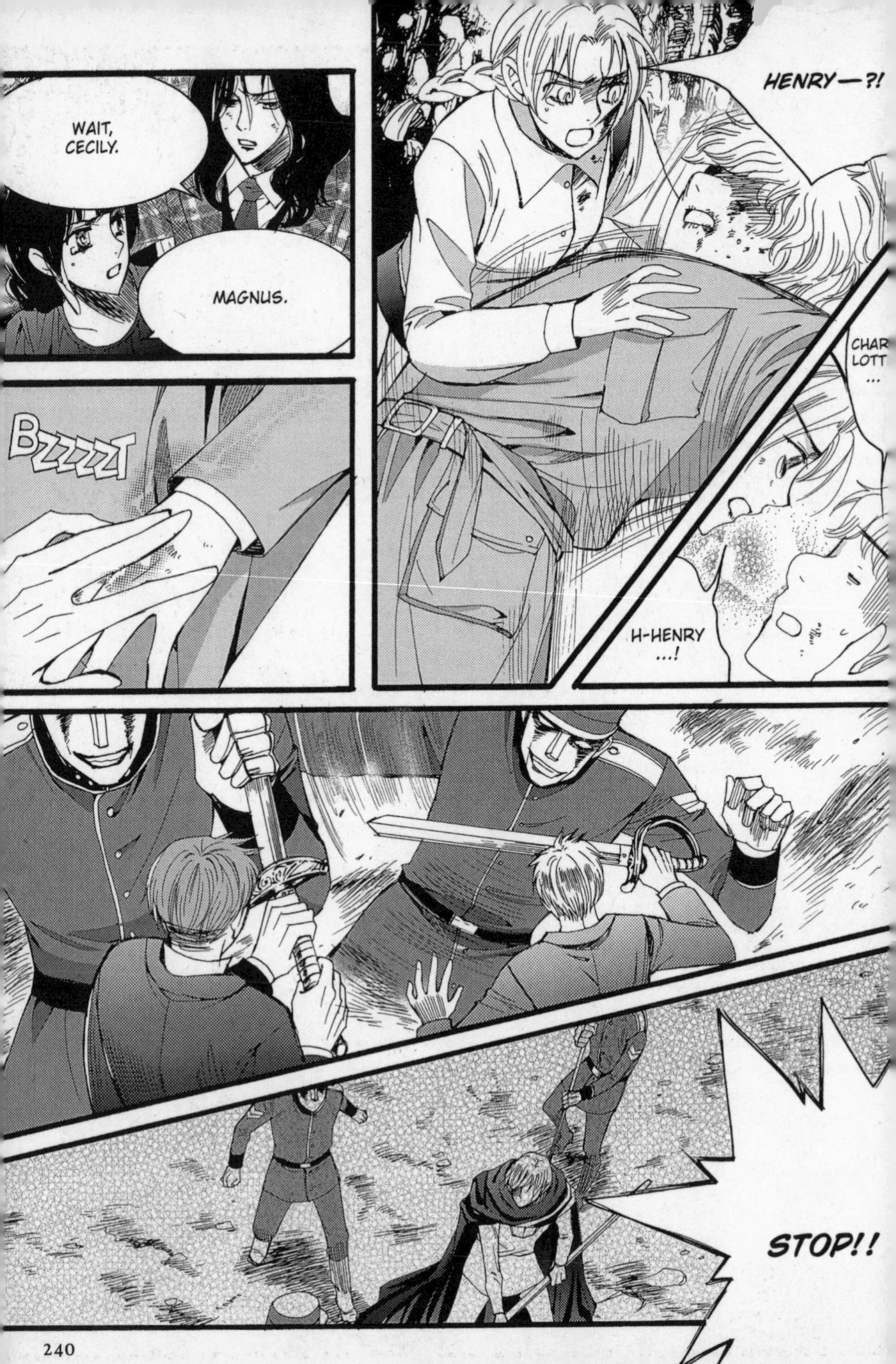
WAIT, CECILY.
MAGNUS.
BZZZZT
HENRY—?!
CHARLOTT...
H-HENRY...!
STOP!!

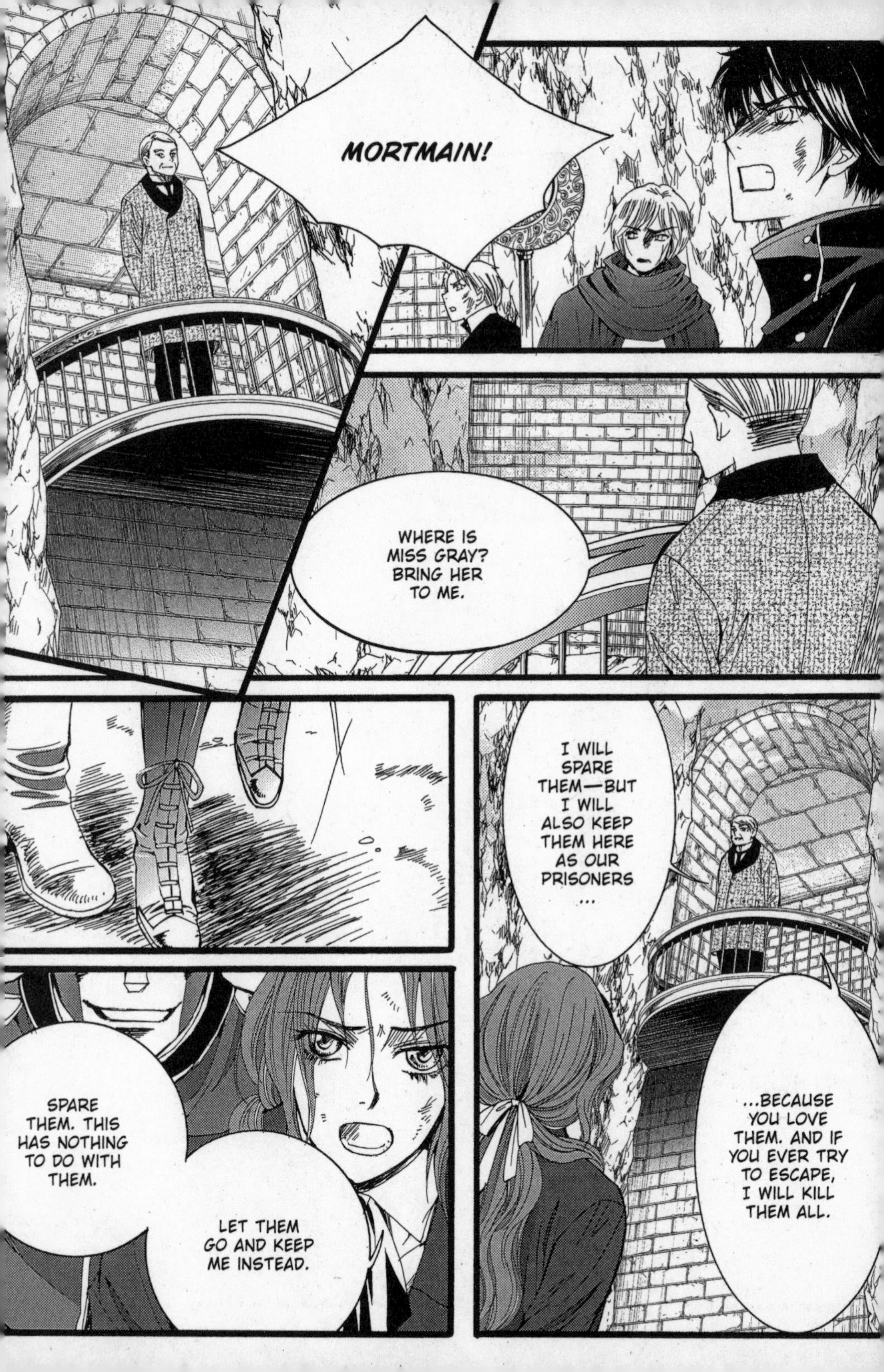
MORTMAIN!
WHERE IS MISS GRAY? BRING HER TO ME.
SPARE THEM. THIS HAS NOTHING TO DO WITH THEM.
LET THEM GO AND KEEP ME INSTEAD.
I WILL SPARE THEM—BUT I WILL ALSO KEEP THEM HERE AS OUR PRISONERS ...
...BECAUSE YOU LOVE THEM. AND IF YOU EVER TRY TO ESCAPE, I WILL KILL THEM ALL.

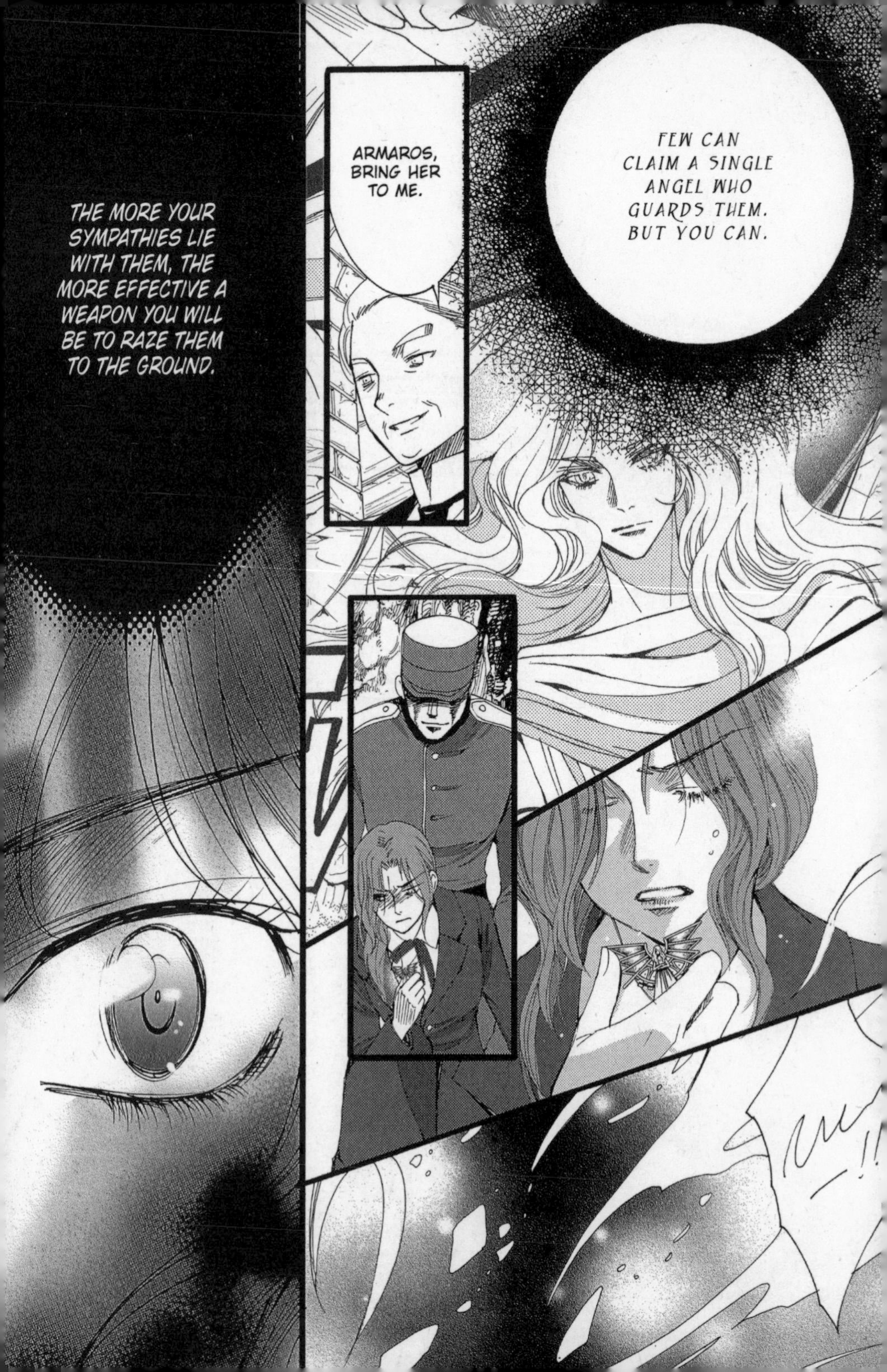
FEW CAN
CLAIM A SINGLE
ANGEL WHO
GUARDS THEM.
BUT YOU CAN.
ARMAROS,
BRING HER
TO ME.
THE MORE YOUR
SYMPATHIES LIE
WITH THEM, THE
MORE EFFECTIVE A
WEAPON YOU WILL
BE TO RAZE THEM
TO THE GROUND.

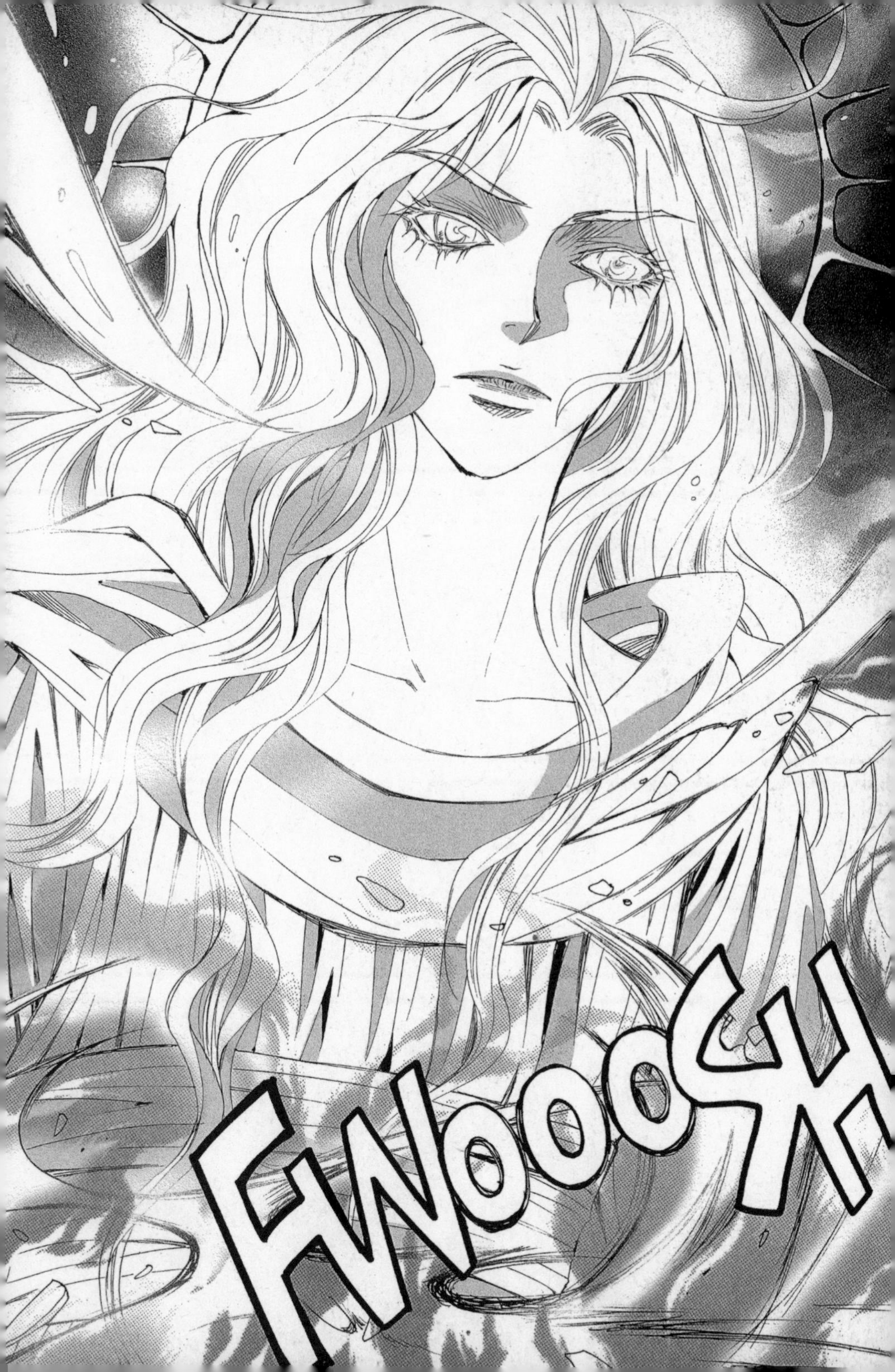
FWOOOSH

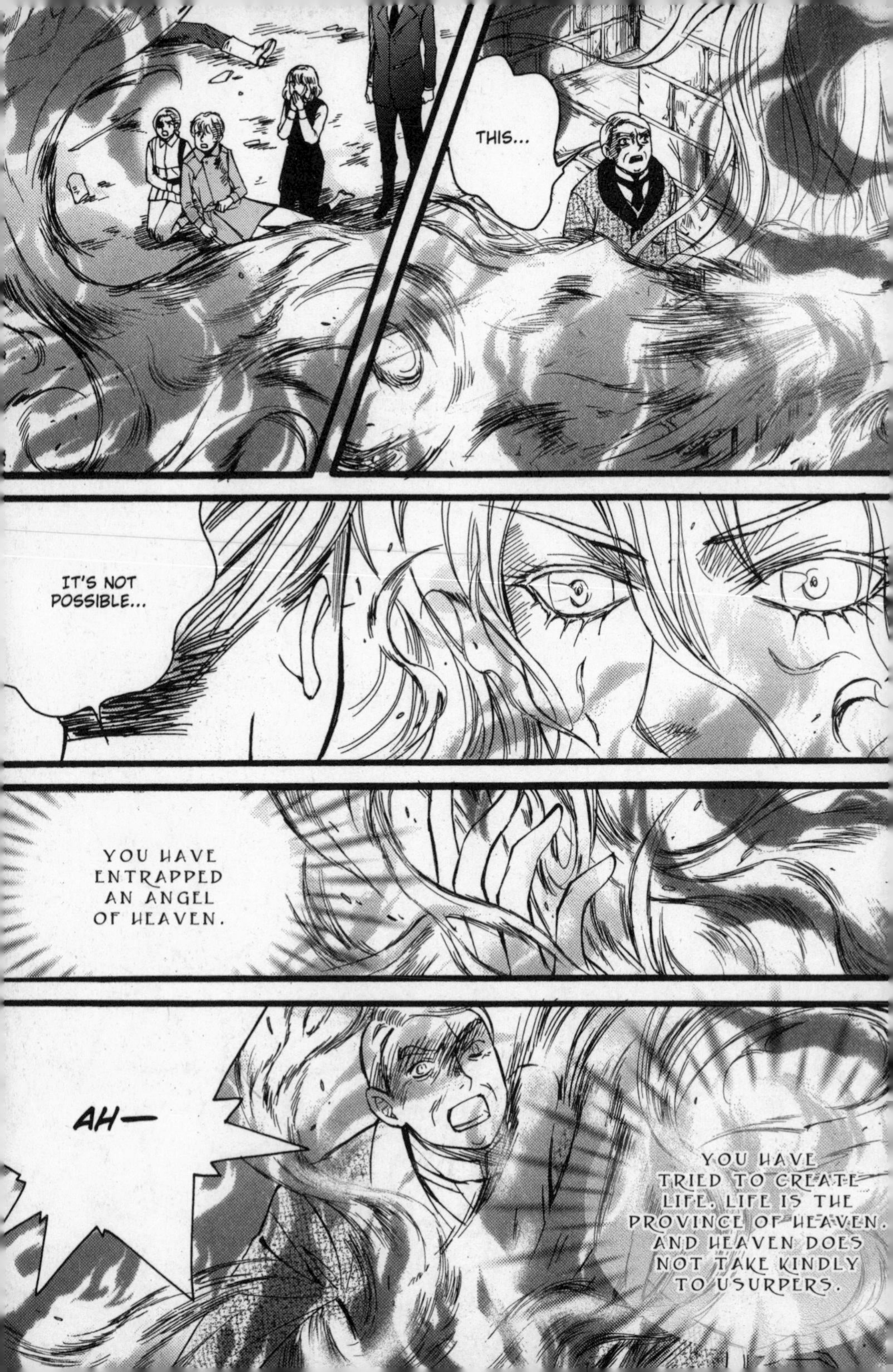
THIS...
IT'S NOT POSSIBLE...
YOU HAVE ENTRAPPED AN ANGEL OF HEAVEN.
AH—
YOU HAVE TRIED TO CREATE LIFE. LIFE IS THE PROVINCE OF HEAVEN. AND HEAVEN DOES NOT TAKE KINDLY TO USURPERS.

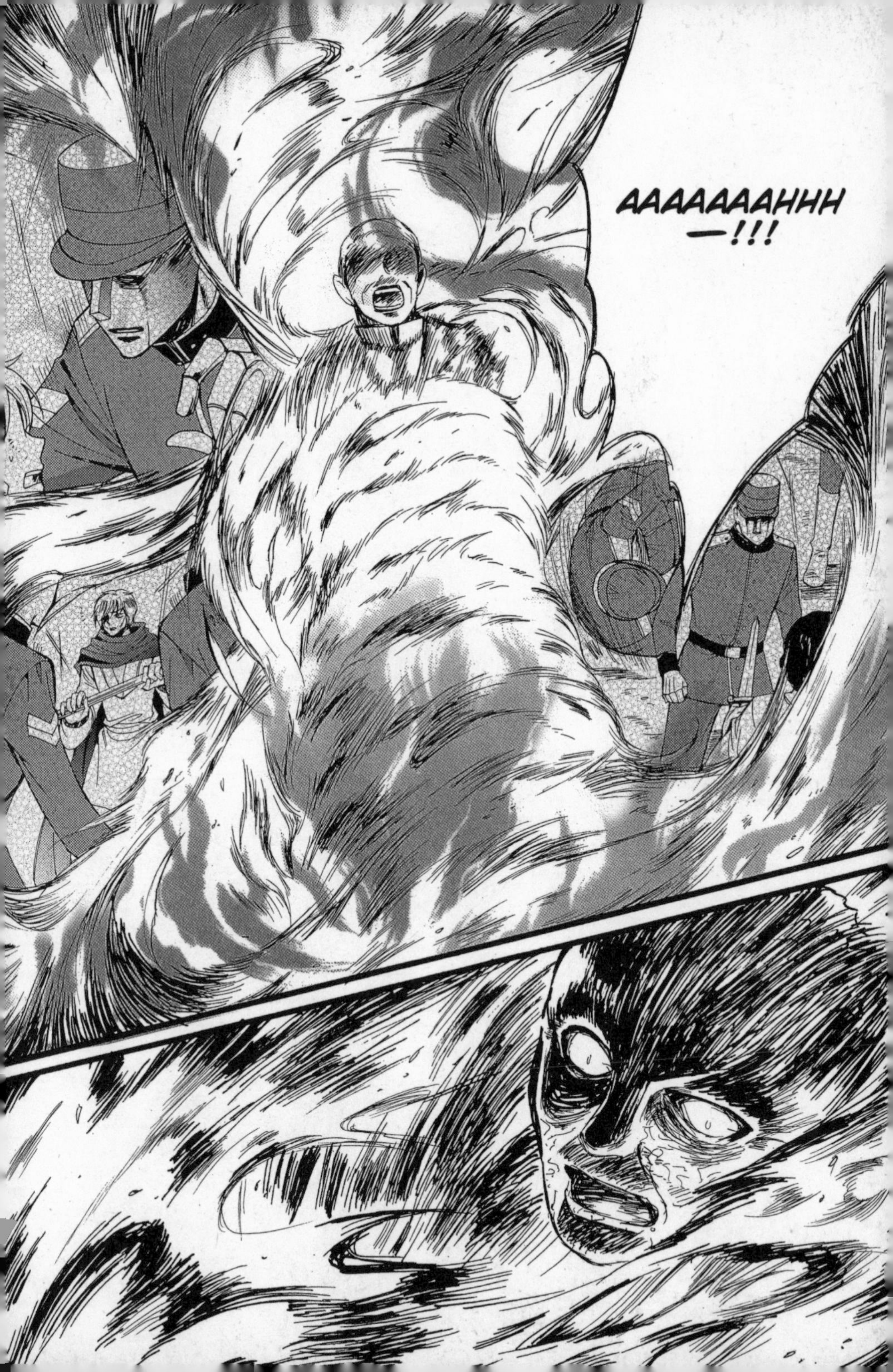
AAAAAAAHHH
—!!!

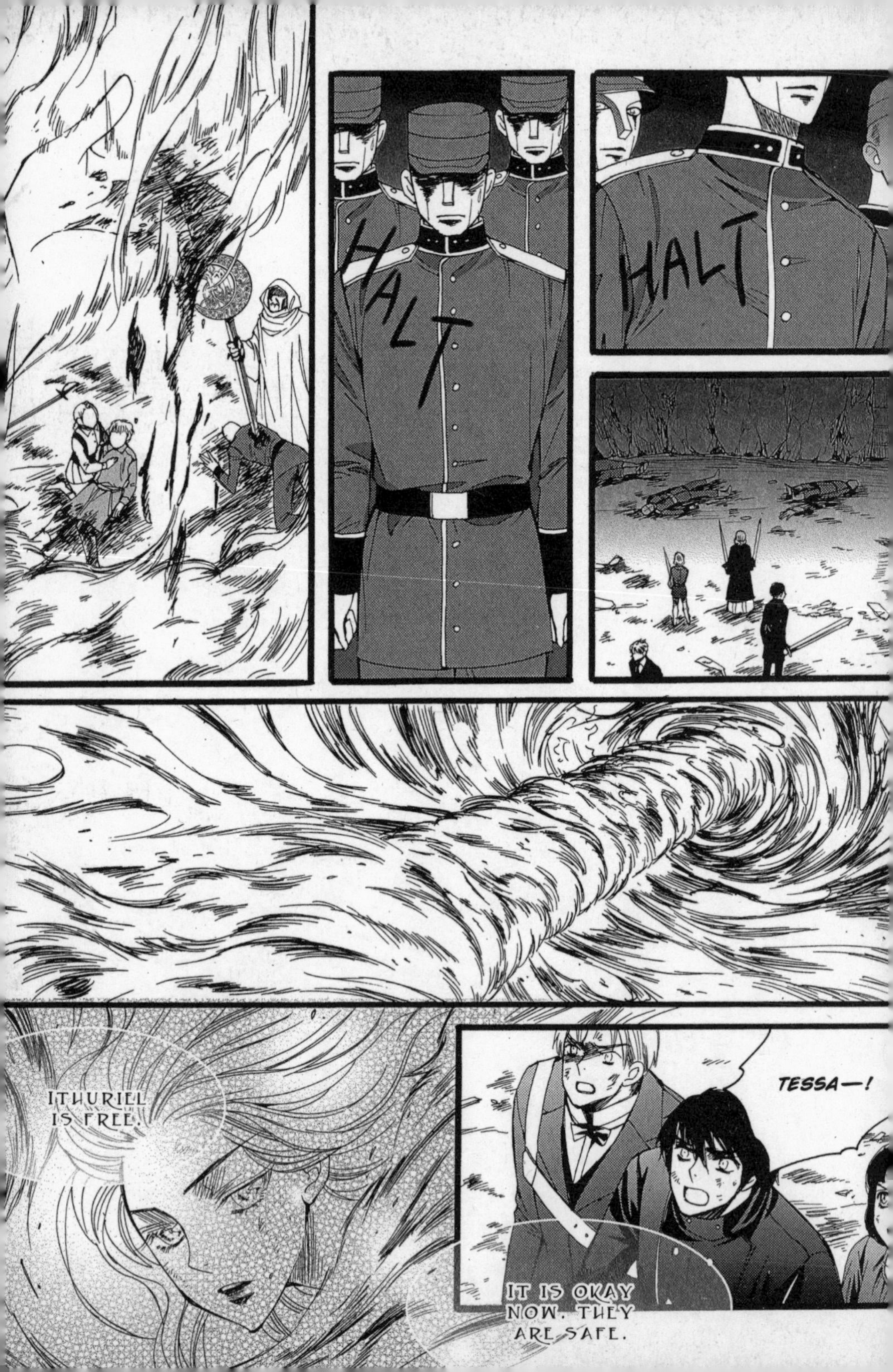
HALT
HALT
ITHURIEL IS FREE.
TESSA—!
IT IS OKAY NOW. THEY ARE SAFE.

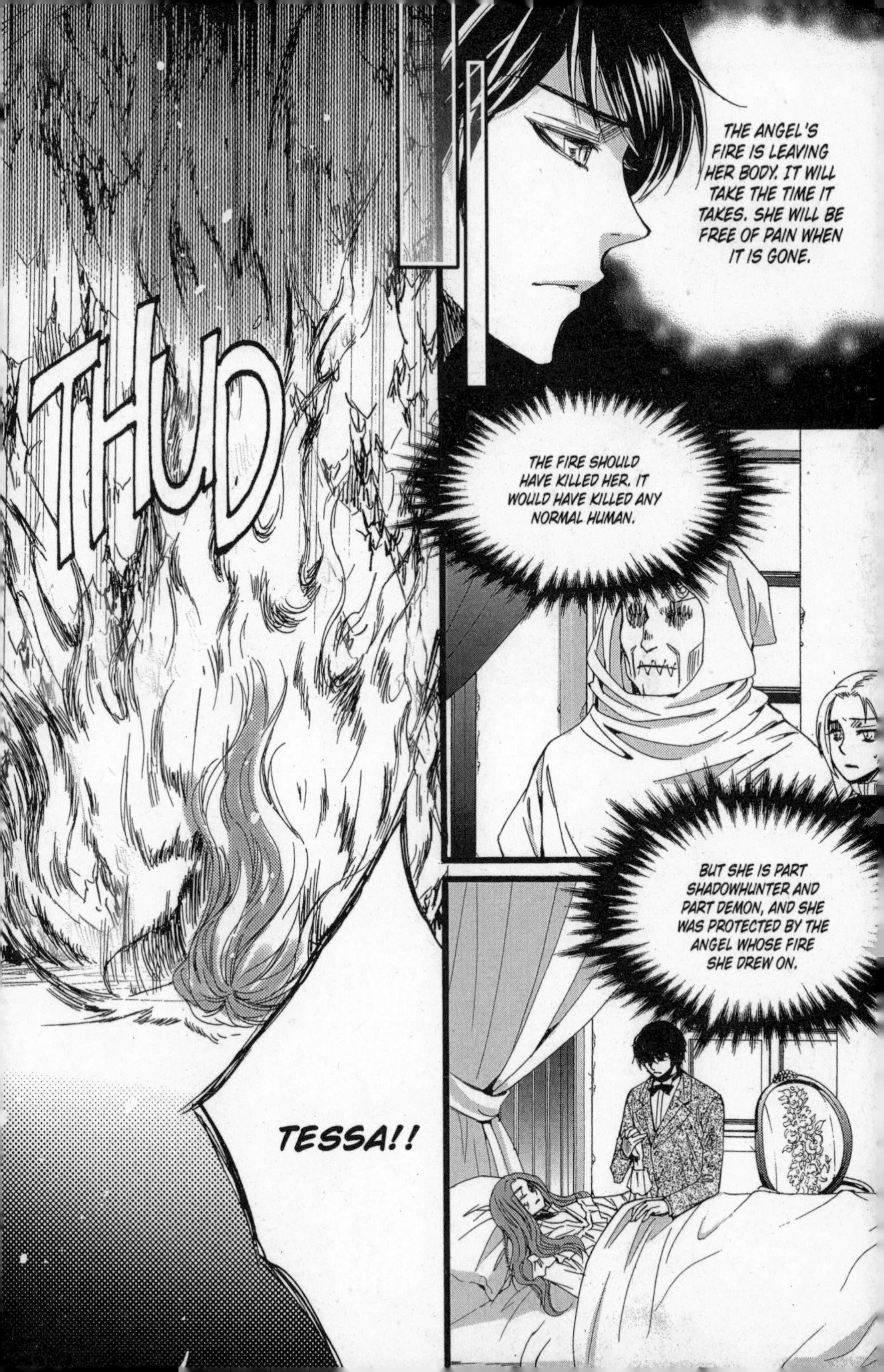
THUD
TESSA!!
THE ANGEL'S FIRE IS LEAVING HER BODY. IT WILL TAKE THE TIME IT TAKES. SHE WILL BE FREE OF PAIN WHEN IT IS GONE.
THE FIRE SHOULD HAVE KILLED HER. IT WOULD HAVE KILLED ANY NORMAL HUMAN.
BUT SHE IS PART SHADOWHUNTER AND PART DEMON, AND SHE WAS PROTECTED BY THE ANGEL WHOSE FIRE SHE DREW ON.

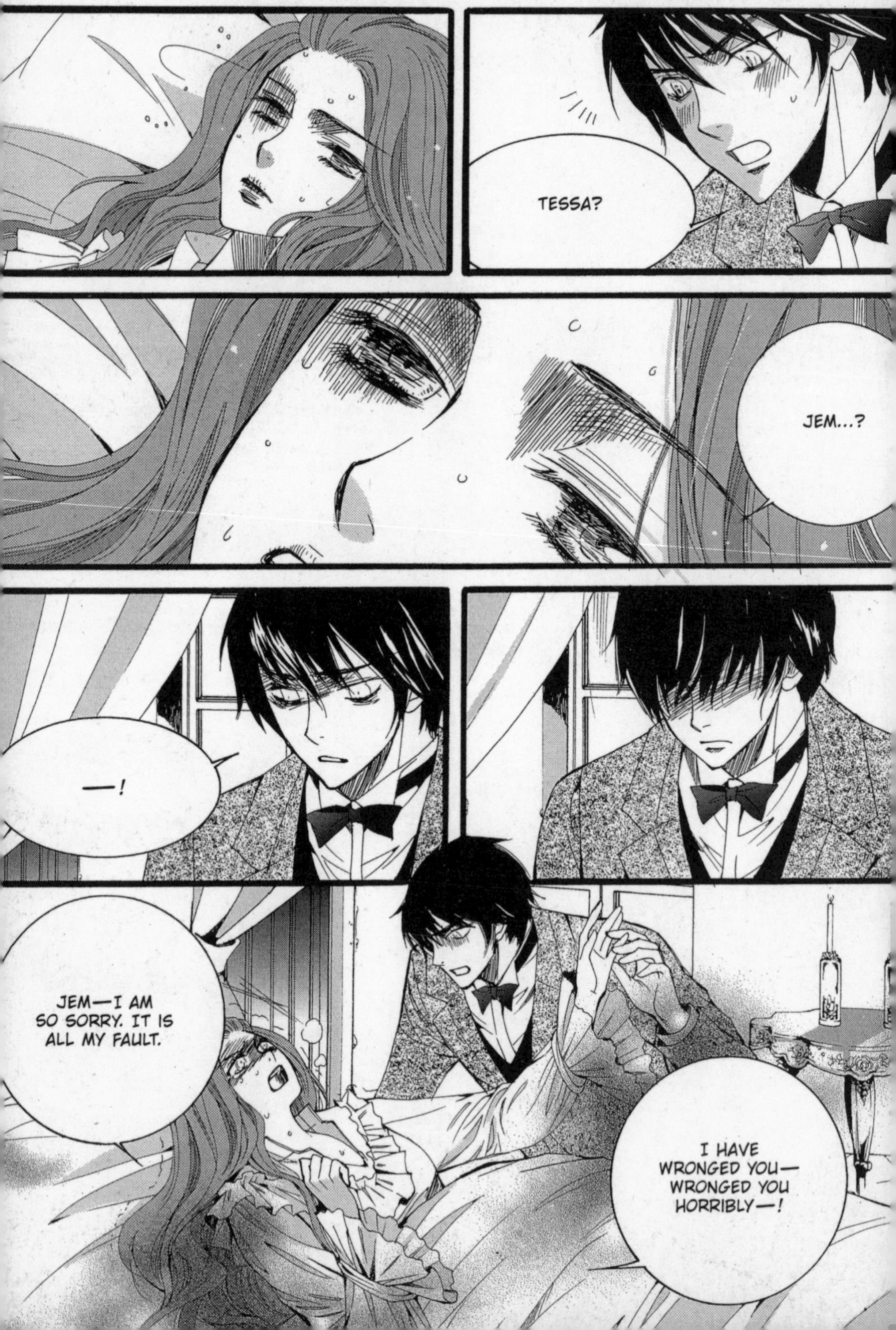
TESSA?
JEM...?
—!
JEM—I AM SO SORRY. IT IS ALL MY FAULT.
I HAVE WRONGED YOU—WRONGED YOU HORRIBLY—!

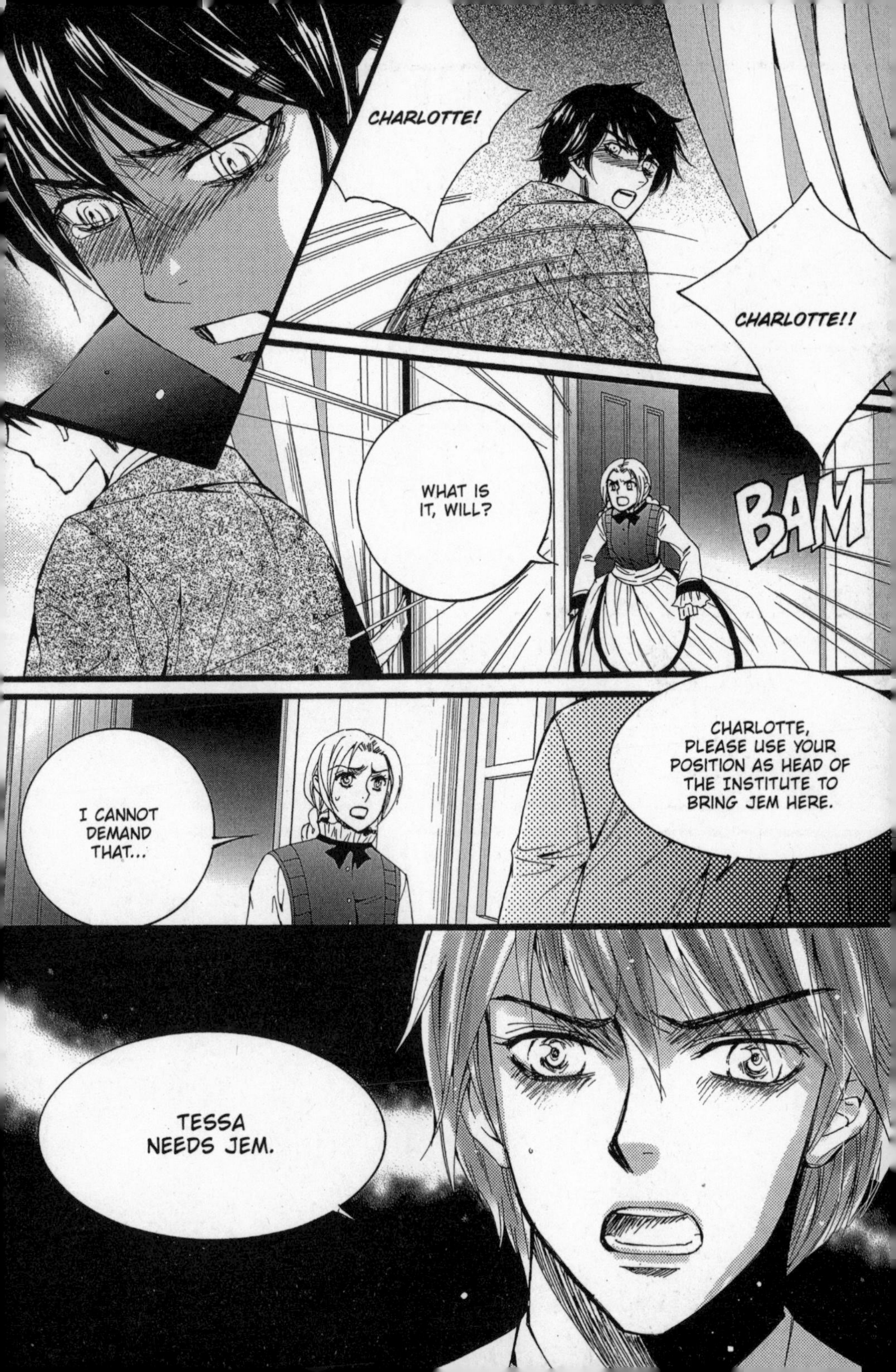
CHARLOTTE!
CHARLOTTE!!
WHAT IS IT, WILL?
BAM
I CANNOT DEMAND THAT...
CHARLOTTE, PLEASE USE YOUR POSITION AS HEAD OF THE INSTITUTE TO BRING JEM HERE.
TESSA NEEDS JEM.

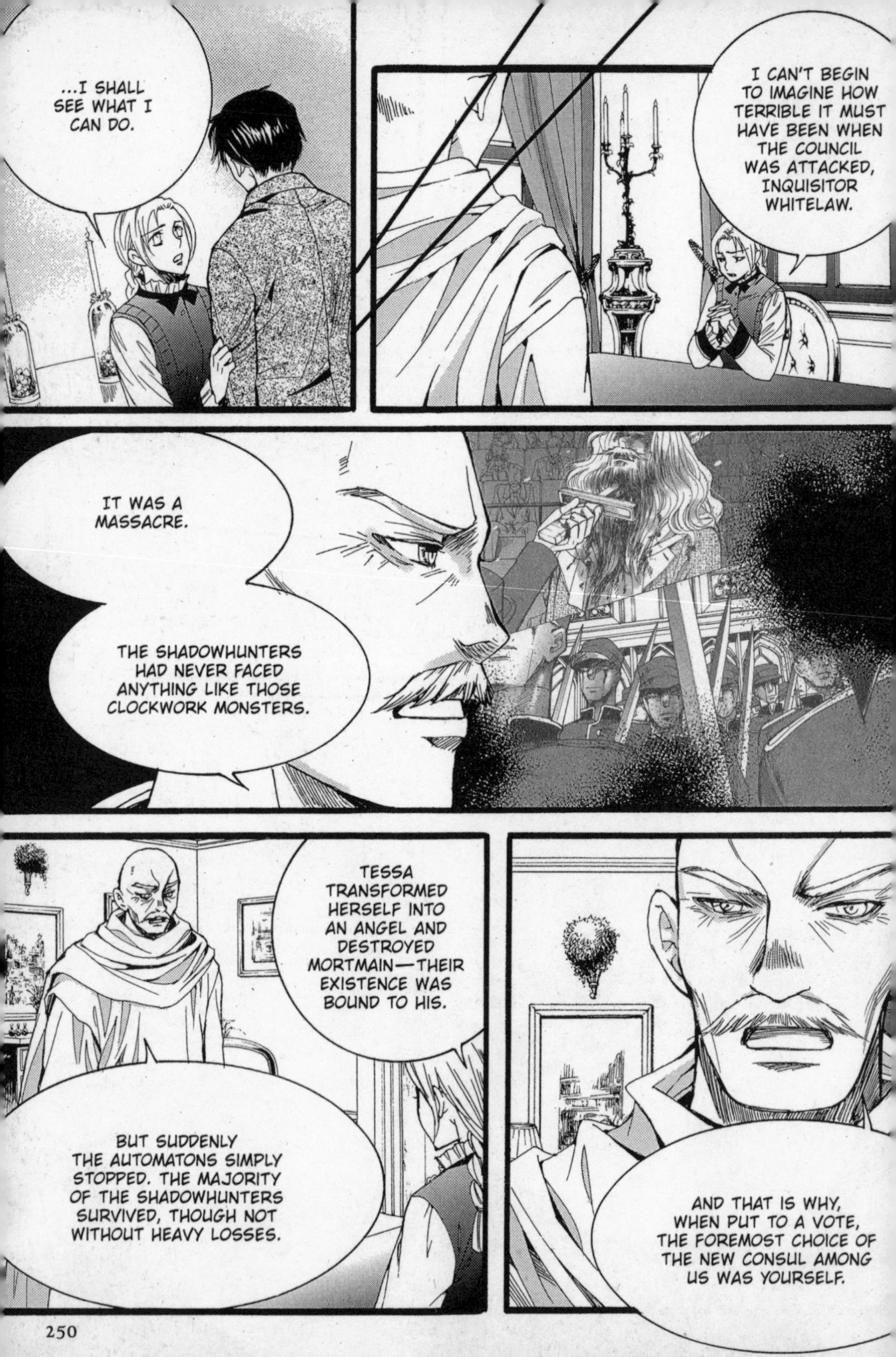
...I SHALL SEE WHAT I CAN DO.
I CAN'T BEGIN TO IMAGINE HOW TERRIBLE IT MUST HAVE BEEN WHEN THE COUNCIL WAS ATTACKED, INQUISITOR WHITELAW.
IT WAS A MASSACRE.
THE SHADOWHUNTERS HAD NEVER FACED ANYTHING LIKE THOSE CLOCKWORK MONSTERS.
BUT SUDDENLY THE AUTOMATONS SIMPLY STOPPED. THE MAJORITY OF THE SHADOWHUNTERS SURVIVED, THOUGH NOT WITHOUT HEAVY LOSSES.
TESSA TRANSFORMED HERSELF INTO AN ANGEL AND DESTROYED MORTMAIN—THEIR EXISTENCE WAS BOUND TO HIS.
AND THAT IS WHY, WHEN PUT TO A VOTE, THE FOREMOST CHOICE OF THE NEW CONSUL AMONG US WAS YOURSELF.

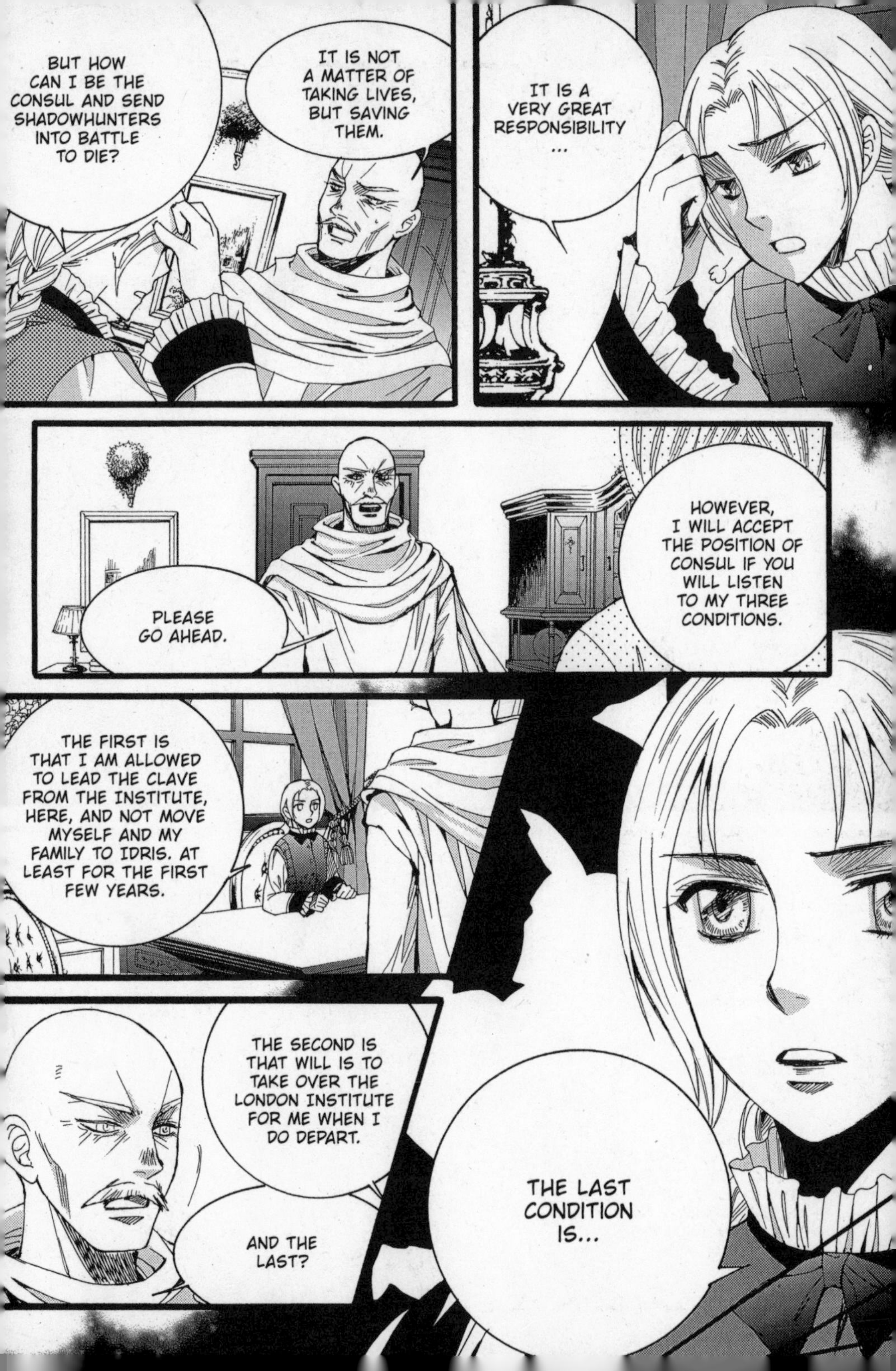
BUT HOW CAN I BE THE CONSUL AND SEND SHADOWHUNTERS INTO BATTLE TO DIE?
IT IS NOT A MATTER OF TAKING LIVES, BUT SAVING THEM.
IT IS A VERY GREAT RESPONSIBILITY ...
HOWEVER, I WILL ACCEPT THE POSITION OF CONSUL IF YOU WILL LISTEN TO MY THREE CONDITIONS.
PLEASE GO AHEAD.
THE FIRST IS THAT I AM ALLOWED TO LEAD THE CLAVE FROM THE INSTITUTE, HERE, AND NOT MOVE MYSELF AND MY FAMILY TO IDRIS. AT LEAST FOR THE FIRST FEW YEARS.
THE SECOND IS THAT WILL IS TO TAKE OVER THE LONDON INSTITUTE FOR ME WHEN I DO DEPART.
AND THE LAST?
THE LAST CONDITION IS...

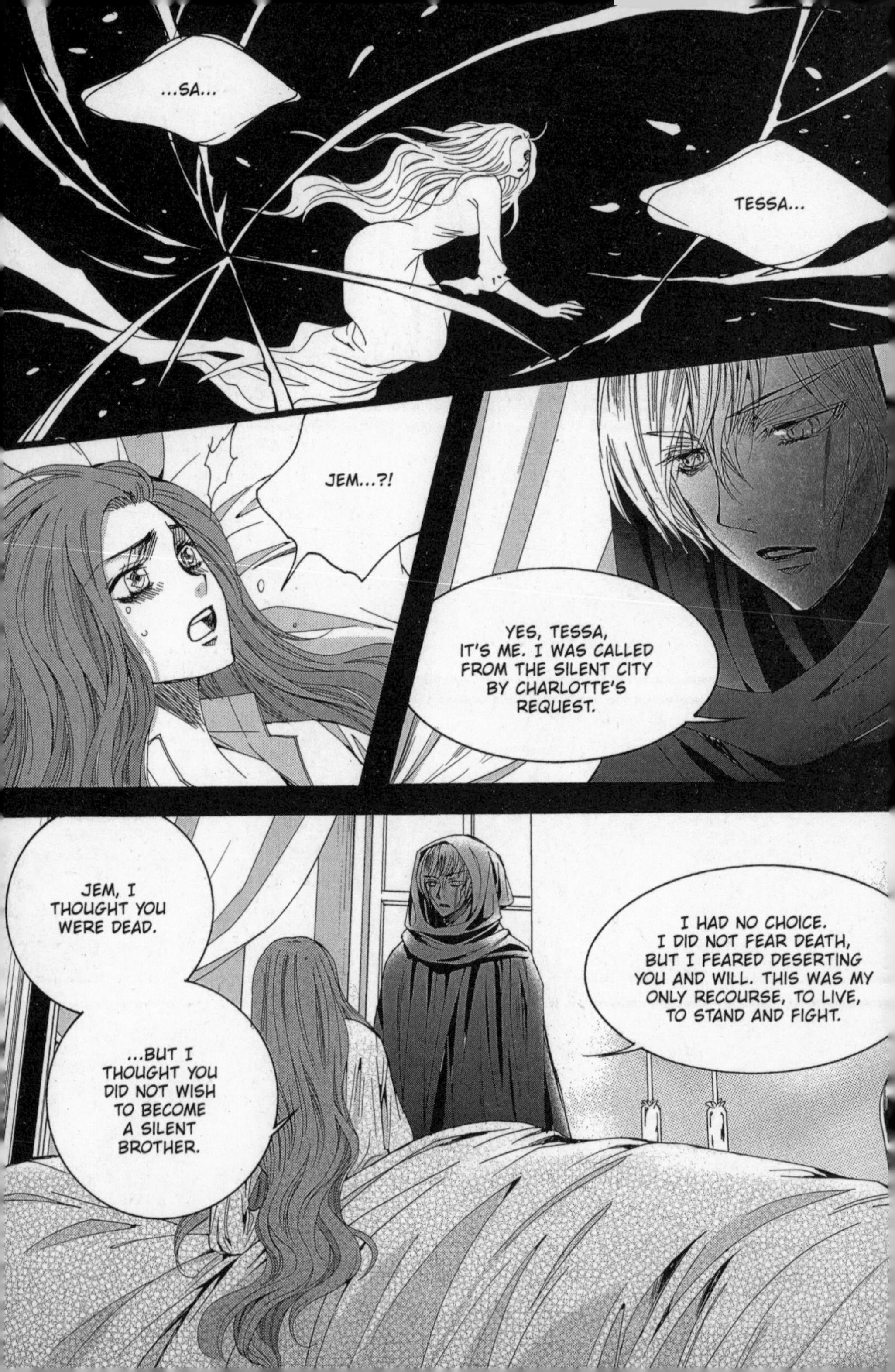
...SA...
TESSA...
JEM...?!
YES, TESSA, IT'S ME. I WAS CALLED FROM THE SILENT CITY BY CHARLOTTE'S REQUEST.
JEM, I THOUGHT YOU WERE DEAD.
...BUT I THOUGHT YOU DID NOT WISH TO BECOME A SILENT BROTHER.
I HAD NO CHOICE. I DID NOT FEAR DEATH, BUT I FEARED DESERTING YOU AND WILL. THIS WAS MY ONLY RECOURSE, TO LIVE, TO STAND AND FIGHT.

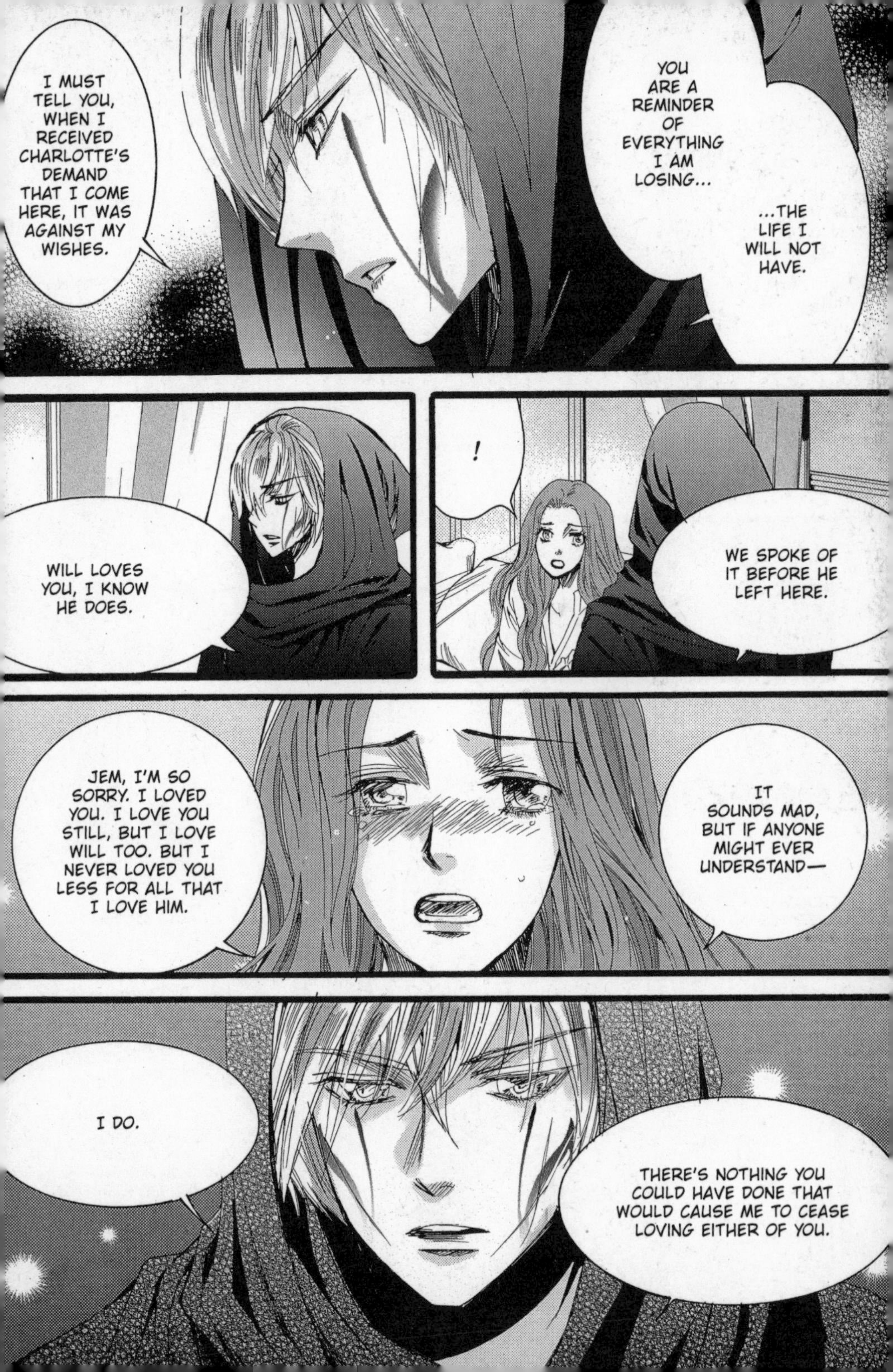
I MUST TELL YOU, WHEN I RECEIVED CHARLOTTE'S DEMAND THAT I COME HERE, IT WAS AGAINST MY WISHES.
YOU ARE A REMINDER OF EVERYTHING I AM LOSING...
...THE LIFE I WILL NOT HAVE.
WILL LOVES YOU, I KNOW HE DOES.
!
WE SPOKE OF IT BEFORE HE LEFT HERE.
JEM, I'M SO SORRY. I LOVED YOU. I LOVE YOU STILL, BUT I LOVE WILL TOO. BUT I NEVER LOVED YOU LESS FOR ALL THAT I LOVE HIM.
IT SOUNDS MAD, BUT IF ANYONE MIGHT EVER UNDERSTAND—
I DO.
THERE'S NOTHING YOU COULD HAVE DONE THAT WOULD CAUSE ME TO CEASE LOVING EITHER OF YOU.

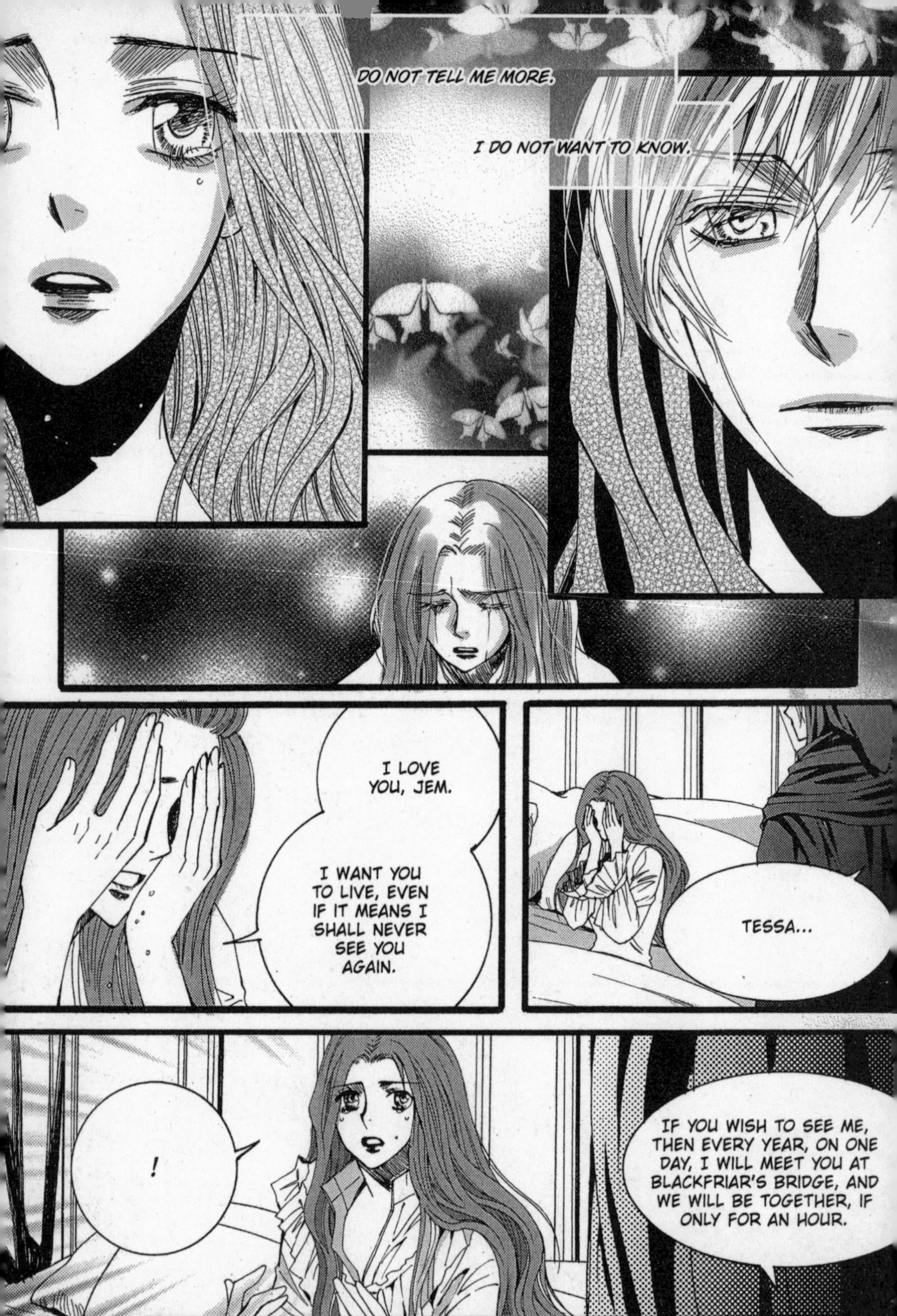
DO NOT TELL ME MORE.
I DO NOT WANT TO KNOW.
I LOVE YOU, JEM.
I WANT YOU TO LIVE, EVEN IF IT MEANS I SHALL NEVER SEE YOU AGAIN.
TESSA...
!
IF YOU WISH TO SEE ME, THEN EVERY YEAR, ON ONE DAY, I WILL MEET YOU AT BLACKFRIAR'S BRIDGE, AND WE WILL BE TOGETHER, IF ONLY FOR AN HOUR.

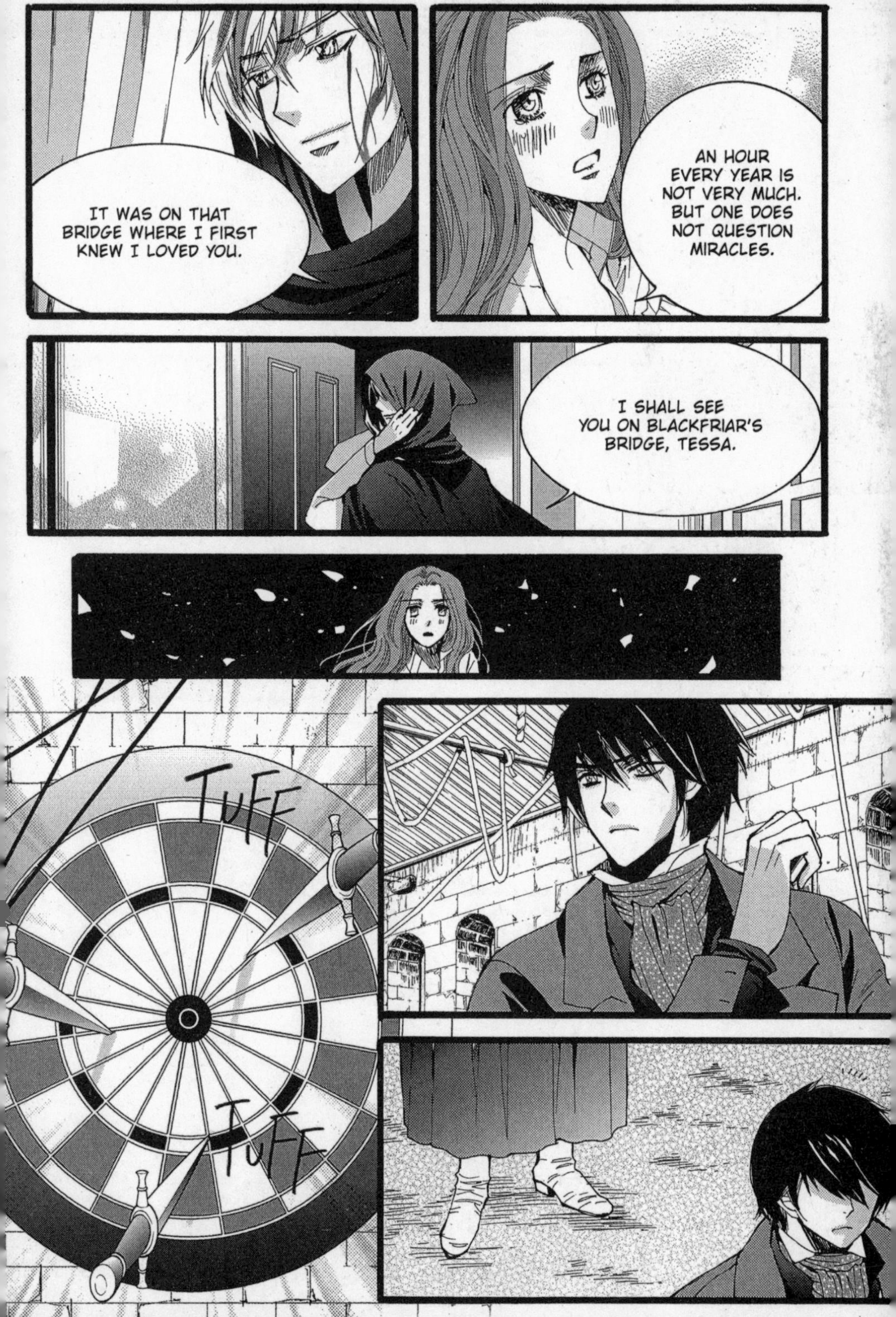
IT WAS ON THAT BRIDGE WHERE I FIRST KNEW I LOVED YOU.
AN HOUR EVERY YEAR IS NOT VERY MUCH. BUT ONE DOES NOT QUESTION MIRACLES.
I SHALL SEE YOU ON BLACKFRIAR'S BRIDGE, TESSA.
TUFF
TUFF

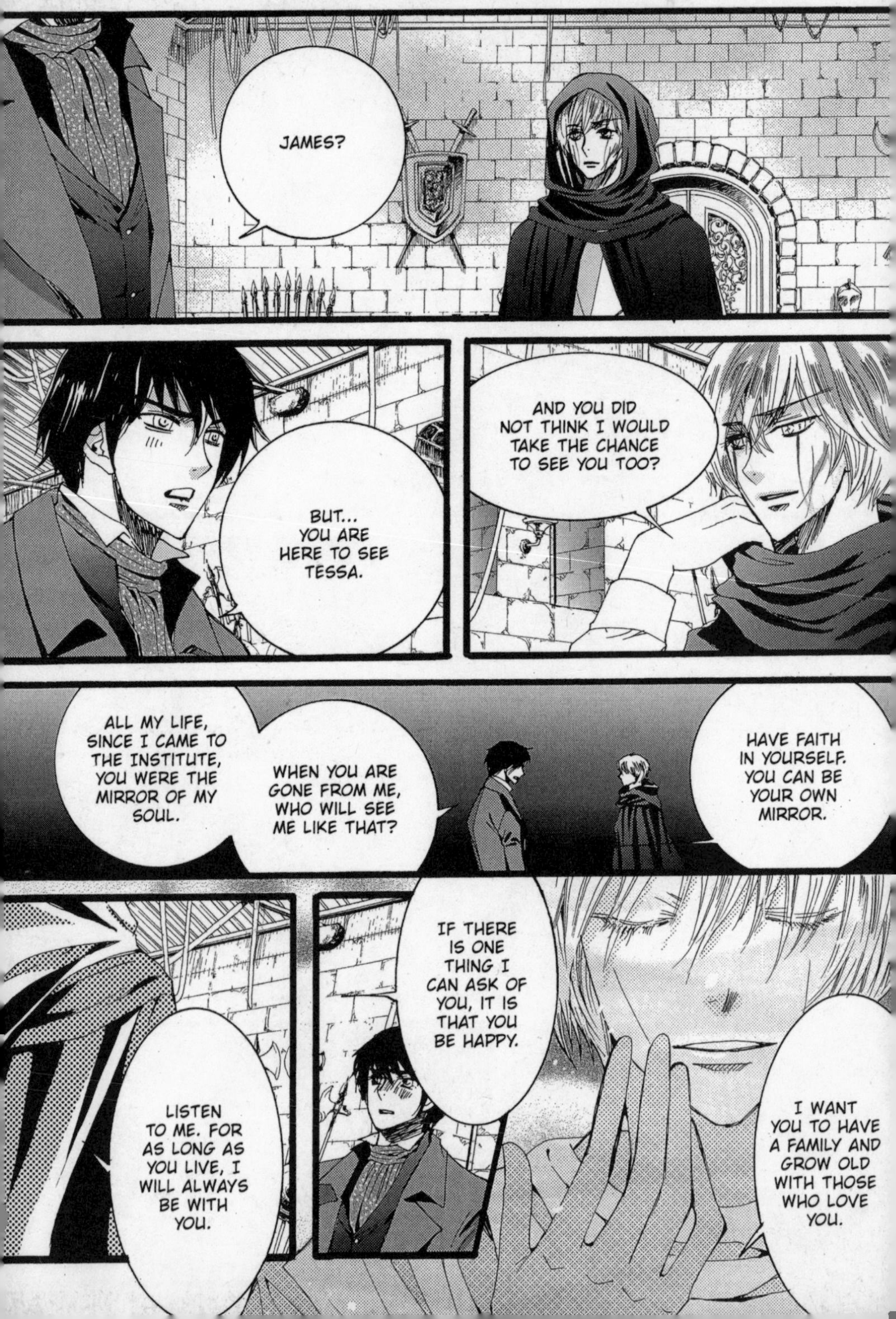
JAMES?
AND YOU DID NOT THINK I WOULD TAKE THE CHANCE TO SEE YOU TOO?
BUT... YOU ARE HERE TO SEE TESSA.
HAVE FAITH IN YOURSELF. YOU CAN BE YOUR OWN MIRROR.
ALL MY LIFE, SINCE I CAME TO THE INSTITUTE, YOU WERE THE MIRROR OF MY SOUL.
WHEN YOU ARE GONE FROM ME, WHO WILL SEE ME LIKE THAT?
IF THERE IS ONE THING I CAN ASK OF YOU, IT IS THAT YOU BE HAPPY.
I WANT YOU TO HAVE A FAMILY AND GROW OLD WITH THOSE WHO LOVE YOU.
LISTEN TO ME. FOR AS LONG AS YOU LIVE, I WILL ALWAYS BE WITH YOU.

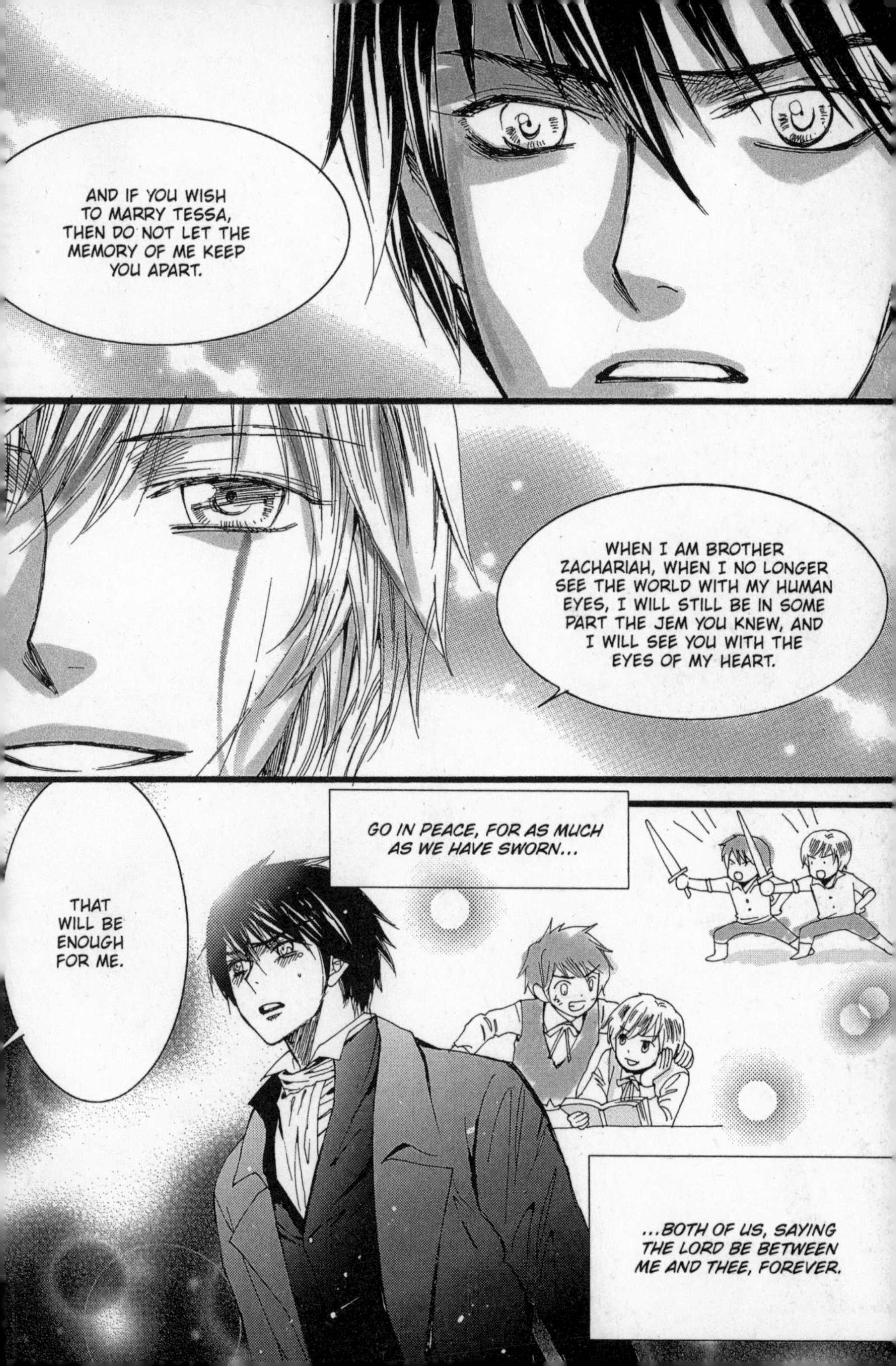
AND IF YOU WISH TO MARRY TESSA, THEN DO NOT LET THE MEMORY OF ME KEEP YOU APART.
WHEN I AM BROTHER ZACHARIAH, WHEN I NO LONGER SEE THE WORLD WITH MY HUMAN EYES, I WILL STILL BE IN SOME PART THE JEM YOU KNEW, AND I WILL SEE YOU WITH THE EYES OF MY HEART.
GO IN PEACE, FOR AS MUCH AS WE HAVE SWORN...
THAT WILL BE ENOUGH FOR ME.
...BOTH OF US, SAYING THE LORD BE BETWEEN ME AND THEE, FOREVER.

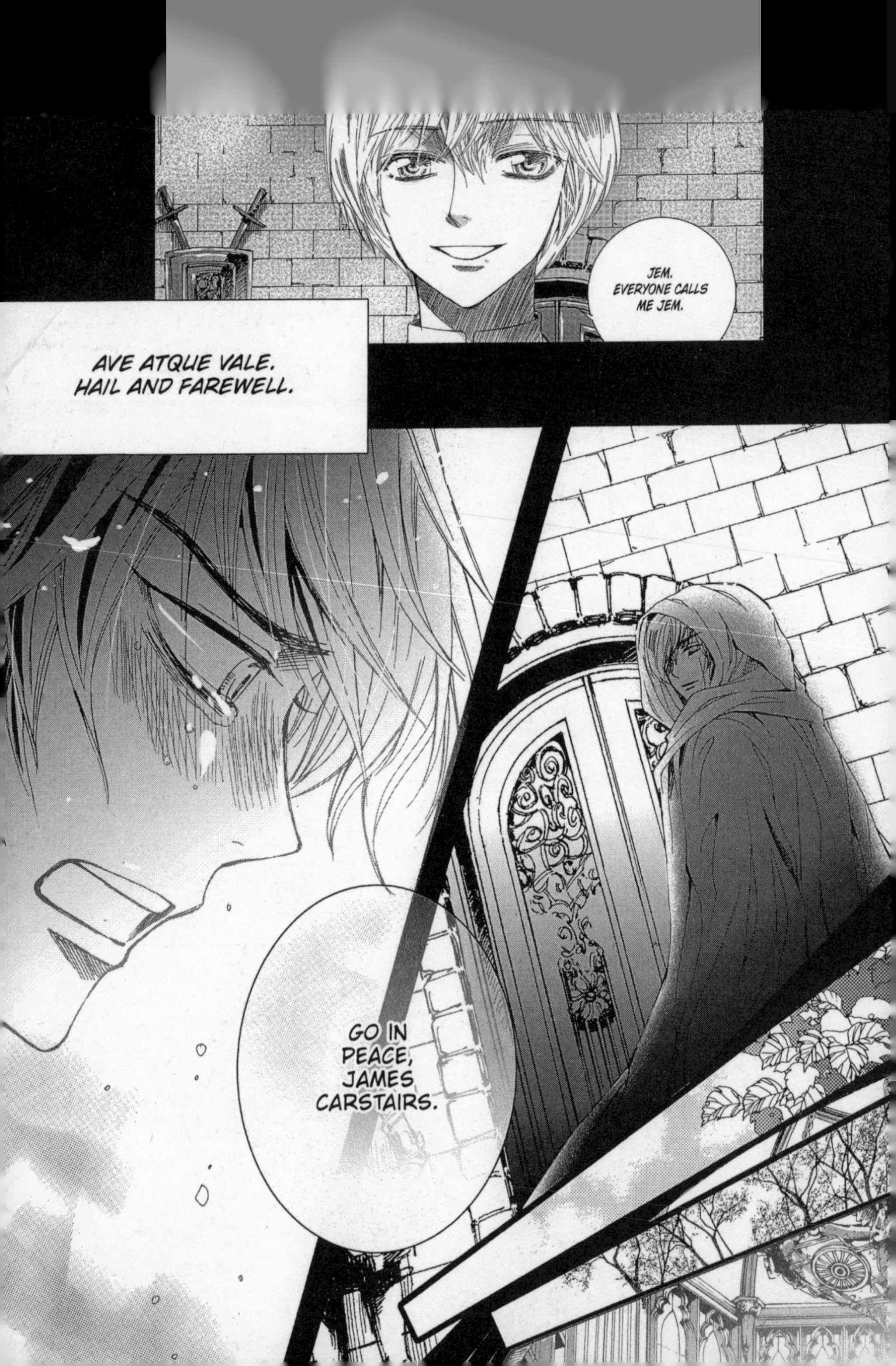

JEM. EVERYONE CALLS ME JEM.
AVE ATQUE VALE. HAIL AND FAREWELL.
GO IN PEACE, JAMES CARSTAIRS.

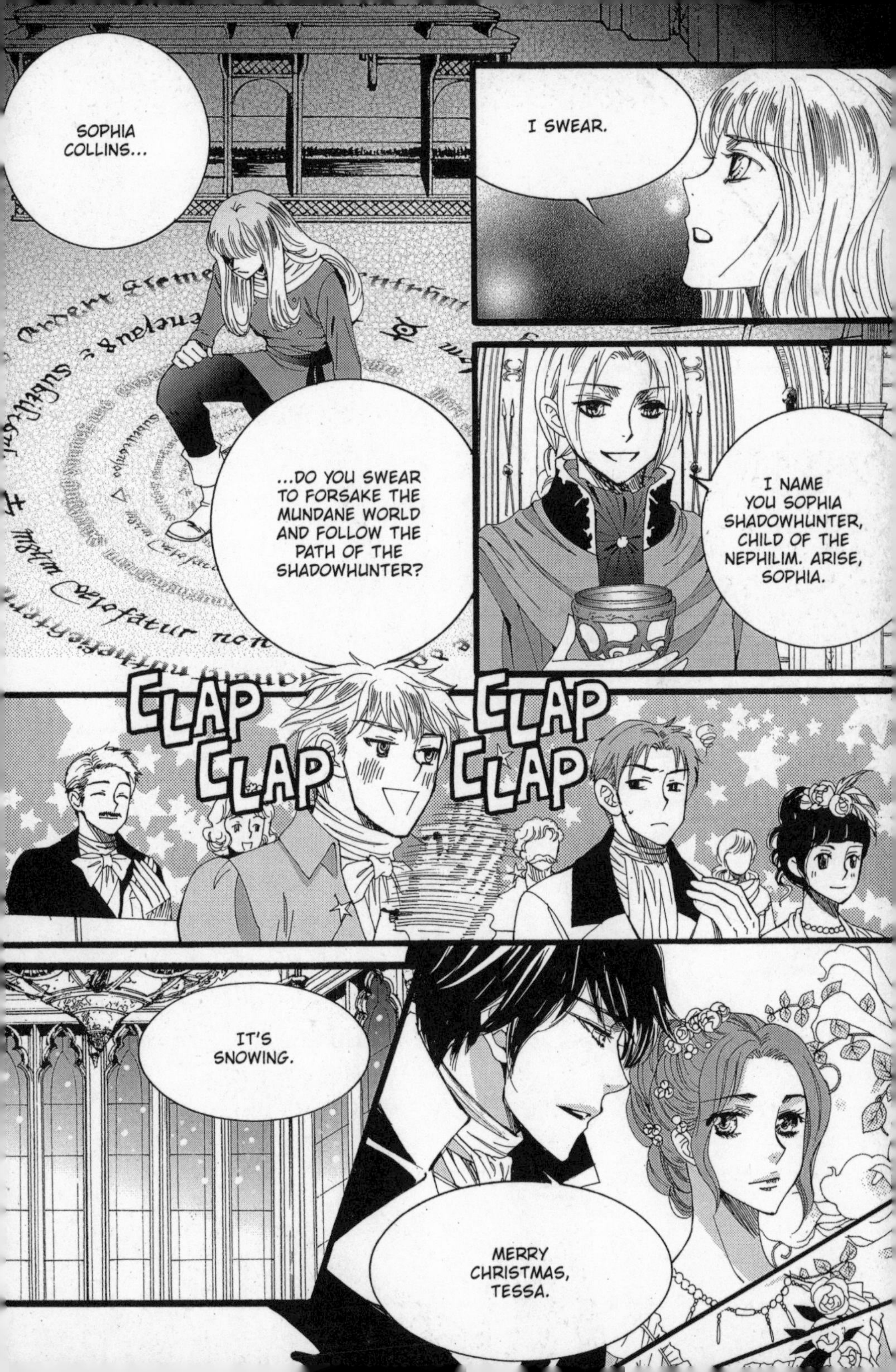
SOPHIA COLLINS...
...DO YOU SWEAR TO FORSAKE THE MUNDANE WORLD AND FOLLOW THE PATH OF THE SHADOWHUNTER?
I SWEAR.
I NAME YOU SOPHIA SHADOWHUNTER, CHILD OF THE NEPHILIM. ARISE, SOPHIA.
CLAP CLAP
CLAP CLAP
IT'S SNOWING.
MERRY CHRISTMAS, TESSA.

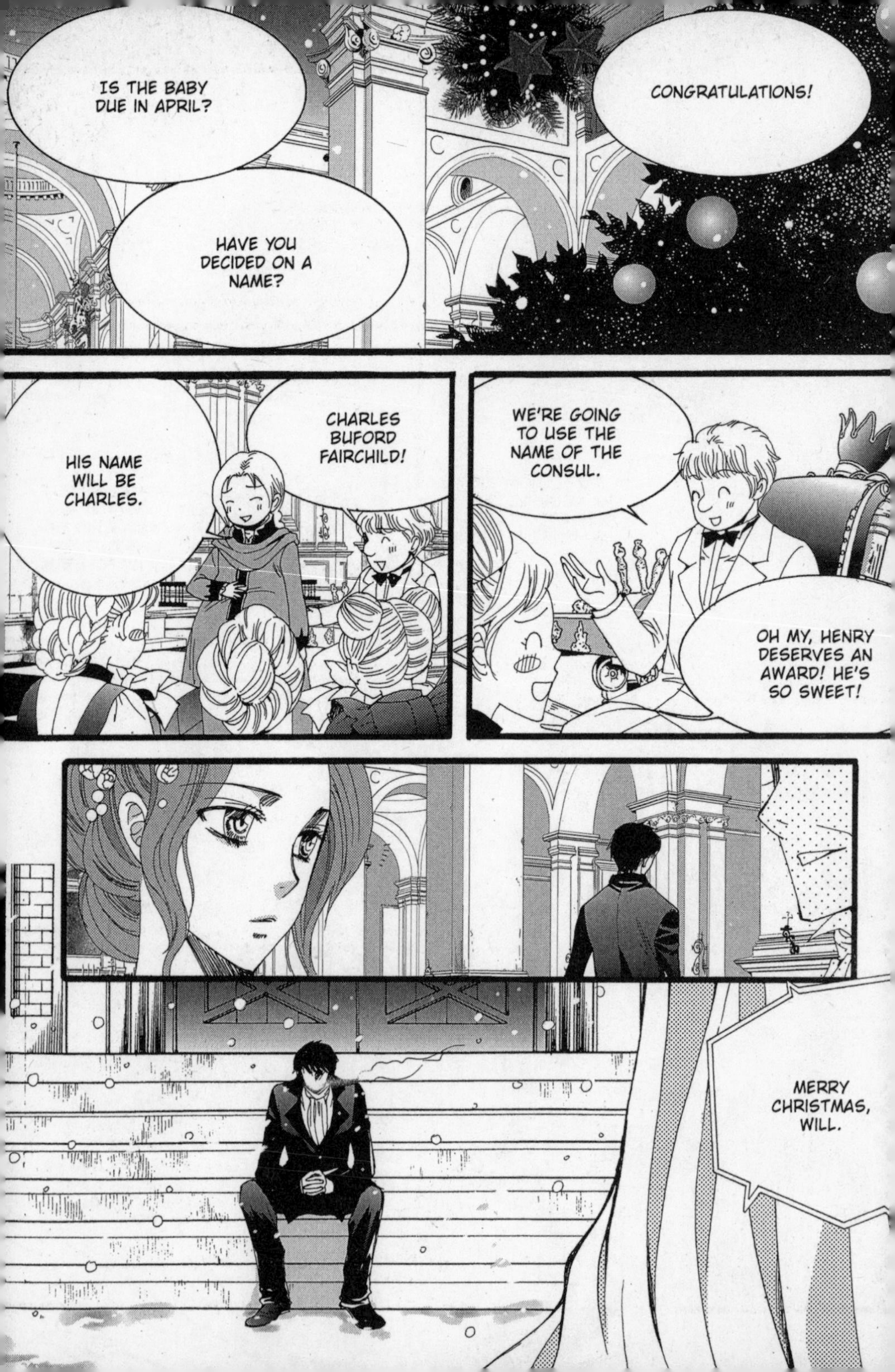
IS THE BABY DUE IN APRIL?
HAVE YOU DECIDED ON A NAME?
CONGRATULATIONS!
HIS NAME WILL BE CHARLES.
CHARLES BUFORD FAIRCHILD!
WE'RE GOING TO USE THE NAME OF THE CONSUL.
OH MY, HENRY DESERVES AN AWARD! HE'S SO SWEET!
MERRY CHRISTMAS, WILL.

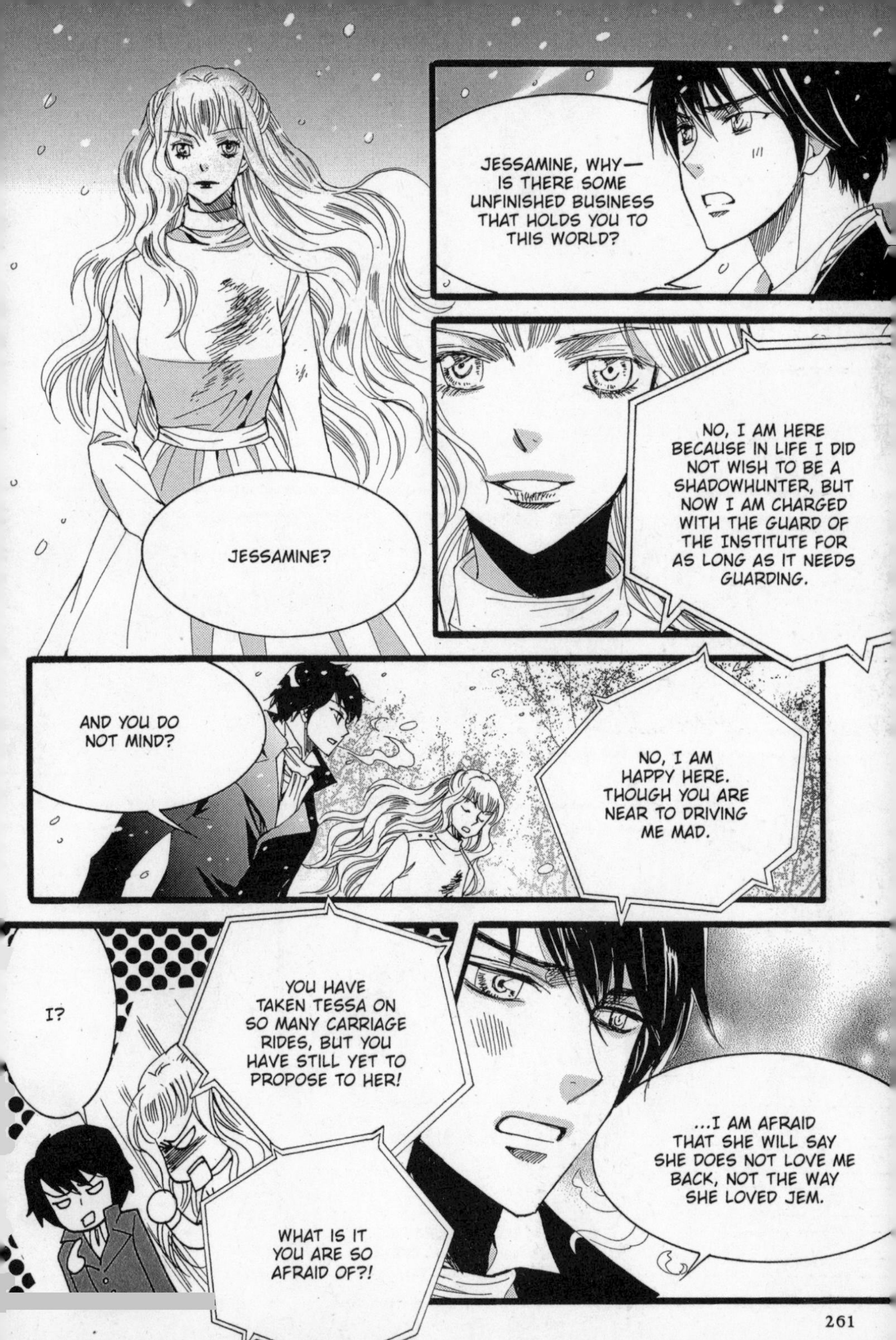
JESSAMINE?
JESSAMINE, WHY— IS THERE SOME UNFINISHED BUSINESS THAT HOLDS YOU TO THIS WORLD?
NO, I AM HERE BECAUSE IN LIFE I DID NOT WISH TO BE A SHADOWHUNTER, BUT NOW I AM CHARGED WITH THE GUARD OF THE INSTITUTE FOR AS LONG AS IT NEEDS GUARDING.
AND YOU DO NOT MIND?
NO, I AM HAPPY HERE. THOUGH YOU ARE NEAR TO DRIVING ME MAD.
I?
YOU HAVE TAKEN TESSA ON SO MANY CARRIAGE RIDES, BUT YOU HAVE STILL YET TO PROPOSE TO HER!
WHAT IS IT YOU ARE SO AFRAID OF?!
...I AM AFRAID THAT SHE WILL SAY SHE DOES NOT LOVE ME BACK, NOT THE WAY SHE LOVED JEM.

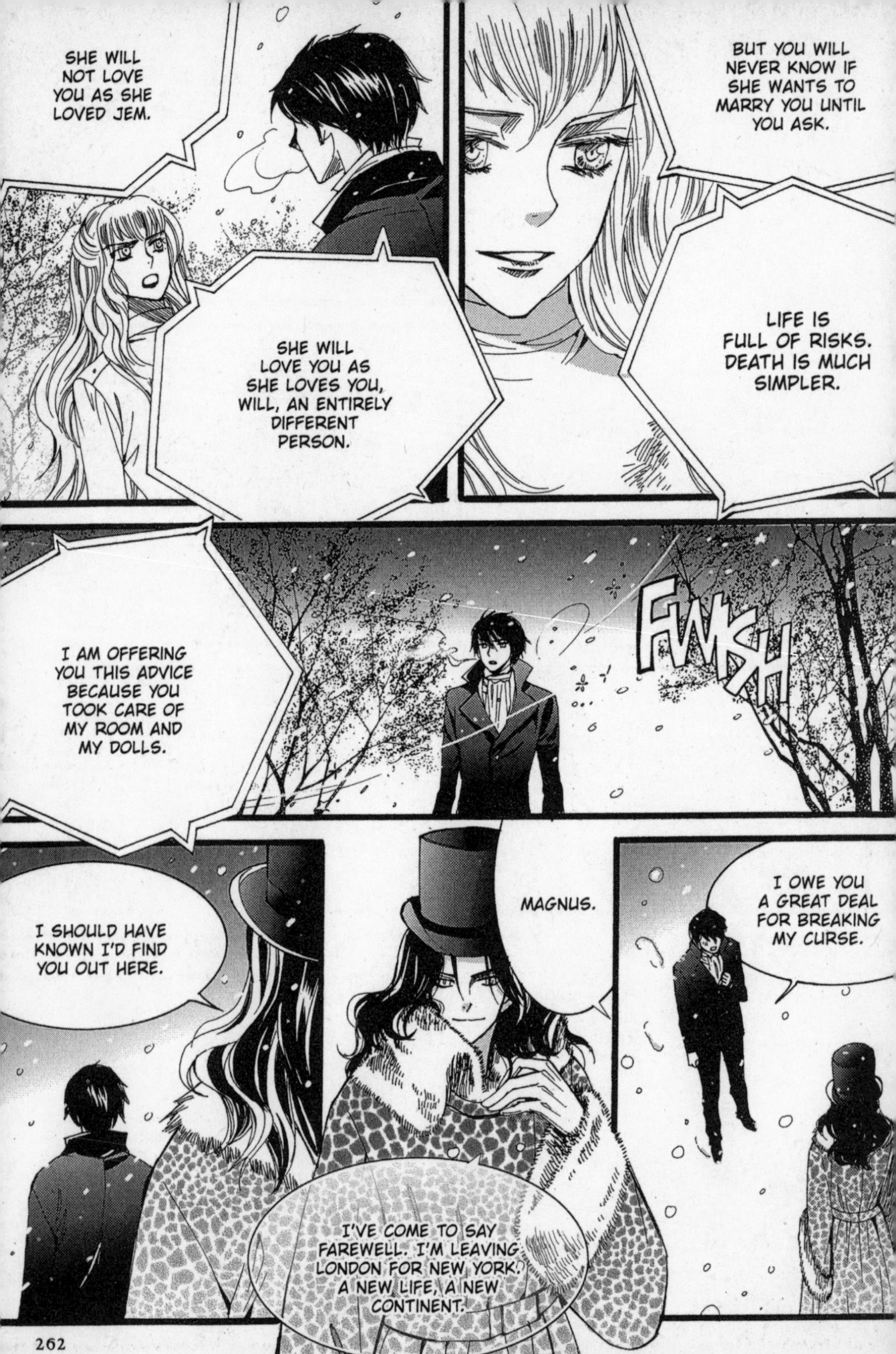
SHE WILL NOT LOVE YOU AS SHE LOVED JEM.
SHE WILL LOVE YOU AS SHE LOVES YOU, WILL, AN ENTIRELY DIFFERENT PERSON.
BUT YOU WILL NEVER KNOW IF SHE WANTS TO MARRY YOU UNTIL YOU ASK.
LIFE IS FULL OF RISKS. DEATH IS MUCH SIMPLER.
I AM OFFERING YOU THIS ADVICE BECAUSE YOU TOOK CARE OF MY ROOM AND MY DOLLS.
FWISH
I SHOULD HAVE KNOWN I'D FIND YOU OUT HERE.
MAGNUS.
I OWE YOU A GREAT DEAL FOR BREAKING MY CURSE.
I'VE COME TO SAY FAREWELL. I'M LEAVING LONDON FOR NEW YORK. A NEW LIFE, A NEW CONTINENT.

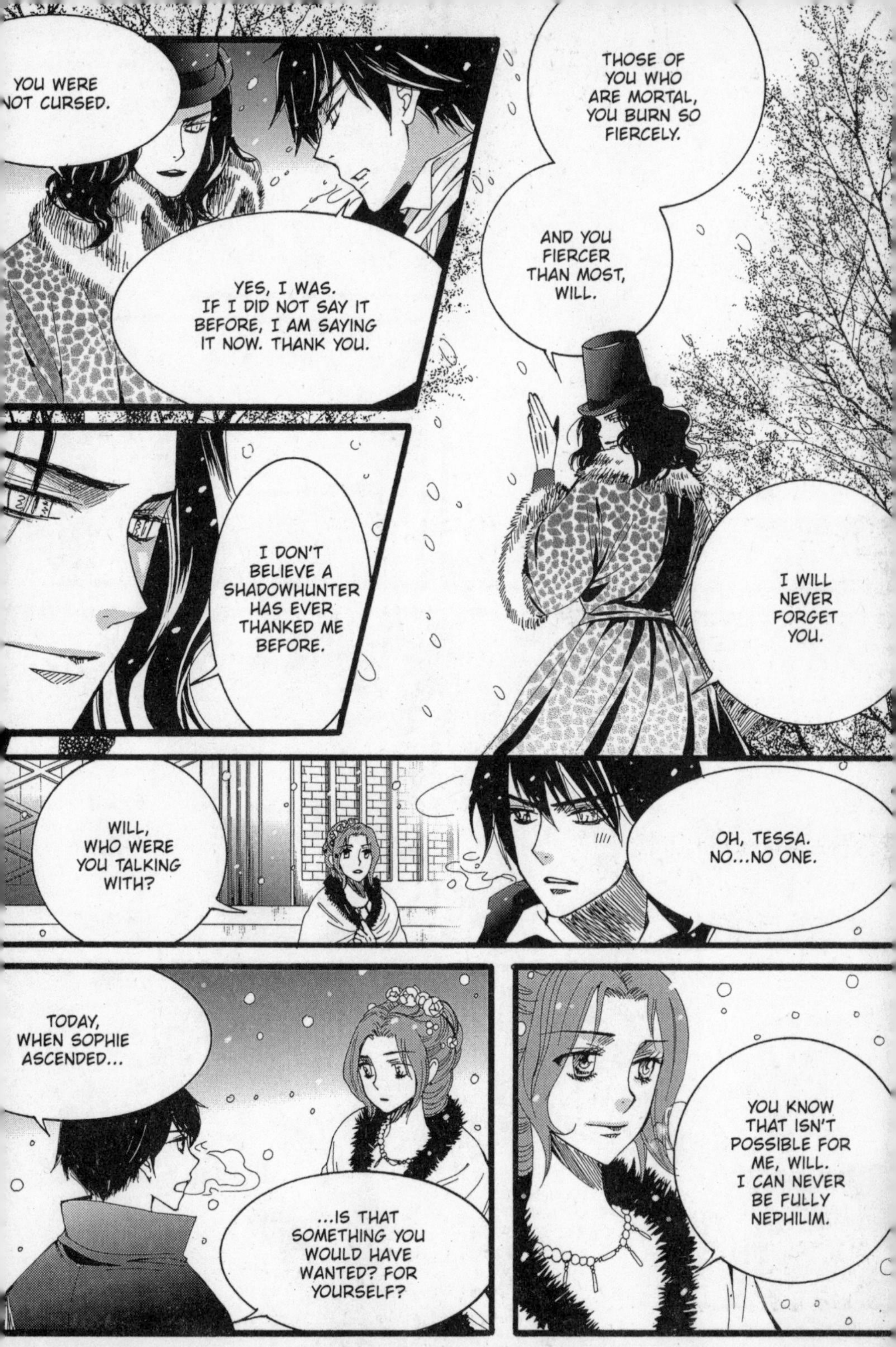

YOU WERE NOT CURSED.
YES, I WAS. IF I DID NOT SAY IT BEFORE, I AM SAYING IT NOW. THANK YOU.
THOSE OF YOU WHO ARE MORTAL, YOU BURN SO FIERCELY.
AND YOU FIERCER THAN MOST, WILL.
I DON'T BELIEVE A SHADOWHUNTER HAS EVER THANKED ME BEFORE.
I WILL NEVER FORGET YOU.
WILL, WHO WERE YOU TALKING WITH?
OH, TESSA. NO...NO ONE.
TODAY, WHEN SOPHIE ASCENDED...
...IS THAT SOMETHING YOU WOULD HAVE WANTED? FOR YOURSELF?
YOU KNOW THAT ISN'T POSSIBLE FOR ME, WILL. I CAN NEVER BE FULLY NEPHILIM.

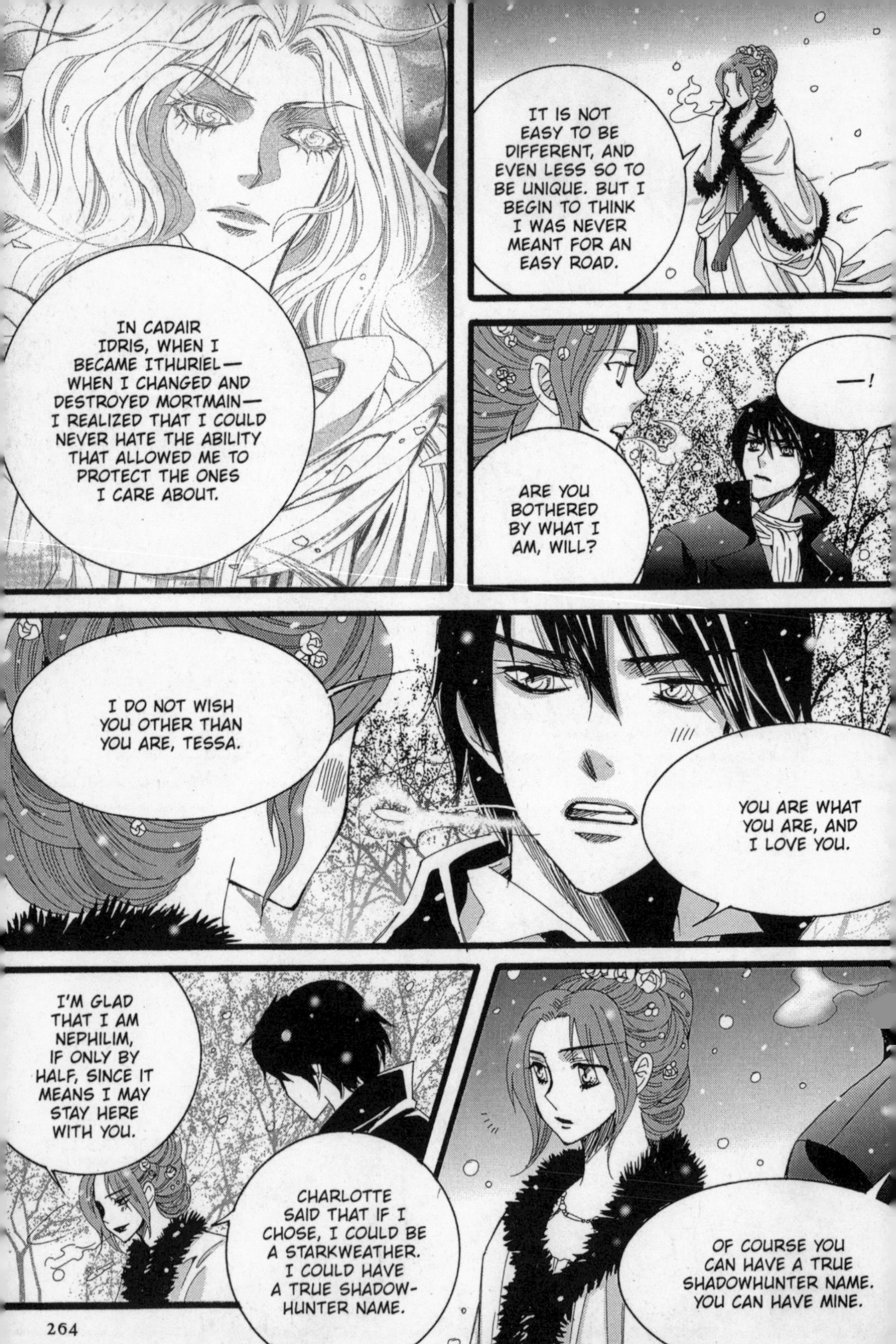
IN CADAIR IDRIS, WHEN I BECAME ITHURIEL— WHEN I CHANGED AND DESTROYED MORTMAIN— I REALIZED THAT I COULD NEVER HATE THE ABILITY THAT ALLOWED ME TO PROTECT THE ONES I CARE ABOUT.
IT IS NOT EASY TO BE DIFFERENT, AND EVEN LESS SO TO BE UNIQUE. BUT I BEGIN TO THINK I WAS NEVER MEANT FOR AN EASY ROAD.
ARE YOU BOTHERED BY WHAT I AM, WILL?
—!
I DO NOT WISH YOU OTHER THAN YOU ARE, TESSA.
YOU ARE WHAT YOU ARE, AND I LOVE YOU.
I'M GLAD THAT I AM NEPHILIM, IF ONLY BY HALF, SINCE IT MEANS I MAY STAY HERE WITH YOU.
CHARLOTTE SAID THAT IF I CHOSE, I COULD BE A STARKWEATHER. I COULD HAVE A TRUE SHADOW-HUNTER NAME.
OF COURSE YOU CAN HAVE A TRUE SHADOWHUNTER NAME. YOU CAN HAVE MINE.

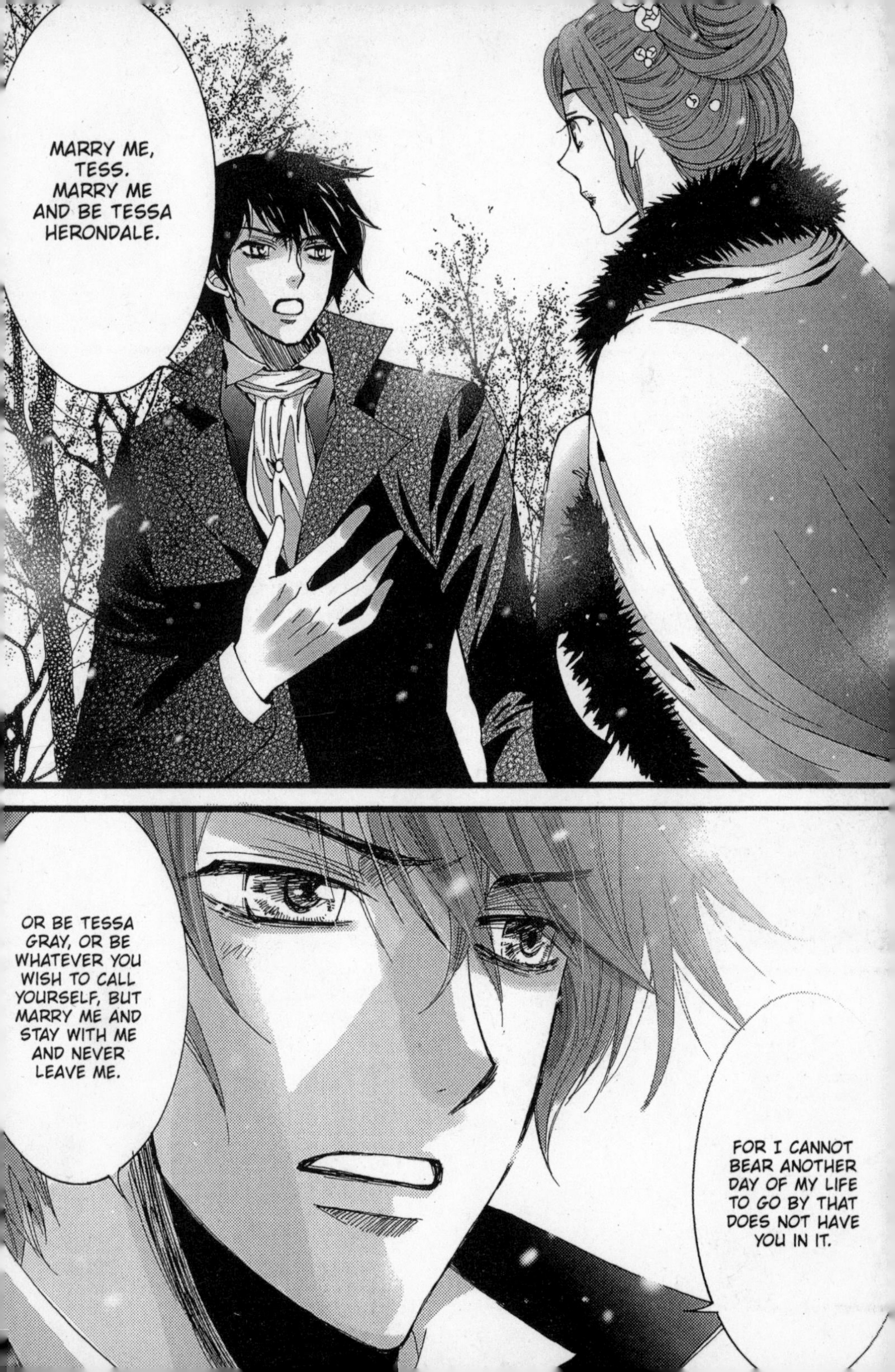
MARRY ME, TESS. MARRY ME AND BE TESSA HERONDALE.
OR BE TESSA GRAY, OR BE WHATEVER YOU WISH TO CALL YOURSELF, BUT MARRY ME AND STAY WITH ME AND NEVER LEAVE ME.
FOR I CANNOT BEAR ANOTHER DAY OF MY LIFE TO GO BY THAT DOES NOT HAVE YOU IN IT.

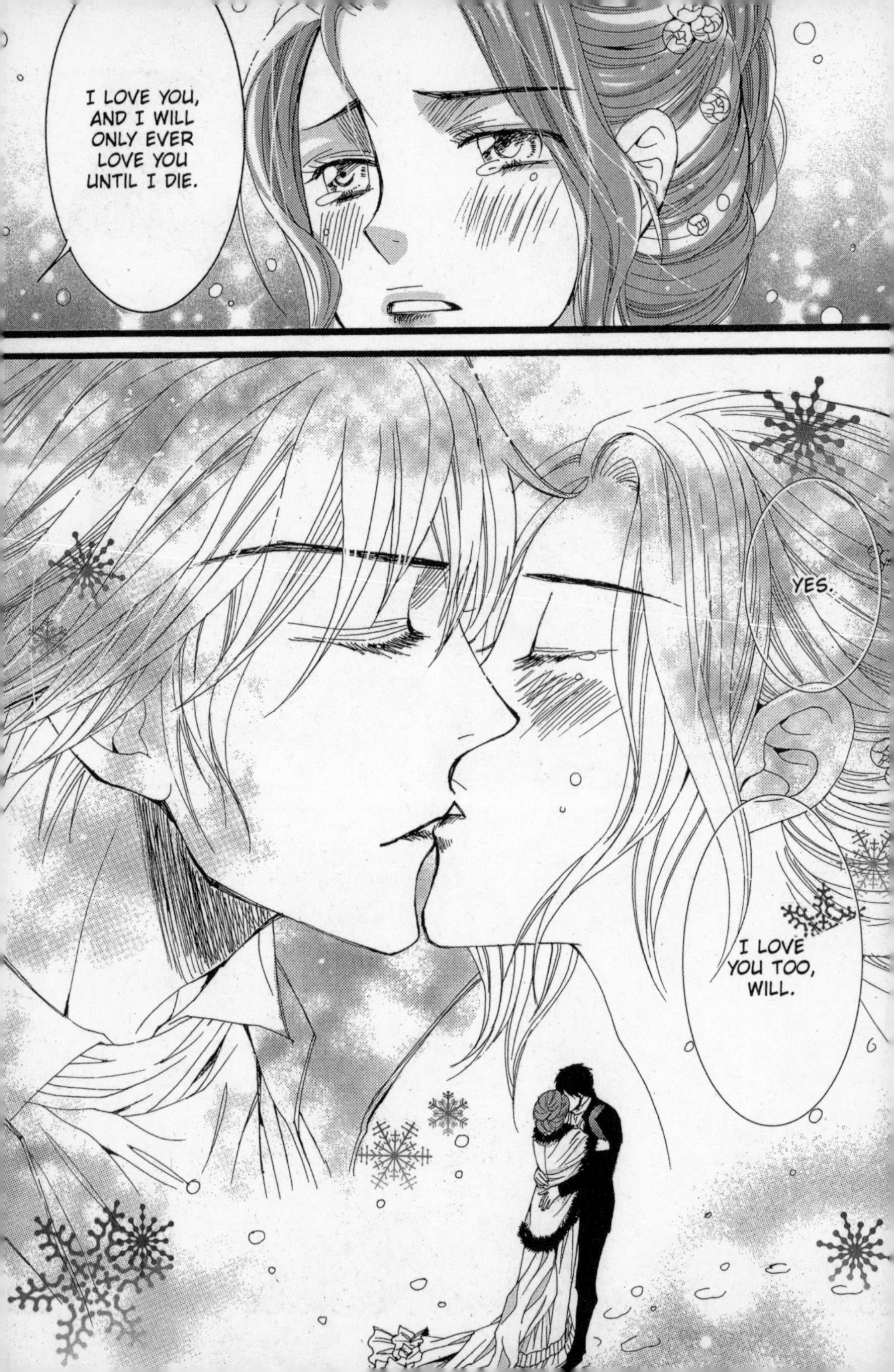
I LOVE YOU, AND I WILL ONLY EVER LOVE YOU UNTIL I DIE.
YES.
I LOVE YOU TOO, WILL.

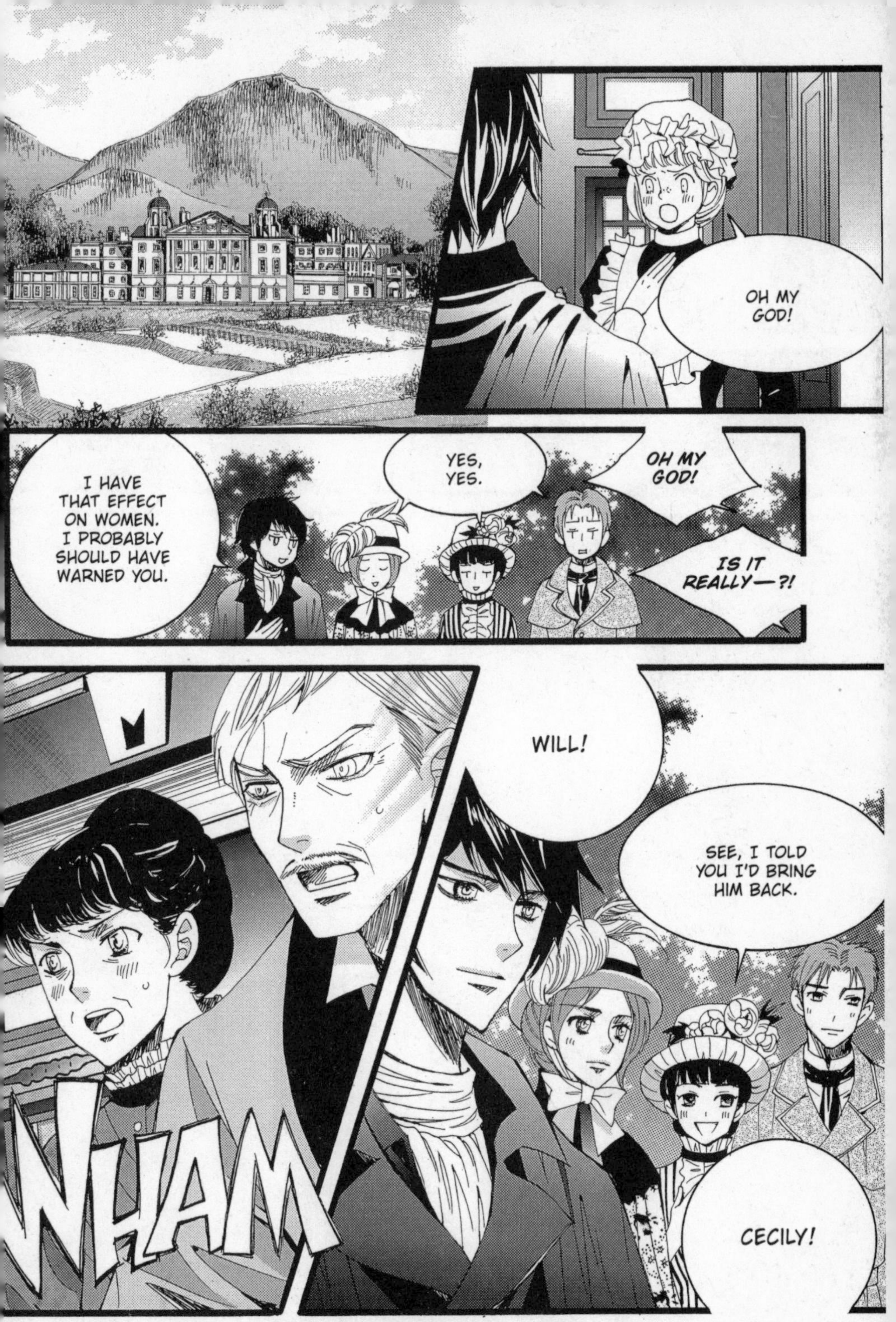
OH MY GOD!
I HAVE THAT EFFECT ON WOMEN. I PROBABLY SHOULD HAVE WARNED YOU.
YES, YES.
OH MY GOD!
IS IT REALLY—?!
WHAM
WILL!
SEE, I TOLD YOU I'D BRING HIM BACK.
CECILY!

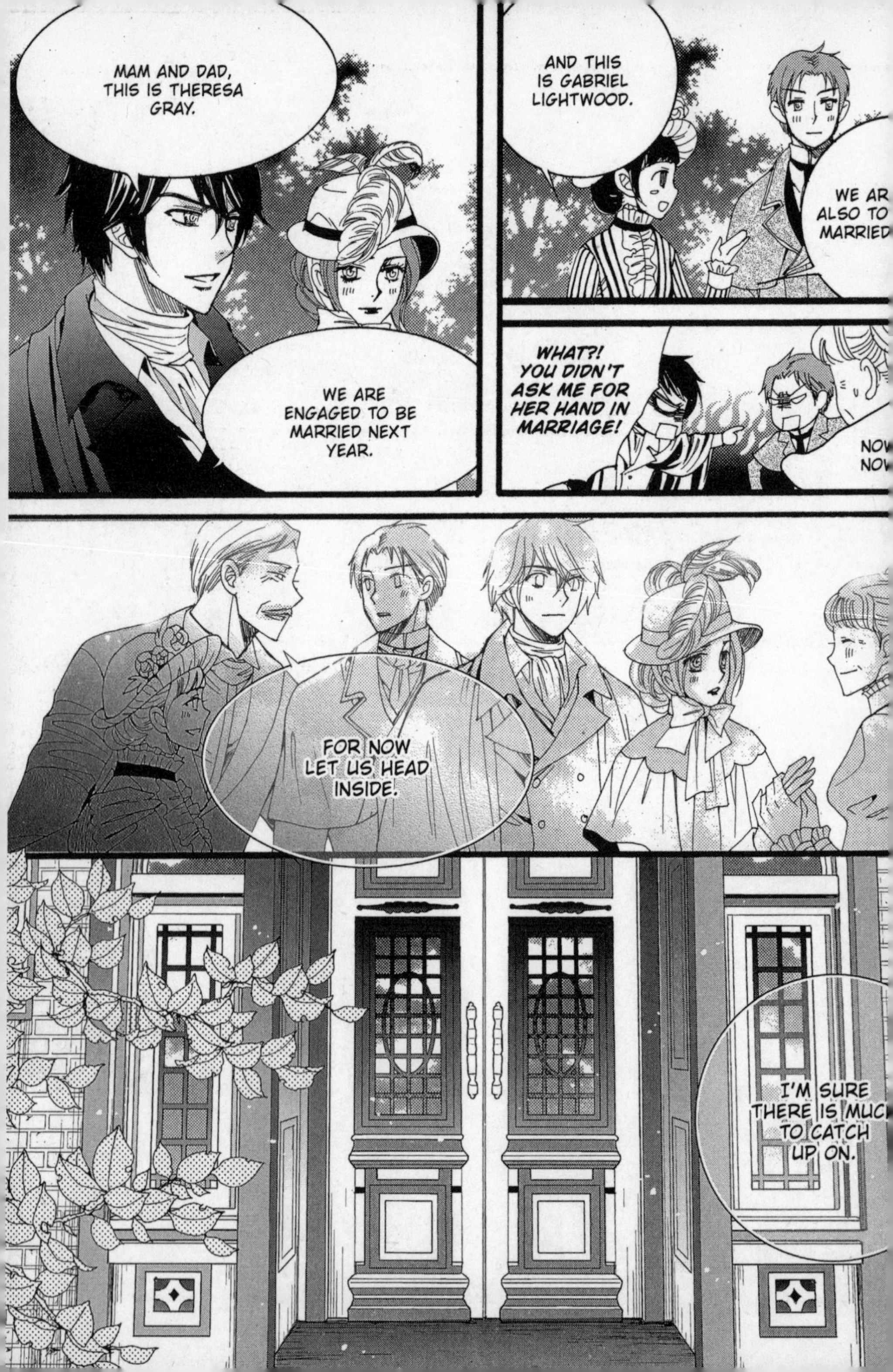
MAM AND DAD, THIS IS THERESA GRAY.
WE ARE ENGAGED TO BE MARRIED NEXT YEAR.
AND THIS IS GABRIEL LIGHTWOOD.
WE AR ALSO TO MARRIED
WHAT?! YOU DIDN'T ASK ME FOR HER HAND IN MARRIAGE!
NOW NOW
FOR NOW LET US HEAD INSIDE.
I'M SURE THERE IS MUC TO CATCH UP ON.

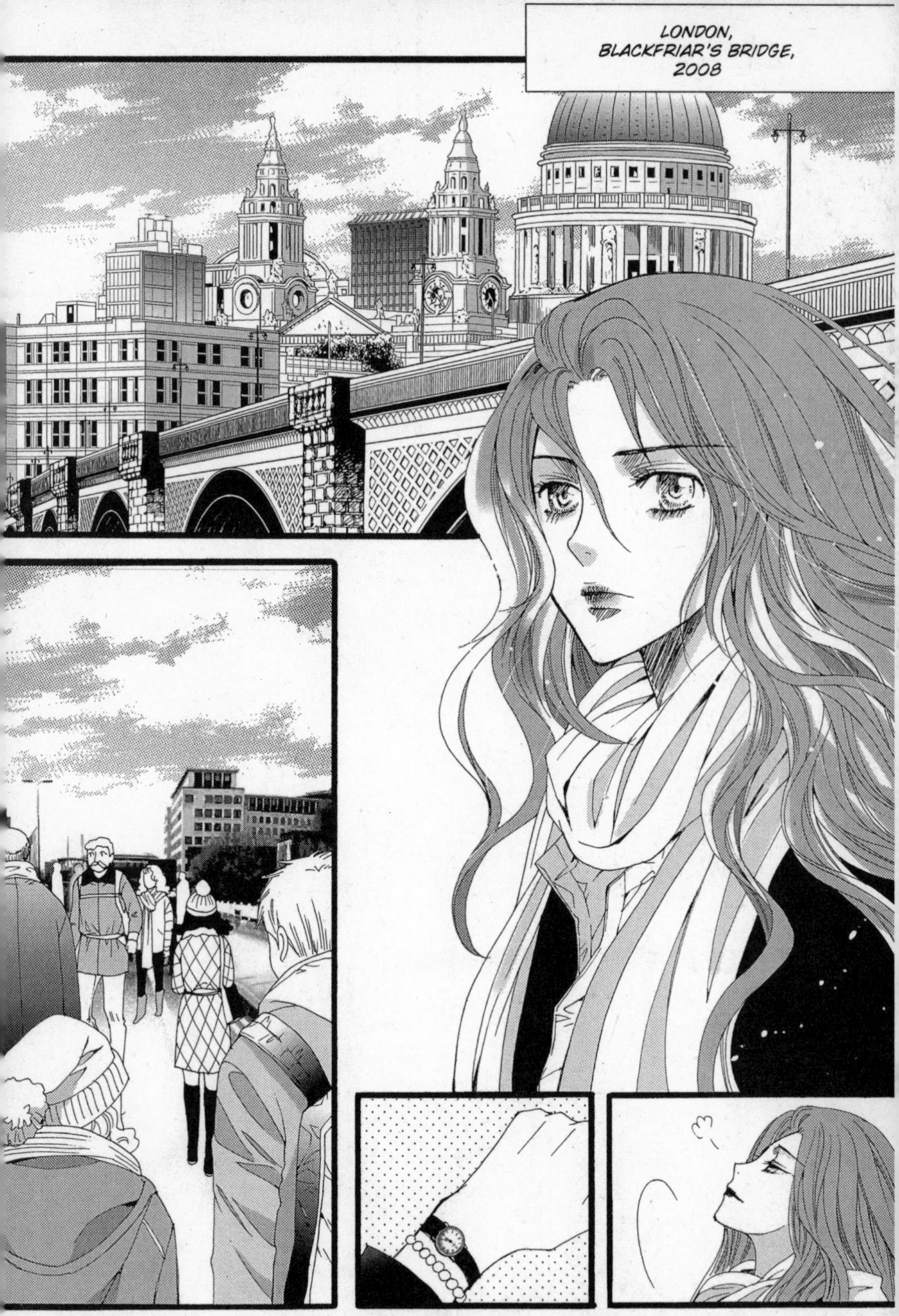
LONDON, BLACKFRIAR'S BRIDGE, 2008

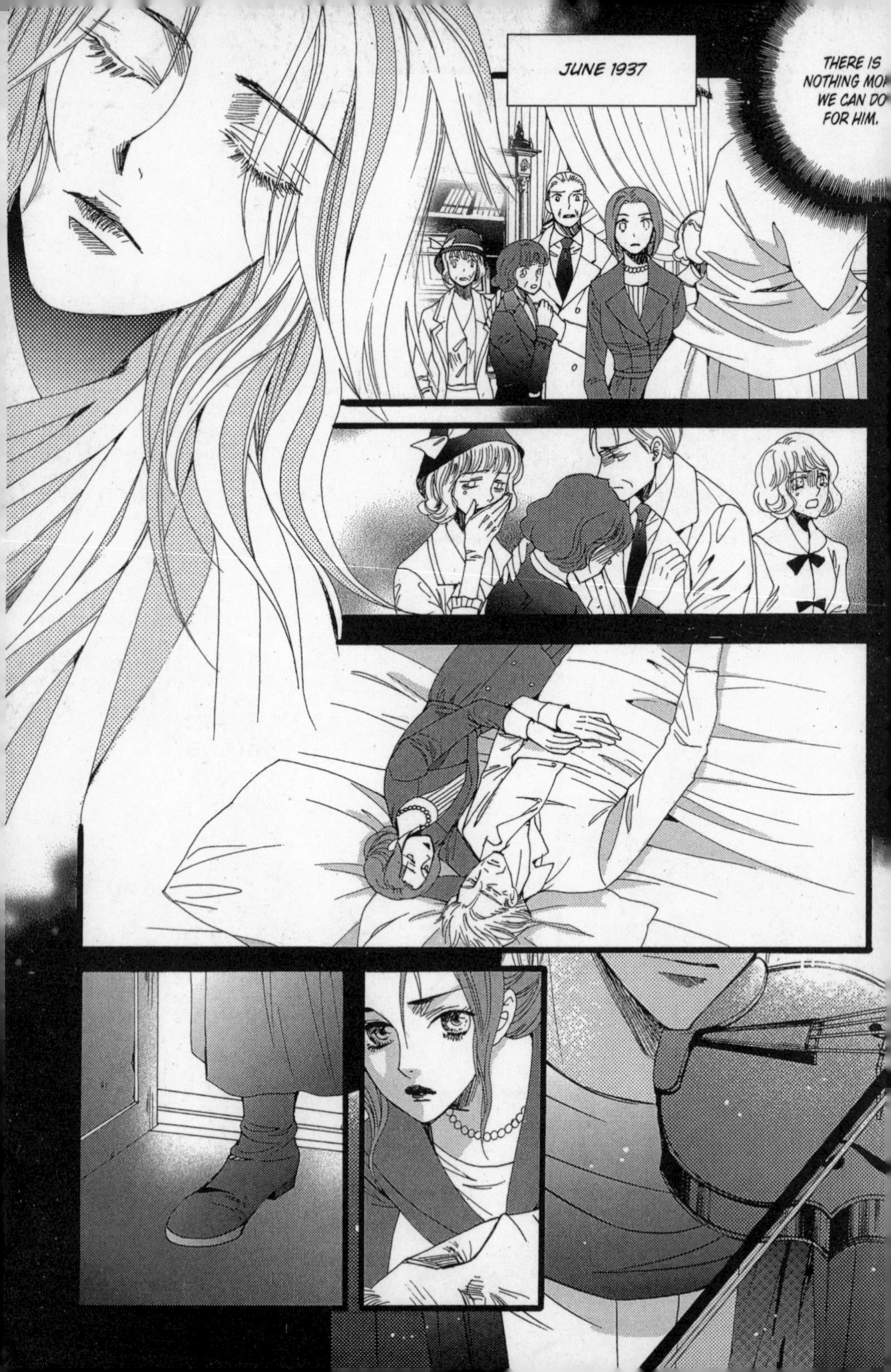
JUNE 1937
THERE IS NOTHING MO WE CAN DO FOR HIM.

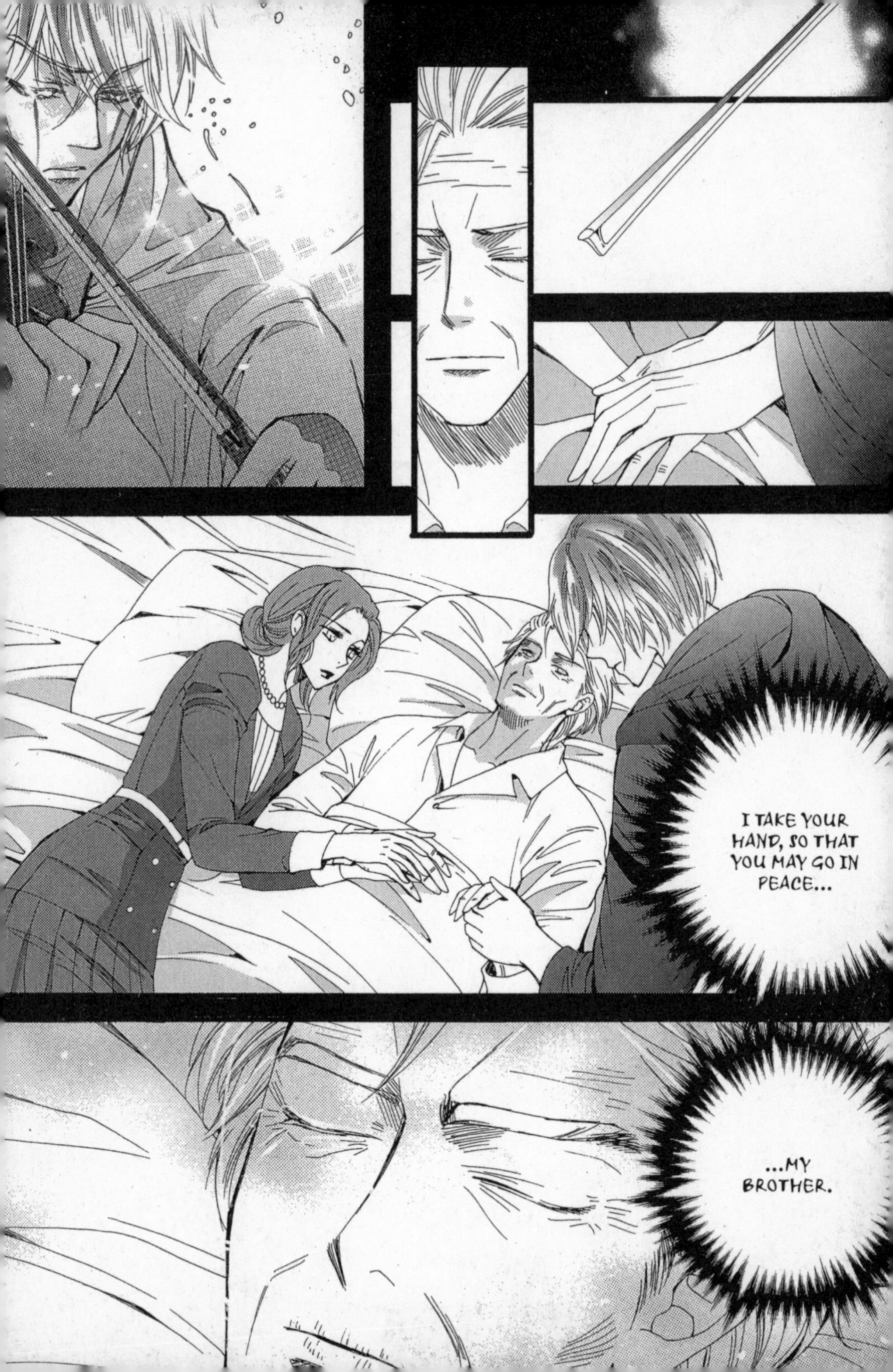
I TAKE YOUR HAND, SO THAT YOU MAY GO IN PEACE...
...MY BROTHER.

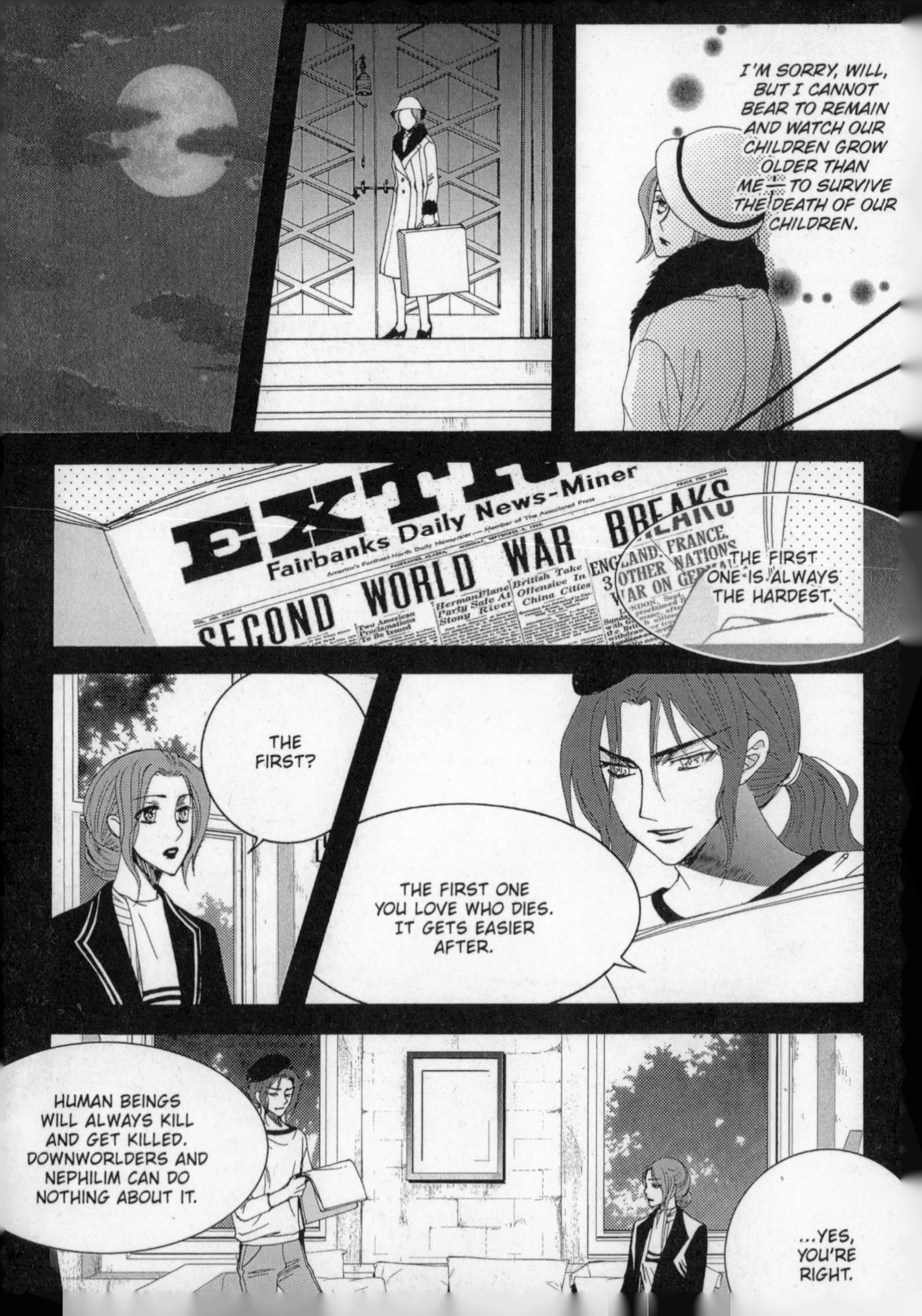
I'M SORRY, WILL, BUT I CANNOT BEAR TO REMAIN AND WATCH OUR CHILDREN GROW OLDER THAN ME — TO SURVIVE THE DEATH OF OUR CHILDREN.
Fairbanks Daily News-Miner
SECOND WORLD WAR BREAKS
ENGLAND, FRANCE, OTHER NATIONS
British Take Offensive In China Cities
Two American Proclamations To Be Issued
THE FIRST ONE IS ALWAYS THE HARDEST.
THE FIRST?
THE FIRST ONE YOU LOVE WHO DIES. IT GETS EASIER AFTER.
HUMAN BEINGS WILL ALWAYS KILL AND GET KILLED. DOWNWORLDERS AND NEPHILIM CAN DO NOTHING ABOUT IT.
...YES, YOU'RE RIGHT.

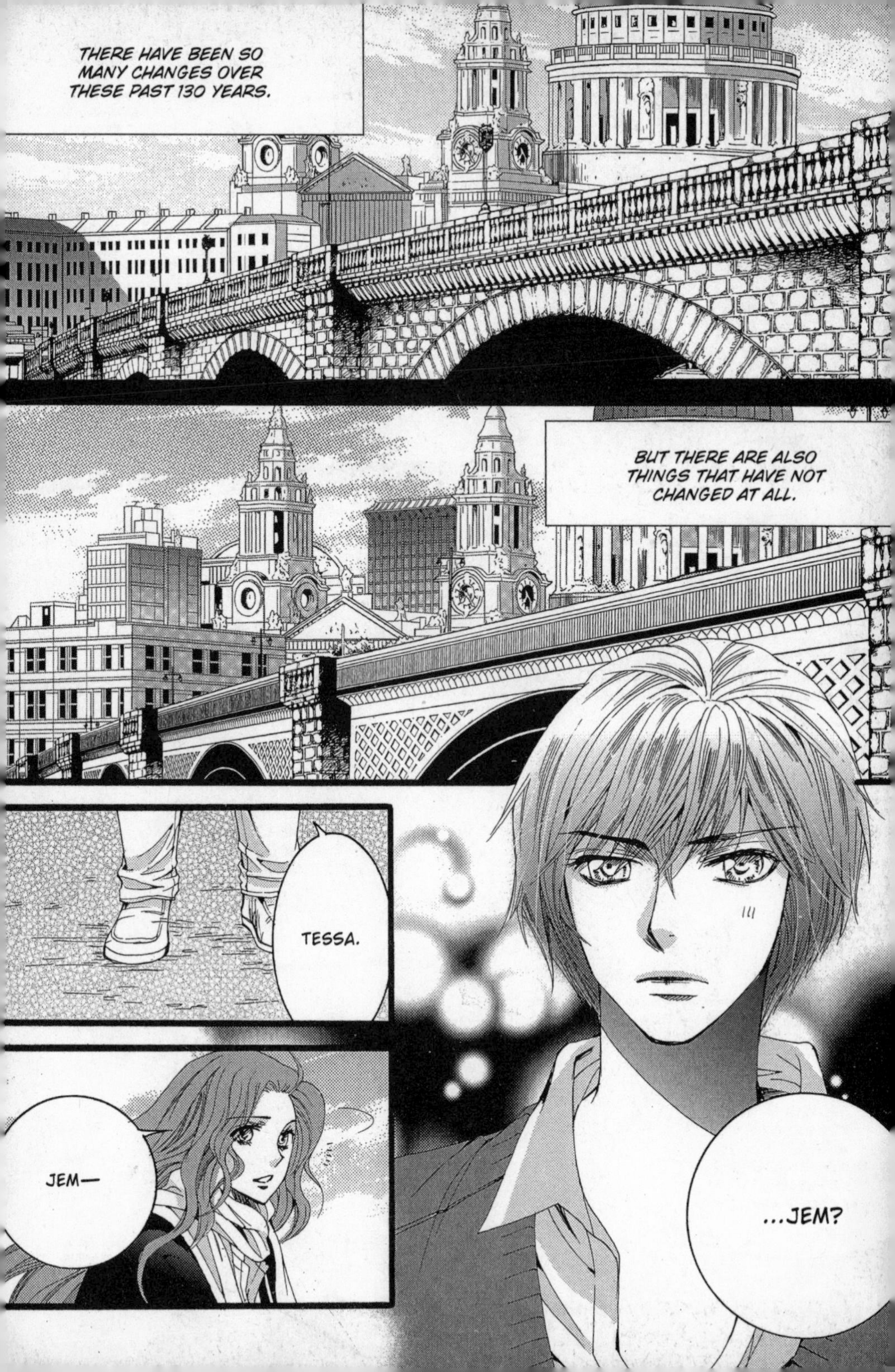
THERE HAVE BEEN SO MANY CHANGES OVER THESE PAST 130 YEARS.
BUT THERE ARE ALSO THINGS THAT HAVE NOT CHANGED AT ALL.
TESSA.
JEM—
...JEM?

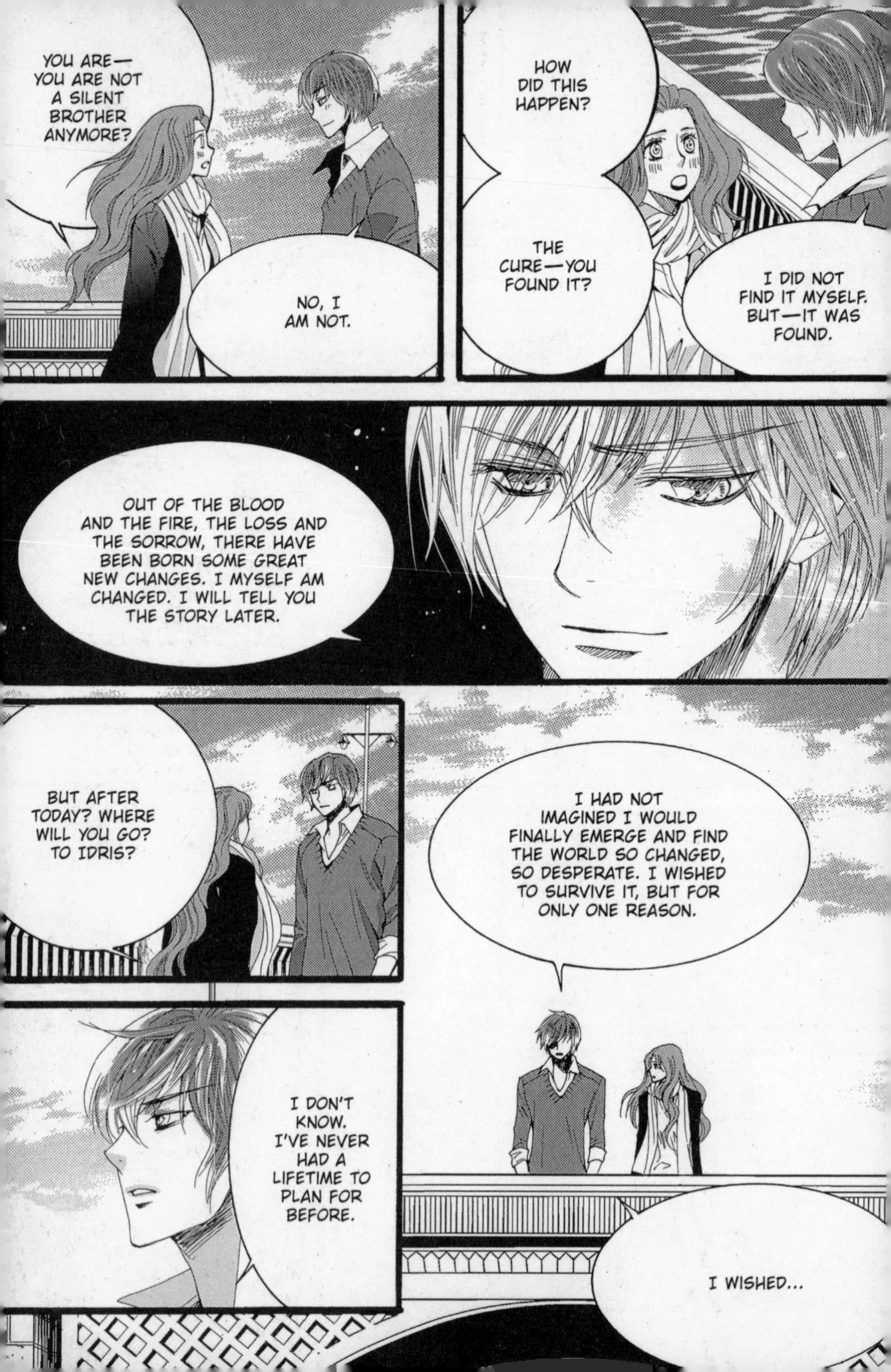
YOU ARE—
YOU ARE NOT A SILENT BROTHER ANYMORE?
NO, I AM NOT.
HOW DID THIS HAPPEN?
THE CURE—YOU FOUND IT?
I DID NOT FIND IT MYSELF. BUT—IT WAS FOUND.
OUT OF THE BLOOD AND THE FIRE, THE LOSS AND THE SORROW, THERE HAVE BEEN BORN SOME GREAT NEW CHANGES. I MYSELF AM CHANGED. I WILL TELL YOU THE STORY LATER.
BUT AFTER TODAY? WHERE WILL YOU GO? TO IDRIS?
I DON'T KNOW. I'VE NEVER HAD A LIFETIME TO PLAN FOR BEFORE.
I HAD NOT IMAGINED I WOULD FINALLY EMERGE AND FIND THE WORLD SO CHANGED, SO DESPERATE. I WISHED TO SURVIVE IT, BUT FOR ONLY ONE REASON.
I WISHED...

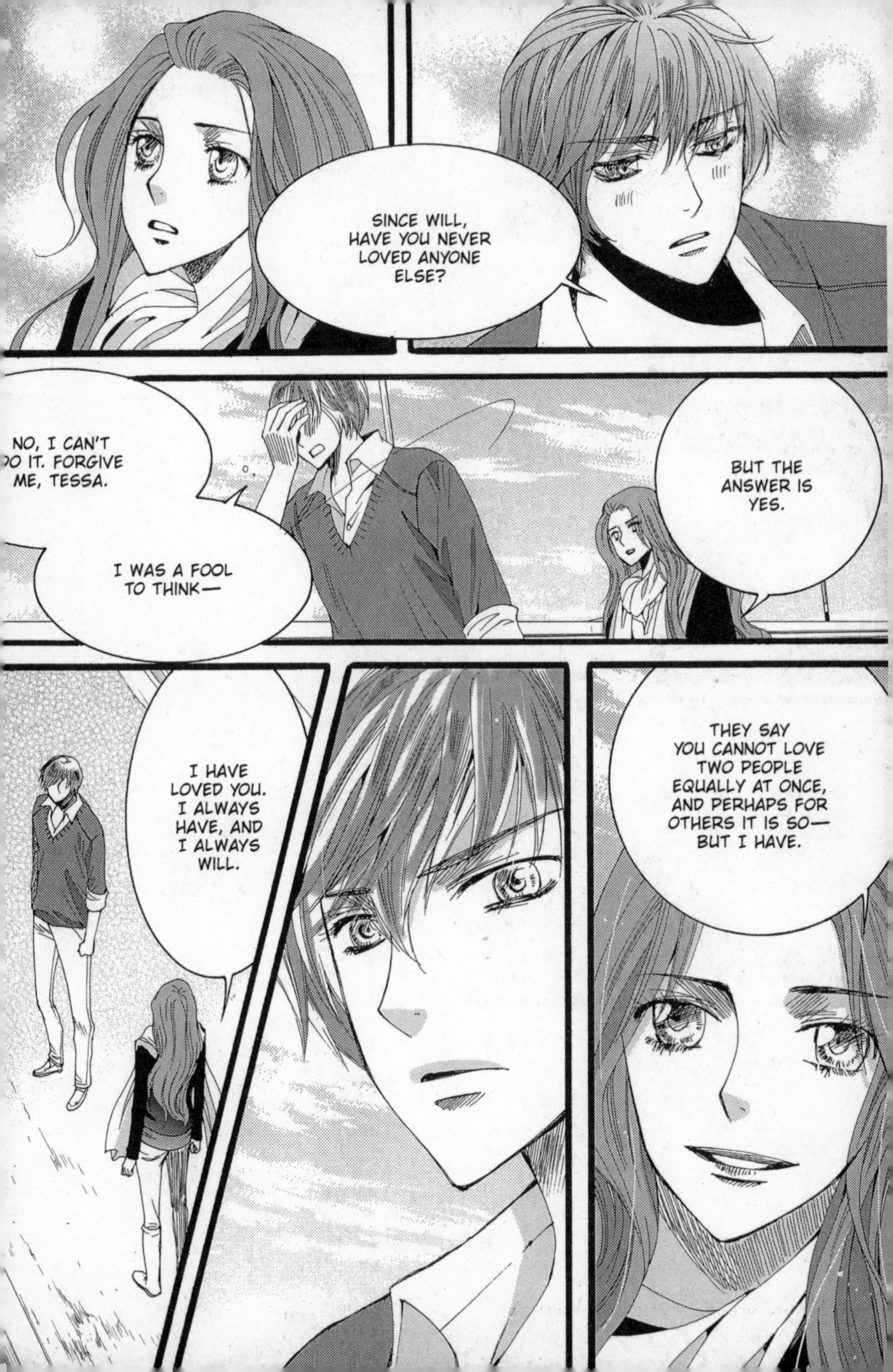
SINCE WILL, HAVE YOU NEVER LOVED ANYONE ELSE?
NO, I CAN'T DO IT. FORGIVE ME, TESSA.
I WAS A FOOL TO THINK—
BUT THE ANSWER IS YES.
I HAVE LOVED YOU. I ALWAYS HAVE, AND I ALWAYS WILL.
THEY SAY YOU CANNOT LOVE TWO PEOPLE EQUALLY AT ONCE, AND PERHAPS FOR OTHERS IT IS SO— BUT I HAVE.

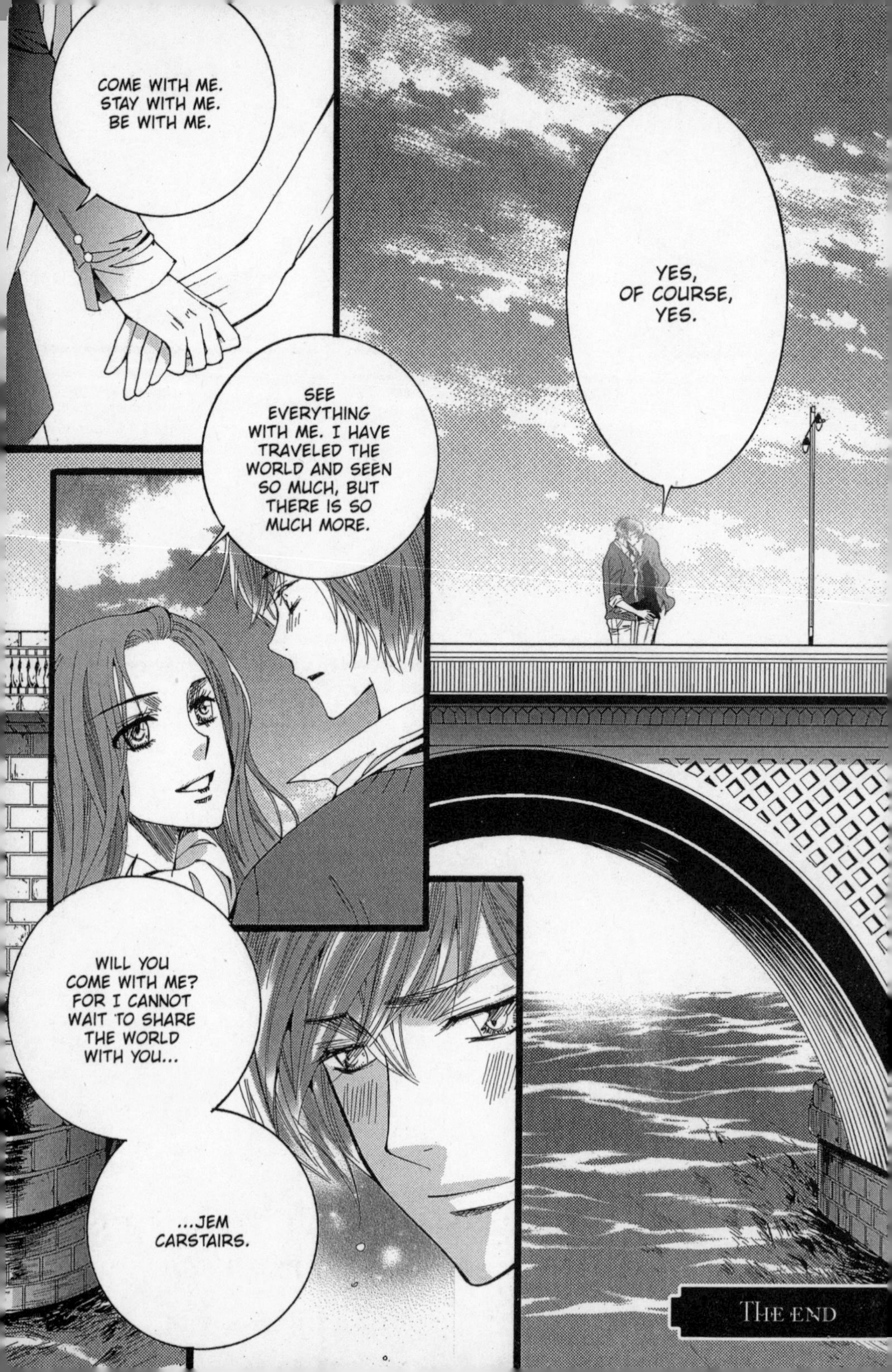
COME WITH ME. STAY WITH ME. BE WITH ME.
SEE EVERYTHING WITH ME. I HAVE TRAVELED THE WORLD AND SEEN SO MUCH, BUT THERE IS SO MUCH MORE.
YES, OF COURSE, YES.
WILL YOU COME WITH ME? FOR I CANNOT WAIT TO SHARE THE WORLD WITH YOU...
...JEM CARSTAIRS.
THE END

The infernal devices
Clockwork princess

THE INFERNAL DEVICES: CLOCKWORK PRINCESS

CASSANDRA CLARE
HYEKYUNG BAEK

Art and Adaptation: HyeKyung Baek

Lettering: Stephanie Lee

Text copyright © Cassandra Claire, LLC 2011

Illustrations © Hachette Book Group, Inc.

Yen Press
Hachette Book Group
1290 Avenue of the Americas, New York, NY 10104

www.HachetteBookGroup.com
www.YenPress.com

Yen Press is an imprint of Hachette Book Group, Inc. The Yen Press name and logo are trademarks of Hachette Book Group, Inc.

First Yen Press Edition: July 2014

ISBN: 978-0-316-20097-4

10 9 8 7 6 5 4 3

BVG

Printed in the United States of America